Contents

II	Driving abroad – a cautionary tale
IV	Driving regulations
VII	Ski resorts

1	**Route planning maps**
1	Key to route planning map pages

24	**Road maps**
24	Key to road map pages · Distance table

201	**City plans and approach maps**

Alicante C	201	Luxembourg C	215
Amsterdam C U	202	Lyon C U	215
Antwerpen C	201	Madrid U C	215
Athina U C	202	Málaga C	216
Barcelona C U	203	Marseille C	216
Basel C	203	Milano C U	217
Beograd C	205	Moskva C U	218
Berlin C U	204	München C U	218
Bordeaux C U	205	Nápoli C U	219
Bruxelles U C	205	Oslo U C	219
Budapest C U	206	Paris C U	220
Dublin C U	207	Praha C U	222
Düsseldorf C U	207	Roma C U	223
Edinburgh C	207	Rotterdam C	222
Firenze Florence C	209	Sankt Peterburg U	222
Frankfurt C	209	Sevilla C	224
Genève Geneva C	209	Stockholm C U	225
Génova Genoa C	209	Strasbourg C U	224
Göteborg C	210	Stuttgart C	224
Granada C	210	Torino U C	226
Hamburg C U	210	Venézia C	226
Helsinki C U	211	Warszawa C U	227
İstanbul U	211	Wien U C	227
København C U	212	Zagreb C	228
Köln Cologne C	212	Zürich C	228
Lisboa C U	213	**C** City street plan	
London C U	213	**U** Urban area map	

229	**Index to road maps**

www.philips-maps.co.uk

First published in 1998 by Philip's,
a division of Octopus Publishing Group Ltd
www.octopusbooks.co.uk
Carmelite House, 50 Victoria Embankment
London EC4Y 0DZ
An Hachette UK Company · www.hachette.co.uk

Twenty-sixth edition 2018, first impression 2018

This product includes mapping data
licensed from Ordnance Survey®, with
the permission of the Controller of
Her Majesty's Stationery Office
© Crown copyright 2018.
All rights reserved. Licence number 100011710

® is a registered Trade Mark of the Northern
Ireland Department of Finance and
Personnel. This product includes mapping
data licensed from Ordnance Survey of
Northern Ireland®, reproduced with the permission of
Land and Property Services under delegated authority
from the Controller of Her Majesty's Stationery Office,
© Crown Copyright 2018.

*Independent research survey, from research carried out by
Outlook Research Limited, 2005/06

Photographic acknowledgements:
Pages II and III: all photographs by Stephen Mesquita

C000285856

Legend to route planning

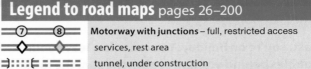

	Motorway with junctions, tunnel, under construction
	Toll motorway, pre-pay motorway
	Main through route
25 56	European road number, motorway number
55	National road number
56	Distances – in kilometres
	International boundary, national boundary
LE HAVRE	Car ferry and destination
✕ ✈ 1089 ▲	Mountain pass, international airport, height (metres)

Town – population

MOSKVA ☐ ▣	5 million +	Gävle ⊙ ◉	50000–100000
BERLIN ☐ ▣	2–5 million	Nybro ⊙ ◉	20000–50000
MINSK ☐ ▣	1–2 million	Ikast ○ ◉	10000–20000
Oslo ◉ ◉	500000–1million	Skjern ○ ◉	5000–10000
Århus ⊙ ◉	200000–500000	Lillesand ○ ●	0–5000
Turku ⊙ ◉	100000–200000		

The green version of the symbol indicates towns with
Low Emission Zones

Scale · pages 2–23

1 : 3 200 000
1 in = 50.51 miles
1 cm = 32km

0	10	20	30	40	50	60	70	80	90	100	110 miles

0	20	40	60	80	100	120	140	160	180 km

Legend to road maps pages 26–200

⑦ ⑧	Motorway with junctions – full, restricted access
◇ ◇	services, rest area
	tunnel, under construction
	Toll Motorway – with toll barrier
A CH CZ H SK	Pre-pay motorway – 'Vignette' must be purchased before travel
	Principal trunk highway – single / dual carriageway
	tunnel, under construction
	Other main highway – single / dual carriageway
	Other important road, other road
E25 A49	European road number, motorway number
135	National road number
Col Bayard 1248	Mountain pass
	Scenic route, gradient – arrow points uphill
143	Distances – in kilometres major
28	minor
	Principal railway with tunnel
	Ferry route
	Short ferry route
	International boundary, national boundary
	National park, natural park

✈	Airport	🎿	Ski resort
🏛	Ancient monument	🎡	Theme park
⌇	Beach	◉	World Heritage site
🏰	Castle or house	1754▲	Spot height
⌂	Cave	**Sevilla**	World Heritage town
✦	Other place of interest	**Verona**	Town of tourist interest
❂	Park or garden	■ ●	City or town with Low Emission Zone
✟	Religious building		

Scale · pages 26–181

1:753 800
1 inch = 12 miles
1 cm = 7.5km

0	2	4	6	8	10	12	14	16	18	20	22	24	26 miles

0	4	8	12	16	20	24	28	32	36	40km

Scale · pages 182–200

1:1 507 600
1 inch = 24 miles
1 cm = 15km

0	4	8	12	16	20	24	28	32	36	40	44	48	52 miles

0	8	16	24	32	40	48	56	64	72	80km

Driving abroad –
a cautionary tale

by Stephen Mesquita,
Philip's On the Road Correspondent

15/06/2016 07:10:39 LS300W   *******

5/06/2016 07:05:10 LS300W   ******* Timeless pastoral scenes

2016 08:54:36 LS300W   ** Wandering down middle of street

15/06/2016 07:01:38 LS300W   *******   Empty beaches

At last, you're on holiday. You can relax, leave your troubles behind you and soak in the sun, the food and the way of life. That's all true, of course – if you don't have to drive.

When you're driving in a strange country, relaxing is the last thing you should be doing. In fact, when you're driving on roads you don't know – and on the 'wrong' side of the road – you need to pay attention at all times and be ultra defensive.

Take one of my favourite places to visit – the very end of the heel of Italy. If you're only used to the UK's roads, driving there is a whole different kettle of fish. Or *'un altro paio di maniche'* (another pair of sleeves), as it should be.

These are the idyllic images you might have :

- Empty roads with great views.
- Timeless pastoral scenes.
- Village locals wandering down the middle of the street.
- Driving down to empty beaches for a swim before breakfast (only if you're really keen).

But the reality's a lot different. It's not that the Southern Italians are any better or worse drivers than we are. But there are different laws, different conventions, different road conditions and different driving styles.

So here is my survival guide. Of course, this is only one small region of Europe. But I'm sure that wherever you're driving, some of this may ring bells – and perhaps even be useful.

Here are my Top 10 Tips from last year's holiday, illustrated with real-time dashcam video...

1 Being overtaken

Overtaking is more of a national sport on the continent than it is in the UK. What's disconcerting is the way that the overtaking car pulls in so sharply after overtaking. It takes a bit of getting used to but it's generally not (quite) as dangerous as it looks.

13/06/2016 08:43:35 LS300W   *******

2 Tailgating

It's probably no worse than in the UK; but tailgating can still be intimidating and distracting. If you feel threatened, try to pull off the road if it's safe to do it. Or try my favourite ploy – go round a roundabout twice to escape your tailgater.

3 Motorway Slip Roads

Beware short slip roads on to motorways. They give merging motorists little chance to join the traffic at anything other than a snail's pace, leading them into narrow lanes of fast traffic. Not for the faint-hearted. Check your mirror as often as you can.

5 Pulling out of side roads and hoping

Pulling out of side roads and hoping. A lot of this goes on at crossroads in small towns and villages. Given the configuration of the roads, there's not much you can do about it – except be very cautious, even when it's your right of way or, as here, the traffic lights only work at certain times of day

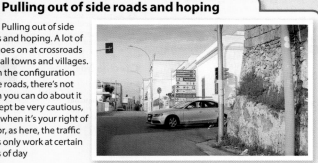

7 Parking Meters

In this region, almost every town has the blue road markings which indicate that, if you want to park here, you'll need to buy a ticket. You'll need coins – many don't accept notes or credit cards. No change is given. If you're lucky, as you put the coins in, the expiry time is shown. If you're unlucky, this panel will be dirty or scratched so that you can't read it. The times you need to pay for vary from town to town, depending on the time of year (always in the tourist season) and the time of day (siesta time is sometimes not charged). A crash course in the language is recommended. In 11 days, I spent over €65 on meters.

10 Cameras

These pictures cost me €200. They show me at the wheel of my stylish Fiat 500 (that's what the website said anyway) being distracted by two cyclists as they went through a red light. The red light is hidden in the hedge. This deserted spot in the middle of the countryside boasts the only traffic camera ever seen in the region. I stupidly had my eye on the cyclists, not the light. First I received a bill from Hertz for €47.90 – which I innocently thought was for the 'offence'. But no, it was for supplying my name and address (with almost every word misspelt) to the local authority. A year later, a bill arrived from said local authority, for €145 if paid within 5 days (or €220 if not).

4 Oncoming traffic driving on your side of the road

On narrow country roads, this is a hazard everywhere. It's probably worse in the UK than it is in Southern Italy. But, as the picture shows, it can produce some heart-stopping moments.

6 Petrol stations

Many country petrol stations are unmanned. Those that are manned sometimes charge you more for the privilege of having someone serve you. It may be worth it: the unmanned ones are not easy to operate. In a richly comic episode, I had to seek assistance to discover that I had paid for €40 of petrol at a pump some distance from the one at which my car was parked.

8 Sat Nav – beware of speed limits

Even though I'm an atlas publisher, I would strongly recommend you take a sat nav – as well as this atlas, of course. It really reduces the stress of navigating on unfamiliar roads (it's not so good for route planning). But beware if your sat nav tells you the speed limit – those on the screen seem to bear little resemblance to the signs at the side of the road.

9 Speed limits Part 2

Even relying on the roadside signs, it can be hard to work out the speed limits. Can you work out what's happening here (answer at the foot of the page)?

And I haven't even got to that most thrilling part of your holiday 'At the Car Hire Desk' (damage waiver rip-off's, not getting the car you ordered, should you photograph the car, and is it worth having another driver), documentation (the code you have to get now from the DVLA if you're hiring a car) and taking a spare pair of glasses. And do watch how much you drink. See the next section for all the rules and regulations for each country, including the alcohol limits. If in doubt, don't drink and drive. Now turn over and read the driving laws of the country you're going to. Buon Viaggio.

Answer to point 9: the speed limit is normally 90kph but it's 50kph when it's foggy or visibility is less than 100m.

Driving regulations

Vehicle A national vehicle identification plate is always required when taking a vehicle abroad.

Fitting headlamp converters or beam deflectors when taking a right-hand drive car to a country where driving is on the right (every country in Europe except the UK and Ireland) is compulsory.

Within the EU, if not driving a locally hired car, it is compulsory to have either Europlates or a country of origin (e.g. GB) sticker. Outside the EU and in Andorra) a sticker is compulsory, even with Europlates.

Documentation All countries require that you carry a valid passport, vehicle registration document, hire certificate or letter of authority for the use of someone else's vehicle, full driving licence/International Driving Permit and insurance documentation (and/or green card outside the EU). Some non-EU countries also require a visa. Minimum driving ages are often higher for people holding foreign licences. New exit checks at the Eurotunnel and ferry terminals mean that drivers taking vehicles from the UK should allow extra time. Drivers of vehicles over three years old should ensure that the MOT is up to date, and take the certificate with them..

EHIC cards are free and give you entitlement to healthcare in other EU countries and Switzerland. www.gov/european-health-insurance-card

Licence A photo licence is preferred; with an old-style paper licence, an International Driving Permit (IDP) should also be carried. In some countries, an IDP is compulsory, whatever form of licence is held. Non-EU drivers should always have both a licence and an IDP. UK (except NI) drivers should check in advance whether a hire company will wish to check for endorsements and vehicle categories. If so, visit www.gov.uk/view-driving-licence to create a digital code (valid for 72 hours) that allows their details to be shared. For more information, contact the DVLA (0300790 6802, www.dft.gov.uk/dvla).

Insurance Third-party cover is compulsory across Europe. Most insurance policies give only basic cover when driving abroad, so you should check that your policy provides at least third-party cover for the countries in which you will be driving and upgrade it to the level that you require. You may have to take out extra cover at the frontier if you cannot produce acceptable proof of adequate insurance. Even in countries in which a green card is not required, carrying one is recommended for extra proof of insurance.

Motorcycles It is compulsory for all motorcyclists and passengers to wear crash helmets.

Other In countries in which visibility vests are compulsory, one for each person should be carried in the passenger compartment, or panniers on a motorbike, where they can be reached easily.

Warning triangles should also be carried in the passenger compartment.

The penalties for infringements of regulations vary considerably from one country to another. In many countries the police may impose on-the-spot fines (ask for a receipt). Penalties can be severe for serious infringements, particularly for exceeding the blood-alcohol limit; in some countries this can result in immediate imprisonment.

In some countries, vignettes for toll roads are being replaced by electronic tags.

Please note that driving regulations may change, and that it has not been possible to cover all the information for every type of vehicle. The figures given for capitals' populations are for the whole metropolitan area.

The symbols used are:

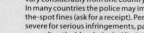

- 🏛 Motorway
- ⚠ Dual carriageway
- ⚠ Single carriageway
- 🚗 Surfaced road
- 🚗 Unsurfaced or gravel road
- 🏭 Urban area
- 🕓 Speed limit in kilometres per hour (kph). These are the maximum speeds for the types of roads listed. In some places and under certain conditions they may be considerably lower. Always obey local signs.

- 🚗 Seat belts
- 🚼 Children
- ♀ Blood alcohol level
- △ Warning triangle
- ⛑ First aid kit
- 🔧 Spare bulb kit
- ⛽ Fire extinguisher
- ⊖ Minimum driving age
- ⬛ Additional documents required
- 📱 Mobile phones
- 🔆 Dipped headlights
- ❄ Winter driving
- **LEZ** Low Emission Zone
- ★ Other information

Andorra Principat d'Andorra (AND)

Area 468 sq km (181 sq miles)
Population 85,500 **Capital** Andorra la Vella (44,000)
Languages Catalan (official), French, Castilian and Portuguese **Currency** Euro = 100 cents
Website http://visitandorra.com

🏛	⚠	⚠	🏭
n/a	90	60/90	50

- 🚗 Compulsory
- 🚼 Under 10 and below 150 cm must travel in an EU-approved restraint system adapted to their size in the rear. Airbag must be deactivated if a child is in the front passenger seat.
- ♀ 0.05% △ Compulsory ⛑ Recommended
- ⛽ Compulsory 🔆 Recommended ⊖ 18
- 📱 Not permitted whilst driving
- 🔆 Compulsory for motorcycles during day and for other vehicles during poor daytime visibility.
- ❄ Winter tyres recommended. Snow chains compulsory in poor conditions or when indicated.
- ★ On-the-spot fines imposed
- ★ Visibility vests compulsory

Austria Österreich (A)

Area 83,859 sq km (32,377 sq miles)
Population 8,794,000 **Capital** Vienna / Wien (1,868,000) **Languages** German (official)
Currency Euro = 100 cents **Website** www.bka.gv.at

🏛	⚠	⚠	🏭
130	100	100	50

If towing trailer under 750kg / over 750 kg

🕓			
100	100	100/80	50

- 🚗 Compulsory
- 🚼 Under 14 and under 150cm cannot travel as a front or rear passenger unless they use a suitable child restraint; under 14 over 150cm must wear adult seat belt
- ♀ 0.049% • 0.01% if licence held less than 2 years
- △ Compulsory 🔆 Compulsory
- ⛽ Recommended 🔆 Recommended
- ⊖ 18 (20 for motorbikes over 50cc)
- 📱 Only allowed with hands-free kit
- ⬛ Paper driving licences must be accompanied by photographic proof of identity.
- **LEZ** Several cities and regions have LEZs affecting HGVs that ban non-compliant vehicles, impose speed restrictions and night-time bans.
- 🔆 Must be used during the day by all road users. Headlamp converters compulsory
- ❄ Winter tyres compulsory 1 Nov–15 Apr
- ★ On-the-spot fines imposed
- ★ Radar detectors and dashcams prohibited
- ★ To drive on motorways or expressways, a motorway sticker must be purchased at the border or main petrol station. These are available for 10 days, 2 months or 1 year. Vehicles 3.5 tonnes or over must display an electronic tag.
- ★ Visibility vests compulsory

Belarus (BY)

Area 207,600 sq km (80,154 sq miles)
Population 9,499,000 **Capital** Minsk (2,101,000)
Languages Belarusian, Russian (both official)
Currency Belarusian ruble = 100 kopek
Website www.belarus.by/en/government

🏛	⚠	⚠	🏭
110	90	90	60*

If towing trailer under 750kg

🕓			
90	70	70	

*In residential areas limit is 20 km/h • Vehicle towing another vehicle 50 kph limit • If full driving licence held for less than two years, must not exceed 70 kph

- 🚗 Compulsory in front seats, and rear seats if fitted
- 🚼 Under 12 not allowed in front seat and must use appropriate child restraint
- ♀ 0.00% △ Compulsory ⛑ Compulsory
- ⛽ Recommended 🔆 Compulsory ⊖ 18
- ⬛ Visa, vehicle technical check stamp, international driving permit, green card, health insurance. Even with a green card, local third-party insurance may be imposed at the border
- 📱 Use prohibited
- 🔆 Compulsory during the day Nov–Mar and at all other times in conditions of poor visibility or when towing or being towed.
- ❄ Winter tyres compulsory; snow chains recommended
- ★ A temporary vehicle import certificate must be purchased on entry and driver must be registered
- ★ It is illegal for vehicles to be dirty
- ★ On-the-spot fines imposed
- ★ Radar-detectors prohibited
- ★ Road tax imposed at the border
- ★ To drive on main motorways and on-board unit must be acquired at the border or a petrol station in order to pay tolls. See **www.beltoll.by/index.php/en**

Belgium Belgique (B)

Area 30,528 sq km (11,786 sq miles)
Population 11,251,000 **Capital** Brussels/Bruxelles (1,175,000) **Languages** Dutch, French, German (all official) **Currency** Euro = 100 cents
Website www.belgium.be/en

🏛	⚠	⚠	🏭
120[1]	120[1]	90[2]	50[3]

If towing trailer

🕓			
90	90	60	50[3]

Over 3.5 tonnes

🕓			
90	90	60	50

[1]Minimum speed of 70 kph may be applied in certain conditions on motorways and some dual carriageways. [2]70 kph in Flanders. [3]20 kph in some residential areas, 30 kph near some schools, hospitals and churches.

- 🚗 Compulsory
- 🚼 All under 18s under 135 cm must wear an appropriate child restraint. Airbags must be deactivated if rear-facing child seat is used in the front
- ♀ 0.049% △ Compulsory ⛑ Recommended
- ⛽ Recommended 🔆 Compulsory ⊖ 18
- 🏍 Motorcyclists must wear fully protective clothing
- 📱 Only allowed with a hands-free kit
- **LEZ** LEZs in operation in Antwerp, Brussels and areas of Flanders. Preregistration necessary and fees payable for most vehicles.
- 🔆 Mandatory at all times for motorcycles and advised during the day in poor conditions for other vehicles
- ★ Cruise control must be deactivated on motorways where indicated ★ On-the-spot fines imposed ★ Radar detectors prohibited ★ Sticker indicating maximum recommended speed for winter tyres must be displayed on dashboard if using them ★Visibility vest compulsory

Bosnia Herzegovina Bosna i Hercegovina (BIH)

Area 51,197 km² (19,767 mi²) **Population** 3,872,000
Capital Sarajevo (643,000) **Languages** Bosnian/Croatian/Serbian **Currency** Convertible Marka = 100 convertible pfenniga
Website www.fbihvlada.gov.ba/english/index.php

🏛	⚠	⚠	🏭
130	100	80	50

- 🚗 Compulsory if fitted
- 🚼 Under 12s must sit in rear using an appropriate child restraint. Under-2s may travel in a rear-facing child seat in the front only if the airbags have been deactivated.
- ♀ 0.03% △ Compulsory ⛑ Compulsory
- ⛽ Compulsory 🔆 Prohibited ⊖ 18
- 🔆 Compulsory for LPG vehicles
- ⬛ Visa, International Driving Permit, green card
- 🔆 Compulsory for all vehicles at all times
- ❄ Winter tyres compulsory 15 Nov–15 Apr; snow chains recommended
- ★ GPS must have fixed speed camera function deactivated; radar detectors prohibited. ★ On-the-spot fines imposed ★Visibility vest, tow rope or tow bar compulsory ★Spare wheel compulsory, except for two-wheeled vehicles

Bulgaria Bulgariya (BG)

Area 110,912 sq km (42,822 sq miles)
Population 7,102,000 **Capital** Sofia (1,682,000)
Languages Bulgarian (official), Turkish **Currency** Lev = 100 stotinki **Website** www.government.bg

🏛	⚠	⚠	🏭
130	90	90	50

If towing trailer

🕓			
100	70	70	50

- 🚗 Compulsory in front and rear seats
- 🚼 Under 3s not permitted in vehicles with no child restraints; 3–10 year olds must sit in rear in an appropriate restraint. Rear-facing child seats may be used in the front only if the airbag has been deactivated
- ♀ 0.049% △ Compulsory ⛑ Compulsory
- ⛽ Recommended 🔆 Compulsory ⊖ 18
- ⬛ Photo driving licence preferred; a paper licence must be accompanied by an International Driving Permit. Green card or insurance specific to Bulgaria.
- 📱 Only allowed with a hands-free kit
- 🔆 Compulsory
- ❄ Winter tyres compulsory. Snow chains should be carried from 1 Nov–1 Mar. Max speed with chains 50 kph
- ★ Fee at border ★ GPS must have fixed speed camera function deactivated; radar detectors prohibited ★ On-the-spot fines imposed ★ Road tax stickers (annual, monthly or weekly) must be purchased at the border and displayed prominently with the vehicle registration number written on them. ★Visibility vest compulsory

---

Croatia Hrvatska (HR)

Area 56,538 km² (21,829 mi²)
Population 4,191,000 **Capital** Zagreb (1,113,000)
Languages Croatian **Currency** Kuna = 100 lipa
Website https://vlada.gov.hr/en

🏛	⚠	⚠	🏭
130	110	90	50

Under 24

🕓			
120	100	80	50

If towing

🕓			
90	90	80	50

- 🚗 Compulsory if fitted
- 🚼 Children under 12 not permitted in front seat and must use appropriate child seat or restraint in rear. Children under 2 may use a rear-facing seat in the front only if the airbag is deactivated
- ♀ 0.05% • 0.00 % for drivers under 24
- △ Compulsory 🔆 Compulsory
- ⛽ Compulsory 🔆 Recommended ⊖ 18
- ⬛ Green card recommended
- 📱 Only allowed with hands-free kit
- 🔆 Compulsory
- ❄ Winter tyres, snow chains and shovel compulsory in winter
- ★ On-the-spot fines imposed ★ Radar detectors prohibited ★ Tow bar and rope compulsory ★ Visibility vest compulsory

Czechia Česko (CZ)

Area 78,864 sq km (30,449 sq miles)
Population 10,554,000 **Capital** Prague/Praha (2,157,000) **Languages** Czech (official), Moravian
Currency Czech Koruna = 100 haler
Website www.vlada.cz/en/

🏛	⚠	⚠	🏭
130	90	90	50

If towing

🕓			
80	80	80	50

- 🚗 Compulsory in front seats and, if fitted, in rear
- 🚼 Children under 36 kg and 150 cm must use appropriate child restraint. Only front-facing child retraints are permitted in the front in vehicles with airbags fitted. Airbags must be deactivated if a rear-facing child seat is used in the front.
- ♀ 0.00% △ Compulsory ⛑ Compulsory
- ⛽ Compulsory 🔆 Compulsory
- ⊖ 18 (17 for motorcycles under 125 cc)
- 📱 Only allowed with a hands-free kit
- **LEZ** Two-stage LEZ in Prague for vehicles over 3.5 and 6 tonnes. Permit system.
- 🔆 Compulsory at all times
- ❄ Winter tyres compulsory November–March, roads are icy/snow-covered or snow is expected. Max speed 50 kph.
- ★ GPS must have fixed speed camera function deactivated; radar detectors prohibited
- ★ On-the-spot fines imposed
- ★ Replacement fuses must be carried
- ★ Spectacles or contact lens wearers must carry a spare pair in their vehicle at all times
- ★ Vignette needed for motorway driving, available for 1 year, 60 days, 15 days. Toll specific to lorries introduced 2006, those over 12 tonnes must buy an electronic tag
- ★ Visibility vest compulsory

Denmark Danmark (DK)

Area 43,094 sq km (16,638 sq miles)
Population 5,749,000 **Capital** Copenhagen / København (2,037,000) **Languages** Danish (official)
Website www.denmark.dk/en

🏛	⚠	⚠	🏭
110-130	80-90	80	50*

If towing

🕓			
80	70	70	50*

*Central Copenhagen 40 kph

- 🚗 Compulsory front and rear
- 🚼 Under 135cm must use appropriate child restraint; in front permitted only in an appropriate rear-facing seat with any airbags disabled.
- ♀ 0.05% △ Compulsory 🔆 Recommended
- ⛽ Recommended 🔆 Recommended ⊖ 17
- 📱 Only allowed with a hands-free kit
- **LEZ** Aalborg, Arhus, Copenhagen, Frederiksberg and Odense. Proofs of emissions compliance or compliant filter needed to obtain sticker. Non-compliant vehicles banned.
- 🔆 Must be used at all times
- ❄ Spiked tyres may be fitted 1 Nov–15 April, if used on all wheels
- ★ On-the-spot fines imposed
- ★ Radar detectors prohibited
- ★ Tolls apply on the Storebaeltsbroen and Oresundsbron bridges.
- ★ Visibility vest recommended

Estonia Eesti (EST)

Area 45,100 sq km (17,413 sq miles)
Population 1,316,000 **Capital** Tallinn (543,000)
Languages Estonian (official), Russian
Currency Euro = 100 cents
Website www.valitsus.ee/en

n/a	90*	90	50
If full driving licence held for less than two years			
90	90	90	50

In summer, the speed limit on some dual carriageways may be raised to 100/110 kph

- Compulsory if fitted
- Children too small for adult seatbelts must wear a seat restraint appropriate to their size. Rear-facing safety seats must not be used in the front if an air bag is fitted, unless this has been deactivated.
- 0.00% △ 2 compulsory Compulsory
- Recommended Compulsory 18
- Only allowed with a hands-free kit
- Compulsory at all times
- Winter tyres are compulsory from Dec–Mar. Studded winter tyres are allowed from 15 Oct–31 Mar, but this can be extended to start 1 Oct and/or end 30 Apr
- ★ A toll system is in operation in Tallinn ★ On-the-spot fines imposed ★ Two wheel chocks compulsory ★ Visibility vest compulsory

Finland Suomi (FIN)

Area 338,145 sq km (130,557 sq miles)
Population 5,506,000 **Capital** Helsinki (1,442,000)
Languages Finnish, Swedish (both official)
Currency Euro = 100 cents
Website http://valtioneuvosto.fi/en/frontpage

120	100	80/100*	20/50
Vans, lorries and if towing			
80	80	60	20/50

*100 in summer • If towing a vehicle by rope, cable or rod, max speed limit 60 kph • Maximum of 80 kph for vans and lorries • Speed limits are often lowered in winter

- Compulsory in front and rear
- Below 135 cm must use a child restraint or seat
- 0.05% △ Compulsory Recommended
- Recommended Recommended
- 18 (motorbikes below 125cc 16)
- Only allowed with hands-free kit
- Must be used at all times
- Winter tyres compulsory Dec–Feb
- ★ On-the-spot fines imposed ★ Radar-detectors are prohibited ★ Visibility vest compulsory

France (F)

Area 551,500 sq km (212,934 sq miles)
Population 66,991,000 **Capital** Paris (12,405,000)
Languages French (official), Breton, Occitan
Currency Euro = 100 cents
Website www.diplomatie.gouv.fr/en/

130	110	90	50
On wet roads or if full driving licence held for less than 3 years			
110	100	80	50
If towing below / above 3.5 tonnes gross			
110/90	100/90	90/80	50

50kph on all roads if fog reduces visibility to less than 50m • Licence will be lost and driver fined for exceeding speed limit by over 50kph

- Compulsory in front seats and, if fitted, in rear
- In rear, 4 or under must have a child safety seat (rear facing if up to 9 months); if 5–10 must use an appropriate restraint system. Under 10 permitted in the front only if rear seats are fully occupied by other under 10s or there are no rear safety belts. In front, if child is in rear-facing child seat, any airbag must be deactivated.
- 0.049% • If towing or with less than 2 years with full driving licence, 0.00% • All drivers/motorcyclists must carry an unused breathalyser to French certification standards, showing an NF number.
- △ Compulsory Recommended
- Recommended
- 18 (16 for motorbikes up to 80cc)
- Use not permitted whilst driving
- LEZ An LEZ operates in the Mont Blanc tunnel and such zones are being progressively introduced across French cities. Non-compliant vehicles are banned during operating hours. See **http://certificat-air.gouv.fr**
- Compulsory in poor daytime visibility and at all times for motorcycles
- Winter tyres recommended. Carrying snow chains recommended in winter as these may have to be fitted if driving on snow-covered roads, in accordance with signage.
- ★ GPS must have fixed speed camera function deactivated; radar-detection equipment is prohibited ★ It is compulsory to carry a French-authority-recognised (NF) breathalyser. ★ Motorcyclists and passengers must have four reflective stickers on their helmets (front, back and both sides) and wear CE-certified gloves. ★ On-the-spot fines imposed ★ Tolls on motorways. Electronic tag needed if using automatic tolls. ★ Visibility vests, to be worn on the roadside in case of emergency or breakdown, must be carried for all vehicle occupants and riders. ★ Wearers of contact lenses or spectacles or lenses should carry a spare pair

Germany Deutschland (D)

Area 357,022 sq km (137,846 sq miles)
Population 82,176,000 **Capital** Berlin (6,005,000)
Languages German (official) **Currency** Euro = 100 cents **Website** www.bundesregierung.de

*	*	100	50
If towing			
80	80	80	50

*no limit, 130 kph recommended

- Compulsory
- Aged 3-12 and under 150cm must use an appropriate child seat or restraint and sit in the rear. In the front, if child is under 3 is in a rear-facing seat, airbags must be deactivated
- 0.049% • 0.0% for drivers 21 or under or with less than two years full licence
- △ Compulsory Compulsory
- Recommended Recommended
- 18 (motorbikes: 16 if under 50cc)
- Use permitted only with hands-free kit – also applies to drivers of motorbikes and bicycles
- LEZ More than 60 cities have or are planning LEZs. Proof of compliance needed to acquire sticker. Non-compliant vehicles banned.
- Compulsory during poor daytime visibility and tunnels; recommended at other times. Compulsory at all times for motorcyclists.
- Winter tyres compulsory in all winter weather conditions; snow chains recommended
- ★ GPS must have fixed speed camera function deactivated; radar detectors prohibited ★ On-the-spot fines imposed ★ Tolls on autobahns for lorries ★ Visibility vest compulsory

Greece Ellas (GR)

Area 131,957 sq km (50,948 sq miles)
Population 10,955,000 **Capital** Athens / Athina (4,174,000) **Languages** Greek (official)
Currency Euro = 100 cents
Website www.primeminister.gr/english

130	110	90	50
Motorbikes, and if towing			
90	70	70	40

- Compulsory in front seats and, if fitted, in rear
- Under 12 or below 135cm must use appropriate child restraint. In front if child is in rear-facing child seat, any airbags must be deactivated.
- 0.05% • 0.00% for drivers with less than 2 years' full licence and motorcyclists
- △ Compulsory Compulsory Recommended
- Compulsory 17 Not permitted.
- Compulsory during poor daytime visibility and at all times for motorcycles
- Snow chains permitted on ice- or snow-covered roads. Max speed 50 kph.
- ★ On-the-spot fines imposed ★ Radar-detection equipment is prohibited ★ Tolls on several newer motorways.

Hungary Magyarország (H)

Area 93,032 sq km (35,919 sq miles)
Population 9,798,000 **Capital** Budapest (3,304,000)
Languages Hungarian (official) **Currency** Forint = 100 filler **Website** www.kormany.hu/en

130	110	90	50*
If towing			
80	70	70	50*

*30 kph zones have been introduced in many cities

- Compulsory
- Under 135cm and over 3 must be seated in rear and use appropriate child restraint. Under 3 allowed in front only in rear-facing child seat with any airbags deactivated.
- 0.00% △ Compulsory Compulsory
- Compulsory Recommended 17
- Only allowed with a hands-free kit
- LEZ Budapest has vehicle restrictions on days with heavy dust and is planning an LEZ.
- Compulsory during the day outside built-up areas; compulsory at all times for motorcycles
- Snow chains compulsory where conditions dictate. Max speed 50 kph.
- ★ Many motorways are toll and operate electronic vignette system with automatic number plate recognition, tickets available for 10 days, 1 month, 13 months ★ On-the-spot fines issued ★ Radar detectors prohibited ★ Tow rope recommended ★ Visibility vest compulsory

Iceland Ísland (IS)

Area 103,000 sq km (39,768 sq miles)
Population 333,000 **Capital** Reykjavik (210,000)
Languages Icelandic **Currency** Krona = 100 aurar
Website www.government.is/

n/a	90	80	50

- Compulsory in front and rear seats
- Under 12 or below 150cm not allowed in front seat and must use appropriate child restraint.
- 0.05% △ Compulsory Compulsory
- Compulsory Compulsory
- 17; 21 to drive a hire car; 25 to hire a jeep
- Only allowed with a hands-free kit
- Compulsory at all times
- Winter tyres compulsory c.1 Nov–14 Apr (variable)
- ★ Driving off marked roads is forbidden ★ Highland roads are not suitable for ordinary cars ★ On-the-spot fines imposed

Ireland Eire (IRL)

Area 70,273 sq km (27,132 sq miles)
Population 4,762,000 **Capital** Dublin (1,905,000)
Languages Irish, English (both official)
Currency Euro = 100 cents **Website** www.gov.ie/en/

120	60–100	60–100	50*
If towing			
80	60	60	50*

* 30 kph zones in Dublin and some other areas

- Compulsory where fitted. Driver responsible for ensuring passengers under 17 comply
- Children 3 and under must be in a suitable child restraint system. Airbags must be deactivated if a rear-facing child seat is used in the front. Those under 150 cm and 36 kg must use appropriate child restraint.
- 0.05% • 0.02% for novice and professional drivers
- △ Compulsory Recommended
- Recommended Recommended
- 17 (16 for motorbikes up to 125cc; 18 for over 125cc; 18 for lorries; 21 bus/minibus)
- Only allowed with a hands-free kit
- Compulsory for motorbikes at all times and in poor visibility for other vehicles
- ★ Driving is on the left ★ GPS must have fixed speed camera function deactivated; radar detectors prohibited ★ On-the-spot fines imposed ★ Tolls are being introduced on some motorways; the M50 Dublin has barrier-free tolling with number-plate recognition.

Italy Italia (I)

Area 301,318 sq km (116,338 sq miles)
Population 60,600,000 **Capital** Rome / Roma (4,356,000) **Languages** Italian (official)
Currency Euro = 100 cents **Website** www.italia.it

130	110	90	50
If towing			
80	70	70	50
Less than three years with full licence			
100	90	90	50
When wet			
110	90	80	50

Some motorways with emergency lanes have speed limit of 150 kph

- Compulsory in front seats and, if fitted, in rear
- Under 12 not allowed in front seats except in child safety seat; children under 3 must have special seat in the back. For foreign-registered cars, the country of origin's legislation applies.
- 0.05% • 0.00% for professional drivers or with less than 3 years full licence
- △ Compulsory Recommended
- Compulsory Recommended
- 18 (14 for mopeds, 16 up to 125cc, 20 up to 350cc)
- Only allowed with hands-free kit
- LEZ Most northern and several southern regions operate seasonal LEZs and many towns and cities have various schemes that restrict access. There is an LEZ in the Mont Blanc tunnel
- Compulsory outside built-up areas, in tunnels, on motorways and dual carriageways and in poor visibility; compulsory at all times for motorcycles
- Snow chains compulsory where signs indicate 15 Oct–15 Apr. Max speed 50 kph
- ★ On-the-spot fines imposed ★ Radar-detection equipment is prohibited ★ Tolls on motorways. Blue lanes accept credit cards; yellow lanes restricted to holders of Telepass pay-toll device. ★ Visibility vest compulsory

Kosovo Republika e Kosoves / Republika Kosovo (RKS)

Area 10,887 sq km (4203 sq miles) **Population** 1,908,000 **Capital** Pristina (504,000) **Languages** Albanian, Serbian (both official), Bosnian, Turkish, Roma **Currency** Euro (Serbian dinar in Serb enclaves)
Website www.kryeministri-ks.net/?page=2,1

130	80	80	50

- Compulsory
- Under 12 must sit in rear seats in an appropriate restraint.
- 0.00% △ Compulsory Compulsory
- Compulsory Compulsory
- 18 (motorbikes under 125 cc – 16, mopeds – 14)
- International driving permit, locally purchased third-party insurance (green card is not recognised), documents with proof of ability to cover costs and valid reason for visiting. Visitors from many non-EU countries require a visa.
- Only allowed with a hands-free kit
- Compulsory at all times
- Winter tyres or snow chains compulsory in poor winter weather conditions

Latvia Latvija (LV)

Area 64,589 sq km (24,942 sq miles)
Population 1,953,000 **Capital** Riga (1,018,000)
Languages Latvian (official), Russian **Currency** Euro = 100 cents **Website** www.mk.gov.lv/en

n/a	100	90	50
If towing			
n/a	80	80	50

In residential areas limit is 20kph • If full driving licence held for less than two years, must not exceed 80 kph

- Compulsory in front seats and if fitted in rear
- If under 12 years and 150cm must use child restraint in front and rear seats
- 0.05% • 0.02% with less than 2 years experience
- △ Compulsory Compulsory
- Recommended Compulsory 18
- Only allowed with hands-free kit
- Must be used at all times all year round
- Winter tyres compulsory for vehicles up to 3.5 tonnes Dec–Feb, but illegal May–Sept
- ★ On-the-spot fines imposed ★ Pedestrians have priority ★ Radar-detection equipment prohibited ★ Visibility vests compulsory

Lithuania Lietuva (LT)

Area 65,200 sq km (25,173 sq miles)
Population 2,822,000 **Capital** Vilnius (805,000)
Languages Lithuanian (official), Russian, Polish
Currency Euro = 100 cents
Website http://lrvk.lrv.lt/en

130	110	70–90	50
If towing			
n/a	70	70	50
If licence held for less than two years			
130	90	70	50

In winter speed limits are reduced by 10–20 km/h

- Compulsory
- Under 12 or below 135 cm not allowed in front seats unless in a child safety seat; under 3 must use appropriate child seat and sit in rear
- 0.04% • 0.00% if full licence held less than 2 years
- △ Compulsory Compulsory
- Recommended Compulsory 18
- Licences without a photograph must be accompanied by photographic proof of identity
- Only allowed with a hands-free kit
- Must be used at all times
- Winter tyres compulsory 10 Nov–1 Apr
- ★ On-the-spot fines imposed
- ★ Visibility vest compulsory

Luxembourg (L)

Area 2,586 sq km (998 sq miles)
Population 576,000 **Capital** Luxembourg (107,000)
Languages Luxembourgian / Letzeburgish (official), French, German **Currency** Euro = 100 cents
Website www.luxembourg.public.lu/en/

130/110	90	90	50*
If towing			
90	75	75	50*

If full driving licence held for less than two years, must not exceed 75 kph • *30 kph zones are progressively being introduced.

🚗 Compulsory

👶 Children under 3 must use an appropriate restraint system. Airbags must be disabled if a rear-facing child seat is used in the front. Children 3–18 and/or under 150 cm must use a restraint system appropriate to their size. If over 36kg a seatbelt may be used in the back only

🍷 0.05%, 0.02 for young drivers, drivers with less than 2 years experience and drivers of taxis and commercial vehicles

△ Compulsory ⊞ Compulsory (buses)

💡 Compulsory ⊖ 18

🧯 Compulsory (buses, transport of dangerous goods)

📱 Use permitted only with hands-free kit

🔦 Compulsory for motorcyclists and in poor visibility for other vehicles

❄ Winter tyres compulsory in winter weather

★ On-the-spot fines ★ Visibility vest compulsory

Macedonia Makedonija (MK)

Area 25,713 sq km (9,927 sq miles)
Population 2,074,000 **Capital** Skopje (507,000)
Languages Macedonian (official), Albanian
Currency Denar = 100 deni **Website**

	🛣	▲▲	▲	🏙
⊙	120	100	80	50
Newly qualified drivers or if towing				
⊙	100	80	60	50

🚗 Compulsory

👶 Under 12 not allowed in front seats

🍷 0.05% • 0.00% for business, commercial and professional drivers and with less than 2 years experience

△ Compulsory ⊞ Compulsory

💡 Compulsory ⊖ 18 (mopeds 16)

🧯 Recommended; compulsory for LPG vehicles

🪪 International driving permit; visa

📱 Use not permitted whilst driving

🔦 Compulsory at all times

❄ Winter tyres or snow chains compulsory 15 Nov–15 Mar. Max speed 70 kph

★ GPS must have fixed speed camera function deactivated; radar detectors prohibited ★ Novice drivers may only drive between 11pm and 5am if there is someone over 25 with a valid licence in the vehicle. ★ On-the-spot fines ★ Tolls apply on many roads ★ Tow rope compulsory ★ Visibility vest must be kept in the passenger compartment and worn to leave the vehicle in the dark outside built-up areas

Moldova (MD)

Area 33,851 sq km (13,069 sq miles)
Population 299,000 **Capital** Chisinau (736,000)
Languages Moldovan / Romanian (official)
Currency Leu = 100 bani
Website www.moldova.md

	🛣	▲▲	▲	🏙
⊙	90	90	90	60
If towing or if licence held under 1 year				
⊙	70	70	70	60

🚗 Compulsory in front seats and, if fitted, in rear

👶 Under 12 not allowed in front seats

🍷 0.00% △ Compulsory ⊞ Compulsory

💡 Recommended 🧯 Compulsory

⊖ 18 (mopeds and motorbikes, 16; vehicles with more than eight passenger places, taxis or towing heavy vehicles, 21)

🪪 International Driving Permit (preferred), visa

📱 Only allowed with hands-free kit

🔦 Must use dipped headlights at all times

❄ Winter tyres recommended Nov–Feb

Montenegro Crna Gora (MNE)

Area 14,026 sq km, (5,415 sq miles)
Population 679,000 **Capital** Podgorica (187,000)
Languages Serbian (of the Ijekavian dialect)
Currency Euro = 100 cents
Website www.gov.me/en/homepage

	🛣	▲▲	▲	🏙
⊙	n/a	100	80	50

80kph speed limit if towing a caravan

🚗 Compulsory in front and rear seats

👶 Under 12 not allowed in front seats. Under-5s must use an appropriate child seat.

🍷 0.03 % △ Compulsory ⊞ Compulsory

💡 Compulsory 🧯 Compulsory

⊖ 18 (16 for motorbikes less than 125cc; 14 for mopeds)

📱 Prohibited

🔦 Must be used at all times

❄ From mid-Nov to March, driving wheels must be fitted with winter tyres ★ An 'eco' tax vignette must be obtained when crossing the border and displayed in the upper right-hand corner of the windscreen ★ On-the-spot fines imposed ★ Tolls on some primary roads and in the Sozina tunnel between Lake Skadar and the sea ★ Visibility vest compulsory

Netherlands Nederland (NL)

Area 41,526 sq km (16,033 sq miles)
Population 17,000,000 **Capital** Amsterdam 2,431,000 • administrative capital 's-Gravenhage (The Hague) 1,051,000 **Languages** Dutch (official), Frisian **Currency** Euro = 100 cents
Website www.government.nl

	🛣	▲▲	▲	🏙
⊙	130	80/100	80/100	50

🚗 Compulsory

👶 Under 3 must travel in the back, using an appropriate child restraint; 3–18 and under 135cm must use an appropriate child restraint. A rear-facing child seat may be used in front only if airbags are deactivated.

🍷 0.05% • 0.02% with less than 5 years experience or moped riders under 24

△ Compulsory ⊞ Recommended

💡 Recommended 🧯 Recommended ⊖ 18

📱 Only allowed with a hands-free kit

LEZ About 20 cities operate or are planning LEZs.

🔦 Recommended in poor visibility and on open roads. Compulsory for motorcycles.

★ On-the-spot fines imposed ★ Radar-detection equipment is prohibited

Norway Norge (N)

Area 323,877 sq km (125,049 sq miles)
Population 5,267,000 **Capital** Oslo (1,718,000)
Languages Norwegian (official), Lappish, Finnish
Currency Krone = 100 øre
Website www.norway.no/en/uk

	🛣	▲▲	▲	🏙
⊙	90–100	80	80	30/50
If towing trailer with brakes				
⊙	80	80	80	50
If towing trailer without brakes				
⊙	60	60	60	50

🚗 Compulsory in front seats and, if fitted, in rear

👶 Children less than 150cm tall must use appropriate child restraint. Children under 4 must use child safety seat or safety restraint (cot). A rear-facing child seat may be used in front only if airbags are deactivated.

🍷 0.01% △ Compulsory ⊞ Recommended

💡 Recommended 🧯 Recommended

⊖ 18 (heavy vehicles 18/21)

📱 Only allowed with a hands-free kit

LEZ Oslo and Bergen (administered through national road-toll scheme), with plans for other cities

🔦 Must be used at all times

❄ Winter tyres or summer tyres with snow chains compulsory for snow- or ice-covered roads

★ On-the-spot fines ★ Radar-detectors prohibited ★ Tolls apply on some bridges, tunnels and access roads into Bergen, Oslo, Trondheim and Stavangar. Several use electronic fee collection only. ★ Visibility vest compulsory

Poland Polska (PL)

Area 323,250 sq km (124,807 sq miles)
Population 38,634,000 **Capital** Warsaw / Warszawa (3,106,000) **Languages** Polish (official)
Currency Zloty = 100 groszy
Website www.premier.gov.pl/en.html

	🛣	▲▲	▲	🏙
Motor-vehicle only roads[1], under/over 3.5 tonnes				
⊙	130[2]/80[2]	110/80	100/80	n/a
Motor-vehicle only roads[1] if towing				
⊙	n/a	80	80	n/a
Other roads, under 3.5 tonnes				
⊙	n/a	100	90	50/60[3]
Other roads, 3.5 tonnes or over				
⊙	n/a	80	70	50/60[3]
Other roads, if towing				
⊙	n/a	60	60	30

[1]Indicated by signs with white car on blue background • [2]Minimum speed 40 kph • [3]50 kph 05.00–23.00; 60 kph 23.00–05.00; 20 kph in marked residential areas

🚗 Compulsory in front seats and, if fitted, in rear

👶 Under 12 and below 150 cm must use an appropriate child restraint. Rear-facing child seats not permitted in vehicles with airbags.

🍷 0.02% △ Compulsory ⊞ Recommended

💡 Recommended 🧯 Compulsory

⊖ 18 (mopeds and motorbikes under 125cc – 16)

📱 Only allowed with a hands-free kit

🔦 Compulsory for all vehicles

❄ Snow chains permitted only on roads completely covered in snow

★ On-the-spot fines imposed ★ Radar-detection equipment is prohibited ★ Vehicles over 3.5 tonnes (including cars towing caravans) must have a VIAbox for the electronic toll system ★ Visibility vests compulsory

Portugal (P)

Area 88,797 sq km (34,284 sq miles)
Population 10,310,000 **Capital** Lisbon / Lisboa (2,822,000) **Languages** Portuguese (official)
Currency Euro = 100 cents
Website www.portugal.gov.pt/en.aspx

	🛣	▲▲	▲	🏙
⊙	120*	90/100	90	50/20
If towing				
⊙	100*	90	80	50

*50kph minimum; 90kph maximum if licence held under 1 year

🚗 Compulsory in front seats and, if fitted, in rear

👶 Under 12 and below 135cm must travel in the rear in an appropriate child restraint; rear-facing child seats permitted in front for under 3s only if airbags deactivated

🍷 0.049%. 0.019% if full licence held less than 3 years

△ Compulsory ⊞ Recommended

💡 Recommended 🧯 Recommended ⊖ 17

🪪 MOT certificate for vehicles over 3 years old, photographic proof of identity must be carried at all times.

📱 Only allowed with hands-free kit

LEZ An LEZ prohibits vehicles without catalytic converters from certain parts of Lisbon. There are plans to extend the scheme city-wide

🔦 Compulsory for motorcycles, compulsory for other vehicles in poor visibility and tunnels

★ On-the-spot fines imposed ★ Radar detectors and dash-cams prohibited ★ Tolls on motorways; do not use green lanes, these are reserved for auto-payment users. Some motorways require an automatic toll device. ★ Visibility vest compulsory ★ Wearers of spectacles or contact lenses should carry a spare pair

Romania (RO)

Area 238,391 sq km (92,042 sq miles) **Population** 19,511,000 **Capital** Bucharest / Bucuresti (2,403,000) **Languages** Romanian (official), Hungarian **Currency** Romanian leu = 100 bani
Website www.gov.ro

	🛣	▲▲	▲	🏙
Cars and motorcycles				
⊙	120/130	100	90	50
Vans				
⊙	110	90	80	40
Motorcycles				
⊙	100	80	80	50

For motor vehicles with trailers or if full driving licence has been held for less than one year, speed limits are 20kph lower than those listed above •Jeep-like vehicles: 70kph outside built-up areas but 60kph in all areas if diesel. For mopeds, the speed limit is 45 kph.

🚗 Compulsory

👶 Under 12s not allowed in front and must use an appropriate restraint in the rear

🍷 0.00% △ Compulsory ⊞ Compulsory

💡 Compulsory 🧯 Compulsory ⊖ 18

📱 Only allowed with hands-free kit

🔦 Compulsory outside built-up areas, compulsory everywhere for motorcycles

❄ Winter tyres compulsory Nov–Mar if roads are snow- or ice-covered, especially in mountainous areas

★ Compulsory road tax can be paid for at the border, post offices and some petrol stations. Price depends on emissions category and length of stay ★ It is illegal for vehicles to be dirty ★ On-the-spot fines imposed ★ Visibility vest compulsory

Russia Rossiya (RUS)

Area 17,075,000 sq km (6,592,800 sq miles) **Population** 144,463,000 **Capital** Moscow / Moskva (17,100,000) **Languages** Russian (official), and many others **Currency** Russian ruble = 100 kopeks **Website** government.ru/en/

	🛣	▲▲	▲	🏙
⊙	110	90	90	60/20
If licence held for under 2 years				
⊙	70	70	70	60/20

🚗 Compulsory if fitted

👶 Under 12s permitted only in an appropriate child restraint

🍷 0.03 % △ Compulsory ⊞ Compulsory

💡 Compulsory 🧯 Compulsory ⊖ 17

🪪 International Driving Permit with Russian translation, visa, green card endorsed for Russia, International Certificate for Motor Vehicles

📱 Only allowed with a hands-free kit

🔦 Compulsory during the day

❄ Winter tyres compulsory 1 Dec–1 Mar

★ On-the-spot fines imposed ★ Picking up hitch-hikers is prohibited ★ Radar detectors/blockers prohibited ★ Road tax payable at the border

Serbia Srbija (SRB)

Area 77,474 sq km, 29,913 sq miles
Population 7,058,000 **Capital** Belgrade / Beograd (1,167,000) **Languages** Serbian **Currency** Dinar = 100 paras **Website** www.srbija.gov.rs

	🛣	▲▲	▲	🏙
⊙	120	100	80	60
If towing				
⊙	80	80	80	60

Novice drivers limited to 90% of speed limit and not permitted to drive 11pm–5am.

🚗 Compulsory in front and rear seats

👶 Age 3–12 must be in rear seats and wear seat belt or appropriate child restraint; under 3 in rear-facing child seat permitted in front only if airbag deactivated

🍷 0.029% • 0.0% for motorcyclists, commercial drivers, or if full licence held less than 1 year

△ Compulsory ⊞ Compulsory

💡 Compulsory 🧯 Compulsory

⊖ 18 (motorbikes under 125cc – 16; mopeds –14)

🪪 International Driving Permit, green card or locally bought third-party insurance

🔦 Compulsory

❄ Winter tyres compulsory Nov–Apr for vehicles up to 3.5 tonnes. Carrying snow chains recommended in winter as these may have to be fitte if driving on snow-covered roads, in accordanc with signage.

★ 3-metre tow bar or rope ★ Spare wheel compulsory ★ On-the-spot fines ★ Radar detecto prohibited ★ Tolls on motorways and some primary roads ★ Visibility vest compulsory

Slovakia Slovenska Republika (SK)

Area 49,012 sq km (18,923 sq miles) **Population** 5,435,000 **Capital** Bratislava (660,000) **Languages** Slovak (official), Hungarian **Currency** Euro = 100 cents **Website** www.vlada.gov.sk

	🛣	▲▲	▲	🏙
⊙	130/90	90	90	50

🚗 Compulsory

👶 Under 12 or below 150cm must be in rear in appropriate child restraint

🍷 0.0% △ Compulsory ⊞ Compulsory

💡 Compulsory 🧯 Recommended

⊖ 18, 17 for motorbikes over 50cc, 15 for mopeds

🪪 International driving permit, proof of health insurance

📱 Only allowed with a hands-free kit

🔦 Compulsory at all times

❄ Winter tyres compulsory

★ On-the-spot fines imposed ★ Radar-detectio equipment is prohibited ★ Tow rope recommended ★ Vignette required for motorways, car valid for 1 year, 30 days, 7 days; lorry vignettes carry a higher charge. ★ Visibility vests compulsory

Slovenia Slovenija (SLO)

Area 20,256 sq km (7,820 sq miles)
Population 2,066,000 **Capital** Ljubljana (280,000)
Languages Slovene **Currency** Euro = 100 cents
Website www.vlada.si/en

	🛣	▲▲	▲	🏙
⊙	130	110[1]	90[1]	50[2]
If towing				
⊙	80	80[1]	80[1]	50[2]

[1] 70 kph in urban areas, [2] 30 kph zones are increasingly common in cities

🚗 Compulsory

👶 Below 150cm must use appropriate child restraint. A rear-facing baby seat may be used i front only if airbags are deactivated.

🍷 0.05% • 0.0% for commercial drivers, under 21s c with less than one year with a full licence

△ Compulsory ⊞ Compulsory

💡 Compulsory 🧯 Recommended

⊖ 18 (motorbikes up to 125cc – 16

🪪 Licences without photographs must be accompanied by an International Driving Perm

📱 Only allowed with hands-free kit

🔦 Must be used at all times

❄ Snow chains or winter tyres compulsory mid-Nov to mid-March, and in wintery conditions at other times. Max speed 50 kph. This limit also applies if visibility is below 50m.

★ On-the-spot fines imposed ★ Radar detectors prohibited ★ Vignettes valid for variety of periods compulsory for vehicles below 3.5 tonnes for toll roads. Write your vehicle registration number on the vignette before displaying it. For heavier vehicles electronic tol ing system applies; several routes are cargo-traffic free during high tourist season. ★ Visibility vest compulsory

Spain España Ⓔ

Area 497,548 sq km (192,103 sq miles) **Population** 46,468,000 **Capital** Madrid (6,530,000) **Languages** Castilian Spanish (official), Catalan, Galician, Basque **Currency** Euro = 100 cents **Website** www.lamoncloa.gob.es/lang/en/Paginas/index.aspx

	🛣	⩓	▲	🏙
⏲	120*	100*	90	50*
If towing				
⏲	80	80	70	50*

Urban motorways and dual carriageways 80 kph. 20 kph zones are being introduced in many cities

- 🔗 Compulsory
- 👶 Under 135cm and below 12 must use appropriate child restraint
- 🍷 0.049% • 0.029% if less than 2 years full licence or if vehicle is over 3.5 tonnes or carries more than 9 passengers
- △ Two compulsory (for in front and behind)
- ⊞ Recommended 🧯 Compulsory
- 💡 Recommended
- ⊖ 18 (heavy vehicles – 21; motorbikes up to 125cc – 16)
- 📱 Hands-free only
- 🔦 Compulsory for motorcycles and in poor daytime visibility for other vehicles.
- ❄ Snow chains recommended for mountainous areas in winter
- ★ Drivers who wear spectacles or contact lenses must carry a spare pair. ★ On-the-spot fines imposed ★ Radar-detection equipment is prohibited ★ Spare wheel compulsory ★ Tolls on motorways ★ Visibility vest compulsory

Sweden Sverige Ⓢ

Area 449,964 sq km (173,731 sq miles) **Population** 10,053,000 **Capital** Stockholm (2,227,000) **Languages** Swedish (official), Finnish **Currency** Swedish krona = 100 ore **Website** www.sweden.gov.se

	🛣	⩓	▲	🏙
⏲	90–120	80	70–100	30–60
If towing trailer with brakes				
⏲	80	80	70	50

- 🔗 Compulsory in front and rear seats
- 👶 Under 15 or below 135cm must use an appropriate child restraint and may sit in the front only if airbag is deactivated; rear-facing baby seat permitted in front only if airbag deactivated.
- 🍷 0.019% △ Compulsory ⊞ Recommended
- 🧯 Recommended 💡 Recommended ⊖ 18
- 📄 Licences without a photograph must be accompanied by photographic proof of identity, e.g. a passport
- LEZ Gothenberg, Helsingborg, Lund, Malmo, Mölndal and Stockholm have LEZs, progressively prohibiting older vehicles.
- 🔦 Must be used at all times
- ❄ 1 Dec–31 Mar winter tyres, anti-freeze, screenwash additive and shovel compulsory
- ★ On-the-spot fines imposed ★ Radar-detection equipment is prohibited

Switzerland Schweiz Ⓒⓗ

Area 41,284 sq km (15,939 sq miles) **Population** 8,401,000 **Capital** Bern (407,000) **Languages** French, German, Italian, Romansch (all official) **Currency** Swiss Franc = 100 centimes / rappen **Website** www.admin.ch

	🛣	⩓	▲	🏙
⏲	120	80	80	30/50
If towing up to 1 tonne / over 1 tonne				
⏲	80	80	60/80	30/50

- 🔗 Compulsory
- 👶 Up to 12 years or below 150 cm must use an appropriate child restraint. Children 6 and under must sit in the rear.
- 🍷 0.05%, but 0.0% for commercial drivers or with less than three years with a full licence
- △ Compulsory ⊞ Recommended
- 🧯 Recommended 💡 Recommended
- ⊖ 18 (mopeds up to 50cc – 16)
- 📱 Only allowed with a hands-free kit
- 🔦 Compulsory
- ❄ Winter tyres recommended Nov–Mar; snow chains compulsory in designated areas in poor winter weather
- ★ GPS must have fixed speed camera function deactivated; radar detectors prohibited ★ Motorways are all toll and for vehicles below 3.5 tonnes a vignette must be purchased at the border. The vignette is valid for one calendar year. Vehicles over 3.5 tonnes must have an electronic tag for travel on any road. ★ On-the-spot fines imposed ★ Pedestrians have right of way ★ Picking up hitchhikers is prohibited on motorways and main roads ★ Spectacles or contact lens wearers must carry a spare pair in their vehicle at all times

Turkey Türkiye Ⓣⓡ

Area 774,815 sq km (299,156 sq miles) **Population** 79,815,000 **Capital** Ankara (5,271,000) **Languages** Turkish (official), Kurdish **Currency** New Turkish lira = 100 kurus **Website** www.mfa.gov.tr/default.en.mfa

	🛣	⩓	▲	🏙
⏲	120	90	90	50
If towing				
⏲	80	80	80	40
Motorbikes				
⏲	80	70	70	50

- 🔗 Compulsory if fitted
- 👶 Under 150 cm and below 36kg must use suitable child restraint. Under 3s can only travel in the front in a rear facing seat if the airbag is deactivated. Children 3–12 may not travel in the front seat.
- 🍷 0.00% ⊞ Compulsory 🧯 Compulsory
- △ Two compulsory (one in front, one behind)
- 💡 Compulsory ⊖ 18
- 📄 International driving permit advised, and required for use with licences without photographs; note that Turkey is in both Europe and Asia, green card/UK insurance that covers whole of Turkey or locally bought insurance, e-visa obtained in advance.
- 📱 Prohibited
- 🔦 Compulsory in daylight hours
- ★ Spare wheel compulsory ★ On-the-spot fines imposed ★ Several motorways, and the Bosphorus bridges are toll roads ★ Tow rope and tool kit must be carried

Ukraine Ukraina Ⓤⓐ

Area 603,700 sq km (233,088 sq miles) **Population** 42,542,000 **Capital** Kiev / Kyviv (3,375,000) **Languages** Ukrainian (official), Russian **Currency** Hryvnia = 100 kopiykas **Website** www.kmu.gov.ua/control/en

	🛣	⩓	▲	🏙
⏲	130	110	90	60
If towing				
⏲	80	80	80	60

If driving licence held less than 2 years, must not exceed 70 kph

- 🔗 Compulsory in front and rear seats
- 👶 Under 12 and below 145cm must use an appropriate child restraint and sit in rear
- 🍷 0.02% – if use of medication can be proved. Otherwise 0.00%
- △ Compulsory ⊞ Compulsory
- 🧯 Optional 💡 Compulsory ⊖ 18
- 📄 International Driving Permit, visa, International Certificate for Motor Vehicles, green card
- 📱 No legislation
- 🔦 Compulsory in poor daytime and from Oct–Apr
- ❄ Winter tyres compulsory Nov–Apr in snowy conditions
- ★ A road tax is payable on entry to the country. ★ On-the-spot fines imposed ★ Tow rope and tool kit recommended

United Kingdom Ⓖⓑ

Area 241,857 sq km (93,381 sq miles) **Population** 65,648,000 **Capital** London (13,880,000) **Languages** English (official), Welsh (also official in Wales), Gaelic **Currency** Sterling (pound) = 100 pence **Website** www.direct.gov.uk

	🛣	⩓	▲	🏙
⏲	112	112	96	48
If towing				
⏲	96	96	80	48

Several cities have introduced 32 kph (20 mph) zones away from main roads

- 🔗 Compulsory in front seats and if fitted in rear
- 👶 Under 3 not allowed in front seats except with appropriate restraint, and in rear must use child restraint if available; in front 3–12 or under 135cm must use appropriate child restraint, in rear must use appropriate child restraint (or seat belt if no child restraint is available, e.g. because two occupied restraints prevent fitting of a third).
- 🍷 0.08% (England, Northern Ireland, Wales) • 0.05% (Scotland)
- △ Recommended ⊞ Recommended
- 🧯 Recommended 💡 Recommended
- ⊖ 17 (16 for mopeds)
- 📱 Only allowed with hands-free kit
- LEZ London's LEZ operates by number-plate recognition; non-compliant vehicles face hefty daily charges. Foreign-registered vehicles must register.
- ★ Driving is on the left ★ On-the-spot fines imposed ★ Smoking banned in all commercial vehicles ★ Some toll motorways, bridges and tunnels

Ski resorts

The resorts listed are popular ski centres, therefore road access to most is normally good and supported by road clearing during snow falls. However, mountain driving is never predictable and drivers should make sure they take suitable snow chains as well as emergency provisions and clothing. Listed for each resort are: the atlas page and grid square; the resort/minimum piste altitude (where only one figure is shown, they are at the same height) and maximum altitude of its own lifts; the number of lifts and gondolas (the total for lift-linked resorts); the season start and end dates (snow cover allowing); whether snow is augmented by cannon; the nearest town (with its distance in km) and, where available, the website and/or telephone number of the local tourist information centre or ski centre ('00' prefix required for calls from the UK).

The ❄ symbol indicates resorts with snow cannon

Andorra

Pyrenees

Pas de la Casa / Grau Roig 146 B2 ❄ 2050–2640m • 31 lifts • Dec–Apr • Andorra La Vella (30km) 💻www.pasdelacasa.com • *Access via Envalira Pass (2407m), highest in Pyrenees, snow chains essential.*

Austria

Alps

Bad Gastein 109 B4 ❄ 1050/1100–2700m • 50 lifts • Dec–Mar • St Johann im Pongau (45km) ✆+43 6432 3393 0 💻www.gastein.com

Bad Hofgastein 109 B4 ❄ 860–2295m • 50 lifts • Dec–Mar • St Johann im Pongau (40km) ✆+43 6432 3393 0 💻www.gastein.com/en/region-villages/bad-hofgastein

Bad Kleinkirchheim 109 C4 ❄ 1070–2310m • 27 lifts • Dec–Mar • Villach (35km) ✆+43 4240 8212 💻www.badkleinkirchheim.at

Ehrwald 108 B1 ❄ 1000–2965m • 24 lifts • Dec–Apr • Imst (30km) ✆+43 5673 2501 💻www.wetterstein-bahnen.at/en

Innsbruck 108 B2 ❄ 574/850–3200m • 59 lifts • Dec–Apr • Innsbruck ✆+ 43 512 56 2000 💻www.innsbruck.info/en/ • *Motorway normally clear. The motorway through to Italy and through the Arlberg Tunnel are both toll roads.*

Ischgl 107 B5 ❄ 1340/1400–2900m • 101 lifts • Dec–May • Landeck (25km) ✆+43 50990 100 💻www.ischgl.com • *Car entry to resort prohibited between 2200hrs and 0600hrs.*

Kaprun 109 B3 ❄ 885/770–3030m, • 25 lifts • Nov–Apr • Zell am See (10km) ✆+43 6542 770 💻www.zellamsee-kaprun.com

Kirchberg in Tirol 109 B3 ❄ 860–2000m • 197 lifts • Nov–Apr • Kitzbühel (6km) ✆+43 57507 2100 💻www.kitzbueheler-alpen.com/en • *Easily reached from Munich International Airport (120 km)*

Kitzbühel (Brixen im Thale) 109 B3 ❄ 800/790–2000m • 197 lifts • Dec–Apr • Wörgl (40km) ✆+43 57057 2000 💻www.kitzbueheler-alpen.com/en

Lech/Oberlech 107 B5 ❄ 1450–2810m • 87 lifts • Dec–Apr • Bludenz (50km) ✆+43 5583 2161 0 💻www.lechzuers.com • *Roads normally cleared but keep chains accessible because of altitude. Linked to the other Arlberg resorts.*

Mayrhofen 108 B2 ❄ 630–2500m • 57 lifts • Dec–Apr • Jenbach (35km) ✆+43 5285 6760 💻www.mayrhofen.at • *Chains rarely required.*

Obertauern 109 B4 ❄ 1740/1640–2350m • 26 lifts • Dec–Apr • Radstadt (20km) ✆+43 6456 7252 💻www.obertauern.com • *Roads normally cleared but chain accessibility recommended. Camper vans and caravans not allowed; park these in Radstadt*

Saalbach Hinterglemm 109 B3 ❄ 1000/1030–2100m • 52 lifts • Nov–Apr • Zell am See (19km) ✆+43 6541 6800-68 💻www.saalbach.com • *Both village centres are pedestrianised and there is a good ski bus service during the daytime*

St Anton am Arlberg 107 B5 ❄ 1300–2810m • 87 lifts • Dec–Apr • Innsbruck (104km) ✆+43 5446 22690 💻www.stantonamarlberg.com • *Linked to the other Arlberg resorts.*

Schladming 109 B4 ❄ 745–1900m • 45 lifts • Dec–Mar • Schladming ✆+ 43 36 87 233 10 💻www.schladming-dachstein.at

Serfaus 108 B1 ❄ 1427/1200–2820m • 68 lifts • Dec–Apr • Landeck (30km) ✆+43 5476 6239 💻www.serfaus-fiss-ladis.at • *Private vehicles banned from village. Use Dorfbahn Serfaus, an underground funicular that runs on an air cushion.*

Sölden 108 C2 ❄ 1380–3250m, • 33 lifts • Oct–Apr • Imst (50km) ✆+43 57200 200 💻www.soelden.com • *Roads normally cleared but snow chains recommended because of altitude. The route from Italy and the south over the Timmelsjoch via Obergurgl is closed Oct–May and anyone arriving from the south should use the Brenner Pass motorway.*

Zell am See 109 B3 ❄ 750–1950m • 53 lifts • Dec–Mar • Zell am See ✆+43 6542 770 💻www.zellamsee-kaprun.com • *Low altitude, so good access and no mountain passes to cross.*

Zell im Zillertal (Zell am Ziller) 109 B3 ❄ 580/930–2410m • 22 lifts • Dec–Apr • Jenbach (25km) ✆+43 5282 7165–226 💻www.zillertalarena.com

Zürs 107 B5 ❄ 1720/1700–2450m • 87 lifts • Dec–Apr • Bludenz (30km) ✆+43 5583 2245 💻www.lechzuers.com • *Roads normally cleared but keep chains accessible because of altitude. Village has garage with 24-hour self-service gas/petrol, breakdown service and wheel chains supply. Linked to the other Arlberg resorts.*

France

Alps

Alpe d'Huez 118 B3 ❄ 1860–3330m • 85 lifts • Dec–Apr • Grenoble (63km) 💻www.alpedhuez.com • *Snow chains may be required on access road to resort.*

Avoriaz 118 A3 ❄ 1800/1100–2280m • 35 lifts • Dec–May • Morzine (14km) ✆+33 4 50 74 02 11 💻www.avoriaz.com/en • *Chains may be required for access road from Morzine. Car-free resort, park on edge of village.*

Chamonix-Mont-Blanc 119 B3 ❄ 1035–3840m • 49 lifts • Dec–Apr • Martigny (38km) ✆+33 4 50 53 99 98 💻www.chamonix.com

Chamrousse 118 B2 ❄ 1700/1420–2250m • 26 lifts • Dec–Apr • Grenoble (30km) 💻www.chamrousse.com • *Roads normally cleared, keep chains accessible because of altitude.*

Châtel 119 A3 ❄ 1200/1110–2200m • 41 lifts • Dec–Apr • Thonon-Les-Bains (35km) ✆+33 4 50 73 22 44 💻www.chatel.com

Courchevel 118 B3 ❄ 1300–2470m • 67 lifts • Dec–Apr • Moûtiers (23km) 💻www.courchevel.com • *Roads normally cleared but keep chains accessible. Traffic 'discouraged' within the four resort bases.*

Flaine 118 A3 ❄ 1600–2500m • 26 lifts • Dec–Apr • Cluses (25km) ✆+33 4 50 90 80 01 💻www.flaine.com • *Keep chains accessible for D6 from Cluses to Flaine. Car access for depositing luggage and passengers only. 1500-space car park outside resort. Near Sixt-Fer-á-Cheval.*

La Clusaz 118 B3 ❄ 1100–2600m • 55 lifts • Dec–Apr • Annecy (32km) 💻www.laclusaz.com • *Roads normally clear but keep chains accessible for final road from Annecy.*

La Plagne 118 B3 ❄ 2500/1250–3250m • 109 lifts • Dec–Apr Moûtiers (32km) 💻www.la-plagne.com • *Ten different centres up to 2100m altitude. Road access via Bozel, Landry or Aime normally cleared. Linked to Les Arcs by cablecar*

Les Arcs 119 B3 ❄ 1600/1200–3230m • 77 lifts • Dec–May • Bourg-St-Maurice (15km) ✆+33 4 79 07 12 57 💻www.lesarcs.com • *Four base areas up to 2000 metres; keep chains accessible. Pay parking at edge of each base resort. Linked to La Plagne by cablecar*

Les Carroz d'Araches 118 A3 ❄ 1140–2500m • 69 lifts • Dec–Apr • Cluses (13km) 💻http://winter.lescarroz.com

Les Deux-Alpes 118 C3 ❄ 1650/1300–3600m • 55 lifts • Dec–Apr • Grenoble (75km) ✆+33 4 76 79 22 00 💻www.les2alpes.com/en • *Roads normally cleared, however snow chains recommended for D213 up from valley road (D1091).*

Les Gets 118 A3 ❄ 1170/1000–2000m • 52 lifts • Dec–Apr • Cluses (18km) ✆+33 4 50 74 74 74 💻www.lesgets.com

Les Ménuires 118 B3 ❄ 1815/1850–3200m • 40 lifts • Dec–Apr • Moûtiers (27km) 💻www.lesmenuires.com • *Keep chains accessible for D117 from Moûtiers.*

Les Sept Laux Prapoutel 118 B3 ❄ 1350–2400m, • 24 lifts • Dec–Apr • Grenoble (38km) 💻www.les7laux.com (in French only) • *Roads normally cleared, however keep chains accessible for mountain road up from the A41 motorway. Near St Sorlin d'Arves.*

Megève 118 B3 1100/1050–2350m • 79 lifts • Dec–Apr • Sallanches (12km) www.megeve.com

Méribel 118 B3 1400/1100–2950m • 61 lifts • Dec–May • Moûtiers (18km) +33 4 79 08 60 01 www.meribel.net • *Keep chains accessible for 18km to resort on D90 from Moûtiers.*

Morzine 118 A3 1000–2460m • 67 lifts, • Dec–Apr • Thonon-Les-Bains (30km) +33 4 50 74 72 72 http://en.morzine-avoriaz.com

Pra Loup 132 A2 1500–2600m • 53 lifts • Dec–Apr • Barcelonnette (10km) www.praloup.com • *Roads normally cleared but chains accessibility recommended.*

Risoul 118 C3 1850/1650–2750m • 59 lifts • Dec–Apr • Briançon (40km) +33 4 92 46 02 60 www.risoul.com • *Keep chains accessible. Near Guillestre. Linked with Vars Les Claux*

St-Gervais Mont-Blanc 118 B3 850/1150–2350m • 27 lifts • Dec–Apr • Sallanches (10km) +33 4 50 47 76 08 www.saintgervais.com/en

Serre Chevalier 118 C3 1350/1200–2800m • 77 lifts • Dec–Apr • Briançon (10km) + 33 4 92 24 98 98 www.serre-chevalier.com • *Made up of 13 small villages along the valley road, which is normally cleared.*

Tignes 119 B3 2100/1550–3450m • 87 lifts • Jan–Dec • Bourg St Maurice (26km) +33 4 79 40 04 40 www.tignes.net • *Keep chains accessible because of altitude. Linked to Val d'Isère.*

Val d'Isère 119 B3 1850/1550–3450m • 87 lifts • Dec–Apr • Bourg-St-Maurice (30km) +33 4 79 06 06 60 www.valdisere.com • *Roads normally cleared but keep chains accessible.*

Val Thorens 118 B3 2300/1850–3200m • 29 lifts • Dec–Apr • Moûtiers (37km) +33 4 79 00 08 08 www.valthorens.com • *Chains essential – highest ski resort in Europe. Obligatory paid parking on edge of resort.*

Valloire 118 B3 1430–2600m • 34 lifts • Dec–Apr • Modane (20km) +33 4 79 59 03 96 www.valloire.net • *Road normally clear up to the Col du Galbier, to the south of the resort, which is closed from 1st November to 1st June. Linked to Valmeinier.*

Valmeinier 118 B3 1500–2600m • 34 lifts • Dec–Apr • St Michel de Maurienne (47km) +33 4 79 59 53 69 www.valmeinier.com • *Access from north on D1006 / D902. Col du Galbier, to the south of the resort closed from 1st November to 1st June. Linked to Valloire.*

Valmorel 118 B3 1400–2550m • 90 lifts • Dec–Apr • Moûtiers (15km) www.valmorel.com • *Near St Jean-de-Belleville. Linked with ski areas of Doucy-Combelouvière and St François-Longchamp.*

Vars Les Claux 118 C3 1850/1650–2750m • 59 lifts • Dec–Apr • Briançon (40km) +33 4 92 46 51 31 www.vars.com/en/winter • *Four base resorts up to 1850 metres. Keep chains accessible. Linked with Risoul.*

Villard de Lans 118 B2 1050/1160–2170m • 28 lifts • Dec–Apr • Grenoble (32km) +33 4 76 95 10 38 www.villarddelans.com

Pyrenees

Font-Romeu 146 B3 1800/1600–2200m • 25 lifts • Nov–Apr • Perpignan (87km) www.font-romeu.fr • *Roads normally cleared but keep chains accessible.*

Saint-Lary Soulan 145 B4 830/1650/1700–2515m • 31 lifts • Dec–Mar • Tarbes (75km) +33 5 62 39 50 81 www.saintlary.com • *Access roads constantly cleared of snow.*

Vosges

La Bresse-Hohneck 106 A1 600–1370m • 33 lifts • Dec–Mar • Cornimont (6km) +33 3 29 25 41 29 www.labresse.net

Germany

Alps

Garmisch-Partenkirchen 108 B2 700–2830m • 38 lifts • Dec–Apr • Munich (95km) +49 8821 180 700 www.gapa.de • *Roads usually clear, chains rarely needed.*

Oberaudorf 108 B3 820/830–2200m • 30 lifts • Dec–Apr • Kufstein (15km) www.oberaudorf.de • *Motorway normally kept clear. Near Bayrischzell.*

Oberstdorf 107 B5 815m • 26 lifts • Dec–Apr • Sonthofen (15km) +49 8322 7000 www.oberstdorf.de/en

Rothaargebirge

Winterberg 81 A4 700/620–830m • 19 lifts • Dec–Mar • Brilon (30km) +49 2981 925 00 www.winterberg.de (German and Dutch only) • *Roads usually cleared, chains rarely required.*

Greece

Central Greece

Mount Parnassos: Kelaria-Fterolakka 182 E4 1640–2260m • 14 lifts • Dec–Apr • Amfiklia www.parnassos-ski.gr

Mount Parnassos: Gerondovrahos 182 E4 1800–1900m • 3 lifts • Dec–Apr • Amfiklia +30 29444 70371

Peloponnisos

Mount Helmos: Kalavrita Ski Centre 184 A3 1650–2100m • 7 lifts • Dec–Mar • Kalavrita +30 276920 24451-2 www.kalavrita-ski.gr (in Greek only)

Mount Menalo: Ostrakina 184 B3 1500–1600m • 4 lifts • Dec–Mar • Tripoli +30 27960 22227

Macedonia

Mount Falakro: Agio Pnevma 183 B6 1720/1620–2230m • 7 lifts • Dec–Apr • Drama + 30 25210 23691

Mount Vermio: Seli 182 C4 1500–1900m • 8 lifts • Dec–Mar • Kozani +30 23310 26237 www.seli-ski.gr (in Greek)

Mount Vermio: Tria-Pente Pigadia 182 C3 1420–2005m • 5 lifts • Dec–Mar • Ptolemaida +30 23320 44464

Mount Verno: Vigla 182 C3 1650–1900m • 5 lifts • Dec–Mar • Florina +30 23850 22354 www.vigla-ski.gr (in Greek)

Mount Vrondous: Lailias 183 B5 1600–1850m • 4 lifts • Dec–Mar • Serres +30 23210 53790

Thessalia

Mount Pilio: Agriolefkes 183 D5 1300–1500m • 5 lifts • Dec–Mar • Volos +30 24280 73719

Italy

Alps

Bardonecchia 118 B3 1312–2750m • 21 lifts • Dec–Apr • Bardonecchia www.bardonecchiaski.com • *Resort reached through the 11km Frejus tunnel from France, roads normally cleared.*

Bórmio 107 C5 1200/1230–3020m • 24 lifts • Dec–Apr • Tirano (40km) www.bormio.com • *Tolls payable in Ponte del Gallo Tunnel, open 0800hrs–2000hrs.*

Breuil-Cervinia 119 B4 2050–3500m • 21 lifts • Jan–Dec • Aosta (54km) +39 166 944311 www.cervinia.it • *Snow chains strongly recommended. Bus from Milan airport.*

Courmayeur 119 B3 1200–2760m • 21 lifts • Dec–Apr • Aosta (40km) www.courmayeurmontblanc.it • *Access through the Mont Blanc tunnel from France. Roads constantly cleared.*

Limone Piemonte 133 A3 1000/1050–2050m • 29 lifts • Dec–Apr • Cuneo (27km) www.limoneturismo.it • *Roads normally cleared, chains rarely required.*

Livigno 107 C5 1800–3000m • 31 lifts • Nov–May • Zernez (CH) (27km) www.livigno.com • *Keep chains accessible. The traffic direction through Munt la Schera Tunnel to/from Zernez is regulated on Saturdays. Check in advance.*

Sestrière 119 C3 2035/1840–2840m • 92 lifts • Dec–Apr • Oulx (22km) www.sestriere-online.com • *One of Europe's highest resorts; although roads are normally cleared keep chains accessible.*

Appennines

Roccaraso – Aremogna 169 B4 1285/1240–2140m • 24 lifts • Dec–Apr • Castel di Sangro (7km) www.roccarasoturismo.it (Italian only)

Dolomites

Andalo – Fai della Paganella 121 A3 1042/1050/2125m • 17 lifts • Dec–Apr • Trento (40km) www.visitdolomitipaganella.it +39 461 585836

Arabba 108 C2 1600/1450–2950m • 29 lifts • Dec–Mar • Brunico (45km) +39 436 79130 www.arabba.it • *Roads normally cleared but keep chains accessible.*

Cortina d'Ampezzo 108 C3 1224/1050–2930m • 37 lifts • Dec–Apr • Belluno (72km) +39 436 869086 www.dolomiti.org/it/cortina • *Access from north on route 51 over the Cimabanche Pass may require chains.*

Corvara (Alta Badia) 108 C2 1568–2500m • 56 lifts • Dec–Apr • Brunico (38km) www.altabadia.it • *Roads normally clear but keep chains accessible.*

Madonna di Campiglio 121 A3 1550/1500–2600m • 72 lifts • Dec–Apr • Trento (60km) +39 465 447501 www.campigliodolomiti.it/homepage • *Roads normally cleared but keep chains accessible. Linked to Folgarida and Marilleva.*

Moena di Fassa (Sorte/Ronchi) 108 C2 1184/1450–2520m • 8 lifts • Dec–Apr • Bolzano (40km) +39 462 609770 www.fassa.com

Selva di Val Gardena/Wolkenstein Groden 108 C2 1563/1570–2450m • 81 lifts • Dec–Apr • Bolzano (40km) +39 471 777777 www.valgardena.it • *Roads normally cleared but keep chains accessible.*

Norway

Hemsedal 47 B5 700/640–1450m • 24 lifts • Nov–May • Honefoss (150km) +47 32 055030 www.hemsedal.com • *Be prepared for extreme weather conditions.*

Slovakia

Chopok (Jasna-Chopok) 99 C3 900/950–1840m • 17 lifts • Dec–Apr • Jasna +421 907 886644 www.jasna.sk

Donovaly 99 C3 913–1360m • 17 lifts • Nov–Apr • Ruzomberok +421 48 4199900 www.paksnow.sk/zima/en

Martinské Hole 98 B2 1250/1150–1456m • 8 lifts • Nov–May • Zilina +421 43 430 6000 http://leto.martinky.com/sk (Slovak only)

Plejsy 99 C4 470–912m • 9 lifts • Dec–Mar • Krompachy +421 53 429 8015 www.plejsy.sk

Strbske Pleso 99 B4 1380–1825m • 7 lifts • Dec–Mar • Poprad +421 917 682 260 www.vt.sk

Slovenia

Julijske Alpe

Kanin (Bovec) 122 A2 460/1600–2389m • 5 lifts • Dec–Apr • Bovec www.boveckanin.si

Kranjska Gora 122 A2 460/1690–2293m • 19 lifts • Dec–Mar • Kranjska Gora +386 4 5809 440 www.kranjska-gora.si

Vogel 122 A2 570–1800m • 8 lifts • Dec–Apr • Bohinjska Bistrica +386 4 5729 712 www.vogel.si

Kawiniške Savinjske Alpe

Krvavec 122 A3 1450–1970m • 10 lifts • Dec–Apr • Kranj 386 4 25 25 911 www.rtc-krvavec.si

Pohorje

Rogla 123 A4 1517/1050–1500m • 13 lifts • Dec–Apr • Slovenska Bistrica +386 3 75 77 100 www.rogla.eu

Spain

Pyrenees

Baqueira-Beret/Bonaigua 145 B4 1500–2500m • 33 lifts • Dec–Apr • Vielha (15km) +34 902 415 415 www.baqueira.es • *Roads normally clear but keep chains accessible. Near Salardú.*

Sistema Penibetico

Sierra Nevada 163 A4 2100–3300m • 24 lifts • Dec–May • Granada (32km) +34 902 70 80 90 http://sierranevada.es • *Access road designed to be avalanche safe and is snow cleared.*

Sweden

Idre Fjäll 199 D9 590–890m • 33 lifts • Nov–Apr • Mora (140km) +46 253 41000 www.idrefjall.se • *Be prepared for extreme weather conditions.*

Sälen 49 A5 360m • 100 lifts • Nov–Apr • Malung (70km) +46 771 84 00 00 www.skistar.com/salen • *Be prepared for extreme weather conditions.*

Switzerland

Alps

Adelboden 106 C2 1353m • 94 lifts • Dec–Apr • Frutigen (15km) +41 33 673 80 80 www.adelboden.ch • *Linked with Lenk.*

Arosa 107 C4 1800/1740–2650m • 16 lifts • Dec–Apr • Chur (30km) +41 81 378 70 20 www.arosa.ch • *Roads cleared but keep chains accessible due to high altitude.*

Crans Montana 119 A4 1500–3000m • 34 lifts • Dec–Apr, Jul–Oct • Sierre (15km) +41 848 22 10 12 www.crans-montana.ch • *Roads normally cleared but keep chains accessible for ascent from Sierre.*

Davos 107 C4 1560/1100–2840m • 38 lifts • Nov–Apr • Davos. +41 81 415 21 21 www.davos.ch

Engelberg 106 C3 1000/1050–3020m • 26 lifts • Nov–May • Luzern (39km) +41 41 639 77 77 www.engelberg.ch • *Straight access road normally cleared.*

Flums (Flumserberg) 107 B4 1400/1000–2220m • 17 lifts • Dec–Apr • Buchs (25km) +41 81 720 18 18 www.flumserberg.ch • *Roads normally cleared, but 1000-metre vertical ascent; keep chains accessible.*

Grindelwald 106 C3 1050–2950m • 39 lifts • Dec–Apr • Interlaken (20km) +41 33 854 12 12 www.jungfrauregion.ch • *Linked with Wengen.*

Gstaad – Saanenland 106 C2 1050/950–3000m • 74 lifts • Dec–Apr • Gstaad +41 33 748 81 81 www.gstaad.ch • *Linked to Anzère.*

Klosters 107 C4 1191/1110–2840m • 52 lifts • Dec–Apr • Davos (10km). +41 81 410 20 20 www.davos.ch/klosters • *Roads normally clear but keep chains accessible.*

Leysin 119 A4 2260–2330m • 16 lifts • Dec–Apr • Aigle (6km) +41 24 493 33 00 www.leysin.ch

Mürren 106 C2 1650–2970m • 12 lifts • Dec–Apr • Interlaken (18km) +41 33 856 86 86 www.mymuerren.ch • *No road access. Park in Strechelberg (1500 free places) and take the two-stage cable car.*

Nendaz 119 A4 1365/1400–3300m • 20 lifts • Nov–Apr • Sion (16km) +41 27 289 55 89 www.nendaz.ch • *Roads normally cleared, however keep chains accessible for ascent from Sion. Near Vex.*

Saas-Fee 119 A4 1800–3500m • 23 lifts • Jan–Dec • Brig (35km) +41 27 958 18 58 www.saas-fee.ch/en/ • *Roads normally cleared but keep chains accessible because of altitude.*

St Moritz 107 C4 1856/1730–3300m • 24 lifts • Nov–May • Chur (89km) +41 81 837 33 33 www.stmoritz.ch • *Roads normally cleared but keep chains accessible.*

Samnaun 107 C5 1846/1400–2900m • 40 lifts • Dec–May • Scuol (30km) +41 81 861 88 30 www.engadin.com/ferienorte/engadin-samnaun • *Roads normally cleared but keep chains accessible.*

Verbier 119 A4 1500–3330m • 17 lifts • Nov–Apr • Martigny (27km) +41 27 775 38 38 www.verbier.ch • *Roads normally cleared.*

Villars-Gryon 119 A4 1253/1200–2100m • 16 lifts • Dec–Apr, Jun–Jul • Montreux (35km) +41 24 495 32 32 www.villars.ch • *Roads normally cleared but keep chains accessible for ascent from N9. Near Bex.*

Wengen 106 C2 1270–2320m • 39 lifts • Dec–Apr • Interlaken (12km) +41 33 856 85 85 http://wengen.ch • *No road access. Park at Lauterbrunnen and take mountain railway. Linked with Grindelwald.*

Zermatt 119 A4 1620–3900m • 40 lifts, • all year • Brig (42km) +41 27 966 81 00 www.zermatt.ch • *Cars not permitted in resort, park in Täsch (3km) and take shuttle train.*

Turkey

North Anatolian Mountains

Uludag 186 B4 1770–2320m • 15 lifts • Dec–Mar • Bursa (36km) +90 224 285 21 11 http://skiingturkey.com/resorts/uludag.html

To the best of the Publisher's knowledge the information in this table was correct at the time of going to press. No responsibility can be accepted for any errors or their consequences.

Skiing near Valmorel, France
Jacques Pierre / hemis.fr / Alamy

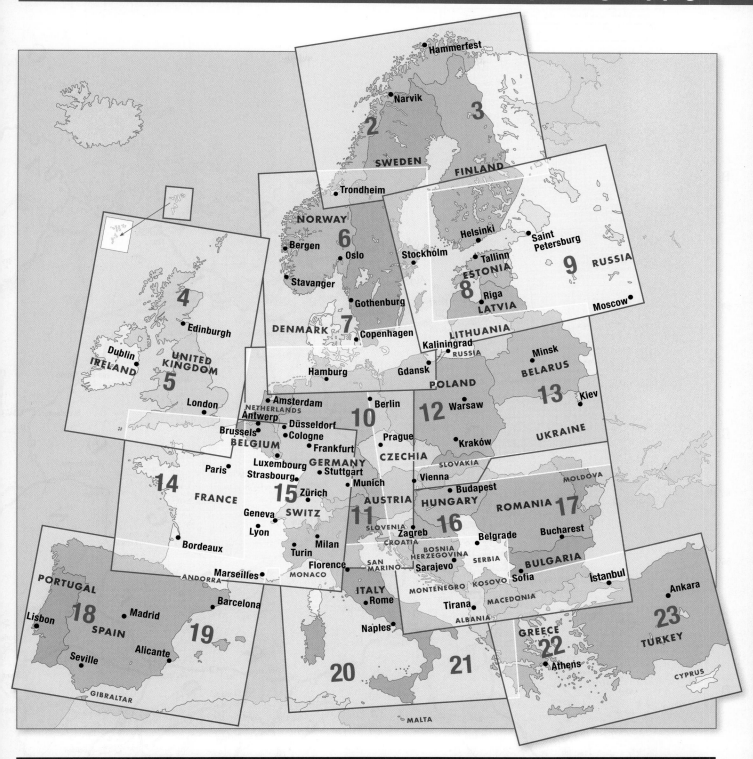

Motorway vignettes

Some countries require you to purchase (and in some cases display) a vignette before using motorways.

In Austria you will need to purchase and display a vignette on the inside of your windscreen. Vignettes are available for purchase at border crossings and petrol stations. More details from www.asfinag.at/toll/toll-sticker

In Belarus all vehicles over 3.5 tonnes and cars and vans under 3.5 tonnes registered outside the Eurasion Economic Union are required to have a *BelToll* unit installed. This device exchanges data with roadside gantries, enabling motorway tolls to be automatically deducted from the driver's account. http://beltoll.by/index.php/en/

In Czechia, you can buy a vignette at the border and also at petrol stations. Make sure you write your vehicle registration number on the vignette before displaying it. The roads without toll are indicated by a traffic sign saying "Bez poplatku". More details from www.motorway.cz

In Hungary a new e-vignette system was introduced in 2008. It is therefore no longer necessary to display the vignette, though you should make doubly sure the information you give on your vehicle is accurate. Vignettes are sold at petrol stations throughout the country. Buy online at http://toll-charge.hu/

In Slovakia, an electronic vignette must purchased before using the motorways. Vignettes may be purchased online, via a mobile app or at Slovak border crossings and petrol stations displaying the 'eznamka' logo. More details from https://eznamka.sk/selfcare/home/

In Switzerland, you will need to purchase and display a vignette before you drive on the motorway. Bear in mind you will need a separate vignette if you are towing a caravan. www.ezv.admin.ch/ezv/en/home/information-individuals/documents-for-travellers-and-road-taxes/motorway-charge-sticker--vignette-.html

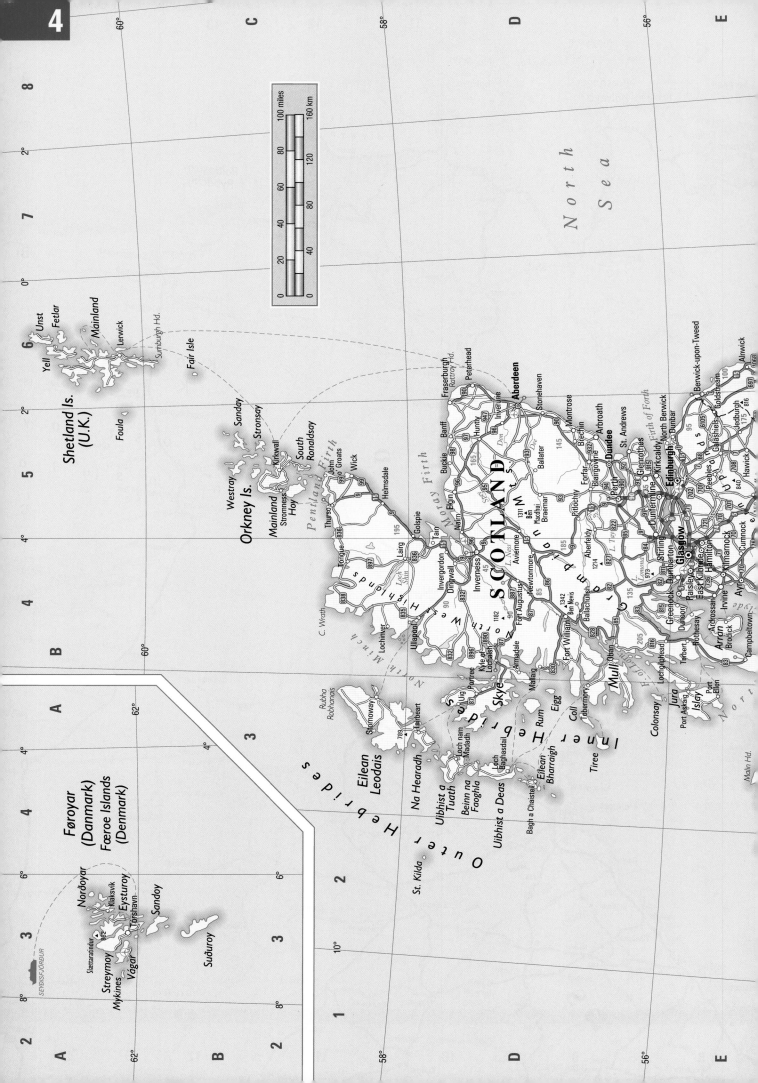

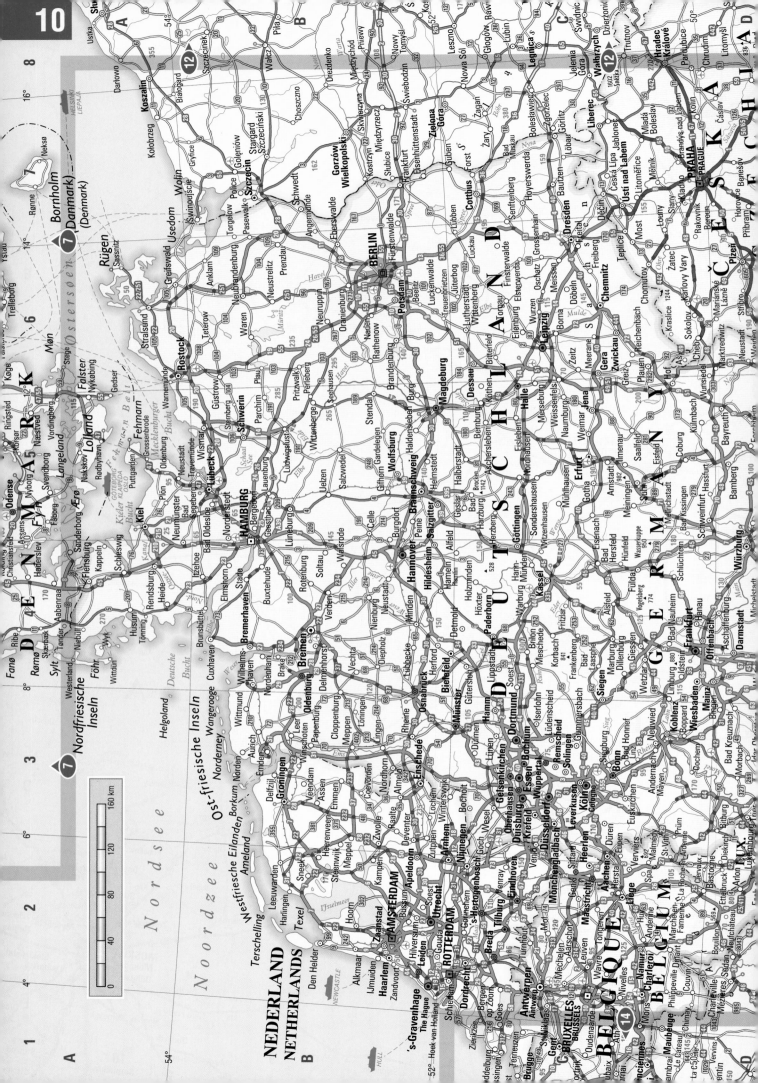

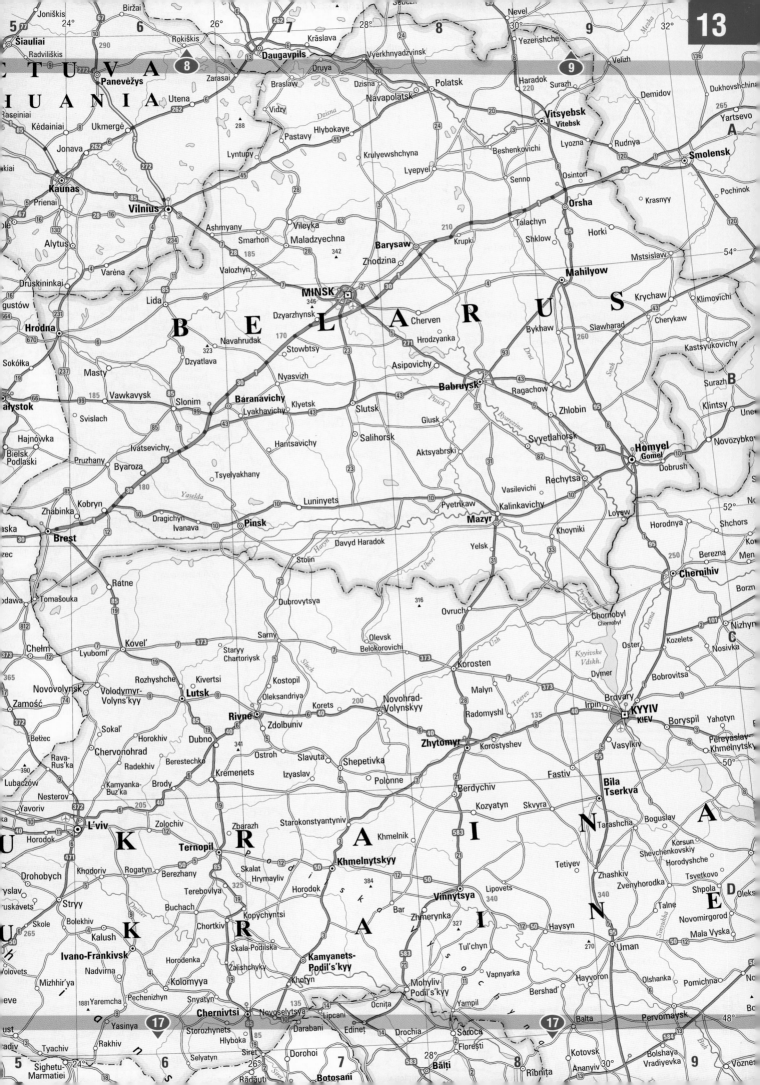

Key to road map pages

● **Florence** City plan
  Firenze
□ **İstanbul** City approach map
■ **Milan** City plan and approach map
  Milano See pages 201–228 for city plans
  and approach maps

97 Map pages at 1:750 000
182 Map pages at 1:1 500 000

Distance table

Amsterdam
2945 **Athina**
1505 3192 **Barcelona**
1484 3742 2803 **Bergen**
650 2412 1863 1309 **Berlin**
197 2895 1308 1586 764 **Bruxelles**
2245 1219 2644 3037 1707 2181 **Bucuresti**
1420 1530 1999 2212 882 1358 852 **Budapest**
367 3100 1269 1783 956 215 2398 1573 **Calais**
533 3630 1817 270 1504 763 3021 2196 548 **Dublin**
1093 3826 1995 176 1696 941 3124 2299 726 346 **Edinburgh**
441 2499 1313 1508 550 383 1804 979 575 1123 1301 **Frankfurt**
1029 3080 2362 819 668 1145 1734 1550 1342 477 176 1067 **Göteborg**
447 2719 1780 1023 286 563 2014 1189 760 477 1486 485 582 **Hamburg**
1560 2539 2338 1063 475 1239 1834 1009 1431 1318 1236 1598 505 1113 **Helsinki**
2756 1145 2990 3653 2223 2706 690 1341 2911 3537 3657 2314 2891 2530 2350 **İstanbul**
965 2782 2090 1103 370 1081 2077 1252 1278 752 479 795 284 518 803 2593 **København**
256 2684 1376 1427 566 198 1983 1158 390 938 1116 180 986 404 1517 2499 714 **Köln**
2331 4460 1268 3723 2869 3141 3917 3222 2069 2617 2795 2400 3282 2700 3817 4342 3014 2339 **Lisboa**
480 3200 1387 458 1074 333 2591 1766 118 430 608 693 122 878 1991 3107 1188 508 2187 **London**
406 2661 1190 1613 749 209 2052 1227 424 972 1150 240 1172 590 1703 2472 900 186 2160 542 **Luxembourg**
1790 3809 617 3183 2364 1600 3262 2622 1528 1634 2254 1930 2742 2160 3276 3589 2473 1798 651 1646 1628 **Madrid**
1210 2683 509 2435 1541 1030 2154 1505 1063 1588 1789 1023 1994 1412 2525 2479 1722 1006 1777 1182 822 1126 **Marseille**
1085 2182 1038 2141 1060 890 1668 992 1072 1620 1798 683 1700 1118 1535 1993 1428 868 2315 1190 679 1655 538 **Milano**
2457 2930 3655 2223 1821 2585 1761 2099 2800 3348 3526 2312 1665 2115 1160 2605 2325 2387 4875 2918 2852 4224 3270 3027 **Moskva**
839 2106 1340 1788 594 789 1497 672 994 1524 1720 398 1347 765 1069 1907 969 580 2545 1094 555 2010 1011 473 2305 **München**
1347 3372 2680 503 960 1463 2667 1842 1660 773 729 1385 316 900 697 3089 590 1304 3604 1778 1490 3063 2312 2018 1823 1559 **Oslo**
510 2917 988 1922 1051 320 2307 1482 281 829 1007 591 1481 899 2012 2727 1209 495 1821 399 351 1280 782 857 2903 810 1799 **Paris**
950 2067 1750 1675 345 888 1362 537 1097 1635 1816 512 1013 652 770 1878 715 690 2870 1205 753 2329 1399 853 1853 388 1305 1061 **Praha**
1691 1140 1385 2706 1502 1520 1904 1263 1678 2226 2404 1289 2265 1683 1977 2237 1993 1474 2653 1796 1285 2002 876 606 3362 918 2583 1389 1309 **Roma**
2347 4223 1031 3736 2894 2150 3709 3010 2078 2626 2804 2344 3295 2713 3826 4034 3023 2318 401 2196 2178 550 1540 2078 4774 2371 3613 1830 2781 2446 **Sevilla**
2206 828 2453 3103 1673 2156 391 790 2361 2891 3087 1764 2341 1980 1800 550 2043 1949 3706 2461 1922 3037 1929 1443 2252 1367 2632 2177 1328 1687 3484 **Sofia**
1393 3418 2726 1063 1006 1509 2713 1888 1673 2254 1069 1431 505 946 167 3185 590 1350 3650 1824 1536 3109 2358 2064 1228 1600 530 1845 1351 2629 3659 2679 **Stockholm**
1256 2128 2366 1909 606 1350 1473 648 1542 2110 2268 1136 1274 886 361 1989 956 1152 3480 1680 1345 2960 2015 1469 1245 996 1506 1677 616 1853 3397 1439 1612 **Warszawa**
1168 1772 1856 1970 640 1114 1067 242 1308 1954 2034 731 1308 947 1088 1583 1010 916 3100 1524 993 2473 1353 818 2137 430 1600 1240 295 1126 2876 1033 1646 727 **Wien**
816 2426 1030 1938 863 619 1810 985 804 1352 1530 464 1497 915 2164 2323 1433 589 2296 922 410 1647 699 292 2552 303 1815 592 691 898 2061 1173 1861 1307 743 **Zürich**

548 **Dublin** ── Dublin ▶ Göteborg = 477 km
726 346 **Edinburgh**
575 1123 1301 **Frankfurt**
1342 477 176 1067 **Göteborg**
760 477 1486 485 582 **Hamburg**

Distances shown in blue involve at least one ferry journey

Istanbul
Ankara
186 **187**
TURKEY
TÜRKIYE
İzmir
Antalya
188 **189**
181
Nicosia **CYPRUS**
KYPROS

km

RUSSIA
ROSSIYA
Moscow
Moskva
Kiev
Kyyiv
UKRAINE
UKRAINA
MOLDOVA

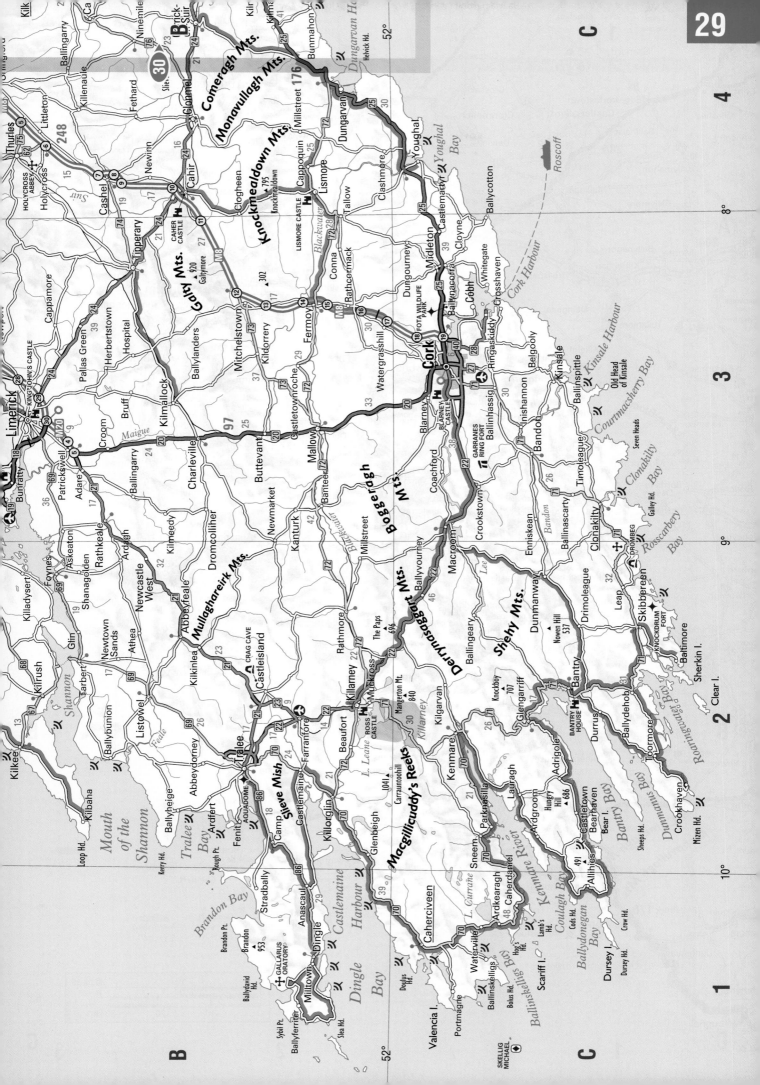

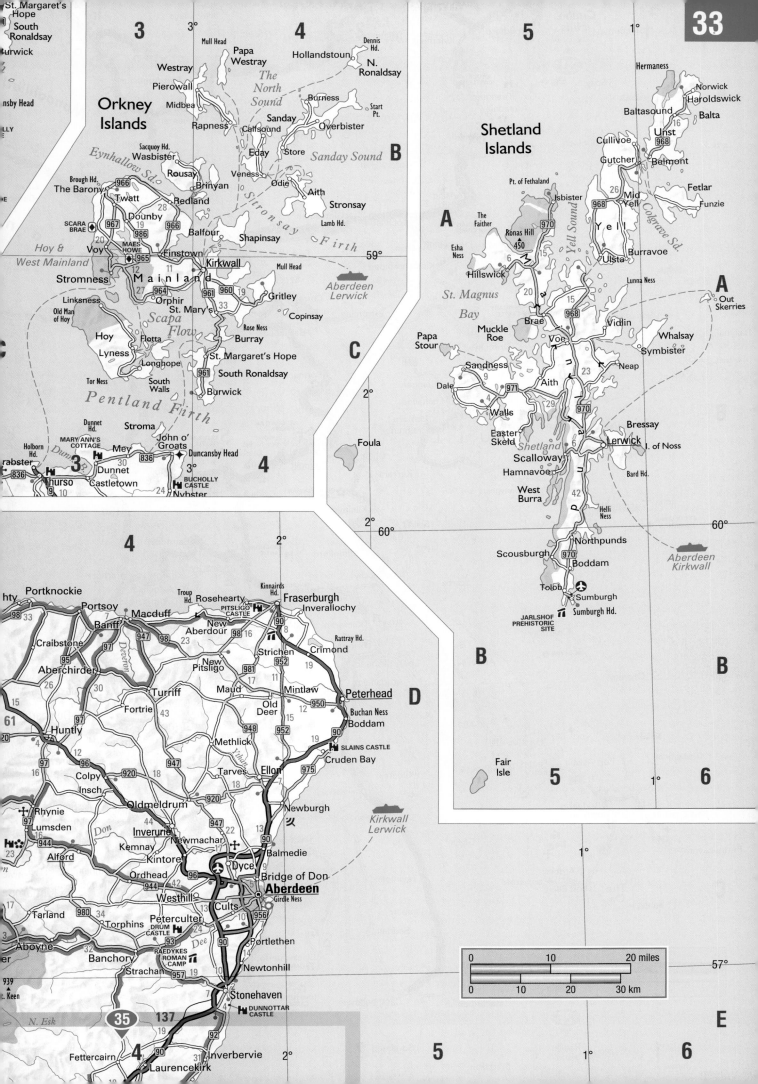

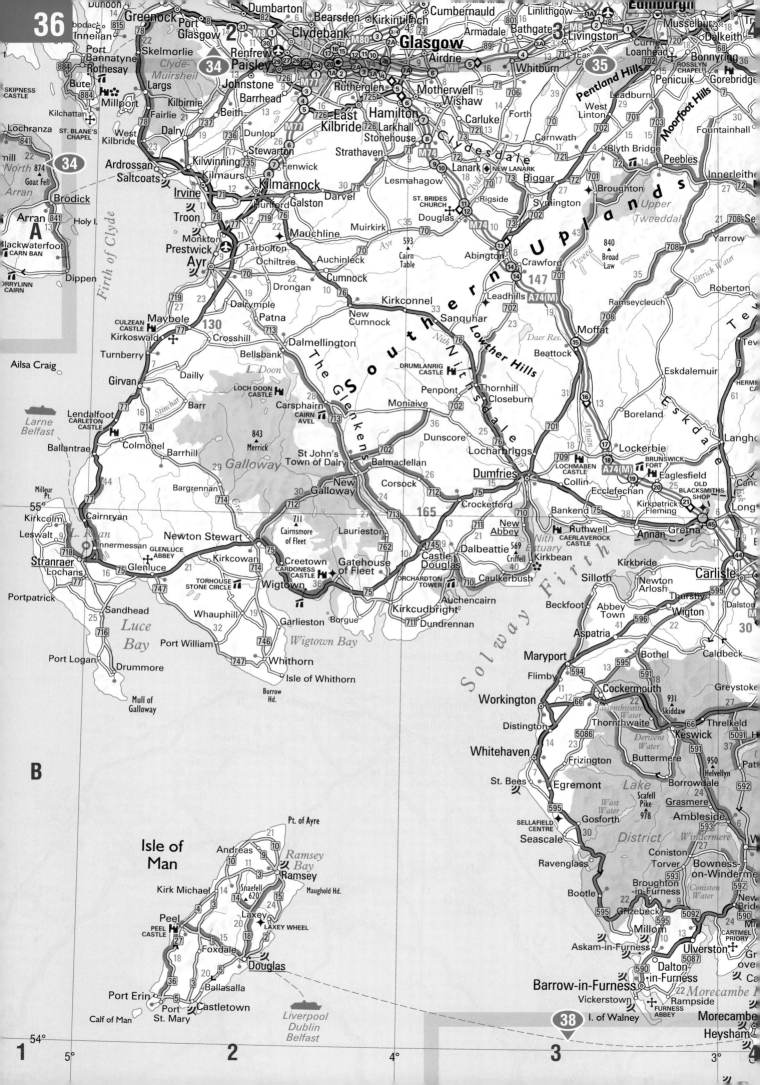

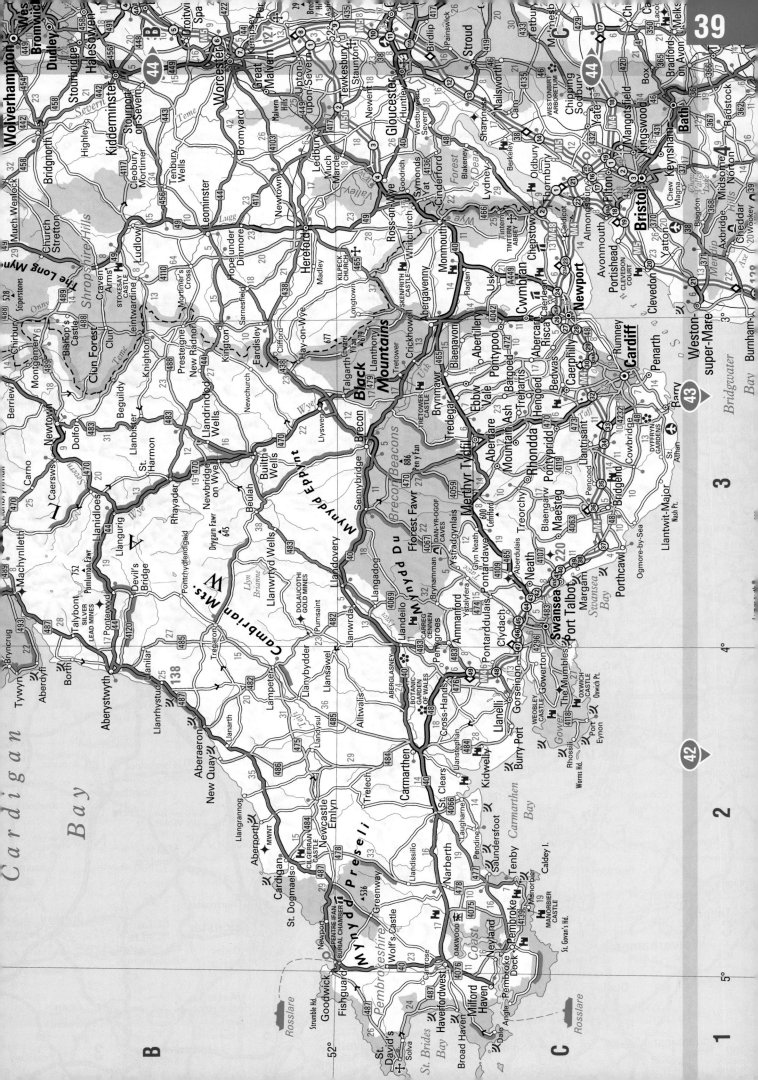

A

B

C

N O R T H

S E A

Filey

Flamborough
165

Bridlington

Bridlington Bay

Skipsea
5

Hornsea
dingham
25

Aldbrough
165
19

Sproatley
Hedon
133
Keyingham
31 1033
Patrington
Immingham
160
Easington

Grimsby
180
Cleethorpes Spurn Hd.
Laceby Humberston
18
North Thoresby
1031 North Somercotes
Binbrook Saltfleet
631 23 41
ST. JAMES CHURCH
Louth 1031
157 21 Mablethorpe
Wragby 153 Withern Sutton-on-Sea
16 157 1104
Scamblesby 1111 Huttoft
20
158 Alford 26
Horncastle 52
oodhall 1028
Spa Partney
Mareham 158 Burgh le Marsh
le Fen 153 155 Skegness
Coningsby Spilsby
33
16 29 Wainfleet All Saints
Sibsey 34 52
Wrangle

The Wash

Norfolk Coast

Benington
12
1121 Brancaster Wells-next- Cley
17 Boston Hunstanton the-Sea Sheringham Cromer
52 Kirton 149 Burnham 149
12 8 Heacham Market 148
Docking Little Holt Mundesley
17 Walsingham 148 140 North
11 Dersingham 34 Saxthorpe 149 Walsham
151 Long 18 SANDRINGHAM Fakenham BICKLING HALL Aylsham Stalham
Spalding Sutton 149 148 26 1067 Reepham 34 149 29
9 Holbeach King's 7 1065 30 Coltishall 151 1064
Lynn Gayton Litcham DINOSAUR 1270 Wroxham Martham
1101 CASTLE ACRE ADVENTURE 140 Acle Caister-on-Sea
1175 Crowland 47 20 PRIORY PARK 47 19 Great Yarmouth
Wisbech 25 47 Dereham 1067 47 Norwich 23 BURGH Gorleston-
24 The Drayton New Costessey CASTLE on-sea
Eye Downham 13 Swaffham 1075 146 The 143
Peterborough Market 1122 Watton Wymondham Broads Oulton
141 Fincham 1065 26 Corton
March Hilgay OXBURGH HALL Attleborough 45
Whittlesey 101 Methwold Stoke Ferry 134 *Breckland* 140 Oulton Broad Lowestoft
Yaxley Fens 20 19 GRIMES 10 11 Bu 45 Beccles
Ramsey 24 10 GRAVES 69 146
141 142 Chatteris Littleport Brandon 1075 23 5
Somersham 20 Lakenheath 20 Thetford 31 143 Harleston 145 Wrenthan
Ely 1065 17 106 Diss 4 12
Mildenhall 1089 Scole Halesworth

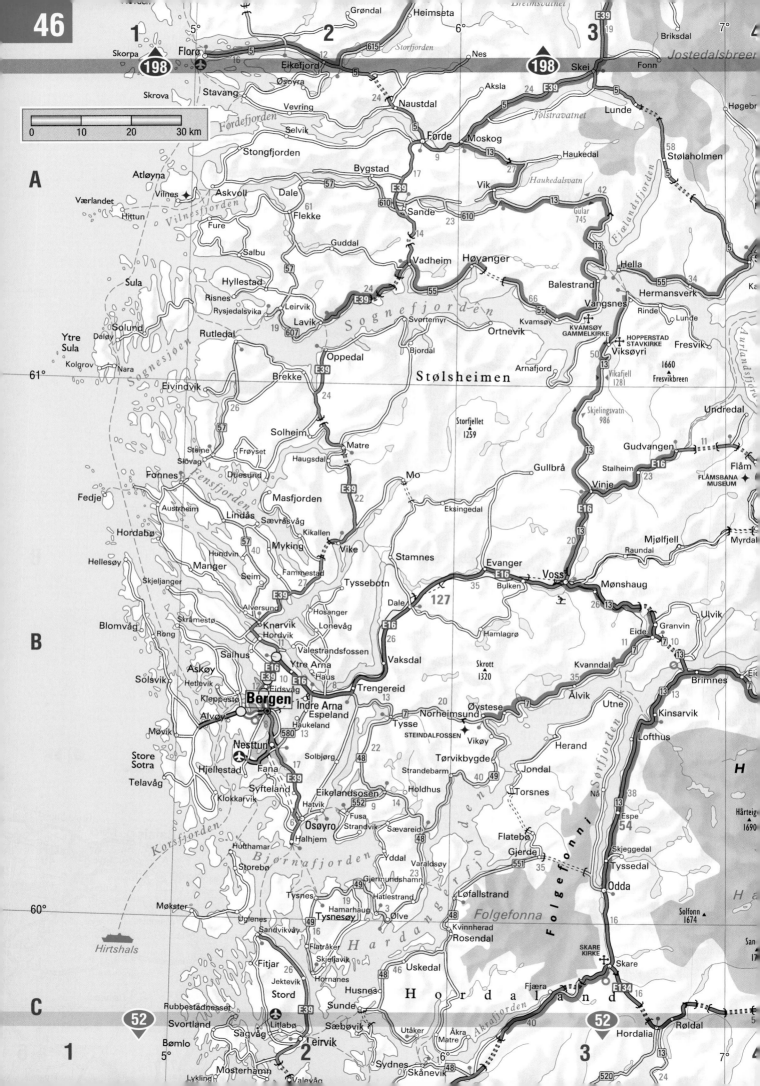

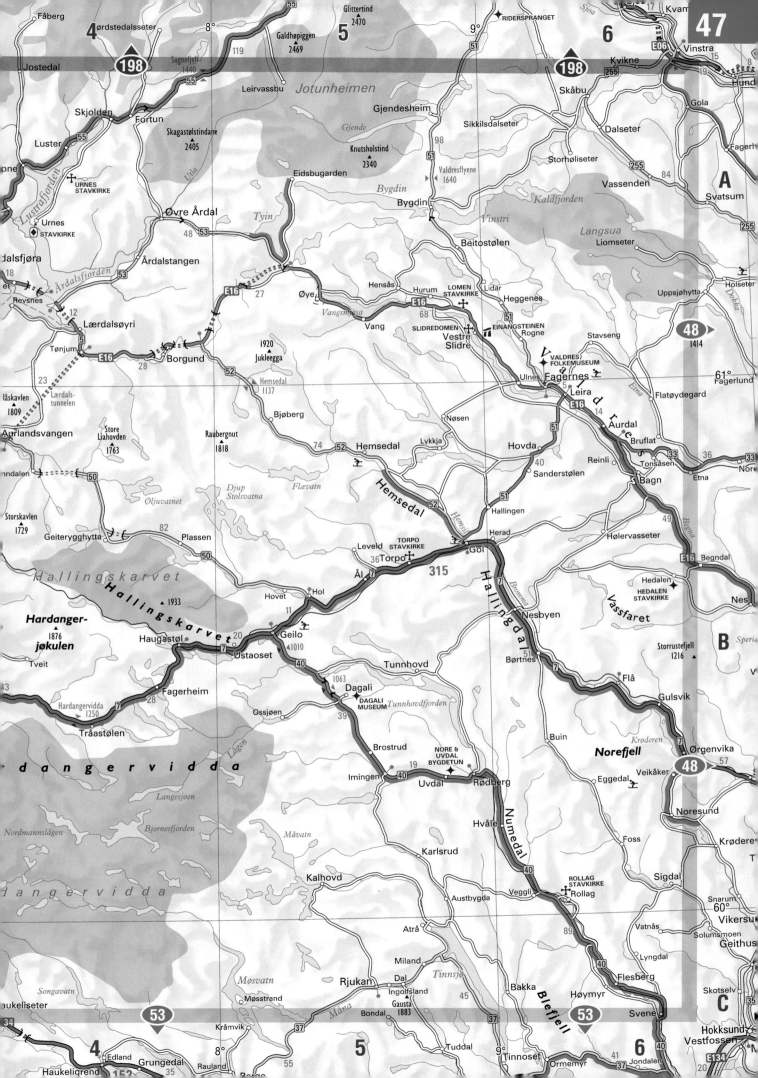

E04
17° Iggesund
Njutånger
Hornslandet
KAPELL
6
20°
Åland (Suomi)
Aland Islands (Finland)
7

48 Enånger
ENÅNGERS
GAMLA KYRKA
Agön
200
Enhammarsfjärden

B
Geta
Näs
Ordals Klint 129
Enklinge
Delet
Teili
B

Trönö
Skarpnätö
19
Saltvik
Sund
Vårdö
Seglinge
Kumlinge

Norrala
Mo
Eckerö
EKERS KYRKA
Godby
16
Finby
Lappo
Torsholma

50
Söderhamn
Storby
HAMMARLANDS KYRKA
Hammarland
Gölby
KASTELHOLMS SLOTT
2

Söderala
Sandarne
Marmen
31
Jomala
14
Lumparn
Lumparland
Överö
Sottunga

Ljusne
2
3
Lemland
3
Degerby
Föglö
Hastersboda

13
83
Storjungfrun
1
Mariehamn
25
Flaka

E04
16
61°
Ål a n d s
h a v
60°
Järsö
60°
Kökar

77
Axmarbruk
Kapellskär
20°
Turku
Helsinki
7
C

Axmarby
18°
5
19°
6

Norrsundet
Bergby
Hagsta
303
Hamrångefjärden

B o t t e n h a v e t
S e l k ä m e r e i
B

16
kland
E04
Trödje
Björke
Åbyggeby
0   10   20   30 km

Öjaren
Gävlebukten
Skutskär
Gårdskär
Lövstabukten
Hållen
Norboda

Högbo
Valbo
199
Gävle
76
Älvkarleby
Hållnäs
Gräsö

11
Forsbäcka
197
E04
Älvkarleö bruk
291
76
Karlholmsbruk
Hålnäs
Graslö

andviken
11
Hästbo
31
196
Storfjärden
12
Marma
29
Skärplinge
Österlövsta
Öregrunds-grepen
Gräsö

torsjön
56
28
Bramsö-fjärden
195
Mehedeby
194
103
13
Åkerby
Strömsberg
Lövstabruk
76
17
Forsmark
Öregrund
Idön

Hedesunda
Söderfors
14
193
Tierp
292
18
18
Norrskedika

n
Gysinge
Hedesunda-fjärdarna
d
29
Tobo
Örbyhus
Tegelsmora
9
290
Valö
14
288
76
Östhammar

56
8
Månkarbo
192
39
Dannemora
Österbybruk
19
Gimo
11
292
Harg
Hökhuvud
8
Boda
Singö

272
Östervåla
191
U
Vendel
290
p
Mörkarla
19
p
l
Ekeby
33
Hargshamn
Herräng

ebofjärdens
Tämnaren
48
Vendel
Viksta
290
p
Alunda
a
76
Grisslehamn
Storby

35
Harbo
Nolnyra
Skyttorp
Tensta
26
Stavby
288
Tuna
Bladåker
Lågbol
n
Edebo
283
Väddö
Björko

56
Rödjebro
65
Huddunge
272
Björklinge
190
Vattholma
Faringe
21
Skebobruk
Älmsta
d
Björko

Östfora
600
Storvreta
273
Edsbo
7
Söderby-Karl
Arholma

by
Morgongåva
Vittinge
Järlåsa
188
Bälinge
288
29
Almunge
282
Knutby
20
Svanberga
Erken
Vätö
Stärbsnäs

254
72
Gamla Uppsala
187
Lännaholm
27
Edsbro
280
Mariehamn
Naantali
C

21
Vänge
Berthåga
Uppsala
Linnes Hammarby
13
Rånäs

70
Fjärdhundra
57
Sävja
LINNES HAMMARBY
273
Rimbo
57
Norrtälje
E18

3
Örsundsbr
VIKS SLOTT
SKOKL STERS SLOTT
Balingsta
Dalby
255
Alsike
184
Knivsta
273
18°
77
18
Rö
12
77
191
190
276
Kapellskär
6

HÄRKEBERGA KYRKA
Skokloster
69
ARLANDA
15
20
14
5
17
8
23
19°

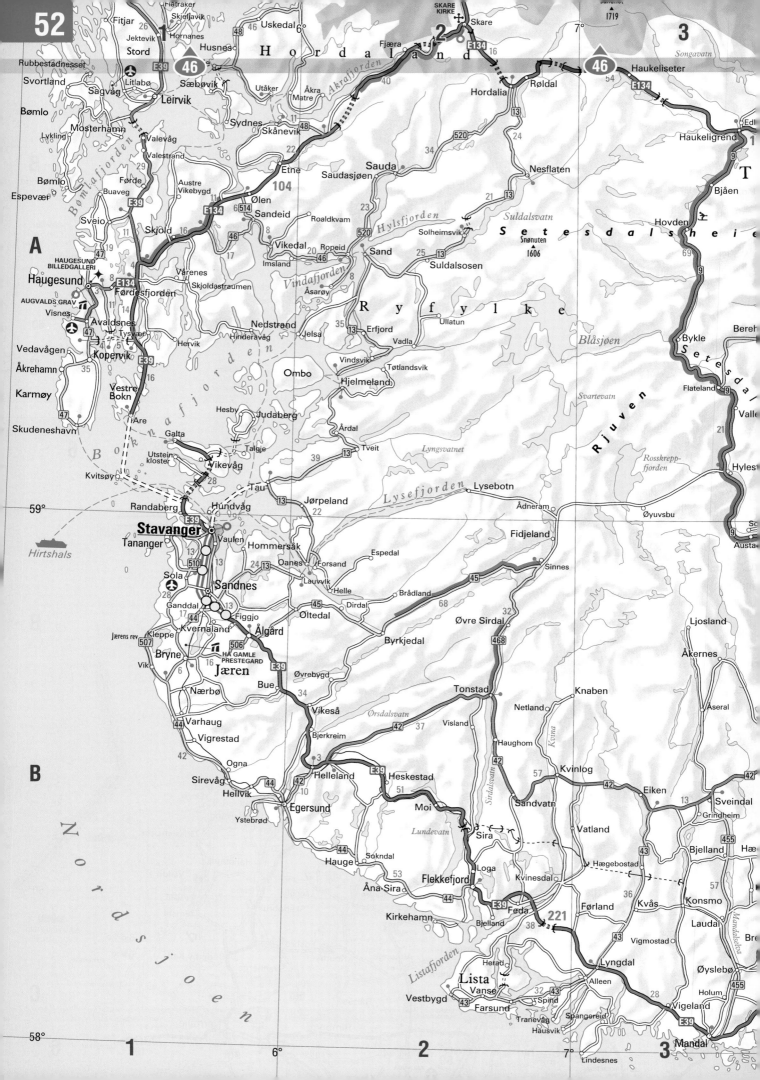

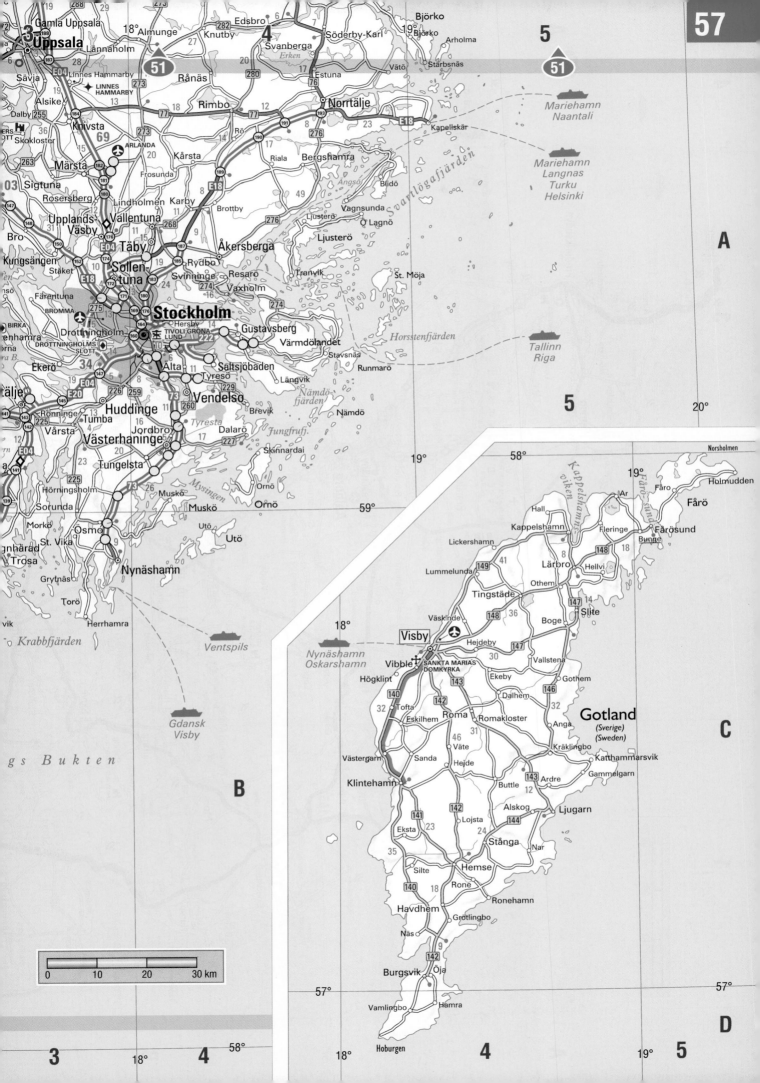

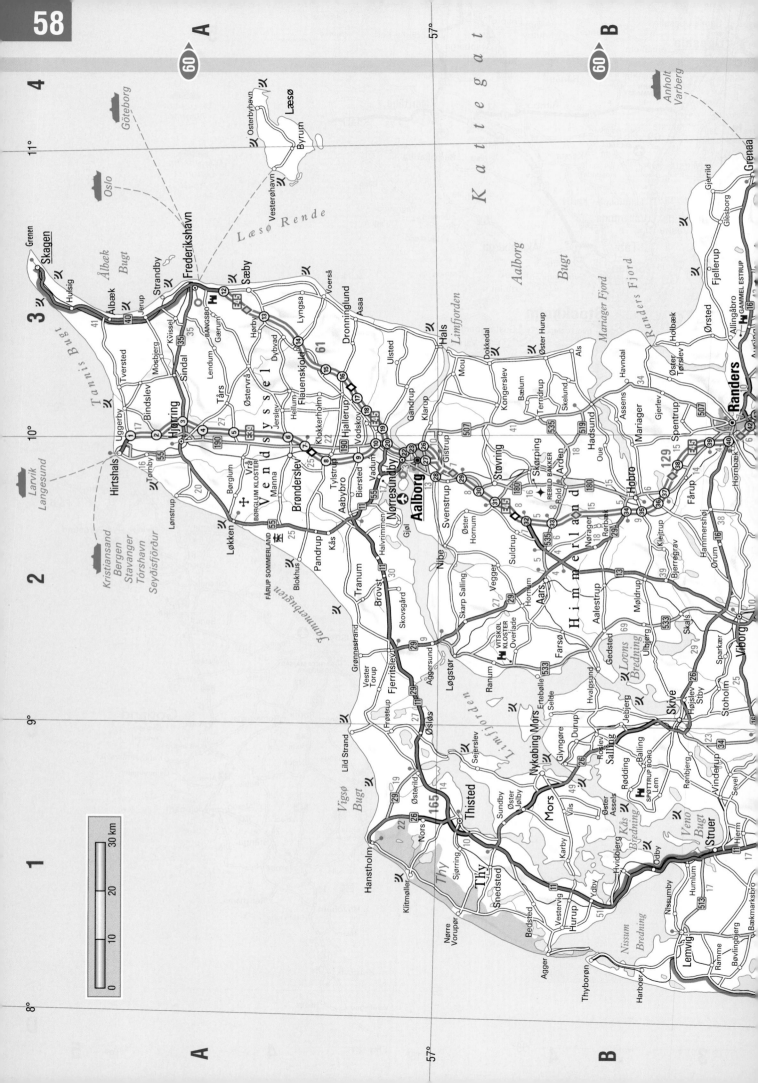

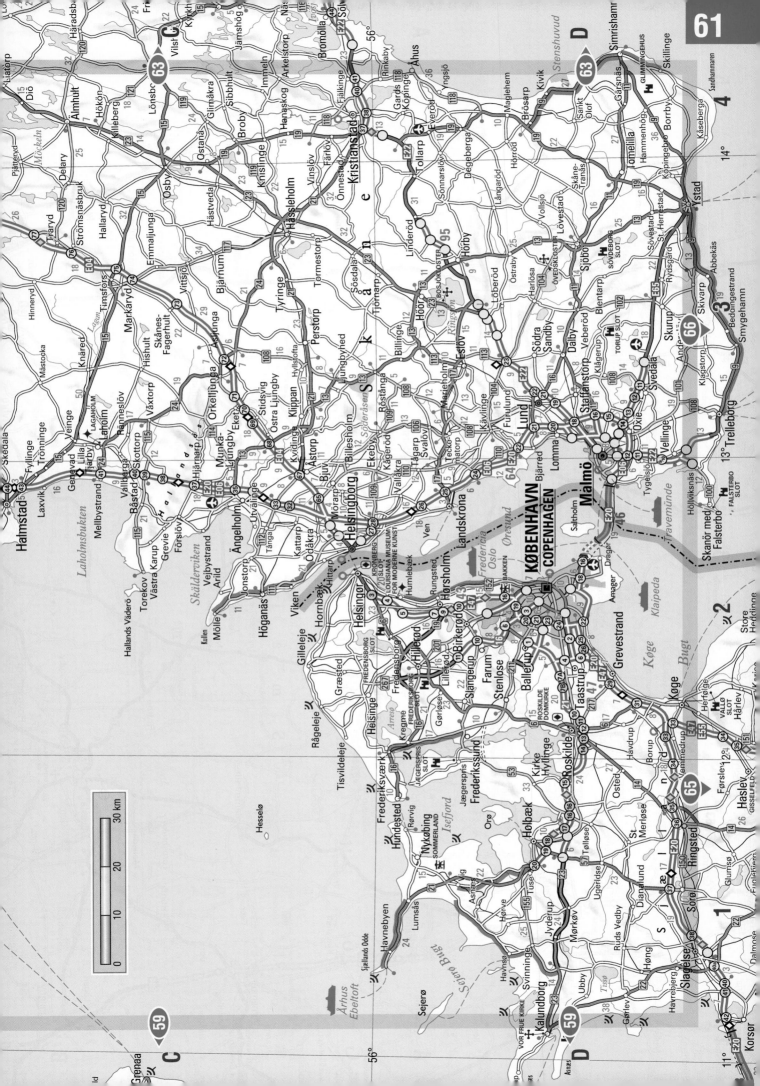

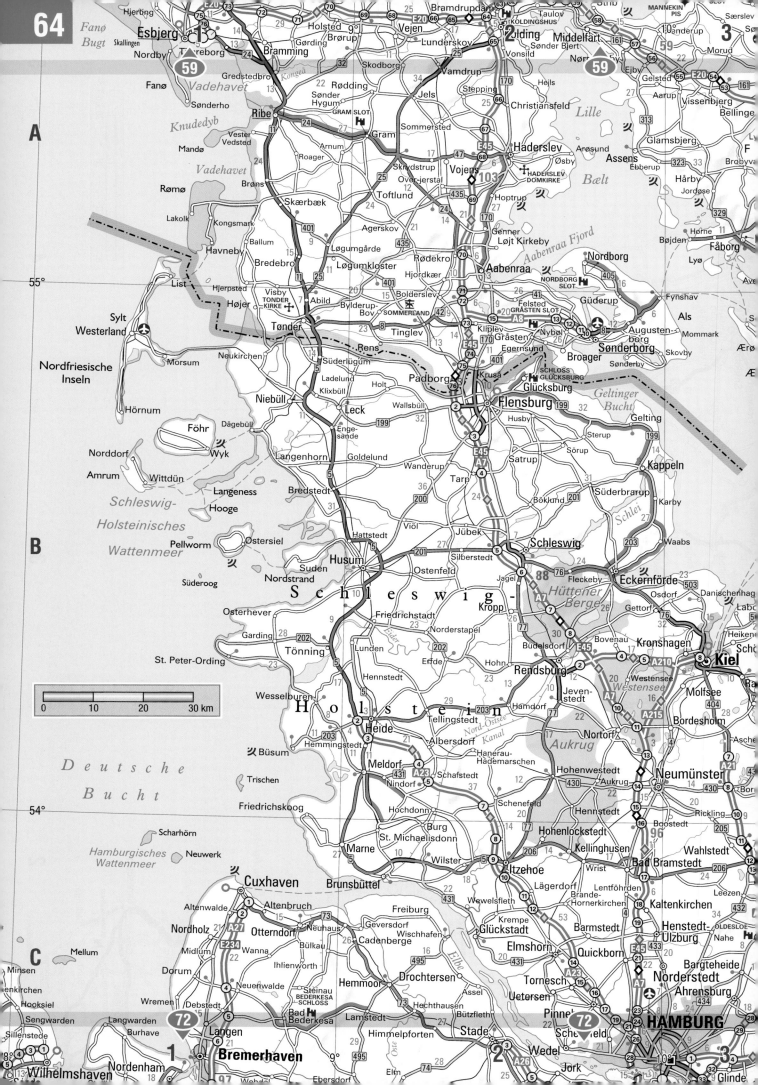

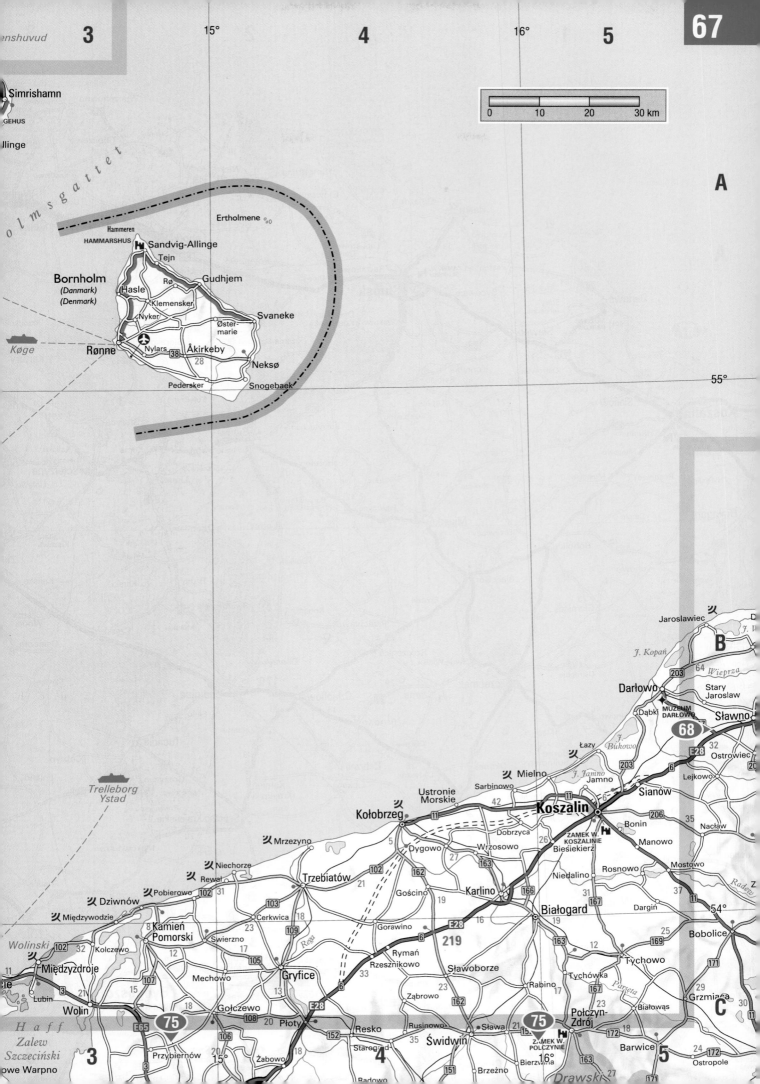

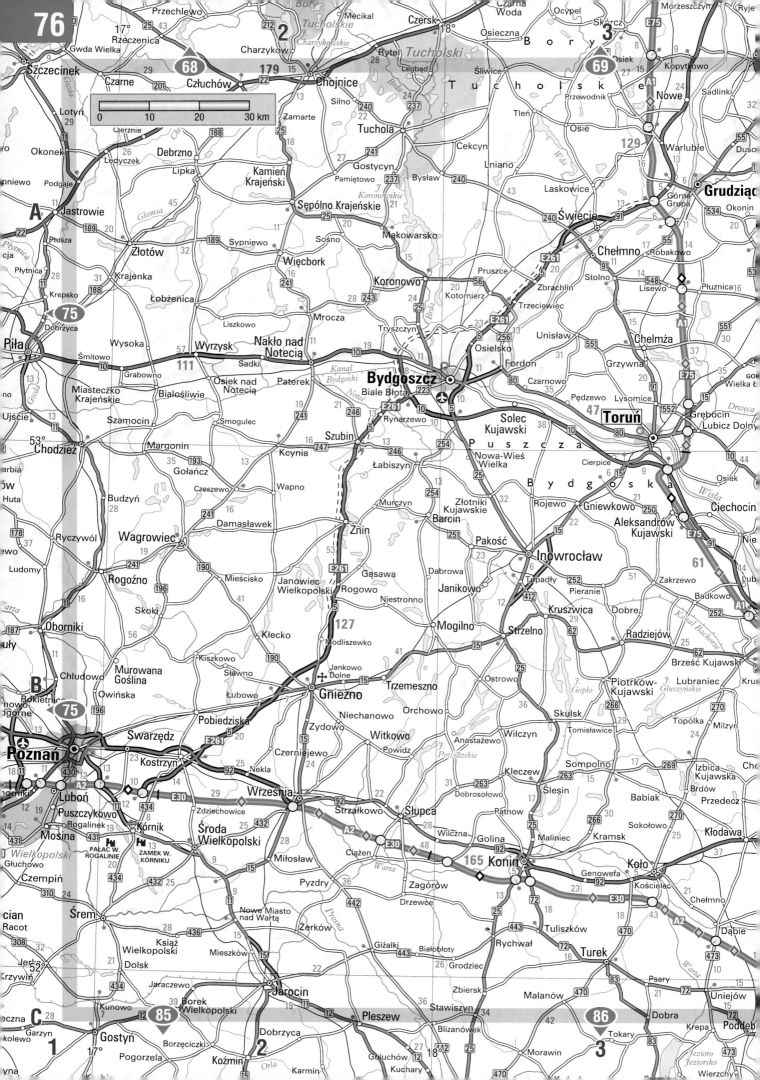

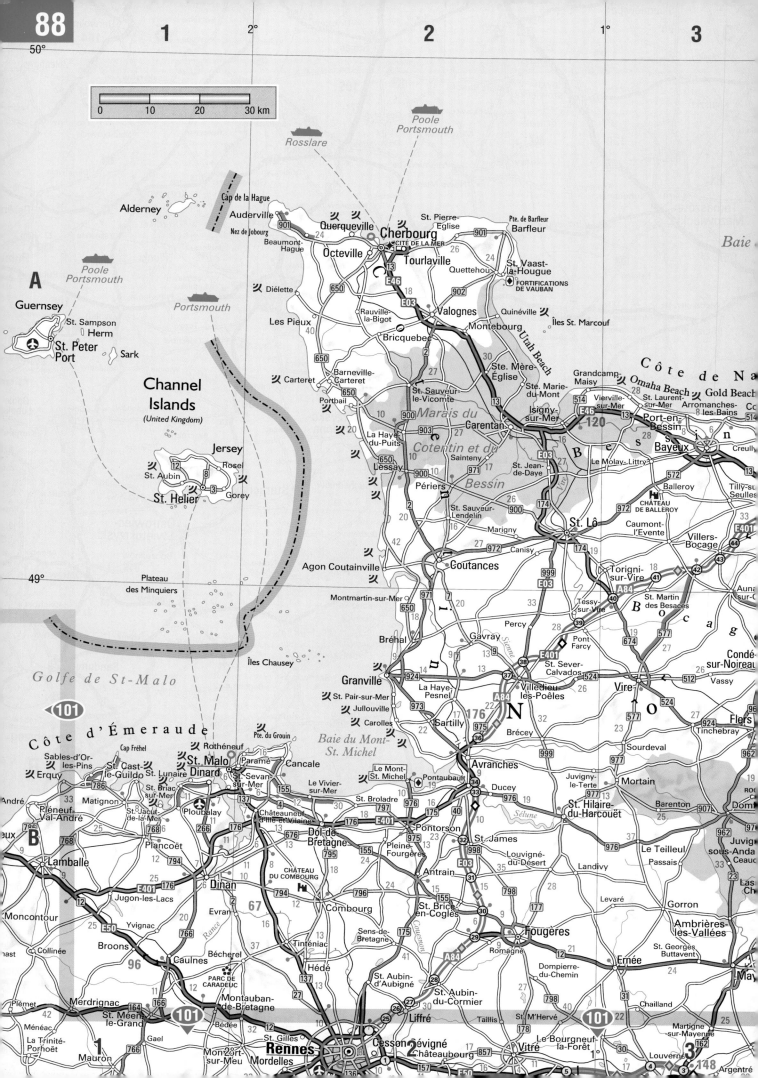

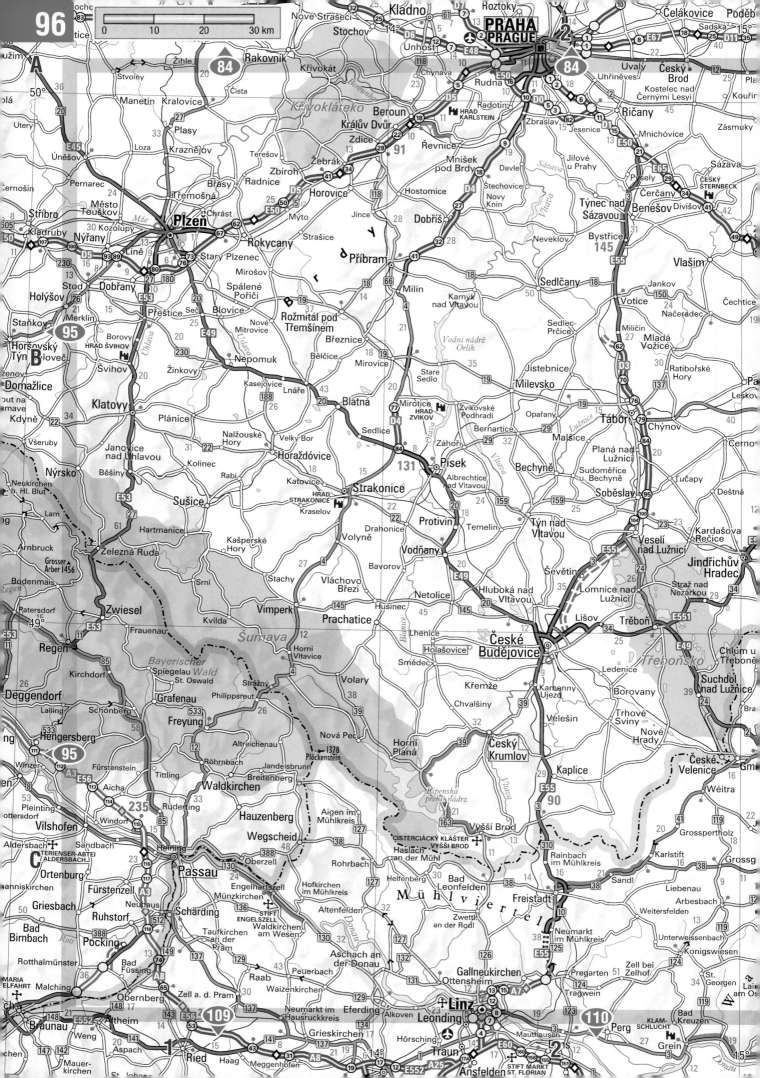

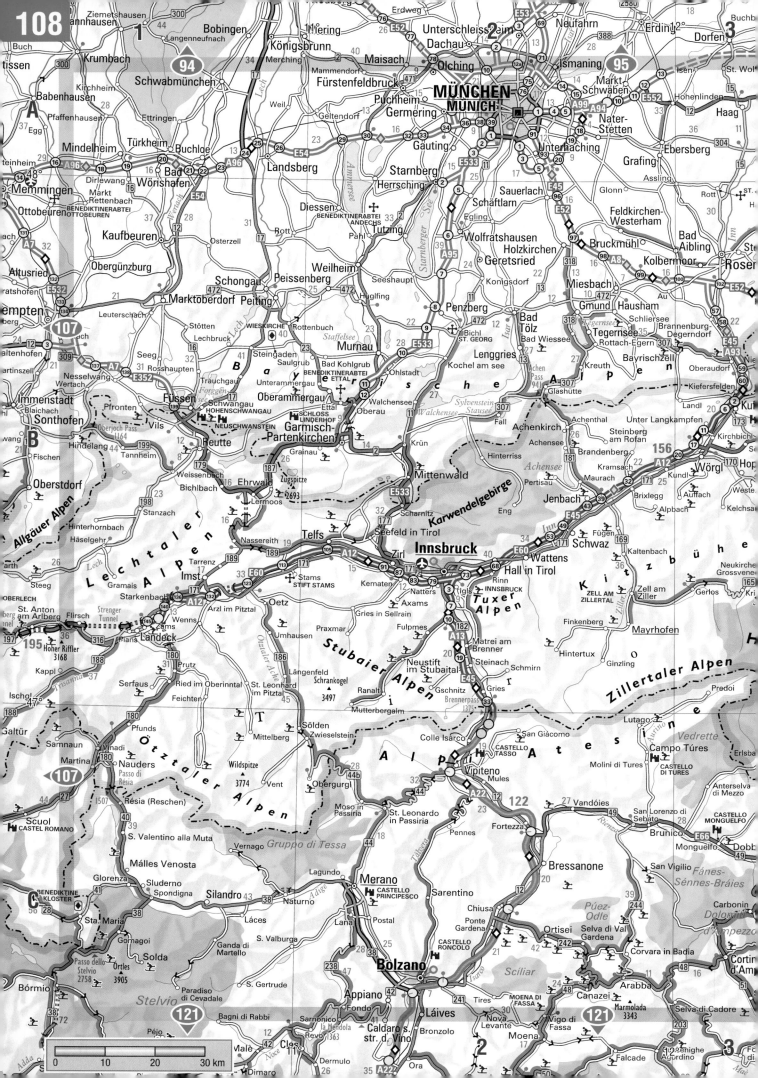

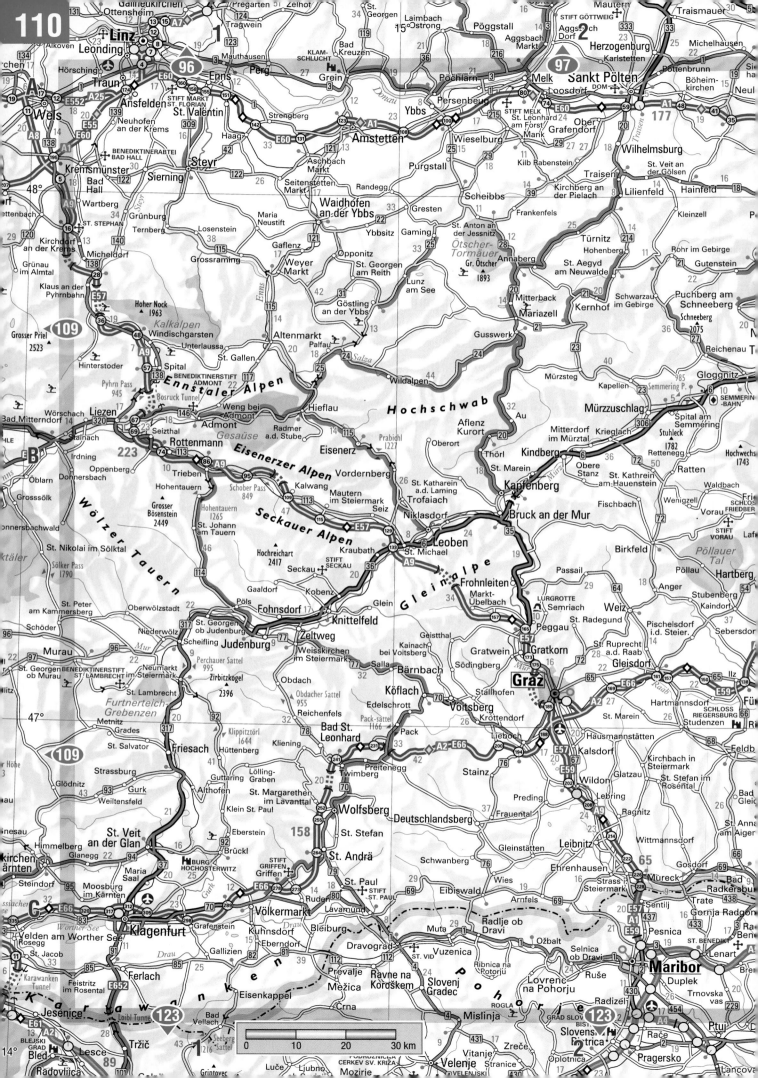

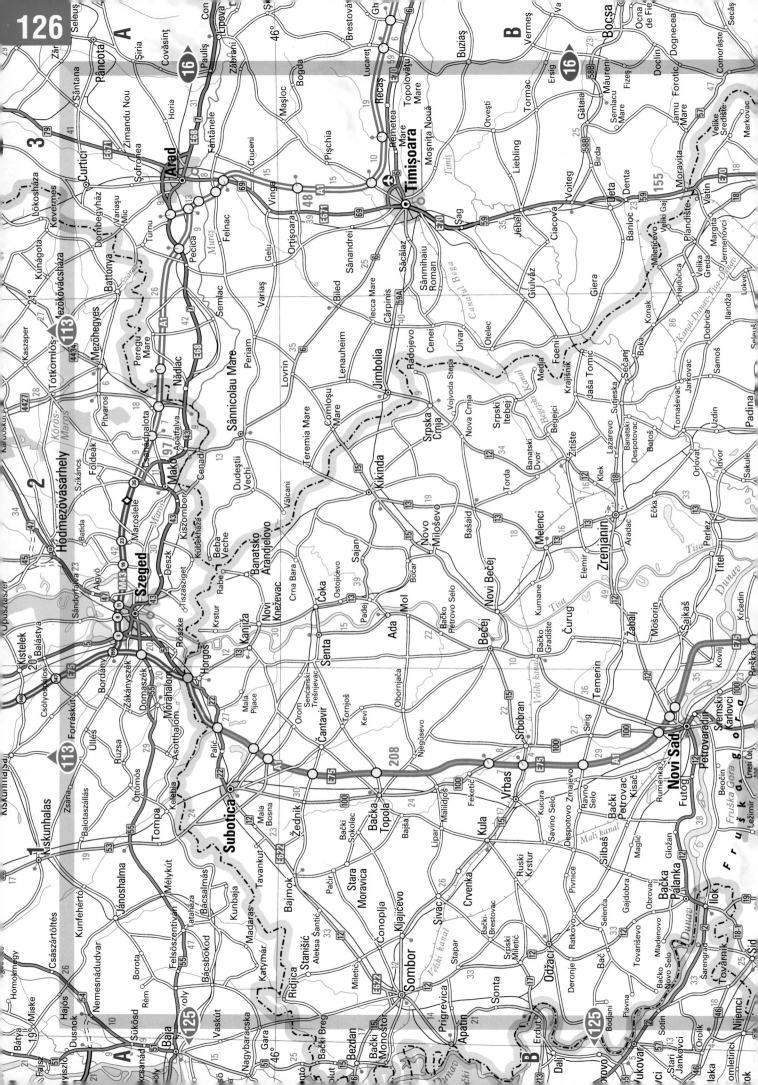

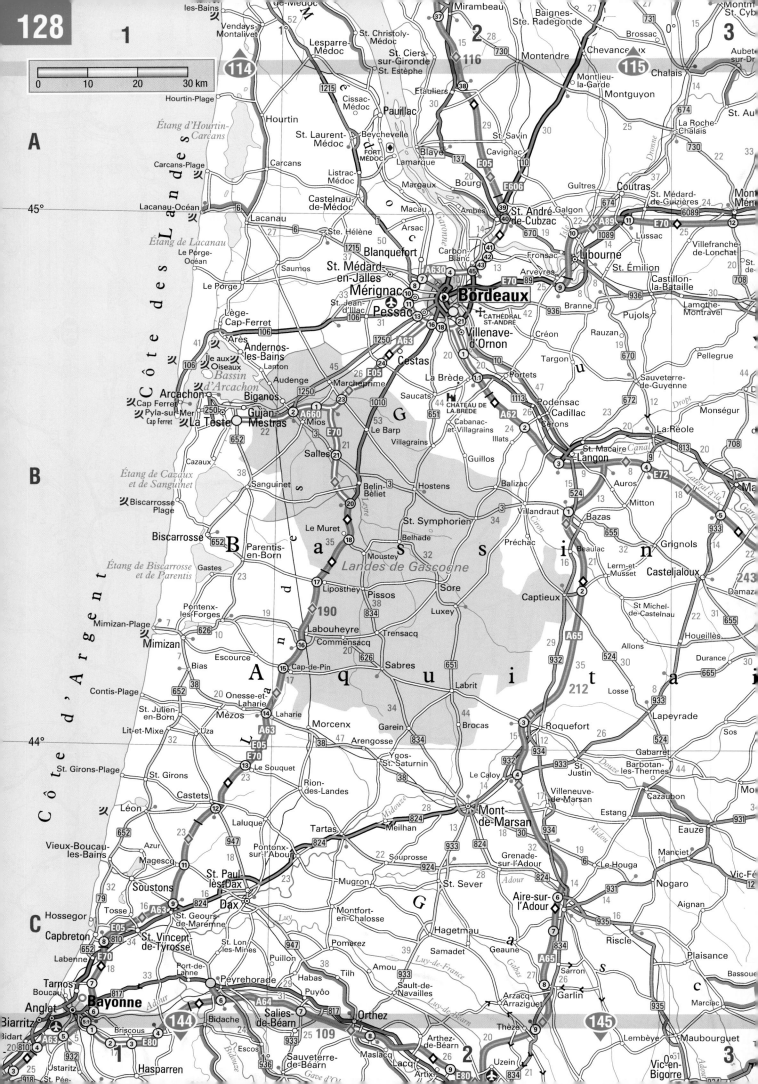

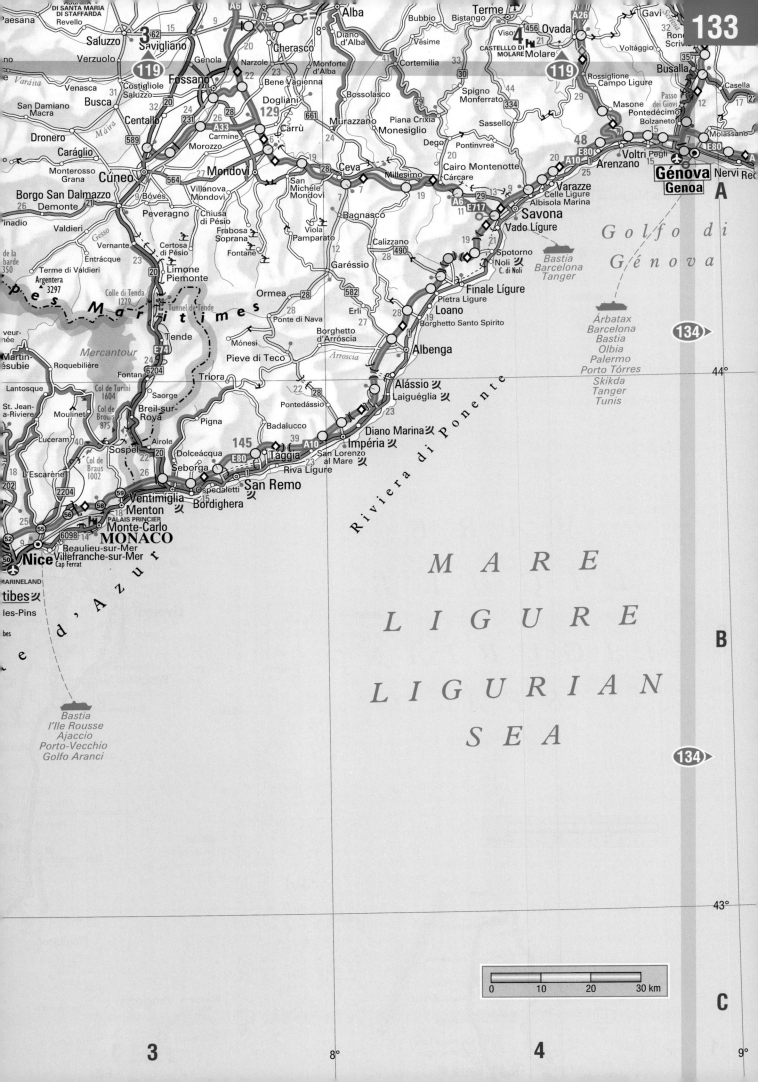

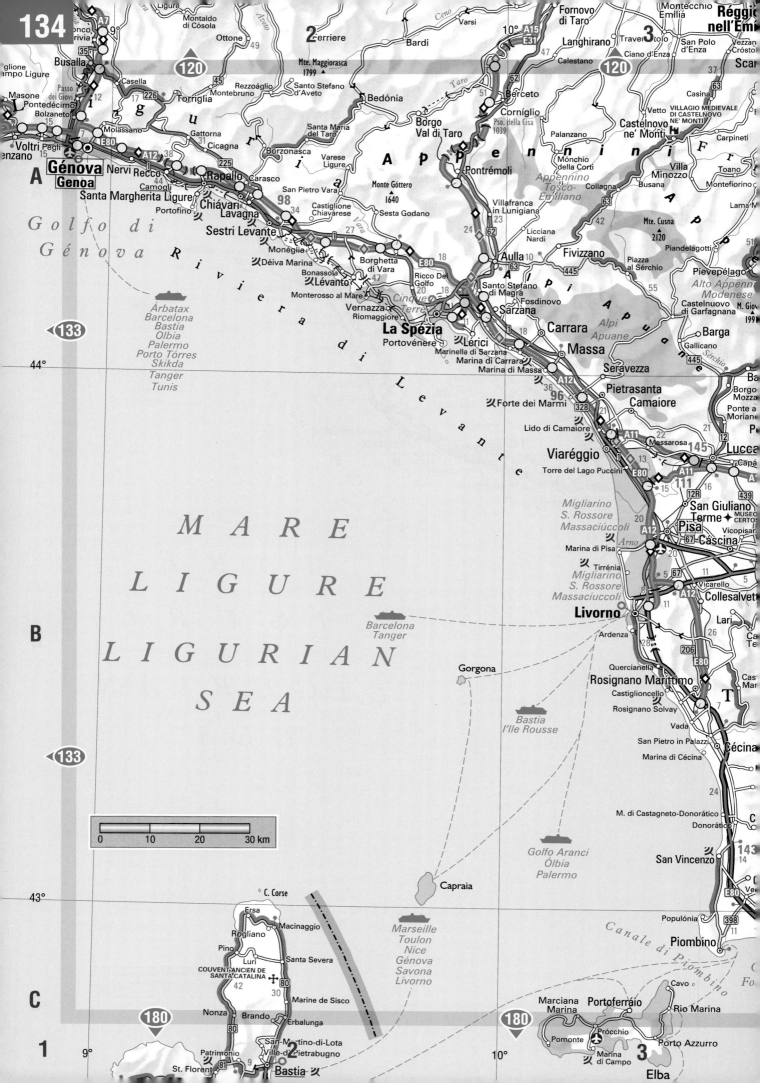

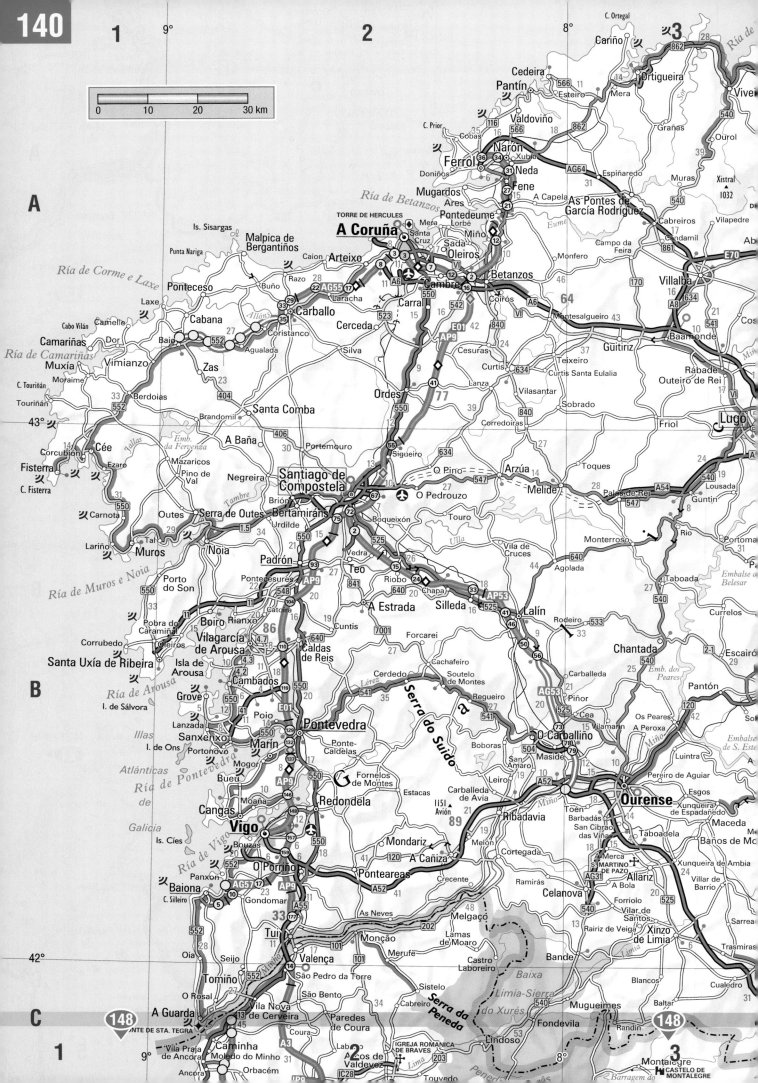

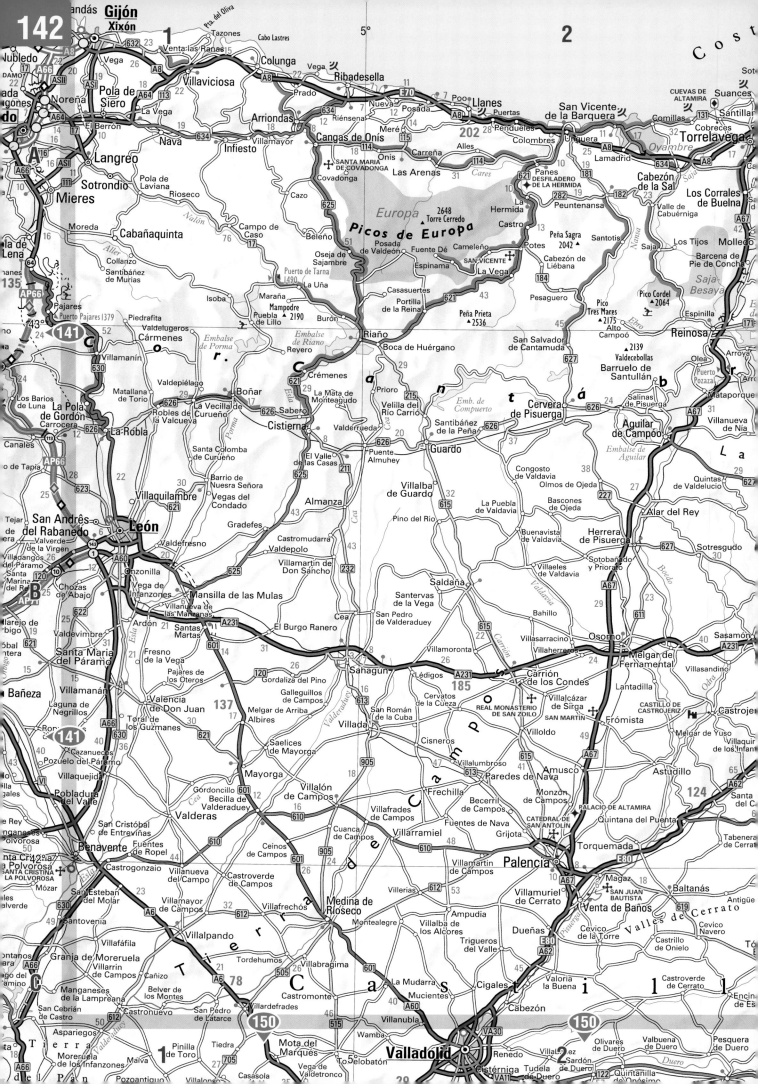

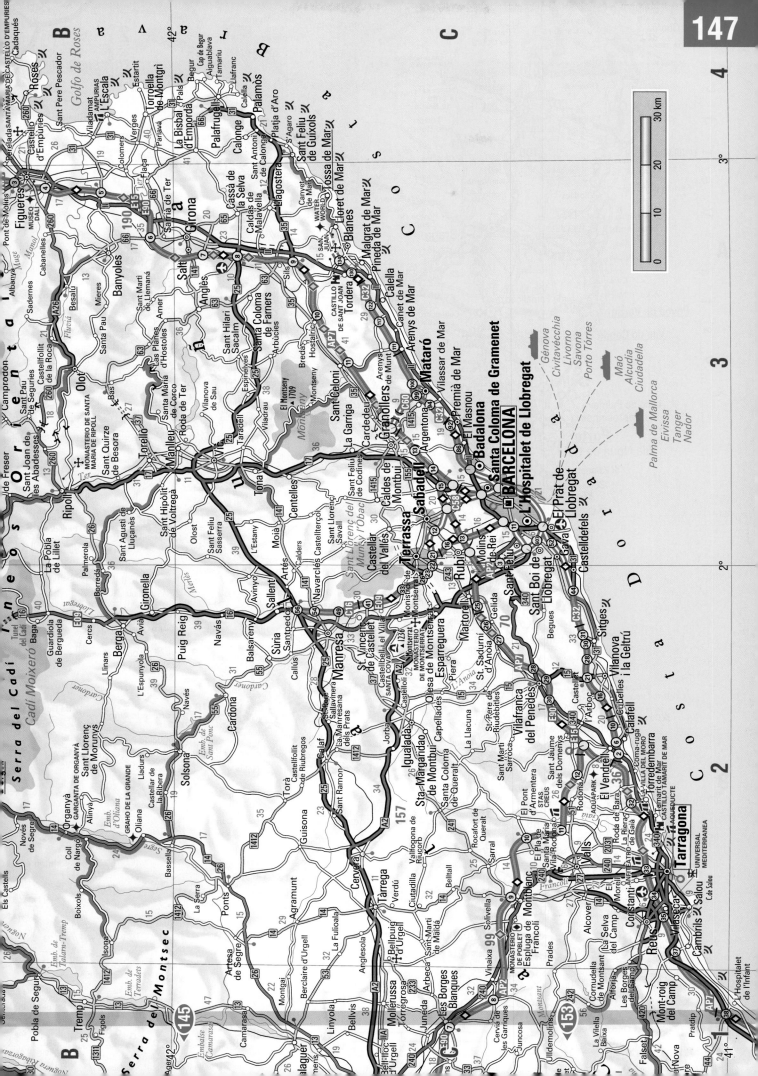

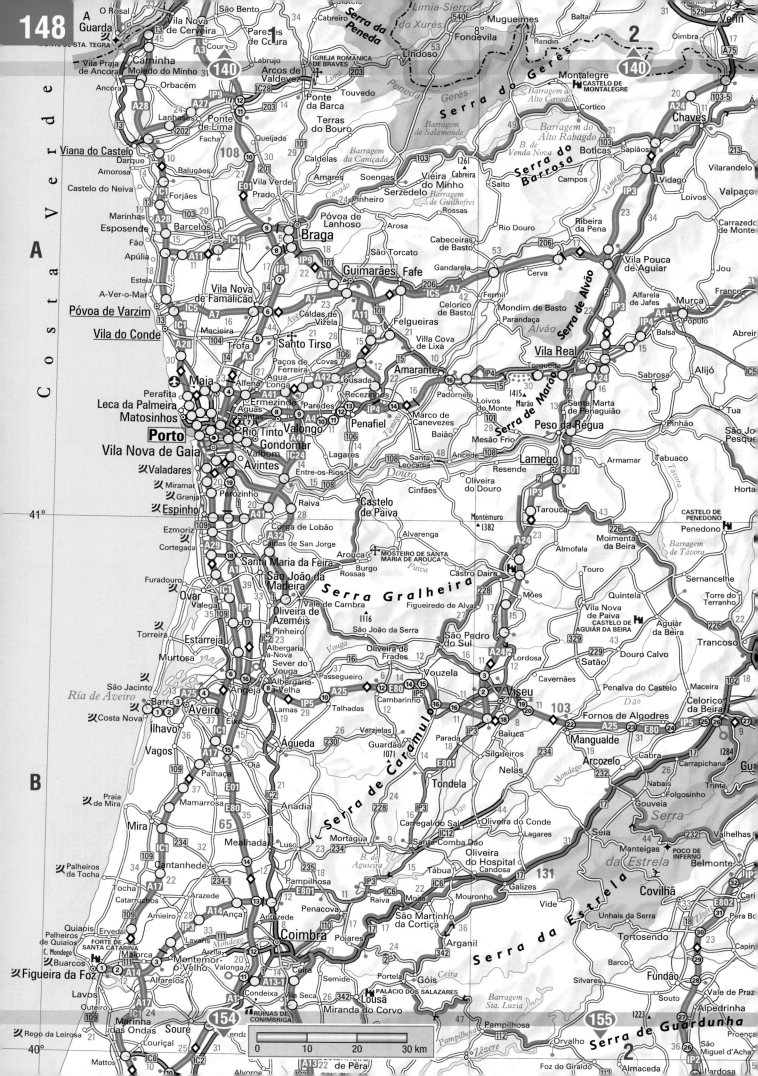

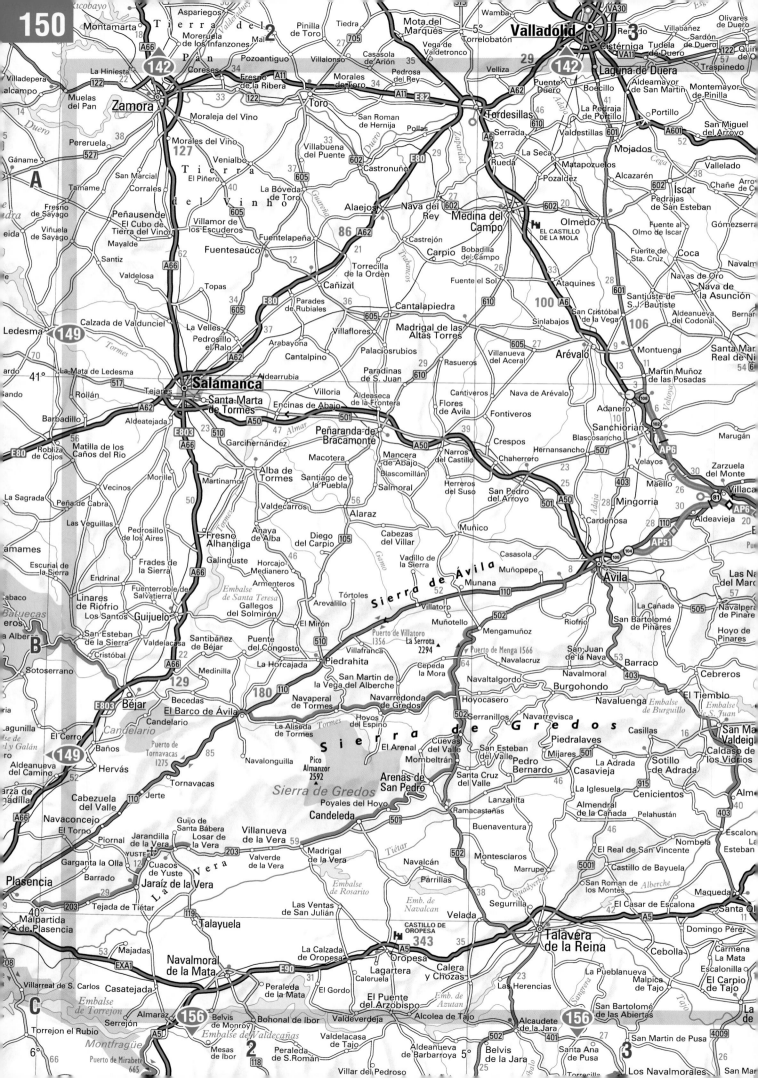

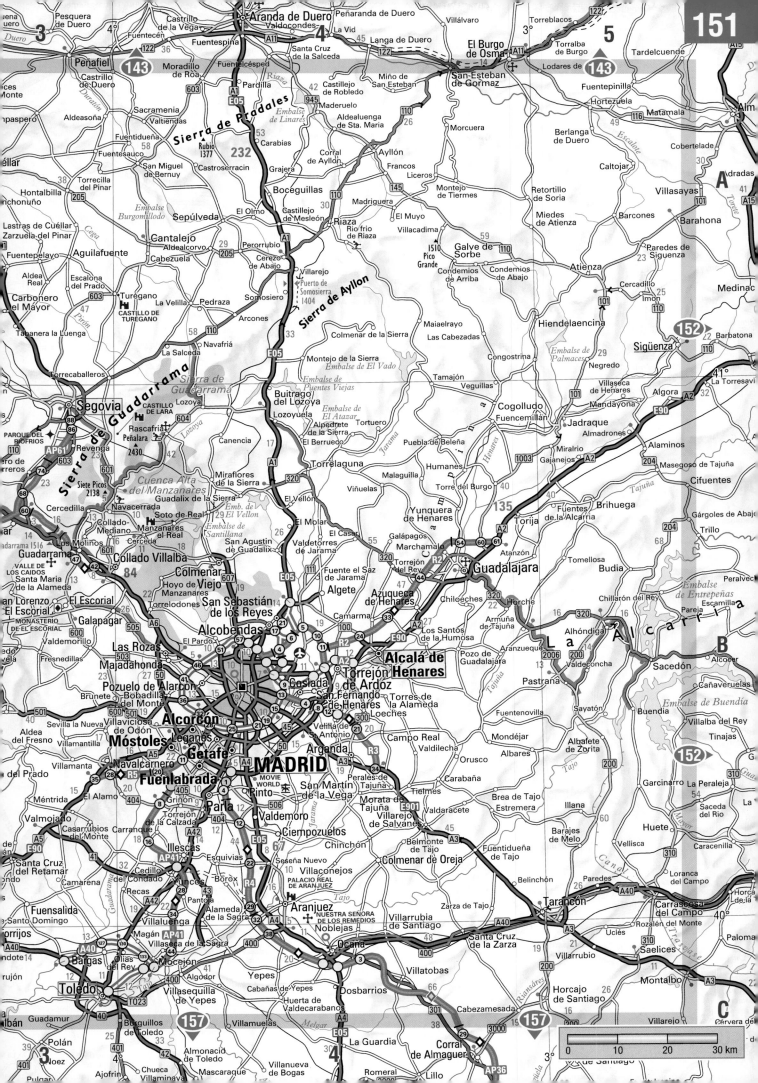

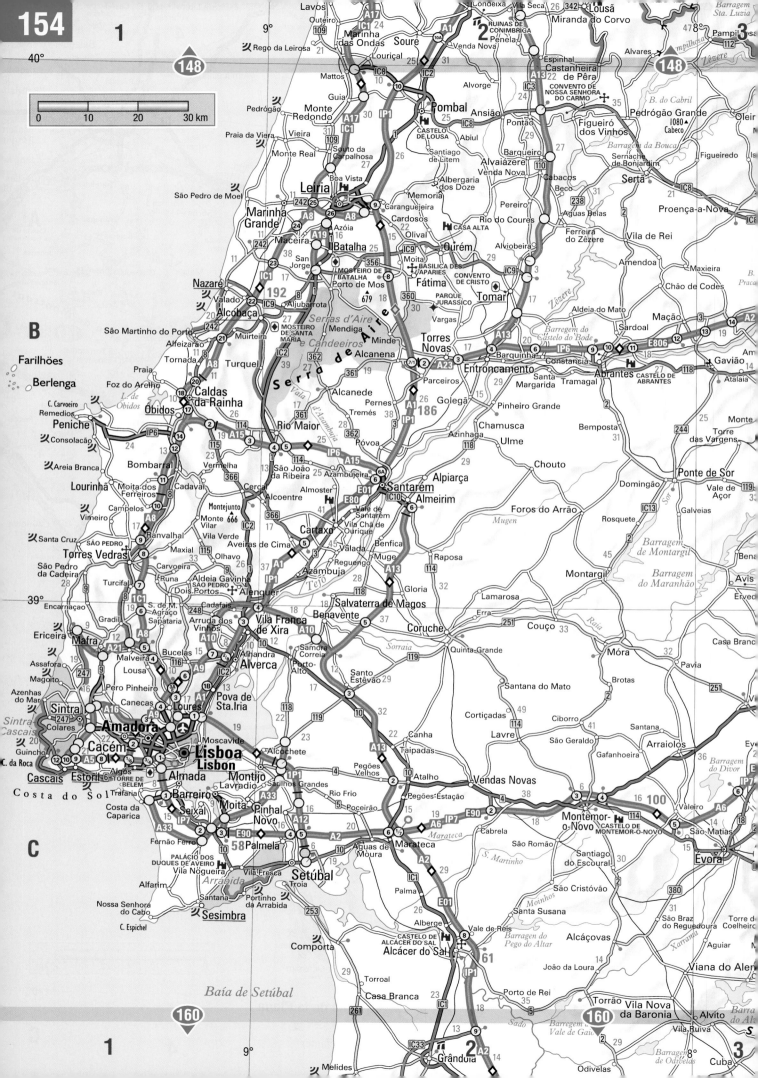

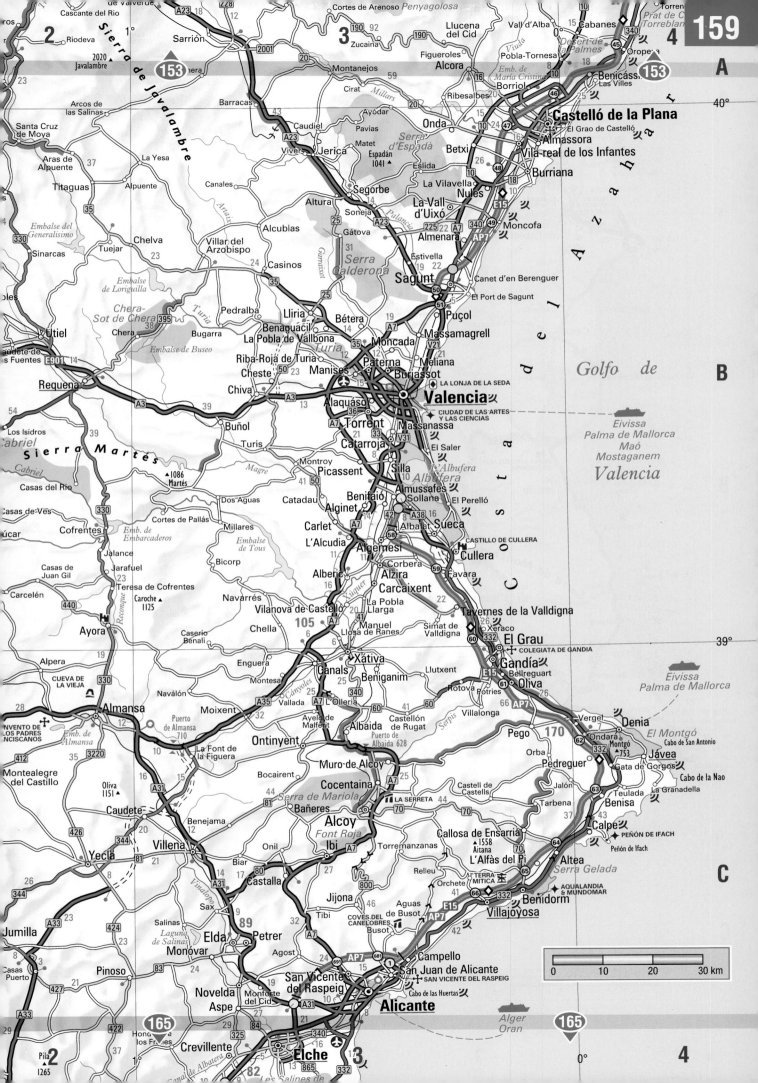

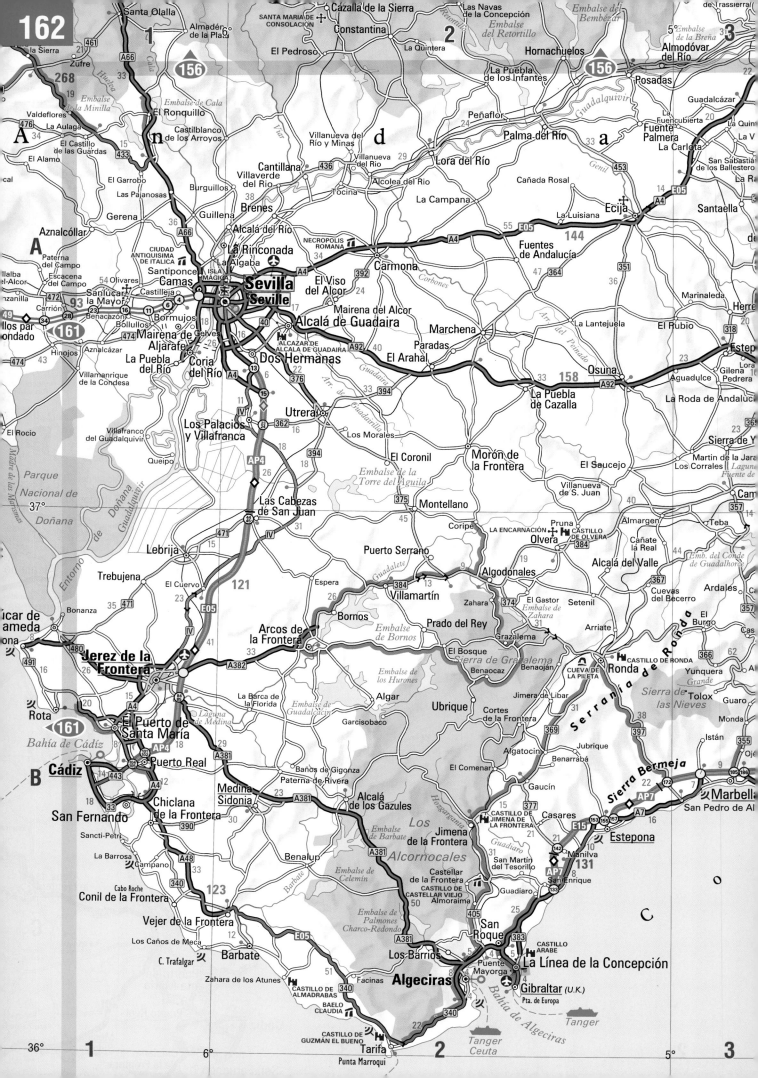

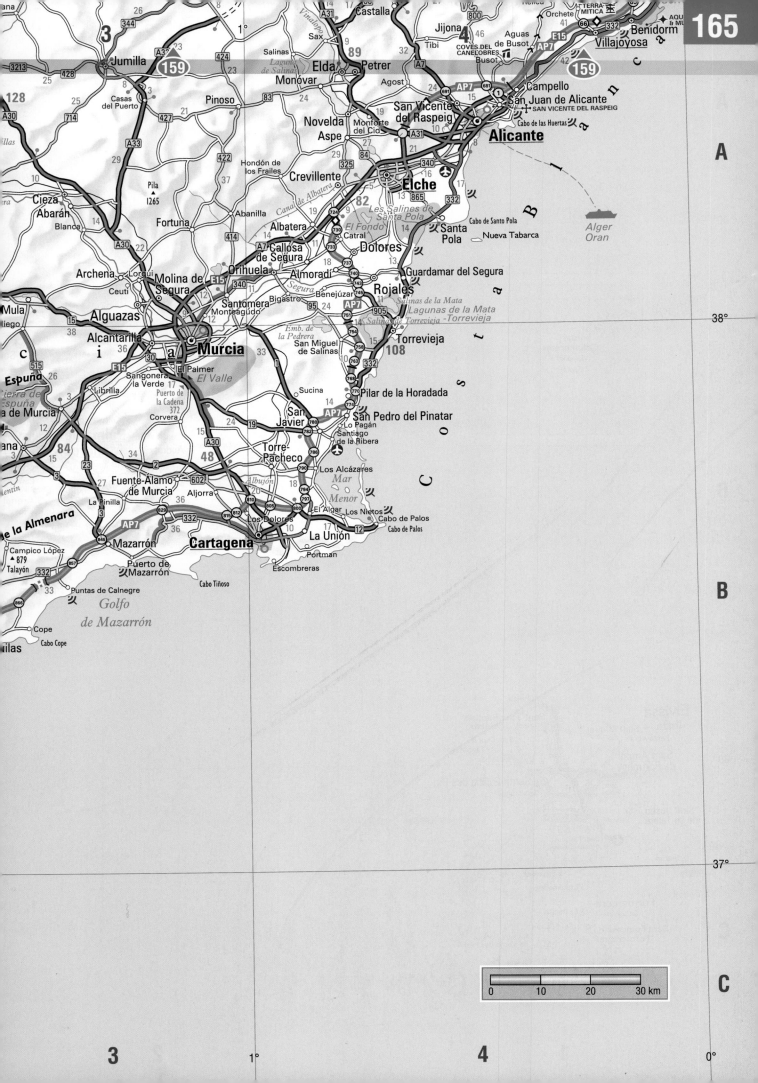

A

40°

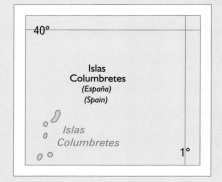

40°

Islas
Columbretes
(España)
(Spain)

*Islas
Columbretes*

1°

B

ISLAS BALEARES
BALEARIC ISLANDS

Port de Sóller
Deià   Sól
Tun Sóll
A
Valldemossa   25
Banyalbufar
Esporles   Bun
Estellencs   39   11   Marrat
Puigpunyent
12
4   8
Sa Dragonera   Andratx   10   **Palma de**
Mallorca
Port d'Andratx   Calviá   MA1   6
Barcelona   15   13   12   10
Peguera   17 14   Palma   Can
Santa Ponça   Nova   Pastilla
Magaluf   S'Arenal
Cap Enderrocat
Cap de Cala Figuera   *Bahía*
Valencia   *de Palma*

Maó

Mallorca
Majorca

Eivissa
Denia

C

39°

Eivissa
Ibiza
Portinatx
Sant Miquel   Sant Joan Baptista
Santa Agnès   8   Pta. Grossa
12   Sant Carlos
Sant Antoni   733   Tagomago
de Portmany   6   Es Caná
Sant   16   11   **Santa Eulàlia des Riu**
Rafel   731   Cala Llonga
Sant Josep   8
de sa Talaia   Eivissa
20   Ibiza
Es Vedrà   Sant Francesc   *Palma de Mallorca*
Cap   de ses Salines   *Barcelona*
Llentrisca   Punta Portás
Denia   S'Espardell
Valencia   S'Espalmador
Formentera
Sa Savina   Es Pujols
Sant Ferran
Sant Francesc de   Nuestra Señora
Formentera   Sa Verge des Pilar
C. de Barbària   Pta. Rotja

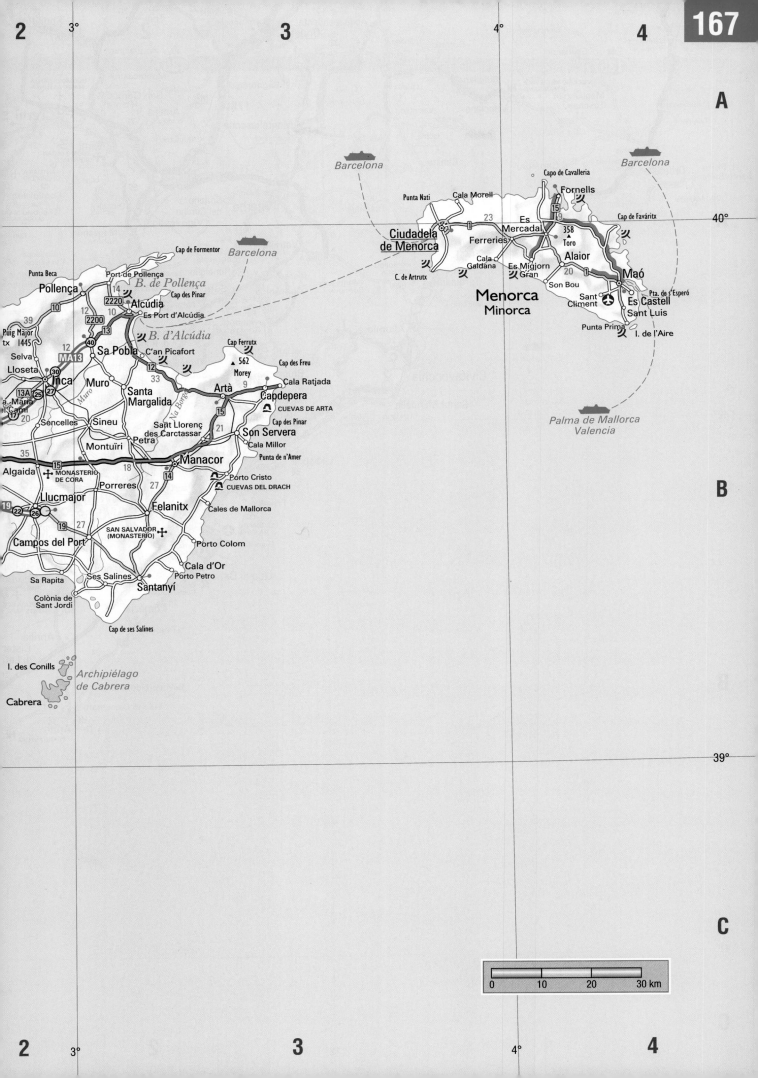

2 3° 3 4° 4

A

40°

Barcelona

Barcelona

Capo de Cavalleria

Punta Nati Cala Morell Fornells

15

Cap de Faváritx

23 Es 9
Mercadal

**Ciudadela
de Menorca** Ferreries 358 Alaior

Toro

Cala Es Migjorn 20 1 **Maó**
Galdana Gran

C. de Artrutx **Menorca** Son Bou Sant **Es Castell**
Minorca Climent Sant Luis

Punta Prima Pta. de s'Esperó

I. de l'Aire

Barcelona

Cap de Formentor

Punta Beca Port-de-Pollença **B. de Pollença**

Pollença 14 Cap des Pinar

10 2220 **Alcúdia**

39 2200 10

Puig Major 13 Es Port d'Alcúdia
tx 1445 12 40 **B. d'Alcúdia**

Selva MA13 **Sa Pobla** Cap Ferrutx

Lloseta 12 C'an Picafort ▲ 562

13A 30 **Inca** 33 Morey Cap des Freu

a. Maria 27 Muro Cala Ratjada
i Camí **Santa** 9
17 20 **Margalida** **Artà** **Capdepera**

Séncelles Sineu 15 **CUEVAS DE ARTA**

Sant Llorenç Cap des Pinar
des Carctassar 21 **Son Servera**
Petra
Cala Millor

35 Montuïri Punta de n'Amer

Algaida 15 **Manacor** Porto Cristo
✝ MONASTERIO 18 14
DE CORA **CUEVAS DEL DRACH**
Porreres 27

Llucmajor **Felanitx** Cales de Mallorca

19 22 26
SAN SALVADOR Porto Colom
19 27 (MONASTERIO) ✝

Campos del Port
Cala d'Or
Porto Petro

Sa Rapita Ses Salines
Santanyí

Colònia de
Sant Jordi

Cap de ses Salines

B

I. des Conills *Archipiélago
de Cabrera*

Cabrera

39°

C

0 10 20 30 km

2 3° 3 4° 4

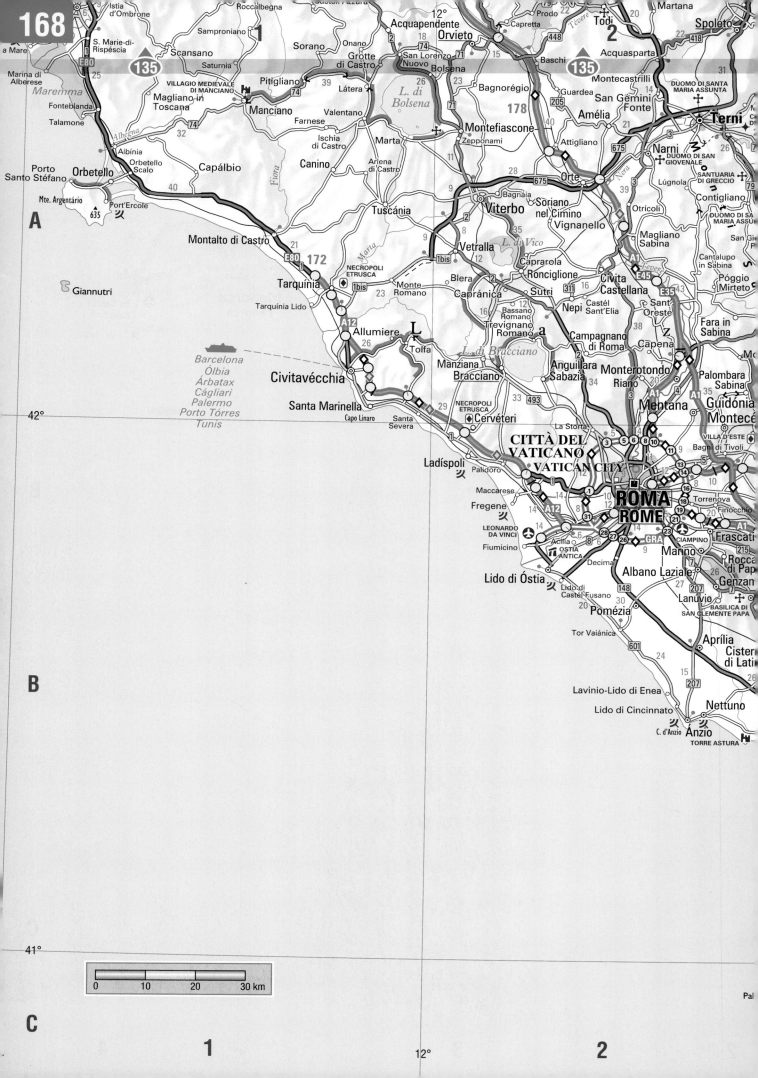

2 17° 3 18° 4

Dubrovnik

Durrës

Kerkyra
Igoumenitsa
Patra

Bari 12
Triggiano Mola di Bari
Capurso Noicáttaro E55 30
Adélfia Rutigliano 16
21 Polignano a Mare
Casamássima Conversano Monópoli
Turi PARCO ARCHEOLOGICO
21 172 GROTTA DI DI EGNAZIA
E843 CASTELLANA Castellana Savelletri
Sammichele Grotte 17
di Bari 100 Torre Canne
Putignano Fasano 23
Gióia del Colle Noci 14 Rosa Marina
604 Villanova
29 172 Locorotondo
Alberobello 172 8 E55
7 Ostuni 379
Cisternino 39 35
Martina Franca 16 Carovigno Torre Guaceto
27 581 Céglie 14
Móttola 24 Messápica San Vito 605 Bríndisi
Crispiano 172 Villa Castelli dei Normanni 13
Montemésola Francavilla 11
106 Massafra Fontana Canale Reale
Palagiano 16 172 Grottáglie E90 23 Mesagne 605
20 7 5 Oria Latiano San Pietro Casa l'Abate
35 E90 603 19 Torre Santa Vernótico Torchiarolo 27
106 Lido Azzurro 29 Susanna Cellino ABBAZIA SANTA
Castellaneta 5 8 11 7 S. Dónaci S. Marco MARIA DI CERRATE
Marina **Táranto** Monteparano Érchie Squinzano
Chéradi San Giórgio Iónico 7ter Fragagnano 17 31 Guagnano Trepuzzi San Cataldo
Marina di Ginosa Talsano Sava 7ter Sálice Cámpi 16 Surbo
PARCO ARCHEOLOGICO Lizzano 24 Mandúria San Pancrázio Salentino Salentina 543 12
METAPONTO Pulsano Torricella Salentino Véglie **Lecce** 366
Lido di Metaponto Avetrana 29 Leverano Léquile Monteroni di Lecce San Foca
Lido Silvana Marúggio 174 Copertino 101 San Cesário Vérnole Torre dell'Orso
Porto Cesáreo 20 367 di Lecce Melendugno
101 Galatina Soleto 30 Calimera 34
Nardò Galátone Martano
Santa Maria al Bagno Cutrofiano 275 Maglie Otranto
101 14 Collepasso 16 15
Gallípoli Alézio Poggiardo Uggiano C. d'Otranto
Sant'Andrea Parábita Nociglia la Chiesa
Casarano Diso Santa
24 Ruffano 38 Castro Cesárea Terme
Taviano Rácale Miggiano 358 43 GROTTA DI 40°
274 Taurisano Tricase ROMANELLI
Ugento Presicce & ZINZULUSA
Alessano
24 Marina di Nováglie
Castrignano del Capo Gagliano del Capo
C. Santa Maria di Léuca Marina di Léuca

G o l f o

d i

T á r a n t o

Kerkyra
Igoumenitsa
Sami
Patra

A

41°

B

40°

C

2 17° 3 18° 4

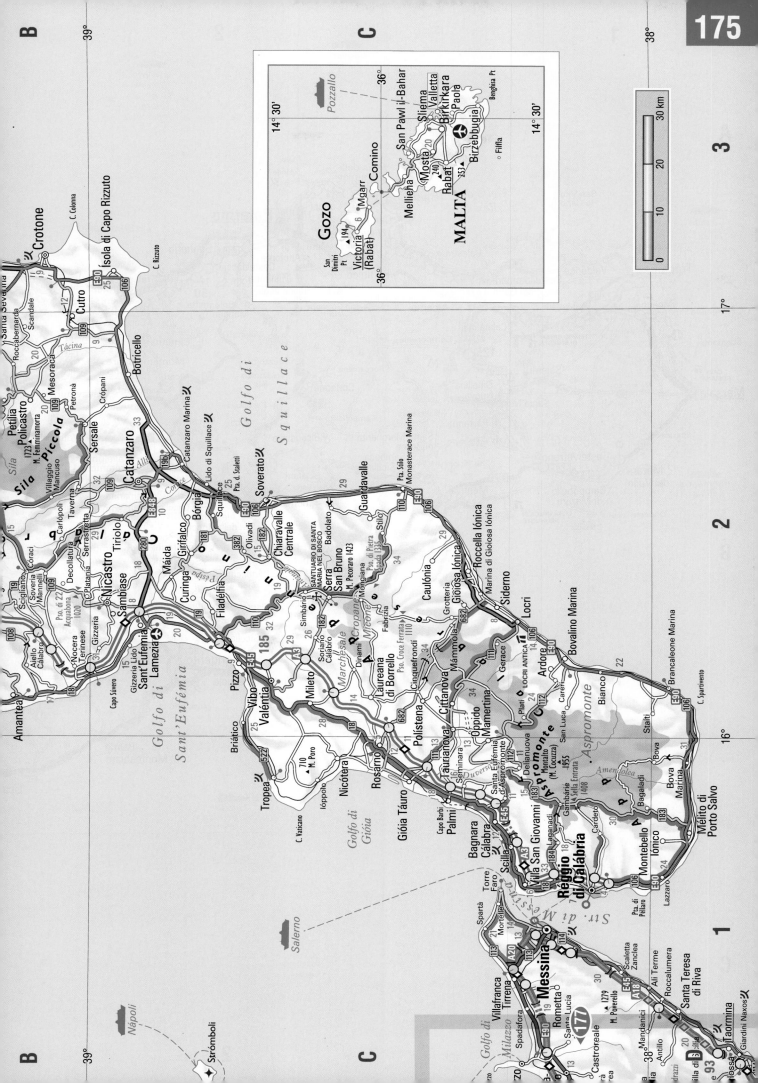

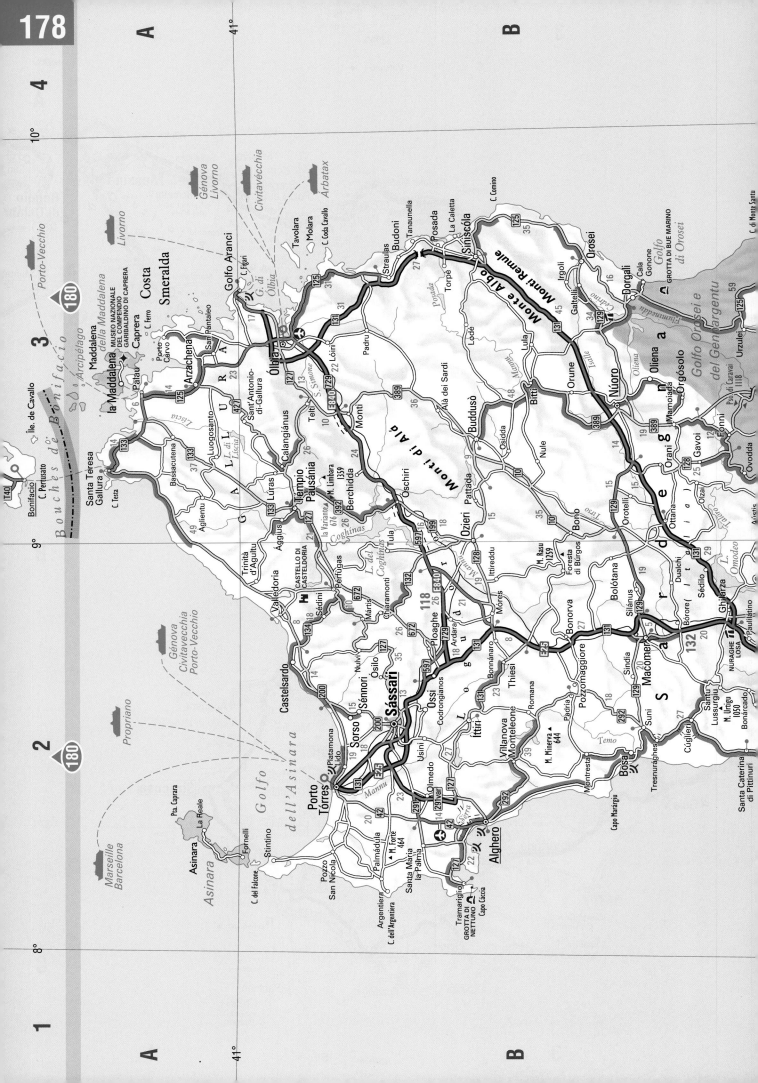

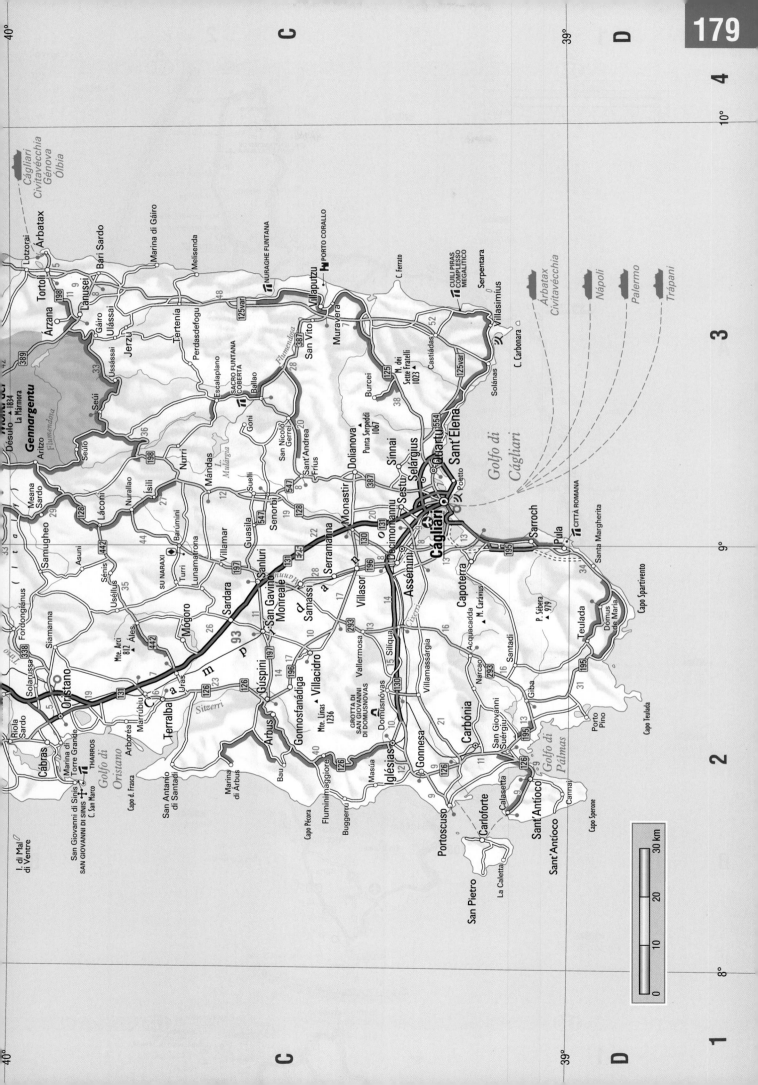

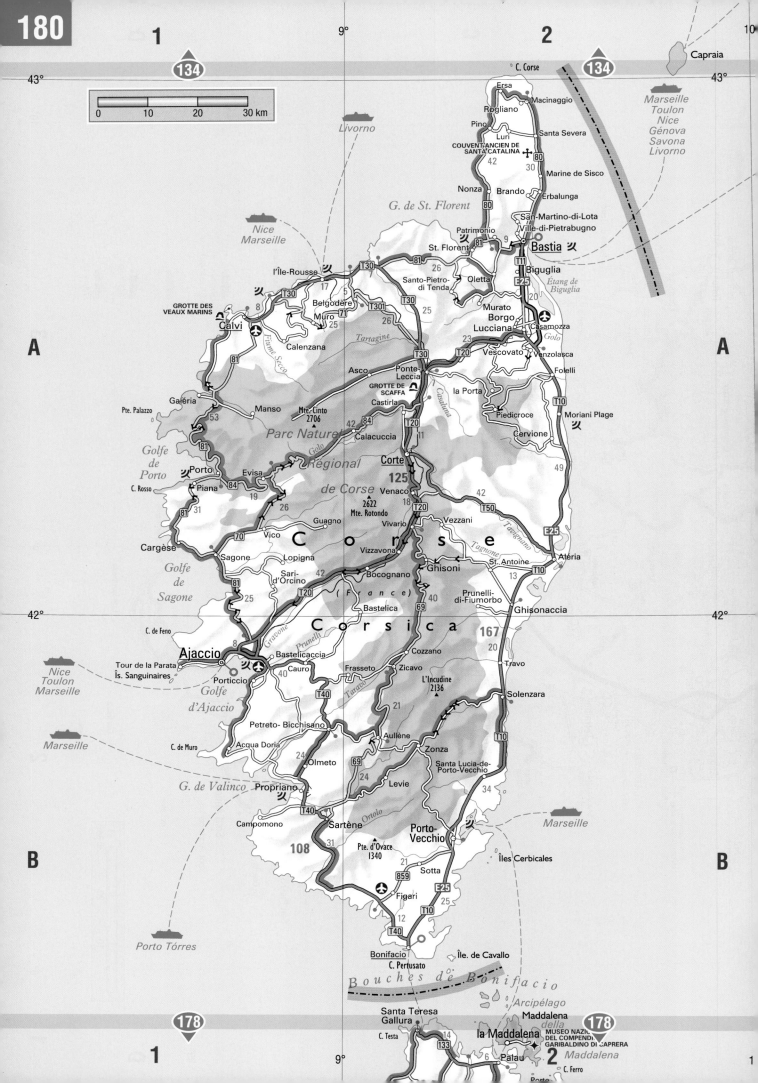

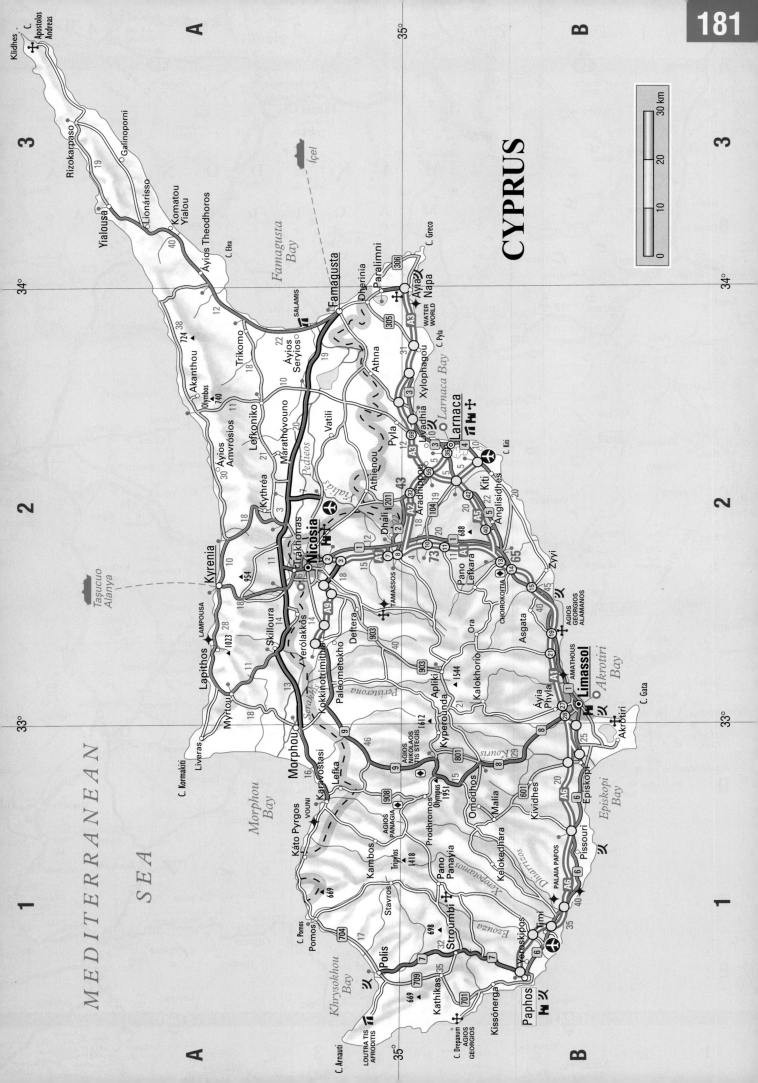

CYPRUS

MEDITERRANEAN

SEA

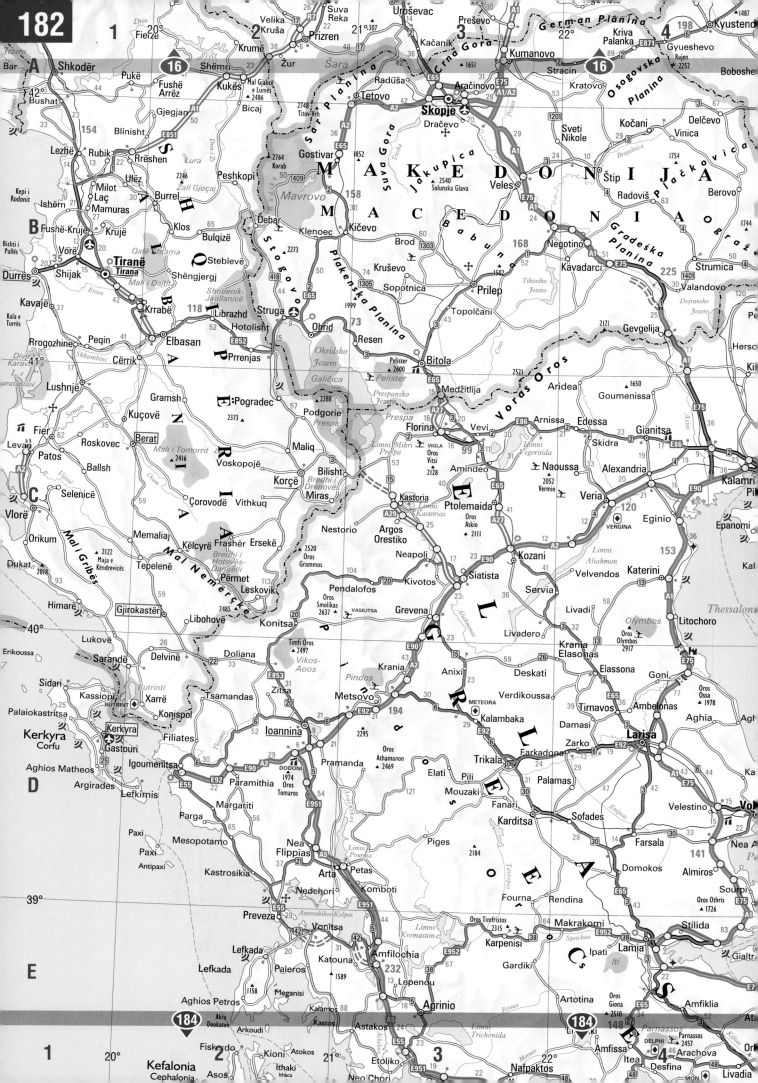

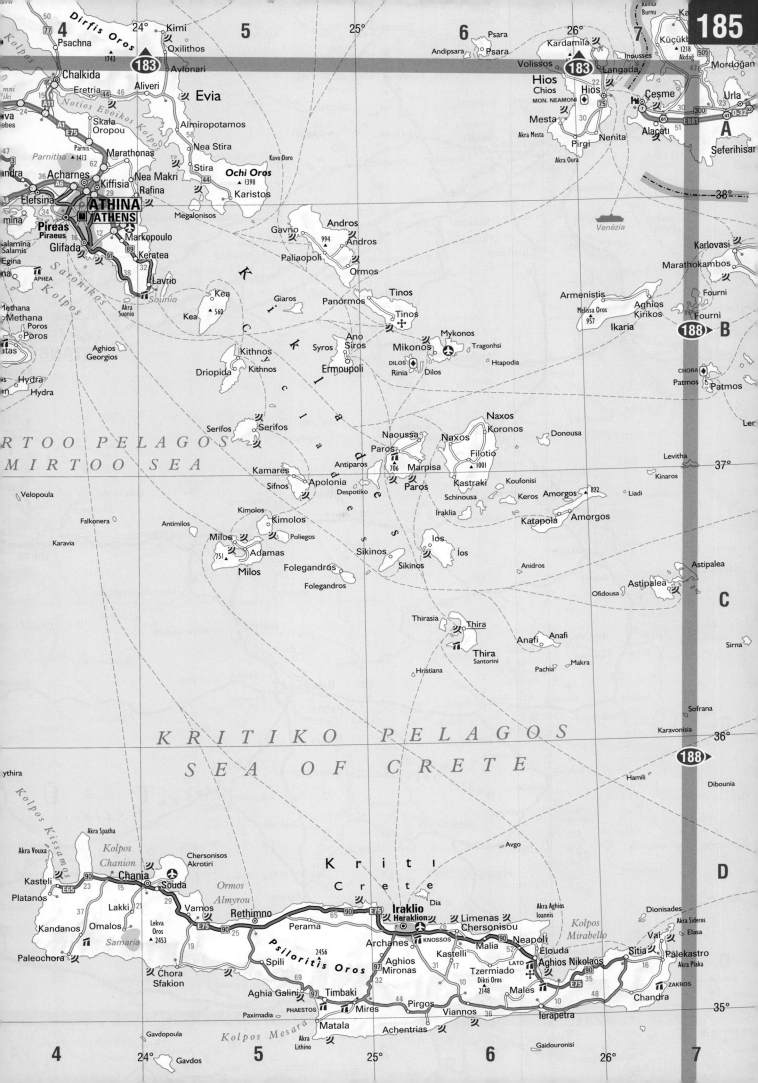

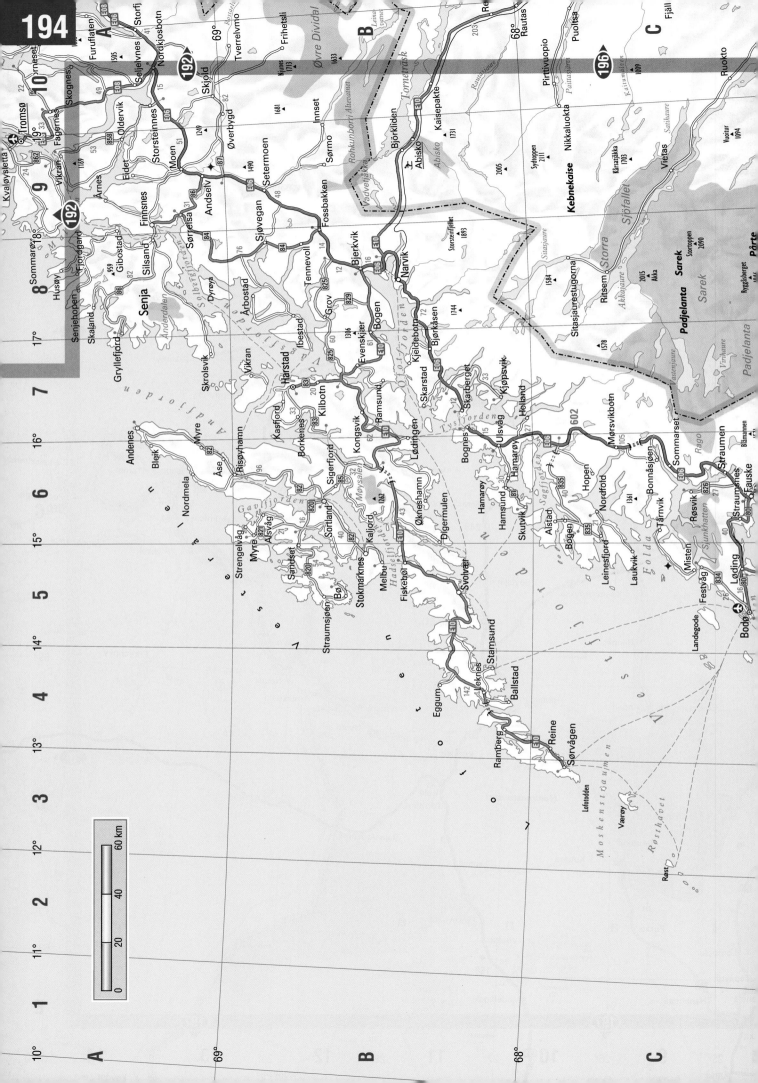

City plans · Plans de villes
Stadtpläne · Piante di città

Motorway	Autoroute	Autobahn	Autostrada
Major through route	Route principale majeur	Hauptstrecke	Strada di grande communicazione
Through route	Route principale	Schnellstrasse	Strada d'importanza regionale
Secondary road	Route secondaire	Nebenstrasse	Strada d'interesse locale
Dual carriageway	Chaussées séparées	Zweispurig Schnellstrasse	Strada a carreggiate doppie
Other road	Autre route	Nebenstrecke	Altra strada
Tunnel	Tunnel	Tunnel	Galleria stradale
Limited access / pedestrian road	Rue réglementée / rue piétonne	Beschränkter Zugang/ Fussgängerzone	Strada pedonale / a accesso limitato
One-way street	Sens unique	Einbahnstrasse	Senso unico
Parking	Parc de stationnement	Parkplatz	Parcheggio
Motorway number A7	Numéro d'autoroute	Autobahnnummer A7	Numero di autostrada
National road number 447	Numéro de route nationale	Nationalstrassennummer 447	Numero di strada nazionale
European road number E45	Numéro de route européenne	Europäische Strassennummer E45	Numero di strada europea
Destination GENT	Destination	Ziel GENT	Destinazione
Car ferry	Bac passant les autos	Autofähre	Traghetto automobili
Railway	Chemin de fer	Eisenbahn	Ferrovia
Rail / bus station	Gare / gare routière	Bahnhof / Busstation	Stazione ferrovia / pullman
Underground, metro station	Station de métro	U-Bahnstation	Metropolitano
Cable car	Téléférique	Drahtseilbahn	Funivia
Abbey, cathedral	Abbaye, cathédrale	Abtei, Kloster, Kathedrale	Abbazia, duomo
Church of interest	Église intéressante	Interessante Kirche	Chiesa da vedere
Synagogue	Synagogue	Synagoge	Sinagoga
Hospital	Hôpital	Krankenhaus	Ospedale
Police station	Police	Polizeiwache POL	Polizia
Post office	Bureau de poste	Postamt	Ufficio postale
Tourist information	Office de tourisme	Informationsbüro	Ufficio informazioni turistiche
Place of interest Theatre	Autre curiosité	Sonstige Sehenswürdigkeit Theatre	Luogo da vedere

Approach maps · Agglomérations
Carte régionale · Regionalkarte

Toll motorway – with motorway number A10	Autoroute à péage – avec numéro d'autoroute	Gebührenpflichtige Autobahn – mit Autobahnnummer A10	Autostrada a pedaggio – con numero
Toll-free motorway – with European road number E51	Autoroute avec numéro de route européenne	Gebührenfreie Autobahn – Europäische Strassennummer E51	Autostrada – con numero di strada europea
Pre-pay motorway – vignette required	Autoroute 'vignette'	Autobahn – 'vignette'	Autostrada – 'vignette'
Motorway services	Aire de service	Autobahnservice	Area di servizio autostradale
Motorway junction full access, restricted access	Échangeur d'autoroute accès libre, accès réglementé	Autobahnkreuz – voller/begrenzter Zugang	Raccordi autostradali – completo/parziali
Under construction	En construction	Im Bau	In construzione
Tunnel	Tunnel	Tunnel	Galleria stradale
Major route dual carriageway 14 single carriageway 14	Route principale chausées séparées chausée sans séparation	Hauptstrecke – zweispurige 14 Schnellstrasse 14	Strada di grande communicazione carreggiata doppia carreggiata unica
Secondary route dual carriageway 96 single carriageway 96	Route secondaire chausées séparées chausée sans séparation	Nebenstrasse – zweispurige 96 Schnellstrasse 96	Strada d'interesse locale – carreggiata doppia carreggiata unica
Other road	Autre route	Nebenstrecke	Altra strada
Car ferry	Bac passant les autos	Autofähre	Traghetto automobili
Destination GIRONA	Destination	Ziel GIRONA	Destinazione
Railway	Chemin de fer	Eisenbahn	Ferrovia
Railway station Estación Central	Gare	Hauptbahnhof Estación Central	Stazione ferrovia
Height – in metres 234	Altitude – en mètres 234	Höhe – über dem Meeresspiegel 234	Altezza in metri 234
Airport	Aéroport principal	Flughafen	Aeroporto
Airfield	Autre aéroport	Flugplatz	Aerodromo/ campo d'aviazione
City plan coverage area	Région de plan de ville	Vom Stadtplan abgedecktes Gebiet	Area della pianta della città

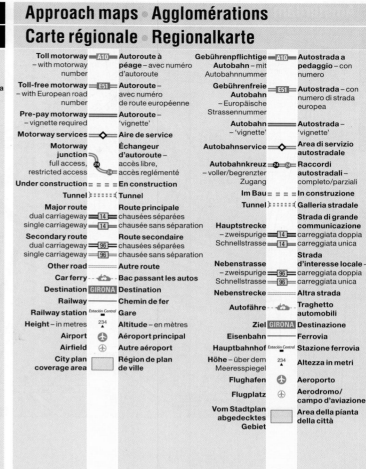

Alicante

0 km 0.5

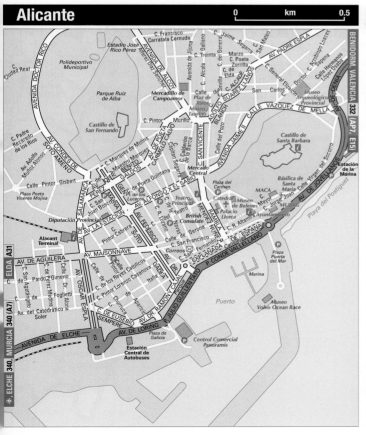

Antwerpen Antwerp

0 km 1

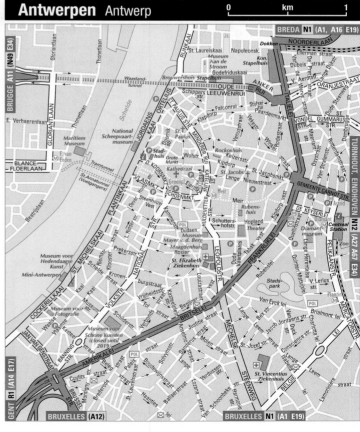

Amsterdam

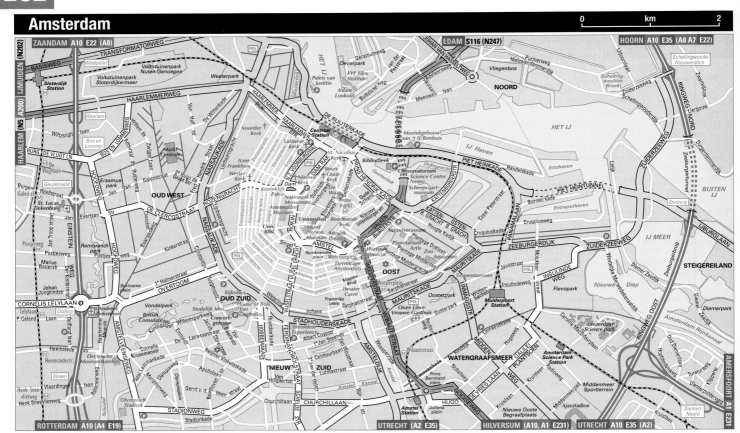

Amsterdam

Athina Athens

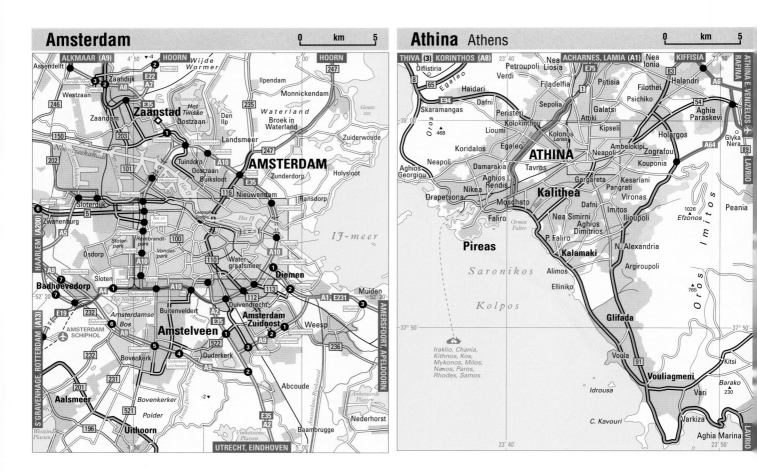

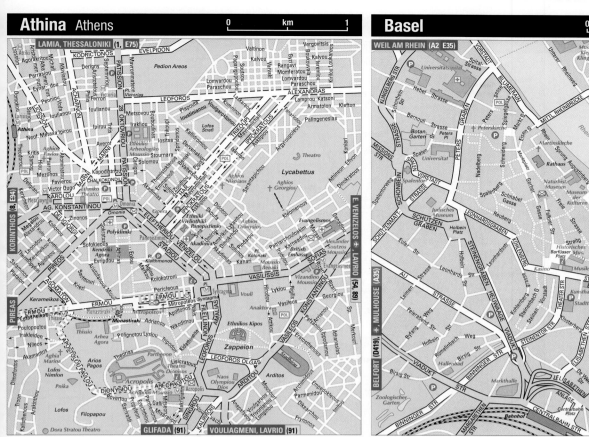

Athina Athens

0 km 1

LAMIA, THESSALONIKI (1, E75)

Basel

0 km 0.5

WEIL AM RHEIN (A2 E35)

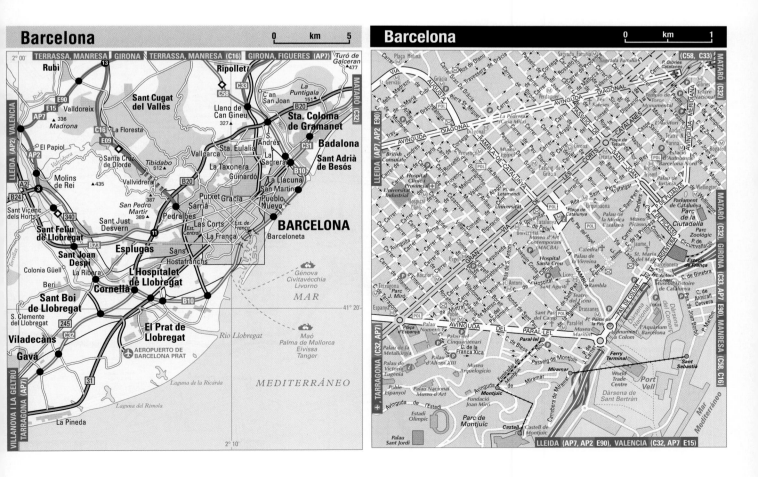

Barcelona

0 km 5

TERRASSA, MANRESA | GIRONA | TERRASSA, MANRESA (C16) | GIRONA, FIGUERES (AP7)

Barcelona

0 km 1

(C58, C33) | MATARÓ

LLEIDA (AP7), AP2 E90, VALENCIA (C32, AP7 E15)

Berlin

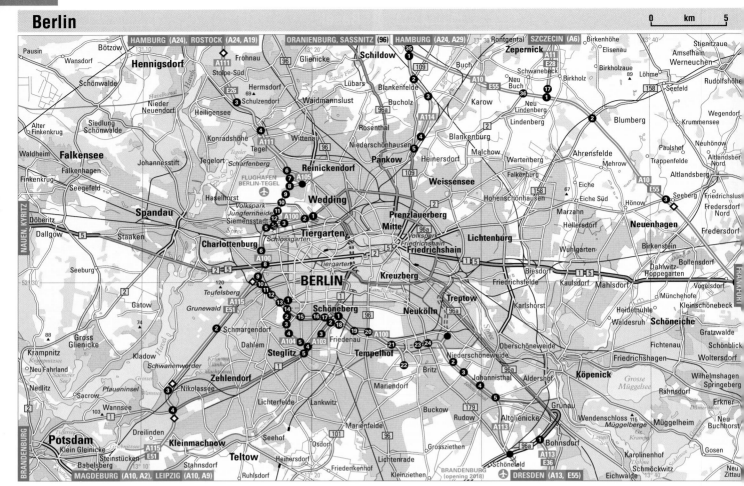

Berlin

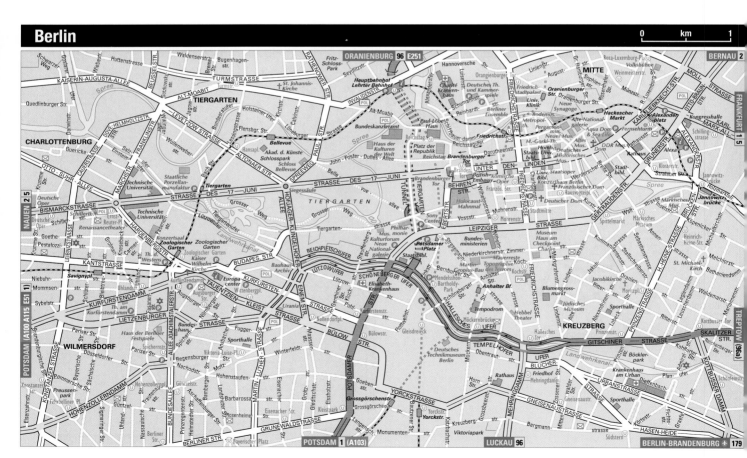

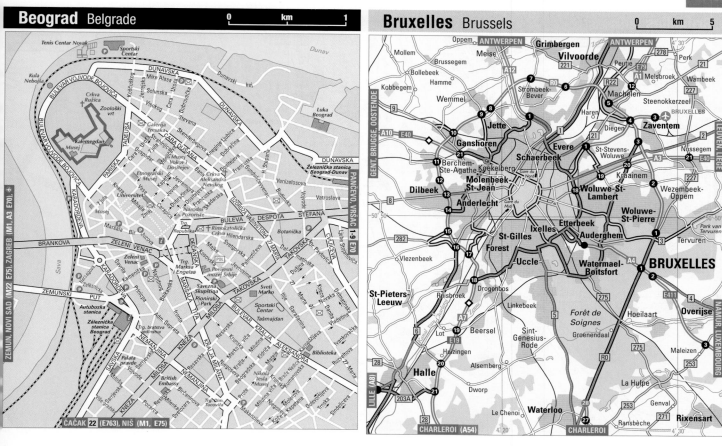

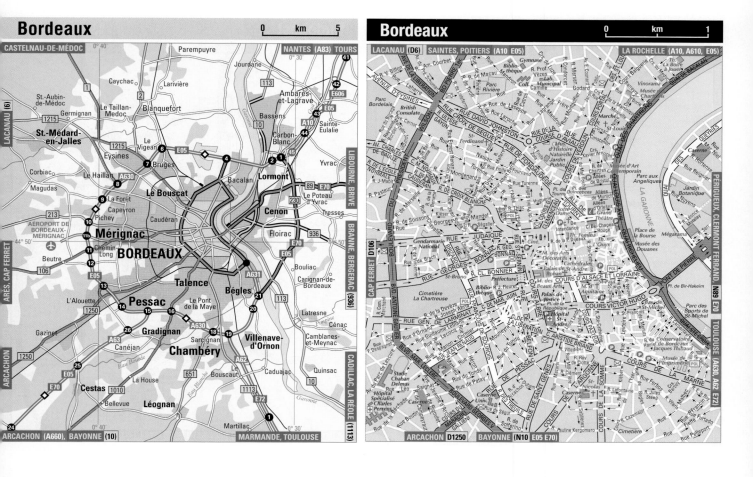

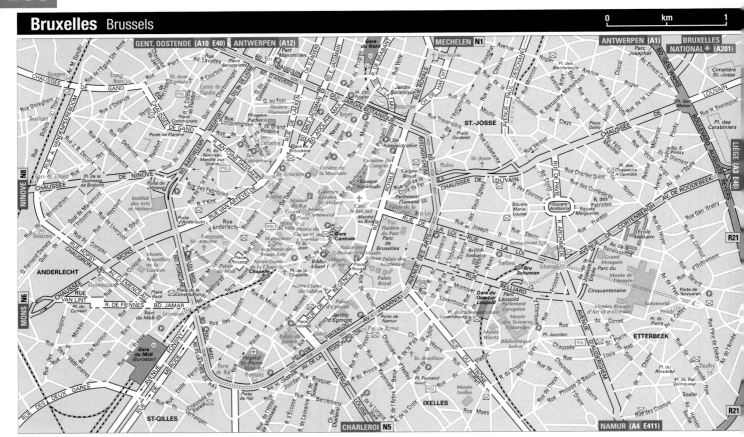

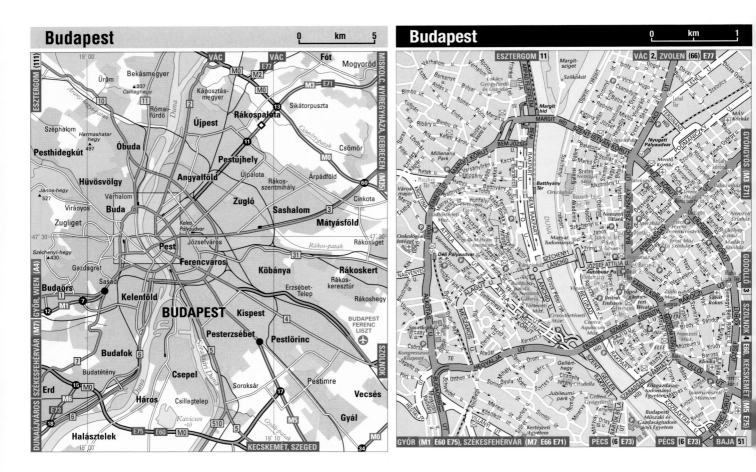

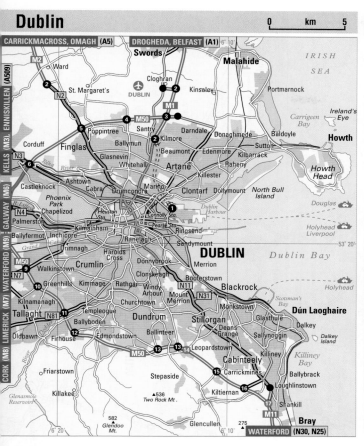

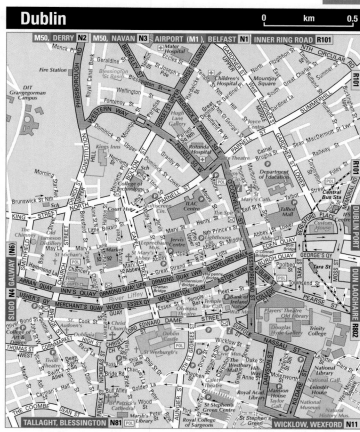

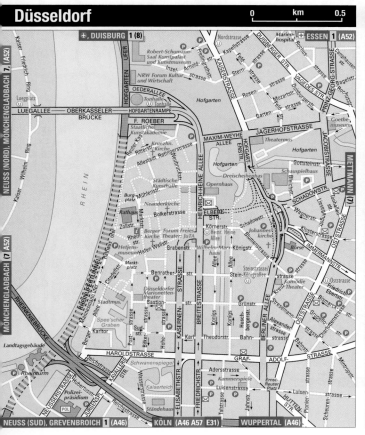

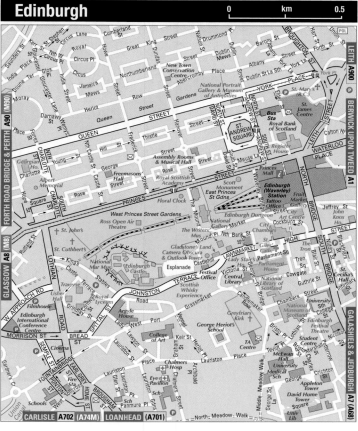

For **Cologne** see page 212
For **Copenhagen** see page 212

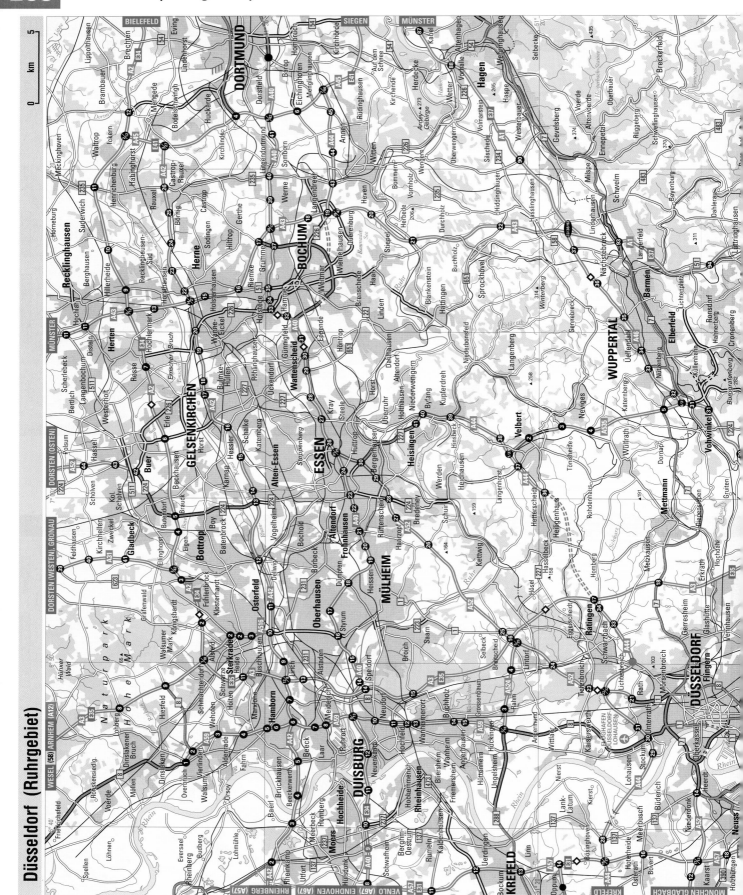

Firenze Florence

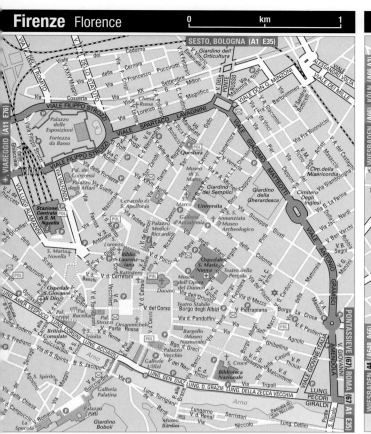

Frankfurt

Genève Geneva

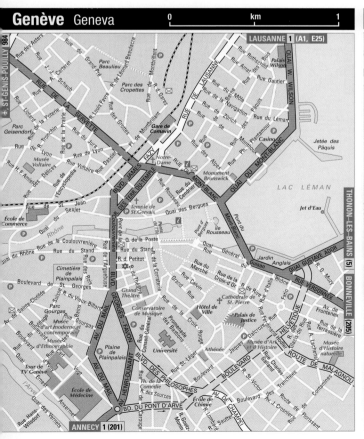

Génova Genoa

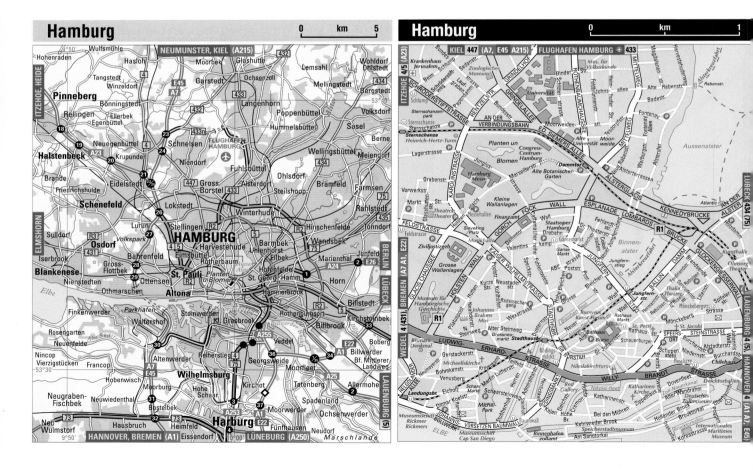

Helsinki

İstanbul

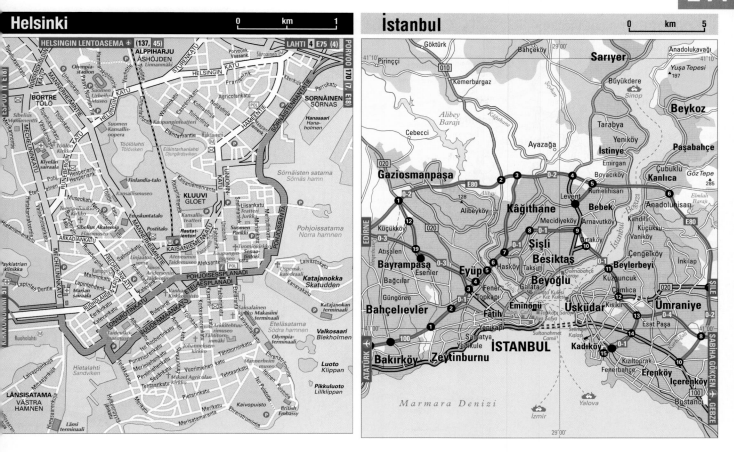

Helsinki

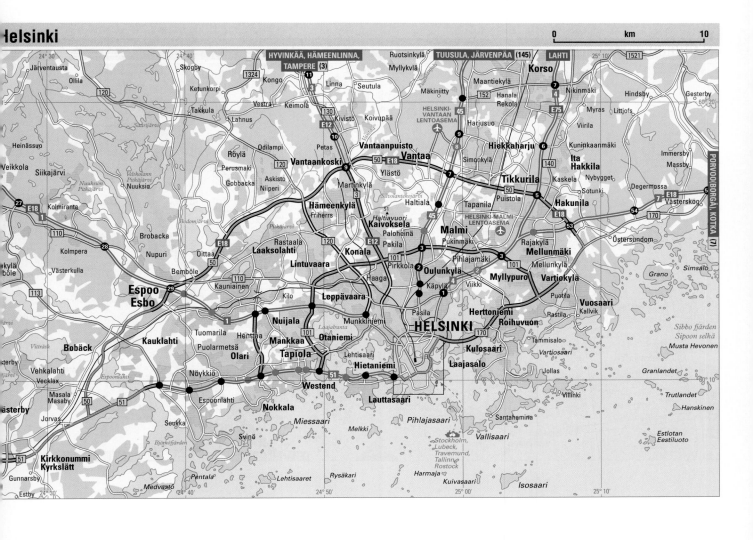

København Copenhagen

0 km 5

HILLERØD
HELSINGØR
Lille Værløse
Kirke Værløse
Furesø
Virum
Brede
Jægersborg Dyrehave
Taarbæk
Frederiksdal
Kongens Lyngby
Klampenborg
Ordrup
Jonstrup
Store Hareskov
Bagsværd
Jægersborg
Skovshoved
Hareskovby
Måløv
Hjortespring
Buddinge
Vangede
Gentofte
Charlottenlund
Pederstrup
Herlev
Gladsakse
Søborg
Hellerup
Oslo Frederica
Ballerup
Ågerup
Skovlunde
Husum
Svanemøllen
Ledøje
Ejby
Brønshøj
Bispebjerg
Fælledparken
KØBENHAVN
Klaipeda
Risby
Vestskoven
Islev
Vanløse
Rosenborg Have
Refshaleøen
Herstedøster
Rødovre
Frederiksberg
Christianshavn
Glostrup
Brøndbyøster
Valby
Sundbyerne
Albertslund
Hvidovre
Taastrup
Vallensbæk
Brøndbyvester
Avedøre
Kastrup
Trængilde
Tårnby
Ishøj Strand
Brøndby Strand
Vallensbæk Strand
KØBENHAVN/ KASTRUP LUFTHAVN
Hundige Strand
Amager
Store Magleby
Greve Strand
Ullerup
Dragør
Sydstranden
Søvang
Køge Bugt
Kongelunden
Aflandshage

HOLBÆK
ODENSE (E20), MARIBO (E47 E55)
MALMÖ

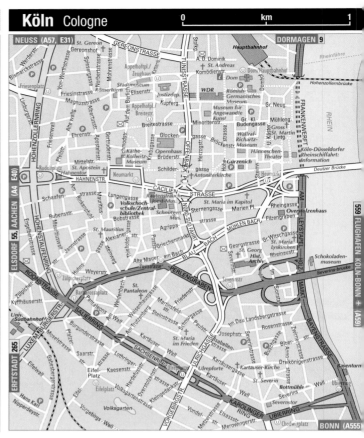

Köln Cologne

0 km 1

NEUSS (A57, E31)
DORMAGEN 9
St. Gereon
Gereonshof
GEREONSTRASSE
Hauptbahnhof
Rheinfähre
Dom/Hauptbahnhof
A. D. Dominik
St. Andreas
Dom
Römisch-Germanisches Museum
WDR
Museum für Angewandte Kunst
Wallraf-Richartz-Museum
Köln-Düsseldorfer Rheinschiffahrt-Information
Opernhaus Brüderstr.
Gürzenich
Hänneschen-Theater
Deutzer Brücke
HAHNENSTR.
Neumarkt
St. Aposteln
St. Antoniterkirche
Overstolzenhaus
RHEIN
CÄCILIEN
STRASSE
ELSDORF 55, AACHEN (A4 E40)
St. Maria im Kapitol
Schokoladenmuseum
Volksschule/Zentral-bibliothek
St. Maria im Frieden
ERFTSTADT 265
St. Pantaleon
Barbarossaplatz
St. Severin
Uni. Südbahnhof
Eifelplatz
Volksgarten
BONN (A555)
FLUGHAFEN KÖLN-BONN (A59)

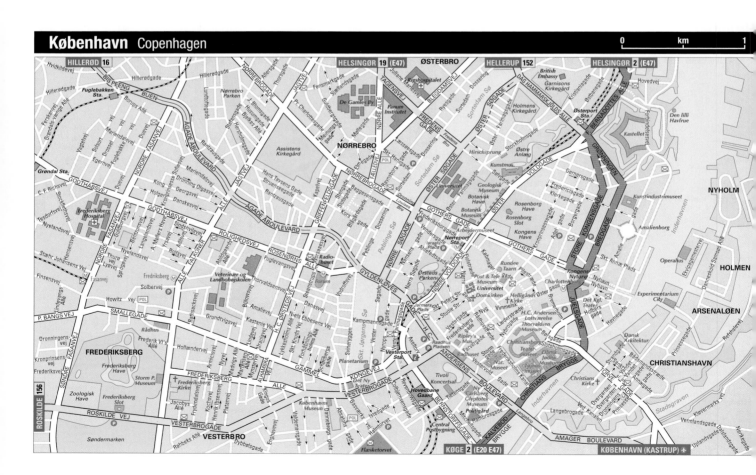

København Copenhagen

0 km 1

HILLERØD 16
HELSINGØR 19 (E47)
ØSTERBRO
HELLERUP 152
HELSINGØR 2 (E47)
British Embassy
Rigshospitalet
Østerport Sta.
Den lille Havfrue
Fuglebakken Sta.
De Gamles By
Panum Institutet
Kastellet
NYHOLM
Grøndal Sta.
Assistens Kirkegård
NØRREBRO
Universitet
Botanisk Have
Rosenborg Slot
Kunstindustrimuseet
HOLMEN
Frederiksberg Hospital
Nørreport Sta.
Rosenborg Have
Kongens Have
Operahus
ARSENALØEN
Forum
Amalienborg
Veterinær- og Landbohøjskolen
Radiohuset
Universitet
Domkirken
Charlottenborg
Dansk Arkitektur
Planetarium
Rådhus
Vesterport Sta.
Ripley's
H.C. Andersens Eventyr
Christiansborg Slot
CHRISTIANSHAVN
FREDERIKSBERG
Zoologisk Have
Frederiksberg Slot
Frederiksberg Have
Tivoli
Ny Carlsberg Glyptotek
Politigård
Christians Kirke
Hovedbane Gaard
Central Postbygning
VESTERBRO
Flæsketorvet
ROSKILDE 156
KØGE 2 (E20 E47)
KØBENHAVN (KASTRUP)

ROSKILDE VEJ
VESTERBROGADE
AMAGER BOULEVARD

Lisboa Lisbon

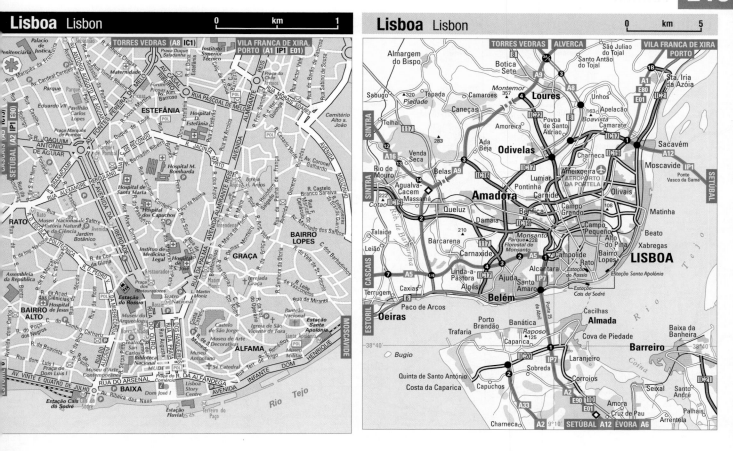

London

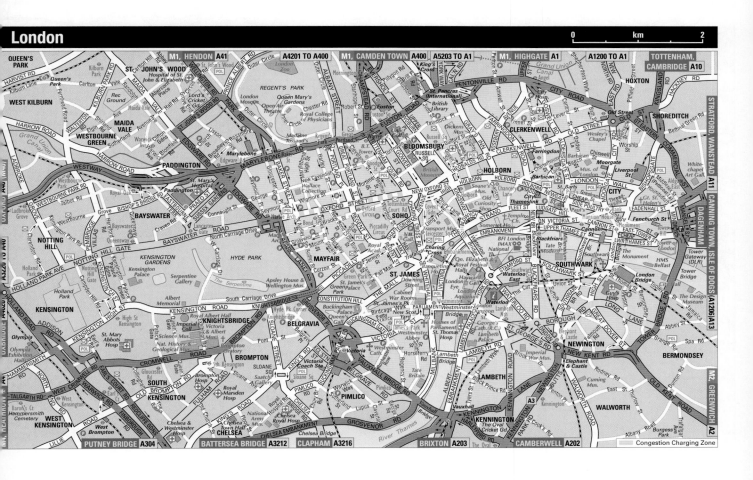

London

0   km

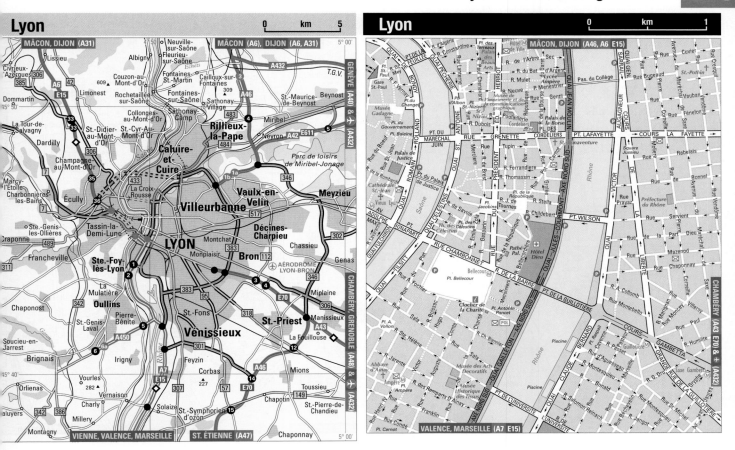

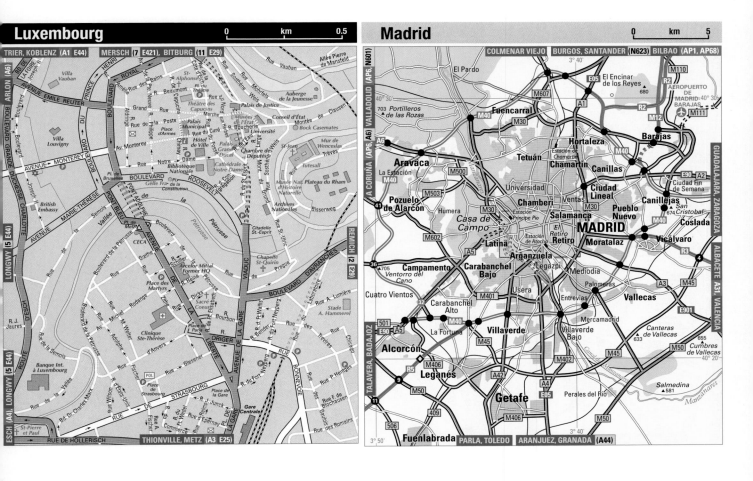

Madrid

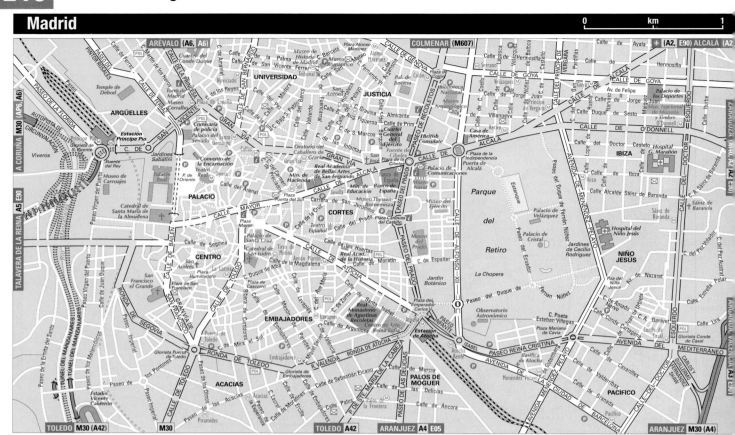

Málaga

Marseille / Marseilles

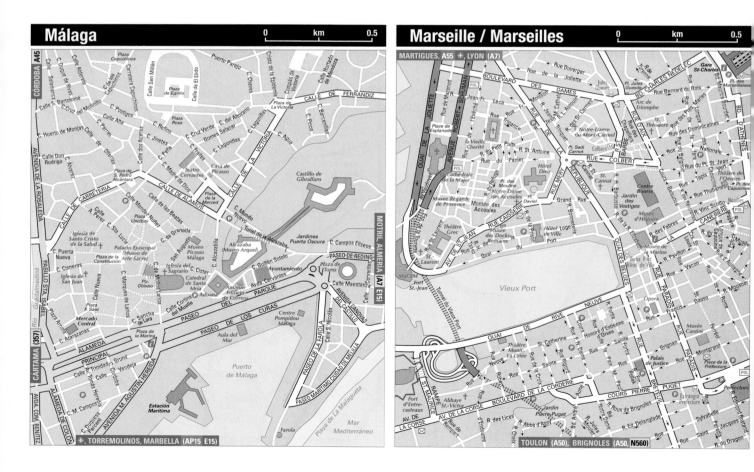

Milano Milan

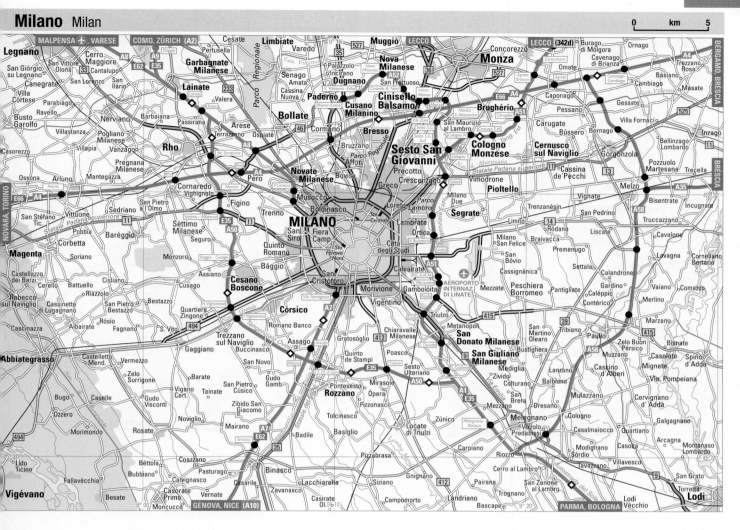

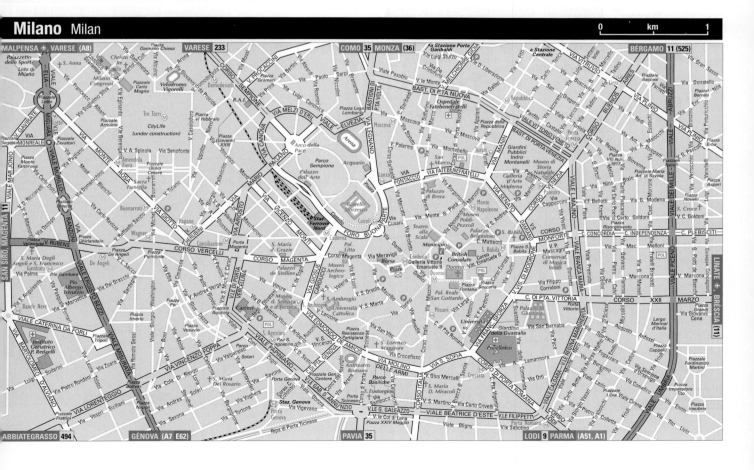

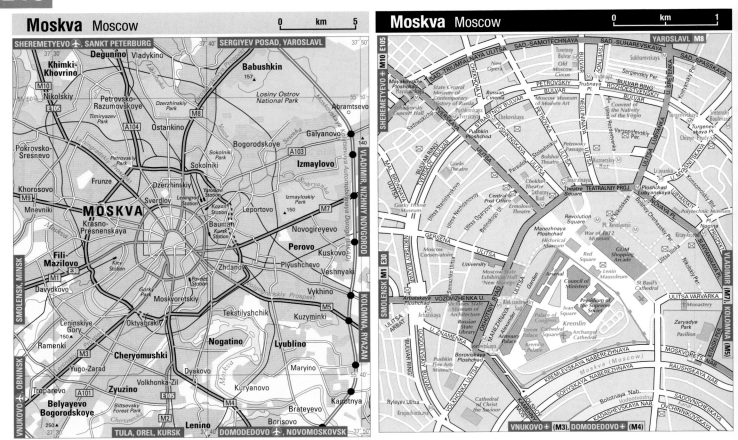

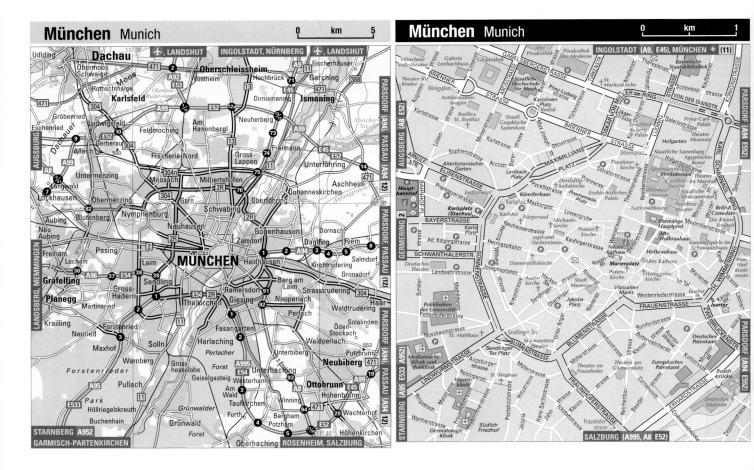

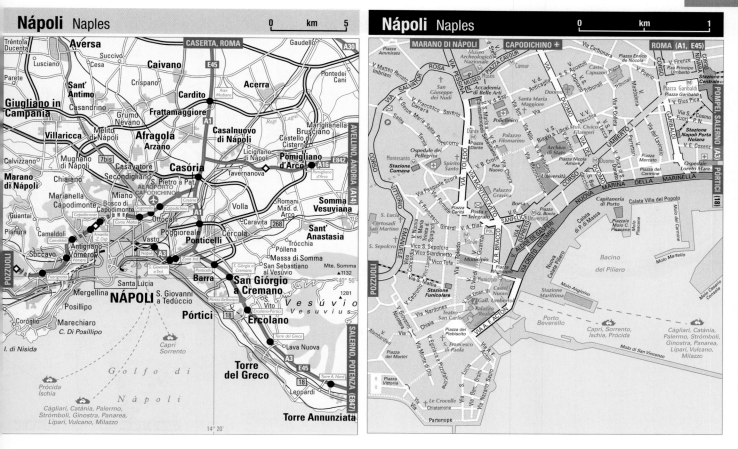

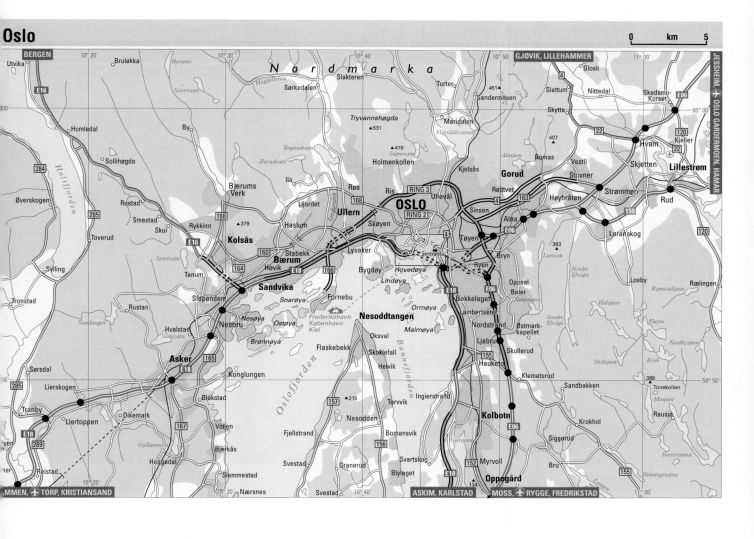

Oslo

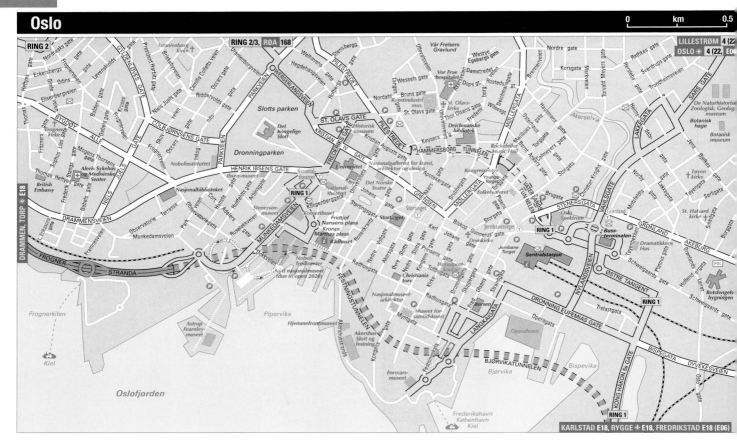

Paris

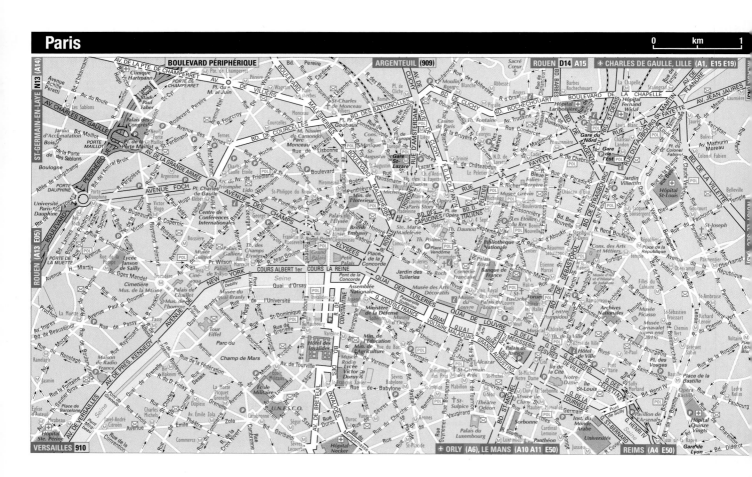

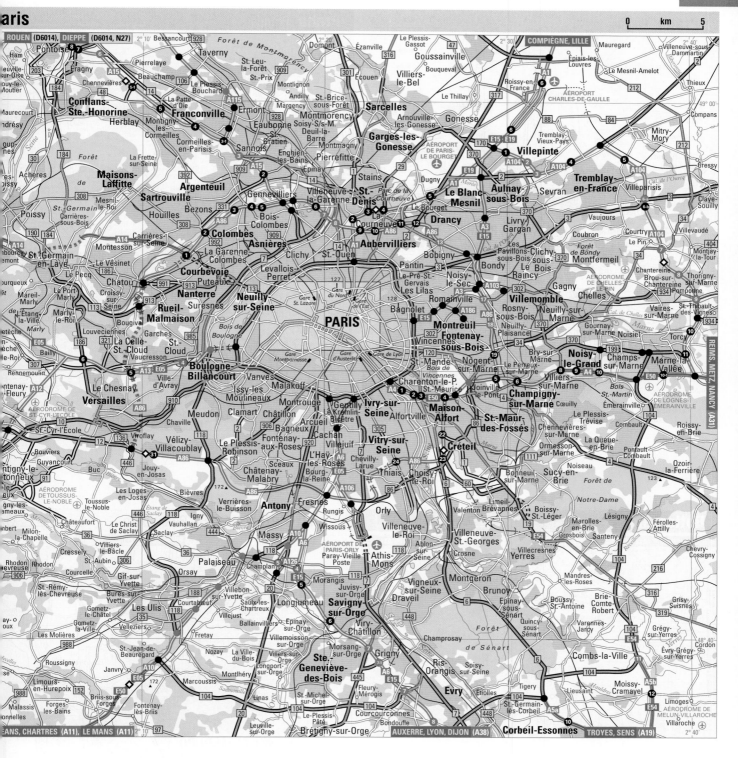

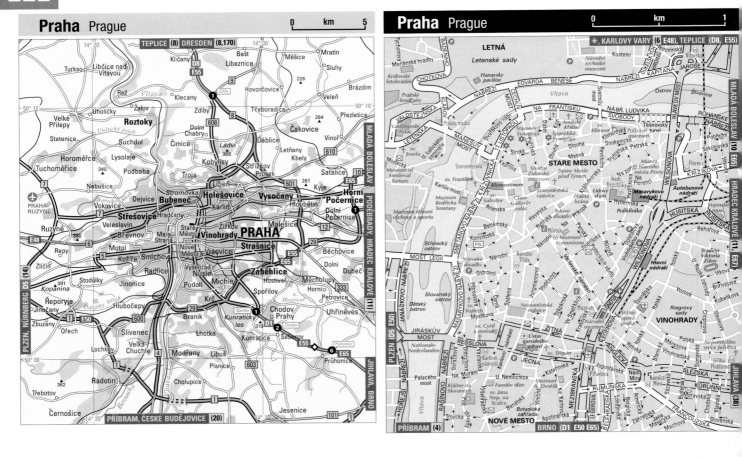

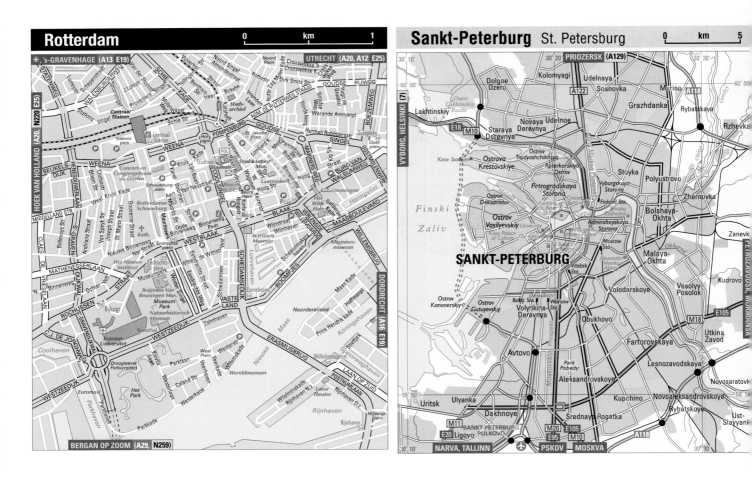

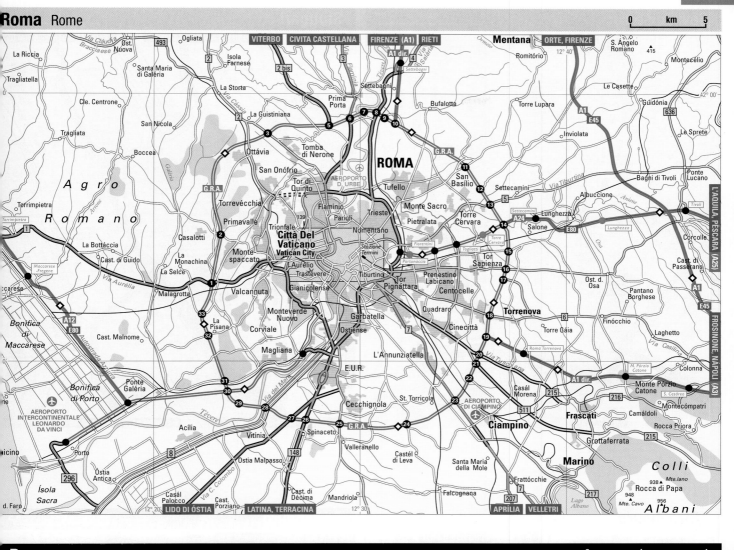

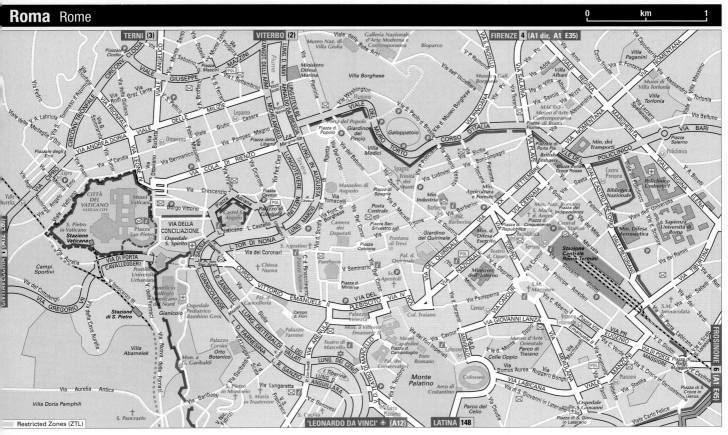

Restricted Zones (ZTL)

Sevilla Seville

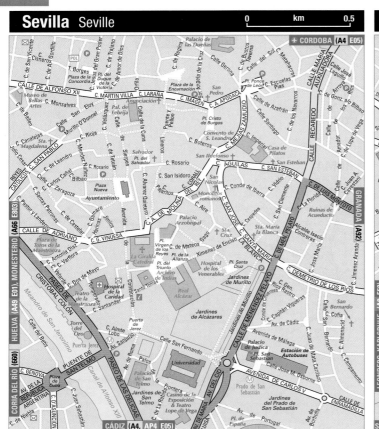

Stuttgart

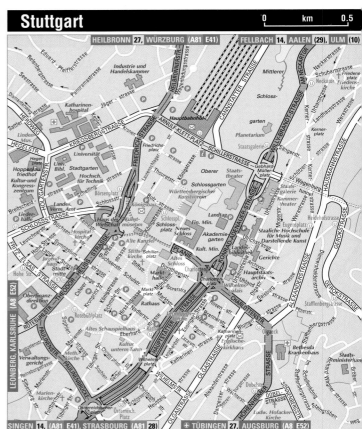

Strasbourg

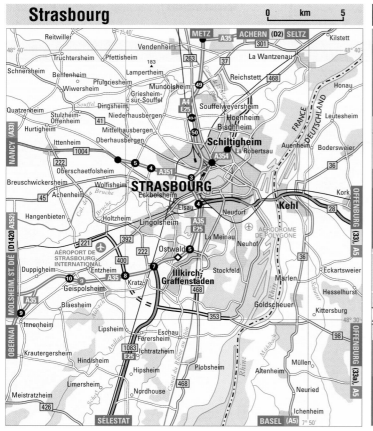

Strasbourg

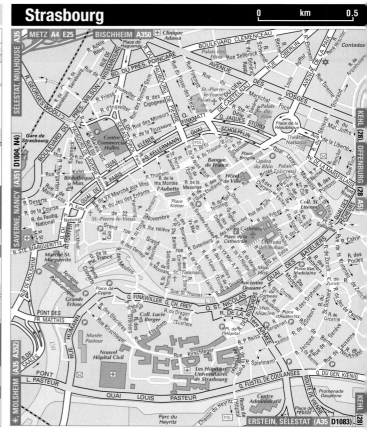

Stockholm

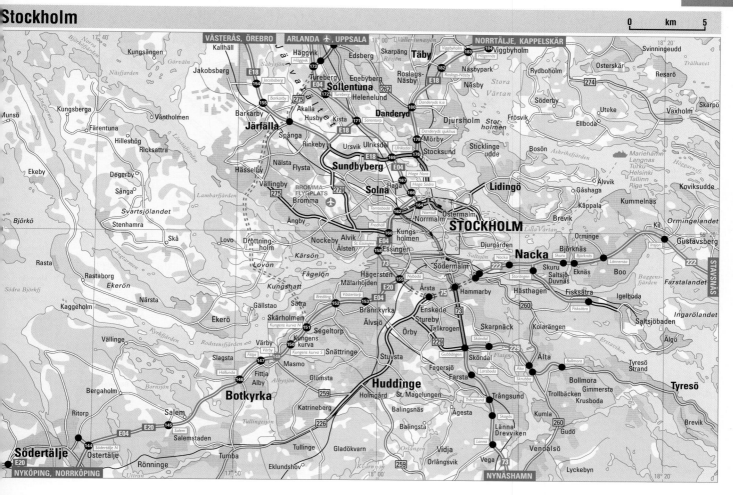

Stockholm

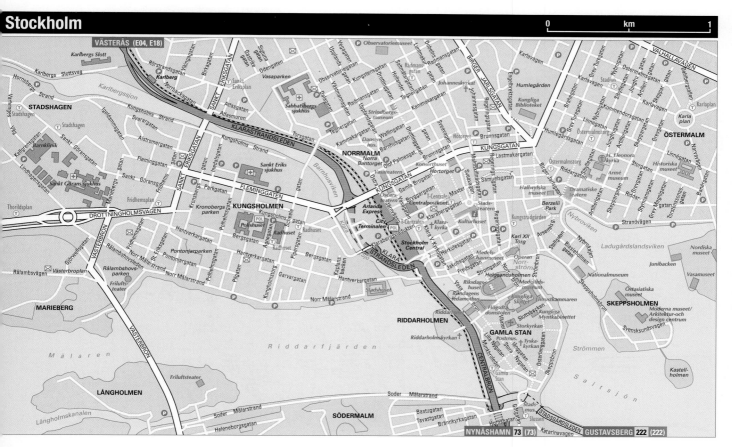

Torino Turin

0 ___ km

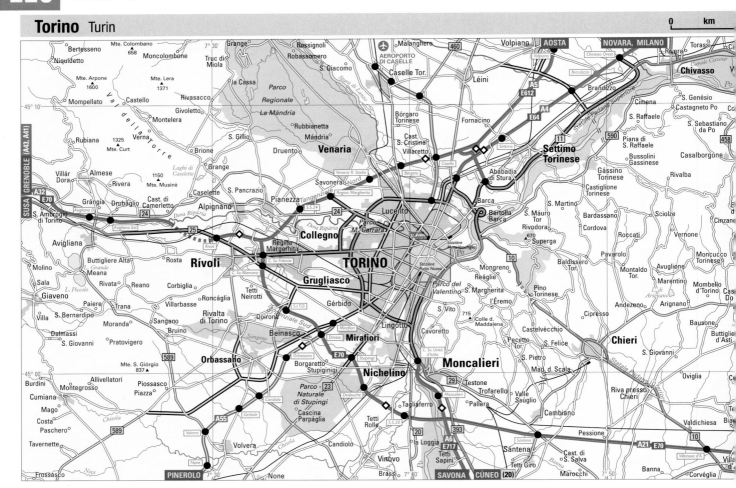

Venézia Venice

0 ___ km ___ 0.

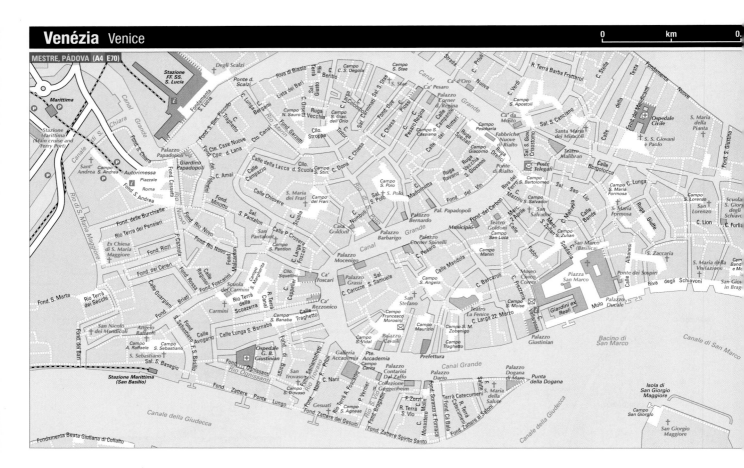

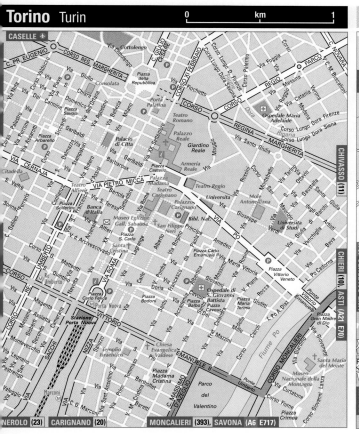

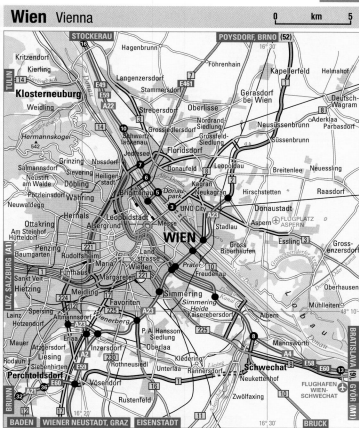

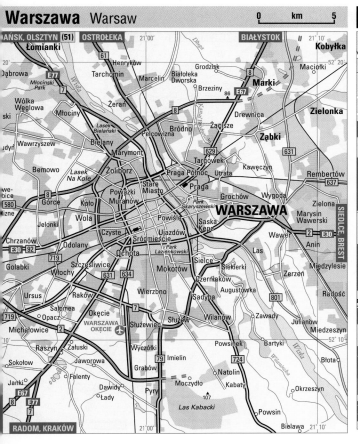

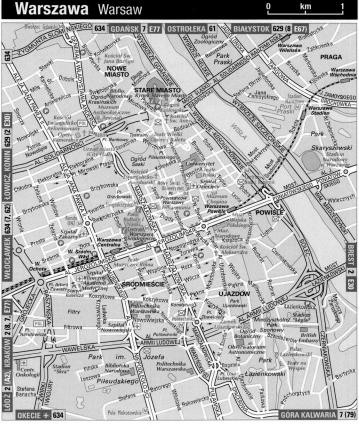

Wien Vienna

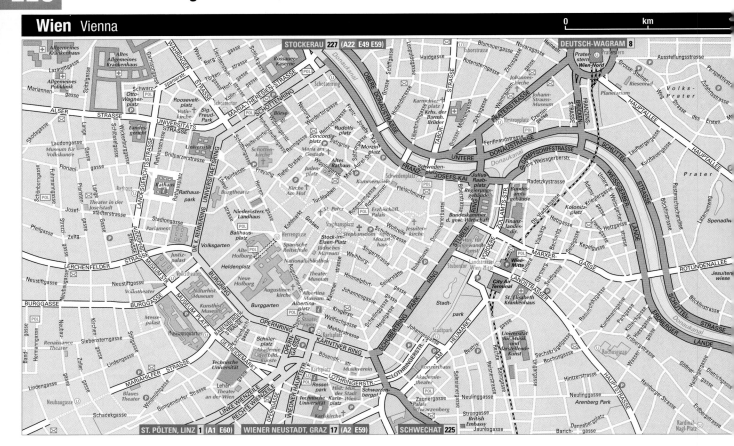

Zagreb

Zürich

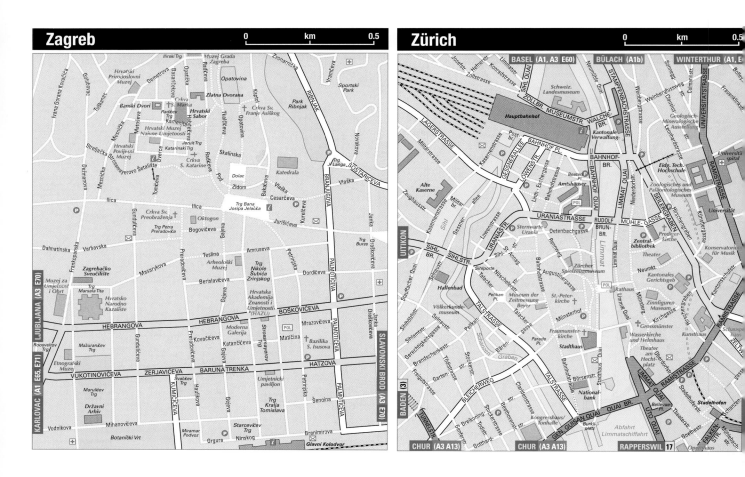

	English	French	German	Italian
(A)	Austria	Autriche	Österreich	Austria
(AL)	Albania	Albanie	Albanien	Albania
(AND)	Andorra	Andorre	Andorra	Andorra
(B)	Belgium	Belgique	Belgien	Belgio
(BG)	Bulgaria	Bulgarie	Bulgarien	Bulgaria
(BIH)	Bosnia-Herzegovin	Bosnie-Herzegovine	Bosnien-Herzegowina	Bosnia-Herzogovina
(BY)	Belarus	Belarus	Weissrussland	Bielorussia
(CH)	Switzerland	Suisse	Schweiz	Svizzera
(CY)	Cyprus	Chypre	Zypern	Cipro
(CZ)	Czechia	République Tchèque	Tschechische Republik	Repubblica Ceca
(D)	Germany	Allemagne	Deutschland	Germania
(DK)	Denmark	Danemark	Dänemark	Danimarca
(E)	Spain	Espagne	Spanien	Spagna
(EST)	Estonia	Estonie	Estland	Estonia
(F)	France	France	Frankreich	Francia
(FIN)	Finland	Finlande	Finnland	Finlandia
(FL)	Liechtenstein	Liechtenstein	Liechtenstein	Liechtenstein
(FO)	Faeroe Islands	Îles Féroé	Färoer-Inseln	Isole Faroe
(GB)	United Kingdom	Royaume Uni	Grossbritannien und Nordirland	Regno Unito
(GBZ)	Gibraltar	Gibraltar	Gibraltar	Gibilterra
(GR)	Greece	Grèce	Greichenland	Grecia
(H)	Hungary	Hongrie	Ungarn	Ungheria
(HR)	Croatia	Croatie	Kroatien	Croazia
(I)	Italy	Italie	Italien	Italia
(IRL)	Ireland	Irlande	Irland	Irlanda
(IS)	Iceland	Islande	Island	Islanda
(KOS)	Kosovo	Kosovo	Kosovo	Kosovo
(L)	Luxembourg	Luxembourg	Luxemburg	Lussemburgo
(LT)	Lithuania	Lituanie	Litauen	Lituania
(LV)	Latvia	Lettonie	Lettland	Lettonia
(M)	Malta	Malte	Malta	Malta
(MC)	Monaco	Monaco	Monaco	Monaco
(MD)	Moldova	Moldavie	Moldawien	Moldavia
(MK)	Macedonia	Macédoine	Makedonien	Macedonia
(MNE)	Montenegro	Monténégro	Montenegro	Montenegro
(N)	Norway	Norvège	Norwegen	Norvegia
(NL)	Netherlands	Pays-Bas	Niederlande	Paesi Bassi
(P)	Portugal	Portugal	Portugal	Portogallo
(PL)	Poland	Pologne	Polen	Polonia
(RO)	Romania	Roumanie	Rumanien	Romania
(RSM)	San Marino	Saint-Marin	San Marino	San Marino
(RUS)	Russia	Russie	Russland	Russia
(S)	Sweden	Suède	Schweden	Svezia
(SK)	Slovakia	République Slovaque	Slowak Republik	Repubblica Slovacca
(SLO)	Slovenia	Slovénie	Slowenien	Slovenia
(SRB)	Serbia	Serbie	Serbien	Serbia
(TR)	Turkey	Turquie	Türkei	Turchia
(UA)	Ukraine	Ukraine	Ukraine	Ucraina

A

Aabenraa DK 64 A2
Aabybro DK 58 A2
Aach D 107 B4
Aachen D 80 B2
Aalborg DK 58 A2
Aalen D 94 C2
Aalestrup DK . . .58 B2
Aalsmeer NL 70 B1
Aalst B 79 B4
Aalten NL 71 C3
Aalter B 79 A3
Äänekoski FIN 8 A4
Aapajärvi FIN . . .197 B10
Aäpınar TR 187 C5
Aarau CH 106 B3
Aarberg CH 106 B2
Aarburg CH 106 B2
Aardenburg NL . . .79 A3
Aars DK 58 B2
Aarschot B 79 B4
Aarup DK 59 C3
Aba H 112 B2
Abádanes E 152 B1
Abades E 151 B3
Abadin E 141 A3
Abádszalók H . . .113 B4
Abaliget H 125 A4
Abana TR 23 A8
A Baña E 140 B2
Abanilla E 165 A3
Abano Terme I . . .121 B4
Abarán E 165 A3
Abasár H 113 B4
Abbadia San Salvatore
I 135 C4
Abbaue D 74 A2
Abbehausen D . . .72 A1
Abbekäs S 66 A2
Abbeville F 90 A1
Abbey IRL 28 A3
Abbeydorney IRL . .29 B2
Abbeyfeale IRL . . .29 B2
Abbeyleix IRL 30 B1
Abbey Town GB . . .36 B3
Abbiategrasso I . . .120 B1
Abborrträsk S . . .196 D2
Abbots Bromley
GB 40 C2
Abbotsbury GB . . .43 B4
Abda H 111 B4
Abejar E 143 C4
Abela P 160 B1
Abelvær N 199 A8
Abenberg D 94 B2
Abenójar E 157 B3
Abensberg D 95 C3
Aberaeron GB 39 B2
Abercarn GB 39 C3
Aberchirder GB . . .33 D4
Aberdare GB 39 C3
Aberdaron GB 38 B2
Aberdeen GB 33 D4
Aberdulais GB 39 C3
Aberdyfi GB 39 B2
Aberfeldy GB 35 B4
Aberffraw GB 38 A2
Aberfoyle GB 34 B3
Abergavenny GB . . .39 C3
Abergele GB 38 A3
Abergynolwyn GB . .38 B3
Aberporth GB 39 B2
Abersoch GB 38 B2
Abertillery GB 39 C3
Abertura E 156 A2
Aberystwyth GB . . .39 B2
Abetone I 135 A3
Abfaltersbach A . . .109 C3
Abide
 Çanakkale TR . . .186 B1
 Kütahya TR 187 D4
Abiego E 145 B3
Abild DK 64 B1
Abingdon-on-Thames
GB 44 B2
Abington GB 36 A3
Abisko S 194 B9
Abiul P 154 B2

Abla E 164 B2
Ablis F 90 C1
A Bola E 140 B3
Abondance F 118 A3
Abony H 113 B4
Aboyne GB 33 D4
Abrantes P 154 B2
Abreiro P 148 A2
Abreschviller F . . .92 C3
Abrest F 117 A3
Abriès F 119 C3
Abrud RO 17 B5
Absdorf A 97 C3
Abtenau A 109 B4
Abtsgmünd D 94 C1
Abusejo E 149 B3
 Kronoberg S 62 A2
Åbyggeby S 56 B2
Åbytorp S 55 A6
A Cañiza E 140 B2
A Capela E 140 A2
Acate I 177 B3
Accadia I 171 B3
Accéglio I 132 A2
Accettura I 172 B2
Acciaroli I 170 C3
Accous F 145 A3
Accrington GB . . .40 B1
Accúmoli I 169 A3
Acedera E 156 A2
Acehuche E 155 B4
Acered E 152 A2
Acerenza I 172 B1
Acerno I 170 C3
Aesch CH 106 B2
Acerra I 170 C2
Aceuchal E 155 C4
Acharacle GB 34 B2
Acharnes GR 185 A4
Achavanich GB . . .32 C3
Achene B 79 B5
Achenkirch A 108 B2
Achensee A 108 B2
Achenthal A 108 B2
Achentrias GR . . .185 E6
Acheux-en-Amienois
 F 90 A2
Achiltibuie GB 32 C1
Achim D 72 A2
Achladokambos
 GR 184 B3
Achnasheen GB . . .32 D1
Achnashellach GB . .32 D1
Achosnich GB 34 B1
Aci Castello I 177 B4
Aci Catena I 177 B4
Acilia I 168 B2
Acipayam TR 189 B4
Acireale I 177 B4
Acle GB 41 C5
A Coruña E 140 A2
Acquacadda I 179 C2
Acqua Doria F 180 B1
Acquanegra sul Chiese
 I 121 B3
Acquapendente I . .168 A1
Acquasanta Terme
 I 136 C2
Acquasparta I . . .168 A2
Acquaviva I 135 B4
Acquaviva delle Fonti
 I 171 C4
Acquaviva Picena
 I 136 C2
Acquigny F 89 A5
Acqui Terme I . . .119 C5
Acri I 174 B2
Acs H 112 B2
Acsa H 112 B3
Ácsteszér H 112 B1
Acy-le-Multien F . .90 B2
Ada SRB 126 B2
Adak S 195 E9
Ådalsbruk N 48 B3
Adamsfjord N . . .193 B10
Adamuz E 157 B3
Adana TR 23 C8

Ádánd H 112 C2
Adanero E 150 B3
Adare IRL 29 B3
Adaševci SRB 125 B5
Adeanueva de Ebro
 E 144 B2
Adelboden CH . . .106 C2
Adelebsen D 82 A1
Adélfia I 173 A2
Adelmannsfelden
 D 94 C2
Adelsheim D 94 B1
Adelsö S 57 A3
Ademuz E 152 B2
Adenau D 80 B2
Adendorf D 72 A3
Adinkerke B 78 A2
Adjud RO 17 B7
Adliswil CH 107 B3
Admont A 110 B1
Ådneram N 52 A2
Adolfsström S . . .195 D7
Adony H 112 B2
Adorf
 Hessen D 81 A4
 Sachsen D 83 B4
Adra E 164 C1
Adradas E 152 A1
Adrall E 147 B2
Adrano I 177 B3
Ádria I 121 B5
Adrigole IRL 29 C2
Adwick le Street
 GB 40 B2
Adzaneta E 153 B3
Aesch CH 106 B2
A Estrada E 140 B2
Afandou GR 188 C3
Åfarnes N 198 C4
Affing D 94 C2
Affoltern CH 106 B3
Aflenz Kurort A . . .110 B2
A Fonsagrada E . . .141 A3
Afragóla I 170 C2
Afritz A 109 C4
Afyonkarahisar
 TR 187 D5
Ågasegyháza H . . .112 C3
Agay F 132 B2
Agazzano I 120 C2
Agde F 130 B2
Agdenes N 198 B6
Agen F 129 B3
Ager E 145 C4
Agerbæk DK 59 C1
Agerskov DK 64 A2
Agger DK 58 B1
Aggersund DK . . .58 A2
Ággius I 178 B3
Aggsbach Dorf A . . .97 C3
Aggsbach Markt A . .97 C3
Aggtelek H 99 C4
Aghalee GB 27 B4
Aghia GR 182 D4
Aghia Anna GR . . .183 E5
Aghia Galini GR . . .185 D5
Aghia Marina GR . .188 D1
Aghia Paraskevi
 GR 186 C1
Aghia Pelagia GR . .184 C3
Aghia Triada GR . . .184 B2
Aghiokambos GR . .182 D4
Aghios Efstratios
 GR 183 D6
Aghios Kirikos
 GR 185 B7
Aghios Matheos
 GR 182 D1
Aghios Mironas
 GR 185 D6
Aghios Nikolaos
 GR 185 D6
Aghios Petros GR . .182 E2
Aghio Theodori
 GR 184 B4
Agía GR 182 E2
Agira I 177 B3
Aglientu I 178 A3

Agnières F 118 C2
Agno CH 120 B1
Agnone I 170 B2
Agolada E 140 B2
Agon Coutainville
 F 88 A2
Ágordo I 121 A5
Agost E 165 A4
Agramón E 158 C2
Agramunt E 147 C2
Agreda E 144 C2
Agria GR 183 D5
Agrigento I 176 B2
Agrinio GR 182 E3
Agrón E 163 A4
Agrópoli I 170 C2
Aguadulce
 Almería E 164 C2
 Sevilla E 162 A3
Agualada E 140 A2
Agua Longa P 148 A1
A Guarda E 140 C2
Aguarón E 152 A2
Aguas E 145 B3
Aguas Belas P . . .154 B2
Aguas de Busot E . .159 C3
Aguas de Moura
 P 154 C2
Águas Frias P . . .148 A2
Aguas Santas P . . .148 A1
Aguaviva E 153 B3
Aguaviva de la Vega
 E 152 A1
A Gudiña E 141 B3
Águeda P 148 B1
Aguessac F 130 A2
Agugliano I 136 B2
Aguiar P 154 C3
Aguiar da Beira P . .148 B2
Aguilafuente E . . .151 A3
Aguilar de Campóo
 E 142 B2
Aguilar de la Frontera
 E 163 A3
Aguilas E 164 B3
Agunnaryd S 60 C4
Ahat TR 187 D4
Ahaus D 71 B3
Åheim N 198 C2
Ahigal E 149 B3
Ahigal de Villarino
 E 149 A3
Ahillones E 156 B2
Ahlbeck
 Mecklenburg-
 Vorpommern D . . .66 C3
 Mecklenburg-
 Vorpommern D . . .74 A3
Ahlen D 81 A3
Ahlhorn D 71 B5
Ahmetbey TR 186 A2
Ahmetler TR 188 A4
Ahmetli TR 188 A2
Ahoghill GB 27 B4
Ahola FIN 197 C11
Ahrensbök D 65 B3
Ahrensburg D 72 A3
Ahrenshoop D 66 B1
Ahun F 116 A2
Åhus S 63 C2
Ahvenselkä FIN . .197 C11
Aibar E 144 B2
Aich D 95 C4
Aicha D 96 C1
Aichach D 94 C3
Aiello Cálabro I . . .175 B2
Aigen im Mühlkreis
 A 96 C1
Aigle CH 119 A3
Aignan F 128 C3
Aignay-le-Duc F . .104 B3
Aigre F 115 C4
Aigrefeuille-d'Aunis
 F 114 B3
Aigrefeuille-sur-Maine
 F 101 B4
Aiguablava E 147 C4
Aiguebelle F 118 B3

Aigueperse F 116 A3
Aigues-Mortes F . .131 B3
Aigues-Vives F . . .130 B1
Aiguilles F 119 C3
Aiguillon F 129 B3
Aigurande F 103 C3
Ailefroide F 118 C3
Aillant-sur-Tholon
 F 104 B2
Ailly-sur-Noye F . .90 B2
Ailly-sur-Somme F .90 B2
Aimargues F 131 B3
Aime F 118 B3
Ainaži LV 8 D4
Ainet A 109 C3
Ainhoa F 144 A2
Ainsa E 145 B4
Airaines F 90 B1
Aird GB 34 B2
Aird Asaig Tairbeart
 GB 31 B2
Airdrie GB 35 C4
Aire-sur-l'Adour F .128 C2
Aire-sur-la-Lys F . .78 B2
Airole I 133 B3
Airolo CH 107 C3
Airvault F 102 C1
Aisey-sur-Seine F .104 B3
Aïssey F 105 B5
Aisy-sur-Armançon
 F 104 B3
Aiterhofen D 95 C4
Aith
 Orkney GB 33 B4
 Shetland GB 33 A5
Aitona E 153 A4
Aitrach D 107 B5
Aiud RO 17 B5
Aix-en-Othe F . . .104 A2
Aix-en-Provence
 F 131 B4
Aixe-sur-Vienne F .115 C5
Aix-les-Bains F . . .118 B2
Aizenay F 114 B2
Aizkraukle LV 8 D4
Aizpute LV 8 D2
Ajac F 146 A3
Ajaccio F 180 B1
Ajain F 116 A1
Ajaureforsen S . . .195 E6
Ajdovščina SLO . .122 B2
Ajka H 111 B4
Ajo E 143 A3
Ajofrin E 157 A4
Ajos FIN 196 D7
Ajuda P 155 C3
Akanthou CY 181 A2
Akarca TR 189 A4
Akasztó H 112 C3
Akçakoca TR 187 A6
Akçaova TR 187 A4
Akçay TR 189 C4
Aken D 83 A4
Åkerby S 51 B4
Åkernes N 52 B3
Åkers styckebruk
 S 56 A3
Åkervik N 195 E4
Akhisar TR 186 D2
Åkirkeby DK 67 A3
Akköy TR 188 B2
Akkrum NL 70 A2
Akören TR 189 B7
Åkra N 52 A2
Akranes IS 190 C3
Åkrehamn N 52 A1
Akrotiri CY 181 B1
Aksaray TR 23 B8
Akşehir TR 189 A6
Akseki TR 189 B6
Aksla N 46 A3
Aksu TR 189 C5
Aktsyabrski BY . . .13 B8
Akureyri IS 191 B7
Akvåg N 53 B5
Akyazı TR 187 B5
Al N 47 B5
Ala I 121 B4
Alaca TR 23 A8

Alacaatlı TR 186 C3
Alaçam TR 23 A8
Alaçatı TR 188 A1
Aladei Sardi I 178 B3
Ala di Stura I 119 B4
Alaejos E 150 A2
Alagna Valsésia I . .119 B4
Alagón E 144 C2
Alaior E 167 B4
Alájar E 161 B3
Alakurtti RUS . . .197 C13
Alakylä FIN 196 B7
Alameda de la Sagra
 E 151 B4
Alamedilla E 163 A4
Alamillo E 156 B3
Alaminos E 151 B5
Ala-Nampa FIN . .197 C9
Alanäs S 199 A12
Alandroal P 155 C3
Alange E 156 B1
Alaniemi FIN 197 D8
Alanís E 156 B2
Alanno I 169 A3
Alansbro S 200 D3
Alanya TR 189 C7
Alap H 112 C2
Alaquáso E 159 B3
Alaraz E 150 B2
Alar del Rey E . . .142 B2
Alarcón E 158 B1
Alaşehir TR 188 A3
Alássio I 133 A4
Alastaro FIN 8 B3
Alava E 143 B4
Alba
 E 152 B2
 I 119 C5
Alba Adriática I . . .136 C2
Albacete E 158 C2
Alba de Tormes E . .150 B2
Alba de Yeltes E . .149 B3
Albaida E 159 C3
Alba-Iulia RO 17 B5
Ålbæk DK 58 A3
Albaladejo E 158 C1
Albala del Caudillo
 E 156 A1
Albalat E 159 B3
Albalate de Cinca
 E 145 C4
Albalate del Arzobispo
 E 153 A3
Albalate de las
 Nogueras E 152 B1
Albalete de Zorita
 E 151 B5
Alban F 130 B1
Albánchez E 164 B2
Albanchez de Ubeda
 E 163 A4
Albano Laziale I . . .168 B2
Albanyà E 147 B3
Albaredo d'Adige
 I 121 B4
Albares E 151 B4
Albarracín E 152 B2
Albatana E 158 C2
Albatàrrec E 153 A4
Albatera E 165 A4
Albbruck D 106 B3
Albedin E 163 A3
Albelda de Iregua
 E 143 B4
Albenga I 133 A4
Albens F 118 B2
Ålberga
 Södermanland S . .56 A2
 Södermanland S . .56 B2
Albergaria-a-Nova
 P 148 B1
Albergaria-a-Velha
 P 148 B1
Albergaria dos Doze
 P 154 B2
Alberge P 154 C2

Aab–Alc

Alberic E 159 B3
Albernoa P 160 B2
Alberobello I 173 B3
Alberoni I 122 B1
Albersdorf D 64 B2
Albersloh D 81 A3
Albert F 90 A2
Albertirsa H 112 B3
Albertville F 118 B3
Alberuela de Tubo
 E 145 C3
Albi F 130 B1
Albidona I 174 B2
Albínia I 168 A1
Albino I 120 B2
Albinshof D 66 C2
Albires E 142 B1
Albisola Marina I . .133 A4
Albocàcer E 153 B4
Albolote E 163 A4
Albondón E 164 C1
Alborea E 158 B2
Albox E 164 B2
Albrechtice nad
 Vitavou CZ 96 B2
Albstadt D 107 A4
Albufeira P 160 B1
Albuñol E 164 C1
Albuñuelas E 163 B4
Alburquerque E . . .155 B3
Alby
 Öland S 63 B4
 Västernorrland S . .200 D1
Alcácer do Sal P . .154 C2
Alcáçovas P 154 C2
Alcadozo E 158 C2
Alcafoces P 155 B3
Alcains P 155 B3
Alcalá de Guadaira
 E 162 A2
Alcalá de Gurrea
 E 144 B3
Alcalá de Henares
 E 151 B4
Alcalá de la Selva
 E 153 B3
Alcalá del Júcar E .158 B2
Alcalá de los Gazules
 E 162 B2
Alcalá del Río E . .162 A2
Alcalá del Valle E . .162 B2
Alcalá la Real E . . .163 A4
Álcamo I 176 B1
Alcampell E 145 C4
Alcanadre E 144 B1
Alcanar E 153 B4
Alcanede P 154 B2
Alcanena P 154 B2
Alcañices E 149 A3
Alcántara E 155 B3
Alcantarilha P . . .160 B1
Alcantarilla E 165 B3
Alcañz E 153 A3
Alcaracejos E 156 B3
Alcara il Fusi I . . .177 A3
Alcaraz E 158 C1
Alcaria Ruiva P . . .160 B2
Alcarraz E 153 A4
Alcaudete E 163 A3
Alcaudete de la Jara
 E 150 C3
Alcázar de San Juan
 E 157 A4
Alcester GB 44 A2
Alcoba E 157 A3
Alcobaça P 154 B1
Alcobendas E 151 B4
Alcocer E 151 B5
Alcochete P 154 C2
Alcoentre P 154 B2
Alcolea
 Almería E 164 C2
 Córdoba E 156 C3
Alcolea de Calatrava
 E 157 B3

Alcolea de Cinca E 145 C4
Alcolea del Pinar E 152 A1
Alcolea del Río E 162 A2
Alcolea de Tajo E 150 C2
Alcollarin E 156 A2
Alconchel E 155 C3
Alconera E 155 C4
Alcontar E 164 B2
Alcora E 153 B3
Alcorcón E 151 B4
Alcorisa E 153 B3
Alcossebre E 153 B4
Alcoutim P 160 B2
Alcover E 147 C2
Alcoy E 159 C3
Alcsútdoboz H 112 B2
Alcubierre E 145 C3
Alcubilla de Avellaneda E 143 C3
Alcubilla de Nogales E 141 B5
Alcubillas E 157 B4
Alcublas E 159 B3
Alcúdia E 167 B3
Alcudia de Guadix E 164 B1
Alcuéscar E 155 B4
Aldbrough GB 41 B3
Aldeacentenera E 156 A2
Aldeadávila de la Ribera E 149 A3
Aldea del Cano E 155 B4
Aldea del Fresno E 151 B3
Aldea del Obispo E 149 B3
Aldea del Rey E 157 B4
Aldea de Trujillo E 156 A2
Aldealcorvo E 151 A4
Aldealuenga de Santa Maria E 151 A4
Aldeamayor de San Martin E 150 A3
Aldeanueva de Barbarroya E 150 C2
Aldeanueva del Camino E 149 B4
Aldeanueva del Codonal E 150 A3
Aldeanueva de San Bartolomé E 156 A2
Aldeapozo E 144 C1
Aldeaquemada E 157 B4
Aldea Real E 151 A3
Aldearrubia E 150 A2
Aldeaseca de la Frontera E 150 B2
Aldeasoña E 151 A3
Aldeatejada E 150 B2
Aldeavieja E 150 B3
Aldeburgh GB 45 A5
Aldehuela E 152 B2
Aldehuela de Calatañazor E 143 C4
Aldeia da Serra P 155 C3
Aldeia do Bispo P 149 B3
Aldeia do Mato P 154 B2
Aldeia Gavinha P 154 B1
Aldeire E 164 B1
Aldenhoven D 80 B2
Aldersbach D 95 C5
Aldershot GB 44 B3
Aldudes F 144 A2
Åled S 60 C2
Aledo E 165 B3
Alegria E 143 B4
Aleksandrovac SRB 127 C3
Aleksandrów Kujawski PL 76 B3
Aleksandrów Łódźki PL 86 A3
Aleksa Šantić SRB 126 B1
Ålem S 62 B4
Alençon F 89 B4
Alenquer P 154 B1
Alenya F 146 B3
Aléria F 180 A2
Alès F 131 A3
Áles I 179 C2
Alessándria I 120 C1
Alessándria della Rocca I 176 B2
Alessano I 173 C4
Ålesund N 198 C3
Alet-les-Bains F 146 B3
Alexandria
GB 34 C3
GR 182 C4
RO 17 D6
Alexandroupoli GR 183 C7
Aleyrac F 131 A3
Alézio I 173 B4
Alfacar E 163 A4
Alfaiates P 149 B3
Alfajarin E 153 A3
Alfambra
E 152 B2
P 160 B1
Alfândega da Fé P 149 A3
Alfarela de Jafes P 148 A2
Alfarelos P 148 B1
Alfarim P 154 C1
Alfarnate E 163 B3
Alfaro E 144 B2
Alfarrás E 145 C4
Alfaz del Pi E 159 C3
Alfedena I 169 B4
Alfeizarão P 154 B1
Alfeld
Bayern D 95 B3
Niedersachsen D 72 C2
Alfena P 148 A1
Alferce P 160 B1
Alfhausen D 71 B4
Alfonsine I 135 A5
Alford
Aberdeenshire GB 33 D4
Lincolnshire GB 41 B4
Alforja E 147 C1
Alfoz E 141 A3
Alfreton GB 40 B2
Alfta S 50 A3
Alfundão P 160 A1
Algaida E 167 B2
Algar E 162 B2
Älgarås S 55 B5
Ålgård N 52 B1
Algarinejo E 163 A3
Algarrobo E 163 B3
Algatocin E 162 B2
Algeciras E 162 B2
Algemesí E 159 B3
Algés P 154 C1
Algete E 151 B4
Alghero I 178 B2
Älghult S 62 A3
Alginet E 159 B3
Algodonales E 162 B2
Algodor
E 151 C4
P 160 B2
Algora E 151 B5
Algoso P 149 A3
Algoz P 160 B1
Älgsjö S 200 B3
Alguaire E 145 C4
Alguazas E 165 A3
Algutsrum S 63 B4
Algyö H 126 A2
Alhama de Almería E 164 C2
Alhama de Aragón E 152 A2
Alhama de Granada E 163 B4
Alhama de Murcia E 165 B3
Alhambra E 157 B4
Alhandra P 154 C1
Alhaurin de la Torre E 163 B3
Alhaurín el Grande E 163 B3
Alhendin E 163 A4
Alhóndiga E 151 B5
Alia E 156 A2
Ália I 176 B2
Aliağa TR 186 D1
Aliaga E 153 B3
Alibunar SRB 127 B2
Alicante E 165 A4
Alicún de Ortega E 164 B1
Alife I 170 B2
Alija del Infantado E 141 B5
Alijó P 148 A2
Alimena I 177 B3
Alingsås S 60 B2
Alinyà E 147 B2
Aliseda E 155 B4
Ali Terme I 177 A4
Aliveri GR 185 A5
Alixan F 117 C5
Aljaraque E 161 B2
Aljezur P 160 B1
Aljorra E 165 B3
Aljubarrota P 154 B2
Aljucen E 155 B4
Aljustrel P 160 B1
Alken B 79 B5
Alkmaar NL 70 B1
Alkoven A 96 C2
Allaines F 103 A3
Allaire F 101 B3
Allanche F 116 B2
Alland A 111 A3
Allariz E 140 B3
Allassac F 129 A4
Allauch F 131 B4
Alleen N 52 B3
Allègre F 117 B3
Allemont F 118 B3
Allendale Town GB 37 B4
Allendorf D 81 B4
Allentsteig A 97 C3
Allepuz E 153 B3
Allersberg D 95 B3
Allershausen D 95 C3
Alles E 142 A2
Allevard F 118 B3
Allgunnen S 62 A3
Allihies IRL 29 C1
Allingåbro DK 58 B3
Allmannsdorf D 107 B4
Allo E 144 B1
Alloa GB 35 B4
Allogny F 103 B4
Ålloluokta S 196 B2
Allones
Eure et Loire F 90 C1
Maine-et-Loire F 102 B2
Allonnes F 102 B2
Allons F 128 B2
Allos F 132 A2
Allstedt D 82 A3
Alltwalis GB 39 C2
Allumiere I 168 A1
Almaceda P 155 B3
Almacelles E 145 C4
Almachar E 163 B3
Almada P 154 C1
Almadén E 156 B3
Almadén de la Plata E 161 B3
Almadenejos E 156 B3
Almadrones E 151 B5
Almagro E 157 B4
Almajano E 144 C1
Almansa E 159 C2
Almansil P 160 B1
Almanza E 142 B1
Almaraz E 150 C2
Almargen E 162 B2
Almarza E 143 C4
Almásfüzitö H 112 B2
Almassora E 159 B3
Almazán E 152 A1
Almazul E 152 A1
Alme D 81 A4
Almedina E 158 C1
Almedinilla E 163 A3
Almeida
E 149 A3
P 149 B3
Almeirim P 154 B2
Almelo NL 71 B3
Almenar E 145 C4
Almenara E 159 B3
Almenar de Soria E 152 A1
Almendra P 149 B2
Almendral E 155 C4
Almendral de la Cañada E 150 B3
Almendralejo E 155 C4
Almenno San Bartolomeo I 120 B2
Almere NL 70 B2
Almería E 164 C2
Almerimar E 164 C2
Almese I 119 B4
Almexial P 160 B2
Älmhult S 63 B2
Almiropotamos GR 185 A5
Almiros GR 182 D4
Almodôvar P 160 B1
Almodóvar del Campo E 157 B3
Almodóvar del Pinar E 158 B2
Almodóvar del Río E 162 A2
Almofala P 148 B2
Almogia E 163 B3
Almoharin E 156 A1
Almonacid de la Sierra E 152 A2
Almonacid de Toledo E 157 A4
Almonaster la Real E 161 B3
Almondsbury GB 43 A4
Almonte E 161 B3
Almoradí E 165 A4
Almoraima E 162 B2
Almorox E 150 B3
Almoster P 154 B2
Almsele S 200 B3
Älmsta S 51 C5
Almudena E 164 A3
Almudévar E 145 B3
Almuñécar E 163 B4
Almunge S 51 C5
Almuradiel E 157 B4
Almussafes E 159 B3
Almvik S 62 A4
Alness GB 32 D2
Alnmouth GB 37 A5
Alnwick GB 37 A5
Åloppe S 51 C4
Álora E 163 B3
Alos d'Ensil E 146 B2
Alosno E 161 B2
Alozaina E 162 B3
Alpbach A 108 B2
Alpedrete de la Sierra E 151 B4
Alpedrinha P 148 B2
Alpen D 80 A2
Alpera E 159 C2
Alphen aan de Rijn NL 70 B1
Alpiarça P 154 B2
Alpignano I 119 B4
Alpirsbach D 93 C4
Alpu TR 187 C5
Alpuente E 159 B2
Alqueva P 160 A2
Alquézar E 145 B4
Als DK 58 B3
Alsasua E 144 B1
Alsdorf D 80 B2
Alselv DK 59 C1
Alsfeld D 81 B5
Alsike S 57 A3
Alskog S 57 C4
Alsleben D 83 A3
Alsónémedi H 112 B3
Alsótold H 112 B3
Alsóújlak H 111 B3
Alstad N 194 C6
Alstätte D 71 B3
Alsterbro S 62 B3
Alstermo S 62 B3
Alston GB 37 B4
Alsvåg N 194 B6
Alsvik N 194 C5
Alta N 192 C7
Älta S 57 A4
Altamura I 172 B2
Altarejos E 158 B1
Altaussee A 109 B4
Altavilla Irpina I 170 B2
Altavilla Silentina I 170 C3
Altdöbern D 84 A2
Altdorf
CH 107 C3
D 95 C4
Altdorf bei Nürnberg D 95 B3
Alte P 160 B1
Altea E 159 C3
Altedo I 121 C4
Altena D 81 A3
Altenau D 82 A2
Altenberg D 84 B1
Altenberge D 71 B4
Altenbruch D 64 C1
Altenburg D 83 B4
Altenfelden A 96 C1
Altengronau D 82 B1
Altenheim D 93 C3
Altenhundem D 81 A4
Altenkirchen
Mecklenburg-Vorpommern D 66 B2
Radom D 81 B3
Altenkunstadt D 82 B3
Altenmarkt
A 110 B1
D 109 A3
Altenmarkt im Pongall A 109 B4
Altensteig D 93 C4
Altentreptow D 74 A2
Altenwalde D 64 C1
Alten-weddingen D 73 B4
Alter do Chão P 155 B3
Altfraunhofen D 95 C4
Altheim
A 109 A4
D 94 B1
Althofen A 110 C1
Altınoluk TR 186 C1
Altınova TR 186 C1
Altıntaş TR 187 C5
Altınyaka TR 189 C5
Altınyayla TR 189 B4
Altkirch F 106 B2
Altlandsberg D 74 B2
Altlewin D 74 B3
Altmannstein D 95 C3
Altmorschen D 82 A1
Altmunster A 109 B4
Altnaharra GB 32 C2
Alto Campoó E 142 A2
Altofonte I 176 A2
Altomonte I 174 B2
Alton
Hampshire GB 44 B3
Staffordshire GB 40 C2
Altopáscio I 135 B3
Altötting D 109 A3
Altreichenau D 96 C1
Alt Ruppin D 74 B1
Altshausen D 107 B4
Altstätten CH 107 B4
Altura E 159 B3
Altusried D 107 B5
Alūksne LV 8 D5
Alunda S 51 B5
Alustante E 152 B2
Alva GB 35 B4
Alvaiázere P 154 B2
Alvalade P 160 B1
Älvängen S 60 B2
Alvarenga P 148 B1
Alvares P 154 A2
Alvdal N 199 C7
Älvdalen S 49 A6
Alverca P 154 C1
Alversund N 46 B2
Alvesta S 62 B2
Alvignac F 129 B4
Alvignano I 170 B2
Ålvik N 46 B3
Alvik S 50 B1
Alvimare F 89 A4
Alviobeira P 154 B2
Alvito P 160 A2
Älvkarleby S 51 B4
Älvkarleöbruk S 51 B4
Alvor P 160 B1
Alvorge P 154 B2
Alvøy N 46 B2
Älvros S 199 C11
Alvsbacka S 55 A4
Älvsbyn S 196 D4
Älvsered S 60 B2
Alwernia PL 86 B3
Alwinton GB 37 A4
Alyth GB 35 B4
Alytus LT 13 A6
Alzénau D 93 A5
Alzey D 93 B4
Alzira E 159 B3
Alzonne F 146 A3
Amadora P 154 C1
Åmål S 55 A3
Amalfi I 170 C2
Amaliada GR 184 B2
Amance F 105 B5
Amancey F 105 B5
Amándola I 136 C2
Amantea I 175 B2
Amarante P 148 A1
Amareleja P 161 A2
Amares P 148 A1
Amaseno I 169 B3
Amasra TR 187 A7
Amatrice I 169 A3
Amay B 79 B5
Ambarnyy RUS 3 D13
Ambazac F 115 C5
Ambelonas GR 182 D4
Amberg D 95 B3
Ambérieu-en-Bugey F 118 B2
Ambérieux-en-Dombes F 117 A4
Ambert F 117 B3
Ambés F 128 A2
Ambjörby S 49 B5
Ambjörnarp S 60 B3
Amble GB 37 A5
Ambleside GB 36 B4
Ambleteuse F 78 B1
Amboise F 102 B2
Ambrières-les-Vallées F 88 B3
Amden CH 107 B4
Amel B 80 B2
Amélia I 168 A2
Amélie-les-Bains-Palalda F 146 B3
Amelinghausen D 72 A3
Amendoa P 154 B2
Amendoeira P 160 B2
Améndola I 171 B3
Amendolara I 174 B2
Amer E 147 B3
A Merca E 140 B3
Amerongen NL 70 B2
Amersfoort NL 70 B2
Amersham GB 44 B3
Amesbury GB 44 B2
Amfiklia GR 182 E4
Amfilochia GR 182 E3
Amfipoli GR 183 C5
Amfissa GR 184 A3
Amièira P 155 C3
Amieira P 154 B3
Amieiro P 148 B1
Amiens F 90 B2
Amindeo GR 182 C3
Åminne S 60 B3
Åmli N 53 B4
Amlwch GB 38 A2
Ammanford GB 39 C3
Ammarnäs S 195 E7
Åmmeberg S 55 B5
Amorbach D 94 B1
Amorebieta E 143 A4
Amorgos GR 185 C6
Amorosa P 148 A1
Amorosi I 170 B2
Åmot
Buskerud N 48 C1
Telemark N 53 A3
S 50 B3
Åmotfors S 54 A3
Åmotsdal N 53 A4
Amou F 128 C2
Ampezzo I 122 A1
Ampfing D 95 C4
Ampflwang A 109 A4
Amplepuis F 117 B4
Amposta E 153 B4
Ampthill GB 44 A3
Ampudia E 142 C2
Ampuero E 143 A3
Amriswil CH 107 B4
Åmsele S 200 B5
Amstelveen NL 70 B1
Amsterdam NL 70 B1
Amstetten A 110 A1
Amtzell D 107 B4
Amulree GB 35 B4
Amurrio E 143 A4
Amusco E 142 B2
Anacapri I 170 C2
Anadia P 148 B1
Anadon E 152 B2
Anafi GR 185 C6
Anagni I 169 B3
Anamur TR 23 C7
Ananyiv UA 17 B8
Anascaul IRL 29 B1
Ånäset S 2 D7
Åna-Sira N 52 B2
Anastaźewo PL 76 B3
Anaya de Alba E 150 B2
Ança P 148 B1
Ancaster GB 40 C3
Ancede P 148 A1
Ancenis F 101 B4
Ancerville F 91 C5
Anchuras E 156 A3
Ancona I 136 B2
Ancora P 148 A1
Ancrum GB 35 C5
Ancy-le-Franc F 104 B3
Andalo I 121 A3
Åndalsnes N 198 C4
Andance F 117 B4
Andau A 111 B4
Andebu N 53 A6
Andeer CH 107 C4
Andelfingen CH 107 B3
Andelot-Blanchville F 105 A4
Andelot-en-Montagne F 105 C4
Andenes N 194 A7
Andenne B 79 B5
Anderlues B 79 B4
Andermatt CH 107 C3
Andernach D 80 B3
Andernos-les-Bains F 128 B1
Anderslöv S 66 A2
Anderstorp S 60 B3
Andijk NL 70 B2
Andoain E 144 A1
Andocs H 112 C1
Andolsheim F 106 A2
Andorra E 153 B3
Andorra La Vella AND 146 B2
Andosilla E 144 B2
Andover GB 44 B2
Andratx E 166 B2
Andreapol RUS 9 D8
Andreas GB 36 B2
Andréspol PL 86 A3
Andrest F 145 A4
Andretta I 172 B1
Andrezieux-Bouthéon F 117 B4
Ándria I 171 B4
Andrijevica MNE 16 D3
Andritsena GR 184 B2
Andros GR 185 B5
Andrychów PL 99 B3
Andselv N 194 A9
Andújar E 157 B3
Anduze F 131 A2
Aneby N 48 B2
Aneby S 62 A2
Añes E 143 A3
Anet F 90 C1
Anfo I 121 B3
Ang S 62 A2
Anga S 57 C4
Angaïs F 145 A3
Änge S 199 B11
Ånge S 200 D1
Angeja P 148 B1
Ängelholm S 61 C2
Angeli FIN 193 D9
Ängelsberg S 50 C3
Anger A 110 B2
Angera I 120 B1
Angermünde D 74 A3
Angern A 97 C4
Angers F 102 B1
Angerville F 90 C2
Anghiari I 135 B5
Angle GB 39 C1
Anglès E 147 C3
Anglés F 130 B1
Angles F 114 B2
Anglesola E 147 C2
Angles sur l'Anglin F 115 B4
Anglet F 128 C1
Anglisidhes CY 181 B2
Anglure F 91 C3
Angoulême F 115 C4
Angoulins F 114 B2
Angsö S 56 A2
Angueira P 149 A3
Angües E 145 B3
Anguiano E 143 B4
Anguillara Sabazia I 168 A2
Anguillara Véneta I 121 B4
Anhée B 79 B4
Anholt DK 60 C1
Aniane F 130 B2
Aniche F 78 B3
Ånimskog S 54 B3
Anina RO 16 C4
Anixi GR 182 D3
Anizy-le-Château F 91 B3
Anjalankoski FIN 8 B5
Anjan S 199 B9
Ankara TR 187 C7
Ankaran SLO 122 B2
Ankarsrum S 62 A4
Ankerlia N 192 C4
Anklam D 66 C2
Ankum D 71 B4
Anlauftal A 109 B4
Anlezy F 104 C2
Ånn S 199 B9
Annaberg A 110 B2
Annaberg-Buchholz D 83 B5
Annaberg im Lammertal A 109 B4
Annaburg D 83 A5
Annahütte D 84 A1
Annalong GB 27 B5
Annan GB 36 B3
Anndalsvågen N 195 E3
Anneberg
Halland S 60 B2
Jönköping S 62 A2
Annecy F 118 B3
Annelund S 60 B3
Annemasse F 118 A3
Annenskiy Most RUS 9 B10
Annerstad S 60 C3
Annestown IRL 30 B1
Annevoie-Rouillon B 79 B4
Annonay F 117 B4
Annot F 132 B2
Annweiler D 93 B3
Ano Poroia GR 183 B5
Añora E 156 B3
Ano Siros GR 185 B5
Anould F 106 A1
Anquela del Ducado E 152 B1
Anröchte D 81 A4
Ans DK 59 B2
Ansager DK 59 C1
Ansbach D 94 B2
Anse F 117 B4
Anseroeul B 79 B3
Ansfelden A 110 A1
Ansião P 154 B2
Ansó E 144 B3
Ansoain E 144 B2
Anstruther GB 35 B5
Antalya TR 189 C5
Antas E 164 B3
Antegnate I 120 B2
Antequera E 163 A3
Anterselva di Mezzo I 108 C3
Antibes F 132 B3
Antigüedad E 142 C2
Antillo I 177 B4
Antirio GR 184 A2
Antnäs S 196 D4
An t-Ob GB 31 B1
Antoing B 79 B3
Antonin PL 86 A1
Antrain F 88 B2
Antrim GB 27 B4
Antrodoco I 169 A3
Antronapiana I 119 A5
Anttis S 196 B5
Antuzede P 148 B1
Antwerp = Antwerpen B 79 A4
Antwerpen = Antwerp B 79 A4
Anversa d'Abruzzi I 169 B3
Anvin F 78 B2
Anzat-le-Luguet F 116 B3
Anzi I 172 B1
Ánzio I 168 B2
Anzola d'Emilia I 135 A4
Anzón E 144 C2
Aoiz E 144 B2
Aosta I 119 B4
Apalhão P 155 B3
Apátfalva H 126 A2
Apatin SRB 125 B5
Apatity RUS 3 C13
Apc H 112 B3
Apécchio I 136 B1
Apeldoorn NL 70 B2
Apen D 71 A4
Apenburg D 73 B4
Apensen D 72 A2
A Peroxa E 140 B3
Apiro I 136 B2
Apliki CY 181 B2
Apolda D 82 A3
Apolonia GR 185 C5
A Pontenova E 141 A3
Apostag H 112 C2
Äppelbo S 49 B6
Appennino I 136 C2
Appenzell CH 107 B4
Appiano I 108 C2
Appingedam NL 71 A3
Appleby-in-Westmorland GB 37 B4
Applecross GB 31 B3
Appledore GB 42 A2
Appoigny F 104 B2
Apremont-la-Forêt F 92 C1
Aprica I 120 A3
Apricena I 171 B3
Aprigliano I 174 B2
Aprilia I 168 B2
Apt F 131 B4
Apúlia P 148 A1
Aquiléia I 122 B2
Aquilónia I 172 B1
Aquino I 169 B3
Ar S 57 C4
Arabayona E 150 A2
Arabba I 108 C2
Araç TR 23 A7
Aracena E 161 B3
Arachova GR 184 A3
Aračinovo MK 182 A3
Arad RO 126 A3
Aradac SRB 126 B2
Aradhippou CY 181 B2
Aragnouet F 145 B4
Aragona I 176 B2
Aramits F 144 A3
Aramon F 131 B3
Aranda de Duero E 143 C3
Aranda de Moncayo E 152 A2
Arandjelovac SRB 127 C2
Aranjuez E 151 B4
Arantzazu E 143 B4
Aranzueque E 151 B4
Aras de Alpuente E 159 B2
Arauzo de Miel E 143 C3
Arazede P 148 B1
Arbas F 145 B4
Árbatax I 179 C3
Arbeca E 147 C1
Arberg D 94 B2
Arbesbach A 96 C2
Arboga S 56 A1
Arbois F 105 C4
Arbon CH 107 B4
Arboréa I 179 C2
Arbório I 119 B5
Årbostad N 194 B8
Arbrå S 50 A3
Arbroath GB 35 B5
Arbùcies E 147 C3
Arbuniel E 163 A4
Arbus I 179 C2
Arcachon F 128 B1
Arce I 169 B3
Arcen NL 80 A2
Arc-en-Barrois F 105 B3
Arces-Dilo F 104 A2
Arc-et-Senans F 105 B4
Arcévia I 136 B1
Arcey F 106 B1
Archanes GR 185 D6
Archangelos GR 188 C3
Archena E 165 A3
Archez E 163 B4
Archiac F 115 C3
Archidona E 163 A3
Archiestown GB 32 D3
Archivel E 164 A3
Arcidosso I 135 C4
Arcille I 135 C4
Arcis-sur-Aube F 91 C4
Arc-lès-Gray F 105 B4
Arco I 121 B3
Arcones E 151 A4
Arcos E 143 B3
Arcos de Jalón E 152 A1
Arcos de la Frontera E 162 B2
Arcos de la Sierra E 152 B1
Arcos de las Salinas E 159 B2
Arcos de Valdevez P 148 A1
Arcozelo P 148 B2
Arc-sur-Tille F 105 B4
Arcusa E 145 B4
Arcy-sur-Cure F 104 B2
Ardagh IRL 29 B2
Årdal N 52 A2
Ardala S 55 B4
Ardales E 162 B3
Årdalstangen N 47 A4
Ardara
I 178 B2
IRL 26 B2
Ardarroch GB 31 B3
Ardbeg GB 34 C1
Ardcharnich GB 32 D1
Ardchyle GB 34 B3
Ardee IRL 27 C4
Arden DK 58 B2

Ardentes F 103 C3
Ardenza I 134 B3
Ardersier GB 32 D2
Ardes F 116 B3
Ardessie GB 32 D1
Ardez CH 107 C5
Ardfert IRL 29 B2
Ardgay GB 32 D2
Ardglass GB 27 B5
Ardgroom IRL 29 C2
Ardhasig GB 31 B2
Ardino BG 183 B7
Ardisa E 144 B3
Ardkearagh IRL 29 C1
Ardlui GB 34 B3
Ardlussa GB 34 B2
Ardón E 142 B1
Ardooie B 78 B3
Ardore I 175 C2
Ardrahan IRL 28 A3
Ardre S 57 C4
Ardres F 78 B1
Ardrishaig GB 34 B2
Ardrossan GB 34 C3
Are N 52 A1
Åre S 199 B10
Areia Branca P 154 B1
Aremark N 54 A2
Arenales de San Gregorio E 157 A4
Arenas E 163 B3
Arenas de Iguña E 142 A2
Arenas del Rey E 163 B4
Arenas de San Juan E 157 A4
Arenas de San Pedro E 150 B2
Arendal N 53 B4
Arendonk B 79 A5
Arengosse F 128 B2
Arentorp S 55 B3
Arenys de Mar E 147 C3
Arenys de Munt E 147 C3
Arenzano I 133 A4
Areo E 146 B2
Areopoli GR 184 C3
Ares E 140 A2
Arès F 128 B1
Ares del Maestrat E 153 B3
Aresvika N 198 B5
Arette F 144 A3
Aretxabaleta E 143 A4
Arevalillo E 150 B2
Arévalo E 150 A3
Arez P 155 B3
Arezzo I 135 B4
Arfeuilles F 117 A3
Argalasti GR 183 D5
Argallón E 156 B2
Argamasilla de Alba E 157 A4
Argamasilla de Calatrava E 157 B3
Arganda E 151 B4
Arganil P 148 B1
Argasion GR 184 B1
Argegno I 120 B2
Argelès-Gazost F 145 A3
Argelès-sur-Mer F 146 B4
Argenta I 121 C4
Argentan F 89 B3
Argentat F 116 B1
Argentera I 132 A2
Argenteuil F 90 C2
Argenthal D 93 B3
Argentiera I 178 B2
Argentona E 147 C3
Argenton-Château F 102 C1
Argenton-sur-Creuse F 103 C3
Argentré F 102 A1
Argentré-du-Plessis F 101 A4
Argent-sur-Sauldre F 103 B4
Argirades GR 182 D1
Argıthanı TR 189 A6
Argos GR 184 B3
Argos Orestiko GR 182 C3
Argostoli GR 184 A1
Argote E 143 B4
Arguedas E 144 B2
Argueil F 90 B1
Arholma S 51 C6
Århus DK 59 B3
Ariano Irpino I 170 B3
Ariano nel Polésine I 121 C5
Aribe E 144 B2
Aridea GR 182 C4
Arienzo I 170 B2
Arild S 61 C2
Arileod GB 34 B1
Arinagour GB 34 B1
Ariño E 153 A3
Arinthod F 118 A2
Arisaig GB 34 B2
Arisgotas E 157 A4
Aritzo I 179 C3
Ariza E 152 A1
Årjäng S 54 A3
Arjeplog S 195 D8
Arjona E 157 C3
Arjonilla E 157 C3
Arkasa GR 188 D2
Arkelstorp S 63 B2
Arklow IRL 30 B2
Arkösund S 56 B2
Ärla S 56 A2
Arlanc F 117 B3
Arlanzón E 143 B3
Arlebosc F 117 B4
Arlena di Castro I 168 A1
Arles F 131 B3
Arles-sur-Tech F 146 B3
Arló H 113 A4
Arlon B 92 B1
Armação de Pera P 160 B1
Armadale *Highland* GB 31 B3
West Lothian GB 35 C4
Armagh GB 27 B4
Armamar P 148 A2
Armenistis GR 185 B7
Armeno I 119 B5
Armenteros E 150 B2
Armentières F 78 B2
Armilla E 163 A4
Armiñón E 143 B4
Armoy GB 27 A4
Armuña de Tajuña E 151 B4
Armutlu *Bursa* TR 186 B3
İzmir TR 188 A2
Arnac-Pompadour F 115 C5
Arnafjord N 46 A3
Arnage F 102 B2
Arnas F 117 A4
Årnäs S 55 B4
Arnay-le-Duc F 104 B3
Arnborg DK 59 B2
Arnbruck D 95 B4
Arnea GR 183 C5
Arneberg *Hedmark* N 48 A2
Hedmark N 49 B4
Arneburg D 73 B5
Arnedillo E 144 B1
Arnedo E 144 B1
Arneguy F 144 A2
Arnés E 153 B4
Árnes IS 190 A4
Årnes *Akershus* N 48 B3
Troms N 194 A9
Arnfels A 110 C2
Arnhem NL 70 C2
Arnissa GR 182 C3
Arno S 56 B3
Arnold GB 40 B2
Arnoldstein A 109 C4
Arnsberg D 81 A4
Arnschwang D 95 B4
Arnsdorf D 84 A1
Årnset N 198 B6
Arnside GB 37 B4
Arnstadt D 82 B2
Arnstein D 94 B1
Arnstorf D 95 C4
Arnum DK 59 C1
Aroche E 161 B3
Ároktő H 113 B4
Arolla CH 119 A4
Arolsen D 81 A5
Arona I 119 B5
Åros N 54 A1
Arosa CH 107 C4
P 148 A1
Ærøskøbing DK 65 B3
Arøsund DK 59 C2
Arouca P 148 B1
Årøysund N 54 A1
Arpajon F 90 C2
Arpajon-sur-Cère F 116 C2
Arpela FIN 196 C7
Arpino I 169 B3
Arquata del Tronto I 136 C2
Arques F 78 B2
Arques-la-Bataille F 89 A5
Arquillos E 157 B4
Arraia-Maeztu E 143 B4
Arraiolos P 154 C2
Arrancourt F 92 C2
Arras F 78 B2
Arrasate E 143 A4
Årre DK 59 C1
Arreau F 145 B4
Arredondo E 143 A3
Arrens-Marsous F 145 B3
Arriate E 162 B2
Arrifana P 160 B1
Arrigorriaga E 143 A4
Arriondas E 142 A1
Arroba de los Montes E 157 A3
Arrochar GB 34 B3
Arromanches-les-Bains F 88 A3
Arronches P 155 B3
Arroniz E 144 B1
Arrou F 103 A3
Arroya E 142 B2
Arroya de Cuéllar E 150 A3
Arroyal E 142 B2
Arroyo de la Luz E 155 B4
Arroyo del Ojanco E 164 A2
Arroyo de San Servan E 155 C4
Arroyomolinos de León E 161 A3
Arroyomolinos de Montánchez E 156 A1
Arruda dos Vinhos P 154 C1
Arsac F 128 B2
Ars-en-Ré F 114 B2
Arsiè I 121 B4
Arsiero I 121 B4
Årslev DK 59 C3
Ársoli I 169 A3
Ars-sur-Moselle F 92 B2
Årsunda S 50 B3
Artà E 167 B3
Arta GR 182 D3
Artajona E 144 B2
Artegna I 122 A2
Arteixo E 140 A2
Artemare F 118 B2
Arten I 121 A4
Artena I 169 B2
Artenay F 103 A3
Artern D 82 A3
Artés E 147 C2
Artesa de Segre E 147 C2
Arth CH 107 B3
Arthez-de-Béarn F 145 A3
Arthon-en-Retz F 101 B4
Arthurstown IRL 30 B2
Artieda E 144 B3
Artix F 145 A3
Artotina GR 182 E4
Artsyz UA 17 B8
Artziniega E 143 A3
A Rúa E 141 B3
Arudy F 145 A3
Arundel GB 44 C3
Arveyres F 128 B2
Arvidsjaur S 196 D2
Arvieux F 118 C3
Arvika S 54 A3
Aryd *Blekinge* S 63 B3
Kronoberg S 62 B2
Arzachena I 178 A3
Arzacq-Arraziguet F 128 C2
Árzana I 179 C3
Arzano F 100 B2
Aržano HR 138 B2
Arzberg D 95 A4
Arzignano I 121 B4
Arzila P 148 B1
Arzl im Pitztal A 108 B1
Arzúa E 140 B2
As B 80 A1
Aš CZ 83 B4
Ås N 54 A1
Åsa S 60 B2
Asaa DK 58 A3
Aşağıçiğil TR 189 A6
Ašanja SRB 127 C2
Åsarna S 199 C11
Åsarøy N 52 A2
Åsarp S 55 B4
Asasp F 145 A3
Åsbro S 55 A6
Åsby S 60 B2
Åsby S 62 A3
Asbygri IS 191 A9
Ascain F 144 A2
Ascea I 172 B1
Ascha D 95 B4
Aschach an der Donau A 96 C2
Aschaffenburg D 93 B5
Aschbach Markt A 110 A1
Ascheberg *Nordrhein-Westfalen* D 81 A3
Schleswig-Holstein D 65 B3
Aschendorf D 71 A4
Aschersleben D 82 A3
Asciano I 135 B4
Ascó E 153 A4
Asco F 180 A2
Áscoli Piceno I 136 C2
Áscoli Satriano I 171 B3
Ascona CH 120 A1
Ascot GB 44 B3
Ascoux F 103 A4
Åse N 194 A6
Åseda S 62 A3
Åsele S 200 B3
Åsen N 199 B8
S 49 A5
Asendorf D 72 B2
Asenovgrad BG 183 A6
Åsensbruk S 54 B3
Åseral N 52 B3
Asfeld F 91 B4
Åsgårdstrand N 54 A1
Ásgarður IS 190 B1
Asgate CY 181 B2
Ash *Kent* GB 45 B5
Surrey GB 44 B3
Åshammar S 50 B3
Ashbourne GB 40 B2
IRL 30 A2
Ashburton GB 43 B3
Ashby-de-la-Zouch GB 40 C2
Ashchurch GB 44 B1
Åsheim N 199 D8
Ashford GB 45 B4
Ashington GB 37 A5
Ashley GB 38 B4
Ashmyany BY 13 A6
Ashton Under Lyne GB 40 B1
Ashwell GB 44 A3
Asiago I 121 B4
Asipovichy BY 13 B8
Aska FIN 197 B9
Askam-in-Furness GB 36 B3
Askeaton IRL 29 B3
Asker N 48 C2
Askersund S 55 B5
Åskilje S 200 B3
Askim N 54 A2
Askland N 53 B4
Äsköping S 56 A2
Askvoll N 46 A2
Åsljunga S 61 C3
Asmunti FIN 197 D9
Asnæs DK 61 D1
As Neves E 140 B2
As Nogaís E 141 B3
Ásola I 120 B3
Asolo I 121 B4
Asos GR 184 A1
Asotthalom H 126 A1
Aspach A 109 A4
Aspang Markt A 111 B3
Aspariegos E 149 A4
Asparn an der Zaya A 97 C4
Aspatria GB 36 B3
Aspberg S 55 A4
Aspe E 165 A4
Aspet F 145 A4
Äspö S 63 B3
As Pontes de García Rodríguez E 140 A3
Aspres-sur-Buëch F 132 A1
Aspsele S 200 C4
Assafora P 154 C1
Asse B 79 B4
Assebakte N 193 C9
Assel D 72 A2
Asselborn L 92 A1
Assémini I 179 C2
Assen NL 71 B3
Assenede B 79 A3
Assens *Aarhus Amt.* DK 58 B3
Fyns Amt. DK 59 C2
Assesse B 79 B5
Assisi I 136 B1
Åsskard N 198 B5
Assling D 108 B3
Asso I 120 B2
Asson F 145 A3
Ássoro I 177 B3
Assumar P 155 B3
Åsta N 48 A3
Astaffort F 129 B3
Astakos GR 184 A2
Asten NL 80 A1
Asti I 119 C5
Astipalea GR 188 C1
Astorga E 141 B4
Åstorp S 61 C2
Åsträsk S 200 B5
Astudillo E 142 B2
Asuni I 179 C2
Asványráró H 111 B4
Aszód H 112 B3
Aszófő H 111 C4
Atabey TR 189 B5
Atalaia P 154 B3
Atalandi GR 182 E4
Atalho P 154 C2
Átány H 113 B4
Atanzón E 151 B4
Ataquines E 150 A3
Atarfe E 163 A4
Atça TR 188 B3
Ateca E 152 A2
A Teixeira E 141 B3
Atella I 172 B1
Atessa I 169 A4
Ath B 79 B3
Athboy IRL 30 A2
Athea IRL 29 B2
Athenry IRL 28 A3
Athens = Athina GR 185 B4
Atherstone GB 40 C2
Athienou CY 181 A2
Athies F 90 B2
Athies-sous-Laon F 91 B3
Athina = Athens GR 185 B4
Athleague IRL 28 A3
Athlone IRL 28 A4
Athna CY 181 A2
Athy IRL 30 B2
Atienza E 151 A5
Atina I 169 B3
Atkár H 113 B3
Atlantı TR 189 A7
Atna N 199 D7
Åtorp S 55 A5
Atrå N 47 C5
Ätran S 60 B2
Atri I 169 A3
Atripalda I 170 C2
Atsiki GR 183 D7
Attendorn D 81 A3
Attichy F 90 B3
Attigliano I 168 A2
Attigny F 91 B4
Attleborough GB 41 C5
Åtvidaberg S 56 B1
Atzendorf D 73 C4
Au *Steiermark* A 110 B2
Vorarlberg A 107 B4
Bayern D 95 C3
Bayern D 108 B2
Aub D 94 B2
Aubagne F 132 B1
Aubange B 92 B1
Aubel B 80 B1
Aubenas F 117 C4
Aubenton F 91 B4
Auberive F 105 B4
Aubeterre-sur-Dronne F 128 A3
Aubiet F 129 C3
Aubigné F 115 B3
Aubigny F 114 B2
Aubigny-au-Bac F 78 B3
Aubigny-en-Artois F 78 B2
Aubigny-sur-Nère F 103 B4
Aubin F 130 A1
Aubonne CH 105 C5
Aubrac F 116 C2
Aubusson F 116 B2
Auch F 129 C3
Auchencairn GB 36 B3
Auchinleck GB 36 A2
Auchterarder GB 35 B4
Auchtermuchty GB 35 B4
Auchtertyre GB 31 B3
Auchy-au-Bois F 78 B2
Audenge F 128 B1
Auderville F 88 A2
Audierne F 100 A1
Audincourt F 106 B1
Audlem GB 38 B4
Audruicq F 78 B2
Audun-le-Roman F 92 B1
Audun-le-Tiche F 92 B1
Aue *Nordrhein-Westfalen* D 81 A4
Sachsen D 83 B4
Auerbach *Bayern* D 95 B3
Sachsen D 83 B4
Auffach A 108 B3
Augher GB 27 B3
Aughnacloy GB 27 B4
Aughrim IRL 30 B2
Augignac F 115 C4
Augsburg D 94 C2
Augusta I 177 B4
Augusten-borg DK 64 B2
Augustfehn D 71 A4
Augustów PL 12 B5
Aukrug D 64 B2
Auktsjaur S 196 D2
Auldearn GB 32 D3
Aulendorf D 107 B4
Auletta I 172 B1
Aulla I 134 A2
Aullène F 180 B2
Aulnay F 115 B3
Aulnoye-Aymeries F 79 B3
Ault F 90 A1
Aultbea GB 31 B3
Aulum DK 59 B1
Aulus-les-Bains F 146 B2
Auma D 83 B3
Aumale F 90 B1
Aumetz F 92 B1
Aumont-Aubrac F 116 C3
Aunay-en-Bazois F 104 B2
Aunay-sur-Odon F 88 A3
Aune N 199 A10
Auneau F 90 C1
Auneuil F 90 B1
Auning DK 58 B3
Aunsetra N 199 A9
Aups F 132 B2
Aura D 82 B1
Auray F 100 B3
Aurdal N 47 B6
Aure N 198 B5
Aurich D 71 A4
Aurignac F 145 A4
Aurillac F 116 C2
Auriol F 132 B1
Auritz-Burguette E 144 B2
Aurlandsvangen N 47 B4
Auronzo di Cadore I 109 C3
Auros F 128 B2
Auroux F 117 C3
Aurskog N 48 C3
Aursmoen N 48 C3
Ausónia I 169 B3
Ausservillgraton A 109 C3
Austad N 52 B3
Austbygda N 47 B5
Aústis I 178 B3
Austmarka N 49 B4
Austre Moland N 53 B4
Austre Vikebygd N 52 A1
Austrheim N 46 B1
Auterive F 146 A2
Autheuil-Authouillet F 89 A5
Authon F 132 A2
Authon-du-Perche F 102 A2
Autol E 144 B2
Autreville F 92 C1
Autrey-lès-Gray F 105 B4
Autti FIN 197 C10
Autun F 104 C3
Auty-le-Châtel F 103 B4
Auvelais B 79 B4
Auvillar F 129 B3
Auxerre F 104 B2
Auxi-le-Château F 78 B2
Auxon F 104 A2
Auxonne F 105 B4
Auxy F 104 C3
Auzances F 116 A2
Auzon F 117 B3
Ağva TR 187 A4
Availles-Limouzine F 115 B4
Avaldsnes N 52 A1
Avallon F 104 B2
Avantas GR 183 C7
Avaviken S 195 E9
Avebury GB 44 B2
A Veiga E 141 B3
Aveiras de Cima P 154 B2
Aveiro P 148 B1
Avelgem B 79 B3
Avellino I 170 C2
Avenches CH 106 C2
A-Ver-o-Mar P 148 A1
Aversa I 170 C2
Avesnes-le-Comte F 78 B2
Avesnes-sur-Helpe F 91 A3
Avesta S 50 B3
Avetrana I 173 B3
Avezzano I 169 A3
Avià E 147 B2
Aviano I 122 A1
Aviemore GB 32 D3
Avigliana I 119 B4
Avigliano I 172 B1
Avignon F 131 B3
Ávila E 150 B3
Avilés E 141 A5
Avilley F 105 B5
Avintes P 148 A1
Avinyo E 147 C2
Àvio I 121 B3
Avioth F 92 B1
Avis P 154 B3
Avize F 91 C4
Avlonari GR 185 A5
Ávola I 177 C4
Avon F 90 C2
Avonmouth GB 43 A4
Avord F 103 B4
Avranches F 88 B2
Avril F 92 B1
Avrillé F 102 B1
Avtovac BIH 139 B4
Awans B 79 B5
Axams A 108 B2
Axat F 146 B3
Axbridge GB 43 A4
Axel NL 79 A3
Ax-les-Thermes F 146 B2
Axmarby S 51 B4
Axmarsbruk S 51 A4
Axminster GB 43 B3
Axvall S 55 B4
Ay F 91 B4
Aya E 144 A1
Ayamonte E 161 B2
Ayancık TR 23 A8
Ayaş TR 187 B7
Aydın TR 188 B2
Ayelo de Malferit E 159 C3
Ayer CH 119 A4
Ayerbe E 144 B3
Ayette F 78 B2
Ayia Napa CY 181 B2
Áyia Phyla CY 181 B2
Áyios Amvrósios CY 181 A2
Áyios Seryios CY 181 A2
Áyios Theodhoros CY 181 A3
Aykirikçi TR 187 C5
Aylesbury GB 44 B3
Ayllón E 151 A4
Aylsham GB 41 C5
Ayna E 158 C1
Ayódar E 159 B3
Ayora E 159 B2
Ayr GB 36 A2
Ayrancı TR 23 C7
Ayrancılar TR 188 A2
Ayron F 115 B4
Aysgarth GB 37 B4
Ayton GB 35 C5
Aytos BG 17 D7
Ayvacık TR 186 C1
Ayvalık TR 186 C1
Aywaille B 80 B1
Azaila E 153 A3
Azambuja P 154 B2
Azambujeira P 154 B2
Azanja SRB 127 C2
Azannes-et-Soumazannes F 92 B1
Azanúy-Alins E 145 C4
Azaruja P 155 C3
Azay-le-Ferron F 115 B5
Azay-le-Rideau F 102 B2
Azcoitia E 143 A4
Azé F 117 A4
Azeiteiros P 155 B3
Azenhas do Mar P 154 C1
Azinhaga P 154 B2
Azinhal P 160 B2
Azinheira dos Bairros P 160 A1
Aznalcázar E 161 B3
Aznalcóllar E 161 B3
Azóia P 154 B2
Azpeitia E 144 A1
Azuaga E 156 B2
Azuara E 153 A3
Azuqueca de Henares E 151 B4
Azur F 128 C1
Azzano Décimo I 122 B1

B

Baad A 107 B5
Baamonde E 140 A3
Baar CH 107 B3
Bağarasi TR 188 B2
Baarle-Nassau B 79 A4
Baarn NL 70 B2
Babadağ TR 188 B3
Babadag RO 17 C8
Babaeski TR 186 A2
Babayevo RUS 9 C9
Babenhausen *Bayern* D 107 A5
Hessen D 93 B4
Babiak PL 76 B3
Babice PL 86 B3
Babigoszcz PL 75 A3
Babimost PL 75 B4
Babina Greda HR 125 B4
Babócsa H 124 A3
Bábolma H 112 B1
Baborów PL 86 B1
Baboszewo PL 77 B5
Babót H 111 B4
Babruysk BY 13 B8
Babsk PL 87 A4
Bac GB 31 A2
Bač SRB 125 B5
Bacares E 164 B2
Bacău RO 17 B7
Baccarat F 92 C2
Bacharach D 93 A3
Backa S 50 B2
Bačka Palanka SRB 126 B1
Backaryd S 63 B3
Bačka Topola SRB 126 B1
Backe S 200 C2
Bäckebo S 62 B4
Bäckefors S 54 B3
Bäckhammar S 55 A5
Bački Breg SRB 125 B4
Bački-Brestovac SRB 126 B1
Bački Monoštor SRB 125 B4
Bački Petrovac SRB 126 B1
Bački Sokolac SRB 126 B1
Backnang D 94 C1
Bačko Gradište SRB 126 B2
Bačko Novo Selo SRB 125 B5
Bačko Petrovo Selo SRB 126 B2
Bácoli I 170 C2
Bacqueville-en-Caux F 89 A5
Bácsalmás H 126 A1
Bácsbokod H 125 A5
Bad Abbach D 95 C4
Badacsonytomaj H 111 C4
Bad Aibling D 108 B3
Badajoz E 155 C4
Badalona E 147 C3
Badalucco I 133 B3
Bad Aussee A 109 B4
Bad Bederkesa D 72 A1
Bad Bentheim D 71 B4
Bad Bergzabern D 93 B3
Bad Berka D 82 B3
Bad Berleburg D 81 A4
Bad Berneck D 95 A3
Bad Bevensen D 73 A3
Bad Bibra D 82 A3
Bad Birnbach D 95 C5
Bad Blankenburg D 82 B3
Bad Bleiberg A 109 C4
Bad Brambach D 83 B4
Bad Bramstedt D 64 C2
Bad Breisig D 80 B3
Bad Brückenau D 82 B1
Bad Buchau D 107 A4
Bad Camberg D 81 B4
Badderen N 192 C6
Bad Doberan D 65 B4
Bad Driburg D 81 A5
Bad Düben D 83 A4
Bad Dürkheim D 93 B4
Bad Dürrenberg D 83 A4
Bad Dürrheim D 107 A3
Bad Elster D 83 B4
Bad Ems D 81 B3
Baden A 111 A3
CH 106 B3
Bádenas E 152 A2
Baden-Baden D 93 C4
Bad Endorf D 109 B3
Badenweiler D 106 B2
Baderna HR 122 B2
Bad Essen D 71 B5
Bad Fischau A 111 B3
Bad Frankenhausen D 82 A3
Bad Freienwalde D 74 B3
Bad Friedrichshall D 93 B5
Bad Füssing D 96 C1
Bad Gandersheim D 82 A2
Bad Gastein A 109 B4
Bad Gleichenberg A 110 C2
Bad Goisern A 109 B4
Bad Gottleuba D 84 B1
Bad Grund D 82 A2
Bad Hall A 110 A1
Bad Harzburg D 82 A2
Bad Herrenalb D 93 C4
Bad Hersfeld D 82 B1
Bad Hofgastein A 109 B4
Bad Homburg D 81 B4
Bad Honnef D 80 B3
Bad Hönningen D 80 B3
Badia Calavena I 121 B4
Badia Polésine I 121 B4
Badia Pratáglia I 135 B4
Badia Tedalda I 135 B5
Bad Iburg D 71 B5
Bad Innerlaterns A 107 B4
Bad Ischl A 109 B4
Bad Karlshafen D 81 A5
Bad Kemmeriboden CH 106 C2
Bądki PL 69 B3
Bad Kissingen D 82 B2
Bad Kleinen D 65 C4
Bad Kohlgrub D 108 B2
Bad König D 93 B5
Bad Königshofen D 82 B2
Bad Köstritz D 83 B4
Badkowo PL 76 B3
Bad Kreuzen A 110 A1
Bad Kreuznach D 93 B3
Bad Krozingen D 106 B2
Bad Laasphe D 81 B4
Bad Langensalza D 82 A2
Bad Lauchstädt D 83 A3
Bad Lausick D 83 A4
Bad Lauterberg D 82 A2
Bad Leonfelden A 96 C2
Bad Liebenwerda D 83 A5
Bad Liebenzell D 93 C4
Bad Lippspringe D 81 A4

Badljevina HR 124 B3
Bad Meinberg D 81 A4
Bad Mergentheim D 94 B1
Bad Mitterndorf A 109 B4
Bad Münder D 72 B2
Bad Münstereifel D 80 B2
Bad Muskau D 84 A2
Bad Nauheim D 81 B4
Bad Nenndorf D 72 B2
Bad Neuenahr-Ahrweiler D 80 B3
Bad Neustadt D 82 B2
Bad Oeynhausen D 72 B1
Badolato I 175 C2
Badolatosa E 163 A3
Bad Oldesloe D 65 C3
Badonviller F 92 C2
Bad Orb D 81 B5
Badovinci SRB 127 C1
Bad Peterstal D 93 C4
Bad Pyrmont D 72 C2
Bad Radkersburg A 110 C2
Bad Ragaz CH 107 C4
Bad Rappenau D 93 B5
Bad Reichenhall D 109 B3
Bad Saarow-Pieskow D 74 B3
Bad Sachsa D 82 A2
Bad Säckingen D 106 B2
Bad Salzdetfurth D 72 B3
Bad Salzig D 81 B3
Bad Salzuflen D 72 B1
Bad Salzungen D 82 B2
Bad Sankt Leonhard A 110 C1
Bad Sassendorf D 81 A4
Bad Schandau D 84 B2
Bad Schmiedeberg D 83 A4
Bad Schönborn D 93 B4
Bad Schussenried D 107 A4
Bad Schwalbach D 81 B4
Bad Schwartau D 65 C3
Bad Segeberg D 64 C3
Bad Soden D 81 B4
Bad Soden-Salmünster D 81 B5
Bad Sooden-Allendorf D 82 A1
Bad Sulza D 83 A3
Bad Sülze D 66 B1
Bad Tatzmannsdorf A 111 B3
Bad Tennstedt D 82 A2
Bad Tölz D 108 B2
Badules E 152 A2
Bad Urach D 94 C1
Bad Vellach A 110 C1
Bad Vilbel D 81 B4
Bad Vöslau A 111 B3
Bad Waldsee D 107 B4
Bad Wiessee D 108 B2
Bad Wildungen D 81 A5
Bad Wilsnack D 73 B4
Bad Windsheim D 94 B2
Bad Wörishafen D 108 A1
Bad Wurzach D 107 B4
Bad Zwesten D 81 A5
Bad Zwischenahn D 71 A5
Baells E 145 C4
Baena E 163 A3
Baesweiler D 80 B2
Baeza E 157 C4
Baflo NL 71 A3
Baga E 147 B2
Bagaladi I 175 C1
Bagenkop DK 65 B3
Baggetorp S 56 A2
Bagh a Chaisteil GB 31 C1
Bagheria I 176 A2
Bagn N 47 B6
Bagnacavallo I 135 A4
Bagnáia I 168 A2
Bagnara Cálabra I 175 C1
Bagnasco I 133 A4
Bagnères-de-Bigorre F 145 A4
Bagnères-de-Luchon F 145 B4
Bagni del Másino I 120 A2
Bagni di Lucca I 134 A3
Bagni di Rabbi I 121 A3
Bagni di Tivoli I 168 B2
Bagno di Romagna I 135 B4
Bagnoles-de-l'Orne F 89 B3
Bagnoli dei Trigno I 170 B2
Bagnoli di Sopra I 121 B4
Bagnoli Irpino I 170 C3
Bagnolo Mella I 120 B3
Bagnols-en-Forêt F 132 B2
Bagnols-sur-Cèze F 131 A3
Bagnorégio I 168 A2
Bagolino I 121 B3
Bagrationovsk RUS 12 A4
Bagrdan SRB 127 C3
Báguena E 152 A2
Bahabón de Esgueva E 143 C3
Bahillo E 142 B2
Báia delle Zágare I 171 B4
Báia Domizia I 169 B3
Baia Mare RO 17 B5
Baiano I 170 C2
Baião P 148 A1
Baiersbronn D 93 C4
Baiersdorf D 94 B3
Baignes-Ste Radegonde F 115 C3
Baigneux-les-Juifs F 104 B3
Baildon GB 40 B2
Bailén E 157 B4
Băileşti RO 17 C5
Baileux B 91 A4
Bailieborough IRL 27 C4
Bailleul F 78 B2
Baillonville B 79 B5
Bailó E 144 B3
Bain-de-Bretagne F 101 B4
Bains F 117 B3
Bains-les-Bains F 105 A5
Bainton GB 40 B3
Baio E 140 A2
Baiona E 140 B2
Bais F 89 B3
Baiso I 134 A3
Baiuca P 148 B2
Baja H 125 A4
Bajánsenye H 111 C3
Bajina Bašta SRB 127 D1
Bajmok SRB 126 B1
Bajna H 112 B2
Bajovo Polje MNE 139 B4
Bajša SRB 126 B1
Bak H 111 C3
Bakar HR 123 B3
Bakewell GB 40 B2
Bakio E 143 A4
Bakka N 47 C6
Bakkafjörður IS 191 A11
Bakkagerði IS 191 B12
Bække DK 59 C2
Bakken N 48 B3
Baklan TR 189 B4
Bækmarksbro DK 58 B1
Bakonybél H 111 B4
Bakonycsernye H 112 B2
Bakonyjákó H 111 B4
Bakonyszentkirály H 111 B4
Bakonyszombathely H 112 B1
Bakov nad Jizerou CZ 84 B2
Bąkowiec PL 87 A5
Baks H 113 C4
Baksa H 125 B4
Bakum D 71 B5
Bala GB 38 B3
Bâlâ TR 23 B7
Balaguer E 145 C4
Balassagyarmat H 112 A3
Balástya H 113 C4
Balatonakali H 111 C4
Balatonalmádi H 112 B2
Balatonboglár H 111 C4
Balatonbozsok H 112 C2
Balatonederics H 111 C4
Balatonfenyves H 111 C4
Balatonföldvár H 112 C1
Balatonfüred H 112 C1
Balatonfüzfő H 112 B2
Balatonkenese H 112 B2
Balatonkiliti H 112 C2
Balatonlelle H 111 C4
Balatonszabadi H 112 C2
Balatonszemes H 111 C4
Balatonszentgyörgy H 111 C4
Balazote E 158 C1
Balbeggie GB 35 B4
Balbigny F 117 B4
Balboa E 141 B4
Balbriggan IRL 30 A2
Balchik BG 17 D8
Balçova TR 188 A2
Baldock GB 44 B3
Bale HR 122 B2
Baleira E 141 A3
Baleizao P 160 A2
Balen B 79 A5
Balerma E 164 C2
Balestrand N 46 A3
Balestrate I 176 A2
Balfour GB 33 B4
Bälganet S 63 B3
Balgari BG 17 D7
Balıkesir TR 186 C2
Balıklıçeşme TR 186 B2
Bälinge S 51 C4
Balingen D 107 A3
Balingsta S 56 A3
Balintore GB 32 D3
Balizac F 128 B2
Balk NL 70 B2
Balkbrug NL 71 B3
Balla IRL 28 A2
Ballachulish GB 34 B2
Ballaghaderreen IRL 26 C2
Ballancourt-sur-Essonne F 90 C2
Ballantrae GB 36 A2
Ballao I 179 C3
Ballasalla GB 36 B2
Ballater GB 32 D3
Ballen DK 59 C3
Ballenstedt D 82 A3
Ballerias E 145 C3
Balleroy F 88 A3
Ballerup DK 61 D2
Ballesteros de Calatrava E 157 B4
Ballı TR 186 B2
Ballina IRL 26 B1
Ballinalack IRL 30 A1
Ballinamore IRL 26 B3
Ballinascarty IRL 29 C3
Ballinasloe IRL 28 A3
Ballindine IRL 28 A3
Balling DK 58 B1
Ballingarry
Limerick IRL 29 B3
Tipperary IRL 30 B1
Ballingeary IRL 29 C2
Ballinhassig IRL 29 C3
Ballinluig GB 35 B4
Ballino I 121 B3
Ballinrobe IRL 28 A2
Ballinskelligs IRL 29 C1
Ballinspittle IRL 29 C3
Ballintra IRL 26 B2
Ballivor IRL 30 A2
Ballobar E 153 A4
Ballon
F 102 A2
IRL 30 B2
Ballószög H 112 C3
Ballsh AL 182 C1
Ballstad N 194 B4
Ballum DK 64 A1
Ballybay IRL 27 B4
Ballybofey IRL 26 B3
Ballybunion IRL 29 B2
Ballycanew IRL 30 B2
Ballycarry GB 27 B5
Ballycastle
GB 27 A4
IRL 26 B1
Ballyclare GB 27 B5
Ballyconneely IRL 28 A1
Ballycotton IRL 29 C3
Ballycroy IRL 26 B1
Ballydehob IRL 29 C2
Ballyferriter IRL 29 B1
Ballygawley GB 27 B3
Ballygowan GB 27 B5
Ballyhaunis IRL 28 A3
Ballyheige IRL 29 B2
Ballyjamesduff IRL 27 C3
Ballylanders IRL 29 B3
Ballylynan IRL 30 B1
Ballymahon IRL 28 A4
Ballymena GB 27 B4
Ballymoe IRL 28 A3
Ballymoney GB 27 A4
Ballymore IRL 28 A4
Ballymote IRL 26 B2
Ballynacorra IRL 29 C3
Ballynagore IRL 30 A1
Ballynahinch GB 27 B5
Ballynure GB 27 B5
Ballyragget IRL 30 B1
Ballysadare IRL 26 B2
Ballyshannon IRL 26 B2
Ballyvaughan IRL 28 A2
Ballyvourney IRL 29 C2
Ballywalter GB 27 B5
Balmaclellan GB 36 A2
Balmaseda E 143 A3
Balmazújváros H 113 B5
Balme I 119 B4
Balmedie GB 33 D4
Balmuccia I 119 B5
Balna-paling GB 32 D2
Balneario de Panticosa E 145 B3
Balotaszállás H 126 A1
Balsa P 148 A2
Balsareny E 147 C2
Balsorano-Nuovo I 169 B3
Bålsta S 57 A3
Balsthal CH 106 B2
Balta UA 17 A8
Baltanás E 142 C2
Baltar E 140 C3
Baltasound GB 33 A6
Bălţi MD 17 B7
Baltimore IRL 29 C2
Baltinglass IRL 30 B2
Baltiysk RUS 69 A4
Baltów PL 87 A5
Balugães P 148 A1
Bælum DK 58 B3
Balve D 81 A3
Balvi LV 8 D5
Balvicar GB 34 B2
Balya TR 186 C2
Balzo I 136 C2
Bamberg D 94 B2
Bamburgh GB 37 A5
Banatska Palanka SRB 127 C3
Banatski Brestovac SRB 127 C2
Banatski Despotovac SRB 126 B2
Banatski Dvor SRB 126 B2
Banatski-Karlovac SRB 127 B3
Banatsko Arandjelovo SRB 126 A2
Banatsko-Novo Selo SRB 127 C2
Banaz TR 187 D4
Banbridge GB 27 B4
Banbury GB 44 A2
Banchory GB 33 D4
Bande
B 79 B5
E 140 B3
Bandholm DK 65 B4
Bandırma TR 186 B2
Bandol F 132 B1
Bandon IRL 29 C3
Bañeres E 159 C3
Banff GB 33 D4
Bangor
F 100 B2
Down GB 27 B5
Gwynedd GB 38 A2
IRL 26 B1
Bangsund N 199 A8
Banie PL 74 A3
Banja Koviljača SRB 127 C1
Banjaloka SLO 123 B3
Banja Luka BIH 124 C3
Banjani SRB 127 C1
Banja Vručica BIH 125 C3
Banka SK 98 C1
Bankekind S 56 B1
Bankend GB 36 A3
Bankeryd S 62 A2
Bankfoot GB 35 B4
Bankso BG 183 B5
Banloc RO 126 B3
Bannalec F 100 B2
Bannes F 91 C3
Bannockburn GB 35 B4
Bañobárez E 149 B3
Bañon E 152 B2
Banon F 132 A1
Baños E 149 B4
Baños de Gigonza E 162 B2
Baños de la Encina E 157 B4
Baños de Molgas E 140 B3
Baños de Rio Tobia E 143 B4
Baños de Valdearados E 143 C3
Bánov CZ 98 C1
Banova Jaruga HR 124 B2
Bánovce nad Bebravou SK 98 C2
Banovići BIH 139 A4
Banovići Selo BIH 139 A4
Bánréve H 99 C4
Bansin D 66 C3
Banská Belá SK 98 C2
Banská Bystrica SK 99 C3
Banská Štiavnica SK 98 C2
Bansko BG 183 B5
Banstead GB 44 B3
Banteer IRL 29 B3
Bantheville F 91 B5
Bantry IRL 29 C2
Bantzenheim F 106 B2
Banyalbufar E 166 B2
Banyoles E 147 B3
Banyuls-sur-Mer F 146 B4
Bapaume F 90 A2
Bar
MNE 16 D3
UA 13 D7
Barabhas GB 31 A2
Barači BIH 138 A2
Baracs H 112 C2
Baracska H 112 B2
Barahona E 151 A5
Barajes de Melo E 151 B5
Barakaldo E 143 A4
Baralla E 141 B3
Barañain E 144 B2
Baranavichy BY 13 B7
Báránd H 113 B5
Baranda SRB 127 B2
Baranello I 170 B2
Baranów Sandomierski PL 87 B5
Baraqueville F 130 A1
Barasoain E 144 B2
Barbacena P 155 C3
Barbadás E 140 B3
Barbadillo E 149 B4
Barbadillo de Herreros E 143 B3
Barbadillo del Mercado E 143 B3
Barbadillo del Pez E 143 B3
Barban HR 123 B3
Barbarano Vicento I 121 B4
Barbariga HR 122 C2
Barbaros TR 186 B2
Barbastro E 145 B4
Barbate E 162 B2
Barbatona E 152 A1
Barbâtre F 114 B1
Barbazan F 145 A4
Barbeitos E 141 A3
Barbentane F 131 B3
Barberino di Mugello I 135 A4
Barbezieux-St Hilaire F 115 C3
Barbonne-Fayel F 91 C3
Barbotan-les-Thermes F 128 C2
Barby D 73 C4
Bárcabo E 145 B4
Barca de Alva P 149 A3
Barcarrota E 155 C4
Barcellona-Pozzo di Gotto I 177 A4
Barcelona E 147 C3
Barcelonette F 132 A2
Barcelos P 148 A1
Bárcena del Monasterio E 141 A4
Barcena de Pie de Concha E 142 A2
Barchfeld D 82 B2
Barcin PL 76 B2
Barcino PL 68 A1
Bárcis I 122 A1
Barco P 148 B2
Barcones E 151 A5
Barcs H 124 B3
Barcus F 144 A3
Bardejov SK 12 D4
Bårdesø DK 59 C3
Bardi I 120 C2
Bardney GB 40 B3
Bardo PL 85 B4
Bardolino I 121 B3
Bardonécchia I 118 B3
Bardoňovo SK 112 A2
Barèges F 145 B4
Barenstein D 83 B5
Barentin F 89 A4
Barenton F 88 B3
Barevo BIH 138 A3
Barfleur F 88 A2
Barga I 134 A3
Bargas E 151 C3
Barge I 119 C4
Bargemon F 132 B2
Barghe I 120 B3
Bargoed GB 39 C3
Bargrennan GB 36 A2
Bargteheide D 64 C3
Barham GB 45 B5
Bari I 173 A2
Barič Draga HR 137 A4
Barilović HR 123 B4
Bari Sardo I 179 C3
Barisciano I 169 A3
Barjac F 131 A3
Barjols F 132 B1
Barjon F 105 B3
Bårkåker N 54 A1
Barkald N 199 D7
Barkowo
Dolnośląskie PL 85 A4
Pomorskie PL 68 B2
Bârlad RO 17 B7
Bar-le-Duc F 91 C5
Barles F 132 A2
Barletta I 171 B4
Barlinek PL 75 B4
Barmouth GB 38 B2
Barmstedt D 64 C2
Barnard Castle GB 37 B5
Barnarp S 62 A2
Bärnau D 95 B4
Bärnbach A 110 B2
Barneberg D 73 B4
Barnenitz D 74 B1
Barnet GB 44 B3
Barnetby le Wold GB 40 B3
Barneveld NL 70 B2
Barneville-Carteret F 88 A2
Barnoldswick GB 40 B1
Barnowko PL 75 B3
Barnsley GB 40 B2
Barnstädt D 83 A3
Barnstaple GB 42 A2
Barnstorf D 72 B1
Barntrup D 72 C2
Baron F 90 B2
Baronissi I 170 C2
Barqueiro P 154 B2
Barquinha P 154 B2
Barr
F 93 C3
GB 36 A2
Barra P 148 B1
Barracas E 159 A3
Barraco E 150 B3
Barrado E 150 B2
Barrafranca I 177 B3
Barranco do Velho P 160 B2
Barrancos P 161 A3
Barrax E 158 B1
Barrbaar D 94 C2
Barre-des-Cevennes F 130 A2
Barreiro P 154 C1
Barreiros E 141 A3
Barrême F 132 B2
Barret-le-Bas F 132 A1
Barrhead GB 34 C3
Barrhill GB 36 A2
Barrio de Nuesra Señora E 142 B1
Barrowford GB 40 B1
Barrow-in-Furness GB 36 B3
Barrow upon Humber GB 40 B3
Barruecopardo E 149 A3
Barruelo de Santullán E 142 B2
Barruera E 145 B4
Barry GB 39 C3
Bårse DK 65 A4
Barsinghausen D 72 B2
Barssel D 71 A4
Bar-sur-Aube F 104 A3
Bar-sur-Seine F 104 A3
Barth D 66 B1
Bartholomä D 94 C1
Bartin TR 187 A7
Barton upon Humber GB 40 B3
Barúmini I 179 C2
Baruth D 74 B2
Barvaux B 80 B1
Barver D 72 B1
Barwatd PL 99 B3
Barwice PL 68 B1
Barysaw BY 13 A8
Barzana E 141 A5
Bârzava RO 16 B4
Bárzio I 120 B2
Bas E 147 B3
Bašaid SRB 126 B2
Basaluzzo I 120 C1
Basarabeasca MD 17 B8
Basauri E 143 A4
Baschi I 168 A2
Baschurch GB 38 B4
Basconcillos del Tozo E 143 B3
Bascones de Ojeda E 142 B2
Basécles B 79 B3
Basel CH 106 B2
Basélice I 170 B2
Basildon GB 45 B4
Basingstoke GB 44 B2
Baška
CZ 98 B2
HR 123 C3
Baška Voda HR 138 B2
Bäsksjö S 200 B3
Baslow GB 40 B2
Başmakçı TR 189 B5
Basovizza I 122 B2
Bassacutena I 178 A3
Bassano del Grappa I 121 B4
Bassano Romano I 168 A2
Bassecourt CH 106 B2
Bassella E 147 B2
Bassevuovdde N 193 D9
Bassou F 104 B2
Bassoues F 128 C3
Bassum D 72 B1
Båstad S 61 C2
Bastardo I 136 C1
Bastelica F 180 A2
Bastelicaccia F 180 B1
Bastia
F 180 A2
I 136 B1
Bastogne B 92 A1
Baston GB 40 C3
Bastuträsk S 200 B6
Bata H 125 A4
Batajnica SRB 127 C2
Batak BG 183 B6
Batalha P 154 B2
Bátaszék H 125 A4
Batea E 153 A4
Batelov CZ 97 B3
Bath GB 43 A4
Bathgate GB 35 C4
Batida H 126 A2
Batignano I 135 C4
Batina HR 125 B4
Bátka SK 99 C4
Batković BIH 125 C5
Batley GB 40 B2
Batnfjordsøra N 198 C4
Batočina SRB 127 C3
Bátonyterenye H 113 B3
Batrina HR 125 B3
Båtsfjord N 193 B13
Båtskärsnäs S 196 D6
Battaglia Terme I 121 B4
Bätterkinden CH 106 B2
Battice B 80 B1
Battipáglia I 170 C2
Battle GB 45 C4
Battonya H 126 A3
Batuša SRB 127 C3
Bátya H 112 C2
Bau I 179 C2
Baud F 100 B2
Baudour B 79 B3
Baugé F 102 B1
Baugy F 103 B4
Bauma CH 107 B3
Baume-les-Dames F 105 B5
Baumholder D 93 B3
Baunatal D 81 A5
Baunei I 178 B3
Bauska LV 8 D4
Bautzen D 84 A2
Bavanište SRB 127 C2
Bavay F 79 B3
Bavilliers F 106 B1
Bavorov CZ 96 B2
Bawdsey GB 45 A5
Bawinkel D 71 B4
Bawtry GB 40 B2
Bayat TR 187 D5
Bayel F 105 A3
Bayeux F 88 A3
Bayındır TR 188 A2
Bayon F 92 C2
Bayonne F 128 C1
Bayons F 132 A2
Bayramiç TR 186 C1
Bayreuth D 95 B3
Bayrischzell D 108 B3
Baza E 164 B2
Bazas F 128 B2
Baziege F 146 A2
Bazoches-les-Gallerandes F 103 A4
Bazoches-sur-Hoëne F 89 B4
Bazzano I 135 A4
Beaconsfield GB 44 B3
Beade E 140 B2
Beadnell GB 37 A5
Beaminster GB 43 B4
Bearsden GB 34 C3
Beas E 161 B3
Beasain E 144 A1
Beas de Segura E 164 A2
Beattock GB 36 A3
Beaubery F 117 A4
Beaucaire F 131 B3
Beaufort
F 118 B3
IRL 29 B2
Beaufort-en Vallée F 102 B1
Beaugency F 103 B3
Beaujeu
Alpes-de-Haute-Provence F 132 A2
Rhône F 117 A4
Beaulac F 128 B2
Beaulieu
F 103 B4
GB 44 C2
Beaulieu-sous-la-Roche F 114 B2
Beaulieu-sur-Dordogne F 129 B4
Beaulieu-sur-Mer F 133 B3
Beaulon F 104 C2
Beauly GB 32 D2
Beaumaris GB 38 A2
Beaumesnil F 89 A4
Beaumetz-lès-Loges F 78 B2
Beaumont
B 79 B4
Beaumont continued
F 129 B3
Beaumont-de-Lomagne F 129 C3
Beaumont-du-Gâtinais F 103 A4
Beaumont-en-Argonne F 91 B5
Beaumont-Hague F 88 A2
Beaumont-la-Ronce F 102 B2
Beaumont-le-Roger F 89 A4
Beaumont-sur-Oise F 90 B2
Beaumont-sur-Sarthe F 102 A2
Beaune F 105 B3
Beaune-la-Rolande F 103 A4
Beaupréau F 101 B5
Beauraing B 91 A4
Beaurepaire F 117 B5
Beaurepaire-en-Bresse F 105 C4
Beaurières F 132 A1
Beauvais F 90 B2
Beauval F 90 A2
Beauville F 129 B3
Beauvoir-sur-Mer F 114 B1
Beauvoir-sur-Niort F 114 B3
Beba Veche RO 126 A2
Bebertal D 73 B4
Bebington GB 38 A3
Bebra D 82 B1
Bebrina HR 125 B3
Beccles GB 45 A5
Becedas E 150 B2
Beceite E 153 B4
Bečej SRB 126 B2
Becerreá E 141 B3
Becerril de Campos E 142 B2
Bécherel F 101 A4
Bechhofen D 94 B2
Bechyně CZ 96 B2
Becilla de Valderaduey E 142 B1
Beckfoot GB 36 B3
Beckingham GB 40 B3
Beckum D 81 A4
Beco P 154 B2
Bécon-les-Granits F 102 B1
Bečov nad Teplou CZ 83 B4
Becsehely H 111 C3
Bedale GB 37 B5
Bedames E 143 A3
Bédar E 164 B3
Bédarieux F 130 B2
Bédarrides F 131 A3
Bedburg D 80 B2
Beddgelert GB 38 A2
Beddingestrand S 66 A2
Bédée F 101 A4
Bedegkér H 112 C2
Beden TR 189 C7
Bedford GB 44 A3
Będków PL 87 A3
Bedlington GB 37 A5
Bedlno PL 77 B4
Bedmar E 163 A4
Bédoin F 131 A4
Bedónia I 134 A2
Bedretto CH 107 C3
Bedsted DK 58 B1
Bedum NL 71 A3
Bedwas GB 39 C3
Bedworth GB 40 C2
Będzin PL 86 B3
Beekbergen NL 70 B2
Beek en Donk NL 80 A1
Beelen D 71 C5
Beelitz D 74 B1
Beer GB 43 B3
Beerfelde D 74 B3
Beerfelden D 93 B4
Beernem B 78 A3
Beeskow D 74 B3
Beetsterzwaag NL 70 A3
Beetzendorf D 73 B4
Beflelay CH 106 B2
Begaljica SRB 127 C2
Bégard F 100 A2
Begejci SRB 126 B2
Begijar E 157 C4
Begijnendijk B 79 A4
Begndal N 48 B1
Begues E 147 C2
Beguildy GB 39 B3
Begur E 147 C4
Beho B 80 B1
Behringen D 82 A2
Beilen NL 71 B3
Beilngries D 95 B3
Beine-Nauroy F 91 B4
Beinwil CH 106 B3
Beiseförth D 82 A1
Beith GB 34 C3
Beitostølen N 47 A5
Beiuş RO 16 B5
Beja P 160 A2
Béjar E 149 B4
Bekçiler TR 189 C4
Békés H 113 C5
Békéscsaba H 113 C5
Bekilli TR 189 A4
Bekkarfjord N 193 B11
Bela SK 98 B2
Bélâbre F 115 B5
Bela Crkva SRB 127 C3
Belacázar E 156 B2
Belánad Radbuzou CZ 95 B4
Belanovica SRB 127 C2
Bélapátfalva H 113 A4

Bělápod Bezdězem CZ 84 B2
Belcaire F 146 B2
Bełchatów PL 86 A3
Belchite E 153 A3
Bělčice CZ 96 B1
Belcoo GB 26 B3
Belecke D 81 A4
Beled H 111 B4
Belej HR 123 C3
Beleño E 142 A1
Bélesta F 146 B2
Belevi TR 188 A2
Belfast GB 27 B5
Belford GB 37 A5
Belfort F 106 B1
Belgentier F 132 B1
Belgern D 83 A5
Belgioioso I 120 B2
Belgodère F 180 A2
Belgooly IRL 29 C3
Belgrade = Beograd SRB 127 C2
Belhade F 128 B2
Belica HR 124 A2
Beli Manastir HR 125 B4
Belin-Bèliet F 128 B2
Belinchón E 151 B4
Belišće HR 125 B4
Bělkovice-Lašt'any CZ 98 B1
Bella I 172 B1
Bellac F 115 B5
Bellágio I 120 B2
Bellananagh IRL 27 C3
Bellano I 120 A2
Bellária I 136 A1
Bellavary IRL 26 C1
Belleau F 90 B3
Belleek GB 26 B2
Bellegarde
Gard F 131 B3
Loiret F 103 B4
Bellegarde-en-Diois F 132 A1
Bellegarde-en-Marche F 116 B2
Bellegarde-sur-Valserine F 118 A2
Belle-Isle-en-Terre F 100 A2
Bellême F 89 B4
Bellenaves F 116 A3
Bellentre F 118 B3
Bellevaux F 118 A3
Bellevesvre F 105 C4
Belleville F 117 A4
Belleville-sur-Vie F 114 B2
Bellevue-la-Montagne F 117 B3
Belley F 118 B2
Bellheim D 93 B4
Bellinge DK 59 C3
Bellingham GB 37 A4
Bellinzago Novarese I 120 B1
Bellinzona CH 120 A2
Bell-lloc d'Urgell E 153 A4
Bello E 152 B2
Bellpuig d'Urgell E 147 C2
Bellreguart E 159 C3
Bellsbank GB 36 A2
Belltall E 147 C2
Belluno I 121 A5
Bellver de Cerdanya E 146 B2
Bellvis E 147 C1
Bélmez E 156 B2
Belmez de la Moraleda E 163 A4
Belmont GB 33 A6
Belmont-de-la-Loire F 117 A4
Belmonte
Asturias E 141 A4
Cuenca E 158 B1
P 148 B2
Belmonte de San José E 153 B3
Belmonte de Tajo E 151 B4
Belmont-sur-Rance F 130 B1
Belmullet IRL 26 B1
Belobreşca RO 127 C3
Beloeil B 79 B3
Belogradchik BG 16 D5
Belokorovichi UA 13 C8
Belorado E 143 B3
Belotič SRB 127 C1
Bělotin CZ 98 B1
Belovo BG 183 A6
Belozersk RUS 9 C10
Belp CH 106 C2
Belpasso I 177 B3
Belpech F 146 A2
Belper GB 40 B2
Belsay GB 37 A5
Belsk Duzy PL 87 A4
Beltinci SLO 111 C3
Beltra IRL 26 C1
Belturbet IRL 27 B3
Beluša SK 98 B2
Belvedere Marittimo I 174 B1
Belver de Cinca E 153 A4
Belver de los Montes E 142 C1
Belvès F 129 B3
Belvezet F 130 A2
Belvis de la Jara E 150 C3
Belvis de Monroy E 150 C2
Belyy RUS 9 E8
Belz F 100 B2
Bełżec PL 13 C5
Belzig D 73 B5
Bembibre E 141 B4
Bembridge GB 44 C2
Bemmel NL 80 A1
Bemposta
Bragança P 149 A3
Santarém P 154 B2
Benabarre E 145 B4
Benacazón E 161 B3
Benaguacil E 159 B3
Benahadux E 164 C2
Benalmádena E 163 B3
Benalúa de Guadix E 164 B1
Benalúa de las Villas E 163 A4
Benalup E 162 B2
Benamargosa E 163 B3
Benamaurel E 164 B2
Benameji E 163 A3
Benamocarra E 163 B3
Benaocaz E 162 B2
Benaoján E 162 B2
Benarrabá E 162 B2
Benasque E 145 B4
Benátky nad Jizerou CZ 84 B2
Benavente
E 142 B1
P 154 C2
Benavides de Órbigo E 141 B5
Benavila P 154 B3
Bendorf D 81 B3
Benedikt SLO 110 C2
Benejama E 159 C3
Benejúzar E 165 A4
Benešov CZ 96 B2
Bénestroff F 92 C2
Benet F 114 B3
Bénévent-l'Abbaye F 116 A1
Benevento I 170 B2
Benfeld F 93 C3
Benfica P 154 B2
Bengtsfors S 54 A3
Bengtsheden S 50 B2
Beničanci HR 125 B4
Benicarló E 153 B4
Benicássim E 153 B4
Benidorm E 159 C3
Benifaió E 159 B3
Beniganim E 159 C3
Benington GB 41 B4
Benisa E 159 C4
Benkovac HR 137 A4
Benllech GB 38 A2
Benneckenstein D 82 A2
Bénodet F 100 B1
Benquerencia de la Serena E 156 B2
Bensafrim P 160 B1
Bensbyn S 196 D5
Bensdorf D 73 B5
Benshausen D 82 B2
Bensheim D 93 B4
Bentley GB 44 B3
Bentwisch D 65 B5
Beočin SRB 126 B1
Beograd = Belgrade SRB 127 C2
Beragh GB 27 B3
Beranga E 143 A3
Berat AL 182 C1
Bérat F 146 A2
Beratzhausen D 95 B3
Bérbaltavár H 111 B3
Berbegal E 145 C3
Berbenno di Valtellina I 120 A2
Berberana E 143 B3
Bercedo E 143 A3
Bercel H 112 B3
Bercenay-le-Hayer F 91 C3
Berceto I 134 A2
Berchem B 79 B3
Berchidda I 178 B3
Berching D 95 B3
Berchtesgaden D 109 B4
Bérchules E 163 B4
Bercianos de Aliste E 149 A3
Berck F 78 B1
Berclaire d'Urgell E 147 C1
Berdoias E 140 A1
Berducedo E 141 A4
Berdún E 144 B3
Berdychiv UA 13 D8
Bere Alston GB 42 B2
Bereguardo I 120 B2
Berehommen N 53 A3
Berehove UA 16 A5
Berek BIH 124 B3
Beremend H 125 B4
Bere Regis GB 43 B4
Berestechko UA 13 C6
Berettyóújfalu H 113 B5
Berezhany UA 13 D6
Berezivka UA 17 B9
Berezna UA 13 C9
Berg
D 95 B3
N 195 E3
S 56 B2
Berga
Sachsen-Anhalt D 82 A3
Thüringen D 83 B4
E 147 B2
S 62 A4
Bergama TR 186 C2
Bérgamo I 120 B2
Bergara E 143 A4
Bergby S 51 B4
Berge
Brandenburg D 74 B1
Niedersachsen D 71 B4
Berge *continued*
Telemark N 53 A4
Telemark N 53 A4
Bergeforsen S 200 D3
Bergen
Mecklenburg-Vorpommern D 66 B2
Niedersachsen D 72 B2
Niedersachsen D 73 B3
N 46 B2
NL 70 B1
Bergen op Zoom NL 79 A4
Bergerac F 129 B3
Bergères-lés-Vertus F 91 C4
Bergeyk NL 79 A5
Berghausen D 93 C4
Bergheim D 80 B2
Berghem S 60 B2
Berg im Gau D 95 C3
Bergisch Gladbach D 80 B3
Bergkamen D 81 A3
Bergkvara S 63 B4
Berglern D 95 C3
Bergnäset S 196 D5
Bergneustadt D 81 A3
Bergsäng S 49 B5
Bergshamra S 57 A4
Bergsjö S 200 E3
Bergs slussar S 56 B1
Bergsviken S 196 D4
Bergtheim D 94 B2
Bergues F 78 B2
Bergum NL 70 A2
Bergün Bravuogn CH 107 C4
Bergwitz D 83 A4
Berhida H 112 B2
Beringel P 160 A2
Beringen B 79 A5
Berja E 164 C2
Berkåk N 199 C7
Berkeley GB 43 A4
Berkenthin D 65 C3
Berkhamsted GB 44 B3
Berkheim D 107 A5
Berkhof D 72 B2
Berkovići BIH 139 B4
Berkovitsa BG 17 D5
Berlanga E 156 B2
Berlanga de Duero E 151 A5
Berlevåg N 193 B13
Berlikum NL 70 A2
Berlin D 74 B2
Berlstedt D 82 A3
Bermeo E 143 A4
Bermillo de Sayago E 149 A3
Bern CH 106 C2
Bernalda I 174 A2
Bernardos E 150 A3
Bernartice
Jihočeský CZ 96 B2
Vychodočeský CZ 85 B3
Bernau
Baden-Württemberg D 106 B3
Bayern D 109 B3
Brandenburg D 74 B2
Bernaville F 90 A2
Bernay F 89 A4
Bernburg D 83 A3
Berndorf A 111 B3
Berne D 72 A1
Bernecebarati H 112 A2
Bernhardsthal A 97 C4
Bernkastel-Kues D 92 B3
Bernolakovo SK 111 A4
Bernsdorf D 84 A2
Bernstadt D 84 A2
Bernstein A 111 B3
Bernués E 145 B3
Beromünster CH 106 B3
Beroun CZ 96 B2
Berovo MK 182 B4
Berre-l'Etang F 131 B4
Berriedale GB 32 C3
Berriew GB 39 B3
Berrocal E 161 B3
Bersenbrück D 71 B4
Bershad' UA 13 D8
Bertamiráns E 140 B2
Berthåga S 51 C4
Berthelming F 92 C2
Bertincourt F 90 A2
Bertinoro I 135 A5
Bertogne B 92 A1
Bertrix B 91 B5
Berufjörður IS 191 C11
Berville-sur-Mer F 89 A4
Berwick-upon-Tweed GB 37 A4
Berzasca RO 16 C4
Berzence H 124 A3
Berzocana E 156 A2
Besalú E 147 B3
Besançon F 105 B5
Besenfeld D 93 C4
Besenyötelek H 113 B4
Besenyszög H 113 B4
Beshenkovichi BY 13 A8
Besigheim D 93 C5
Běšiny CZ 96 B1
Beška SRB 126 B2
Beşkonak TR 189 B6
Besle F 101 B4
Besnyö H 112 B2
Bessais-le-Fromental F 103 C4
Bessan F 130 B2
Besse-en-Chandesse F 116 B2
Bessèges F 131 A3
Bessé-sur-Braye F 102 B2
Bessines-sur-Gartempe F 115 B5
Best NL 79 A5
Bestorp S 56 B1
Betanzos E 140 A2
Betelu E 144 A2
Bétera E 159 B3
Beteta E 152 B1
Béthenville F 91 B4
Bethesda GB 38 A2
Béthune F 78 B2
Beton-Bazoches F 90 C3
Bettembourg L 92 B2
Betterdorf L 92 B2
Bettna S 56 B2
Béttola I 120 C2
Bettona I 136 B1
Bettyhill GB 32 C2
Betws-y-Coed GB 38 A3
Betxi E 159 B3
Betz F 90 B2
Betzdorf D 81 B3
Beuil F 132 A2
Beulah GB 39 B3
Beuzeville F 89 A4
Bevagna I 136 C1
Bevens-bruk S 56 A1
Beveren B 79 A4
Beverley GB 40 B3
Bevern D 81 A5
Beverstedt D 72 A1
Beverungen D 81 A5
Beverwijk NL 70 B1
Bex CH 119 A4
Bexhill GB 45 C4
Beyazköy TR 186 A2
Beychevelle F 128 A2
Beydağ TR 188 A3
Beyeğaç TR 188 B3
Beykoz TR 186 A4
Beynat F 129 A4
Beyoğlu TR 186 A4
Beypazarı TR 187 B6
Beyşehir TR 189 B6
Bezas E 152 B2
Bezau A 107 B4
Bezdan SRB 125 B4
Bèze F 105 B4
Bezenet F 116 A2
Bezhetsk RUS 9 D10
Béziers F 130 B2
Bezzecca I 121 B3
Biadki PL 85 A5
Biała
Łódzkie PL 77 C4
Opolskie PL 85 B5
Białaczów PL 87 A4
Biała Podlaska PL 13 B5
Biała Rawska PL 87 A4
Biale Błota PL 76 A2
Białobłoty PL 76 B2
Białobrzegi PL 87 A4
Białogard PL 67 C4
Białośliwie PL 76 A2
Białowąs PL 68 B1
Biały Bór PL 68 B1
Białystok PL 13 B5
Biancavilla I 177 B3
Bianco I 175 C2
Biandrate I 119 B5
Biar E 159 C3
Biarritz F 144 A2
Bias F 128 B1
Biasca CH 120 A1
Biatorbágy H 112 B2
Bibbiena I 135 B4
Bibbona I 134 B3
Biberach
Baden-Württemberg D 93 C4
Baden-Württemberg D 107 A4
Bibinje HR 137 A4
Bibione I 122 B2
Biblis D 93 B4
Bibury GB 44 B2
Bicaj AL 182 B2
Biccari I 171 B3
Bicester GB 44 B2
Bichl D 108 B2
Bichlbach A 108 B1
Bicorp E 159 B3
Bicos P 160 B1
Bicske H 112 B2
Bidache F 128 C1
Bidart F 144 A2
Biddinghuizen NL 70 B2
Biddulph GB 40 B1
Bideford GB 42 A2
Bidford-on-Avon GB 44 A2
Bidjovagge N 192 C6
Bie S 56 A2
Bieber D 81 B5
Biebersdorf D 74 C2
Biedenkopf D 81 B4
Biel E 144 B3
Bielany Wroclawskie PL 85 A4
Bielawa PL 85 B4
Bielawy PL 77 B4
Biel / Bienne CH 106 B2
Bielefeld D 72 B1
Biella I 119 B5
Bielsa E 145 B4
Bielsk PL 77 B4
Bielsko-Biała PL 99 B3
Bielsk Podlaski PL 13 B5
Bienenbuttel D 72 A3
Bieniow PL 84 A3
Bienservida E 158 C1
Bienvenida E 156 B1
Bierdzany PL 86 B2
Bierné F 102 B1
Biersted DK 58 A2
Bierun PL 86 B3
Bierutów PL 85 A5
Bierwart B 79 B5
Bierzwina PL 75 A4
Bierzwnik PL 75 A4
Biescas E 145 B3
Biesenthal D 74 B2
Biesiekierz PL 67 B5
Bietigheim-Bissingen D 93 C5
Bièvre B 91 B5
Bieżuń PL 77 B4
Biga TR 186 B2
Bigadiç TR 186 C3
Biganos F 128 B2
Bigas P 148 B2
Bigastro E 165 A4
Bigbury GB 42 B3
Biggar GB 36 A3
Biggin Hill GB 45 B4
Biggleswade GB 44 A3
Bignasco CH 119 A5
Biguglia F 180 A2
Bihać BIH 124 C1
Biharnagybajom H 113 B5
Bijeljani BIH 139 B4
Bijeljina BIH 125 C5
Bijuesca E 152 A2
Bilaj HR 137 A4
Bila Tserkva UA 13 D9
Bilbao E 143 A4
Bilcza PL 87 B4
Bíldudalur IS 190 B2
Bileća BIH 139 C4
Bilecik TR 187 B4
Biled RO 126 B2
Biłgoraj PL 12 C5
Bilhorod-Dnistrovskyy UA 17 B9
Bílina CZ 84 B1
Bilisht AL 182 C2
Bilje HR 125 B4
Billdal S 60 B1
Billerbeck D 71 C4
Billericay GB 45 B4
Billesholm S 61 C2
Billingborough GB 40 C3
Billinge S 61 D3
Billingham GB 37 B5
Billinghay GB 41 B3
Billingsfors S 54 B3
Billingshurst GB 44 B3
Billom F 116 B3
Billsta S 200 C4
Billund DK 59 C2
Bílovec CZ 98 B2
Bilstein D 81 A4
Bilthoven NL 70 B2
Bilto N 192 C5
Bilzen B 80 B1
Bíňa SK 112 B2
Binaced E 145 C4
Binasco I 120 B2
Binbrook GB 41 B3
Binche B 79 B4
Bindlach D 95 B3
Bindslev DK 58 A3
Binefar E 145 C4
Bingen D 93 B3
Bingham GB 40 C3
Bingley GB 40 B2
Bingsjö S 50 A2
Binic F 100 A3
Binz D 66 B2
Biograd na Moru HR 137 B4
Bionaz I 119 B4
Bioska SRB 127 D1
Birda RO 126 B3
Birdlip GB 44 B1
Biri N 48 B2
Birkeland N 53 B4
Birkenfeld
Baden-Württemberg D 93 C4
Rheinland-Pfalz D 92 B3
Birkenhead GB 38 A3
Birkerød DK 61 D2
Birkfeld A 110 B2
Birkirkara M 175 C3
Birmingham GB 40 C2
Birr IRL 28 A4
Birresborn D 80 B2
Birstein D 81 B5
Biržai LT 8 D4
Birzebbugia M 175 C3
Bisáccia I 172 A1
Bisacquino I 176 B2
Bisbal de Falset E 153 A4
Biscarosse F 128 B1
Biscarosse Plage F 128 B1
Biscarrués E 144 B3
Biscéglie I 171 B4
Bischheim F 93 C3
Bischofsheim D 82 B1
Bischofshofen A 109 B4
Bischofswerda D 84 A2
Bischofswiesen D 109 B3
Bischofszell CH 107 B4
Bischwiller F 93 C3
Bisenti I 169 A3
Bishop Auckland GB 37 B5
Bishop's Castle GB 39 B4
Bishops Lydeard GB 43 A3
Bishop's Stortford GB 45 B4
Bishop's Waltham GB 44 C2
Bisignano I 174 B2
Bisingen D 93 C4
Biskupice-Oławskie PL 85 A5
Biskupiec PL 69 B4
Bismark D 73 B4
Bismo N 198 D5
Bispgården S 200 C2
Bispingen D 72 A2
Bissen L 92 B2
Bissendorf D 71 B5
Bisserup DK 65 A4
Bistango I 119 C5
Bistarac Donje BIH 139 A4
Bistrica BIH 124 C3
Bistrica ob Sotli SLO 123 A4
Bistriţa RO 17 B6
Bitburg D 92 B2
Bitche F 93 B3
Bitetto I 171 B4
Bitola MK 182 B3
Bitonto I 171 B4
Bitschwiller F 106 B2
Bitterfeld D 83 A4
Bitti I 178 B3
Biville-sur-Mer F 89 A5
Bivona I 176 B2
Biwer L 92 B2
Bizeljsko SLO 123 A4
Bizovac HR 125 B4
Bjåen N 52 A3
Bjärnum S 61 C3
Bjärred S 61 D3
Bjästa S 200 C4
Bjelland
Vest-Agder N 52 B2
Vest-Agder N 52 B3
Bjelovar HR 124 B2
Bjerkreim N 52 B2
Bjerkvik N 194 B8
Bjerreby DK 65 B3
Bjerregrav DK 58 B2
Bjerringbro DK 59 B2
Bjøberg N 47 B5
Bjøllånes N 195 D5
Björbo S 50 B1
Bjordal N 46 A2
Björg IS 191 B8
Bjørkåsen N 194 B7
Björke
Gävleborg S 51 B4
Östergötland S 56 B1
Bjørkelangen N 48 C3
Björketorp S 60 B2
Björkholmen S 196 C2
Björkliden S 194 B9
Björklinge S 51 B4
Björko S 51 C6
Björkö S 60 B1
Björköby S 62 A2
Björkvik S 56 B2
Bjørn N 195 D3
Björna S 200 C4
Björneborg S 55 A5
Björnerod S 54 A2
Bjørnevatn N 193 C13
Björnlunda S 56 A3
Bjørnstad N 193 C14
Björsäter S 56 B2
Bjurberget S 49 B4
Bjurholm S 200 C5
Bjursås S 50 B2
Bjurtjärn S 55 A5
Bjuv S 61 C2
Blachownia PL 86 B2
Blackburn GB 38 A4
Blackpool GB 38 A3
Blackstad S 62 A4
Blackwater IRL 30 B2
Blackwaterfoot GB 34 C2
Blacy F 91 C4
Bladåker S 51 B5
Blaenau Ffestiniog GB 38 B3
Blaenavon GB 39 C3
Blaengarw GB 39 C3
Blagaj
BIH 124 B2
BIH 139 B3
Blagdon GB 43 A4
Blagnac F 129 C4
Blagoevgrad BG 183 A5
Blaichach D 107 B5
Blain F 101 B4
Blainville-sur-l'Eau F 92 C2
Blair Atholl GB 35 B4
Blairgowrie GB 35 B4
Blajan F 145 A4
Blakeney GB 39 C4
Blakstad N 53 B4
Blâmont F 92 C2
Blanca E 165 A3
Blancos E 140 C3
Blandford Forum GB 43 B4
Blanes E 147 C3
Blangy-sur-Bresle F 90 B1
Blankaholm S 62 A4
Blankenberge B 78 A3
Blankenburg D 82 A2
Blankenfelde D 74 B2
Blankenhain D 82 B3
Blankenheim D 80 B2
Blanquefort F 128 B2
Blansko CZ 97 B4
Blanzac F 115 C4
Blanzy F 104 C3
Blaricum NL 70 B2
Blarney IRL 29 C3
Blascomillán E 150 B2
Blascosancho E 150 B3
Błaszki PL 86 A2
Blatná CZ 96 B1
Blatné SK 111 A4
Blatnice CZ 98 C1
Blatnika BIH 139 A3
Blato HR 138 C2
Blato na Cetini HR 138 B2
Blatten CH 119 A4
Blattnicksele S 195 E8
Blatzheim D 80 B2
Blaubeuren D 94 C1
Blaufelden D 94 B1
Blaustein D 94 C1
Blaydon GB 37 B5
Blaye F 128 A2
Blaye-les-Mines F 130 A1
Blázquez E 156 B2
Bleckede D 73 A3
Blecua E 145 B3
Bled SLO 123 A3
Bleiburg A 110 C1
Bleichenbach D 81 B5
Bleicherode D 82 A2
Bleik N 194 A6
Bleikvassli N 195 E4
Bléneau F 104 B1
Blentarp S 61 D3
Blera I 168 A2
Blérancourt F 90 B3
Bléré F 102 B2
Blesle F 116 B3
Blessington IRL 30 A2
Blet F 103 C4
Bletchley GB 44 B3
Bletterans F 105 C4
Blidö S 57 A4
Blidsberg S 60 B3
Blieskastel D 92 B3
Bligny-sur-Ouche F 104 B3
Blikstorp S 55 B5
Blinisht AL 182 B1
Blinja HR 124 B2
Blizanówek PL 76 C3
Bliżyn PL 87 A4
Blois F 103 B3
Blokhus DK 58 A2
Blokzijl NL 70 B2
Blombacka S 55 A4
Blomberg D 72 C2
Blomskog S 54 A3
Blomstermåla S 62 B4
Blomvåg N 46 B1
Blönduós IS 190 B5
Błonie PL 77 B5
Blonville-sur-Mer F 89 A4
Blötberget S 50 B2
Blovice CZ 96 B1
Bloxham GB 44 A2
Blšany CZ 83 B5
Bludenz A 107 B4
Bludov CZ 97 B4
Blumberg D 107 B3
Blyberg S 49 A6
Blyth
Northumberland GB 37 A5
Nottinghamshire GB 40 B2
Blyth Bridge GB 35 C4
Blythburgh GB 45 A5
Blythe Bridge GB 40 C1
Bø
Nordland N 194 B5
Telemark N 53 A5
Boal E 141 A4
Boan MNE 139 C5
Boario Terme I 120 B3
Boat of Garten GB 32 D3
Boa Vista P 154 B2
Boğazkale TR 23 A8
Boğazlıyan TR 23 B8
Boba H 111 B4
Bobadilla
Logroño E 143 B4
Málaga E 163 A3
Bobadilla del Campo E 150 A2
Bobadilla del Monte E 151 B4
Bóbbio I 120 C2
Bóbbio Pellice I 119 C4
Bobigny F 90 C2
Bobingen D 94 C2
Böblingen D 93 C5
Bobolice PL 68 B1
Boboras E 140 B2
Boboshevo BG 182 A4
Bobowa PL 99 B4
Bobrová CZ 97 B4
Bobrovitsa UA 13 C9
Bobrowice PL 75 C4
Bobrówko PL 75 B4
Boca de Huérgano E 142 B2
Bocairent E 159 C3
Bočar SRB 126 B2
Bocchigliero I 174 B2
Boceguillas E 151 A4
Bochnia PL 99 B4
Bocholt
B 80 A1
D 80 A2
Bochov CZ 83 B5
Bochum D 80 A3
Bockara S 62 A4
Bockenem D 72 B3
Bockfliess A 97 C4
Bockhorn D 71 A5
Bočna SLO 123 A3
Bocognano F 180 A2
Boconád H 113 B4
Bőcs H 113 A4
Boczów PL 75 B3
Boda S 50 A2
Böda S 62 A5
Boda
Stockholm S 51 B5
Värmland S 55 A4
Västernorrland S 200 D2
Bodafors S 62 A2
Boda Glasbruk S 63 B3
Bodajk H 112 B2
Boddam
Aberdeenshire GB 33 D5
Shetland GB 33 B5
Boddin D 73 A4
Bödefeld-Freiheit D 81 A4
Boden S 196 D4
Bodenmais D 95 B5
Bodenteich D 73 B3
Bodenwerder D 72 C2
Bodiam GB 45 B4
Bodinnick GB 42 B2

Bodio CH 120 A1
Bodjani SRB 125 B5
Bodmin GB 42 B2
Bodø N 194 C5
Bodonal de la Sierra E 161 A3
Bodrum TR 188 B2
Bodstedt D 66 B1
Bodträskfors S 196 C3
Bodzanów PL 77 B5
Bodzanowice PL 86 B2
Bodzechów PL 87 B5
Bodzentyn PL 87 B4
Boecillo E 150 A3
Boëge F 118 A3
Boën F 117 B3
Bogács H 113 B4
Bogadmindszent H 125 B4
Bogajo E 149 B3
Bogarra E 158 C1
Bogarre E 163 A4
Bogatić SRB 127 C1
Bogatynia PL 84 B2
Bogda RO 126 B3
Bogdaniec PL 75 B4
Boge S 57 C4
Bogen
D 95 C4
Nordland N 194 B7
Nordland N 194 C6
S 49 B4
Bogense DK 59 C3
Bognanco Fonti I 119 A5
Bognelv N 192 B6
Bognes N 194 B7
Bogno CH 120 A2
Bognor Regis GB 44 C3
Bogoria PL 87 B5
Bograngen S 49 B4
Boguchwaly PL 69 B5
Bogumiłowice PL 86 A3
Boguslav UA 13 D9
Boguszów-Gorce PL 85 B4
Bogyiszló H 112 C2
Bohain-en-Vermandois F 91 B3
Böheimkirchen A 110 A2
Bohinjska Bistrica SLO 122 A2
Böhlen D 83 A4
Böhmenkirch D 94 C1
Bohmte D 71 B5
Bohonal de Ibor E 150 C2
Böhönye H 124 A3
Bohumin CZ 98 B2
Boiro E 140 B2
Bois-d'Amont F 105 C5
Boisseron F 131 B3
Boitzenburg D 74 A2
Boixols E 147 B2
Boizenburg D 73 A3
Bojadła PL 75 C4
Bojano I 170 B2
Bojanowo PL 85 A4
Bøjden DK 64 A3
Bojkovice CZ 98 B1
Bojná SK 98 C2
Bojnice SK 98 C2
Boka SRB 126 B2
Böklund D 64 B2
Bokod H 112 B2
Böksholm S 62 A2
Boksitogorsk RUS 9 C8
Bol HR 138 B2
Bolaños de Calatrava E 157 B4
Bolayır TR 186 B1
Bolbec F 89 A4
Bölcske H 112 C2
Bolderslev DK 64 B2
Boldog H 112 B3
Boldva H 113 A4
Böle S 196 D4
Bolea E 145 B3
Bolekhiv UA 13 D5
Bolesławiec PL 84 A3
Boleszkowice PL 74 B3
Bolewice PL 75 B5
Bólgheri I 134 B3
Bolhrad UA 17 C8
Boliden S 200 B6
Bolimów PL 77 B5
Boliqueime P 160 B1
Boljevci SRB 127 C2
Boljkovci SRB 127 C2
Bolków PL 85 B4
Bollebygd S 60 B2
Bollène F 131 A3
Bólliga E 152 B1
Bollnäs S 50 A3
Bollstabruk S 200 D3
Bollullos E 161 B3
Bollullos par del Condado E 161 B3
Bologna I 135 A4
Bologne F 105 A4
Bolognetta I 176 B2
Bolognola I 136 C2
Bologoye RUS 9 D9
Bolótana I 178 B2
Bolsena I 168 A1
Bolshaya Vradiyevka UA 17 B9
Bolsover GB 40 B2
Bolstad S 54 B3
Bolsward NL 70 A2
Boltaña E 145 B4
Boltenhagen D 65 C4
Boltigen CH 106 C2
Bolton GB 38 A4
Bolu TR 187 B6
Bolungarvík IS 190 A2
Bolvadin TR 187 D6
Bóly H 125 B4
Bolzaneto I 133 A4
Bolzano I 108 C2
Bomba I 169 A4
Bombarral P 154 B1
Bömenzien D 73 B4
Bomlitz D 72 B2
Bømlo N 52 A1
Bøn N 48 B3
Bona F 104 B2
Bonaduz CH 107 C4
Bonanza E 161 C3
Boñar E 142 B1
Bonarbridge GB 32 D2
Bonárcado I 178 B2
Bonares E 161 B3
Bonäs S 50 A1
Bonassola I 134 A2
Bonawe GB 34 B2
Bondal N 53 A4
Bondeno I 121 C4
Bondorf D 93 C4
Bondstorp S 60 B3
Bon-Encontre F 129 B3
Bo'ness GB 35 B4
Bonete E 158 C2
Bonifacio F 180 B2
Bonigen CH 106 C2
Bonin PL 67 B5
Bonn D 80 B3
Bonnánaro I 178 B2
Bonnåsjøen N 194 C6
Bonnat F 116 A1
Bonndorf D 106 B3
Bonnétable F 102 A2
Bonnétage F 106 B1
Bonneuil-les-Eaux F 90 B2
Bonneuil-Matours F 115 B4
Bonneval F 103 A3
Bonneval-sur-Arc F 119 B4
Bonneville F 118 A3
Bonnières-sur-Seine F 90 B1
Bonnieux F 131 B4
Bönnigheim D 93 B5
Bonnyrigg GB 35 C4
Bonny-sur-Loire F 103 B4
Bono
E 145 B4
I 178 B3
Bonorva I 178 B2
Bønsnes N 48 B2
Bonyhád H 125 A4
Boom B 79 A4
Boos F 89 A5
Boostedt D 64 B3
Bootle
Cumbria GB 36 B3
Merseyside GB 38 A3
Bopfingen D 94 C2
Boppard D 81 B3
Boqueixón E 140 B2
Bor
CZ 95 B4
S 62 A2
SRB 16 C5
TR 23 C8
Boran-sur-Oise F 90 B2
Borås S 60 B2
Borba P 155 C3
Borbona I 169 A3
Borča SRB 127 C2
Borci BIH 139 B4
Borculo NL 71 B3
Bordány H 126 A1
Bordeaux F 128 B2
Bordeira P 160 B1
Bordesholm D 64 B3
Borðeyri IS 190 B4
Bordighera I 133 B3
Bording DK 59 B2
Bordón E 153 B3
Bore I 120 C2
Borehamwood GB 44 B3
Borek Strzeliński PL 85 B5
Borek Wielkopolski PL 76 C2
Boreland GB 36 A3
Borello I 135 A5
Borensberg S 56 B1
Borgafjäll S 199 A12
Borgarnes IS 190 C4
Borgentreich D 81 A5
Börger D 71 B4
Borger NL 71 B3
Borggård S 56 B1
Borghamn S 55 B5
Borghetta di Vara I 134 A2
Borghetto d'Arróscia I 133 A3
Borghetto Santo Spirito I 133 A4
Borgholm S 62 B4
Borghorst D 71 B4
Bórgia I 175 C2
Borgloon B 79 B5
Børglum DK 58 A2
Borgo F 180 A2
Borgo alla Collina I 135 B4
Borgo a Mozzano I 134 B3
Borgoforte I 121 B3
Borgofranco d'Ivrea I 119 B4
Borgomanero I 119 B5
Borgomasino I 119 B4
Borgonovo Val Tidone I 120 B2
Borgo Pace I 135 B5
Borgorose I 169 A3
Borgo San Dalmazzo I 133 A3
Borgo San Lorenzo I 135 B4
Borgosésia I 119 B5
Borgo Val di Taro I 134 A2
Borgo Valsugana I 121 A4
Borgo Vercelli I 119 B5
Borgstena S 60 B3
Borgue GB 36 B2
Borgund N 47 A4
Borgvik S 55 A3
Borja E 144 C2
Bork D 80 A3
Borken D 80 A2
Borkenes N 194 B7
Børkop DK 59 C2
Borkowice PL 87 A4
Borkowo PL 77 B5
Borkum D 71 A3
Borlänge S 50 B2
Borlu TR 186 D3
Bormes-les-Mimosas F 132 B2
Bórmio I 107 C5
Bormujos E 161 B3
Borna D 83 A4
Borne NL 71 B3
Bornes P 149 A2
Borne Sulinowo PL 68 B1
Bornheim D 80 B2
Bornhöved D 64 B3
Börnicke D 74 B1
Bornos E 162 B2
Borobia E 152 A2
Borodino RUS 9 E9
Borohrádek CZ 85 B4
Boronów PL 86 B2
Bórore I 178 B2
Borosźow PL 86 B2
Borota H 126 A1
Boroughbridge GB 40 A2
Borovany CZ 96 C2
Borovichi RUS 9 C8
Borovnica SLO 123 B3
Borovo HR 125 B4
Borovsk RUS 9 E10
Borovy CZ 96 B1
Borowa PL 85 A5
Borox E 151 B4
Borrby S 66 A3
Borre
DK 65 B5
N 54 A1
Borredá E 147 B2
Borrenes E 141 B4
Borriol E 159 A3
Borris
DK 59 C1
IRL 30 B2
Borris-in-Ossory IRL 28 B4
Borrisokane IRL 28 B3
Borrisoleigh IRL 28 B4
Borrowdale GB 36 B3
Børrud N 49 C4
Borşa RO 17 B6
Borsdorf D 83 A4
Børselv N 193 B9
Borsfa H 111 C3
Borský Mikuláš SK 98 C1
Borsodivánka H 113 B4
Borsodnádasd H 113 A4
Börte N 53 A3
Borth GB 39 B2
Bort-les-Orgues F 116 B2
Börtnan S 199 C10
Børtnes N 47 B6
Borup DK 61 D1
Boryslav UA 13 D5
Boryspil UA 13 C9
Boryszyn PL 75 B4
Borzęciczki PL 85 A5
Borzęcin PL 77 B5
Borzonasca I 134 A2
Borzyszkowy PL 68 A2
Borzytuchom PL 68 A2
Bosa I 178 B2
Bošáca SK 98 C1
Bosanci HR 123 B4
Bosanska Dubica BIH 124 B2
Bosanska Gradiška BIH 124 B3
Bosanska Kostajnica BIH 124 B2
Bosanska Krupa BIH 124 C2
Bosanski Brod BIH 125 B3
Bosanski Novi BIH 124 B2
Bosanski Petrovac BIH 124 C2
Bosanski Šamac BIH 125 B4
Bosansko Grahovo BIH 138 A2
Bošany SK 98 C2
Bösárkány H 111 B4
Bosau D 65 B3
Bósca H 112 C3
Boscastle GB 42 B2
Bosco I 120 C1
Bosco Chiesanuova I 121 B4
Bösdorf D 65 B3
Bösel D 71 A4
Bosham GB 44 C3
Bösingfeld D 72 B2
Bosjön S 49 C5
Boskoop NL 70 B1
Boskovice CZ 97 B4
Bošnjaci HR 125 B4
Bošnjane SRB 127 D3
Bossast E 145 B4
Bossolasco I 133 A4
Boštanj SLO 123 A4
Boston GB 41 C3
Bostrak N 53 A4
Böszénfa H 125 A3
Bot E 153 A4
Botajica BIH 125 C4
Bøte By DK 65 B4
Bothel GB 36 B3
Boticas P 148 A2
Botilsäter S 55 A4
Botngård N 198 B6
Botoš SRB 126 B2
Botoşani RO 17 B7
Botricello I 175 C2
Botsmark S 200 B6
Bottendorf D 81 A4
Bottesford GB 40 C3
Bottnaryd S 60 B3
Bottrop D 80 A2
Botunje SRB 127 C3
Bötzingen D 106 A2
Bouaye F 101 B4
Bouça P 149 A2
Boucau F 128 C1
Bouchain F 78 B3
Bouchoir F 90 B2
Boudreville F 105 B3
Boudry CH 106 C1
Bouesse F 103 C3
Bouguenais F 101 B4
Bouhy F 104 B2
Bouillargues F 131 B3
Bouillon B 91 B5
Bouilly F 104 A2
Bouin F 114 B2
Boulay-Moselle F 92 B2
Boulazac F 129 A3
Boule-d'Amont F 146 B3
Bouligny F 92 B1
Boulogne-sur-Gesse F 145 A4
Boulogne-sur-Mer F 78 B1
Bouloire F 102 B2
Bouquemaison F 78 B2
Bourbon-Lancy F 104 C2
Bourbon-l'Archambault F 104 C2
Bourbonne-les-Bains F 105 B4
Bourbourg F 78 B2
Bourbriac F 100 A2
Bourcefranc-le-Chapus F 114 C2
Bourdeaux F 131 A4
Bouresse F 115 B4
Bourg F 128 A2
Bourg-Achard F 89 A4
Bourganeuf F 116 B1
Bourg-Argental F 117 B4
Bourg-de-Péage F 117 B5
Bourg-de-Thizy F 117 A4
Bourg-de-Visa F 129 B3
Bourg-en-Bresse F 118 A2
Bourges F 103 B4
Bourg-et-Comin F 91 B3
Bourg-Lastic F 116 B2
Bourg-Madame F 146 B2
Bourgneuf-en-Retz F 114 A2
Bourgogne F 91 B4
Bourgoin-Jallieu F 118 B2
Bourg-St Andéol F 131 A3
Bourg-St Maurice F 119 B3
Bourgtheroulde F 89 A4
Bourgueil F 102 B2
Bourmont F 105 A4
Bourne GB 40 C3
Bournemouth GB 43 B5
Bourneville F 89 A4
Bournezeau F 114 B2
Bourran F 129 B3
Bourret F 129 C4
Bourron-Marlotte F 90 C2
Bourton-on-The-Water GB 44 B2
Boussac F 116 A2
Boussens F 145 A4
Boutersem B 79 B4
Bouttencourt F 90 B1
Bouvières F 131 A4
Bouvron F 101 B4
Bouxwiller F 93 C3
Bouzas E 140 B2
Bouzonville F 92 B2
Bova I 175 D1
Bovalino Marina I 175 C2
Bovallstrand S 54 B2
Bova Marina I 175 D1
Bovec SLO 122 A2
Bóveda E 141 B3
Bóvegno I 120 B3
Bovenau D 64 B2
Bovenden D 82 A1
Bøverdal N 198 D5
Boves F 90 B2
Bóves I 133 A3
Bovey Tracey GB 43 B3
Bovino I 171 B3
Bøvlingbjerg DK 58 B1
Bovolenta I 121 B4
Bovolone I 121 B4
Bowes GB 37 B5
Bowmore GB 34 C1
Bowness-on-Windermere GB 36 B4
Box GB 43 A4
Boxberg
Baden-Württemberg D 94 B1
Sachsen D 84 A2
Boxholm S 55 B6
Boxmeer NL 80 A1
Boxtel NL 79 A5
Boyabat TR 23 A8
Boyalıca TR 187 B4
Boyle IRL 26 C2
Bozan TR 187 C6
Božava HR 137 A3
Bozburun TR 188 C3
Bozcaada TR 186 C1
Bozdoğan TR 188 B3
Bożepole Wielkie PL 68 A2
Boževac SRB 127 C3
Božice CZ 97 C4
Boži Dar CZ 83 B4
Bozkır TR 189 B7
Bozouls F 130 A1
Bozova TR 189 B5
Bozüyük TR 187 C5
Bòzzolo I 121 B3
Bra I 119 C4
Braås S 62 A3
Brabrand DK 59 B3
Bracadale GB 31 B2
Bracciano I 168 A2
Bracieux F 103 B3
Bräcke S 199 C12
Brackenheim D 93 B5
Brackley GB 44 A2
Bracklin IRL 27 C4
Bracknell GB 44 B3
Brackwede D 72 C1
Braco GB 35 B4
Brad RO 16 B5
Bradford GB 40 B2
Bradford on Avon GB 43 A4
Bradina BIH 139 B4
Brådland N 52 B2
Brædstrup DK 59 C2
Brae GB 33 A5
Braemar GB 32 D3
Braemore GB 32 D1
Braga P 148 A1
Bragança P 149 A3
Brăila RO 17 C7
Braine F 91 B3
Braine-le-Comte B 79 B4
Braintree GB 45 B4
Braives B 79 B5
Brake D 72 A1
Brakel
B 79 B3
D 81 A5
Bräkne-Hoby S 63 B3
Brålanda S 54 B3
Bralin PL 86 A1
Brallo di Pregola I 120 C2
Bram F 146 A3
Bramafan F 132 B2
Bramberg am Wildkogel A 109 B3
Bramdrupdam DK 59 C2
Bramming DK 59 C1
Brampton GB 37 B4
Bramsche D 71 B4
Branca I 136 B1
Brancaleone Marina I 175 D2
Brancaster GB 41 C4
Brand
Nieder Östereich A 96 C3
Vorarlberg A 107 B4
Brandbu N 48 B2
Brande DK 59 C2
Brande-Hornerkirchen D 64 C2
Brandenberg A 108 B2
Brandenburg D 73 B5
Brand-Erbisdorf D 83 B5
Brandis D 83 A4
Brando F 180 A2
Brandomil E 140 A2
Brandon GB 45 A4
Brandshagen D 66 B2
Brandval N 49 B4
Brandýs nad Labem CZ 84 B2
Branice PL 98 A1
Braničevo SRB 127 C3
Braniewo PL 69 A4
Branik SLO 122 B2
Brankovina SRB 127 C1
Branky CZ 98 B1
Branne F 128 B2
Brannenburg-Degerndorf D 108 B3
Brantôme F 115 C4
Branzi I 120 A2
Bras d'Asse F 132 B2
Braskereidfoss N 48 B3
Braslaw BY 13 A7
Braşov RO 17 C6
Brasparts F 100 A2
Brassac F 130 B1
Brassac-les-Mines F 116 B3
Brasschaat B 79 A4
Brastad S 54 B2
Břasy CZ 96 B1
Brąszewice PL 86 A2
Bratislava SK 111 A4
Brattfors S 55 A5
Brattvåg N 198 C3
Bratunac BIH 127 C1
Braubach D 81 B3
Braunau A 95 C5
Braunfels D 81 B4
Braunlage D 82 A2
Braunsbedra D 83 A3
Braunschweig D 73 B3
Bray IRL 30 A2
Bray Dunes F 78 A2
Bray-sur-Seine F 90 C3
Bray-sur-Somme F 90 B2
Brazatortas E 157 B3
Brazey-en-Plaine F 105 B4
Brbinj HR 137 A4
Brčko BIH 125 C4
Brdani SRB 127 D2
Brdów PL 76 B3
Brea de Tajo E 151 B4
Brécey F 88 B2
Brechen D 81 B4
Brechin GB 35 B5
Brecht B 79 A4
Brecketfeld D 80 A3
Břeclav CZ 97 C4
Brecon GB 39 C3
Brécy F 103 B4
Breda
E 147 C3
NL 79 A4
Bredaryd S 60 B3
Bredbyn S 200 C4
Breddin D 73 B5
Bredebro DK 64 A1
Bredelar D 81 A4
Bredenfelde D 74 A2
Bredsjö S 50 C1
Bredstedt D 64 B1
Bredsten DK 59 C2
Bredträsk S 200 C4
Bredviken S 195 D5
Bree B 80 A1
Bregana HR 123 B4
Breganze I 121 B4
Bregenz A 107 B4
Bréhal F 88 B2
Brehna D 83 A4
Breiðdalsvík IS 191 C11
Breidenbach F 93 B3
Breil-sur-Roya F 133 B3
Breisach D 106 A2
Breitenbach
CH 106 B2
D 81 B5
Breitenberg D 96 C1
Breitenfelde D 73 A3
Breitengussbach D 94 B2
Breivikbotn N 192 B6
Brejning DK 59 C2
Brekke N 46 A2
Brekken N 199 C8
Brekkestø N 53 B4
Brekkvasselv N 199 A10
Brekstad N 198 B6
Breland N 53 B3
Bremanger N 198 D1
Bremen D 72 A1
Bremerhaven D 72 A1
Bremervörde D 72 A2
Bremgarten CH 106 B3
Bremsnes N 198 B4
Brem-sur-Mer F 114 B2
Brenderup DK 59 C2
Brenes E 162 A2
Brengova SLO 110 C2
Brenna PL 98 B2
Breno I 120 B3
Brénod F 118 A2
Brensbach D 93 B4
Brentwood GB 45 B4
Brescello I 121 C3
Bréscia I 120 B3
Breskens NL 79 A3
Bresles F 90 B2
Bresnica SRB 127 D2
Bressana I 120 B2
Bressanone I 108 C2
Bressuire F 102 C1
Brest
BY 13 B5
F 100 A1
HR 122 B2
Brestač SRB 127 C1
Brestanica SLO 123 A4
Brestova HR 123 B3
Brestovac HR 125 B3
Bretenoux F 129 B4
Breteuil
Eure F 89 B4
Oise F 90 B2
Brétigny-sur-Orge F 90 C2
Bretten D 93 B4
Bretteville-sur-Laize F 89 A3
Brettheim D 94 B2
Breuil-Cervínia I 119 B4
Breukelen NL 70 B2
Brevik
N 53 A5
Stockholm S 57 A4
Västra Götaland S 55 B5
Breza BIH 139 A4
Brežice SLO 123 B4
Bréziers F 132 A2
Breznica HR 124 A2
Breznica Našička HR 125 B4
Březnice CZ 96 B1
Brezno SK 99 C3
Brezolles F 89 B5
Březovánad Svitavou CZ 97 B4
Brezovápod Bradlom SK 98 C1
Brezovica
SK 99 B4
SLO 123 A3
Brezovo Polje Selo BIH 125 C4
Briançon F 118 C3
Brianconnet F 132 B2
Briare F 103 B4
Briatexte F 129 C4
Briático I 175 C2
Briaucourt F 105 A4
Bribir HR 123 B3
Bricquebec F 88 A2
Bridgend
Argyll & Bute GB 34 C1
Bridgend GB 39 C3
Bridge of Cally GB 35 B4
Bridge of Don GB 33 D4
Bridge of Earn GB 35 B4
Bridge of Orchy GB 34 B3
Bridgnorth GB 39 B4
Bridgwater GB 43 A4
Břidličná CZ 98 B1
Bridlington GB 41 A3
Bridport GB 43 B4
Briec F 100 A1
Brie-Comte-Robert F 90 C
Brienne-le-Château F 91 C
Brienon-sur-Armançon F 104 B
Brienz CH 106 C
Brienza I 172 B
Briesen D 74 B
Brieskow Finkenheerd D 74 B
Brietlingen D 72 A
Brieva de Cameros E 143 B
Briey F 92 B
Brig CH 119 A
Brigg GB 40 B
Brighouse GB 40 B
Brightlingsea GB 45 B
Brighton GB 44 C
Brignogan-Plage F 100 A
Brignoles F 132 B
Brigstock GB 40 C
Brihuega E 151 B
Brijuni HR 122 C
Brillon-en-Barrois F 91 C
Brilon D 81 A
Brimnes N 46 B
Brinches P 160 A
Brindisi I 173 B
Brinje HR 123 B
Brinon-sur-Beuvron F 104 B
Brinon-sur-Sauldre F 103 B
Brinyan GB 33 B
Brión E 140 B
Briones E 143 B
Brionne F 89 A
Brioude F 117 B
Brioux-sur-Boutonne F 115 B
Briouze F 89 B
Briscous F 144 A
Brisighella I 135 A
Brissac-Quincé F 102 B
Brissago CH 120 A
Bristol GB 43 A
Brive-la-Gaillarde F 129 A
Briviesca E 143 B
Brixham GB 43 B
Brixlegg A 108 B
Brjánslækur IS 190 B
Brka BIH 125 C
Brnaze HR 138 B
Brněnec CZ 97 B
Brno CZ 97 B
Bro S 57 A
Broadclyst GB 43 B
Broadford
GB 31 B
IRL 28 B
Broad Haven GB 39 C
Broadstairs GB 45 B
Broadstone GB 43 B
Broadway GB 44 A
Broager DK 64 B
Broaryd S 60 B
Broby S 61 C
Brobyværk DK 59 C
Bročanac BIH 138 B
Brocas F 128 B
Brock D 71 B
Brockel D 72 A
Brockenhurst GB 44 C
Broczyno PL 75 A
Brod MK 182 B
Brodalen S 54 B
Broddbo S 50 C
Brodek u Přerova CZ 98 B
Broden-bach D 80 B
Brodick GB 34 C
Brod na Kupi HR 123 B
Brodnica PL 69 B
Brodnica Graniczna PL 68 A
Brodowe Łąki PL 77 A
Brody
Lubuskie PL 75 B
Lubuskie PL 84 A
Mazowieckie PL 77 B
UA 13 C
Broglie F 89 B
Brójce PL 75 B
Brokind S 56 B
Brolo I 177 A
Brome D 73 B
Bromley GB 45 B
Bromölla S 63 B
Bromont-Lamothe F 116 B
Brömsebro S 63 B
Bromsgrove GB 44 A
Bromyard GB 39 B
Bronchales E 152 B
Bronco E 149 B
Brønderslev DK 58 A
Broni I 120 B
Brønnøysund N 195 E
Brøns DK 59 C
Bronte I 177 B
Bronzani Mejdan BIH 124 C
Bronzolo I 121 A
Broons F 101 A
Broquies F 130 A
Brora GB 32 C
Brørup DK 59 C
Brösarp S 63 C
Brossac F 115 C
Brostrud N 47 B
Brotas P 154 C
Brötjärna S 50 B
Broto E 145 B
Brottby S 57 A
Brøttum N 48 A

Brou F 103 A3
Brouage F 114 C2
Brough GB 37 B4
Broughshane GB 27 B4
Broughton GB 35 C4
Broughton-in-Furness GB 36 B3
Broumov CZ 85 B4
Broût-Vernet F 116 A1
Brouvelieures F 106 A1
Brouwershaven NL 79 A3
Brovary UA 13 C9
Brovst DK 58 A2
Brownhills GB 40 C2
Brozas E 155 B4
Brozzo I 120 B3
Brtnice CZ 97 B3
Brtonigla HR 122 B2
Bruay-la-Buissière F 78 B2
Bruchhausen-Vilsen D 72 B2
Bruchsal D 93 B4
Bruck D 95 B4
Brück D 74 B1
Bruck an der Grossglocknerstrasse A 109 B3
Bruck an der Leitha A 111 A3
Bruck an der Mur A 110 B2
Brückl A 110 C1
Bruckmühl D 108 B2
Brue-Auriac F 132 B1
Brüel D 65 C4
Bruen CH 107 C3
Bruère-Allichamps F 103 C4
Bruff IRL 29 B3
Bruflat N 47 B6
Brugg CH 106 B3
Brugge B 78 A3
Brüggen D 80 A2
Brühl D 80 B2
Bruinisse NL 79 A4
Brûlon F 102 B1
Brumano I 120 B2
Brumath F 93 C3
Brummen NL 70 B3
Brumov-Bylnice CZ 98 B2
Brumunddal N 48 B2
Brunau D 73 B4
Brunehamel F 91 B4
Brünen D 80 A2
Brunete E 151 B3
Brunflo S 199 B11
Brunico I 108 C2
Brunkeberg N 53 A4
Brunn D 74 A2
Brunnen CH 107 C3
Brunsbüttel D 64 C2
Brunssum NL 80 B1
Bruntál CZ 98 B1
Brušane HR 137 A4
Brusasco I 119 B5
Brusio CH 120 A3
Brusno SK 99 C3
Brusque F 130 B1
Brussels = Bruxelles B 79 B4
Brusson I 119 B4
Brüssow D 74 A3
Brusy PL 68 B2
Bruton GB 43 A4
Bruvno HR 138 A1
Bruvoll N 48 B3
Bruxelles = Brussels B 79 B4
Bruyères F 106 A1
Bruz F 101 A4
Bruzaholm S 62 A3
Brwinów PL 77 B5
Brynamman GB 39 C3
Bryncrug GB 39 B2
Bryne N 52 B1
Brynmawr GB 39 C3
Bryrup DK 59 B2
Brzeg PL 85 B5
Brzeg Dolny PL 85 A4
Brześć Kujawski PL 76 B3
Brzesko PL 99 B4
Brzeszcze PL 99 B3
Brzezie PL 68 B1
Brzeziny
Łódzkie PL 87 A3
Wielkopolskie PL 86 A2
Brzeźnica PL 84 A3
Brzeźnica Nowa PL 86 A3
Brzeźno PL 75 A4
Brzotin SK 99 C4
Brzozie Lubawskie PL 69 B4
Bua S 60 B2
Buarcos P 148 B1
Buavåg N 52 A1
Bubbio I 119 C5
Bubry F 100 B2
Buca TR 188 A2
Bucak TR 189 B5
Buccheri I 177 B3
Buccino I 172 B1
Bucelas P 154 C1
Buch
Bayern D 94 C2
Bayern D 95 C4
Buchach UA 13 D6
Bucharest = Bucureşti RO 17 C7
Buchbach D 95 C4
Buchboden A 107 B4
Buchen D 94 B1
Büchen D 73 A3
Buchenberg D 107 B5
Buchères F 104 A3
Buchholz D 72 A2
Buchloe D 108 A1

Buchlovice CZ 98 B1
Buchlyvie GB 34 B3
Bucholz D 73 A5
Buchs CH 107 B4
Buchy F 89 A5
Bückeburg D 72 B2
Buckfastleigh GB 42 B3
Buckhaven GB 35 B4
Buckie GB 33 D4
Buckingham GB 44 A3
Buckley GB 38 A3
Bučovice CZ 97 B5
Bucsa H 113 B5
Bucureşti = Bucharest RO 17 C7
Bucy-lès-Pierrepont F 91 B3
Buczek PL 86 A3
Bud N 198 C3
Budakalasz H 112 B3
Budakeszi H 112 B3
Budal N 199 C7
Budaörs H 112 B2
Budapest H 112 B3
Búðardalur IS 190 B4
Budča SK 99 C3
Buddusò I 178 B3
Bude GB 42 B2
Budeč CZ 97 B3
Büdelsdorf D 64 B2
Budens P 160 B1
Budia E 151 B5
Budimlić-Japra BIH 124 C2
Büdingen D 81 B5
Budišov CZ 98 B1
Budleigh Salterton GB 43 B3
Budmerice SK 98 C1
Budoni I 178 B3
Búdrio I 135 A4
Budva MNE 16 D3
Budynën Ohŕi CZ 84 B2
Budziszewice PL 87 A3
Budzyń PL 76 B1
Bue N 52 B1
Bueña E 152 B2
Buenache de Alarcón E 158 B1
Buenache de la Sierra E 152 B2
Buenaventura E 150 B3
Buenavista de Valdavia E 142 B2
Buendia E 151 B5
Bueu E 140 B2
Buezo E 143 B3
Bugac H 112 C3
Bugarra E 159 B3
Bugeat F 116 B1
Buggerru I 179 C2
Bugojno BIH 138 A3
Bugøyfjord N 193 C13
Bugøynes N 193 C13
Bugyi H 112 B3
Buharkent TR 188 B3
Bühl
Baden-Württemberg D 93 C4
Bayern D 107 B5
Bühlertal D 93 C4
Bühlertann D 94 B1
Buia I 122 A2
Builth Wells GB 39 B3
Buin N 47 B6
Buis-les-Baronnies F 131 A4
Buitenpost NL 70 A3
Buitrago del Lozoya E 151 B4
Bujalance E 157 C3
Bujaraloz E 153 A3
Buje HR 122 B2
Bujedo E 143 B3
Bük H 111 B3
Buk PL 75 B5
Bükkösd H 125 A3
Bükkzsérc H 113 B4
Bukovci SLO 124 A1
Bukowiec PL 75 B5
Bukowina Tatrzańska PL 99 B4
Bukownica PL 86 A2
Bukowno PL 86 B3
Bülach CH 107 B3
Buldan TR 188 A3
Bulgnéville F 105 A4
Bülkau D 64 C1
Bulken N 46 B3
Bulkowo PL 77 B5
Bullas E 164 A3
Bulle CH 106 C2
Büllingen B 80 B2
Bullmark S 200 B6
Bulqizë AL 182 B2
Buna BIH 139 B3
Bunahowen IRL 26 B1
Bunbeg IRL 26 A2
Bunclody IRL 30 B2
Buncrana IRL 27 A3
Bunde D 71 A4
Bünde D 72 B1
Bundoran IRL 26 B2
Bunessan GB 34 B1
Bungay GB 45 A5
Bunge S 57 C5
Bunić HR 123 C4
Bunmahon IRL 30 B1
Bunnyconnellan IRL 26 B1
Buño E 140 A2
Buñol E 159 B3
Bunratty IRL 29 B3
Bunskeek B 79 B4
Buñuel E 144 C2

Bunyola E 166 B2
Buonabitácolo I 172 B1
Buonalbergo I 170 B2
Buonconvento I 135 B4
Buonvicino I 174 B1
Burano I 122 B1
Burbach D 81 B4
Burcei I 179 C3
Burdons-sur-Rognon F 105 A4
Burdur TR 189 B5
Bureå S 2 D7
Burela E 141 A3
Büren D 81 A4
Büren an der Aare CH 106 B2
Burford GB 44 B2
Burg
Cottbus D 84 A2
Magdeburg D 73 B4
Schleswig-Holstein D 64 C2
Burgau
A 111 B3
D 94 C2
P 160 B1
Burg auf Fehmarn D 65 B4
Burgbernheim D 94 B2
Burgdorf
CH 106 B2
D 72 B3
Burgebrach D 94 B2
Bürgel D 83 B3
Burgess Hill GB 44 C3
Burghaslach D 94 B2
Burghausen D 109 A3
Burghead GB 32 D3
Burgheim D 94 C3
Burgh le Marsh GB 41 B4
Búrgio I 176 B2
Burgkirchen D 109 A3
Burgkunstadt D 82 B3
Burglengenfeld D 95 B4
Burgo P 148 B1
Burgoberbach D 94 B2
Burgohondo E 150 B3
Burgos E 143 B3
Burgsinn D 82 B1
Burgstädt D 83 B4
Burgstall D 73 B4
Burg Stargard D 74 A2
Burgsvik S 57 C4
Burgui E 144 B3
Burguillos E 162 A2
Burguillos del Cerro E 155 C4
Burguillos de Toledo E 151 C4
Burhaniye TR 186 C1
Burhave D 71 A5
Burie F 114 C3
Burjassot F 159 B3
Burk D 94 B2
Burkhardtsdorf D 83 B4
Burlada E 144 B2
Burladingen D 107 A4
Burlage D 71 A4
Burness GB 33 B4
Burnham GB 44 B3
Burnham Market GB 41 C4
Burnham-on-Crouch GB 45 B4
Burnham-on-Sea GB 43 A4
Burniston GB 40 A3
Burnley GB 40 B1
Burntisland GB 35 B4
Burón E 142 A1
Buronzo I 119 B5
Burovac SRB 127 C3
Burow D 74 A2
Burravoe GB 33 A5
Burrel AL 182 B2
Burret F 146 B2
Burriana E 159 B3
Burry Port GB 39 C2
Bürs A 107 B4
Bursa TR 186 B4
Burseryd S 60 B3
Burton GB 37 B4
Burton Agnes GB 41 A3
Burton Bradstock GB 43 B4
Burton Latimer GB 44 A3
Burton upon Stather GB 40 B3
Burton upon Trent GB 40 C2
Burträsk S 200 B6
Burujón E 151 C3
Burwell GB 45 A4
Burwick GB 33 C4
Bury GB 40 B1
Bury St Edmunds GB 45 A4
Burzenin PL 86 A2
Busachi I 179 B2
Busalla I 134 A1
Busana I 134 A3
Busano I 119 B4
Busca I 133 A3
Busch D 73 B4
Buševec HR 124 B2
Bushat AL 182 B1
Bushey GB 44 B3
Bushmills GB 27 A4
Bušince SK 112 A3
Buskhyttan S 56 B3
Busko-Zdrój PL 87 B4
Busot E 159 C3
Busovača BIH 139 A3
Busquistar E 163 B4
Bussang F 106 B1
Busseto I 120 C3
Bussière-Badil F 115 C4

Bussière-Poitevine F 115 B4
Bussolengo I 121 B3
Bussoleno I 119 B4
Bussum NL 70 B2
Busto Arsízio I 120 B1
Butera I 177 B3
Butgenbach B 80 B2
Butler's Bridge IRL 27 B3
Butryny PL 77 A5
Bütschwil CH 107 B4
Buttermere GB 36 B3
Buttevant IRL 29 B3
Buttle S 57 C4
Buttstädt D 82 A3
Butzbach D 81 B4
Bützfleth D 72 A2
Bützow D 65 C4
Buxières-les-Mines F 104 C1
Buxtehude D 72 A2
Buxton GB 40 B2
Buxy F 104 C3
Büyükçekmece TR 186 A3
Büyükkarıştıran TR 186 A2
Büyükorhan TR 186 C3
Buzançais F 103 C3
Buzancy F 91 B4
Buzău RO 17 C7
Buzet HR 122 B2
Buziaş RO 126 B3
Buzsák H 111 C4
Buzy F 145 A3
By S 50 B3
Byala BG 17 D6
Byaroza BY 13 B6
Byczyna PL 86 A2
Bydalen S 199 B10
Bydgoszcz PL 76 A3
Bygdin N 47 A5
Bygdsiljum S 200 B6
Bygland N 53 B3
Byglandsfjord N 53 B3
Bygstad N 46 A2
Bykhaw BY 13 B9
Bykle N 52 A3
Bylderup-Bov DK 64 B2
Byremo N 52 B3
Byrkjedal N 52 B2
Byrkjelo N 198 D3
Byrum DK 58 A3
Byšice CZ 84 B2
Byske S 2 D7
Býškovice CZ 98 B1
Bysław PL 76 A2
Bystré CZ 97 B4
Bystřice CZ 96 B2
Bystřice CZ 96 B2
Bystřice nad Pernštejnem CZ 97 B4
Bystřice pod Hostýnem CZ 98 B1
Bystrzyca Kłodzka PL 85 B4
Bytča SK 98 B2
Bytnica PL 75 B4
Bytom PL 86 B2
Bytom Odrzański PL 85 A3
Byxelkrok S 62 A5
Bzenec CZ 98 C1
Bzince SK 98 C1

C

Çağa TR 187 B7
Cabacos P 154 B2
Cabaj-Čápor SK 98 C2
Cabana E 140 A2
Cabanac-et-Villagrains F 128 B2
Cabañaquinta E 142 A1
Cabanas P 160 B2
Cabañas del Castillo E 156 A2
Cabañas de Yepes E 151 C4
Cabanelles E 147 B3
Cabanes E 153 B4
Cabanillas E 144 B2
Cabar HR 123 B3
Cabasse F 132 B2
Cabdella E 146 B2
Cabeceiras de Basto P 148 A1
Cabeço de Vide P 155 B3
Cabella Ligure I 120 C2
Cabeza del Buey E 156 B2
Cabeza la Vaca E 161 A3
Cabezamesada E 151 C4
Cabezarados E 157 B3
Cabezarrubias del Puerto E 157 B3
Cabezas del Villar E 150 B2
Cabezas Rubias E 161 B2
Cabezón E 142 C2
Cabezón de la Sal E 142 A2
Cabezón de Liébana E 142 A2
Cabezuela E 151 A4
Cabezuela del Valle E 149 B4
Cabo de Gata E 164 C2
Cabo de Palos E 165 B4
Cabolafuente E 152 A1
Cabourg F 89 A3
Cabra
E 163 A3
P 148 B2
Cabra del Santo Cristo E 163 A4
Cábras I 179 C2

Cabreiro P 140 C2
Cabreiros E 140 A3
Cabrejas E 152 B1
Cabrela P 154 C2
Cabrillas E 149 B3
Cabuna HR 125 B3
Cacabelos E 141 B4
Čačak SRB 127 D2
Cáccamo I 176 B2
Caccuri I 174 B2
Cacela P 160 B2
Cacém P 154 C1
Cáceres E 155 B4
Cachafeiro E 140 B2
Cachopo P 160 B2
Čachtice SK 98 C1
Cacin E 163 A4
Čačinci HR 125 B3
Cadafais P 154 C1
Cadalen F 129 C5
Cadalso E 149 B3
Cadaqués E 147 B4
Cadaval P 154 B1
Cadavedo E 141 A4
Čadavica BIH 138 A2
Cadéac F 145 B4
Cadelbosco di Sopra I 121 C3
Cadenazzo CH 120 A1
Cadenberge D 64 C2
Cadenet F 131 B4
Cadeuil F 114 C3
Cádiar E 164 C1
Cadillac F 128 B2
Cádiz E 162 B1
Čadjavica HR 125 B3
Cadouin F 129 B3
Cadours F 129 C4
Cadrete E 152 A3
Caen F 89 A3
Caerleon GB 39 C4
Caernarfon GB 38 A2
Caerphilly GB 39 C3
Caersws GB 39 B3
Cafede P 155 B3
Caggiano I 172 B1
Cagli I 136 B1
Cágliari I 179 C3
Čaglin HR 125 B3
Cagnano Varano I 171 B3
Cagnes-sur-Mer F 132 B3
Caher IRL 29 B4
Caherciveen IRL 29 C1
Caherdaniel IRL 29 C1
Cahors F 129 B4
Cahul MD 17 C8
Caiazzo I 170 B2
Caion E 140 A2
Cairndow GB 34 B3
Cairnryan GB 36 B1
Cairo Montenotte I 133 A4
Caister-on-Sea GB 41 C5
Caistor GB 41 B3
Caivano I 170 C2
Cajarc F 129 B4
Čajniče BIH 139 B5
Çakırlar TR 189 C5
Çakmak TR 187 C6
Čakovec HR 124 A2
Çal TR 189 A4
Cala E 161 B3
Calabritto I 172 B1
Calaceite E 153 B4
Calacuccia F 180 A2
Cala d'Or E 167 B3
Calaf E 147 C2
Calafat RO 17 C5
Calafell E 147 C2
Cala Galdana E 167 B3
Cala Gonone I 178 B3
Calahonda
Granada E 163 B4
Málaga E 163 B3
Calahorra E 144 B2
Calais F 78 B1
Cala Llonga E 166 C1
Calalzo di Cadore I 109 C3
Cala Millor E 167 B3
Calamocha E 152 B2
Calamonte E 155 C4
Cala Morell E 167 A3
Calanais GB 31 A2
Calañas E 161 B3
Calanda E 153 B3
Calangiánus I 178 B3
Călăraşi RO 17 C7
Calascibetta I 177 B3
Calasetta I 179 C2
Calasparra E 164 A3
Calatafimi I 176 B1
Calatayud E 152 A2
Calatorao E 152 A2
Calau D 84 A1
Calbe D 73 C4
Calcena E 152 A2
Calcinelli I 136 B1
Calco I 120 B2
Caldaralo I 136 B2
Caldaro sulla strada del Vino I 121 A4
Caldas da Rainha P 154 B1
Caldas de Bo i E 145 B4
Caldas de Malavella E 147 C3
Caldas de Reis E 140 B2
Caldas de San Jorge P 148 B1
Caldas de Vizela P 148 A1
Caldaso de los Vidrios E 150 B3
Caldbeck GB 36 B3
Caldearenas E 145 B3
Caldelas P 148 A1
Calders E 147 C2

Caldes de Montbui E 147 C3
Caldicot GB 39 C4
Caldirola I 120 C2
Caledon GB 27 B4
Calella
Barcelona E 147 C3
Girona E 147 C4
Calenzana F 180 A1
Calera de León E 161 A3
Calera y Chozas E 150 C3
Caleruega E 143 C3
Caleruela E 150 C2
Cales de Mallorca E 167 B3
Calestano I 134 A3
Calfsound GB 33 B4
Calgary GB 34 B1
Calimera I 173 B4
Calitri I 172 B1
Calizzano I 133 A4
Callac F 100 A2
Callan IRL 30 B1
Callander GB 35 B3
Callas F 132 B2
Calliano
Piemonte I 119 B5
Trentino Alto Adige I 121 B4
Callington GB 42 B2
Callosa de Ensarriá E 159 C3
Callosa de Segura E 165 A4
Callús E 147 C2
Čalma SRB 127 B1
Calmbach D 93 C4
Calne GB 43 A5
Calolziocorte I 120 B2
Calonge E 147 C4
Čalovec SK 112 B1
Calpe E 159 C4
Caltabellotta I 176 B2
Caltagirone I 177 B3
Caltanissetta I 177 B3
Caltavuturo I 176 B2
Çaltılıbük TR 186 C3
Caltojar E 151 A5
Caluire-et-Cuire F 117 B4
Caluso I 119 B4
Calvello I 172 B1
Calvi F 180 A1
Calviá E 166 B2
Calvinet F 116 C2
Calvisson F 131 B3
Calvörde D 73 B4
Calw D 93 C4
Calzada de Calatrava E 157 B4
Calzada de Valdunciel E 150 A2
Calzadilla de los Barros E 155 C4
Cam GB 43 A4
Camaiore I 134 B3
Camarasa E 145 C4
Camarena E 151 B3
Camarès F 130 B1
Camaret-sur-Aigues F 131 A3
Camaret-sur-Mer F 100 A1
Camarillas E 153 B3
Camariñas E 140 A1
Camarma E 151 B4
Camarzana de Tera E 141 B4
Camas E 162 A1
Camastra I 176 B2
Cambados E 140 B2
Cambarinho P 148 B1
Camberley GB 44 B3
Cambil E 163 A4
Cambligeu F 78 B2
Cambo-les-Bains F 144 A2
Camborne GB 42 B1
Cambrai F 78 B3
Cambre E 140 A2
Cambridge GB 45 A4
Cambrils E 147 C2
Cambs D 65 C4
Camburg D 83 A3
Camden GB 44 B3
Cameleño E 142 A2
Camelford GB 42 B2
Camelle E 140 A1
Camerano I 136 B2
Camerino I 136 B2
Camerota I 172 B1
Camigliatello Silano I 174 B2
Caminha P 148 A1
Caminomorisco E 149 B3
Caminreal E 152 B2
Camisano Vicentino I 121 B4
Camlidere TR 187 B7
Cammarata I 176 B2
Camogli I 134 A2
Camors F 100 B3
Camp IRL 29 B2
Campagna I 172 B1
Campagnano di Roma I 168 A2
Campagnático I 135 C4
Campan F 145 A4
Campana I 174 B2
Campanario E 156 B2
Campanillas E 163 B3
Campano E 162 B1
Camparañón E 143 C4
Campaspero E 151 A3
Campbeltown GB 34 C2
Campello E 165 A4
Campelos P 154 B1
Campi Bisénzio I 135 B4
Campico López E 165 B3

Campíglia Maríttima I 134 B3
Campillo de Altobuey E 158 B2
Campillo de Aragón E 152 A2
Campillo de Arenas E 163 A4
Campillo de Llerena E 156 B2
Campillos E 162 A3
Câmpina RO 17 C6
Campi Salentina I 173 B4
Campli I 136 C2
Campo E 145 B4
Campobasso I 170 B2
Campobello di Licata I 176 B2
Campobello di Mazara I 176 B1
Campo da Feira E 140 B3
Campodársego I 121 B4
Campo de Bacerros E 141 B3
Campo de Caso E 142 A1
Campo de Criptana E 157 A4
Campodolcino I 120 A2
Campofelice di Roccella I 176 B2
Campofiorito I 176 B2
Campofórmido I 122 A2
Campofranco I 176 B2
Campofrio E 161 B3
Campogalliano I 121 C3
Campo Ligure I 133 A4
Campolongo I 109 C3
Campo Lugar E 156 A2
Campo Maior P 155 B3
Campomanes E 141 A5
Campomarino I 170 B3
Campo Molino I 133 A3
Campomono I 180 B1
Campo Real E 151 B4
Camporeale I 176 B2
Camporells E 145 C4
Camporrobles E 158 B2
Campos E 148 A2
Camposa P 148 A1
Camposampiero I 121 B4
Camposanto I 121 C4
Campos del Port E 167 B3
Camposines E 153 A4
Campotéjar E 163 A4
Campotosto I 169 A3
Campo Túres I 108 C2
Camprodón E 147 B3
Campsegret F 129 B3
Camrose GB 39 C1
Camuñas E 157 A4
Çamyolu TR 189 C7
Çan TR 186 B2
Cañada del Hoyo E 158 B2
Cañadajuncosa E 158 B1
Cañada Rosal E 162 A2
Čanak HR 123 C4
Çanakkale TR 186 B1
Canale I 119 C4
Canales
Asturias E 141 B5
Castellón de la Plana E 159 B3
Canals E 159 C3
Canal San Bovo I 121 A4
Cañamares E 152 B1
Cañamero E 156 A2
Cañar E 163 B4
Cañate la Real E 162 B2
Cañaveral E 155 B4
Cañaveral de León E 161 A3
Cañaveras E 152 B1
Cañaveruelas E 151 B5
Canazei I 108 C2
Cancale F 88 B2
Cancellara I 172 B1
Cancello ed Arnone I 170 B2
Cancon F 129 B3
Canda E 141 B4
Candamil E 140 A3
Candanchu E 145 B3
Çandarlı TR 186 D1
Candas E 141 A5
Candasnos E 153 A4
Candé F 101 B4
Candela I 172 A1
Candelario E 150 B2
Candeleda E 150 B2
Cándia Lomellina I 120 B1
Candide
Casamazzagno I 109 C3
Candin E 141 B4
Candosa P 148 B2
Canecas P 154 C1
Canelli I 119 C5
Canena E 157 B4
Canencia E 151 B4
Canero E 141 A4
Canet F 130 B2
Canet de Mar E 147 C3
Canet d'en Berenguer E 159 B3
Cañete E 158 B2
Cañete de las Torres E 163 A3
Canet-Plage F 146 B4
Canfranc E 145 B3
Cangas
Lugo E 141 A3
Pontevedra E 140 B2

Cangas de Narcea E . . . 141 A4
Cangas de Onís E 142 A1
Canha P 154 C2
Canhestros P . . . 160 A1
Canicattì I 176 B2
Canicattini Bagni I 177 B4
Canicosa de la Sierra E . . . 143 C3
Caniles E 164 B2
Canillas de Aceituno E . . . 163 B3
Canino I 168 A1
Canisy F 88 A2
Cañizal E 150 A2
Cañizo E 142 C1
Canjáyar E 164 C2
Çankırı TR 23 A7
Çannai I 179 C2
Cannara I 136 B1
Cánnero Riviera I . . . 120 A1
Cannes F 132 B3
Canneto
  Sicilia I 177 A3
  Toscana I 135 B3
Canneto sull'Oglio I 120 B3
Cannich GB 32 D2
Cannóbio I 120 A1
Cannock GB 40 C1
Canonbie GB 36 A4
Canosa di Púglia I 171 B4
Can Pastilla E . . . 166 B2
C'an Picafort E . . . 167 B3
Cantalapiedra E . . . 150 A2
Cantalejo E 151 A4
Cantalgallo E 161 A3
Cantalice I 169 A2
Cantalpino E 150 A2
Cantalupo in Sabina I 168 A2
Cantanhede P . . . 148 B1
Çantavieja E 153 B3
Čantavir SRB 126 B1
Canterbury GB 45 B5
Cantiano I 136 B1
Cantillana E 162 A2
Cantiveros E 150 B3
Cantoria E 164 B2
Cantù I 120 B2
Canvey GB 45 B4
Cany-Barville F . . . 89 A4
Canyet de Mar E . . . 147 C3
Caol GB 34 B2
Cáorle I 122 B1
Caorso I 120 B2
Capáccio I 172 B1
Capaci I 176 A2
Capálbio I 168 A1
Capánnori I 134 B3
Caparde BIH 139 A4
Caparroso E 144 B2
Capbreton F 128 C1
Capdenac-Gare F . . . 116 C2
Capdepera E 167 B3
Cap-de-Pin F 128 B2
Capel Curig GB 38 A3
Capellades E 147 C2
Capena I 168 A2
Capendu F 146 A3
Capestang F 130 B2
Capestrano I 169 A3
Cap Ferret F 128 B1
Capileira E 163 B4
Capinha P 148 B2
Ca'Pisani I 122 C1
Capistrello I 169 B3
Capizzi I 177 B3
Čaplje BIH 124 C2
Čapljina BIH 139 B3
Capo di Ponte I . . . 120 A3
Caposile I 122 B1
Capoterra I 179 C2
Cappadócia I 169 A3
Cappamore IRL 29 B3
Cappeln D 71 B5
Cappoquin IRL 29 B4
Capracotta I 169 B4
Capránica I 168 A2
Caprarola I 168 A2
Capretta I 135 C5
Capri I 170 C2
Capriati a Volturno I 170 B2
Caprino Veronese I 121 B3
Captieux F 128 B2
Cápua I 170 B2
Capurso I 173 A2
Capvern F 145 A4
Carabaña E 151 B4
Carabias E 151 A4
Caracal RO 17 C6
Caracenilla E 152 B1
Carágio I 133 A3
Caraman F 146 A2
Caramánico Terme I 169 A4
Caranga E 141 A4
Caranguejeira P . . . 154 B2
Caransebeş RO . . . 16 C5
Carantec F 100 A2
Carapelle I 171 B3
Carasco I 134 A2
Carate Brianza I 120 B2
Caravaca de la Cruz E 164 A3
Caravággio I 120 B2
Carbajal E 163 B3
Carbajo E 155 B3
Carballeda E 140 B3
Carballeda de Avia E 140 B2
Carballo E 140 A2
Carbis Bay GB 42 B1
Carbon-Blanc F . . . 128 B2

Carbonera de Frentes E 143 C4
Carboneras E 164 C3
Carboneras de Guadazaón E 158 B2
Carbonero el Mayor E 151 A3
Carboneros E 157 B4
Carbónia I 179 C2
Carbonin I 108 C3
Carbonne F 146 A2
Carbost
  Highland GB 31 B2
  Highland GB 31 B2
Carcaboso E 149 B3
Carcabuey E 163 A3
Carcaixent E 159 B3
Carcans F 128 A1
Carcans-Plage F . . . 128 A1
Carção P 149 A3
Carcar E 144 B2
Cárcare I 133 A4
Carcassonne F 146 A3
Carcastillo E 144 B2
Carcedo de Burgos E 143 B3
Carcelén E 159 B2
Carcès F 132 B2
Carchelejo E 163 A4
Çardak
  Çanakkale TR . . . 186 B1
  Denizli TR 189 B4
Cardedeu E 147 C3
Cardeña E 157 B3
Cardenete E 158 B2
Cardeñosa E 150 B3
Cardeto I 175 C1
Cardiff GB 39 C3
Cardigan GB 39 B2
Cardona E 147 C2
Cardosos P 154 B2
Carei RO 16 B5
Carentan F 88 A2
Carentoir F 101 B3
Careri I 175 C2
Carevdar HR 124 A2
Cargèse F 180 A1
Carhaix-Plouguer F 100 A2
Caria P 148 B2
Cariati I 174 B2
Carignan F 91 B5
Carignano I 119 C4
Cariñena E 152 A2
Carini I 176 A2
Cariño E 140 A3
Carínola I 170 B1
Carisbrooke GB 44 C2
Carlabhagh GB 31 A2
Carlepont F 90 B3
Carlet E 159 B3
Carlingford IRL 27 B4
Carlisle GB 36 B4
Carloforte I 179 C2
Carlópoli I 175 B2
Carlow
  D 65 C3
  IRL 30 B2
Carlton GB 40 C2
Carluke GB 35 C4
Carmagnola I 119 C4
Carmarthen GB 39 C2
Carmaux F 130 A1
Carmena E 150 C3
Cármenes E 142 B1
Carmine I 133 A3
Carmona E 162 A2
Carmonita E 155 B4
Carmyllie GB 35 B5
Carnac F 100 B2
Carndonagh IRL . . . 27 A3
Carnew IRL 30 B2
Carnforth GB 37 B4
Cárnia I 122 A2
Carnlough GB 27 B5
Carno GB 39 B3
Carnon Plage F . . . 131 B2
Carnota I 140 B1
Carnoustie GB 35 B5
Carnwath GB 35 C4
Carolei I 174 B2
Carolinensiel D . . . 71 A4
Carolles F 88 B2
Carona I 120 A2
Caronía I 177 A3
Carovigno I 173 B3
Carovilli I 170 B2
Carpaneto Piacentino I 120 C2
Carpegna I 135 B5
Carpenédolo I 121 B3
Carpentras F 131 A4
Carpi I 121 C3
Carpignano Sésia I 119 B5
Carpineti I 134 A3
Carpineto Romano I 169 B3
Cărpinis RO 126 B2
Carpino I 171 B3
Carpinone I 170 B2
Carpio E 150 A2
Carquefou F 101 B4
Carqueiranne F 132 B2
Carral E 140 A2
Carranque E 151 B4
Carrapichana P . . . 148 B2
Carrara I 134 A3
Carraroe IRL 28 A2
Carrascalejo E 156 A2
Carrascosa del Campo E 151 B5
Carratraca E 162 B3
Carrazeda de Ansiães P 148 A2
Carrazedo de Montenegro P 148 A2
Carrbridge GB 32 D3
Carregal do Sal P . . . 148 B1
Carreña E 142 A2

Carrick IRL 26 B2
Carrickart IRL 26 A3
Carrickfergus GB 27 B5
Carrickmacross IRL 27 C4
Carrick-on-Shannon IRL 26 C2
Carrick-on-Suir IRL 30 B1
Carrigallen IRL . . . 27 C3
Carrión E 161 B3
Carrión de Calatrava E 157 A4
Carrión de los Condes E 142 B2
Carrizo de la Ribera E 141 B5
Carrizosa E 157 B5
Carro F 131 B4
Carrocera E 142 B1
Carros F 133 B3
Carrouge CH 106 C1
Carrouges F 89 B3
Carrù I 133 A3
Carryduff GB 27 B5
Carry-le-Rouet F . . . 131 B4
Carsóli I 169 A3
Carsphairn GB 36 A2
Cartagena E 165 B4
Cártama E 163 B3
Cartaxo P 154 B2
Cartaya E 161 B2
Carteret F 88 A2
Cartes E 142 A2
Carúnchio I 170 B2
Carviões P 149 A3
Carvin F 78 B2
Carvoeira P 154 B1
Carvoeiro P 160 B1
Casabermeja E 163 B3
Casa Branca
  Portalegre P 154 C3
  Setúbal P 154 C2
Casacalenda I 170 B2
Casa Castalda I 136 B1
Casaio E 141 B4
Casa l'Abate I 173 B4
Casalarreina E 143 B4
Casalbordino I 169 A4
Casalborgone I 119 B4
Casalbuono I 174 A1
Casalbuttano ed Uniti I 120 B2
Casàl di Principe I 170 B2
Casalécchio di Reno I 135 A4
Casale Monferrato I 119 B5
Casalina I 136 C1
Casalmaggiore I . . . 121 C3
Casalnuovo Monterotaro I . . . 170 B3
Casaloldo I 121 B3
Casalpusterlengo I 120 B2
Casamássima I . . . 173 B2
Casamicciola Terme I 170 C1
Casamozza F 180 A2
Casarabonela E . . . 162 B3
Casarano I 173 B4
Casar de Cáceres E . . . 155 B4
Casar de Palomero E 149 B3
Casarejos E 143 C3
Casares E 162 B2
Casares de las Hurdes E 149 B3
Casariche E 163 A3
Casarrubios del Monte E 151 B3
Casas de Don Pedro E 156 A2
Casas de Fernando Alonso E 158 B1
Casas de Haro E 158 B1
Casas de Juan Gil E 159 B2
Casas del Juan Núñez E 158 B2
Casas del Puerto E 159 C2
Casas del Río E 159 B2
Casas de Millán E . . . 155 B4
Casas de Reina E . . . 156 B2
Casas de Ves E 159 B2
Casas-Ibáñez E 158 B2
Casasimarro E 158 B1
Casas Nuevas E 164 B3
Casasola E 150 B3
Casasola de Arión E 150 A2
Casasuertes E 142 A2
Casatejada E 150 C2
Casavieja E 150 B3
Casazza I 120 B2
Cascais P 154 C1
Cascante E 144 C2
Cascante del Rio E 152 B2
Cáscia I 169 A3
Casciana Terme I . . . 134 B3
Cáscina I 134 B3
Cáseda E 144 B2
Casekow D 74 A3
Casella I 134 A2
Caselle Torinese I 119 B4
Casemurate I 135 A5
Casenove I 136 C1
Caseres E 153 A4
Caserío Benali E . . . 159 B3
Caserta I 170 B2
Casével P 160 B1
Cashel IRL 29 B4
Casillas E 150 B3
Casillas de Coria E . . . 155 B4
Casina I 134 A3
Casinos E 159 B3

Čáslav CZ 97 B3
Cásola Valsénio I . . . 135 A4
Cásole d'Elsa I . . . 135 B4
Cásoli I 169 A4
Casória I 170 C2
Caspe E 153 A3
Cassàde la Selva I 147 C3
Cassagnas F 130 A2
Cassagnes-Bégonhès F 130 A1
Cassano allo Iónio I 174 B2
Cassano d'Adda I . . . 120 B2
Cassano delle Murge I 171 C4
Cassano Magnago I 120 B1
Cassano Spínola I . . . 120 C1
Cassel F 78 B2
Cássibile I 177 C4
Cassine I 119 C5
Cassino I 169 B3
Cassis F 132 B1
Cassolnovo I 120 B1
Cassuéjouls F 116 C2
Častá SK 98 C1
Castagnaro I 121 B4
Castagneto Carducci I 134 B3
Castagnola CH 120 A1
Castalla E 159 C3
Castañar de Ibor E . . . 156 A2
Castanheira de Pêra P 154 A2
Cástano Primo I . . . 120 B1
Castasegna CH 120 A2
Castéggio I 120 B2
Casteição P 148 B2
Castejón E 144 B2
Castejón de Monegros E 153 A3
Castejón de Sos E 145 B4
Castejón de Valdejasa E 144 C2
Castèl Baronia I . . . 172 A1
Castèl Bolognese I 135 A4
Castelbuono I 177 B3
Casteldáccia I 176 A2
Castel d'Aiano I 135 A4
Castel d'Ario I 121 B3
Castel de Cabra E . . . 153 B3
Castèl del Monte I 169 A3
Castèl del Piano I 135 C4
Castèl di Iúdica I . . . 177 B3
Castèl di Rio I 135 A4
Castèl di Sangro I . . . 169 B4
Castèl di Tora I 169 A2
Castelfidardo I 136 B2
Castelfiorentino I 135 B3
Castelforte I 169 B3
Castelfranco Emília I 121 C4
Castelfranco in Miscano I . . . 170 B3
Castelfranco Véneto I 121 B4
Castèl Frentano I . . . 169 A4
Casteljaloux F 128 B3
Castellabate I 170 C2
Castellammare del Golfo I . . . 176 A1
Castellammare di Stábia I . . . 170 C2
Castellamonte I . . . 119 B4
Castellana Grotte I 173 B3
Castellane F 132 B2
Castellaneta I 173 B2
Castellaneta Marina I 173 B2
Castellar E 157 B4
Castellarano I 135 A3
Castellar de la Frontera E . . . 162 B2
Castellar de la Ribera E 147 B2
Castellar del Vallès E 147 C3
Castellar de Santiago E 157 B4
Castellbell i Villar E 147 C2
Castelldans E 153 A4
Castell de Cabres E 153 B4
Castell de Castells E 159 C3
Castelldefels E 147 C2
Castell de Ferro E 163 B4
Castelleone I 120 B2
Castellet E 147 C2
Castelletto di Brenzone I . . . 121 B3
Castellfollit de la Roca E 147 B3
Castellfollit de Riubregos E . . . 147 C2
Castellfort E 153 B3
Castellina in Chianti I . . . 135 B4
Castellina Marittima I 134 B3
Castellóde Farfaña E 145 C4
Castellóde la Plana E 159 B3
Castelloli E 147 C2
Castellón de Rugat E 159 C3

Castellote E 153 B3
Castello Tesino I . . . 121 A4
Castellterçol E 147 C3
Castellúcchio I 121 B3
Castellúccio de'Sáuri I 171 B3
Castelluccio Inferiore I 174 B1
Castelluccio Valmaggiore I 171 B3
Castelmassa I 121 B4
Castelmáuro I 170 B2
Castelmoron-sur-Lot F 129 B3
Castelnaudary F . . . 146 A2
Castelnau-de-Médoc F 128 A2
Castelnau-de-Montmirail F 129 C4
Castelnau-Magnoac F 145 A4
Castelnau-Montratier F 129 B4
Castelnovo ne'Monti I 134 A3
Castelnuovo Berardenga I 135 B4
Castelnuovo della Dáunia I 170 B3
Castelnuovo di Garfagnana I 134 A3
Castelnuovo di Val di Cécina I 135 B3
Castelnuovo Don Bosco I 119 B4
Castelnuovo Scrivia I 120 C1
Castelo Branco
  Bragança P . . . 149 A3
  Castelo Branco P 155 B3
Castelo de Paiva P 148 A1
Castelo de Vide P . . . 155 B3
Castelo do Neiva P 148 A1
Castelraimondo I . . . 136 B2
Castel San Gimignano I 135 B4
Castèl San Giovanni I 120 B2
Castèl San Pietro Terme I . . . 135 A4
Castelsantángelo I 136 C2
Castèl Sant'Elia I 168 A2
Castelsaraceno I 174 A1
Castelsardo I 178 B2
Castelserás E 153 B3
Casteltérmini I 176 B2
Castelvecchio Subéquo I 169 A3
Castelvetrano I 176 B1
Castèl Volturno I 170 B1
Castenédolo I 120 B3
Castets F 128 C1
Castiádas I 179 C3
Castiglioncello I . . . 134 B3
Castiglione I 169 A3
Castiglione Chiavarese I 134 A2
Castiglione d'Adda I 120 B2
Castiglione dei Pepoli I 135 A4
Castiglione del Lago I 135 B5
Castiglione della Pescáia I 135 C3
Castiglione delle Stiviere I 121 B3
Castiglione di Sicília I 177 B4
Castiglione d'Órcia I 135 B4
Castiglione Messer Marino I . . . 170 B2
Castiglione Messer Raimondo I . . . 169 A3
Castiglion Fibocchi I 135 B4
Castiglion Fiorentino I 135 B4
Castilblanco E 156 A2
Castilblanco de los Arroyos E 161 B4
Castil de Peones E . . . 143 B3
Castilfrío de la Sierra E 144 C1
Castilgaleu E 145 B4
Castilisar E 144 B2
Castillazuelo E 145 B4
Castilléjar E 164 B2
Castillejo de Martín Viejo E 149 B3
Castillejo de Mesleón E 151 A4
Castillejo de Robledo E 151 A4
Castillo de Bayuela E 150 B3
Castillo de Locubín E 163 A4
Castillonès E 129 B3
Castillon-la-Bataille F 128 B2
Castillon-Len-Couserans F . . . 146 B2
Castillonroy E 145 C4
Castilruiz E 144 C1
Castione CH 120 A2
Castions di Strada I 122 B2
Castirla F 180 A2
Castlebar IRL 28 A2
Castlebellingham IRL 27 C4
Castleblaney IRL 27 B4
Castlebridge IRL . . . 30 B2

Castle Cary GB 43 A4
Castlecomer IRL 30 B1
Castlederg GB 27 B3
Castle Douglas GB . . . 36 B3
Castleford GB 40 B2
Castleisland IRL 29 B2
Castlemaine IRL 29 B2
Castlemartyr IRL 29 C3
Castlepollard IRL 30 A1
Castlerea IRL 28 A3
Castleton GB 40 B2
Castletown
  Highland GB 32 C3
  Isle of Man GB 36 B2
Castletown Bearhaven IRL 29 C2
Castletownroche IRL 29 B3
Castlewellan GB 27 B5
Casto I 120 B3
Castrejón E 150 A2
Castrelo del Valle E 141 B3
Castres F 130 B1
Castricum NL 70 B1
Castries F 131 B2
Castril E 164 B2
Castrillo de Duero E 151 A4
Castrillo de la Vega E 143 C3
Castrillo de Onielo E 142 C2
Castro
  León E 142 A2
  Orense E 140 B3
Castrocabón E 141 B5
Castrocaro Terme I 135 A4
Castrocontrigo E . . . 141 B4
Castro Daire P 148 B2
Castro dei Volsci I . . . 169 B3
Castro del Río E . . . 163 A3
Castro de Rey E 141 A3
Castrofilippo I 176 B2
Castrogonzaio E 142 B1
Castrojeriz E 142 B2
Castro Laboreiro P 140 B2
Castro Marim P 160 B2
Castromonte E 142 C1
Castromudarra E 142 B1
Castronuevo E 142 C1
Castronuño E 150 A2
Castropol E 141 A3
Castroreale I 177 A4
Castroserracin E 151 A4
Castro-Urdiales E 143 A3
Castroverde E 141 A3
Castro Verde P 160 B1
Castroverde de Campos E 142 C1
Castroverde de Cerrato E 142 C2
Castrovillari I 174 B2
Castuera E 156 B2
Catadau E 159 B3
Cataéggio I 120 A2
Çatalca TR 186 A3
Catallar TR 189 C5
Çatalzeytin TR 23 A8
Catánia I 177 B4
Catanzaro I 175 C2
Catanzaro Marina I 175 C2
Catarroja E 159 B3
Catarruchos P 148 B1
Catcleugh GB 37 A4
Caterham GB 44 B3
Cati E 153 B4
Čatići BIH 139 A4
Catignano I 169 A3
Catillon F 91 A3
Catoira E 140 B2
Caton GB 37 B4
Catral E 165 A4
Catterick GB 37 B5
Cáttólica I 136 B1
Cáttólica Eraclea I 176 B2
Catton GB 37 B4
Caudebec-en-Caux F 89 A4
Caudete E 159 C3
Caudete de las Fuentes E 159 B2
Caudiel E 159 B3
Caudiès-de-Fenouillèdes F . . . 146 B3
Caudry F 91 A3
Caulkerbush GB 36 B3
Caulnes F 101 A3
Caulónia I 175 C2
Caumont-l'Évente F 88 A3
Caunes-Minervois F 146 A3
Cauro F 180 B1
Caussade F 129 B4
Causse-de-la-Selle F 130 B2
Cauterets F 145 B3
Cava de Tirreni I . . . 170 C2
Cavaglia I 119 B5
Cavaillon F 131 B4
Cavalaire-sur-Mer F 132 B2
Cavaleiro P 160 B1
Cavalese I 121 A4
Cavallermaggiore I 119 C4
Cavallino I 122 B1
Cavan IRL 27 C3
Cávarzere I 121 B5
Çavdarhisar TR 187 C4

Çavdır TR 189 B4
Cavernães P 148 B2
Cavezzo I 121 C4
Cavignac F 128 A2
Çavle HR 123 B3
Cavo I 134 C3
Cavour I 119 C4
Cawdor GB 32 D3
Çay TR 187 D6
Çaycuma TR 187 A4
Cayeux-sur-Mer F . . . 78 B1
Çayıralan TR 23 B8
Caylus F 129 B4
Cayres F 117 C3
Cazalilla E 157 C4
Cazalla de la Sierra E 156 C2
Cazals F 129 B4
Cazanuecos E 142 B1
Cazaubon F 128 C2
Cazaux F 128 B1
Cazavet F 146 A2
Cazères F 146 A2
Cazin BIH 124 C1
Cazis CH 107 C4
Čazma HR 124 B2
Cazo E 142 A1
Cazorla E 164 B2
Cazouls-lès-Béziers F 130 B2
Cea
  León E 142 B1
  Orense E 140 B2
Ceánuri E 143 A4
Ceauce F 88 B3
Cebolla E 150 C3
Čebovce SK 112 A3
Cebreros E 150 B3
Čečava BIH 125 C3
Ceccano I 169 B3
Cece H 112 C2
Cecenowo PL 68 A2
Čechtice CZ 96 B3
Čechtín CZ 97 B3
Cécina I 134 B3
Ceclavín E 155 B4
Cedégolo I 120 A3
Cedeira E 140 A2
Cedillo E 155 B3
Cedillo del Condado E 151 B4
Cedrillas E 153 B3
Cedynia PL 74 B3
Cée E 140 B1
Cefalù I 177 A3
Céglia I 122 B2
Céglied H 113 B3
Céglie Messápica I 173 B3
Cehegín E 164 B3
Ceilhes-et-Rocozels F 130 B2
Ceinos de Campos E 142 B1
Ceira P 148 B1
Čejč CZ 97 C2
Cekcyn PL 76 A3
Cela BIH 124 C2
Čelákovice CZ 84 B2
Celano I 169 A3
Celanova E 140 B3
Celbridge IRL 30 A2
Čelebić BIH 138 B2
Celenza Valfortore I 170 B2
Čelić BIH 125 C4
Čelinac Donji BIH 124 C2
Celje SLO 123 A4
Cella E 152 B2
Celldömölk H 111 B4
Celle D 72 B3
Celle Ligure I 133 A4
Celles B 79 B3
Celles-sur-Belle F 115 B3
Cellino San Marco I 173 B3
Celorico da Beira P 148 B2
Celorico de Basto P 148 A2
Çeltik TR 187 C6
Çeltikçi TR 189 B5
Cemaes GB 38 A2
Cembra I 121 A4
Čemerno BIH 139 B4
Cenad RO 126 A2
Cencenighe Agordino I 121 A4
Cenei RO 126 B2
Ceneselli I 121 B4
Cenicero E 143 B4
Cenicientos E 150 B3
Censeau F 105 C5
Čenta SRB 126 B2
Centallo I 133 A3
Centelles E 147 C3
Cento I 121 C4
Centúripe I 177 B3
Cepeda la Mora E 150 B2
Cépet F 129 C4
Čepin HR 125 B4
Čepinski Martinci HR 125 B4
Cepovan SLO 122 A2
Čeralije HR 125 B3
Ceprano I 169 B3
Cerami I 177 B3
Cerano I 120 B1
Cérans Foulletourte F 102 B2
Ceraso I 172 B1
Cerbaia I 135 B4
Cerbère F 146 B4
Cercadillo E 151 A5
Cercal
  Lisboa P 154 B1
  Setúbal P 160 B1
Čerčany CZ 96 B2

Cerceda E 151 B4
Cercedilla E 151 B3
Cercemaggiore I . .170 B2
Cercs E 147 B2
Cercy-la-Tour F . . .104 C2
Cerdá I 176 B2
Cerdedo E 140 B2
Cerdeira P 149 B2
Cerdon F 103 B4
Cerea I 121 B4
Ceres
  GB 35 B5
  I 119 B4
Cerese I 121 B3
Ceresole-Reale I . .119 B4
Cereste F 132 B1
Céret F 146 B3
Cerezo de Abajo
  E 151 A4
Cerezo de Riotirón
  E 143 B3
Cerfontaine B 79 B4
Cergy F 90 B2
Cerignola I 171 B3
Cerilly F 103 C4
Cerisiers F 104 A2
Cerizay F 114 B3
Cerkeş TR 23 A7
Cerkezköy TR 186 A3
Cerkije SLO 123 A3
Cerklje SLO 123 B3
Cerknica SLO 123 B3
Cerkno SLO 122 A2
Cerkwica PL 67 B4
Cerná HR 125 B4
Cerná Hora CZ 97 B4
Cernavodă RO 17 C8
Cernay F 106 B2
Cerne Abbas GB . . .43 B4
Cernégula E 143 B3
Cernik HR 124 B3
Cernóbbio I 120 B2
Cernošin CZ 95 B4
Cernovice CZ 96 B2
Cérons F 128 B2
Cerovlje HR 123 B3
Cerovo SK 99 C3
Cerqueto I 135 C5
Cerralbo E 149 B3
Cerreto d'Esi I 136 B1
Cerreto Sannita I . .170 B2
Cerrigydrudion GB .38 A3
Cerro Muriano E . . .156 B3
Certaldo I 135 B4
Certosa di Pésio I . .133 A3
Cerva E 148 A2
Cervaro I 169 B3
Cervatos de la Cueza
  E 142 B2
Cervera E 147 C2
Cervera de la Cañada
  E 152 A2
Cervera del Llano
  E 158 B1
Cervera del Río Alhama
  E 144 B2
Cervera de Pisuerga
  E 142 B2
Cervéteri I 168 B2
Cérvia I 135 A5
Cerviáde les Garrigues
  E 147 C1
Cervignano del Friuli
  I 122 B2
Cervinara I 170 B2
Cervione F 180 A2
Cervon F 104 B2
Cesana Torinese I . .119 C3
Cesarica HR 137 A4
Cesarò I 177 B3
Cesena I 135 A5
Cesenático I 135 A5
Cēsis LV 8 D4
Ceská Belá CZ 97 B3
Ceská Kamenice
  CZ 84 B2
Ceská Lípa CZ 84 B2
Ceská Skalice CZ . .85 B3
Ceská Trebová CZ . .97 B4
České Budějovice
  CZ 96 C2
České Velenice CZ . .96 C2
Ceský Brod CZ 96 A2
Ceský Dub CZ 84 B2
Ceský Krumlov CZ . .96 C2
Ceský Tĕšín CZ 98 B2
Cešljeva Bara
  SRB 127 C3
Ceşme TR 188 A1
Cessenon F 130 B2
Cesson-Sévigné
  F 101 A4
Cestas F 128 B2
Cestobrodica SRB 127 D2
Cesuras E 140 A2
Cetina E 152 A2
Cetin Grad HR 123 B4
Cetinje MNE 16 D3
Cetraro I 174 B1
Ceuti E 165 A3
Ceva I 133 A4
Cevico de la Torre
  E 142 C2
Cevico Navero E . .142 C2
Cevins F 118 B3
Cévio CH 119 A5
Cevizli TR 189 B6
Cewice PL 68 A2
Ceylan TR 189 C4
Ceyrat F 116 B3
Ceyzériat F 118 A2
Chaam NL 79 A4
Chabanais F 115 C4
Chabeuil F 117 C5

Chabielice PL 86 A3
Chablis F 104 B2
Chábons F 118 B2
Chabówka PL 99 B3
Chabreloche F 117 B3
Chabris F 103 B3
Chagford GB 42 B3
Chagny F 105 C3
Chagoda RUS 9 C9
Chaherrero E 150 B3
Chailland F 88 B3
Chaillé-les-Marais
  F 114 B2
Chailles F 103 B3
Chailley F 104 A2
Chalabre F 146 B3
Chalamont F 118 B2
Châlette-sur-Loing
  F 103 A4
Chalindrey F 105 B4
Chalkida GR 185 A4
Challacombe GB . . .42 A3
Challans F 114 B2
Challes-les-Eaux
  F 118 B2
Chalmazel F 117 B3
Chalmoux F 104 C2
Chalonnes-sur-Loire
  F 102 B1
Châlons-en-
  Champagne F . . .91 C4
Chalon-sur-Saône
  F 105 C3
Chalupy PL 69 A3
Châlus F 115 C4
Cham
  CH 106 B3
  D 95 B4
Chamberet F 116 B1
Chambéry F 118 B2
Chambilly F 117 A4
Chambley F 92 B1
Chambly F 90 B2
Chambois F 89 B4
Chambon-sur-Lac
  F 116 B2
Chambon-sur-Voueize
  F 116 A2
Chambord F 103 B3
Chamborigaud F . .131 A2
Chamboulive F 116 B1
Chamerau D 95 B4
Chamonix-Mont Blanc
  F 119 B3
Chamoux-sur-Gelon
  F 118 B2
Champagnac-le-Vieux
  F 117 B3
Champagney F 106 B1
Champagnole F . . .105 C4
Champagny-Mouton
  F 115 B4
Champaubert F 91 C3
Champdeniers-St Denis
  F 114 B3
Champdieu F 117 B4
Champdôtre F 105 B4
Champeix F 116 B3
Champéry CH 119 A3
Champigne F 102 B1
Champignelles F . .104 B2
Champigny-sur-Veude
  F 102 B2
Champlitte-et-le-Prelot
  F 105 B4
Champoluc I 119 B4
Champoly F 117 B3
Champorcher I 119 B4
Champrond-en-Gâtine
  F 89 B5
Champs-sur-Tarentaine
  F 116 B2
Champs-sur-Yonne
  F 104 B2
Champtoceaux F . .101 B4
Chamrousse F 118 B2
Chamusca P 154 B2
Chanac F 130 A2
Chanaleilles F 117 C3
Chandler's Ford
  GB 44 C2
Chandra GR 185 D7
Chandrexa de Queixa
  E 141 B3
Chañe E 150 A3
Changy F 117 A3
Chania GR 185 D5
Channes F 104 B3
Chantada E 140 B3
Chantelle F 116 A3
Chantenay-St Imbert
  F 104 C2
Chanteuges F 117 B3
Chantilly F 90 B2
Chantonnay F 114 B2
Chão de Codes P . .154 B2
Chaource F 104 A3
Chapa E 140 B2
Chapareillan F 118 B2
Chapel en le Frith
  GB 40 B2
Chapelle Royale F 103 A3
Chapelle-St Laurent
  F 102 C1
Charbonnat F 104 C3
Chard GB 43 B4
Charenton-du-Cher
  F 103 C4
Charlbury GB 44 B2
Charleroi B 79 B4
Charlestown
  GB 42 B3
  IRL 26 C2
Charlestown of
  Aberlour GB 32 D3
Charleville IRL 29 B3
Charleville-Mézières
  F 91 B4
Charlieu F 117 A4

Charlottenberg S . .49 C4
Charlton Kings GB . .44 B1
Charly F 90 C3
Charmes F 92 C2
Charmes-sur-Rhône
  F 117 C4
Charmey CH 106 C2
Charminster GB . . .43 B4
Charmont-en-Beauce
  F 103 A4
Charmont-en-Vexin
  F 90 B1
Charnwolles F 117 A4
Chârost F 103 C4
Charquemont F . . .106 B1
Charrin F 104 C2
Charroux F 115 B4
Chartres F 90 C1
Charzykow PL 68 B2
Chasseneuil-sur-
  Bonnieure F 115 C4
Chassigny F 105 B4
Château-Arnoux
  F 132 A2
Châteaubernard
  F 115 C3
Châteaubourg F . . .101 A4
Châteaubriant F . . .101 B4
Château-Chinon
  F 104 B2
Château-d'Oex
  CH 106 C2
Château-d'Olonne
  F 114 B2
Château-du-Loir
  F 102 B2
Châteaudun F 103 A3
Châteaugiron F . . .101 A4
Château-Gontier
  F 102 B1
Château-Landon
  F 103 A4
Château-la-Vallière
  F 102 B2
Château-l'Evêque
  F 129 A3
Châteaulin F 100 A1
Châteaumeillant
  F 103 C4
Châteauneuf
  Nièvre F 104 B2
  Saône-et-Loire F .117 A4
Châteauneuf-de-
  Randon F 117 C3
Châteauneuf-d'Ille-et-
  Vilaine F 88 B2
Châteauneuf-du-Faou
  F 100 A2
Châteauneuf-du-Pape
  F 131 A3
Châteauneuf-en-
  Thymerais F 89 B5
Châteauneuf la-Forêt
  F 116 B1
Châteauneuf-le-Rouge
  F 132 B1
Châteauneuf-sur-
  Charente F 115 C3
Châteauneuf-sur-Cher
  F 103 C4
Châteauneuf-sur-Loire
  F 103 B4
Châteauneuf-sur-
  Sarthe F 102 B1
Châteauponsac F .115 B5
Château-Porcien F .91 B4
Châteauredon F . .132 A2
Châteaurenard
  Bouches du Rhône
  F 131 B3
  Loiret F 104 B1
Château-Renault
  F 102 B2
Châteauroux F . . .103 C3
Châteauroux-les-Alpes
  F 118 C3
Château-Salins F . .92 C2
Château-Thierry F .91 B3
Châteauvillain F . . .105 A3
Châtel F 119 A3
Châtelaillon-Plage
  F 114 B2
Châtelaudren F . . .100 A3
Châtel-Censoir F . .104 B2
Châtel-de-Neuvre
  F 116 A3
Châtelet B 79 B4
Châtelguyon F 116 B3
Châtellerault F 115 B4
Châtel-Montagne
  F 117 A3
Châtel-St Denis
  CH 106 C1
Châtel-sur-Moselle
  F 92 C2
Châtelus-Malvaleix
  F 116 A2
Châtenois F 105 A4
Châtenois-les-Forges
  F 106 B1
Chatham GB 45 B4
Châtillon I 119 B4
Châtillon-Coligny
  F 103 B4
Châtillon-en-Bazois
  F 104 B2
Châtillon-en-Diois
  F 118 C2
Châtillon-sur
  Chalaronne F . . .117 A4
Châtillon-sur-Indre
  F 103 B3
Châtillon-sur-Loire
  F 103 B4
Châtillon-sur-Marne
  F 91 B3
Châtillon-sur-Seine
  F 104 B3
Châtres F 91 C3
Chatteris GB 45 A4
Chatton GB 37 A5

Chauchina E 163 A4
Chaudes-Aigues
  F 116 C3
Chaudrey F 91 C4
Chauffailles F 117 A4
Chaulnes F 90 B2
Chaument Gistoux
  B 79 B4
Chaumergy F 105 C4
Chaumont F 105 A4
Chaumont-en-Vexin
  F 90 B1
Chaumont-Porcien
  F 91 B4
Chaumont-sur-Aire
  F 91 C5
Chaumont-sur-Loire
  F 103 B3
Chaunay F 115 B4
Chauny F 90 B3
Chaussin F 105 C4
Chauvigny F 115 B4
Chavagnes-en-Paillers
  F 114 B2
Chavanges F 91 C4
Chaves P 148 A2
Chavignon F 91 B3
Chazelles-sur-Lyon
  F 117 B4
Chazey-Bons F . . .118 B2
Cheadle
  Greater Manchester
  GB 40 B1
  Staffordshire GB . 40 C2
Cheb CZ 83 B4
Chebsara RUS 9 C11
Checa E 152 B2
Checiny PL 87 B4
Cheddar GB 43 A4
Cheddleton GB 40 B2
Chef-Boutonne F . .115 B3
Cheles E 155 C3
Chella E 159 B3
Chelles F 90 C2
Chełm PL 13 C5
Chełmno
  Kujawsko-Pomorskie
  PL 76 A3
  Wielkopolskie PL . .76 B3
Chelmsford GB 45 B4
Chelmuzhi RUS 9 A9
Chełmża PL 76 A3
Cheltenham GB . . .44 B1
Chelva E 159 B3
Chémery F 103 B3
Chemery-sur-Bar F .91 B4
Chemillé F 102 B1
Chemin F 105 C4
Chemnitz D 83 B4
Chénerailles F 116 A2
Cheniménil F 105 A5
Chenonceaux F . . .103 B3
Chenôve F 105 B3
Chepelare BG 183 B6
Chepstow GB 39 C4
Chera E 159 B3
Cherasco I 119 C4
Cherbonnières F . .115 C3
Cherbourg F 88 A2
Cherchiara di Calábria
  I 174 B2
Cherepovets RUS . .9 C10
Chernihiv UA 13 C9
Chernivtsi UA 17 A6
Chernobyl = Chornobyl
  UA 13 C9
Chernyakhovsk
  RUS 12 A4
Chéroy F 104 A1
Cherven BY 13 B8
Chervonohrad UA . .13 C6
Cherykaw BY 13 B9
Chesham GB 44 B3
Cheshunt GB 44 B3
Chessy-lès-Pres
  F 104 A2
Cheste E 159 B3
Chester GB 38 A4
Chesterfield GB . . .40 B2
Chester-le-Street
  GB 37 B5
Chevagnes F 104 C2
Chevanceaux F . . .115 C3
Chevillon F 91 C5
Chevilly F 103 A3
Chew Magna GB . . .43 A4
Chézery-Forens F 118 A2
Chialamberto I 119 B4
Chiampo I 121 B4
Chianale I 119 C4
Chianciano Terme
  I 135 B4
Chiaramonte Gulfi
  I 177 B3
Chiaramonti I 178 B2
Chiaravalle I 136 B2
Chiaravalle Centrale
  I 175 C2
Chiaréggio I 120 A2
Chiari I 120 B2
Chiaromonte I 174 A2
Chiasso CH 120 B2
Chiávari I 134 A2
Chiché F 102 C1
Chichester GB 44 C3
Chiclana de la Frontera
  E 162 B1
Chiclana de Segura
  E 164 A1
Chiddingfold GB . . .44 B3
Chieri I 119 B4
Chiesa in Valmalenco
  I 120 A2
Chieti I 169 A4
Chieti Scalo I 169 A4
Chiéuti I 171 B3
Chigwell GB 45 B4
Chiliomodi GR 184 B3

Chillarón de Cuenca
  E 152 B1
Chillarón del Rey
  E 151 B5
Chilleurs-aux-Bois
  F 103 A4
Chillón E 156 B3
Chilluevar E 164 B1
Chiloeches E 151 B4
Chimay B 91 A4
Chimeneas E 163 A4
Chinchilla de Monte
  Aragón E 158 C2
Chinchón E 151 B4
Chingford GB 45 B4
Chinon F 102 B2
Chióggia I 122 B1
Chiomonte I 119 B3
Chipiona E 161 C3
Chippenham GB . . .43 A4
Chipping Campden
  GB 44 A2
Chipping Norton
  GB 44 B2
Chipping Ongar
  GB 45 B4
Chipping Sodbury
  GB 43 A4
Chirac F 130 A2
Chirbury GB 39 B3
Chirens F 118 B2
Chirivel E 164 B2
Chirk GB 38 B3
Chirnside GB 35 C5
Chişinău = Khisinev
  MD 17 B8
Chişineu Criş RO .113 C5
Chissey-en-Morvan
  F 104 B3
Chiusa I 108 C2
Chiusa di Pésio I . .133 A3
Chiusaforte I 122 A2
Chiusa Sclafani I . .176 B2
Chiusi I 135 B4
Chiva E 159 B3
Chivasso I 119 B4
Chlewiska PL 87 A4
Chludowo PL 75 B5
Chlumec nad Cidlinou
  CZ 84 B3
Chlum u Třeboně
  CZ 96 C2
Chmielnik PL 87 B4
Chobienia PL 85 A4
Chobienice PL 75 B4
Choceń E 97 A4
Choceń PL 77 B4
Chochołow PL 99 B3
Chociw PL 86 A3
Chociwel PL 75 A4
Choczewo PL 68 A2
Chodaków PL 77 B5
Chodecz PL 77 B4
Chodov CZ 83 B4
Chodzież PL 75 B5
Chojna PL 74 B3
Chojnice PL 68 B2
Chojno
  Kujawsko-Pomorskie
  PL 77 B4
  Wielkopolskie PL . .75 B5
Chojnów PL 85 A3
Cholet F 114 A3
Chomérac F 117 C4
Chomutov CZ 83 B5
Chop UA 12 D5
Chora GR 184 B2
Chora Sfakion GR 185 D5
Chorges F 132 A2
Choristanco E 140 A2
Chorley GB 38 A4
Chornobyl = Chernobyl
  UA 13 C9
Chortkiv UA 13 D6
Chorzele PL 77 A5
Chorzów PL 86 B2
Choszczno PL 75 A4
Chotěboř CZ 97 B3
Chouilly F 91 B4
Chouto P 154 B2
Chouzy-sur-Cisse
  F 103 B3
Chozas de Abajo
  E 142 B1
Chrast CZ 97 B3
Chrást CZ 96 B1
Chrastava CZ 84 B2
Chřibská CZ 84 B2
Christchurch GB . . .44 C2
Christiansfeld DK . .59 C2
Chroberz PL 87 B4
Chropyně CZ 98 B1
Chrudim CZ 97 B3
Chrzanów PL 86 B3
Chtelnica SK 98 C1
Chudovo RUS 9 C7
Chueca E 157 A4
Chulmleigh GB 42 B3
Chur CH 107 C4
Church Stretton
  GB 39 B4
Churriana E 163 B3
Churwalden CH . . .107 C4
Chvalšiny CZ 96 C2
Chwaszczyno PL . . .69 A3
Chynava CZ 96 A2
Chýnov CZ 96 B2
Ciacova RO 126 B3
Ciadîr-Lunga MD . .17 B8
Cianciana I 176 B2
Ciano d'Enza I 134 A3
Ciążen PL 76 B2
Cibakhaza H 113 C4
Ciborro P 154 C2
Cicagna I 134 A2
Cicciano I 170 C2
Ciciliano I 169 B2

Cicognolo I 120 B3
Cidadelhe P 149 B2
Cide TR 23 A7
Cidones E 143 C4
Ciechanów
  Dolnośląskie PL . .85 A4
  Mazowieckie PL . .77 B5
Ciechocinek PL 76 B3
Cieladz PL 87 A4
Ciemnik PL 75 A4
Ciempozuelos E . .151 B4
Ciepielów PL 87 A5
Cierny Balog SK . . .99 C3
Cierp-Gaud F 145 B4
Cierpice PL 76 B3
Ciervana E 143 A3
Cierznie PL 68 B2
Cieslé PL 77 B5
Cieszyn PL 98 B2
Cieutat F 145 A4
Cieza E 165 A3
Cifer SK 98 C1
Çifteler TR 187 C6
Cifuentes E 151 B5
Cigales E 142 C2
Cigliano I 119 B5
Cihanbeyli TR 23 B7
Cillas E 152 B2
Cilleros E 149 B3
Cilleruelo de Arriba
  E 143 C3
Cilleruelo de Bezana
  E 143 B3
Cimalmotto CH . . .119 A5
Cimanes del Tejar
  E 141 B5
Ciminna I 176 B2
Cimişlia MD 17 B8
Cimoláis I 122 A1
Cîmpulung RO 17 C6
Çinarcik TR 186 B4
Cinctorres E 153 B3
Cinderford GB 39 C4
Çine TR 188 B3
Cinéves CZ 84 B3
Ciney B 79 B5
Cinfães P 148 A1
Cingia de Botti I . . .120 B3
Cíngoli I 136 B2
Cinigiano I 135 C4
Cinobaňa SK 99 C3
Cinq-Mars-la-Pile
  F 102 B2
Cinquefrondi I 175 C2
Cintegabelle F 146 A2
Cintruénigo E 144 B2
Ciólkowo PL 77 B4
Ciperez E 149 B3
Cirat E 153 B3
Cirella I 174 B1
Cirencester GB 44 B2
Cirey-sur-Vezouze
  F 92 C2
Ciria E 152 A2
Ciriè I 119 B4
Cirigliano I 174 A2
Ciró I 174 B3
Ciró Marina I 174 B3
Ciry-le-Noble F . . .104 C3
Cislău RO 17 C7
Cismon del Grappa
  I 121 B4
Cisneros E 142 B2
Cissac-Médoc F . .128 A2
Cista CZ 96 A1
Cisterna di Latina
  I 169 B2
Cistérniga E 150 A3
Cisternino I 173 B3
Cistierna E 142 B1
Čitluk BIH 139 B3
Citov CZ 84 B2
Cittadella I 121 B4
Cittádel Pieve I . . .135 C5
Cittádel Vaticano =
  Vatican City I . . .168 B2
Cittádi Castello I . .135 B5
Cittaducale I 169 A2
Cittanova I 175 C2
Città Sant'Angelo
  I 169 A4
Cittareale I 169 A3
Cittá Sant'Angelo .136 B2
Civezzano I 121 A4
Cívita I 169 A3
Cívita Castellana I 168 A2
Civitanova Alta I . .136 B2
Civitanova Marche
  I 136 B2
Civitavécchia I 168 A1
Civitella di Romagna
  I 135 A4
Civitella di Tronto
  I 136 C2
Civitella Roveto I . .169 B3
Civray F 115 B4
Çivril TR 189 A4
Cizur Mayor E 144 B2
Clabhach GB 34 B1
Clachan GB 31 B2
Clachan na Luib
  GB 31 B1
Clacton-on-Sea GB .45 B5
Cladich GB 34 B2
Claggan GB 34 B2
Clairvaux-les-Lacs
  F 105 C4
Clamecy F 104 B2
Claonaig GB 34 C2
Clarecastle IRL 28 B3
Claregalway IRL . . .28 A3
Claremorris IRL 28 A2
Clarinbridge IRL . . .28 A3
Clashmore
  GB 32 D2
  IRL 29 B4

Claudy GB 27 B3
Clausthal-Zellerfeld
  D 82 A2
Cláut I 122 A1
Clay Cross GB 40 B2
Claye-Souilly F 90 C2
Cléder F 100 A1
Cleethorpes GB . . .41 B3
Clefmont F 105 A4
Cléguérec F 100 A2
Clelles F 118 C2
Clenze D 73 B3
Cleobury Mortimer
  GB 39 B4
Cléon-d'Andran F 117 C4
Cléré-les-Pins F . .102 B2
Clères F 89 A5
Clermont F 90 B2
Clermont-en-Argonne
  F 91 B5
Clermont-Ferrand
  F 116 B3
Clermont-l'Hérault
  F 130 B2
Clerval F 105 B5
Clervaux L 92 A2
Cléry-St André F . .103 B3
Cles I 121 A4
Clevedon GB 43 A4
Cleveleys GB 38 A3
Cley GB 41 C5
Clifden IRL 28 A1
Clifford GB 39 B3
Clisson F 101 B4
Clitheroe GB 40 B1
Clogh IRL 30 B1
Cloghan
  Donegal IRL 26 B3
  Offaly IRL 28 A4
Clogheen IRL 29 B4
Clogher GB 27 B3
Cloghjordan IRL . . .28 B3
Clohars-Carnoët
  F 100 B2
Clonakilty IRL 29 C3
Clonaslee IRL 30 A1
Clondalkin IRL 30 A2
Clones IRL 27 B3
Clonmany IRL 27 A4
Clonmel IRL 29 B4
Clonmellon IRL 30 A1
Clonord IRL 30 A1
Clonroche IRL 30 B2
Cloone IRL 26 C3
Cloppenburg D 71 B5
Closeburn GB 36 A3
Clough GB 27 B5
Clova GB 35 B4
Clovelly GB 42 B2
Clowne GB 40 B2
Cloyes-sur-le-Loir
  F 103 B3
Cloyne IRL 29 C3
Cluis F 103 C3
Cluj-Napoca RO . . .17 B5
Clun GB 39 B3
Clunes GB 34 B3
Cluny F 117 A4
Cluses F 118 A3
Clusone I 120 B2
Clydach GB 39 C3
Clydebank GB 34 C3
Coachford IRL 29 C3
Coagh GB 27 B4
Coalisland GB 27 B4
Coalville GB 40 C2
Coaña E 141 A4
Cobas E 140 A2
Cóbdar E 164 B2
Cobertelade E 151 A5
Cobeta E 152 B1
Cóbh IRL 29 C3
Cobreces E 142 A2
Coburg D 82 B2
Coca E 150 A3
Cocentaina E 159 C3
Cochem D 80 B3
Cockburnspath GB 35 C5
Cockermouth GB . .36 B3
Codigoro I 121 C5
Codogno I 120 B2
Codos E 152 A2
Codróipo I 122 B1
Codrongianos I . . .178 B2
Coelhoso P 149 A3
Coesfeld D 71 C4
Coevorden NL 71 B3
Cofrentes E 159 B2
Cogeces del Monte
  E 150 A3
Coggeshall GB 45 B4
Cognac F 115 C3
Cogne I 119 B4
Cognin F 118 B2
Cogolin F 132 B2
Cogollos de Guadix
  E 164 B1
Cogollos-Vega E . .163 A4
Cogolludo E 151 B4
Coimbra P 148 B1
Coín E 163 B3
Coirós E 140 A2
Čoka SRB 126 B2
Col SLO 123 B3
Colares P 154 C1
Cölbe D 81 B4
Colbitz D 73 B4
Colchester GB 45 B4
Coldingham GB 35 C5
Colditz D 83 A4
Coldstream GB 35 C5
Colebrooke GB 43 B3
Colera E 146 B4
Coleraine GB 27 A4
Colfiorito I 136 B1
Cólico I 120 A2
Coligny F 118 A2

Colindres E 143 A3
Collado-Mediano
  E 151 B3
Collado Villalba E .151 B4
Collagna I 134 A3
Collanzo E 142 A1
Collat F 117 B3
Coll de Nargó E . . .147 B2
Collécchio I 120 C3
Colledimezzo I 169 B4
Colle di Val d'Elsa
  I 135 B4
Colleferro I 169 B3
Colle Isarco I 108 C2
Collelongo I 169 B3
Collepasso I 173 B4
Collepepe I 136 C1
Collesalvetti I 134 B3
Colle Sannita I 170 B2
Collesano I 176 B2
Colli a Volturno I . .169 B4
Collin GB 36 A3
Collinée F 101 A3
Collingham
  Nottinghamshire
    GB. 40 B2
  West Yorkshire
    GB. 40 B3
Collinghorst D. 71 A4
Cóllio I 120 B3
Collobrières F 132 B2
Collon IRL 27 C4
Collooney IRL 26 B2
Colmar F 106 A2
Colmars F 132 A2
Colmenar E 163 B3
Colmenar de la Sierra
  E 151 A4
Colmenar de Oreja
  E 151 B4
Colmenar Viejo E .151 B4
Colmonel GB. 36 A2
Colne GB 40 B1
Colobraro I 174 A2
Cologna Véneta I . .121 B4
Cologne = Köln D . .80 B2
Cologne F 129 C3
Cologne al Serio I .120 B2
Colombey-les-Belles
  F. 92 C1
Colombey-les-deux-
  Églises F 105 A3
Colombres E 142 A2
Colomera E 163 A4
Colomers E 147 B3
Colomiers F 129 C4
Colònia de Sant Jordi
  E 167 B3
Colorno I 120 C3
Colos P 160 B1
Cölpin D. 74 A2
Colpy GB 33 D4
Colsterworth GB. . .40 C3
Coltishall GB 41 C5
Colunga E 142 A1
Colwell GB. 37 A4
Colwyn Bay GB 38 A3
Colyford GB. 43 B3
Comácchio I 121 C5
Coma-ruga E 147 C2
Combarros E 141 B4
Combeaufontaine
  F. 105 B4
Comber GB 27 B5
Comblain-au-Pont
  B 80 B1
Combloux F 118 B3
Combourg F 88 B2
Combronde F 116 B3
Comeglians I 109 C3
Comillas E 142 A2
Comines F 78 B3
Cómiso I 177 C3
Comloşu Mare RO .126 B2
Commensacq F . . .128 B2
Commentry F 116 A2
Commerau D 84 A2
Commercy F 92 C1
Como I 120 B2
Cómpeta E 163 B4
Compiègne F. 90 B2
Comporta P 154 C2
Comps-sur-Artuby
  F. 132 B2
Comrat MD 17 B8
Comrie GB 35 B4
Comunanza I 136 C2
Cona
  Emilia Romagna
    I. 121 C4
  Veneto I 121 B5
Concarneau F 100 B2
Conceição P 160 B1
Conches-en-Ouche
  F. 89 B4
Concordia Sagittária
  I 122 B1
Concordia sulla
  Sécchia I 121 C3
Concots F 129 B4
Condat F 116 B2
Condé-en-Brie F . .91 C3
Condeixa P 148 B1
Condemios de Abajo
  E 151 A4
Condemios de Arriba
  E 151 A4
Condé-sur-l'Escaut
  F. 79 B3
Conde-sur-Marne F 91 B4
Condé-sur-Noireau
  F. 88 B3
Condino I 121 B3
Condom F 129 C3
Condove I 119 B4
Condrieu F. 117 B4
Conegliano I 122 B1

Conflans-sur-Lanterne
  F. 105 B5
Confolens F. 115 B4
Conforto E 141 A3
Cong IRL 28 A2
Congleton GB 40 B1
Congosto E 141 B4
Congosto de Valdavia
  E 142 B2
Congostrina E. 151 A4
Conil de la Frontera
  E 162 B1
Coningsby GB. 41 B3
Coniston GB 36 B3
Conlie F 102 A1
Conliège F 105 C4
Conna IRL 29 B3
Connah's Quay GB 38 A3
Connantre F 91 C3
Connaugh IRL. 28 B3
Connaux F 131 A3
Connel GB 34 B2
Connerré F 102 A2
Cononbridge GB. . . .32 D2
Čonoplja SRB 126 B1
Conques F 116 C2
Conques-sur-Orbiel
  F. 146 A3
Conquista E 157 B3
Conquista de la Sierra
  E 156 A2
Consándolo I 121 C4
Consélice I 135 A4
Conselve I 121 B4
Consenvoye F. 91 B5
Consett GB 37 B5
Consolação P 154 B1
Constancia P. 154 B2
Constanța RO 17 C8
Constanti E. 147 C2
Constantina E 162 A2
Consuegra E 157 A4
Consuma I 135 B4
Contarina I 122 B1
Contay F 90 B2
Conthey CH 119 A4
Contigliano I 168 A2
Contis-Plage F 128 B1
Contres F 103 B3
Contrexéville F 105 A4
Controne I 172 B1
Contursi Termi I . . .172 B1
Conty F 90 B2
Conversano I 173 B3
Conwy GB 38 A3
Cookstown GB 27 B4
Coole F 91 C4
Coolgreany IRL 30 B2
Cooneen GB 27 B3
Cootehill IRL 27 B3
Cope E 165 B3
Copenhagen =
  København DK . . .61 D2
Copertino I 173 B4
Copparo I 121 C4
Coppenbrugge D . .72 B2
Corabia RO 17 D6
Córaci I 175 B2
Coralići BIH 124 C1
Corato I 171 B4
Coray F 100 A2
Corbeil-Essonnes
  F. 90 C2
Corbeny F 91 B3
Corbera E 159 B3
Corbie F 90 B2
Corbigny F 104 B2
Corbion B 91 B4
Corbridge GB 37 B4
Corby GB 40 C3
Corcieux E 143 A3
Corcubión E 140 B1
Corcumello I 169 A3
Cordenòns I. 122 B1
Cordes-sur-Ciel F .129 B4
Córdoba E. 156 C3
Cordobilla de Lácara
  E 155 B4
Cordovado I 122 B1
Corella E 144 B2
Coreses E 150 A2
Corfe Castle GB . . .43 B4
Corga de Lobão
  P 148 B1
Cori I 169 B2
Coria E 155 B4
Coria del Río E 162 A1
Corigliano Cálabro
  I 174 B2
Corinaldo I 136 B1
Corinth = Korinthos
  GR 184 B3
Cório I 119 B4
Coripe E 162 B2
Cork IRL 29 C3
Corlay F 100 A2
Corleone I 176 B2
Corleto Monforte I .172 B1
Corleto Perticara I .174 A2
Çorlu TR 186 A2
Cormainville F 103 A3
Cormatin F 104 C3
Cormeilles F 89 A4
Cormery F 102 B2
Cormòns I 122 B2
Cornago E 144 B1
Cornberg D 82 A1
Cornellana E 141 A4
Corníglio I 134 A3
Cornimont F 106 B1
Corniolo I 135 B4
Cornuda I 121 B5
Cornudella de
  Montsant E 147 C1
Cornudilla E 143 B3
Cornus F 130 B2
Çorovodë AL 182 C2

Corpach GB. 34 B2
Corps F 118 C2
Corps Nuds F 101 B4
Corral de Almaguer
  E 157 A4
Corral de Ayllon E .151 A4
Corral de Calatrava
  E 157 B3
Corrales E 149 A4
Corral-Rubio E 158 C2
Corran GB 34 B2
Corredoiras E 140 A2
Corréggio I 121 C3
Corrèze F 116 B1
Corridónia I 136 B2
Corris GB 38 B3
Corrubedo E 140 B1
Córsico I 120 B2
Corsock GB 36 A3
Corte F 180 A2
Corteconceptión
  E 161 B3
Corte de Peleas E 155 C4
Cortegaca P 148 B1
Cortegada E 140 B2
Cortegana E 161 B3
Cortemaggiore I . . .120 B2
Cortemília I 133 A4
Corte Pinto P 160 B2
Cortes E 144 C2
Cortes de Aragón
  E 153 B3
Cortes de Arenoso
  E 153 B3
Cortes de Baza E .164 B2
Cortes de la Frontera
  E 162 B2
Cortes de Pallás
  E 159 B3
Cortiçadas P 154 C2
Cortico P 148 A2
Cortijo de Arriba
  E 157 A3
Cortijos Nuevos E 164 A2
Cortina d'Ampezzo
  I 108 C3
Corton GB 41 C5
Cortona I 135 B4
Coruche P 154 C2
Corullón E 141 B4
Çorum TR 23 A8
Corvara in Badia I .108 C2
Corvera E 165 B3
Corwen GB 38 B3
Cosham GB 44 C2
Coslada E 151 B4
Cosne-Cours-sur-Loire
  F. 104 B1
Cosne d'Allier F . . .103 C4
Cospeito E 140 A3
Cossato I 119 B5
Cossaye F 104 C2
Cossé-le-Vivien F .101 B5
Cossonay CH 105 C5
Costa da Caparica
  P 154 C1
Costa de Santo André
  P 160 A1
Costalpino I 135 B4
Costa Nova P. 148 B1
Costaros F 117 C3
Costeşti RO 17 C6
Costigliole d'Asti
  I 119 C5
Costigliole Saluzzo
  I 133 A3
Coswig
  Sachsen D 83 A5
  Sachsen-Anhalt D .83 A4
Cotherstone GB . . .37 B5
Cotronei I 175 B2
Cottbus D 84 A2
Cottenham GB 45 A4
Cottingham GB 40 B3
Coublanc F 105 B4
Couches F 104 C3
Couço P 154 C2
Coucouron F 117 C3
Coucy-le-Château-
  Auffrique F 90 B3
Couëron F 101 B4
Couflens F 146 B2
Couhé F 115 B4
Couiza F 146 B3
Coulags GB. 31 B3
Coulanges F 104 C2
Coulanges-la-Vineuse
  F. 104 B2
Coulanges-sur-Yonne
  F. 104 B2
Couleuvre F 104 C1
Coulmier-le-Sec F 104 B3
Coulommiers F 90 C3
Coulonges-sur-l'Autize
  F. 114 B3
Coulounieix-Chamiers
  F. 129 A3
Coulport GB 34 B3
Coupar Angus GB. .35 B4
Coupéville F 91 C4
Couptrain F 89 B3
Coura P 140 C2
Courcelles B 79 B4
Courcelles-Chaussy
  F. 92 B2
Courchevel F 118 B3
Cour-Cheverny F .103 B3
Courçôme F 115 C4
Courçon F 114 B3
Cour-et-Buis F 117 B4
Courgenay CH 106 B2
Courmayeur I 119 B3
Cournon-d'Auvergne
  F. 116 B3
Cournonterral F . . .130 B2
Courpière F 117 B3
Coursan F 130 B2

Courseulles-sur-Mer
  F. 89 A3
Cours-la-Ville F 117 A4
Courson-les-Carrières
  F. 104 B2
Courtalain F 103 A3
Courtenay F 104 A2
Courtomer F 89 B4
Courville
  Eure-et-Loire F . .89 B5
  Marne F 91 B3
Coussac-Bonneval
  F. 115 C5
Coutances F 88 A2
Couterne F 89 B3
Coutras F. 128 A2
Couvet CH 106 C1
Couvin B 91 A4
Couzon F 104 C2
Covadonga E. 142 A1
Covaleda E 143 C4
Covarrubias E 143 B3
Covas P 148 A1
Cove GB. 31 B3
Coventry GB 44 A2
Coverack GB 42 B1
Covigliáio I 135 A4
Covilhã P 148 B2
Cowbridge GB 39 C3
Cowdenbeath GB . .35 B4
Cowes GB 44 C2
Cox F 129 C4
Cózar E 157 B4
Cozes F 114 C3
Cozzano F 180 B2
Craco I 174 A2
Cracow = Kraków
  PL 99 A3
Craibstone GB. 33 D4
Craighouse GB 34 C2
Craignure GB 34 B2
Crail GB 35 B5
Crailsheim D 94 B2
Craiova RO 17 C5
Cramlington GB . . .37 A5
Cranleigh GB. 44 B3
Craon F 101 B5
Craonne F 91 B3
Craponne F 117 B3
Craponne-sur-Arzon
  F. 117 B3
Crathie GB 32 D3
Crato P 155 B3
Craughwell IRL 28 A3
Craven Arms GB . .39 B4
Crawford GB 36 A3
Crawinkel D. 82 B2
Crawley GB 44 B3
Creag Ghoraidh
  GB 31 B1
Crecente E 140 B2
Crèches-sur-Saône
  F. 117 A4
Crécy-en-Ponthieu
  F. 78 B1
Crécy-la-Chapelle
  F. 90 C2
Crécy-sur-Serre F .91 B3
Crediton GB 43 B3
Creeslough IRL 26 A3
Creetown GB. 36 B2
Creeve GB 27 B4
Creglingen D 94 B2
Creil F 90 B2
Creissels F 130 A2
Crema I 120 B2
Cremeaux F 117 B3
Crémenes E 142 B1
Crémieu F 118 B2
Cremlingen D 73 B3
Cremona I 120 B3
Creney F 91 C4
Črenšovci SLO 111 C3
Créon F 128 B2
Crepaja SRB 127 B2
Crépey F 92 C1
Crépy F 91 B3
Crépy-en-Valois F .90 B2
Cres HR 123 C3
Crescentino I 119 B5
Crespino I 121 C4
Crespos E 150 B3
Cressage GB 39 B4
Cressensac F 129 A4
Cressia F 105 C4
Crest F 117 C5
Cresta CH 107 C4
Créteil F 90 C2
Creully F 88 A3
Creussen D. 95 B3
Creutzwald F 92 B2
Creuzburg D 82 A2
Crevalcore I 121 C4
Crèvecoeur-le-Grand
  F. 90 B2
Crevillente E 165 A4
Crévola d'Ossola
  I 119 A5
Crewe GB. 38 A4
Crewkerne GB. 43 B4
Criales E 143 B3
Crianlarich GB. 34 B3
Criccieth GB. 38 B2
Crickhowell GB 39 C3
Cricklade GB. 44 B2
Crieff GB 35 B4
Criel-sur-Mer F 90 A1
Crikvenica HR 123 B3
Crillon F 90 B1
Crimmitschau D . . .83 B4
Crimond GB. 33 D5
Crinitz D. 84 A1
Cripán E 143 B4
Criquetot-l'Esneval
  F. 89 A4
Crispiano I 173 B3
Crissolo I 119 C4
Cristóbal E. 149 B4
Crivitz D 73 A4
Črna SLO 110 C1

Crna Bara
  Srbija SRB 127 C1
  Vojvodina SRB. . .126 B2
Crnac HR 125 B3
Crnča SRB. 127 C1
Crni Lug
  BIH 138 A2
  HR 123 B3
Črni Vrh SLO 123 B3
Crnjelov Donje
  BIH. 125 C5
Črnomelj SLO 123 B4
Crocketford GB 36 A3
Crocq F 116 B2
Crodo I 119 A5
Croglin GB. 37 B4
Crolly IRL 26 A2
Cromarty GB 32 D2
Cromer GB 41 C5
Cronat F. 104 C2
Crookhaven IRL . . .29 C2
Crookstown IRL . . .29 C3
Croom IRL 29 B3
Cropalati I 174 B2
Crópani I 175 C2
Crosbost GB 31 A2
Crosby GB 38 A3
Crosía I 174 B2
Crossakiel IRL 27 C3
Cross-Hands GB . . .39 C2
Crosshaven IRL . . .29 C3
Crosshill GB 36 A2
Crossmolina IRL . . .26 B1
Crotone I 175 B3
Crottendorf D 83 B4
Crouy F 90 B3
Crowborough GB . .45 B4
Crowland GB 41 C3
Crowthorne GB 44 B3
Croyde GB 42 A2
Croydon GB 44 B3
Crozant F 116 A1
Crozon F 100 A1
Cruas F 117 C4
Cruceni RO 126 A3
Crúcoli I 174 B3
Cruden Bay GB 33 D5
Crudgington GB . . .38 B4
Cruis F 132 A1
Crumlin GB 27 B4
Cruseilles F 118 A3
Crusheen IRL. 28 B3
Cruz de Incio E . . .141 B3
Črvenka SRB 126 B1
Crveny Kamen SK. .98 B2
Csabacsüd H 113 C4
Csabrendek H 111 B4
Csákánydoroszló
  H 111 C3
Csanádapáca H . . .113 C4
Csanádpalota H . . .126 A2
Csány H 113 B3
Csanytelek H 113 C4
Csapod H 111 B3
Császár H 112 B2
Császártöltés H. . . .112 C3
Csávoly H 125 A5
Csemő H 113 B3
Csengöd H 112 C3
Csépa H. 113 C4
Cséphreg H 111 B3
Cserkeszölö H 113 C4
Csernely H. 113 A4
Csesztreg H 111 C3
Csökmö H 113 B5
Csököly H 124 A3
Csokonyavisonta
  H 124 A3
Csólyospálos H. . . .113 C3
Csongrád H 113 C4
Csopak H 112 C1
Csorna H. 111 B4
Csorvás H 113 C4
Csurgo H 124 A3

Cuacos de Yuste
  E 150 B2
Cualedro E. 140 C3
Cuanca de Campos
  E 142 B1
Cuba P 160 A2
Cubel E 152 A2
Cubelles E 147 C2
Cubillos E 143 B4
Cubillos del Sil E .141 B4
Cubjac F 129 A3
Cubo de la Solana
  E 152 A1
Çubuk TR. 23 A7
Cuckfield GB. 44 B3
Cucuron F 131 B4
Cudillero E. 141 A4
Cuéllar E 151 A3
Cuenca E 152 B1
Cuers F 132 B2
Cuerva E 157 A3
Cueva de Agreda
  E 144 C2
Cuevas Bajas E. . .163 A3
Cuevas del Almanzora
  E 164 B3
Cuevas del Becerro
  E 162 B2
Cuevas del Campo
  E 164 B2
Cuevas del Valle
  E 150 B3
Cuevas de San
  Clemente E 143 B3
Cuevas de San Marcos
  E 163 A3
Cuges-les-Pins F .132 B1
Cúglieri I 178 B2
Cugnaux F 129 C4
Cuijk NL 80 A1
Cuinzier F 117 A4
Cuiseaux F 105 C4
Cuisery F 105 C4
Culan F 103 C4
Culemborg NL 79 A5

Dağ TR 189 B5
Daaden D 81 B3
Dabas H 112 B3
Dąbie PL 76 B3
Dąbki PL. 67 B5
Dabo F 92 C3
Dabrowa PL 76 B2
Dąbrowa Górnicza
  PL. 86 B3
Dąbrowa Tarnowska
  PL. 87 B4
Dąbrowice PL 77 B4
Dabrowno PL 77 A5
Dachau D 108 A2
Dačice CZ 97 B3
Daday TR 23 A7
Dagali N. 47 B5
Dägebüll D 64 B1
Dagmersellen CH .106 B2
Dahlen D 83 A4
Dahlenburg D 73 A3
Dahme D 83 A5
Dahn D 93 B3
Dähre D 73 B3
Daikanvik S 195 E7
Dail bho Dheas GB .31 A2
Dailly GB 36 A2
Daimiel E 157 A4
Daingean IRL 30 A1
Đakovica KOS 16 D4
Đakovo HR 125 B4
Dal
  Akershus N 48 B3
  Telemark N 47 C5
Dalaas A. 107 B5
Dalabrog GB 31 B1
Dala-Floda S 50 B1
Dala-Husby S 50 B2
Dala-Järna S 50 B1
Dalaman TR 188 C3
Dalarö S 57 A4
Dalbeattie GB 36 B3

Dalby
  DK . . . . .59 C
  Skåne S . . . . .61 D
  Uppsala S . . . . . . .57 A
  Värmland S . . . . . .49 B
Dale
  Pembrokeshire
    GB. . . . . .39 C
  Shetland GB . . . .33 A
  Hordaland N . . . . .46 B
  Sogn og Fjordane
    N . . . . .46 A
Dalen
  Akershus N . . . . .48 C
  Telemark N . . . . .53 A
Daleszyce PL. . . . . .87 B
Dalhalvaig GB . . . . .32 C
Dalheim L. . . . . .92 B
Dalhem S . . . . .57 C
Dalias E . . . . .164 C
Dalj HR . . . . .125 B
Dalkeith GB . . . . . . .35 C
Dalkey IRL . . . . . . .30 A
Dalmally GB . . . . . . .34 B
Dalmellington GB . .36 A
Dalmose DK. . . . . . .65 A
Daløy N . . . . .46 A
Dalry
  Dumfries & Galloway
    GB. . . . . .36 A
  North Ayrshire GB 36 A
Dalrymple GB . . . . .36 A
Dalseter N . . . . .47 A
Dalsjöfors S. . . . . . .60 B
Dalskog S . . . . .54 B
Dals Långed S . . . .54 B
Dals Rostock S . . . .54 B
Dalston GB . . . . . . .36 B
Dalstorp S . . . . .60 B
Dalton-in-Furness
  GB . . . . .36 B
Daluis F . . . . .132 A
Dalum
  D . . . . .71 B
  S . . . . .60 B
Dalvík IS. . . . . .191 B
Dalwhinnie GB . . . .32 E
Dalyan TR . . . . .188 C
Damasi GR . . . . . . .182 D
Damasławek PL . . .76 B
Damazan F . . . . . . .129 B
Damgan F . . . . .101 B
Dammarie-les-Lys
  F. . . . . .90 C
Dammartin-en-Goële
  F. . . . . .90 B
Damme D . . . . .71 B
Damnica PL . . . . . . .68 A
Dampierre F. . . . . . .105 B
Dampierre-sur-Salon
  F. . . . . .105 B
Damüls A . . . . .107 B
Damville F . . . . .89 B
Damvillers F . . . . . .92 B
Damwoude NL. . . . .70 A
Danasjö S . . . . .195 E
Danbury GB. . . . . . .45 B
Dångebo S. . . . . . . .63 B
Dangers F . . . . .89 B
Dangé-St Romain
  F. . . . . .102 C
Dangeul F . . . . .89 B
Danilovgrad MNE . .16 D
Danischenhagen D 64 B
Daniszyn PL. . . . . . .85 A
Danjoutin F . . . . . . .106 B
Dannas S . . . . .60 B
Dannemare DK . . . .65 B
Dannemora S . . . . .51 B
Dannenberg D . . . .73 A
Dánszentmiklós
  H . . . . .112 B
Dány H . . . . .112 B
Daoulas F . . . . .100 A
Darabani RO . . . . . .17 A
Darány H . . . . .125 B
Darda HR . . . . .125 B
Dardesheim D . . . . .73 C
Darfeld D . . . . .71 B
Darfo I . . . . .120 B
Dargin PL. . . . . .68 A
Dargun D . . . . .66 C
Darlington GB . . . . .37 B
Darłowo PL . . . . . . .68 A
Darmstadt D . . . . . .93 B
Darney F . . . . .105 A
Daroca E . . . . .152 A
Darque P . . . . .148 A
Darragh IRL . . . . . .28 B
Dartford GB. . . . . . .45 B
Dartington GB . . . . .43 B
Dartmouth GB . . . . .43 B
Darton GB . . . . .40 B
Daruvar HR . . . . . . .124 B
Darvas H . . . . .113 B
Darvel GB . . . . .36 A
Darwen GB . . . . . . .38 A
Dassel D . . . . .82 A
Dassow D . . . . .65 C
Datça TR . . . . .188 C
Datteln D . . . . .80 A
Dattenfeld D . . . . . .81 B
Daugard DK. . . . . . .59 C
Daugavpils LV . . . . .8 E
Daumeray F . . . . . .102 B
Daun D . . . . .80 B
Daventry GB . . . . . .44 A
Davle CZ . . . . .96 B
Davor HR . . . . .124 B
Davos CH. . . . . . . .107 C
Davutlar TR . . . . . .188 B
Davyd Haradok BY .13 B
Dawlish GB . . . . . . .43 B
Dax F . . . . .128 C
Dazkırı TR . . . . . . .189 B
Deal GB . . . . .45 B
Deauville F. . . . . . . .89 A
Deba E . . . . .143 A
Debar MK . . . . .182 B
Dębe PL . . . . .77 B

Dębica PL 87 B5
Dębnica Kaszubska
PL. 68 A2
Dębno PL 74 B3
Dębołęka PL 86 A2
Dębowa Łąka PL . .69 B4
Debrc SRB 127 C1
Debrecen H 113 B5
Debrznica PL 75 B4
Debrzno PL 68 B2
Debstedt D 72 A1
Decazeville F 130 A1
Dechtice SK. 98 C1
Decima I 168 B2
Decimomannu I . .179 C2
Děčín CZ. 84 B2
Decize F 104 C2
De Cocksdorp NL . .70 A1
Decollatura I 175 B2
Decs H 125 A4
Deddington GB 44 B2
Dedeler TR. 187 B5
Dedelow D 74 A2
Dedemli TR 189 B7
Dedemsvaart NL . .71 B3
Dedestapolcsány
H 113 A4
Dedovichi RUS 9 D6
Deeping St Nicholas
GB. 41 C4
Deftera CY 181 A2
Dég H 112 C2
Degaña E 141 B4
Degeberga S 61 D4
Degerby FIN 51 B7
Degerfors S 55 A5
Degerhamn S 63 B4
Degernes N 54 A2
Deggendorf D 95 C4
Deggingen D 94 C1
Dego I 133 A4
Degolados P 155 B3
De Haan B 78 A3
Dehesas de Guadix
E 164 B1
Dehesas Viejas E .163 A4
Deia E. 166 B2
Deining D 95 B3
Deinze B 79 B3
Deiva Marina I . . .134 A2
Dej RO 17 B5
Deje S. 55 A4
De Koog NL 70 A1
Delabole GB 42 B2
Delary S 61 C3
Delbrück D 81 A4
Delčevo MK 182 B4
Delden NL 71 B3
Deleitosa E 156 A2
Delekovec HR . . .124 A2
Delémont CH 106 B2
Delft NL 70 B1
Delfzijl NL 71 A3
Délia I 176 B2
Delianuova I 175 C1
Deliblato SRB 127 C3
Delice TR 23 B7
Deliceto I 171 B3
Dellach A 109 C4
Delle F 106 B2
Delme F 92 C2
Delmenhorst D . . .72 A1
Delnice HR. 123 B3
Delsbo S 200 E2
Delvin IRL 30 A1
Delvinë AL 182 D2
Demandice SK. . . .112 A2
Demen D 73 A4
Demidov RUS 13 A9
Demigny F 105 C3
Demirci TR. 186 C3
Demirköy TR 186 A2
Demirtaş TR. 186 B4
Demmin D 66 C2
Demonte I 133 A3
Demyansk RUS 9 D8
Denain F 78 B3
Denbigh GB. 38 A3
Den Burg NL 70 A1
Den Ham NL. 71 B3
Den Helder NL 70 B1
Denholm GB 35 C5
Denia E 159 C4
Denizli TR 188 B4
Denkendorf D 95 C3
Denklingen D. 81 B3
Denny GB 35 B4
Den Oever NL 70 B2
Denta RO 126 B3
Déols F 103 C3
De Panne B 78 A2
Denby GB. 40 C2
Derby GB 40 B2
Derecske H 113 B5
Dereköy TR 186 A2
Derenberg D 82 A2
Derinkuyu TR 23 B8
Dermbach D 82 B2
Dermulo I 121 A4
Deronje SRB 125 B5
Derrygonnelly GB .26 B3
Derrylin GB 27 B3
Derry/Londonderry
GB 27 B3
Dersingham GB. . .41 C4
Deruta I 136 C1
Dervaig GB 34 B1
Derval F 101 B4
Derveni GR 184 A3
Derventa BIH 125 C3
Dervock GB. 27 A4
Desana I 119 B5
Descartes F 102 C2
Desenzano del Garda
I. 121 B3
Deset N 48 A3
Deševa BIH 139 B4

Desfina GR 184 A3
Desimirovac SRB .127 C2
Désio I 120 B2
Deskati GR 182 D3
Deskle SLO 122 A2
Desná CZ. 84 B3
Dešov CZ 97 C3
Despotovac SRB .127 C3
Despotovo SRB. .126 B1
Dessau D 83 A4
Deštná CZ 96 B2
Destriana E 141 B4
Désulo I 179 B3
Desvres F 78 B1
Deszk H 126 A2
Deta RO 126 B3
Detmold D 72 C1
Dětřichov CZ 98 B1
Dettelbach D 94 B2
Dettingen
Baden-Württemberg
D 94 C1
Baden-Württemberg
D 107 B4
Dettwiller F 93 C3
Detva SK 99 C3
Deurne NL 80 A1
Deutschkreutz A .111 B3
Deutschlandsberg
A 110 C2
Deutsch Wagram
A 111 A3
Deva RO. 16 C5
Dévaványa H 113 B4
Devecikonağı TR .186 C3
Devecser H 111 B4
Develi TR. 23 B8
Deventer NL 70 B3
Devil's Bridge GB .39 B3
Devin BG 183 B6
Devinska Nova Ves
SK 111 A3
Devizes GB 43 A5
Devonport GB 42 B2
Devrek TR 187 A6
Devrekâni TR. 23 A7
Đevrske HR 137 B4
De Wijk NL 71 B3
Dewsbury GB 40 B2
Deza E 152 A1
Dežanovac HR. . .124 B3
Dezzo I 120 B3
Dhali CY 181 A2
Dherinia CY 181 A2
Diamante I 174 B1
Diano d'Alba I . . .119 C5
Diano Marina I . . .133 B4
Dicomano I 135 B4
Didcot GB 44 B2
Didim TR 188 B2
Didimoticho GR . .186 A1
Die F 118 C2
Diebling F 92 B2
Dieburg D 93 B4
Diego del Carpio
E 150 B2
Diekirch L. 92 B2
Diélette F 88 A2
Diemelstadt D 81 A5
Diémoz F 118 B2
Dienten am Hochkönig
A 109 B3
Diepenbeek B 79 B5
Diepholz D 71 B5
Dieppe F 89 A5
Dierberg D 74 A1
Dierdorf D 81 B3
Dieren NL 70 B3
Dierhagen D 66 B1
Diesdorf D 73 B3
Diessen D 108 B2
Diest B 79 B5
Dietenheim D. 94 C2
Dietfurt D 95 B3
Dietikon CH. 106 B3
Dietzenbach D. . . .93 A4
Dieue-sur-Meuse F .92 B1
Dieulefit F 131 A4
Dieulouard F 92 C2
Dieuze F 92 C2
Diever NL 71 B3
Diez D. 81 B4
Diezma E 163 A4
Differdange F 92 B1
Digermulen N 194 B6
Dignac F 115 C4
Dignano I 122 A1
Digne-les-Bains F 132 A2
Digny F 89 B5
Digoin F 104 C2
Dijon F 105 B4
Dikanäs S 195 E7
Dikili TR 186 C1
Diksmuide B 78 A2
Dilar E 163 A4
Dillenburg D 81 B4
Dillingen
Bayern D 94 C2
Saarland D 92 B2
Dilsen B 80 A1
Dimaro I 121 A3
Dimitrovgrad BG .183 A7
Dimitsana GR 184 B3
Dinami I 175 C2
Dinan F 101 A3
Dinant B 79 B4
Dinar TR 189 A5
Dinard F 101 A3
Dinek TR. 187 C6
Dingelstädt D 82 A2
Dingle
IRL 29 B1
S 54 B2
Dingolfing D 95 C4
Dingtuna S. 56 A2
Dingwall GB. 32 D2
Dinkelsbühl D 94 B2
Dinkelscherben D. .94 C2

Dinklage D 71 B5
Dinslaken D. 80 A2
Dinxperlo NL. 80 A2
Diö S 63 B2
Diou F 104 C2
Dippen GB 34 C2
Dipperz D. 82 B1
Dippoldiswalde D .84 B1
Dirdal N 52 B2
Dirksland NL 79 A4
Dirlewang D 108 B1
Dischingen D. 94 C2
Disentis CH 107 C3
Diso I 173 B4
Diss GB 45 A5
Dissen D 71 B5
Distington GB 36 B3
Ditzingen D 93 C5
Ditzum D 71 A4
Divača SLO 122 B2
Dives-sur-Mer F . .89 A3
Divín SK 99 C3
Divin BG 183 B6
Divion F 78 B2
Divišov CZ. 96 B2
Divonne les Bains
F 118 A3
Dixmont F 104 A2
Dizy-le-Gros F. . . .91 B4
Djúpivogur IS . . .191 C11
Djupvasshytta N .198 C4
Djura S 50 B1
Djurås S 50 B2
Djurmo S 50 B2
Djursdala S 62 A3
Dlouhá Loucka CZ .98 B1
Długowola PL 87 A5
Dmitrov RUS 9 D10
Dno RUS 9 D6
Doade E 141 B3
Doğanhisar TR . .189 A6
Dobanovci SRB. .127 C2
Dobbertin D 73 A5
Dobbiaco I 108 C3
Dobczyce PL 99 B4
Dobele LV. 8 D3
Döbeln D 83 A5
Doberlug-Kirchhain
D 83 A5
Dobern D 84 A2
Dobersberg A 97 C3
Dobiegniew PL . . .75 B4
Dobieszyn PL 87 A5
Doboj BIH 125 C4
Dobošnica BIH . .125 C4
Dobra
Wielkopolskie PL . 76 C3
Zachodnio-Pomorskie
PL 74 A3
Zachodnio-Pomorskie
PL 75 A4
Dobrá Niva SK. . . .99 C3
Dobřany CZ. 96 B1
Dobre PL 76 B3
Dobre Miasto PL . .69 B5
Dobreta-Turnu-Severin
RO 16 C5
Dobri H 111 C3
Dobrica SRB 126 B2
Dobrich BG 17 D7
Dobrinishte BG . .183 B5
Dobříš CZ. 96 B2
Dobro E 143 B3
Dobrodzień PL. . . .86 B2
Döbrököz H 112 C2
Dobromierz PL. . . .85 B4
Dobrosołowo PL. .76 B3
Dobroszyce PL. . . .85 A5
Dobrovnik SLO . .111 C3
Dobruška CZ. 85 B4
Dobrzany PL 75 A4
Dobrzen Wielki PL. .86 B1
Dobrzyca
Wielkopolskie PL. .85 A5
Wielkopolskie PL. .85 A5
Zachodnio-Pomorskie
PL 67 B4
Dobrzyńnad Wisłą
PL 77 B4
Dobšiná SK. 99 C4
Dobwalls GB 42 B2
Dochamps B 80 B1
Docking GB 41 C4
Docksta S 200 C4
Doddington GB . . .37 A4
Döderhult S 62 A4
Doesburg NL 70 B3
Doetinchem NL . . .71 C3
Dogliani I 133 A3
Dogueno P 160 B2
Doische B 91 A4
Dois Portos P 154 B1
Dojč SK 98 C1
Dokka N 48 B2
Dokkedal DK 58 B3
Dokkum NL 70 A2
Dokleževje SLO . .111 C3
Doksy CZ. 84 B2
Dokuz TR 189 A7
Dol-de-Bretagne F .88 B2
Dole F 105 B4
Dølemo N 53 B4
Dolenjske Toplice
SLO 123 B4
Dolenji vas SLO . .123 B3
Dolfor GB 39 B3
Dolgarrog GB 38 A3
Dolgellau GB 38 B3
Doliana GR 182 D2
Dolianova I 179 C3
Dolice PL 75 A4
Doljani HR 138 A2
Döllach im Mölltal
A 109 C3

Dolle D 73 B4
Dollnstein D 94 C3
Dollot F 104 A2
Döllstädt D 82 A2
Dolná Strehová
SK 99 C3
Dolné Saliby SK . .111 A4
Dolné Beňšov CZ. .98 B2
Dolni Bousov CZ. .84 B3
Dolni Kounice CZ. .97 B4
Dolni Kralovice CZ.97 B3
Dolni Újezd CZ . . .97 B4
Dolni Žandov CZ. .95 A4
Dolný Kubín SK. . .99 B3
Dolo I 121 B5
Dolores E 165 A4
Dolovo SRB 127 C2
Dölsach A. 109 C3
Dolsk PL 76 B2
Dolwyddelan GB. .38 A3
Domanic TR 187 C4
Domaniža SK. 98 B2
Domaszék H 126 A1
Domaszków PL. . . .85 B4
Domaszowice PL. .86 A1
Domat-Ems CH . .107 C4
Domažlice CZ. 95 B4
Dombås N 198 C6
Dombasle-sur-Meurthe
F 92 C2
Dombegyház H . . .126 A3
Dombóvár H 112 C2
Domène F 118 B2
Domérat F 116 A2
Domfessel F 92 C3
Domfront F. 88 B3
Domfront-en-
Champagne F . . .102 A2
Domingão P. 154 B2
Domingo Pérez
Granada E. 163 A4
Toledo E 150 C3
Dömitz D 73 A4
Dommartin-le-Franc
F 91 C4
Domme F 129 B4
Dommitzsch D. . . .83 A4
Domodóssola I . . .119 A5
Domokos GR. . . .182 D4
Domoszló H 113 B4
Dompaire F 105 A5
Dompierre-du-Chemin
F 88 B2
Dompierre-sur-Besbre
F 104 C2
Dompierre-sur-Mer
F 114 B2
Domrémy-la-Pucelle
F 92 C1
Dömsöd H 112 B3
Domsure F 118 A2
Dómus de Maria I .179 D2
Domusnóvas I . . .179 C2
Domvena GR. . . .184 A3
Domžale SLO. . . .123 A3
Donado E. 141 B4
Donaghadee GB . .27 B5
Don Alvaro E 155 C4
Doña Mencía E . .163 A3
Donaueschingen
D 106 B3
Donauwörth D 94 C2
Don Benito E 156 B2
Doncaster GB 40 B2
Donegal IRL 26 B2
Donestebe-
Santesteban E . .144 A2
Donges F 101 B3
Dongo I 120 A2
Donington GB 41 C3
Doniños E 140 A2
Donja Bebrina HR .125 B4
Donja Brela HR . .138 B2
Donja Dubica BIH .125 B4
Donja Dubrava
HR 124 A2
Donja Kupčina
HR 123 B4
Donja Šatornja
SRB 127 C2
Donja Stubica HR .124 B1
Donje Brišnik BIH .138 B3
Donje Stative HR. .123 B4
Donji-Andrijevci
HR 125 B4
Donji Kazanci BIH 138 B2
Donji Koričáni
BIH 138 A3
Donji Lapac HR . .124 C1
Donji Malovan
BIH 138 B3
Donji Miholjac HR .124 B3
Donji Mosti HR . . .124 A2
Donji Poloj HR . . .123 B4
Donji-Rujani BIH . .138 B2
Donji Svilaj BIH . .125 B4
Donji Tovarnik
SRB 127 C1
Donji Vakuf BIH . .138 A3
Donnalucata I 177 C3
Donnemarie-Dontilly
F 90 C3
Donnersbach A . .110 B1
Donnersbachwald
A 109 B5
Donnerskirchen A .111 B3
Donorático I 134 B3
Donostia-San
Sebastián E 144 A2
Donovaly SK 99 C3
Donzac F 129 A4
Donzère F 131 A3
Donzy F 104 B2
Doonbeg IRL 29 B2
Doorn NL 70 B2

Dor E 140 A1
Dørdal N. 53 B5
Dorchester GB 43 B4
Dörenthe D 71 B4
Dores GB 32 D2
Dorfen D 95 C4
Dorfgastein A 109 B4
Dorfmark D 72 B2
Dorf Mecklenburg
D 65 C4
Dorgali I 178 B3
Dorking GB 44 B3
Dormagen D 80 A2
Dormánd H 113 B4
Dormans F 91 B3
Dornava SLO 124 A1
Dornbirn A. 107 B4
Dornburg D. 83 A3
Dorndorf D 82 B2
Dornecy F 104 B2
Dornes F 104 C2
Dornhan D 93 C4
Dornie GB. 31 B3
Dornoch GB. 32 D2
Dornum D 71 A4
Dorog H 112 B2
Dorohoi RO 17 B7
Dorotea S. 200 B2
Dorotowo PL 69 B5
Dörpen D 71 B4
Dorsten D 80 A2
Dortan F 118 A2
Dortmund D. 80 A3
Doruchów PL. 86 A2
Dorum D 64 C1
Dörverden D 72 B2
Dörzbach D 94 B1
Dos Aguas E 159 B3
Dosbarrios E 151 C4
Dos Hermanas E. .162 A2
Dospat BG 183 B6
Dos-Torres E 156 B3
Dötlingen D 72 B1
Dottignies B. 78 B3
Döttingen CH. . . .106 B3
Douai F 78 B3
Douarnenez F . . .100 A1
Douchy F 104 B2
Douchy-les-Mines
F 78 B3
Doucier F 105 C4
Doudeville F 89 A4
Doué-la-Fontaine
F 102 B1
Douglas
Isle of Man GB. . .36 B2
South Lanarkshire
GB. 36 A3
Doulaincourt-Saucourt
F 91 C5
Doulevant-le-Château
F 91 C4
Doullens F 90 A2
Dounby GB. 33 B3
Doune GB. 35 B3
Dounreay GB. 32 C3
Dour B 79 B3
Dourdan F 90 C2
Dourgne F 146 A3
Dournazac F 115 C4
Douro Calvo P . . .148 B2
Douvaine F 118 A3
Douvres-la-Délivrande
F 89 A3
Douzy F 91 B5
Dover GB 45 B5
Dovje SLO 109 C4
Dovre N 198 D6
Doxato GR. 183 B6
Doyet F 116 A2
Dozule F 89 A3
Drača SRB 127 C2
Dračevo
BIH 139 C4
MK 182 B3
Drachten NL 70 A3
Draga SLO 123 B3
Drăgăşani RO 17 C6
Dragatuš SLO . . .123 B4
Dragichyn BY 13 B6
Draginja SRB. . . .127 C1
Dragocvet SRB . .127 C3
Dragolovci BIH . .125 C3
Dragoni I 170 B2
Dragør DK 61 D2
Dragotina HR. . . .124 B2
Dragotinja BIH . . .124 B2
Dragozetići HR . .123 B3
Draguignan F. . . .132 B2
Drahnsdorf D. 74 C2
Drahonice CZ 96 B2
Drahovce SK. 98 C1
Drama GR 183 B6
Drammen N 54 A1
Drangedal N 53 A5
Drangsnes IS 190 B4
Dransfeld D 82 A1
Dranske D 66 B2
Draperstown GB. .27 B4
Drassburg A 111 B3
Dravaszabolcs H. .125 B4
Dravograd SLO . .110 C2
Drawno PL. 75 A4
Drawsko Pomorskie
PL 75 A4
Drayton GB 41 C5
Drążdżewo PL 77 A6
Draženov CZ 95 B4
Draževac SRB . . .127 C2
Dražice HR. 123 B3
Drebkau D 84 A2
Dreieich D. 93 A4
Dreisen D 93 B4

Drenovci HR 125 C4
Drensteinfurt D . . .81 A3
Dresden D 84 A1
Dretyń PL. 68 A1
Dřevohostice CZ. .98 B1
Drevsjø N. 199 D9
Drewitz D 73 B5
Drezdenko PL 75 B4
Drežnica HR 123 B4
Drežnik-Grad HR. .123 C4
Drietona SK. 98 C1
Driffield GB 40 A3
Drimnin GB 34 B2
Drimoleague IRL . .29 C2
Dringenberg D. . . .81 A5
Drinić BIH 138 A2
Drinjača BIH 139 A5
Drinovci BIH 138 B3
Driopida GR. 185 B5
Drivstua N 198 C6
Drlače SRB 127 C1
Drnholec CZ 97 C4
Drniš HR 138 B2
Drnje HR 124 A2
Drnovice CZ. 97 B4
Dro I 121 B3
Drøbak N 54 A1
Drobin PL. 77 B5
Drochia MD 17 A7
Drochtersen D 64 C2
Drogheda IRL 30 A2
Drohobych UA. . . .13 D5
Droitwich Spa GB .44 A1
Droltowice PL. 85 A5
Dromahair IRL. . . .26 B2
Dromcolliher IRL. .29 B3
Dromore
Down GB. 27 B4
Tyrone GB 27 B3
Dromore West IRL .26 B2
Dronero I 133 A3
Dronfield GB 40 B2
Drongan GB. 36 A2
Dronninglund DK . .58 A3
Dronrijp NL 70 A2
Dronten NL 70 B2
Drosendorf A. 97 C3
Drösing A 97 C4
Drottningholm S . .57 A3
Droué F 103 A3
Drulingen F 92 C3
Drumbeg GB 32 C1
Drumcliff IRL 26 B2
Drumgask GB 32 D2
Drumkeeran IRL . .26 B2
Drummore GB 36 B2
Drumnadrochit GB .32 D2
Drumquin GB 27 B3
Drumshanbo IRL. .26 B2
Drumsna IRL. 26 C2
Drunen NL 79 A5
Druskininkai LT . . .13 A5
Druten NL. 80 A1
Druya BY 9 A7
Družetići SRB . . .127 C2
Drvar BIH 138 A2
Drvenik HR 138 B3
Drwalew PL 77 C6
Drymen GB 34 B3
Drynoch GB. 31 B2
Drzewce PL 76 B2
Drzewiany PL. 68 B1
Drzewica PL. 87 A4
Dualchi I. 178 B2
Duas Igrejas P . .149 A3
Dub SRB 127 C1
Dubá CZ. 84 B2
Dubăsari MD 17 B8
Duben D 74 C2
Dübendorf CH . . .107 B3
Dubi CZ. 84 B1
Dubica HR 124 B2
Dublin IRL 30 A2
Dubna RUS 9 D10
Dubňany CZ 98 C1
Dubnica nad Váhom
SK 98 C2
Dubnik SK 112 B2
Dubno UA. 13 C6
Dubodiel SK 98 C2
Dubona SRB. 127 C3
Dubovac SRB . . .127 C3
Dubovic BIH 124 B2
Dubranec HR. . . .124 B1
Dubrava HR 124 B2
Dubrave BIH 125 C4
Dubravica
HR 124 B1
SRB 127 C3
Dubrovnik HR . . .139 C4
Dubrovytsya UA . .13 C7
Ducey F 88 B2
Duchcov CZ. 84 B1
Ducherow D. 74 A2
Dučina SRB 127 C2
Duclair F 89 A4
Dudar H. 112 B1
Duddington GB . . .40 C3
Duderstadt D. 82 A2
Dudeştii Vechi RO 126 A2
Dudley GB. 40 C1
Dueñas E 142 C2
Duesund N 46 B2
Dueville I 121 B4
Duffel B 79 A4
Duffield GB 40 C2
Dufftown GB 32 D3
Duga Resa HR . . .123 B4
Dugi Rat HR. 138 B2
Dugny-sur-Meuse
F 92 B1
Dugo Selo HR . . .124 B2
Duino I 122 B2
Duisburg D 80 A2
Dukat AL. 182 C1
Dukovany CZ. 97 B4
Duleek IRL 30 A2
Dülken D 80 A2

Dülmen D 80 A3
Dulovo BG 17 D7
Dulpetorpet N 49 B4
Dulverton GB. 43 A3
Dumbarton GB. . . .34 C3
Dümerek TR. 187 C6
Dumfries GB. 36 A3
Dumlupınar TR . .187 D4
Dümpelfeld D 80 B2
Dunaalmás H 112 B2
Dunabogdány H . .112 B3
Dunafalva H 125 A4
Dunaföldvár H . . .112 C2
Dunaharaszti H . .112 B3
Dunajská Streda
SK 111 B4
Dunakeszi H 112 B3
Dunakiliti H 111 B4
Dunakömlöd H . . .112 C2
Dunapataj H 112 C2
Dunaszekcsö H . .125 A4
Dunaszentgyorgy
H 112 C2
Dunatetétlen H . .112 C3
Dunaújváros H . .112 C2
Dunavecse H 112 C2
Dunbar GB. 35 B5
Dunbeath GB 32 C3
Dunblane GB 35 B4
Dunboyne IRL 30 A2
Dundalk IRL. 27 B4
Dundee GB 35 B5
Dundrennan GB . .36 B3
Dundrum GB 27 B5
Dunfanaghy IRL . .26 A3
Dunfermline GB . .35 B4
Dungannon GB . . .27 B4
Dungarvan IRL . . .29 B4
Dungiven GB 27 B4
Dunglow IRL 26 B2
Dungourney IRL . .29 C3
Duninowo PL 68 A1
Dunkeld GB 35 B4
Dunker S 56 A2
Dunkerque = Dunkirk
F 78 A2
Dunkineely IRL . . .26 B2
Dunkirk = Dunkerque
F 78 A2
Dun Laoghaire IRL .30 A2
Dunlavin IRL. 30 A2
Dunleer IRL 27 C4
Dun-le-Palestel F .116 A1
Dun-les-Places F .104 B3
Dunlop GB. 36 A2
Dunloy GB. 27 A4
Dunmanway IRL . .29 C2
Dunmore IRL 28 A3
Dunmore East IRL .30 B2
Dunmurry GB 27 B4
Dunnet GB. 32 C3
Dunningen D 107 A3
Dunoon GB 34 C3
Duns GB 35 C5
Dunscore GB. 36 A3
Dunsford GB 43 B3
Dunshaughlin IRL. .30 A2
Dunstable GB 44 B3
Dunster GB 43 A3
Dun-sur-Auron F. .103 C4
Dun-sur-Meuse F .91 B5
Dunvegan GB 31 B2
Duplek SLO 110 C2
Dupnitsa BG 17 D5
Durağan TR 23 A8
Durach D 107 B5
Durak TR 186 C3
Durana E 143 B4
Durance F 128 B3
Durango E 143 A4
Durankulak BG . . .17 D8
Duras F 128 B3
Durban-Corbières
F 146 B3
Dürbheim D 107 A3
Durbuy B 79 B5
Dúrcal E 163 B4
Đurđenovac HR . .125 B3
Đurđevac HR 124 A3
Đurđevik BIH 139 A4
Düren D 80 B2
Durham GB 37 B5
Đurinci SRB. 127 C2
Durlach D. 93 C4
Đurmanec HR . . .124 A1
Durness GB 32 C2
Dürnkrut A. 97 C4
Dürrboden CH. . . .107 C4
Dürres AL. 182 B1
Durrow IRL. 30 B1
Durrus IRL. 29 C2
Dursunbey TR. . . .186 C3
Durtal F 102 B1
Durup DK 58 B1
Durusu TR. 186 A3
Dusina BIH. 139 B3
Dusnok H 112 C2
Dusocin PL. 69 B3
Düsseldorf D 80 A2
Dusslingen D. 93 C5
Duszniki PL 75 B5
Duszniki-Zdrój PL. .85 B4
Dutovlje SLO 122 B2
Duvebo S 55 B5
Duved S 199 B9
Düzağaç TR 187 D5
Dvärsätt S 199 B11
Dvor HR 124 B2
Dvorce CZ. 98 B1
Dvorníky SK 98 C1
Dvory nad Žitavou
SK 112 B2
Dvůr Králvénad
Labem CZ 85 B3
Dybvad DK. 58 A3

Dyce GB 33 D4
Dygowo PL 67 B4
Dykehead GB 35 B4
Dymchurch GB 45 B5
Dymer UA. 13 C9
Dyrnes N 198 B4
Dywity PL 69 B5
Džanići BIH 139 B3
Dziadowa Kłoda
 PL. 86 A1
Działdowo PL. 77 A5
Działoszyce PL . . .87 B4
Działoszyn PL 86 A2
Dziemiany PL. 68 A2
Dzierżążnia PL 77 B5
Dzierzgoń PL 69 B4
Dzierzgowo PL 77 A5
Dzierżoniów PL . . .85 B4
Dzisna BY 13 A8
Dziwnów PL 67 B3
Dźwierzuty PL 77 A5
Dzyarzhynsk BY . . .13 B7
Dzyatlava BY 13 B6

E

Ea E 143 A4
Eaglesfield GB 36 A3
Ealing GB. 44 B3
Eardisley GB 39 B3
Earls Barton GB . . .44 A3
Earl Shilton GB . . .40 C2
Earlston GB 35 C5
Easington GB 41 B4
Easky IRL 26 B2
Eastbourne GB 45 C4
East Calder GB 35 C4
East Dereham GB . .41 C4
Easter Skeld GB . . .33 A5
East Grinstead GB .45 B4
East IIsley GB 44 B2
East Kilbride GB . . .36 A2
Eastleigh GB 44 C2
East Linton GB 35 C5
East Markham GB . .40 B3
Easton GB 43 B4
East Wittering GB . .44 C3
Eaton Socon GB . . .44 A3
Eaux-Bonnes F . . .145 B3
Eauze F 128 C3
Ebberup DK 59 C2
Ebbs A 108 B3
Ebbw Vale GB 39 C3
Ebeleben D 82 A2
Ebeltoft DK 59 B3
Ebene Reichenau
 A. 109 C4
Eben im Pongau
 A. 109 A4
Ebensee A 109 B4
Ebensfeld D. 94 A2
Eberbach D 93 B4
Ebergötzen D 82 A2
Ebermann-Stadt D .94 B3
Ebern D 82 B2
Eberndorf A 110 C1
Ebersbach D 84 A2
Ebersberg D 108 A2
Ebersdorf
 Bayern D 82 B3
 Niedersachsen D .72 A2
Eberstein A 110 C1
Eberswalde D 74 B2
Ebnat-Kappel CH .107 B4
Éboli I 170 C3
Ebrach D 94 B2
Ebreichsdorf A . . .111 B3
Ebreuil F 116 A3
Ebstorf D 72 A3
Ecclefechan GB . . .36 A3
Eccleshall GB 40 C1
Eceabat TR 186 B1
Echallens CH. 106 C1
Echauri E 144 B2
Echinos GR 183 B7
Echiré F 114 B3
Échirolles F 118 B2
Echourgnac F 128 A3
Echt NL 80 A1
Echte D 82 A2
Echternach L 92 B2
Ecija E 162 A2
Ečka SRB 126 B2
Eckartsberga D 82 A3
Eckelshausen D . . .81 B4
Eckental D 94 B3
Eckernförde D 64 B2
Eckington GB 40 B2
Éclaron F 91 C4
Écommoy F 102 B2
Écouché F 89 B3
Écouis F 90 B1
Ecséd H 113 B3
Ecsegfalva H 113 B4
Écueillé F 103 B3
Ed S 54 B2
Eda E 49 C4
Eda glasbruk S 49 C4
Edam NL 70 B2
Edane S 55 A3
Edderton GB 32 D2
Ede NL 70 B2
Edebäck S 49 B5
Edebo S 51 B5
Edelény H 99 C4
Edelschrott A 110 B2
Edemissen D 72 B3
Edenbridge GB 45 B4
Edenderry IRL 30 A1
Edenkoben D. 93 B4
Edesheim D 93 B4
Edessa GR. 182 C4
Edewecht D 71 A4
Edgeworthstown
 IRL 30 A1
Edinburgh GB 35 C4
Edineţ MD 17 A7
Edirne TR. 186 A1
Edland N 52 A3
Edolo I 120 A3
Edøy N 198 B5
Edremit TR. 186 C2
Edsbro S 51 C5
Edsbruk S 56 B2
Edsbyn S 50 A2
Edsele S. 200 C2
Edsleskog S 54 A3
Edsvalla S 55 A4
Eekloo B 79 A3
Eemshaven NL 71 A3
Eerbeek NL 70 B3
Eersel NL 79 A5
Eferding A 96 C2
Effiat F 116 A3
Efteløt N 53 A5
Egeln D 73 C4
Eger H 113 B4
Egerbakta H. 113 B4
Egernsund DK 64 B2
Egersund N 52 B2
Egerszólát H 113 B4
Egervár H 111 C3
Egg
 A. 107 B4
 D. 107 A5
Eggby S 55 B4
Eggedal N 47 B6
Eggenburg A 97 C3
Eggenfelden D 95 C4
Eggesin D 74 A3
Eggum N 194 B4
Egham GB. 44 B3
Éghezée B 79 B4
Egiertowo PL. 68 A3
Egilsstaðir IS 191 B11
Egina GR 185 B4
Eginio GR 182 C4
Egio GR 184 A3
Égletons F 116 B2
Egling D. 108 B2
Eglinton GB 27 A3
Eglisau CH 107 B3
Égliseneuve-
 d'Entraigues F . .116 B2
Eglofs D 107 B4
Egmond aan Zee
 NL 70 B1
Egna I 121 A4
Egosthena GR. . . .184 A4
Egremont GB. 36 B3
Egtved DK 59 C2
Éguilles F 131 B4
Eguilly-sous-Bois
 F 104 A3
Éguzon-Chantôme
 F 103 C3
Egyek H 113 B4
Egyházasrádóc
 H 111 B3
Ehekirchen D 94 C3
Ehingen D 94 C1
Ehra-Lessien D . . .73 B3
Ehrang D 92 B2
Ehrenfriedersdorf
 D 83 B4
Ehrenhain D 83 B4
Ehrenhausen A 110 C2
Ehringshausen D . .81 B4
Ehrwald A. 108 B1
Eibar E 143 A4
Eibelstadt D 94 B2
Eibenstock D 83 B4
Eibergen NL. 71 B3
Eibiswald A 110 C2
Eichenbarleben D . .73 B4
Eichendorf D 95 C4
Eichstätt D 95 C3
Eickelborn D 81 A4
Eid
 Hordaland N 46 B3
 Møre og Romsdal
 N 198 C4
Eidfjord N 46 B4
Eidsberg N. 54 A2
Eidsbugarden N . . .47 A5
Eidsdal N. 198 C4
Eidsfoss N 53 A6
Eidskog N 49 B4
Eidsvåg
 Hordaland N 46 B2
 Møre og Romsdal
 N 198 C5
Eidsvoll N 48 B3
Eikefjord N 46 A2
Eikelandsosen N. . .46 B2
Eiken N 52 B3
Eikesdal N 198 C5
Eikstrand N 53 A5
Eilenburg D 83 A4
Eilsleben D 73 B4
Eina N 48 B2
Einbeck D 82 A1
Eindhoven NL 79 A5
Einsiedeln CH 107 B3
Einville-au-Jard F . .92 C2
Eisenach D 82 B2
Eisenberg
 Rheinland-Pfalz
 D. 93 B4
 Thüringen D 83 B3
Eisenerz A 110 B1
Eisenhüttenstadt D .74 B3
Eisenkappel A 110 C1
Eisenstadt A 111 B3
Eisentratten A 109 C4
Eisfeld D 82 B2
Eisleben D 82 A3
Eislingen D 94 C1
Eitensheim D 95 C3
Eiterfeld D 82 B1
Eitorf D 80 B3
Eivindvik N 46 B2
Eivissa = Ibiza E .166 C1
Eixo P 148 B1

Ejby DK 59 C2
Ejea de los Caballeros
 E 144 B2
Ejstrupholm DK. . . .59 C2
Ejulve E 153 B3
Eke B 79 B3
Ekeby
 Gotland S. 57 C4
 Skåne S 61 D2
 Uppsala S 51 B5
Ekeby-Almby S 56 A1
Ekenäs S 55 B4
Ekenässjön S 62 A3
Ekerö S 57 A3
Eket S. 61 C3
Eketorp S 63 B4
Ekevik S 56 B2
Ekkerøy N 193 B14
Ekshärad S 49 B5
Eksjö S. 62 A2
Eksta S. 57 C4
Ekträsk S 200 B5
Ekeby
El Alamo
 Madrid E 151 B4
 Sevilla E 161 B3
El Algar E 165 B4
El Almendro E 161 B2
El Alquián E 164 C2
El Arahal E 162 A2
El Arenal E 150 B2
El Arguellite E 164 A2
Elassona GR 182 D4
El Astillero E 143 A3
Elati GR 182 D3
Żelazno PL 85 B4
El Ballestero E. . . .158 C1
El Barco de Ávila
 E 150 B2
Elbasan AL 182 B2
El Berrón E 142 A1
El Berrueco E 151 B4
Elbeuf F 89 A4
Elbigenowe D 82 A2
Elbingerode D 82 A2
Elbląg PL 69 A4
El Bodón E 149 B3
El Bonillo E 158 C1
El Bosque E 162 B2
El Bullaque E 157 A3
Elburg NL. 70 B2
El Burgo E 162 B3
El Burgo de Ebro
 E 153 A3
El Burgo de Osma
 E 151 A4
El Burgo Ranero
 E 142 B1
El Buste E 144 C2
El Cabaco E 149 B3
El Callejo E 143 A3
El Campillo E 161 B3
El Campillo de la Jara
 E 156 A2
El Cañavete E 158 B1
El Carpio E 157 C3
El Carpio de Tajo
 E 150 C3
El Casar E 151 B4
El Casar de Escalona
 E 150 B3
El Castillo de las
 Guardas E 161 B3
El Centenillo E 157 B4
El Cerro E 149 B4
El Cerro de Andévalo
 E 161 B3
Elche E 165 A4
Elche de la Sierra
 E 158 C1
Elchingen D 94 C2
El Comenar E 162 B2
El Coronil E 162 A2
El Crucero E 141 A4
El Cubo de Tierra del
 Vino E 149 A4
El Cuervo E 162 B1
Eldagsen D 72 B2
Eldena D 73 A4
Eldingen D 72 B3
Elefsina GR 185 A4
El Ejido E 164 C2
Elek H 113 C5
Elemir SRB 126 B2
El Escorial E 151 B3
El Espinar E 151 B3
Eleutheroupoli
 GR 183 C6
El Frago E 144 B3
El Franco E 141 A4
El Frasno E 152 A2
Elgå N 199 C8
El Garrobo E 161 B3
El Gastor E 162 B2
Elgin GB. 32 D3
Elgoibar E 143 A4
Elgol GB. 31 B2
El Gordo E 150 C2
El Grado E 145 B4
El Granado E 161 B2
El Grao de Castelló
 E 159 B4
El Grau E 159 C3
Elgshøa N 49 A4
El Higuera E 163 A3
El Hijate E 164 B2
El Hontanar E 152 B2
Elhovo BG 17 D7
El Hoyo E 157 B4
Elie GB 35 B5
Elizondo E 144 A2
Elk PL 12 B5
Ellenberg D 94 B2
Ellesmere GB 38 B4
Ellesmere Port GB .38 A4
Ellingen D 94 B2
Ellmau A 109 B3
Ellon GB. 33 D4
Ellös S 54 B2

Ellrich D. 82 A2
Ellwangen D 94 C2
Elm
 CH 107 C4
 D 72 A2
Elmadağ TR. 23 B7
El Madroño E. 161 B3
El Maíllo E 149 B3
Elmalı TR. 189 C4
El Masnou E 147 C3
El Mirón E 150 B2
El Molar E 151 B4
El Molinillo E 157 A3
El Morell E 147 C2
El Muyo E 151 A4
Elne F 146 B3
El Olmo E 151 A4
Elorrio E 143 A4
Elouda GR 185 D6
El Palo E 163 B3
El Pardo E 151 B4
El Payo E 149 B3
El Pedernoso E . . .158 B1
El Pedroso E 162 A2
El Peral E 158 B2
El Perelló
 Tarragona E 153 B4
 Valencia E 159 B3
Elphin GB 32 C1
El Picazo E 158 B1
El Pinell de Bray
 E 153 A4
El Piñero E 150 A2
El Pla de Santa Maria
 E 147 C2
El Pobo E 153 B3
El Pobo de Dueñas
 E 152 B2
El Pont d'Armentera
 E 147 C2
El Port de la Selva
 E 147 B4
El Port de Llançà
 E 146 B4
El Port de Sagunt
 E 159 B3
El Prat de Llobregat
 E 147 C3
El Provencio E. . . .158 B1
El Puente E 143 A3
El Puente del
 Arzobispo E 150 C2
El Puerto E 141 A4
El Puerto de Santa
 María E 162 B1
El Real de la Jara
 E 161 B3
El Real de San Vincente
 E 150 B3
El Robledo E 157 A3
El Rocio E 161 B3
El Rompido E 161 B2
El Ronquillo E 161 B3
El Royo E 143 C4
El Rubio E 162 A3
El Sabinar E 164 A2
El Saler E 159 B3
El Salobral E 158 C2
El Saucejo E 162 A2
Els Castells E 147 B2
Elsdorf D 80 B2
Elsenfeld D 93 B5
El Serrat AND. 146 B2
Elsfleth D. 72 A1
Elspeet NL 70 B2
Elst NL 70 B2
Elstead GB. 44 B3
Elster D 83 A4
Elsterberg D 83 B4
Elsterwerda D 83 A5
Elstra D 84 A2
El Temple E 144 C3
El Tiemblo E 150 B3
Eltmann D 94 B2
El Toboso E 157 A5
El Tormillo E 145 C3
El Torno E 149 B4
Eltville D 93 A4
El Valle de las Casas
 E 142 B1
El Vellón E 151 B4
Elven F 101 B3
El Vendrell E 147 C2
Elverum N 48 B3
El Villar de Arnedo
 E 144 B1
Elvington GB. 40 B3
El Viso E 156 B3
El Viso del Alcor
 E 162 A2
Elxleben D 82 A2
Ely GB 45 A4
Elzach D. 106 A3
Elze D. 72 B2
Emådalen S 50 A1
Embleton GB 37 A5
Embonas GR 188 C2
Embrun F 132 A2
Embún E 144 B3
Emden D 71 A4
Emecik TR. 188 C2
Emet TR. 186 C4
Emirdağ TR. 187 C6
Emlichheim D 71 B3
Emmaboda S 63 B3
Emmaljunga S 61 C3
Emmeloord NL 70 B2
Emmen
 CH 106 B3
 NL 71 B3
Emmendingen D . . .106 A2
Emmer-Compascuum
 NL 71 B4

Emmerich D. 80 A2
Emmern D 72 B2
Emöd H 113 B4
Émpoli I 135 B3
Emsbüren D 71 B4
Emsdetten D 71 B4
Emsfors S 62 A4
Emskirchen D 94 B2
Emstek D. 71 B5
Emsworth GB 44 C3
Emyvale IRL 27 B4
Enafors S 199 B9
Enånger S 51 A4
Encamp AND. 146 B2
Encarnaçao P 154 C1
Encinas de Abajo
 E 150 B2
Encinas de Esgueva
 E 142 C2
Encinasola E 161 A3
Encinas Reales E . .163 A3
Encio E 143 B3
Enciso E 144 B1
Enden N 199 D7
Endingen D 106 A2
Endrinal E 149 B4
Endröd H 113 C4
Enebakk N 54 A2
Eneryda S 63 B2
Enese H 111 B4
Enez TR 183 C8
Enfield IRL 30 A2
Eng A 108 B2
Engelberg CH 106 C3
Engelhartszell A . . .96 C1
Engelskirchen D . . .80 B3
Engen D 107 B3
Enger N 48 B2
Engerdal N 199 D8
Engerneset N 49 A4
Enge-sande D 64 B1
Engesvang DK 59 B2
Enghien B 79 B4
Engstingen D 94 C1
Engter D. 71 B5
Enguera E 159 C3
Enguidanos E 158 B2
Enkenbach D. 93 B3
Enkhuizen NL 70 B2
Enklinge FIN 51 B7
Enköping S 56 A3
Enna I 177 B3
Ennezat F 116 B3
Ennigerloh D 81 A4
Enningdal N. 54 B2
Ennis IRL 28 B3
Enniscorthy IRL . . .30 B2
Enniskean IRL 29 C3
Enniskillen GB 27 B3
Ennistimon IRL 28 B2
Enns A 110 A1
Eno FIN 9 A7
Enontekiö FIN. 196 A6
Ens NL 70 B2
Enschede NL 71 B3
Ensdorf D 95 B3
Ensisheim F 106 B2
Enstaberga S. 56 B2
Enstone GB. 44 B2
Entlebuch CH 106 B3
Entrácque I 133 A3
Entradas P. 160 B1
Entrains-sur-Nohain
 F 104 B2
Entrambasaguas
 E 143 A3
Entrambasmestas
 E 143 A3
Entraygues-sur-
 Truyère F 116 C2
Entre-os-Rios P. . .148 A1
Entrevaux F 132 B2
Entrin Bajo E. 155 C4
Entroncamento P .154 B2
Entzheim F 93 C3
Envermeu F 89 A5
Enviken S 50 B2
Enying H 112 C2
Enzingerboden A. .109 B3
Enzklösterle D 93 C4
Épagny F 90 B3
Epalinges CH 106 C1
Epannes F 114 B3
Epanomi GR 182 C4
Epe
 D 71 B4
 NL 70 B2
Épernay F 91 B3
Épernon F 90 C1
Epfig F 93 C3
Epierre F 118 B3
Épila E 152 A2
Épinac F 104 C3
Épinal F 105 A5
Episcopia I 174 A2
Episkopi CY 181 B1
Epitalio GR 184 B2
Epoisses F 104 B3
Eppenbrunn D. 93 B3
Eppendorf D 83 B5
Epping GB 45 B4
Eppingen D 93 B4
Epsom GB. 44 B3
Epworth GB. 40 B3
Eraclea I 122 B1
Eraclea Mare I 122 B1
Erba I 120 B2
Erbach
 Baden-Württemberg
 D 94 C1
 Hessen D 93 B4
Erbalunga F 180 A2
Erbendorf D 95 B4
Érchie I 173 B3
Ercolano I 170 C2
Ercsi H 112 B2
Érd H 112 B2
Erdek TR 186 B2
Erdemli TR. 23 C8
Erdevik SRB 126 B1

Erding D. 95 C3
Erdőtelek H 113 B4
Erdut HR 125 B5
Erdweg D 95 C3
Ereğli
 Konya TR. 23 C8
 Zonguldak TR . . .187 A6
Erenkaya TR 23 C8
Eresfjord N 198 C5
Eresos GR 186 C1
Eretria GR 185 A4
Erfde D 64 B2
Erfjord N 52 A2
Erfstadt D 80 B2
Erfurt D 82 B3
Ergli LV. 8 D4
Ergoldsbach D 95 C4
Eriboll GB 32 C2
Érice I. 176 A1
Ericeira P. 154 C1
Eğridir TR 189 B5
Eriksberg S 195 E6
Eriksmåla S 62 B3
Eringsboda S 63 B3
Eriswil CH 106 B2
Erithres GR 185 A4
Erkelenz D 80 A2
Erkner D. 74 B2
Erkrath D 80 A2
Erla E. 144 B3
Erlangen D. 94 B3
Erli I 133 A4
Erlsbach A. 109 C3
Ermelo NL 70 B2
Ermenak TR. 23 C7
Ermenonville F 90 B2
Ermezinde P 148 A1
Ermidas P 160 A1
Ermioni GR 184 B4
Ermoupoli GR 185 B5
Ermsleben D 82 A3
Erndtebrück D 81 B4
Ernée F 88 B3
Ernestinovo HR. . . .125 B4
Ernstbrunn A. 97 C4
Erolzheim D. 107 A5
Erquelinnes B 79 B4
Erquy F 101 A3
Erra P 154 C2
Erratzu E 144 A2
Errindlev DK 65 B4
Erro E. 144 B2
Ersa F 180 A2
Érsekcsanád H . . .125 A4
Érsekë AL. 182 C2
Érsekvadkert H . . .112 B3
Ersmark S 200 C6
Erstein F 93 C3
Erstfeld CH 107 C3
Ertebølle DK 58 B2
Ertingen D 107 A4
Ervedal
 Coimbra P 148 B1
 Portalegre P. 154 B3
Ervenik HR. 138 A1
Ervidel P 160 B1
Ervy-le-Châtel F . .104 A2
Erwitte D 81 A4
Erxleben D 73 B4
Erzsébet H 125 A4
Esbjerg DK. 59 C1
Esbly F 90 C2
Escacena del Campo
 E 161 B3
Escairón E 140 B3
Escalada E 143 B3
Escalante E 143 A3
Escalaplano I 179 C3
Escalona E 150 B3
Escalona del Prado
 E 151 A3
Escalonilla E 150 C3
Escalos de Baixo
 P 155 B3
Escalos de Cima
 P 155 B3
Escamilla E 152 B1
Es Caná E 166 B1
Escañuela E 157 C3
Es Castell E 167 B4
Escatrón E 153 A3
Escharch D 107 B4
Eschau D 94 B1
Eschede D 72 B3
Eschenau D 95 B3
Eschenbach D. 95 B3
Eschenz CH 107 B3
Eschershausen D . .72 C2
Esch-sur-Alzette L .92 B1
Esch-sur-Sûre L . . .92 B1
Eschwege D 82 A2
Eschweiler D. 80 B2
Escobasa de Almazán
 E 152 A1
Escœuilles F. 78 B1
Escombreras E . . .165 B4
Escos F 144 A2
Escource F 128 B1
Escragnolles F 132 B2
Escrick GB. 40 B2
Escurial E 156 A2
Escurial de la Sierra
 E 149 B4
Esens D 71 A4
Esgos E 140 B3
Esher GB 44 B3
Eskdalemuir GB . . .36 A3
Eskifjörður IS 191 B12
Eskilhem S 57 C4
Eskilsäter S 55 B4
Eskilstrup DK 65 B4
Eskilstuna S 56 A2
Eskipazar TR 187 B7
Eskişehir TR 187 C5
Eslarn D 95 B4
Eslava E 144 B2
Eslida E 159 B3
Eslohe D. 81 A4
Eslöv S. 61 D3
Eşme TR 188 A3

Es Mercadal E 167 B4
Es Migjorn Gran E .167 B4
Espa N 48 B3
Espalion F 130 A1
Esparragalejo E . . .155 C4
Esparragosa del
 Caudillo E 156 B2
Esparragossa de la
 Serena E 156 B2
Esparreguera E . . .147 C2
Esparron F 132 B1
Espe N 46 B3
Espedal N 52 B2
Espejo
 Álava E 143 B3
 Córdoba E 163 A3
Espeland N 46 B2
Espelkamp D 72 B1
Espeluche F 131 A3
Espeluy E 157 B4
Espera E 162 B2
Esperança P 155 B3
Esperia I 169 B3
Espevær N 52 A1
Espiel E 156 B3
Espinama E 142 A2
Espiñaredo E 140 A3
Espinasses F 132 A2
Espinelves E 147 C3
Espinhal P. 154 A2
Espinho P 148 A1
Espinilla E 142 A2
Espinosa de Cerrato
 E 143 C3
Espinosa de los
 Monteros E 143 A3
Espinoso del Rey
 E 156 A3
Espírito Santo P . . .160 B2
Espluga de Francolí
 E 147 C2
Esplús E 145 C4
Espolla E 146 B3
Espoo FIN 8 B4
Esporles E 166 B2
Es Port d'Alcúdia
 E 167 B3
Esposende P 148 A1
Espot E 146 B2
Es Pujols E 166 C1
Esquedas E 145 B3
Esquivias E 151 B4
Essay F 89 B4
Essen
 B 79 A4
 Niedersachsen D .71 B4
 Nordrhein-Westfalen
 D. 80 A3
Essenbach D 95 C4
Essertaux F 90 B2
Essingen D 94 C2
Esslingen D 94 C1
Es Soleràs E 153 A4
Essoyes F 104 A3
Estacas E 140 B2
Estadilla E 145 B4
Estagel F 146 B3
Estaires F 78 B2
Estang F 128 C2
Estarreja P 148 B1
Estartit E 147 B4
Estavayer-le-Lac
 CH 106 C1
Este I 121 B4
Esteiro E 140 A2
Estela P 148 A1
Estella E 144 B1
Estellencs E 166 B2
Estepa E 162 A3
Estépar E 143 B3
Estepona E 162 B2
Esternay F 91 C3
Esterri d'Aneu E . .146 B2
Esterwegen D 71 B4
Estissac F 104 A2
Estivadas E 140 B3
Estivareilles F 116 A2
Estivella E 159 B3
Estói P 160 B2
Estopiñán E 145 C4
Estoril P 154 C1
Estoublon F 132 B2
Estrée-Blanche F . .78 B2
Estrées-St Denis F .90 B2
Estrela P 155 C3
Estremera E 151 B4
Estremoz P 155 C3
Estuna S 51 C5
Esyres F 102 B2
Esztergom H 112 B2
Étables-sur-Mer F .100 A3
Étain F 92 B1
Étalans F 105 B5
Étalle B 92 B1
Étampes F 90 C2
Étang-sur-Arroux
 F 104 C3
Étaples F 78 B1
Etauliers F 128 A2
Etili TR 186 C1
Etne N 52 A1
Etna N 48 B2
Etoges F 91 C3
Etoliko GR 184 A2
Eton GB. 44 B3
Étréaupont F 91 B3
Étréchy F 90 C2
Étrépagny F 90 B1
Étretat F 89 A4
Étreux F 91 A3
Étroubles I 119 B4
Ettal D 108 B2
Ettelbruck L 92 B2
Etten NL 79 A4
Ettenheim D 106 A2
Ettlingen D 93 C4
Ettringen D 108 A1
Etuz F 105 B4

txarri-Aranatz E . 144 B1
tyek H 112 B2
u F 90 A1
uerdorf D 82 B2
ulate E 144 B1
upen B 80 B2
uropoort NL . . 79 A4
uskirchen D . . . 80 B2
utin D 65 B3
vanger N 46 B3
vaux-les-Bains F 116 A2
vciler
  Afyon TR 189 A4
  Çanakkale TR . . 186 C1
venskjær N . . . 194 B7
venstad N 48 A3
vercreech GB . . 43 A4
vergem B 79 A3
veröd S 61 D4
versberg D 81 A4
verswinkel D . . 71 C4
vertsberg S . . . 49 A5
vesham GB . . . 44 A2
vian-les-Bains F 118 A3
visa F 180 A1
vje N 53 B3
volène CH 119 A4
vora F 154 C3
voramonte P . . 155 C3
vran F 101 A4
vrecy F 89 A3
vreux F 89 A5
vron F 102 A1
vry F 90 C2
well GB 44 B3
wersbach D . . . 81 B4
xcideuil F 115 C5
xeter GB 43 B3
xmes F 89 B4
xminster GB . . . 43 B3
xmouth GB . . . 43 B3
ydehamn N . . . 53 B4
ye
  Peterborough
  GB. 41 C3
  Suffolk GB . . . 45 A5
yemouth GB . . . 35 C5
yguians F 132 A1
yguières F 131 B4
ygurande F . . . 116 B2
ylie F 145 B4
ymet F 129 B3
ymouriers F . . . 116 B1
ynsham GB . . . 44 B2
yrarbakki IS . . 190 D4
ystrup D 72 B2
zaro E 140 B1
zcaray E 143 B4
zcároz E 144 B2
zine TR 186 C1
zmoriz P 148 B3

F

abara E 153 A4
ábbrico I 121 C3
åberg N 48 A2
abero E 141 B4
ábiánsebestyén
  H 113 C4
åborg DK 64 A3
abrègues F . . . 130 B2
abriano I 136 B1
abrizia I 175 C2
acha P 148 A1
acinas E 162 B2
ačkov SK 98 B2
adagosa P 155 B3
add H 112 C2
aédis I 122 A2
aenza I 135 A4
afe P. 148 A1
agagna I 122 A1
ágáras RO 17 C6
ágelberget S . . 199 A11
ágelfors S 62 A3
ágelmara S . . . 63 B3
ágelsta S 55 B6
agerås S 55 A4
agerheim N . . . 47 B4
agerhøy N 48 A1
agerhult S 62 A3
agerlund S 48 B2
agernes
  Oppland N . . . 47 B6
  Troms N 192 C3
agersanna S . . . 55 B5
agersta S 50 B2
áglavik S 55 B4
agnano Castello
  I 174 B2
agnières F 91 C4
aido CH 107 C3
ains-Véel F . . . 91 C5
airford GB 44 B2
airlie GB. 34 C3
ajsz H 112 C2
akenham GB . . 41 C4
åker S 199 B11
akse DK 65 A5
akse Ladeplads
  DK 65 A5
alaise F 89 B3
alcade I 121 A4
alces E 144 B2
álciu RO 17 B8
alconara Marittima
  I 136 B2
alcone I 177 A4
aldingworth GB. . 40 B3
alerum S 56 B2
áleşti MD 17 B7
alkenberg
  Bayern D 95 B4
  Bayern D 95 C4
  Brandenburg D . 83 A5
  S 60 C2

Falkensee D 74 B2
Falkenstein
  Bayern D 95 B4
  Sachsen D . . . 83 B4
Falkenthal D . . . 74 B2
Falkirk GB 35 B4
Falkland GB . . . 35 B4
Falköping S . . . 55 B4
Fall D 108 B2
Falla S 56 B1
Fallingbostel D . 72 B2
Falmouth GB . . . 42 B1
Falset E 147 C1
Fălticeni RO . . . 17 B7
Falun S 50 B2
Famagusta CY . . 181 A2
Fammestad N . . 46 B2
Fana I 146 B2
Fanano I 135 A3
Fanari GR 182 D3
Fanjeaux F 146 A3
Fano I 136 B2
Fântânele RO . . 126 A3
Fão P 148 A1
Fara in Sabina I . 168 A2
Faramontanos de
  Tábara E 149 A4
Fara Novarese I . 119 B5
Farasdues E . . . 144 B2
Fårbo S 62 A4
Fareham GB . . . 44 C2
Färentuna S . . . 57 A3
Färgelanda S . . 54 B2
Färila S 200 E1
Faringdon GB . . 44 B2
Faringe S 51 C5
Fariza E 149 A3
Farkadona GR . . 182 D4
Farkasfa H 111 C3
Farlete E 153 A3
Färlöv S 61 C4
Farmos H 113 B3
Farná SK 112 B2
Färnäs S 50 B1
Farnborough GB. . 44 B3
Farnese I 168 A1
Farnham GB . . . 44 B3
Farnroda D 82 B2
Faro P 160 B2
Fåro S 57 C5
Fårösund S . . . 57 C5
Farra d'Alpago I . 122 A1
Farranfore IRL . . 29 B2
Farre DK 59 B2
Farsala GR . . . 182 D4
Farsø DK 58 B2
Farsund N 52 B2
Farum DK 61 D2
Fårup DK 58 B2
Fasana I 172 B1
Fasano I 173 B3
Fáskrúðsfjörður
  IS 191 C11
Fassberg D . . . 72 B3
Fastiv UA 13 C8
Fastnäs S 49 B5
Fátima P 154 B2
Fatmomakke S . . 195 E6
Fättjaur S 195 E6
Faucogney-et-la-Mer
  F 105 B5
Fauguerolles F . . 128 B3
Faulenrost D . . . 74 A1
Faulquemont F . . 92 B2
Fauquembergues F 78 B2
Fauske N 194 C6
Fauville-en-Caux F . 89 A4
Fauvillers B . . . 92 B1
Fåvang N 48 A2
Favara
  E 159 B3
  I 176 B2
Faverges F 118 B3
Faverney F 105 B5
Favignana I . . . 176 B1
Fawley GB 44 C2
Fay-aux-Loges F . 103 B4
Fayence F 132 B2
Fayet F 130 B1
Fayl-Billot F . . . 105 B4
Fayón E 153 A4
Fearn GB 32 D3
Fécamp F 89 A4
Feda N 52 B2
Fedje N 46 B1
Feeny GB 27 B3
Fegen S 60 B3
Fegyvernek H . . 113 B4
Fehrbellin D . . . 74 B1
Fehring A 111 C3
Feichten A 108 B1
Feiring N 48 B3
Feistritz im Rosental
  A 110 C1
Feketić SRB . . . 126 B1
Felanitx E 167 B3
Feld am See A . . 109 C4
Feldbach A 110 C2
Feldberg D 74 A2
Feldkirch A . . . 107 B4
Feldkirchen in Kärnten
  A 109 C5
Feldkirchen-Westerham
  D 108 B2
Felgueiras P . . . 148 A1
Felitto I 172 B1
Félix E 164 C2
Felixstowe GB. . 45 B5
Felletin F 116 B2
Fellingsbro S . . 56 A1
Felnac RO 126 A3
Felnémet H . . . 113 B4
Felpéc H. 111 B4
Fels am Wagram A . 97 C3
Felsberg D 81 A5
Felsönyék H . . . 112 C2

Felsöszentiván H . 126 A1
Felsöszentmárton
  H 125 B3
Felsözsolca H . . 113 A4
Felsted DK 64 B2
Feltre I 121 A4
Femsjö S 60 C3
Fenagh IRL . . . 26 B3
Fene E 140 A2
Fenestrelle I . . . 119 B4
Fénétrange F . . 92 C3
Feneu F 102 B1
Fengersfors S . . 54 B3
Fenit IRL 29 B2
Fensmark DK . . 65 A4
Fenwick GB . . . 36 A2
Feolin Ferry GB. . 34 C1
Ferbane IRL . . . 28 A4
Ferdinandovac
  HR 124 A3
Ferdinandshof D . 74 A2
Fère-Champenoise
  F 91 C3
Fère-en-Tardenois
  F 91 B3
Ferentillo I 168 A2
Ferentino I 169 B3
Feres GR 183 C8
Feria E 155 C4
Feričanci HR . . . 125 B3
Ferizli TR 187 B5
Ferla I 177 B3
Fermil P 148 A2
Fermo I 136 B2
Fermoselle E . . 149 A3
Fermoy IRL . . . 29 B3
Fernancaballero E 157 A4
Fernán Nuñéz E . 163 A3
Fernán Peréz E . 164 C2
Fernão Ferro P . . 154 C1
Fernay-Voltaire F . 118 A3
Ferndown GB . . 43 B5
Fernhurst GB . . 44 B3
Ferns IRL 30 B2
Ferpécle CH . . . 119 A4
Ferrals-les-Corbières
  F 146 A3
Ferrandina I . . . 172 B2
Ferrara I 121 C4
Ferrara di Monte Baldo
  I 121 B3
Ferreira E 141 A3
Ferreira do Alentejo
  P 160 A1
Ferreira do Zêzere
  P 154 B2
Ferreras de Abajo
  E 141 C4
Ferreras de Arriba
  E 141 C4
Ferreruela E . . . 152 A2
Ferreruela de Tabara
  E 149 A3
Ferret CH 119 B4
Ferrette F 106 B2
Ferriere I 120 C2
Ferrière-la-Grande
  F 79 B3
Ferrières
  Hautes-Pyrénées
    F 145 A4
  Loiret F 103 A4
  Oise F 90 B2
Ferrières-sur-Sichon
  F 117 A3
Ferrol E 140 A2
Ferryhill GB . . . 37 B5
Fertörakos H . . 111 B3
Fertöszentmiklós
  H 111 B3
Ferwerd NL . . . 70 A2
Festieux F 91 B3
Festøy N 198 C3
Festvåg N 194 C5
Feteşti RO 17 C7
Fethard
  Tipperary IRL . . 29 B4
  Wexford IRL. . . 30 B2
Fethiye TR 188 C4
Fetsund N 48 C3
Fettercairn GB. . 35 B5
Feucht D 95 B3
Feuchtwangen D . 94 B2
Feudingen D . . . 81 B4
Feuges F 91 C4
Feuquières F . . 90 B1
Feurs F 117 B4
Fevik N 53 B4
Ffestiniog GB . . 38 B3
Fiamignano I . . 169 A3
Fiano I 119 B4
Ficarazzi I 176 A2
Ficarolo I 121 C4
Fichtelberg D. . . 95 A3
Ficulle I 135 C5
Fidenza I 120 C3
Fidjeland N . . . 52 B2
Fieberbrunn A . . 109 B3
Fier AL 182 C1
Fiera di Primiero I . 121 A4
Fiesch CH 119 A5
Fiesso Umbertiano
  I 121 C4
Figari F 180 B2
Figeac F 116 C2
Figeholm S . . . 62 A4
Figgjo N 52 B1
Figline Valdarno I . 135 B4
Figols E 145 B4
Figueira da Foz P . 148 B1
Figueira de Castelo
  Rodrigo P . . . 149 B3
Figueira dos Caveleiros
  P 160 A1
Figueiredo P . . 154 B3
Figueiredo de Alva
  P 148 B2

Figueiródos Vinhos
  P 154 B2
Figueres E 147 B3
Figueroles E . . . 153 B3
Figueruela de Arriba
  E 141 C4
Filadélfia I 175 C2
Fil'akovo SK . . . 99 C3
Filderstadt D . . . 94 C1
Filey GB 41 A3
Filiaşi RO 17 C5
Filiates GR 182 D2
Filiatra GR 184 B2
Filipstad S 55 A5
Fillan N 198 B5
Filotio GR 185 B6
Filottrano I 136 B2
Filskov DK 59 C2
Filton GB 43 A4
Filtvet N 54 A1
Filzmoos A 109 B4
Finale Emília I . . 121 C4
Finale Lígure I . . 133 A4
Fiñana E 164 B2
Fincham GB . . . 41 C4
Finchingfield GB. . 45 B4
Findhorn GB . . . 32 D3
Findochty GB . . 33 D4
Finike TR 189 C5
Finkenberg A . . 108 B2
Finnea IRL 27 C3
Finneidfjord N . . 195 D4
Finnerödja S . . . 55 B5
Finnskog N . . . 49 B4
Finnsnes N . . . 194 A9
Finntorp S 54 A3
Finócchio I 168 B2
Finsjö S 62 A4
Finsland N 52 B3
Finspång S 56 B1
Finsterwalde D . . 84 A1
Finsterwolde NL . 71 A4
Finstown GB . . . 33 B3
Fintona GB 27 B3
Fionnphort GB . . 34 B1
Fiorenzuola d'Arda
  I 120 C2
Firenze = Florence
  I 135 B4
Firenzuola I . . . 135 A4
Firmi F 130 A1
Firminy F 117 B4
Firmo I 174 B2
Fischamend Markt
  A 111 A3
Fischbach
  A 110 B2
  D 93 B3
Fischbeck D . . . 73 B5
Fishbourne GB . . 44 C2
Fishguard GB . . 39 C2
Fiskardo GR . . . 184 A1
Fiskebäckskil S . 54 B2
Fiskebøl N 194 B5
Fismes F 91 B3
Fisterra E 140 B1
Fitero E 144 B2
Fitjar N 46 C2
Fiuggi I 169 B3
Fiumata I 169 A3
Fiumefreddo Brúzio
  I 174 B2
Fiumefreddo di Sicilia
  I 177 B4
Fiumicino I 168 B2
Fivemiletown GB. . 27 B3
Fivizzano I 134 A3
Fjälkinge S 63 B2
Fjällåsen S 196 B3
Fjällbacka S . . . 54 B2
Fjæra N 46 C3
Fjärdhundra S . . 56 A2
Fjellerup DK . . . 58 B3
Fjerritslev DK . . 58 A2
Fjordgard N . . . 194 A8
Fjugesta S 55 A5
Flå N 47 B6
Flåbygd N 53 A4
Flaça E 147 B3
Fladungen D . . . 82 B2
Flaine F 118 A3
Flaka FIN 51 B7
Flåm N 46 B4
Flamatt CH . . . 106 C2
Flamborough GB. . 41 A3
Flammersfeld D. . 81 B3
Flassans-sur-Issole
  F 132 B2
Flatdal N 53 A4
Flatebø N 46 B3
Flateby N 48 C3
Flateland N . . . 52 A3
Flateyri IS 190 A2
Flatøydegard N . . 47 B6
Flatråker N 46 C2
Flattach A 109 C4
Flatvarp S 62 A4
Flauenskjold DK . 58 A3
Flavigny-sur-Moselle
  F 92 C2
Flavy-le-Martel F . 90 B3
Flawil CH 107 B4
Flayosc F 132 B2
Flechtingen D . . 73 B4
Fleckeby D 64 B2
Fleet GB. 44 B3
Fleetmark D . . . 73 B4
Fleetwood GB . . 38 A3
Flehingen D . . . 93 B4
Flekke N 46 A2
Flekkefjord N . . 52 B2
Flen S 56 A2
Flensburg D . . . 64 B2
Fleringe S 57 C4

Flerohopp S . . . 62 B3
Flers F 88 B3
Flesberg N 47 C6
Fleurance F . . . 129 C3
Fleuré F 115 B4
Fleurier CH 105 C5
Fleurus B 79 B4
Fleury
  Hérault F 130 B2
  Yonne F 104 B2
Fleury-les-Aubrais
  F 103 B3
Fleury-sur-Andelle
  F 89 A5
Fleury-sur-Orne F . 89 A3
Flieden D 81 B5
Flimby GB 36 B3
Flims CH 107 C4
Flines-lèz-Raches
  F 78 B3
Flint GB 38 A3
Flirey F 92 C1
Flirsch A 108 B1
Flisa N 49 B4
Flisby S 62 A2
Fliseryd S 62 A4
Flix E 153 A4
Flixecourt F . . . 90 A2
Flize F 91 B4
Flobecq B 79 B3
Floby S 55 B4
Floda S 60 B2
Flodden GB . . . 37 A4
Flogny-la-Chapelle
  F 104 B2
Flöha D 83 B5
Flonheim D 93 B4
Florac F 130 A2
Floreffe B 79 B4
Florence = Firenze
  I 135 B4
Florennes B . . . 79 B4
Florensac F . . . 130 B2
Florentin F 129 C5
Florenville B . . . 91 B5
Flores de Avila E . 150 B2
Floresta I 177 B3
Floreşti MD . . . 17 B8
Florídia I 177 B4
Florina GR 182 C3
Flörsheim D . . . 93 A4
Floss D 95 B4
Fluberg N 48 B2
Flúðir IS 190 C5
Flühli CH 106 C3
Flumet F 118 B3
Fluminimaggiore I . 179 C2
Flums CH 107 B4
Flyeryd S 63 B3
Flygsfors S . . . 62 B3
Foča BIH 139 B4
Fochabers GB . . 32 D3
Focşani RO . . . 17 C7
Foel GB 38 B3
Foeni RO 126 B2
Fogdö S 56 A2
Fóggia I 171 B3
Foglianise I . . . 170 B2
Föglö FIN 51 B7
Fohnsdorf A . . . 110 B1
Foiano della Chiana
  I 135 B4
Foix F 146 B2
Fojnica
  BIH. 139 B3
  BIH. 139 B4
Fokstua N 198 C6
Foldereid N . . . 199 A9
Foldingbro DK . . 59 C2
Folegandros GR . 185 C5
Folelli F 180 A2
Folgaria I 121 B4
Folgosinho P . . 148 B2
Folgoso de la Ribera
  E 141 B4
Folgoso do Courel
  E 141 B3
Foligno I 136 C1
Folkärna S 50 B3
Folkestad N . . . 198 C3
Folkestone GB . . 45 B5
Follafoss N . . . 199 B8
Folldal N 198 C6
Follebu N 48 A2
Follina I 121 B5
Föllinge S 199 B11
Follónica I 135 C3
Folsbyn S 54 A3
Foncebadón E . . 141 B4
Foncine-le-Bas F. . 105 C5
Fondevila E . . . 140 C2
Fondi I 169 B3
Fondo I 121 A4
Fonelas E 164 B1
Fonfría
  Teruel E 152 B2
  Zamora E 149 A3
Fonn N 46 A3
Fonnes N 46 B1
Fonni I 178 B3
Fontaine F 91 C4
Fontainebleau F . 90 C2
Fontaine de Vaucluse
  F 131 B4
Fontaine-Française
  F 105 B4
Fontaine-le-Dun F. . 89 A4
Fontan F 133 A3
Fontanarejo E . . 157 A3
Fontane I 133 A3
Fontanélice I . . . 135 A4
Fontanières F . . 116 A2
Fontanosas E . . 157 B3
Fonteblanca I . . . 168 A1
Fontenay-le-Comte
  F 114 B3

Fontenay-Trésigny
  F 90 C2
Fontevrault-l'Abbaye
  F 102 B2
Fontiveros E . . . 150 B3
Fontoy F 92 B1
Fontpédrouse F . . 146 B3
Font-Romeu F . . 146 B3
Fontstown IRL. . . 30 A2
Fonyód H 111 C4
Fonz E 145 B4
Fonzaso I 121 A4
Fóppolo I 120 A2
Föra S 62 A4
Forbach
  D 93 C4
  F 92 B2
Forcall E 153 B3
Forcalquier F . . 132 B1
Forcarei E 140 B2
Forchheim D . . . 94 B3
Forchtenau A . . 111 B3
Forchtenberg D. . 94 B1
Ford GB 34 B2
Førde
  Hordaland N . . 52 A1
  Sogn og Fjordane
  N 46 A2
Förderstedt D . . 83 A3
Førdesfjorden N . 52 A1
Fordham GB . . . 45 A4
Fordingbridge GB. . 44 C2
Fordon PL 76 A3
Fordongiánus I . . 179 C2
Forenza I 172 B1
Foresta di Búrgos
  I 178 B2
Forfar GB 35 B5
Forges-les-Eaux F . 90 B1
Foria I 172 B1
Forío I 170 C1
Forjães P 148 A1
Førland N 52 B3
Forl ì I 135 A5
Forlimpopoli I . . 135 A5
Formazza I 119 A5
Formby GB 38 A3
Formerie F 90 B1
Fórmia I 169 B3
Formígine I 135 A3
Formigliana I . . . 119 B5
Formiguères F . . 146 B3
Fornalutx E . . . 166 B2
Fornåsa S 56 B1
Fornelli I 178 B2
Fornells E 167 A4
Fornelos de Montes
  E 140 B2
Fornes E 163 B4
Forneset N 192 C3
Forni Avoltri I . . 109 C3
Forni di Sopra I . 122 A1
Forni di Sotto I . 122 A1
Forno
  Piemonte I . . . 119 B4
  Piemonte I . . . 119 B5
Forno Alpi-Gráie I . 119 B4
Forno di Zoldo I . 121 A5
Fornos de Algodres
  P 148 B2
Fornovo di Taro I . 120 C3
Foros do Arrão P . 154 B2
Forráskút H . . . 126 A1
Forres GB 32 D3
Forriolo E 140 B3
Fors S 50 B3
Forsand N 52 B2
Forsbacka S . . . 51 B3
Forserum S . . . 62 A2
Forshaga S . . . 55 A4
Forsheda S . . . 60 B3
Forsinain GB . . . 32 C3
Førslev DK 65 A4
Förslöv S 61 C2
Forsmark
  Uppsala S . . . 51 B5
  Västerbotten S . . 195 E6
Forsmo N 200 C3
Forsnäs S 195 D9
Forsnes N 198 B5
Forssa FIN 8 B3
Forssjöbruk S . . 56 B2
Forst D 84 A2
Forsvik S 55 B5
Fortanete E . . . 153 B3
Fort Augustus GB. . 32 D2
Forte dei Marmi I . 134 B3
Fortezza I 108 C2
Forth GB 35 C4
Fort-Mahon-Plage
  F 78 B1
Fortrie GB 33 D4
Fortrose GB . . . 32 D2
Fortun N 47 A4
Fortuna E 165 A3
Fortuneswell GB . 43 B4
Fort William GB . . 34 B2
Forvik N 195 E3
Fos F 145 B4
Fosdinovo I . . . 134 A3
Foss N 47 B6
Fossacésia I . . . 169 A4
Fossano I 133 A3
Fossato di Vico I . 136 B1
Fossbakken N . . 194 B8
Fossby N 54 A2
Fosse-la-Ville B . 79 B4
Fossombrone I . . 136 B1
Fos-sur-Mer F . . 131 B3
Fot H 112 B3
Fouchères F . . . 104 A3
Fouesnant F . . . 100 B1
Foug F 92 C1
Fougères F 88 B2
Fougerolles F . . 105 B5
Foulain F 105 B4
Fountainhall GB . 35 C5
Fouras F 114 C2
Fourchambault F . 104 B2
Fourmies F 91 A4
Fourna GR 182 D3

Fournels F 116 C3
Fourni GR 188 B1
Fournols F 117 B3
Fourques F 146 B3
Fourquevaux F . . 146 A2
Fours F 104 C2
Fowey GB 42 B2
Foxdale GB . . . 36 B2
Foxford IRL . . . 26 C1
Foyers GB 32 D2
Foynes IRL . . . 29 B2
Foz E 141 A3
Foza I 121 B4
Foz do Arelho P. . 154 B1
Foz do Giraldo P . 155 B3
Frabosa Soprana
  I 133 A3
Frades de la Sierra
  E 149 B4
Fraga E 153 A4
Fragagnano I . . 173 B3
Frailes E 163 A4
Fraire B 79 B4
Fraize F 106 A1
Framlingham GB. . 45 A5
Frammersbach D . 94 A1
Framnes N 54 A1
França P 141 C4
Francaltroff F . . 92 C2
Francavilla al Mare
  I 169 A4
Francavilla di Sicília
  I 177 B4
Francavilla Fontana
  I 173 B3
Francavilla in Sinni
  I 174 A2
Francescas F . . 129 B3
Franco P 148 A2
Francofonte I . . 177 B3
Francos E 151 A4
Frändefors S . . . 54 B3
Franeker NL . . . 70 A2
Frangy F 118 A2
Frankenau D . . . 81 A4
Frankenberg
  Hessen D 81 A4
  Sachsen D . . . 83 B5
Frankenburg A . . 109 A4
Frankenfels A . . 110 B2
Frankenmarkt A. . 109 B4
Frankenthal D . . 93 B4
Frankfurt
  Brandenburg D . 74 B3
  Hessen D 81 B4
Frankrike S . . . 199 B10
Fränsta S 200 D2
Františkovy Lázně
  CZ 83 B4
Franzburg D . . . 66 B1
Frascati I 168 B2
Frasdorf D 109 B3
Fraserburgh GB . . 33 D4
Frashër AL 182 C2
Frasne F 105 C5
Frasnes-lez-Anvaing
  B 79 B3
Frasseto F 180 B2
Frastanz A 107 B4
Fratel P 155 B3
Fratta Todina I . . 135 C5
Frauenau D . . . 96 C1
Frauenfeld CH . . 107 B3
Frauenkirchen A . 111 B3
Frauenstein D . . 83 B5
Frauental A . . . 110 C2
Frayssinet F . . . 129 B4
Frayssinet-le-Gélat
  F 129 B4
Frechas P 149 A2
Frechen D 80 B2
Frechilla E 142 B2
Freckenhorst D . . 71 C4
Fredeburg D . . . 81 A4
Fredelsloh D . . . 82 A1
Fredeng N 48 B2
Fredensborg DK . 61 D2
Fredericia DK . . 59 C2
Frederiks DK . . 59 B2
Frederikshavn DK. . 58 A3
Frederikssund DK. . 61 D2
Frederiksværk DK. . 61 D2
Fredrika S 200 B4
Fredriksberg S . . 50 B1
Fredriksdal S . . 62 A2
Fredrikstad N . . 54 A1
Fregenal de la Sierra
  E 161 A3
Fregene I 168 B2
Freiberg D 83 B5
Freiburg
  Baden-Württemberg
  D 106 B2
  Niedersachsen D . 64 C2
Freienhagen D . . 81 A5
Freienhufen D . . 84 A1
Freiensteinau D . 81 B5
Freihung D 95 B3
Freilassing D . . 109 B3
Freisen D 92 B3
Freising D 95 C3
Freistadt A 96 C2
Freital D 84 A1
Freixedas P . . . 149 B2
Freixo de Espada à
  Cinta P. 149 A3
Fréjus F 132 B2
Fremdingen D . . 94 C2
Frenštát pod
  Radhoštěm CZ . 98 B2
Freren D 71 B4
Freshford IRL . . 30 B1
Freshwater GB . . 44 C2
Fresnay-sur-Sarthe
  F 89 B4
Fresneda de la Sierra
  E 152 B1

Fresneda de la Sierra
Tiron E 143 B3
Fresnedillas E 151 B3
Fresnes-en-Woevre
F 92 B1
Fresne-St Mamès
F 105 B4
Fresno Alhandiga
E 150 B2
Fresno de la Ribera
E 150 A2
Fresno de la Vega
E 142 B1
Fresno de Sayago
E 149 A4
Fresnoy-Folny F 90 B1
Fresnoy-le-Grand F 91 B3
Fressenville F 90 A1
Fresvik N 46 A3
Fréteval F 103 B3
Fretigney F 105 B4
Freudenberg
Baden-Württemberg
D 94 B1
Nordrhein-Westfalen
D 81 B3
Freudenstadt D 93 C4
Freux B 92 B1
Frévent F 78 B2
Freyburg D 83 A3
Freyenstein D 73 A5
Freyming-Merlebach
F 92 B2
Freystadt D 95 B3
Freyung D 96 C1
Frias de Albarracin
E 152 B2
Fribourg CH 106 C2
Frick CH 106 B3
Fridafors S 63 B2
Fridaythorpe GB 40 A3
Friedberg
A 111 B3
Bayern D 94 C2
Hessen D 81 B4
Friedeburg D 71 A4
Friedewald D 82 B1
Friedland
Brandenburg D 74 B3
Mecklenburg-Vorpommern D 74 A2
Niedersachsen D 82 A1
Friedrichroda D 82 B2
Friedrichsdorf D 81 B4
Friedrichshafen D 107 B4
Friedrichskoog D 64 B1
Friedrichstadt D 64 B2
Friedrichswalde D 74 A2
Friesach A 110 C1
Friesack D 73 B5
Friesenheim D 93 C3
Friesoythe D 71 A4
Friggesund S 200 E2
Frigiliana E 163 B4
Frihetsli N 192 D3
Frillesås S 60 B2
Frinnaryd S 62 A2
Frinton-on-Sea GB 45 B5
Friockheim GB 35 B5
Friol E 140 A3
Fristad S 60 B2
Fritsla S 60 B2
Fritzlar D 81 A5
Frizington GB 36 B3
Frödinge S 62 A4
Froges F 118 B2
Frohburg D 83 A4
Frohnhausen D 81 B4
Frohnleiten A 110 B2
Froissy F 90 B2
Frombork PL 69 A4
Frome GB 43 A4
Frómista E 142 B2
Fröndenberg D 81 A3
Fronsac F 128 B2
Front I 119 B4
Fronteira P 155 B3
Frontenay-Rohan-Rohan F 114 B3
Frontenhausen D 95 C4
Frontignan F 130 B2
Fronton F 129 C4
Fröseke S 62 B3
Frosinone I 169 B3
Frosolone I 170 B2
Frosta N 199 B7
Frøstrup DK 58 A1
Frosunda S 57 A4
Frouard F 92 C2
Frövi S 56 A1
Frøyset N 46 B2
Fruges F 78 B2
Frutigen CH 106 C2
Frýdek-Místek CZ 98 B2
Frýdlant CZ 84 B3
Frydlant nad Ostravicí
CZ 98 B2
Frygnowo PL 77 A5
Fryšták CZ 98 B1
Fucécchio I 135 B3
Fuencaliente
Ciudad Real E 157 A4
Ciudad Real E 157 B3
Fuencemillán E 151 B4
Fuendejalón E 144 C2
Fuengirola E 163 B3
Fuenlabrada E 151 B4
Fuenlabrada de los Montes E 156 A3
Fuensalida E 151 B3
Fuensanta E 164 B3
Fuensanta de Martos
E 163 A4
Fuente-Alamo E 158 C2
Fuente-Álamo de Murcia E 165 B3
Fuentealbilla E 158 B2
Fuente al Olmo de Iscar
E 150 A3
Fuentecén E 151 A4
Fuente Dé E 142 A2
Fuente de Cantos
E 155 C4
Fuente del Arco E 156 B2
Fuente del Conde
E 163 A3
Fuente del Maestre
E 155 C4
Fuente de Santa Cruz
E 150 A3
Fuente el Fresno
E 157 A4
Fuente el Saz de Jarama E 151 B4
Fuente el Sol E 150 A3
Fuenteguinaldo E 149 B3
Fuentelapeña E 150 A2
Fuentelcésped E 151 A4
Fuentelespino de Haro
E 158 B1
Fuentelespino de Moya
E 158 B2
Fuentenovilla E 151 B4
Fuente Obejuna E 156 B2
Fuente Palmera E 162 A2
Fuentepelayo E 151 A3
Fuentepinilla E 151 A5
Fuenterroble de Salvatierra E 150 B2
Fuenterrobles E 158 B2
Fuentes E 158 B1
Fuentesauco E 151 A3
Fuentesaúco E 150 A2
Fuentes de Andalucía
E 162 A2
Fuentes de Ebro
E 153 A3
Fuentes de Jiloca
E 152 A2
Fuentes de la Alcarria
E 151 B5
Fuentes de León
E 161 A3
Fuentes de Nava
E 142 B2
Fuentes de Oñoro
E 149 B3
Fuentes de Ropel
E 142 B1
Fuentespalda E 153 B4
Fuentespina E 151 A4
Fuente-Tójar E 163 A3
Fuente Vaqueros
E 163 A4
Fuentidueña E 151 A4
Fuentidueña de Tajo
E 151 B4
Fuerte del Rey E 157 C4
Fügen A 108 B2
Fuglebjerg DK 65 A4
Fuglevik N 54 A1
Fuhrberg D 72 B2
Fulda D 82 B1
Fulgatore I 176 B1
Fully CH 119 A4
Fulnek CZ 98 B1
Fülöpszállás H 112 C3
Fulpmes A 108 B2
Fulunäs S 49 A5
Fumay F 91 B4
Fumel F 129 B3
Funäsdalen S 199 C9
Fundão P 148 B2
Funzie GB 33 A6
Furadouro P 148 B1
Fure N 46 A2
Fürstenau D 71 B4
Fürstenau D 81 A5
Förstenberg D 74 A2
Fürstenfeld A 111 B3
Fürstenfeldbruck
D 108 A2
Fürstenstein D 96 C1
Fürstenwalde D 74 B3
Fürstenwerder D 74 A2
Fürstenzell D 96 C1
Furta H 113 B5
Fürth
Bayern D 94 B2
Hessen D 93 B4
Furth im Wald D 95 B4
Furtwangen D 106 A3
Furuby S 62 B3
Furudal S 50 A2
Furuflaten N 192 C4
Furulund S 61 D3
Furusjö S 60 B3
Fusa N 46 B2
Fuscaldo I 174 B2
Fusch an der Grossglocknerstrasse
A 109 B3
Fushë Arrëz AL 182 A2
Fushë-Krujë AL 182 B1
Fusina I 122 B1
Fusio CH 107 C3
Füssen D 108 B1
Fustiñana E 144 B2
Futog SRB 126 B1
Futrikelv N 192 C3
Füzesabony H 113 B4
Füzesgyarmat H 113 B5
Fužine HR 123 B3
Fyllinge S 61 C2
Fynshav DK 64 B2
Fyresdal N 53 A4

G

Gaaldorf A 110 B1
Gabaldón E 158 B2
Gabarret F 128 C2
Gabčíkovo SK 111 B4
Gąbin PL 77 B4
Gabriac F 130 A1
Gabrovo BG 17 D6
Gaby I 119 B4
Gacé F 89 B4
Gacko BIH 139 B4
Gäddede S 199 A11
Gadebusch D 65 C4
Gadmen CH 106 C3
Gádor E 164 C2
Gádoros H 113 C4
Gael F 101 A3
Găeşti RO 17 C6
Gaeta I 169 B3
Gafanhoeira P 154 C2
Gaflenz A 110 B1
Gagarin RUS 9 E9
Gaggenau D 93 C4
Gagliano Castelferrato
I 177 B3
Gagliano del Capo
I 173 C4
Gagnet S 50 B2
Gaibanella I 121 C4
Gaildorf D 94 B1
Gaillac F 129 C4
Gaillefontaine F 90 B1
Gaillon F 89 A5
Gainsborough GB 40 B3
Gairloch GB 31 B3
Gairlochy GB 34 B3
Gáiro I 179 C3
Gaj
HR 124 B3
SRB 127 C3
Gaja-la-Selve F 146 A2
Gajanejos E 151 B5
Gajary SK 97 C4
Gajdobra SRB 126 B1
Galan F 145 A4
Galanta SK 111 A4
Galapagar E 151 B3
Galápagos E 151 B4
Galaroza E 161 B3
Galashiels GB 35 C5
Galatas GR 185 B4
Galați RO 17 C8
Galatina I 173 B4
Galatista GR 183 C5
Galátone I 173 B4
Galaxidi GR 184 A3
Galdakao E 143 A4
Galeata I 135 B4
Galende E 141 B4
Galera E 164 B2
Galéria F 180 A1
Galgamácsa H 112 B3
Galgate GB 38 A4
Galgon F 128 B2
Galinduste E 150 B2
Galinoporni CY 181 A3
Galisteo E 155 B4
Galizes P 148 B2
Galków PL 87 A3
Gallarate I 120 B1
Gallardon F 90 C1
Gallegos de Argañán
E 149 B3
Gallegos del Solmirón
E 150 B2
Galleguillos de Campos
E 142 B1
Galleno I 135 B3
Galliate I 120 B1
Gallicano I 134 A3
Gállio I 121 B4
Gallipoli = Gelibolu
TR 186 B1
Gallípoli I 173 B3
Gällivare S 196 B3
Gallizien A 110 C1
Gallneukirchen A 96 C2
Gällö S 199 C12
Gallocanta E 152 B2
Gällstad S 60 B3
Gallur E 144 C2
Galmisdale GB 31 C2
Galmpton GB 43 B3
Galston GB 36 A2
Galta N 52 A1
Galtelli I 178 B3
Galten DK 59 B2
Galtür A 107 C5
Galve de Sorbe E 151 A4
Galveias P 154 B2
Gálvez E 157 A3
Galway IRL 28 A2
Gamaches F 90 B1
Gámbara I 120 B3
Gambárie I 175 C1
Gambassi Terme I 135 B3
Gambatesa I 170 B2
Gambolò I 120 B1
Gaming A 110 B2
Gamla Uppsala S 51 C4
Gamleby S 62 A4
Gamlingay GB 44 A3
Gammelgarn S 57 C4
Gammelstad S 196 D5
Gammertingen D 107 A4
Gams CH 107 B4
Gamvik
Finnmark N 192 B6
Finnmark N 193 A12
Gan F 145 A3
Gáname E 149 A3
Ganda di Martello
I 108 C1
Gandarela P 148 A1
Ganddal N 52 B1
Ganderkesee D 72 A1
Gandesa E 153 A4
Gandía E 159 C3
Gandino I 120 B2
Gandrup DK 58 A3
Ganges F 130 B2
Gånghester S 60 B3
Gangi I 177 B3
Gangkofen D 95 C4
Gannat F 116 A3
Gannay-sur-Loire
F 104 C2
Gänserdorf A 97 C4
Ganzlin D 73 A5
Gap F 132 A2
Gara H 125 A5
Garaballa E 158 B2
Garaguso I 172 B2
Garbayuela E 156 A2
Garbhallt GB 34 B2
Garbsen D 72 B2
Garching D 109 A3
Garciaz E 156 A2
Garcihernández E 150 B2
Garcillán E 151 B3
Garcinarro E 151 B5
Garcisobaco E 162 B2
Garda I 121 B3
Gardanne F 131 B4
Gärdås S 49 B5
Gårdby S 63 B4
Gardeja PL 69 B3
Gardelegen D 73 B4
Gardermoen N 48 B3
Gardiki GR 182 E3
Garding D 64 B1
Gardone Riviera I 121 B3
Gardone Val Trómpia
I 120 B3
Gárdony H 112 B2
Gardouch F 146 A2
Gårdsjö S 55 B5
Gårdskär S 51 B4
Gards Köpinge S 63 C2
Garein F 128 B2
Garelochhead GB 34 B3
Garéoult F 132 B2
Garešnica HR 124 B2
Garéssio I 133 A4
Garforth GB 40 B2
Gargaliani GR 184 B2
Gargaligas E 156 A2
Gargallo E 153 B3
Garganta la Olla E 150 B2
Gargantiel E 156 B3
Gargellen A 107 C4
Gargilesse-Dampierre
F 103 C3
Gargnano I 121 B3
Gargnäs S 195 E8
Gárgoles de Abajo
E 152 B1
Gargrave GB 40 B1
Garitz D 73 C5
Garlasco I 120 B1
Garlieston GB 36 B2
Garlin F 128 C2
Garlitos E 156 B2
Garmisch-Partenkirchen D 108 B2
Garnat-sur-Engièvre
F 104 C2
Garpenberg S 50 B3
Garphyttan S 55 A5
Garray E 143 C4
Garrel D 71 B5
Garriguella E 146 B4
Garrison GB 26 B2
Garrovillas E 155 B4
Garrucha E 164 B3
Gars-am-Kamp A 97 C3
Garsås S 50 B1
Garsdale Head GB 37 B4
Gärsnäs S 63 C2
Garstang GB 38 A4
Gartow D 73 A4
Gartz D 74 A3
Gærum DK 58 A3
Garvagh GB 27 B4
Garvão P 160 B1
Garve GB 32 D2
Garwolin PL 12 C4
Garz D 66 B2
Garzyn PL 85 A4
Gąsawa PL 76 B2
Gåsborn S 49 C6
Gaschurn A 107 C5
Gascueña E 152 B1
Gasny F 90 B1
Gąsocin PL 77 B5
Gastes F 128 B1
Gastouni GR 184 B2
Gastouri GR 182 D1
Gata
E 149 B3
HR 138 B2
Gata de Gorgos E 159 C4
Gătaia RO 126 B3
Gatchina RUS 9 C7
Gatehouse of Fleet
GB 36 B2
Gátér H 113 C3
Gateshead GB 37 B5
Gátova E 159 B3
Gattendorf A 111 A3
Gatteo a Mare I 136 A1
Gattinara I 119 B5
Gattorna I 134 A2
Gaucín E 162 B2
Gaulstad N 199 B9
Gaupne N 47 A4
Gautefall N 53 A4
Gauting D 108 A2
Gauto S 195 D7
Gava E 147 C3
Gavardo I 121 B3
Gavarnie F 145 B3
Gávavencsello H 113 A5
Gavi I 120 C1
Gavião P 154 B3
Gavirate I 120 B1
Gävle S 51 B4
Gavoi I 178 B3
Gavorrano I 135 C3
Gavray F 88 B2
Gavrio GR 185 B5
Gävunda S 49 B6
Gaweinstal A 97 C4
Gaworzyce PL 85 A3
Gawroniec PL 75 A5
Gaydon GB 44 A2
Gayton GB 41 C4
Gazipaşa TR 189 C7
Gazoldo degli Ippoliti
I 121 B3
Gazzuolo I 121 B3
Gbelce SK 112 B2
Gdańsk PL 69 A3
Gdinj HR 138 B2
Gdov RUS 8 C5
Gdów PL 99 B4
Gdynia PL 69 A3
Gea de Albarracin
E 152 B2
Geary GB 31 B2
Géaudot F 91 C4
Geaune F 128 C2
Gebesee D 82 A2
Gebiz TR 189 B5
Gebze TR 187 B4
Géderlak H 112 C2
Gedern D 81 B5
Gedinne B 91 B4
Gediz TR 187 D4
Gèdre F 145 B4
Gedser DK 65 B4
Gedsted DK 58 B2
Geel B 79 A4
Geesthacht D 72 A3
Geetbets B 79 B5
Gefell D 83 B3
Gehrden D 72 B2
Gehren D 82 B3
Geilenkirchen D 80 B2
Geilo N 47 B5
Geinsheim D 93 B4
Geisa D 82 B1
Geiselhöring D 95 C4
Geiselwind D 94 B2
Geisenfeld D 95 C3
Geisenhausen D 95 C4
Geisenheim D 93 B4
Geising D 84 B1
Geisingen D 107 B3
Geislingen D 94 C1
Geistthal A 110 B2
Geiteryggyhtta N 47 B4
Geithain D 83 A4
Geithus N 48 C1
Gela I 177 B3
Geldermalsen NL 79 A5
Geldern D 80 A2
Geldrop NL 80 A1
Geleen NL 80 B1
Gelembe TR 186 C2
Gelendost TR 189 A6
Gelibolu = Gallipoli
TR 186 B1
Gelida E 147 C2
Gelnhausen D 81 B5
Gelnica SK 99 C4
Gelsa E 153 A3
Gelse H 111 C3
Gelsenkirchen D 80 A3
Gelsted DK 59 C2
Geltendorf D 108 A2
Gelterkinden CH 106 B2
Gelting D 64 B2
Gelu RO 126 A3
Gelves E 162 A1
Gembloux B 79 B4
Gemeaux F 105 B4
Gémenos F 132 B1
Gemerská Poloma
SK 99 C4
Gemerská Ves SK 99 C4
Gemert NL 80 A1
Gemla S 62 B2
Gemlik TR 186 B4
Gemmenich B 80 B1
Gemona del Friuli
I 122 A2
Gémozac F 114 C3
Gemund D 80 B2
Gemünden
Bayern D 94 A1
Hessen D 81 B4
Rheinland-Pfalz D 93 B3
Genappe B 79 B4
Génave E 164 A2
Genazzano I 169 B2
Gençay F 115 B4
Gencsapáti H 111 B3
Gendringen NL 80 A2
Genelard F 104 C3
Genemuiden NL 70 B3
Generalski Stol
HR 123 B4
Geneva = Genève
CH 118 A3
Genevad S 61 C3
Genève = Geneva
CH 118 A3
Genevriéres F 105 B4
Gengenbach D 93 C4
Genillé F 103 B3
Genk B 80 B1
Genlis F 105 B4
Gennep NL 80 A1
Genner DK 64 A2
Gennes F 102 B1
Genoa = Génova I 134 A1
Genola I 133 A3
Génova = Genoa I 134 A1
Genowefa PL 76 B3
Gensingen D 93 B3
Gent = Ghent B 79 A3
Genthin D 73 B5
Gentioux F 116 B1
Genzano di Lucánia
I 172 B2
Genzano di Roma
I 168 B2
Georgenthal D 82 B2
Georgsmarienhütte
D 71 B5
Gera D 83 B4
Geraards-bergen B 79 B3
Gerace I 175 C2
Geraci Sículo I 177 B3
Geraki GR 184 C3
Gérardmer F 106 A1
Geras A 97 C3
Gerbéviller F 92 C2
Gerbini I 177 B3
Gerbstedt D 83 A3
Gerði IS 191 C9
Gerede TR 187 B7
Gerena E 161 B3
Geretsried D 108 B2
Gérgal E 164 B2
Gergy F 105 C3
Gerindote E 150 C3
Gerjen H 112 C2
Gerlos A 108 B3
Germay F 92 C1
Germencik TR 188 B2
Germering D 108 A2
Germersheim D 93 B4
Gernika-Lumo E 143 A4
Gernrode D 82 A3
Gernsbach D 93 C4
Gernsheim D 93 B4
Geroda D 82 B1
Gerola Alta I 120 A2
Geroldsgrun D 83 B3
Gerolsbach D 95 C3
Gerolstein D 80 B2
Gerolzhofen D 94 B2
Gerovo HR 123 B3
Gerpinnes B 79 B4
Gerrards Cross GB 44 B3
Gerri de la Sal E 147 B2
Gersfeld D 82 B1
Gerstetten D 94 C2
Gersthofen D 94 C2
Gerstungen D 82 B2
Gerswalde D 74 A2
Gerzat F 116 B3
Gerze TR 23 A8
Gerzen D 95 C4
Gescher D 71 C4
Geseke D 81 A4
Geslau D 94 B2
Gespunsart F 91 B4
Gesté F 101 B4
Gestorf D 72 B2
Gesualda I 170 C3
Gesunda S 50 B1
Gesztely H 113 A4
Geta FIN 51 B6
Getafe E 151 B4
Getinge S 60 C2
Getxo E 143 A4
Geversdorf D 64 C2
Gevgelija MK 182 B4
Gevora del Caudillo
E 155 C4
Gevrey-Chambertin
F 105 B3
Gex F 118 A3
Gey D 80 B2
Geyikli TR 186 C1
Geysir IS 190 C5
Geyve TR 187 B5
Gföhl A 97 C3
Ghedi I 120 B3
Ghent = Gent B 79 A3
Gheorgheni RO 17 B6
Ghigo I 119 C4
Ghilarza I 178 B2
Ghisonaccia F 180 A2
Ghisoni F 180 A2
Gialtra GR 182 E4
Gianitsa GR 182 C4
Giardinetto Vécchio
I 171 B3
Giardini Naxos I 177 B4
Giarratana I 177 B3
Giarre I 177 B4
Giat F 116 B2
Giaveno I 119 B4
Giazza I 121 B4
Giba I 179 C2
Gibellina Nuova I 176 B1
Gibostad N 194 A9
Gibraleón E 161 B3
Gibraltar GBZ 162 B2
Gic H 111 B4
Gideå S 200 C5
Gideåkroken S 200 B3
Gidle PL 86 B3
Giebelstadt D 94 B1
Gieboldehausen D 82 A2
Gielniów PL 87 A4
Gielow D 74 A1
Gien F 103 B4
Giengen D 94 C2
Giens F 132 B2
Giera RO 126 B2
Gieselwerder D 81 A5
Giessen D 81 B4
Gieten NL 71 A3
Giethoorn NL 70 B3
Giffaumont-Champaubert F 91 C4
Gifford GB 35 C5
Gifhorn D 73 B3
Gige H 125 A3
Gignac F 130 B2
Gijón = Xixón E 142 A1
Gilena E 162 A3
Gilford GB 27 B4
Gillberga S 55 A3
Gilleleje DK 61 C2
Gilley F 105 B5
Gilley-sur-Loire F 104 C2
Gillingham
Dorset GB 43 A4
Medway GB 45 B4
Gilocourt F 90 B2
Gilserberg D 81 B5
Gilsland GB 37 B4
Gilze NL 79 A4
Gimåt S 200 C4
Gimo S 51 B5
Gimont F 129 C3
Ginasservis F 132 B1
Gingelom B 79 B5
Gingst D 66 B2
Ginosa I 171 C4
Ginzling A 108 B2
Giões P 160 B2
Gióia dei Marsi I 169 B3
Gióia del Colle I 173 B2
Gióia Sannitica I 170 B2
Gióia Táuro I 175 C1
Gioiosa Iónica I 175 C2
Gioiosa Marea I 177 A3
Giosla GB 31 A2
Giovinazzo I 171 B4
Girifalco I 175 C2
Giromagny F 106 B1
Girona E 147 C3
Gironcourt-sur-Vraine
F 92 C1
Gironella E 147 B2
Gironville-sous-les-Côtes F 92 C1
Girvan GB 36 A2
Gislaved S 60 B3
Gislev DK 59 C3
Gisors F 90 B1
Gissi I 170 A2
Gistad S 56 B1
Gistel B 78 A2
Gistrup DK 58 B3
Giswil CH 106 C3
Githio GR 184 C3
Giugliano in Campania
I 170 C2
Giulianova I 136 C2
Giulvăz RO 126 B2
Giurgiu RO 17 D6
Give DK 59 C2
Givet F 91 A4
Givors F 117 B4
Givry
B 79 B4
F 104 C3
Givry-en-Argonne
F 91 C4
Givskud DK 59 C2
Giżalki PL 76 B2
Gizeux F 102 B2
Giżycko PL 12 A4
Gizzeria I 175 C2
Gizzeria Lido I 175 C2
Gjedved DK 59 C2
Gjegjan AL 182 B2
Gjendesheim N 47 A5
Gjerde N 46 B3
Gjerlev DK 58 B3
Gjermundshamn N 46 B2
Gjerrild DK 58 B3
Gjerstad N 53 B5
Gjesås N 49 B4
Gjesvær N 193 A9
Gjirokastër AL 182 C2
Gjøfjell N 54 A1
Gjøl DK 58 A2
Gjøra N 198 C6
Gjøvik N 48 B2
Gladbeck D 80 A2
Gladenbach D 81 B4
Gladstad N 195 E2
Glamis GB 35 B4
Glamoč BIH 138 A2
Glamsbjerg DK 59 C3
Gland CH 105 C5
Glandorf D 71 B4
Glanegg A 110 C1
Glanshammar S 56 A1
Glarus CH 107 B4
Glasgow GB 35 C3
Glashütte
Bayern D 108 B2
Sachsen D 84 B1
Glastonbury GB 43 A4
Glatzau A 110 C2
Glauchau D 83 B4
Glava S 54 A3
Glavatičevo BIH 139 B4
Glavičice BIH 127 C1
Glŭbovo BG 183 A7
Glein
A 110 B1
N 195 D3
Gleinstätten A 110 C2
Gleisdorf A 110 B2
Glenamoy IRL 26 B1
Glenarm GB 27 B5
Glenavy GB 27 B4
Glenbarr GB 34 C2
Glenbeigh IRL 29 B2
Glenbrittle GB 31 B2
Glencoe GB 34 B2
Glencolumbkille
IRL 26 B2
Glendalough IRL 30 A2
Glenealy IRL 30 B2
Glenelg GB 31 B3
Glenfinnan GB 34 B2
Glengarriff IRL 29 C2
Glenluce GB 36 B2
Glennamaddy IRL 28 A3
Glenrothes GB 35 B4
Glenties IRL 26 B2
Glesborg DK 58 B3
Glesien D 83 A4
Gletsch CH 106 C3
Glewitz D 66 B1
Glifada GR 185 B4
Glimåkra S 63 B2
Glin IRL 29 B2
Glina HR 124 B2
Glinde D 72 A3
Glinojeck PL 77 B5
Glinsk IRL 28 A1
Gliwice PL 86 B2
Glödnitz A 109 C5
Gloggnitz A 110 B2
Głogoczów PL 99 B3
Glogonj SRB 127 C2
Glogovac SRB 127 C3
Głogów PL 85 A4
Głogówek PL 86 B1
Glomel F 100 A2
Glomfjord N 195 D4
Glommen S 60 C2
Glommersträsk S 196 D2
Glonn D 108 B3
Glorenza I 108 C1

loria P 154 B2
losa GR 183 D5
lossop GB 40 B2
loucester GB 39 C4
łowaczów PL 87 A5
łówczyce PL 68 A2
löwen D 73 B5
łowno PL 77 C4
łożan SRB 126 B1
łubczyce PL 86 B1
łucholazy PL 85 B5
łuchów PL 87 A4
łuchowo PL 75 B5
lücksburg D 64 B2
lückstadt D 64 C2
lumina BIH 139 A5
lumsø DK 65 A4
lušci SRB 127 C1
lusk BY 13 B8
łuszyca PL 85 B4
lyngøre DK 58 B1
lyn Neath GB. 39 C3
münd
Kärnten A. 109 C4
Nieder Österreich
A. 96 C2
mund D 108 B2
munden A 109 B4
narp S 200 D3
nesau A 109 C4
nesta S 56 A3
nięchowice PL 85 A4
niew PL 69 B3
niewkowo PL 76 B3
nioto PL 76 B2
noien D 66 C1
nojnice BIH 139 B3
nojno PL 87 B4
nosall GB 40 C1
nosjö S 60 B3
öbel TR 186 B3
öçbeyli TR. 186 C2
och D 80 A2
ochsheim D 94 A2
öd H. 112 B3
odalming GB. 44 B3
odby FIN 51 B6
oddalir IS 190 B6
oddelsheim D. 81 A4
ódega di Sant'Urbano
. . . . .122 B1
odegård S 56 B1
odelheim D 81 A4
oderville F. 89 A4
odiasco I 120 C2
odič SLO. 123 A3
odkowo PL 69 A4
odmanchester
GB 44 A3
ödöllő H 112 B3
ödre H 125 A3
odshill GB. 44 C2
odzikowice PL 85 B5
odziszewo PL 69 A3
oes NL 79 A3
oetzenbrück F 93 C3
óglio I 119 A5
ogolin PL. 86 B2
öhren D 66 B2
oirle NL 79 A5
óis P 148 B1
óito I 121 B3
oizueta E. 144 A2
ojna Gora SRB . .127 D2
ojsk PL 77 B4
ökçedağ TR. 186 C3
ökçen TR. 188 A2
ökçeören TR. 188 A3
ökçeyazı TR 186 C1
öktepe TR 188 B3
ol N 47 B5
ola
HR 124 A3
N 48 A1
ołańcz PL 76 B2
ölbaşı TR. 23 B7
ölby FIN. 51 B6
ölcük
Kocaeli TR. 187 B4
Niğde TR 23 B8
ölčův Jeníkov CZ .97 B3
ołczewo PL. 67 C3
oldach CH. 107 B4
oldbach D 93 A5
oldbeck D 73 B4
oldberg D 73 A5
oldelund D 64 B2
oldenstedt D 72 B1
ołdrowo PL 69 A3
olegå P 154 B2
oleniów PL 75 A3
olfo Aranci I 178 B3
ölhisar TR 189 B4
olina PL. 76 B3
ölle H 112 C2
öllersdorf A. 97 C4
olling an der Salzach
A. 109 B4
ölmarmara TR. 186 D2
olnice PL. 84 A3
olnik SLO. 123 A3
ölova TR 189 C5
ölpazarı TR. 187 B5
ols A. 111 B3
olspie GB 32 D3
olssen P 154 B2
olub-Dobrzyń PL . .77 A4
olubinci SRB. 127 C2
ołuchów PL. 86 A1
olmin-Ośrodek
PL. 77 B5
ölzow D. 73 B5
omagoi P. 108 C1
ómara E. 152 A1
omaringen D. 93 C3
ömbe TR 189 C4
omel = Homyel
BY 13 B9

Gomes Aires P . . .160 B1
Gómezserracin E . .150 A3
Gommern D 73 B4
Gomulin PL 86 A3
Gonäs S. 50 B2
Goncelin F. 118 B2
Gończyce PL. 87 A5
Gondomar
E. 140 B2
P 148 A1
Gondrecourt-le-
Château F 92 C1
Gondrin F 128 C3
Gönen
Balıkesir TR. . . .186 B2
İsparta TR 189 B5
Gonfaron F 132 B2
Goñi E 144 B2
Goni
GR 182 D4
I 179 C2
Gonnesa I 179 C2
Gonnosfanádiga I 179 C2
Gönyü H. 111 B4
Gonzaga I 121 C3
Goodrich GB 39 C4
Goodwick GB 39 B1
Gooik B 79 B4
Goole GB 40 B3
Goor NL 71 B3
Göpfritz an der Wild
A. 97 C3
Goppenstein CH . .119 A4
Göppingen D 94 C1
Gor E 164 B2
Góra
Dolnośląskie PL. .85 A4
Mazowieckie PL. .77 B5
Gorafe E. 164 B1
Gorawino PL 67 C4
Goražde BIH 139 B4
Görbeháza H 113 B5
Gordaliza del Pino
E. 142 B1
Gördes TR 186 D3
Gørding DK. 59 C1
Górdola CH 120 A1
Gordon GB 35 C5
Gordoncillo E 142 B1
Gorenja Vas SLO. .123 A3
Gorenje Jelenje
HR 123 B3
Gorey
GB 88 A1
IRL 30 B2
Gorgonzola I 120 B2
Gorica HR 137 A4
Gorican HR 124 A2
Gorinchem NL. 79 A4
Goring GB 44 B2
Goritsy RUS 9 C10
Göritz D 74 A2
Gorízia I 122 B2
Górki PL 77 B4
Gorleben D 73 A4
Gorleston-on-sea
GB 41 C5
Gørlev DK 61 D1
Görlitz D. 84 A2
Görliz F 143 A4
Görmin D 66 C2
Górna Grupa PL . . .69 B3
Gorna Oryahovitsa
BG 17 D6
Gorna Ploča HR . .137 A4
Gornja Radgona
SLO 110 C2
Gornja Sabanta
SRB 127 D3
Gornja Trešnjevica
SRB 127 C2
Gornja Tuzla BIH . .125 C4
Gornje Polje MNE .139 C4
Gornje Ratkovo
BIH. 124 C2
Gornji Grad SLO . .123 A3
Gornji Humac HR .138 B2
Gornji Jasenjani
BIH. 139 B3
Gornji Kamengrad
BIH. 124 C2
Gornji Kneginec
HR 124 A2
Gornji Kosinj HR. .123 C4
Gornji Milanovac
SRB 127 C2
Gornji Podgradci
BIH. 124 B3
Gornji Ravno BIH .138 B3
Gornji Sjenicak
HR 124 B1
Gornji Vakuf BIH .138 B3
Górno PL 87 B4
Görömböly H 113 A4
Górowo Iławeckie
PL. 69 A5
Gorran Haven GB . .42 B2
Gorredijk NL 70 A2
Gorron F 88 B3
Gorseinon GB 39 C2
Gort IRL 28 A3
Gortin GB. 27 B3
Görzke D 73 B5
Gorzkowice PL. 86 A3
Górzno
Kujawsko-Pomorskie
PL. 77 A4
Zachodnio-Pomorskie
PL. 75 A4
Gorzów Śląski PL . .86 A2
Gorzów Wielkopolski
PL. 75 B4
Górzyca PL 74 B3
Gorzyce PL 98 B2
Górzyn PL. 84 A2
Gorzyń PL 75 B4
Gorzyno PL 68 A2

Gosaldo I 121 A4
Gosau A 109 B4
Gosberton GB 41 C3
Gościcino PL 68 A3
Gościęcin PL. 86 B2
Gościm PL. 75 B4
Gościno PL. 67 B4
Gosdorf A. 110 C2
Gosforth GB 36 B3
Goslar D 82 A2
Goslice PL. 77 B4
Gospič HR. 137 A4
Gosport GB 44 C2
Gössäter S. 55 B4
Gossau CH 107 B4
Goss Ilsede D 72 B3
Gössnitz D. 83 B4
Gössweinstein D. . .95 B3
Gostivar MK. 182 B2
Gostkow PL. 77 C4
Göstling an der Ybbs
A. 110 B1
Gostomia PL 75 A5
Gostycyn PL 76 A2
Gostyń PL. 85 A5
Gostynin PL 77 B4
Goszczyn PL. 87 A4
Göta S 54 B3
Göteborg =
Gothenburg S. . . .60 B1
Götene S. 55 B4
Gotha D 82 B2
Gothem S. 57 C4
Gothenburg =
Göteborg S. 60 B1
Gotse Delchev BG 183 B5
Gottersdorf D 95 C4
Göttingen D 82 A1
Gottne S 200 C4
Götzis A. 107 B4
Gouarec F 100 A2
Gouda NL 70 B1
Goudhurst GB 45 B4
Goumenissa GR . .182 C4
Goura GR. 184 B3
Gourdon F 129 B4
Gourgançon F 91 C4
Gourin F 100 A2
Gournay-en-Bray F 90 B1
Gourock GB 34 C3
Gouveia P 148 B2
Gouvy B 80 B1
Gouzeacourt F 90 A3
Gouzon F 116 A2
Govedari HR 138 C3
Govérnolo I 121 B3
Gowarczów PL 87 A4
Gowerton GB 39 C2
Gowidlino PL. 68 A2
Gowran IRL 30 B1
Goyatz D 74 B3
Göynük
TR 187 B5
Antalya TR 189 C5
Gozdnica PL 84 A3
Gozdowo PL 77 B4
Gozee B 79 B4
Graal-Müritz D 65 B5
Grabenstätt D 109 B3
Grabhair GB 31 A2
Gråbo S 60 B2
Grabovac
HR 138 B2
SRB 127 C1
Grabow D 73 A4
Grabów PL 77 B4
Grabow nad Pilicą
PL. 87 A5
Grabów nad Prosną
PL. 86 A2
Grabowno PL. 76 A2
Grabs CH 107 B4
Gračac HR 138 A1
Gračanica BIH 125 C4
Graçay F 103 B3
Grad SLO 111 C3
Gradac
BIH 139 C4
HR 138 B3
MNE 139 B5
Gradačac BIH 125 C4
Gradec HR 124 B2
Gradefes E. 142 B1
Grades A 110 C1
Gradil P 154 C1
Gradina
HR 124 B3
MNE 139 B5
Gradisca d'Isonzo
I 122 B2
Gradište HR 125 B4
Grado
E 141 A4
I 122 B2
Grafenau D 96 C1
Gräfenberg D. 95 B3
Gräfenhainichen D .83 A4
Grafenschlag A. . . .97 C3
Grafenstein A. 110 C1
Gräfenthal D 82 B3
Grafentonna D 82 A2
Grafenwöhr D. 95 B3
Grafing D 108 A2
Grafling D 95 C4
Gräfsnäs S. 54 B3
Gragnano I 170 C2
Grahovo SLO. 122 A2
Graiguenamanagh
IRL. 30 B2
Grain GB 45 B4
Grainau D 108 B2
Graja de Iniesta E .158 B2
Grajera E 151 A4
Gram DK 59 C2
Gramais A. 108 B1
Gramat F 129 B4
Gramatneusiedl A 111 A3
Grambow D 74 A3
Grammichele I. 177 B3

Gramsh AL. 182 C2
Gramzow D 74 A3
Gran N 48 B2
Granada E 163 A4
Granard IRL 27 C3
Grañas E 140 A3
Granátula de Calatrava
E 157 B4
Grancey-le-Château
F 105 B4
Grandas de Salime
E 141 A4
Grandcamp-Maisy
F 88 A2
Grand-Champ F . .100 B3
Grand Couronne F .89 A5
Grand-Fougeray F 101 B4
Grândola P. 160 A1
Grandpré F 91 B4
Grandrieu
B 79 B4
F 117 C3
Grandson CH 106 C1
Grandvillars F 106 B1
Grandvilliers F 90 B1
Grañén E 145 C3
Grängärde S 50 B1
Grange IRL 26 B2
Grangemouth GB . .35 B4
Grange-over-Sands
GB 36 B4
Grängesberg S 50 B1
Granges-de Crouhens
F 145 B4
Granges-sur-Vologne
F 106 A1
Grängsjö S 200 E3
Granitola-Torretta
I 176 B1
Granja
Évora P 155 C3
Porto P 148 A1
Granja de Moreruela
E 142 C1
Granja de
Torrehermosa E 156 B2
Gränna S 55 B5
Grannäs
Västerbotten S. .195 E7
Västerbotten S. .195 E8
Granö S 200 B5
Granollers E 147 C3
Granowiec PL. 85 A5
Granowo PL. 75 B5
Gransee D 74 A2
Gransherad N 53 A5
Grantham GB 40 C3
Grantown-on-Spey
GB 32 D3
Grantshouse GB . .35 C5
Granville F 88 B2
Granvin N 46 B3
Graal S 51 B5
Grasbakken N 193 B12
Grasberg D 72 A2
Grasmere GB. 36 B3
Gräsmyr S 200 C5
Grasö S 51 B5
Grassano I 172 B2
Grassau D 109 B3
Grasse F 132 B2
Grassington GB 40 A2
Græsted DK 61 C2
Gråsten DK 64 B2
Grästorp S 54 B3
Gratkorn A 110 B2
Gråträsk S 196 D2
Gratwein A 110 B2
Graulhet F 129 C4
Graus E 145 B4
Grávalos E 144 B2
Gravedona I 120 A2
Gravelines F 78 A2
Gravellona Toce I .119 B5
Gravendal S. 50 B1
Gravens DK. 59 C2
Gravesend GB. 45 B4
Graveson F 131 B3
Gravina in Púglia
I 172 B2
Gray F 105 B4
Grayrigg GB 37 B4
Grays GB. 45 B4
Grayshott GB 44 B3
Graz A. 110 B2
Grazalema E 162 B2
Grazzano Visconti
I 120 C2
Greåker N 54 A2
Great Dunmow GB .45 B4
Great Malvern GB . .39 B4
Great Torrington
GB 42 B2
Great Waltham GB .45 B4
Great Yarmouth
GB 41 C5
Grebbestad S 54 B2
Grebenstein D 81 A5
Grebocice PL. 85 A4
Grebocin PL. 76 A3
Greding D 95 B3
Gredstedbro DK . . .59 C1
Greencastle IRL. . . .27 A4
Greenhead GB. 37 B4
Greenisland GB. . . .27 B5
Greenlaw GB. 35 C5
Greenock GB. 34 C3
Greenway GB 39 C2
Greenwich GB 45 B4
Grefrath D. 80 A2
Greifenburg A 109 C4
Greiffenberg D 74 A2
Greifswald D 66 B2
Grein A. 110 A1
Greipstad N 53 B3
Greiz D 83 B4

Grenaa DK 58 B3
Grenade F 129 C4
Grenade-sur-l'Adour
F. 128 C2
Grenchen CH. 106 B2
Grendi N 53 B3
Grenivík IS 191 B7
Grenoble F 118 B2
Gréoux-les-Bains
F. 132 B1
Gresenhorst D. 66 B1
Gressoney-la-Trinité
I 119 B4
Gressoney-St.Jean
I 119 B4
Gressthal D 82 B2
Gressvik N 54 A1
Gresten A. 110 B2
Gretna GB 36 B3
Greussen D 82 A2
Greve in Chianti I .135 B4
Greven
Mecklenburg-
Vorpommern D . .73 A3
Nordrhein-Westfalen
D. 71 B4
Grevená GR. 182 C3
Grevenbroich D 80 A2
Grevenbrück D 81 A4
Grevenmacher L . . .92 B2
Grevesmühlen D. . .65 C4
Grevestrand DK . . .61 D2
Grevie S. 61 C2
Greystoke GB 36 B4
Greystones IRL. . . .30 A2
Grez-Doiceau B. . . .79 B4
Grez-en-Bouère F 102 B1
Grezzana I 121 B4
Grgar SLO 122 A2
Grgurevci SRB 127 B1
Gries A 108 B2
Griesbach D 96 C1
Griesheim D 93 B4
Gries in Sellrain A .108 B2
Grieskirchen A 109 A4
Griffen A 110 C1
Grignan F 131 A3
Grignano I 122 B2
Grigno I 121 A4
Grignols F 128 B2
Grignon F 118 B3
Grijota E 142 B2
Grijpskerk NL 71 A3
Grillby S. 56 A3
Grimaud F 132 B2
Grimbergen B 79 B4
Grimma D 83 A4
Grimmen D 66 B2
Grimmialp CH 106 C2
Grimsås S 60 B3
Grimsby GB. 41 B3
Grimslöv S 62 B2
Grímsstaðir IS 191 B9
Grimstad N 53 B4
Grimstorp S 62 A2
Grindavík IS 190 D3
Grindelwald CH. . .106 C3
Grindheim N 52 B3
Grindsted DK. 59 C1
Griñón E 151 B4
Gripenberg S 62 A2
Gripsholm S 56 A3
Grisolles F 129 C4
Grisslehamn S 51 B5
Gritley GB. 33 C4
Grizebeck GB 36 B3
Grndina BIH 124 C2
Gröbming A 109 B4
Gröbzig D 83 A3
Grocka SRB. 127 C2
Gröditz D. 83 A5
Gródki PL. 77 A5
Gródek PL. 85 B5
Grodziec PL 76 B3
Grodzisk Mazowiecki
PL. 77 B5
Grodzisk Wielkoposki
PL. 75 B5
Groenlo NL 71 B3
Groesbeek NL. 80 A1
Grohote HR 138 B2
Groitzsch D 83 A4
Groix F 100 B2
Grójec PL. 77 C5
Grom PL 77 A5
Gromiljca BIH 139 B4
Grömitz D 65 B3
Gromnik PL. 99 B4
Gromo I 120 B2
Gronau
Niedersachsen D .72 B2
Nordrhein-Westfalen
D. 71 B4
Grönenbach D. . . .107 B5
Grong N 199 A9
Grönhögen S 63 B4
Groningen
D 73 C4
NL 71 A3
Grønnestrand DK. .58 A2
Grono CH. 120 A2
Grönskåra S 62 A3
Grootegast NL. 71 A3
Gropello Cairoli I. .120 B1
Grorud N 48 C2
Grósio I 120 A3
Grošnica SRB 127 D2
Grossalmerode D .82 A1
Grossarl A 109 B4
Gross Beeren D. . . .74 B2
Gross Berkel D 72 B2
Grossbodungen D. .82 A2
Gross-botwar D. . . .94 C1
Grossbreitenbach D 82 B3
Grossburgwedel D .72 B2
Grosschönau D 84 B2
Gross-Dölln D. 74 B2
Grossenbrode D . . .65 B4
Grossenehrich D. . .82 A2

Grossengottern D. .82 A2
Grossenhain D 83 A5
Grossenkneten D . .71 B5
Grossenlüder D. . . .81 B5
Grossensee D 72 A3
Grossenzersdorf
A. 111 A3
Grosseto I 135 C4
Gross-Gerau D 93 B4
Grossgerungs A . . .96 C2
Grossglobnitz A . . .97 C3
Grosshabersdorf D 94 B2
Grossharras A. 97 C3
Grosshartmansdorf
D. 83 B5
Grosshöchstetten
CH 106 C2
Gross Kreutz D 74 B1
Grosskrut A 97 C4
Gross Lafferde D. . .72 B3
Gross Leutheb D. . .74 B3
Grosslohra D. 82 A2
Grossmehring D . . .95 C3
Gross Muckrow D. . .74 B3
Gross Oesingen D .72 B3
Grossostheim D . . .93 B5
Grosspertholz A . . .96 C2
Grosspetersdorf
A. 111 B3
Grosspostwitz D. . .84 A2
Grossraming A 110 B1
Grossräschen D . . .84 A2
Gross Reken D 80 A3
Grossrinderfeld D. .94 B1
Grossröhrsdorf D. . .84 A2
Gross Sarau D. 65 C3
Gross Särchen D. . .84 A2
Grossschirma D . . .83 B5
Gross Schönebeck
D. 74 B2
Grossschweinbarth
A. 97 C4
Grosssiegharts A . .97 C3
Grosssölk A. 109 B4
Gross Umstadt D . .93 B4
Grosswarasdorf A 111 B3
Gross Warnow D. . .73 A4
Gross-Weikersdorf
A. 97 C3
Gross-Welle D. 73 A5
Grosswilfersdorf
A. 110 B2
Gross Wokern D . . .65 C5
Grostenquin F 92 C2
Grosuplje SLO. . . .123 B3
Grotli N 198 C4
Grótlingbo S 57 C4
Grottáglie I 173 B3
Grottaminarda I. . .170 B3
Grottammare I 136 C2
Grotte di Castro I .168 A1
Grotteria I 175 C2
Gróttole I 172 B2
Grouw NL. 70 A2
Grov N 194 B8
Grova N 53 A4
Grove E 140 B2
Grua N 48 B2
Grube D 65 B4
Grubišno Polje
HR 124 B3
Grude BIH 138 B3
Grudusk PL. 77 A5
Grudziądz PL. 69 B3
Grue N 49 B4
Gruissan F 130 B2
Grullos E 141 A4
Grumăzeşti RO. . . .17 B7
Grumello del Monte
I 120 B2
Grumento Nova I. .174 A1
Grumo Áppula I . . .171 B4
Grums S 55 A4
Grünau im Almtal
A. 109 B4
Grünberg D 81 B4
Grünburg A 110 B1
Grundarfjörður IS 190 B2
Gründau D 81 B5
Gründelhardt D 94 B1
Grundforsen S 49 A4
Grundlsee A. 109 B4
Grundsund S. 54 B2
Grunewald D 84 A1
Grungedal N. 53 A4
Grunow D 74 B3
Grünstadt D 93 B4
Gruvberget S 50 A3
Gruyères CH 106 C2
Gruža SRB 127 D2
Grybów PL. 99 B4
Grycksbo S 50 B2
Gryfice PL 67 C4
Gryfino PL 74 A3
Gryfów Śląski PL. . .84 A3
Gryllefjord N 194 A8
Grymyr N 48 B2
Gryt S. 56 B2
Grytgöl S 56 B1
Grythyttan S 55 A5
Grytnäs S. 57 B3
Grzmiąca PL. 68 B1
Grzywna PL 76 A3
Gschnitz A. 108 B2
Gschwend D. 94 C1
Gstaad CH 119 A4
Gstadt D 109 B3
Guadahortuna E . .163 A4
Guadalajara E 151 B4
Guadalaviar E 152 B2
Guadalcanal E. . . .156 B2
Guadalcázar E. . . .162 A3
Guadalix de la Sierra
E. 151 B4
Guadálmez E. 156 B3
Guadalupe E 156 A2
Guadamur E 151 C3
Guadarrama E. . . .151 B3
Guadiaro E. 162 B2
Guadix E 164 B1
Guagnano I 173 B3
Guagno F 180 A1
Guajar-Faragüit E 163 B4

Glo–Gun 243

Gualchos E 163 B4
Gualdo Tadino I. . .136 B1
Gualtieri I 121 C3
Guarcino I 169 B3
Guarda P 149 B2
Guardamar del Segura
E 165 A4
Guardão P. 148 B1
Guardavalle I 175 C2
Guardea I 168 A2
Guárdia I 172 B1
Guardiagrele I. . . .169 A4
Guardiarégia I. . . .170 B2
Guárdia Sanframondi
I. 170 B2
Guardias Viejas E 164 C2
Guardiola de Berguada
E 147 B2
Guardo E 142 B2
Guareña E 156 B1
Guaro E 162 B3
Guarromán E. 157 B4
Guasila I. 179 C3
Guastalla I 121 C3
Gubbhögen S 199 A12
Gúbbio I 136 B1
Guben D. 74 C3
Gubin PL 74 C3
Gudå N 199 B8
Gudavac BIH 124 C2
Guddal N. 46 A2
Gudhem S 55 B4
Gudhjem DK 67 A3
Gudovac HR 124 B2
Gudow D 73 A3
Güdül TR 187 B7
Gudvangen N 46 B3
Guebwiller F 106 B2
Guéjar-Sierra E. . .163 A4
Guéméné-Penfao
F. 101 B4
Guéméné-sur-Scorff
F. 100 A2
Güeñes E. 143 A3
Guer F 101 B3
Guérande F 101 B3
Guéret F 116 A1
Guérigny F. 104 B2
Gueugnon F 104 C3
Guglionesi I. 170 B2
Gühlen Glienicke
D. 74 A1
Guia P 154 B2
Guichen F 101 B4
Guidizzolo I 121 B3
Guidónia-Montecélio
I. 168 B2
Guiglia I 135 A3
Guignes F 90 C2
Guijo E 156 B3
Guijo de Coria E . .149 B3
Guijo de Santa Bábera
E 150 B2
Guijuelo E 150 B2
Guildford GB. 44 B3
Guillaumes F 132 A2
Guillena E 162 A1
Guillestre F 118 C3
Guillos F 128 B2
Guilsfield GB. 38 B3
Guilvinec F 100 B1
Guimarães P 148 A1
Guincho P. 154 C1
Guînes F 78 B1
Guingamp F. 100 A2
Guipavas F 100 A1
Guisborough GB. . .37 B5
Guiscard F 90 B3
Guiscriff F 100 A2
Guise F 91 B3
Guisona E 147 C2
Guitiriz E 140 A3
Guîtres F 128 A2
Gujan-Mestras F .128 B1
Gulbene LV 8 D5
Gülçayır TR. 187 C6
Gulçayır TR 187 C6
Guldborg DK. 65 B4
Gullabo S. 63 B3
Gullane GB 35 B5
Gullbrå N 46 B3
Gullbrandstorp S . .61 C2
Gulleråsen S 50 A2
Gullhaug N 53 A6
Gullringen S. 62 A3
Gullspång S 55 B5
Gullstein N. 198 B5
Güllük TR 188 B2
Gülnar TR. 23 C7
Gülpınar TR 186 C1
Gülşehir TR 23 B8
Gulsvik N. 48 B1
Gumiel de Hizán
E 143 C3
Gummersbach D. . .81 A3
Gümüldür TR. 188 A2
Gümüşhacıköy TR .23 A8
Gümüşova TR 187 B5
Gundelfingen D . . .94 C2
Gundelsheim D 93 B5
Gunderschoffen F. .93 C3
Gundertshausen
A. 109 A3
Gundinci HR 125 B4
Gündoğmuş TR. . .189 C7
Güney
Burdur TR 189 B4
Denizli TR 188 A4
Günlüce TR 188 C3
Gunnarn S. 195 E8
Gunnarsbyn S 196 C4
Gunnarskog S 49 C4
Gunnebo S 62 A4
Gunnislake GB 42 B2

Günselsdorf A 111 B3
Guntersblum D . . 93 B4
Guntersdorf A 97 C4
Guntín E. 140 B3
Günyüzü TR. 187 C6
Günzburg D. 94 C2
Gunzenhausen D . .94 B2
Güre
  Balıkesir TR 186 C1
  Uşak TR. 186 D4
Gurk A 110 C1
Gurrea de Gállego
  E. 144 B3
Gürsu TR. 186 B4
Gušće TR. 124 B2
Gusev RUS. 12 A5
Gúspini I 179 C2
Gusselby S 56 A1
Güssing A 111 B3
Gusswerk A 110 B2
Gustav Adolf S 49 B5
Gustavsberg S 57 A4
Gustavsfors S 54 C3
Güstrow D. 65 C5
Gusum S. 56 B2
Gutcher GB. 33 A5
Gutenstein A 110 B2
Gütersloh D. 81 A4
Guttannen CH . . . 106 C3
Guttaring A 110 C1
Guttau D. 84 A2
Güttingen CH 107 B4
Gützkow D. 66 C2
Guzów PL. 77 B5
Gvardeysk RUS. . . .12 A4
Gvarv N 53 A5
Gvozd MNE 139 C5
Gvozdansko HR . 124 B2
Gwda Wielka PL . . .68 B2
Gwennap GB. 42 B1
Gy F 105 B4
Gyál H 112 B3
Gyarmat H 111 B4
Gyékényes H 124 A3
Gye-sur-Seine F . . 104 A3
Gyljen S. 196 C5
Gylling DK. 59 C3
Gyoma H 113 C4
Gyömöre H 111 B4
Gyömrő H 112 B3
Gyón H. 112 B3
Gyöngyfa H 125 B3
Gyöngyös H 113 B3
Gyöngyöspata H . . 113 B3
Gyönk H. 112 C2
Györ H 111 B4
Györszemere H . . . 111 B4
Gypsera CH 106 C2
Gysinge S 51 B3
Gyttorp S. 55 A5
Gyula H 113 C5
Gyulafirátót H . . . 112 B1
Gyulaj H. 112 C2

H

Haacht B 79 B4
Haag
  Nieder Östereich
    A. 110 A1
  Ober Östereich A 109 A4
  D. 108 A2
Haaksbergen NL . . .71 B3
Haamstede NL. 79 A3
Haan D. 80 A3
Haapajärvi FIN. 3 E9
Haapsalu EST 8 C3
Haarlem NL 70 B1
Habas F 128 C2
Habay B 92 B1
Habo S 62 A2
Håbol S 54 B3
Habry CZ 97 B3
Habsheim F 106 B2
Hachenburg D. 81 B3
Hacıbektaş TR 23 B8
Hacılar TR 23 B8
Hacinas E 143 C3
Hackås S 199 C11
Hacketstown IRL. . .30 B2
Hackthorpe GB 37 B4
Hadamar D. 81 B4
Hädanberg S 200 C4
Haddington GB. . . .35 C5
Hadersdorf am Kamp
  A. 97 C3
Haderslev DK 59 C2
Haderup DK. 59 B1
Hadım TR. 23 C7
Hadleigh
  Essex GB. 45 B4
  Suffolk GB 45 A4
Hadlow GB. 45 B4
Hadmersleben D . . .73 B4
Hadsten DK. 59 B3
Hadsund DK. 58 B3
Hadžići BIH 139 B4
Hafnarfjörður IS . . 190 C4
Hafnir IS. 190 D1
Hafslo N. 47 A4
Haganj HR 124 B2
Hagby S. 63 B4
Hage D 71 A4
Hægebostad N 52 B3
Hægeland N. 53 B3
Hagen
  Niedersachsen D . .72 A1
  Nordrhein-Westfalen
    D. 80 A3
Hagenbach D. 93 B4
Hagenow D 73 A4
Hagetmau F. 128 C2
Hagfors S. 49 B5
Häggenås S 199 B11
Hagondange F. 92 B2
Hagsta S. 51 B4

Haguenau F 93 C3
Hahnbach D. 95 B3
Hahnslätten D 81 B4
Hahót H 111 C3
Haiger D. 81 B4
Haigerloch D 93 C4
Hailsham GB 45 C4
Hainburg A 111 A3
Hainfeld A 110 A2
Hainichen D. 83 B5
Hajdúböszörmény
  H 113 B5
Hajdučica SRB . . . 126 B2
Hajdúdorogo H . . . 113 B5
Hajdúnánás H 113 B5
Hajdúszoboszló
  H 113 B5
Hajnácka SK 113 A3
Hajnówka PL 13 B5
Hajós H 112 C3
Håkafot S 199 A11
Håkåböl S 50 B2
Håksberg S 50 B2
Halaszi H 111 B4
Halberstadt D 82 A3
Halberton GB. 43 B3
Hald Ege DK 58 B2
Haldem D. 71 B5
Halden N 54 A2
Haldensleben D. 73 B4
Halenbeck D 73 A5
Halesowen GB. 40 C1
Halesworth GB. 45 A5
Halfing D 109 B3
Halhjem N 46 B2
Håliden S 49 B5
Halifax GB. 40 B2
Häljelöt S 56 B2
Halkirk GB 32 C3
Hall S 57 C4
Hälla S 200 C3
Hallabro S. 63 B3
Hallabrottet S. 56 A1
Halland GB 45 C4
Hällaryd S 63 B2
Hällaryd S 61 C3
Hällberga S 56 A2
Hällbybrunn S 56 A2
Halle
  B. 79 B4
  Nordrhein-Westfalen
    D. 72 B1
  Sachsen-Anhalt D .83 A3
Hålleberga S 62 B3
Hällefors S. 55 A5
Hälleforsnäs S. 56 A2
Hallein A 109 B4
Hällekis S. 55 B4
Hallen S 199 B11
Hållen S 51 B4
Hallenberg D 81 A4
Hällestad S 56 B1
Hallevik N 52 B2
Hällevadsholm S 54 B2
Hällevik S. 63 B2
Hälleviksstrand S 54 B2
Hallingby N 48 B2
Hallingeberg S 62 A4
Hallingen N 47 B6
Hallsberg S 56 A1
Hållsta S 56 A2
Hallstahammar S 56 A2
Hallstatt A 109 B4
Hallstavik S. 51 B5
Halltorp S 63 B4
Halluin F 78 B3
Hallviken S 199 B12
Hallworthy GB. 42 B2
Halmstad S 61 C2
Hals DK 58 A3
Halsa N 198 B5
Halstead GB. 45 B4
Haltdalen N 199 C8
Haltern D. 80 A3
Haltwhistle GB 37 B4
Halvarsgårdarna S .50 B2
Halver D 80 A3
Halvrimmen DK 58 A2
Ham F. 90 B3
Hamar N. 48 B3
Hamarhaug N 46 B2
Hamarøy N 194 B6
Hambach F 92 B3
Hambergen D 72 A1
Hambergsund S 54 B2
Hambledon GB. 44 C2
Hambuhren D 72 B2
Hamburg D 72 A2
Hamdibey TR 186 C2
Hamdorf D. 64 B2
Hämeenlinna FIN 8 B4
Hameln = Hamlin D 72 B2
Hamersleben D 73 B4
Hamidiye TR 187 C5
Hamilton GB 36 A2
Hamina FIN 8 B5
Hamlagrø N 46 B2
Hamlin = Hameln D 72 B2
Hamm D. 81 A3
Hammar S 55 B5
Hammarland FIN 51 B6
Hammarö S 55 A4
Hammarstrand S . . . 200 C2
Hamme B 79 A4
Hammel DK 59 B2
Hammelburg D 82 B1
Hammelspring D 74 A2
Hammenhög S 66 A3
Hammerdal S 199 B12
Hammerfest N 192 B7
Hammershøj DK 58 B2
Hammerum DK 59 B2
Hamminkeln D 80 A2
Hamnavoe GB 33 A5
Hamneda S 60 C3

Hamningberg N . .193 B14
Hamoir B 80 B1
Hamont B 80 A1
Hámor H 113 A4
Hamra
  Gävleborg S . . . 199 D12
  Gotland S 57 D4
Hamrångefjärden
  S 51 B4
Hamstreet GB 45 B4
Hamsund N 194 B6
Han TR. 187 C5
Hanaskog S. 61 C4
Hanau D 81 B4
Händelöp S 62 A4
Handlová SK. 98 C2
Hanerau-
  Hademarschen D 64 B2
Hånger S 60 B3
Hanhimaa FIN 197 B8
Hanken S 55 B5
Hankensbüttel D 73 B3
Han Knežica BIH . . 124 B2
Hanko FIN 8 C3
Hannover D 72 B2
Hannut B 79 B5
Han Pijesak BIH. . . 139 A4
Hansnes N 192 C3
Hanstedt D 72 A3
Hanstholm DK 58 A1
Hantsavichy BY 13 B7
Hanušovice CZ. 85 B4
Haparanda S 196 D7
Haradok BY 13 A8
Harads S 196 C4
Häradsbäck S 63 B2
Häradsbygden S 50 B2
Harbo S 51 B4
Harboør DK. 58 B1
Harburg
  Bayern D 94 C2
  Hamburg D 72 A2
Hårby DK. 59 C3
Harc H 112 C2
Hardegarijp NL 70 A2
Hardegsen D 82 A1
Hardelot Plage F . . .78 B1
Hardenbeck D 74 A2
Hardenberg NL 71 B3
Harderwijk NL 70 B2
Hardheim D 94 B1
Hardt D 106 A3
Hareid N 198 C3
Haren
  D 71 B4
  NL 71 A3
Harestua N 48 B2
Harfleur F. 89 A4
Harg S 51 B5
Hargicourt F 90 B3
Hargnies F. 91 A4
Hargshamn S 51 B5
Härja S 55 B4
Harkány H 125 B4
Härkeberga S 56 A3
Harkebrügge D 71 A4
Harlech GB 38 B2
Harleston GB. 45 A5
Hårlev DK. 65 A5
Harlingen NL 70 A2
Harlösa S 61 D3
Harlow GB. 45 B4
Harmanck TR 186 C4
Harmånger S. 200 E3
Harmanli BG 183 B7
Härnevi S. 56 A3
Härnösand S 200 D3
Haro E 143 B4
Haroldswick GB 33 A6
Háromfa H 124 A3
Haroué F 92 C2
Harpenden GB. 44 B3
Harplinge S 60 C2
Harpstedt D 72 B1
Harrogate GB. 40 A2
Harrow GB. 44 B3
Härryda S 60 B2
Harsefeld D 72 A2
Harsewinkel D 71 C5
Hârşova 17 C7
Harstad N 194 B7
Harsum D. 72 B2
Harsvik N 199 A7
Harta H 112 C3
Hartberg A 110 B2
Hartburn GB 37 A5
Hartennes F. 90 B3
Hartest GB. 45 A4
Hartha D 83 A4
Hartland GB. 42 B2
Hartlepool GB 37 B5
Hartmanice CZ 96 B1
Hartmannsdorf A . .110 B2
Harvassdal N. 195 E5
Harwell GB. 44 B2
Harwich GB. 45 B5
Harzgerode D 82 A3
Häselgärn A 108 B1
Haselünne D 71 B4
Haslev DK. 65 A4
Hasloch D 94 B1
Haslach an der Mühl
  A. 96 C2
Hasle DK. 67 A3
Haslemere GB. 44 B3
Haslev DK. 65 A4
Hasloch D 94 B1
Hassfurt D 94 A2
Hässleholm S 61 C3
Hasslö S 63 B3
Hassloch D 93 B4

Hästbo S 51 B4
Hastersboda FIN 51 B7
Hästholmen S 55 B5
Hastière-Lavaux B . .79 B4
Hastigrow GB 32 C3
Hastings GB. 45 C4
Hästveda S 61 C3
Hasvik N 192 B6
Hatfield
  Hertfordshire GB . .44 B3
  South Yorkshire
    GB. 40 B3
Hatherleigh GB 42 B2
Hathersage GB. 40 B2
Hatlestrand N 46 B2
Hattem NL 70 B3
Hatten
  D 71 A5
  F. 93 C3
Hattfjelldal N 195 E4
Hatting DK. 59 C2
Hattingen D 80 A3
Hattstedt D 64 B2
Hatvan H 112 B3
Hatvik N 46 B2
Hau D 80 A2
Haudainville F 92 B1
Hauganes IS. 191 B7
Haugastøl N 47 B4
Hauge N 52 B2
Haughom N 52 B2
Haugsdal N 46 B2
Haugsdorf A. 97 C4
Haukedal N 46 A3
Haukeland N 46 B2
Haukeligrend N 52 A3
Haukeliseter N. 52 A3
Haukipudas FIN 3 D9
Haulerwijk NL 71 A3
Haunersdorf D 95 C4
Haus A 109 B4
Hausach D 106 A3
Hausham D 108 B2
Hausmannstätten
  A. 110 C2
Hausvik N 52 B2
Hautajärvi FIN 197 C12
Hautefort F 129 A4
Hauterives F 117 B5
Hauteville-Lompnès
  F. 118 B2
Haut-Fays F 91 A5
Hautmont F 79 B3
Hautrage B. 79 B3
Hauzenberg D 96 C1
Havant GB. 44 C3
Havári DK 59 B4
Havdrup DK 61 D2
Havelange B 79 B5
Havelberg D 73 B5
Havelte NL 70 B3
Haverfordwest GB .39 C2
Haverhill GB. 45 A4
Havering GB 45 B4
Håverud S 54 B3
Havdhem S 57 C4
Havixbeck D 71 C4
Havlíčkův Brod CZ .97 B3
Havndal DK. 58 B3
Havneby DK 64 A1
Havnebyen DK. 61 D1
Havnsø DK. 61 D1
Havøysund N 193 A8
Havran TR 186 C2
Havrebjerg DK. 61 D1
Havsa TR 186 A1
Havstenssund S 54 B2
Hawes GB. 37 B4
Hawick GB. 35 C5
Hawkhurst GB. 45 B4
Hawkinge GB. 45 B5
Haxey GB. 40 B3
Hayange F 92 B2
Haydarlı TR 189 A5
Haydon Bridge GB .37 B4
Hayle GB 42 B1
Haymana TR 187 C7
Hay-on-Wye GB. . . .39 B3
Hayrabolu TR 186 A2
Haysyn UA 13 D8
Hayvoron UA. 13 D8
Haywards Heath
  GB. 44 C3
Hazebrouck F 78 B2
Hazlov CZ. 83 B4
Heacham GB. 41 C4
Headcorn GB. 45 B4
Headford IRL 28 A2
Heanor GB. 40 B2
Héas F 145 B4
Heathfield GB. 45 C4
Hebden Bridge GB .40 B1
Heberg S 60 C2
Heby S 51 C3
Hechingen D 93 C4
Hechlingen D. 94 C2
Hecho E 145 B3
Hechtel B 79 A5
Hechthausen D 72 A2
Heckelberg D 74 B2
Heckington GB 41 C3
Hecklingen D 73 C4
Hed S 56 A1
Hedalen N 48 B1
Hedared S 60 B2
Heddal N 53 A5
Hédé F 101 A4
Hede S 199 C10
Hedekas S 54 B2
Hedemora S 50 B2
Hedenäset S 196 C6
Hedensted DK. 59 C2
Hedersleben D 82 A3
Hedesunda S 51 B4
Hedge End GB. 44 C2
Hedon GB. 41 B3
Heede D 71 B4

Heek D 71 B4
Heemstede NL. 70 B1
Heerde D. 70 B3
Heerenveen NL 70 B2
Heerhugowaard NL 70 B1
Heerlen NL. 80 B1
Heeze NL. 80 A1
Heggenes N. 47 A6
Hegra N 199 B8
Hegyeshalom H . . . 111 B4
Hegyközség H 111 B3
Heia N 199 A9
Heide D 64 B2
Heidelberg D 93 B4
Heiden D 80 A2
Heidenau D 84 B1
Heidenheim D 94 C2
Heidenreichstein A .97 C3
Heikendorf D 64 B3
Heikkilä FIN 197 C12
Heilam GB 32 C2
Heiland D 53 B4
Heilbad Heiligenstadt
  D. 82 A2
Heilbronn D 93 B5
Heiligenblut A 109 B3
Heiligendamm D . . .65 B4
Heiligendorf D 73 B3
Heiligengrabe D 73 A5
Heiligenhafen D 65 B3
Heiligenhaus D 80 A2
Heiligenkreuz A . . . 111 C3
Heiligenstadt D 94 B3
Heiloo NL 70 B1
Heilsbronn D 94 B2
Heim N 198 B6
Heimburg D 82 A2
Heimdal N 199 B7
Heinerscheid L 92 A2
Heinersdorf D 74 B3
Heining D 96 C1
Heiningen D 94 C1
Heinola FIN 8 B5
Heinsberg D 80 A2
Heist-op-den-Berg
  B 79 A4
Hejde S 57 C4
Hejdeby S 57 C4
Hejls DK. 59 C2
Hejnice CZ. 84 B3
Hel PL. 69 A3
Helchteren B 79 A5
Heldburg D 82 B2
Helechosa E 156 A3
Helensburgh GB . . .34 B3
Helfenberg A. 96 C2
Helgen N 53 A5
Helgeroa N 53 B5
Hella
  IS 190 D5
  N 46 A3
Helland N 194 B7
Hellas S. 55 B4
Helle N. 52 B2
Helleland N. 52 B2
Hellendoorn NL 71 B3
Hellenthal D. 80 B2
Hellesøy N. 46 B1
Hellesylt N 198 C3
Hellevoetsluis NL . . .79 A4
Helligskogen N . . . 192 C4
Hellín E 158 C2
Hellissandur IS . . . 190 C2
Hellnar IS. 190 C2
Hellum DK 58 A3
Hellvi S 57 C4
Hellvik N. 52 B1
Helm-brechts D 83 B3
Helmond NL. 80 A1
Helmsdale GB. 32 C3
Helmsley GB 37 B5
Helmstedt D. 73 B3
Hel'pa SK. 99 C3
Helsa D 82 A1
Helsby GB 38 A4
Helsinge DK. 61 C2
Helsingør DK. 61 C2
Helsinki FIN 8 B4
Helston GB 42 B1
Hemau D 95 B3
Hemel Hempstead
  GB. 44 B3
Hemer D. 81 A3
Héming F 92 C2
Hemmet DK 59 C1
Hemmingstedt D 64 B2
Hemmoor D 64 C2
Hemnes N 54 A2
Hemnesberget N . . 195 D4
Hemse S 57 C4
Hemsedal N 47 B5
Hemslingen D 72 A2
Hemsworth GB 40 B2
Hen N 48 B2
Henån S 54 B2
Hendaye F. 144 A2
Hendek TR. 187 B5
Hendungen D 82 B2
Henfield GB. 44 C3
Hengelo
  Gelderland NL. . . .71 B3
  Overijssel NL. 71 B3
Hengersberg D 95 C5
Hengoed GB 39 C3
Hénin-Beaumont F .78 B2
Henley-on-Thames
  GB. 44 B3
Hennan S. 200 D1
Henneberg D 82 B2
Hennebont F 100 B2
Henne Strand DK . . .59 C1
Hennigsdorf D 74 B2
Hennet N. 198 B5
Hennstedt
  Schleswig-Holstein
    D. 64 B2

Hennstedt continued
  Schleswig-Holstein
    D. 64 B2
Henrichemont F . 103 B4
Henryków PL. 85 B5
Henrykowo PL. 69 A5
Hensås N 47 A5
Henstedt-Ulzburg
  D. 64 C2
Heppenheim D 93 B4
Herad
  Buskerud N 47 B6
  Vest-Agder N. 52 B2
Heradsbygd N 48 B3
Heraklion = Iraklio
  GR. 185 D6
Herálec CZ. 97 B3
Herand N. 46 B3
Herbault F 103 B3
Herbern D. 81 A3
Herbertstown IRL . . .29 B3
Herbeumont B 91 B5
Herbignac F 101 B3
Herbisse F 91 C4
Herbitzheim F 92 B3
Herbolzheim D 106 A2
Herborn D 81 B4
Herbrechtingen D . . .94 C2
Herby PL. 86 B2
Herceg-Novi MNE . .16 D3
Hercegovać HR . . . 124 B3
Hercegszántó H . . . 125 B4
Herchen D. 80 B3
Heréd H 112 B3
Hereford GB 39 B4
Herefoss N. 53 B4
Hereke TR 187 B4
Herencia E. 157 A4
Herend H 111 B4
Herentals B 79 A4
Herépian F 130 B2
Herford D. 72 B1
Herguijuela E 156 A2
Héric F. 101 B4
Héricourt F 106 B1
Héricourt-en-Caux
  F. 89 A4
Hérimoncourt F . . . 106 B1
Heringsdorf D 65 B4
Herisau CH 107 B4
Hérisson F 103 C4
Herk-de-Stad B 79 B5
Herlufmagle DK 64 A4
Hermagor A 109 C4
Hermannsburg D . .72 B3
Hermansverk N 46 A3
Heřmanův Městec
  CZ. 97 B3
Herment F 116 B2
Hermeskeil D 92 B2
Hermisende E 141 C4
Hermonville F 91 B3
Hermsdorf D. 83 B3
Hernani E 144 A2
Hernansancho E . . 150 B3
Herne D 80 A3
Herne Bay GB 45 B5
Hernes N 48 B3
Herning DK 59 B1
Herøya N 53 A5
Herramelluri E 143 B3
Herräng S 51 B5
Herre N 53 A5
Herrenberg D 93 C4
Herrera E 162 A3
Herrera de Alcántara
  E. 155 B3
Herrera del Duque
  E. 156 A2
Herrera de los Navarros
  E. 152 A2
Herrera de Pisuerga
  E. 142 B2
Herreros del Suso
  E. 150 B2
Herrestad S 54 B2
Herrhamra S 57 B3
Herritslev DK. 65 B4
Herrljunga S 55 B4
Herrnhut D 84 A2
Herrsching D 108 A2
Hersbruck D 95 B3
Hersby S 57 A4
Herscheid D 81 A3
Herschhorn D. 93 B4
Herselt B 79 A4
Herso GR 182 B4
Herstal B 80 B1
Herstmonceux GB .45 C4
Herten D. 80 A3
Hertford GB. 44 B3
Hervás E 149 B4
Hervik N 52 A1
Herxheim D 93 B4
Herzberg
  Brandenburg D . . .74 B1
  Brandenburg D . . .83 A3
  Niedersachsen D .82 A2
Herzebrock D 81 A4
Herzfelde D. 74 B2
Herzlake D 71 B4
Herzogenaurach D .94 B2
Herzogenbuchsee
  CH 106 B2
Herzogenburg A . . .110 A2
Herzsprung D 73 A5
Hesby N 52 A1
Hesdin F 78 B2
Hesel D 71 A4
Heskestad N 52 B2
Heslington GB 199 C8
Hesselager DK. 65 A3
Hessen D 82 A1
Hesseng N 193 C13
Hessisch Lichtenau
  D. 82 A1
Hessisch-Oldendorf
  D. 72 B2
Hestra S. 60 B3

Heswall GB 38 A3
Hetlevik N 46 B2
Hettange-Grande F .92 B2
Hetton-le-Hole GB . .37 B5
Hettstedt D 82 A3
Heuchin F. 78 B2
Heudicourt-sous-les-
  Côtes F. 92 C1
Heunezel F. 105 A4
Heuqueville F 89 A4
Heves H. 113 B4
Héviz H 111 C4
Hexham GB 37 B4
Heysham GB 36 B4
Heytesbury GB. 43 A4
Hidas H 125 A4
Hieflau A. 110 B1
Hiendelaencina E . 151 A4
Hiersac F. 115 C4
High Bentham GB . .37 B4
Highclere GB 44 B2
High Hesket GB. 37 B4
Highley GB 39 B4
High Wycombe GB .44 B3
Higuera de Arjona
  E 157 C4
Higuera de Calatrava
  E 163 A3
Higuera de la Serena
  E 156 B2
Higuera de la Sierra
  E 161 B3
Higuera de Vargas
  E 155 C4
Higuera la Real E . 161 A3
Higuers de Llerena
  E 156 B1
Higueruela E 158 C2
Híjar E 153 A3
Hilchenbach D. 81 A4
Hildburghausen D . .82 B2
Hilden D. 80 A2
Hilders D 82 B1
Hildesheim D 72 B2
Hilgay GB. 41 C4
Hillared S 60 B3
Hille D 72 B1
Hillegom NL 70 B1
Hillerød DK 61 D2
Hillerstorp S 60 B3
Hillesheim D 80 B2
Hillestad N 53 A6
Hillmersdorf D 83 A5
Hillsborough GB . . .27 B5
Hillswick GB 33 A5
Hilpoltstein D 95 B3
Hiltpoltstein D 94 B3
Hilvarenbeek NL . . .79 A5
Hilversum NL. 70 B2
Himarë AL 182 C1
Himbergen D 73 A3
Himeshaza H 125 A4
Himmelberg A 109 C2
Himmelpforten D . . .72 A2
Himód H 111 B4
Hinckley GB. 40 C2
Hindås S 60 B2
Hindelang D 108 B1
Hindelbank CH . . . 106 B2
Hinderavåg N 52 A1
Hindhead GB. 44 B3
Hinojosa del Valle
  E 156 B1
Hinnerup DK 59 B3
Hinneryd S 61 C3
Hinojal E. 155 B4
Hinojales E 161 B3
Hinojos E 161 B3
Hinojosa del Duque
  E 156 B2
Hinojosas de Calatrava
  E 157 B3
Hinterhornbach A . 108 B1
Hinterriss A 108 B2
Hintersee
  A. 109 B3
  D. 74 A3
Hinterstoder A. . . . 110 B1
Hintertux A 108 B2
Hinterweidenthal D 93 B3
Hinwil CH. 107 B3
Hios GR. 185 A7
Hippolytushoef NL .70 B1
Hirschaid D 94 B2
Hirschau D 95 B3
Hirschfeld D 83 A5
Hirschhorn D. 93 B4
Hirsingue F 106 B2
Hirson F 91 B4
Hirtshals DK 58 A2
Hirvaskoski FIN . . 197 D10
Hirzenhain D 81 B5
Hisarcık TR 186 C4
Hishult S 61 C3
Hissjön S 200 C6
Hitchin GB 44 B3
Hitra N 198 B5
Hittarp S. 61 C2
Hittisau A 107 B4
Hittun N 46 A1
Hitzacker D 73 A4
Hjallerup DK 58 A3
Hjällstad S 49 B5
Hjältevad S 62 A3
Hjärnarp S 61 C2
Hjartdal N 53 A4
Hjellestad N 46 B2
Hjelmeland N 52 A2
Hjelset N 198 C4
Hjerkinn N 198 C6
Hjerm DK 58 B1
Hjerpsted DK 64 A1
Hjerting DK. 59 C1
Hjo S 55 B5
Hjordkær DK 64 A2
Hjørring DK 58 A3
Hjorted S 62 A4
Hjortkvarn S. 56 B1
Hjortnäs S 50 B1
Hjortsberga S 62 B2

Hjukse N 53 A5
Hjuksebø N 53 A5
Hjulsjö S 55 A5
Hliník nad Hronom SK 98 C2
Hlinsko CZ 97 B3
Hlío IS 191 A10
Hlohovec SK 98 C1
Hlubokánad Vltavou CZ 96 B2
Hlučín CZ 98 B2
Hlyboka UA 17 A6
Hlybokaye BY 13 A7
Hniezdne SK 99 B4
Hnilec SK 99 C4
Hnúšt'a SK 99 C3
Hobol H 125 A3
Hobro DK 58 B2
Hobscheid D 92 B1
Hocalar TR. 189 A4
Hochdonn D 64 B2
Hochdorf CH 106 B3
Hochfelden F 93 C3
Hochspeyer D 93 B3
Hochstadt D 94 B2
Höchstädt D 94 C2
Hochstenbach D . . 81 B3
Höchst im Odenwald 93 B5
Höckendorf D 83 B5
Hockenheim D 93 B4
Hoddesdon GB . . . 44 B3
Hodejov SK 99 C3
Hodenhagen D 72 B2
Hodkovice CZ 84 B3
Hódmezóvásárhely 113 C4
Hodnet D. 38 B4
Hodonín CZ. 98 C1
Hodslavice CZ 98 B2
Hoedekenskerke NL 79 A3
Hoegaarden B 79 B4
Hoek van Holland NL 79 A4
Hoenderlo NL 70 B2
Hof D 83 B3
N 53 A6
Hofbieber D 82 B1
Hoff GB 37 B4
Hofgeismar D 81 A5
Hofheim Bayern D. 82 B2
Hessen D. 93 A4
Hofkirchen im Mühlkreis A. . . . 96 C1
Höfn IS 191 C10
Hofors 50 B3
Hofsós IS 190 B6
Hofstad N. 199 A7
Höganäs S 61 C2
Högbo S 51 B3
Högdal S 54 A2
Høgebru N 46 A4
Högfors S 50 C2
Högklint S 57 C4
Högsäter S. 54 B3
Högsjö S 62 A4
Högsjö S 56 A1
Hogstad S 55 B6
Högyész H 112 C2
Hohenau A 97 C4
Hohenberg A 110 B2
Hohenbucko D 83 A5
Hohenburg D 95 B3
Hohendorf D 66 B1
Hohenems A 107 B4
Hohenhameln D . . . 72 B3
Hohenhausen D . . . 72 B1
Hohenkirchen D . . . 71 A4
Hohenlinden D . . . 108 A2
Hohenlockstedt D . 64 C2
Hohenmölsen D . . . 83 A4
Hohennauen D 73 B5
Hohen Neuendorf 74 B2
Hohenseeden D . . . 73 B5
Hohentauern A . . . 110 B1
Hohentengen D . . . 106 B3
Hohenwepel D 81 A5
Hohenwestedt D . . 64 B2
Hohenwutzen D . . . 74 B3
Hohenzieritz D 74 A2
Hohne D. 64 B2
Hohne D. 72 B3
Hohnstorf D 73 A3
Hojer DK 64 B1
Højslev Stby DK . . . 58 B2
Hok S 62 A2
Hökerum S. 60 B3
Hokhuvud S. 51 B5
Hokksund S 53 A5
Hökön S. 63 B2
Hol N 47 B5
Hólar S 190 B6
Holašovice CZ. . . . 96 C2
Holbæk Aarhus Amt. DK. . 58 B3
Vestsjællands Amt. DK. 61 D1
Holbeach GB. 41 C4
Holdenstedt D 73 B3
Holdhus N 46 B2
Holdorf D 71 B5
Holeby DK 65 B4
Holen N. 54 A1
Holervasseter N . . . 47 B6
Holešov CZ 98 B1
Holguera E. 155 B4
Holič SK. 98 C1
Holice CZ 97 A3
SK 111 B4
Höljes S 49 B4
Hollabrunn A 97 C4
Hollandstoun GB . 33 B4
Hollen N. 53 B3
Hollfeld D 95 B3
Hollókő H. 112 B3

Hollstadt D 82 B2
Hollum NL 70 A2
Höllviksnäs S 66 A1
Holm N 195 E3
Hólmavík IS 190 B4
Holmbukt N 192 B5
Holmedal S 54 A2
Holmegil N 54 A2
Holmen N 48 B2
Holme-on-Spalding-Moor GB 40 B3
Holmes Chapel GB 38 A4
Holmestrand N . . . 54 A1
Holmfirth GB 40 B2
Holmfoss N 193 C14
Holmsbu N 54 A1
Holmsjö S 63 B3
Holmsund S 200 C6
Holmsveden S 50 A3
Holmudden S 57 C5
Hölö S 57 A3
Holøydal N 199 C8
Holsbybrunn S 62 A3
Holseter N 48 A1
Holsljunga S 60 B2
Holstebro DK 59 B1
Holsted DK 59 C1
Holsworthy GB 42 B2
Holt D 64 B2
Norfolk GB 41 C5
Wrexham GB . . . 38 A4
Holten NL 71 B3
Holtwick D 71 B4
Holum N 52 B3
Holwerd NL 70 A2
Holycross IRL 29 B4
Holyhead GB 38 A2
Holýšov CZ 95 B5
Holywell GB 38 A3
Holywood GB 27 B5
Holzdorf D 83 A5
Holzhausen D 72 B1
Holzheim D 94 C2
Holzkirchen D 108 B2
Holzminden D 81 A5
Holzthaleben D . . . 82 A2
Homberg Hessen D 81 A5
Hessen D 81 B5
Homburg D 93 B3
Hommelstø N 195 E3
Hommersåk N 52 B1
Homokmegy H 112 C3
Homokszentgyörgy H 124 A3
Honaz TR 188 B4
Hondarribia E 144 A2
Hondón de los Frailes E 165 A4
Hondschoote F . . . 78 B2
Hönebach D 82 B1
Hønefoss N 48 B2
Honfleur F 89 A4
Høng DK 61 D1
Honiton GB 43 B3
Hönningen D 80 B2
Honningsvåg N . . . 193 B9
Hönö S 60 B1
Honrubia E 158 B1
Hontalbilla E 151 A3
Hontheim D 92 A2
Hontianske-Nemce SK 98 C2
Hontoria de la Cantera E 143 B3
Hontoria del Pinar E 143 C3
Hontoria de Valdearados E . . . 143 C3
Hoofddorp NL 70 B1
Hoogerheide NL . . 79 A4
Hoogeveen NL . . . 71 B3
Hoogezand-Sappemeer NL 71 A3
Hoogkarspel NL . . . 70 B2
Hoogkerk NL 71 A3
Hoogstede D 71 B3
Hoogstraten B 79 A4
Hook GB 44 B3
Hooksiel D 71 A5
Höör S 61 D3
Hoorn NL 70 B2
Hope GB 38 A3
Hopen N 194 C6
Hope under Dinmore GB 39 B4
Hopfgarten A 108 B3
Hopfgarten in Defereggen A . . . 109 C3
Hopseidet N 193 B11
Hopsten D 71 B4
Hoptrup DK 59 C2
Hora Svatého Sebestiána CZ . . . 83 B5
Horaždovice CZ . . . 96 B1
Horb am Neckar D . 93 C4
Horbelev DK 65 B5
Hørby DK 58 A3
Hörby S 61 D3
Horcajada de la Torre E 158 A1
Horcajo de los Montes E 156 A3
Horcajo de Santiago E 151 C4
Horcajo-Medianero E 150 B2
Horche E 151 B4
Horda S 62 A2
Hordabø N 46 B1
Hordalia N 52 A2
Hordvik N 46 B2
Hořesedly CZ 83 B5
Horezu RO 17 C6
Horgen CH 107 B3

Horgoš SRB 126 A1
Horia RO 126 A3
Hořice CZ 84 B3
Horjul SLO 123 A3
Horka D 84 A2
Hörken S 50 B1
Horki BY 13 A9
Hörle S 60 B4
Horn A 97 C3
D 81 A4
N 48 B2
S 62 A3
Horna E 158 C2
Hornachos E 156 B1
Hornachuelos E . . . 162 A2
Horná Mariková SK 98 B2
Hornanes N 46 C2
Horná Streda SK . . 98 C1
Horná Štrubna SK . 98 C2
Horná Súča SK . . . 98 C1
Hornbæk Aarhus Amt. DK. . 58 B2
Frederiksværk DK 61 C2
Hornberg D 106 A3
Hornburg D 73 B3
Horncastle GB 41 B3
Horndal S 50 B3
Horndean GB. 44 C2
Horne Fyns Amt. DK. . . . 64 A3
Ribe Amt. DK. . . . 59 C1
Hornebo S 55 B5
Horneburg D 72 A2
Hörnefors S 200 C5
Horní Bečva CZ . . . 98 B2
Horní Benešov CZ . 98 B1
Horní Cerekev CZ . 97 B3
Horní Jiřetín CZ . . . 83 B5
Horní Lomná CZ . . . 98 B2
Horní Maršov CZ . . 85 B3
Hornindal N 198 D3
Hørning DK 59 B3
Hörningsholm S . . . 57 A3
Horní Planá CZ . . . 96 C2
Horní Slavkov CZ . . 83 B4
Horní Vltavice CZ . . 96 C1
Hornnes N 53 B3
Horno D 84 A2
Hornos E 164 A2
Hornoy-le-Bourg F . 90 B1
Hornsea GB 41 B3
Hornsjø N 48 A2
Hornslet DK 59 B3
Hornstein A 111 B3
Hörnum D 64 B1
Hornum DK 58 B2
Horný Tisovnik SK . 99 C3
Horodenka UA 13 D6
Horodnya UA 13 C9
Horodok Khmelnytskyy UA . . . 13 D7
Lviv UA 13 D5
Horokhiv UA 13 C6
Horovice CZ 96 B1
Horred S 60 B2
Hörröd S 61 D4
Hörsching A 110 A1
Horsens DK 59 C2
Horsham GB 44 B3
Hørsholm DK 61 D2
Horslunde DK 65 B4
Horšovský Týn CZ . 95 B4
Horst NL 80 A2
Horstel D 71 B4
Horsten D 71 A4
Horstmar D 71 B4
Hort H 113 B3
Horten N 54 A1
Hortezuela E 151 A4
Hortiguela E 143 B3
Hortobágy H 113 B5
Horton in Ribblesdale GB 37 B4
Hørve DK 61 D1
Hörvik S 63 B2
Horwich GB 38 A4
Hosanger N 46 B2
Hösbach D 93 A5
Hosena D 84 A2
Hosenfeld D 81 B5
Hosingen L 92 A2
Hosio FIN 197 D8
Hospental CH 107 C3
Hospital IRL 29 B3
Hossegor F 128 C1
Hosszuhetény H . . . 125 A4
Hostal de Ipiés E . . 145 B3
Hoštálková CZ 98 B1
Hostalric E 147 C3
Hostens F 128 B2
Hostěradice CZ . . . 97 C4
Hostinné CZ 85 B3
Hostomice CZ 96 B2
Hostouň CZ 95 B4
Hotagen S 199 B11
Hoting S 200 B2
Hotolisht AL 182 B2
Hotton B 79 B5
Houdain F 78 B2
Houdan F 90 C1
Houdelaincourt F . . 92 C1
Houeillès F 128 B2
Houffalize B 92 A1
Houghton-le-Spring GB 37 B5
Houlberg DK 59 B2
Houlgate F 89 A3
Hounslow GB 44 B3
Hourtin F 128 A1
Hourtin-Plage F . . . 128 A1
Houthalen B 79 A5
Houyet B 79 B4
Hov DK 59 C3
N 48 B2
Hova S 55 B5

Høvåg N 53 B4
Hovborg DK 59 C1
Hovda N 47 B6
Hovden N 52 A3
Hove GB 44 C3
Hovedgård DK 59 C2
Hovelhof D 81 A4
Hoven DK 59 C1
Hoven N 47 B5
Hovingham GB 40 A3
Hovmantorp S 62 B3
Hovsta S 56 A1
Howden GB 40 B3
Howe D 72 A3
Höxter D 81 A5
Hoya D 72 B2
Hoya de Santa Maria E 161 B3
Hoya-Gonzalo E . . 158 C2
Høyanger N 46 A3
Hoyerswerda D . . . 84 A2
Høyjord N 53 A6
Hoylake GB 38 A3
Høylandet N 199 A9
Hoym D 82 A3
Høymyr N 47 C6
Hoyocasero E 150 B3
Hoyo de Manzanares E 151 B4
Hoyo de Pinares E 150 B3
Hoyos E 149 B3
Hoyos del Espino E 150 B2
Hrabušiče SK 99 C4
Hradec Králové CZ 85 B3
Hradec nad Moravicí CZ 98 B1
Hrádek CZ 97 C4
Hrádek nad Nisou CZ 84 B2
Hradište SK 98 C2
Hrafnagil IS 191 B7
Hrafnseyri IS 190 B2
Hranice Severomoravsky CZ. . . 98 B1
Západočeský CZ . 83 B4
Hranovnica SK 99 C4
Hrasnica BIH 139 B4
Hrastnik SLO 123 A4
Hřensko CZ 84 B2
Hriňová SK 99 C3
Hrisoupoli GR 183 C6
Hrochov CZ 97 B4
Hrochův Tynec CZ . 97 B3
Hrodna BY 13 B5
Hrodzyanka BY . . . 13 B8
Hronov CZ 85 B4
Hronský Beňadik SK 98 C2
Hrotovice CZ 97 B4
Hrtkovci SRB 127 C1
Hrun IS 190 A5
Hrušov SK 112 A3
Hrušovany nad Jevišovkou CZ . . . 97 C4
Hřuštin SK 99 B3
Hrvaćani BIH 124 C3
Hrvace HR 138 B2
Hrymayliv UA. 13 D7
Huben A 109 C3
Hückel-hoven D . . . 80 A2
Hückeswagen D . . . 80 A3
Hucknall GB 40 B2
Hucqueliers F 78 B1
Huddersfield GB . . 40 B2
Huddinge S 57 A3
Huddunge S 51 B3
Hude D 72 A1
Hudiksvall S 200 E3
Huélago E 163 A4
Huélamo E 152 B2
Huelgoat F 100 A2
Huelma E 163 A4
Huelva E 161 B3
Huéneja E 164 B2
Huércal de Almeria E 164 C2
Huércal-Overa E . . 164 B3
Huerta de Abajo E 143 B3
Huerta del Rey E . . 143 C3
Huerta de Valdecarabanos E 151 C4
Huertahernando E 152 B1
Huesa E 164 B1
Huesca E 145 B3
Huéscar E 164 B2
Huete E 151 B5
Huétor Tájar E 163 A3
Hüfingen D 106 B3
Hufthamar N 46 B2
Hugh Town GB 42 B1
Huglfing D 108 B2
Huissen NL 70 C2
Huittinen FIN 8 B3
Huizen NL 70 B2
Hulín CZ 98 B1
Hüls D 80 A2
Hulsig DK 58 A3
Hulst NL 79 A4
Hult S 62 A3
Hulteby S 55 A5
Hultsfred S 62 A3
Humanes E 151 B4
Humberston GB . . . 41 B3
Humble DK 65 B3
Humenné SK 12 D4
Humilladero E 163 A3
Humlebæk DK 61 D2
Humlum DK 58 B1
Hummelsta S 56 A2
Humpolec CZ 97 B3
Humshaugh GB . . . 37 A4
Hundåla N 195 E3
Hundested DK 61 D1
Hundorp N 48 A1

Hundvåg N 52 A1
Hundvin N 46 B2
Hunedoara RO . . . 17 C5
Hünfeld D 82 B1
Hungen D 81 B4
Hungerford GB 44 B2
Hunndalen N 48 B2
Hunnebostrand S . . 54 B2
Hunstanton GB . . . 41 C4
Huntingdon GB . . . 44 A3
Huntley GB 39 C4
Huntly GB 33 D4
Hünxe D 80 A2
Hurbanovo SK 112 B2
Hürbel D 107 A4
Hurdal N 48 B3
Hurezani RO 17 C5
Hurlford GB 36 A2
Hurstbourne Tarrant GB 44 B2
Hurstpierpoint GB . 44 C3
Hürth D 80 B2
Hurum N 47 A5
Hurup DK 58 B1
Húsafell IS 190 C5
Húsavík IS 191 A8
Husbands Bosworth GB 44 A2
Husby D 64 B2
DK 59 B1
Husey IS 191 B11
Huşi RO 17 B8
Husina BIH 139 A4
Husinec CZ 96 B1
Husinish GB 31 B1
Huskvarna S 62 A2
Husnes N 46 C2
Husøy N 194 A8
Hustad N 198 C4
Hüsten D 81 A3
Hustopeče CZ 97 C4
Hustopeče nad Bečvou CZ 98 B1
Husum D 64 B2
S 200 C5
Husvika N 195 E3
Huta PL 75 B5
Hutovo BIH 139 C3
Hüttenberg A 110 C1
Hüttlingen D 94 C2
Huttoft GB 41 B4
Hutton Cranswick GB 40 B3
Hüttschlag A 109 B4
Hüttisheim D 94 C1
Huttwil CH 106 B2
Huy B 79 B5
Hüyük TR 189 B6
Hval N 48 B2
Hvåle N 47 B6
Hvaler N 54 A2
Hvalpsund DK 58 B2
Hvammstangi IS . . . 190 B5
Hvammur IS 190 B6
Hvanneyri IS 190 C4
Hvar HR 138 B2
Hvidbjerg DK 58 B1
Hvide Sande DK . . . 59 C1
Hvittingfoss N 53 A6
Hvolsvöllur IS 190 D5
Hybe SK 99 B3
Hyckinge S 62 A3
Hydra GR 185 B4
Hyen N 198 D2
Hyères F 132 B2
Hyères Plage F . . . 132 B2
Hylestad N 52 A3
Hylke DK 59 C2
Hyllestad N 46 A2
Hyllstofta S 61 C3
Hyltebruk S 60 B3
Hynnekleiv N 53 B4
Hythe Hampshire GB . . 44 C2
Kent GB 45 B5
Hyvinkää FIN 8 B4

I

Iam RO 127 B3
Iaşi RO 17 B7
Iasmos GR 183 B7
Ibahernando E 156 A2
Ibarranguelua E . . . 143 A4
Ibbenbüren D 71 B4
Ibeas de Juarros E 143 B3
Ibestad N 194 B8
Ibi E 159 C3
Ibiza = Eivissa E . . 166 C1
Ibradı TR 189 B6
İbriktepe TR 186 A1
Ibros E 157 B4
Ibstock GB 40 C2
İçel TR 23 C8
Ichenhausen D . . . 94 C2
Ichtegem B 78 A3
Ichtershausen D . . . 82 B2
Idanha-a-Novo P . . 155 B3
Idar-Oberstein D . . 93 B3
Idd N 54 A2
Idiazábal E 144 B1
Idivuoma S 196 A4
Idkerberget S 50 B2
Idön S 51 B5
Idre S 199 D9
Idrija SLO 123 A3
Idritsa RUS 9 D6
Idstein D 81 B4
Idvor SRB 126 B2
Iecca Mare RO . . . 126 B2
Ielsi I 170 B2
Ierapetra GR 185 D6
Ierissos GR 183 C5
If F 12 D4

Ig SLO 123 B3
Igal H 112 C1
Igea I 144 B1
Igea Marina I 136 A1
Igelfors S 56 B1
Igersheim D 94 B1
Iggesund S 200 E3
Iglésias I 143 B3
Iglésias I 179 C2
Igls A 108 B2
Igny-Comblizy F . . . 91 B3
Igorre E 143 A4
Igoumenitsa GR . . . 182 D2
Igries E 145 B3
Igualada E 147 C2
Igüeña E 141 B4
Iguerande F 117 A4
Iharosberény H 124 A3
Ihl'any SK 99 B4
Ihlienworth D 64 C1
Ihringen D 106 A2
Ihrlerstein D 95 C3
Ihsaniye TR 187 C5
Ii FIN 197 D8
Iijärvi FIN 193 C11
Iisalmi FIN 3 E10
IJmuiden NL 70 B1
IJsselmuiden NL . . . 70 B2
IJzendijke NL 79 A3
Ikast DK 59 B2
Ikervár H 111 B3
Ilandža SRB 126 B2
Ilanz CH 107 C4
Ilava SK 98 C2
Iława PL 69 B4
Ilche E 145 C4
Ilchester GB 43 B4
Ilfeld D 82 A2
Ilfracombe GB 42 A2
Ilgaz TR 23 A7
Ilgın TR 189 A6
Ilhavo P 148 B1
Ilica TR 186 C2
Ilidža BIH 139 B4
Ilijaš BIH 139 B4
Ilirska Bistrica SLO 123 B3
Ilkeston GB 40 C2
Ilkley GB 40 B2
Illana E 151 B5
Illano E 141 A4
Illar E 164 C2
Illas E 141 A5
Illats F 128 B2
Illertissen D 94 C2
Illescas E 151 B4
Ille-sur-Têt F 146 B3
Illfurth F 106 B2
Illichivsk UA 17 B10
Illiers-Combray F . . 89 B5
Illkirch-Graffenstaden F 93 C3
Illmersdorf D 74 C2
Illmitz A 111 B3
Illora E 163 A4
Illueca E 152 A2
Ilmajoki FIN 8 A3
Ilmenau D 82 B2
Ilminster GB 43 B4
Ilok HR 126 B1
Ilomantsi FIN 9 A7
Iłow PL 77 B5
Iłowa PL 84 A3
Iłowo-Osada PL . . . 77 A5
Ilsenburg D 82 A2
Ilshofen D 94 B1
Ilz A 110 B2
Iłża PL 87 A5
Imatra FIN 9 B6
Imielin PL 86 B3
Imingen N 47 B5
Immeln S 63 B2
Immenhausen D . . . 81 A5
Immenstaad D 107 B4
Immenstadt D 107 B5
Immingham GB 41 B3
Imola I 135 A4
Imon E 151 A5
Imotski HR 138 B3
Impéria I 133 B4
Imphy F 104 C2
İmroz TR 183 C7
Imsland N 52 A1
Imst A 108 B1
Inagh IRL 28 B2
Inari FIN 193 D10
Inca E 167 B2
Inchnadamph GB . . 32 C2
Incinillas E 143 B3
Indal S 200 D3
Indjija SRB 127 B2
Indre Arna N 46 B2
Indre Billefjord N . . 193 B9
Indre Brenna N . . . 193 B9
İğneada TR 186 A2
İnebolu TR 23 A7
İnecik TR 186 B2
İnegöl TR 187 B4
Inerthal CH 107 B3
Infiesto E 142 A1
Ingatorp S 62 A3
Ingedal N 54 A2
Ingelheim D 93 B4
Ingelmunster B . . . 78 B3
Ingelstad S 62 B2
Ingleton GB 37 B4
Ingolfsland N 47 C5
Ingolstadt D 95 C3
Ingrandes Maine-et-Loire F . . 101 B5
Vienne F 102 C2
Ingwiller F 93 C3
İnhisar TR 187 B5
Iniesta E 158 B2
Inishannon IRL 29 C3
Inishcrone IRL 26 B1
Inke H 124 A3
Inndyr N 195 C5
Innellan GB 34 C3

Innerleithen GB . . . 35 C4
Innermessan GB . . 36 B2
Innertkirchen CH . . 106 C3
Innervillgraten A . . . 109 C3
Innsbruck A 108 B2
Innset N 194 B9
Innvik N 198 D3
İnönü TR 187 C5
Inowłódz PL 87 A4
Inowrocław PL 76 B3
Ins CH 106 B2
Insch GB 33 D4
Insjön S 50 B2
Ińsko PL 75 A4
Instow GB 42 A2
İntepe TR 186 B1
Interlaken CH 106 C2
Intragna CH 120 A1
Introbio I 120 B2
Inveran GB 32 D2
IRL 28 D2
Inveraray GB 34 B2
Inverbervie GB 35 B5
Invergarry GB 32 D2
Invergordon GB . . . 32 D2
Invergowrie GB 35 B4
Inverkeilor GB 35 B5
Inverkeithing GB . . . 35 B4
Invermoriston GB . . 32 D2
Inverness GB 32 D2
Inveruno I 120 B1
Inverurie GB 33 D4
Ioannina GR 182 D2
Iolanda di Savoia I 121 C4
Ion Corvin RO 17 C7
Ióppolo I 175 C1
Ios GR 185 C6
Ipati GR 182 E4
Ipsala TR 186 B1
Ipswich GB 45 A5
Iraklia GR 183 B5
Iraklio = Heraklion GR 185 D6
Irdning A 110 B1
Iregszemcse H 112 C2
Irgoli I 178 B3
Irig SRB 127 B1
Ironbridge GB 39 B4
Irpin UA 13 C9
Irrel D 92 B2
Irsina I 172 B2
Irsta S 56 A2
Irthlingborough GB 44 A3
Iruela E 141 B4
Irún E 144 A2
Irurita E 144 A2
Irurzun E 144 A2
Irvine GB 36 A2
Irvinestown GB . . . 27 B3
Isaba E 144 B3
Isabela I 157 B4
Ísafjörður IS 190 A2
Isane N 198 D2
Isaszeg H 112 B3
Isbister GB 33 A5
Iscar E 150 A3
İscehisar TR 187 D5
Ischgl A 107 B5
Ischia I 170 C1
Ischia di Castro I . . 168 A1
Ischitella I 171 B3
Isdes F 103 B4
Ise N 54 A2
Iselle I 119 A5
Iseltwald CH 106 C2
Isen D 108 A3
Isenbüttel D 73 B3
Iseo I 120 B3
Iserlohn D 81 A3
Isérnia I 170 B2
Isfjorden N 198 C4
Ishëm AL 182 B1
Isigny-sur-Mer F . . 88 A2
Işıklı TR 189 A4
İsili I 179 C3
İskilip TR 23 A8
Isla Canela E 161 B2
Isla Cristina E 161 B2
Islares E 143 A3
Isleham GB 45 A4
Isle of Whithorn GB 36 B2
Ismaning D 108 A2
Isna P 154 B3
Isnestoften N 192 B6
Isny D 107 B5
Isoba E 142 A1
Isokylä FIN 197 C10
S 196 B5
Isola F 132 A2
Isola d'Asti I 119 C5
Isola del Gran Sasso d'Itália I 169 A3
Ísola della Scala I . 121 B4
Isola delle Fémmine I 176 A2
Ísola del Liri I 169 B3
Ísola di Capo Rizzuto I 175 C3
Isona E 147 B2
Ispagnac F 130 A2
Ísparta TR 189 B5
Isperih BG 17 C7
Íspica I 177 C3
Isselburg D 80 A2
Issigeac F 129 B3
Issogne I 119 B4
Issoire F 116 B3
Issoncourt F 91 C5
Issoudun F 103 C4
Is-sur-Tille F 105 B4
Issy-l'Evêque F . . . 104 C2

Istán E 162 B3
İstanbul TR 186 A3
Istebna PL 98 B2
Ìstia d'Ombrone I .135 C4
Istiea GR 183 E5
Istres F 131 B3
Istvándi H 125 A3
Itea GR 184 A3
Ithaki GR 184 A1
Itoiz E 144 B2
Ítrabo E 163 B4
Itri I 169 B3
Ittireddu I 178 B2
Íttiri I 178 B2
Itzehoe D 64 C2
Ivalo FIN 193 D11
Iván H 111 B3
Ivanava BY 13 B6
Ivančice CZ 97 B4
Ivančna Gorica
  SLO 123 B3
Iváncsa H 112 B2
Ivanec HR 124 A2
Ivanić Grad HR 124 B2
Ivanjska BIH 124 C3
Ivanka SK 98 C2
Ivankovo HR 125 B4
Ivano-Frankivsk
  UA 13 D6
Ivanovice na Hané
  CZ 98 B1
Ivanska HR 124 B2
Ivatsevichy BY 13 B6
Ivaylovgrad BG 183 B8
Iveland N 53 B3
Ivoz Ramet B 79 B5
Ivrea I 119 B4
Ìvrindi TR 186 C2
Ivry-en-Montagne
  F. 104 B3
Ivry-la-Bataille F . . .90 C1
Ivybridge GB 42 B3
Iwaniska PL 87 B5
Iwiny PL 85 A3
Iwuy F 78 B3
Ixworth GB. 45 A4
Izarra E 143 B4
Izbica Kujawska PL 76 B3
Izbište SRB 127 B3
Izeda P 149 A3
Izegem B 78 B3
Izernore F 118 A2
Izmayil UA 17 C8
İzmir TR 188 A2
İzmit = Kocaeli
  TR 187 B4
Iznájar E 163 A3
Iznalloz E 163 A4
Iznatoraf E 164 A1
İznik TR 187 B4
Izola SLO 122 B2
Izsák H 112 C3
Izsófalva H. 99 C4
Izyaslav UA 13 C7

J

Jabalquinto E 157 B4
Jablanac HR 123 C3
Jablanica BIH 139 B3
Jablonec nad Jizerou
  CZ 84 B3
Jablonec nad Nisou
  CZ 84 B3
Jablonica SK 98 C1
Jablonka PL. 99 B3
Jabłonna PL 77 B5
Jablonnad Orlicí
  CZ 97 A4
Jablonne Podještědi
  CZ 84 B2
Jablonov nad Turňou
  SK 99 C4
Jabłonowo Pomorskie
  PL 69 B4
Jablúnka CZ 98 B1
Jablunkov CZ 98 B2
Jabučje SRB 127 C2
Jabugo E 161 B3
Jabuka SRB 127 C2
Jabukovac HR 124 B2
Jaca E 145 B3
Jáchymov CZ 83 B4
Jacobidrebber D . . .72 B1
Jade D 71 A5
Jäderfors S 50 B3
Jädraås S. 50 B3
Jadraque E 151 B5
Jaén E 163 A4
Jagare BIH 124 C3
Jagel D 64 B2
Jagenbach A 96 C3
Jægerspris DK 61 D1
Jagodina SRB 127 C3
Jagodnjak HR 125 B4
Jagodzin PL 84 A3
Jagstheim D 94 B2
Jagstzell D 94 B2
Jahodna SK 111 A4
Jajce BIH 138 A3
Ják H 111 B3
Jakabszálbs H 112 C3
Jäkkvik S 195 D8
Jakobsnes N 193 C14
Jakovlje HR 124 B1
Jakšic HR 125 B3
Jalasjärvi FIN 3 E9
Jalance E 159 B2
Jalasjärvi FIN 8 E18
Jalhay B 80 B1
Jaligny-sur-Besbre
  F. 117 A3
Jallais F 102 B1
Jalón E. 159 C3
Jâlons F 91 C4
Jamena SRB 125 C5

Jamilena E 163 A4
Jämjö S 63 B3
Jamnička Kiselica
  HR 124 B1
Jamno PL. 67 B5
Jamoigne B 92 B1
Jämsä FIN 8 B4
Jämshög S 63 B2
Jamu Mare RO. 126 B3
Janakkala FIN. 8 B4
Jandelsbrunn D 96 C1
Jänickendorf D 74 B2
Janikowo PL 76 B3
Janja BIH 125 C5
Janjina HR 138 C3
Janki
  Łódzkie PL. 86 A3
  Mazowieckie PL . .77 B5
Jankov CZ 96 B2
Jankowo Dolne PL .76 B2
Jánoshalma H 126 A1
Jánosháza H 111 B4
Jánoshida H 113 B4
Jánossomorja H . . .111 B4
Janovice nad Uhlavou
  CZ. 96 B1
Janów PL 86 B3
Janowiec Wielkopolski
  PL. 76 B2
Janowo PL 77 A5
Jänsmässholmen
  S. 199 B10
Janville F. 103 A3
Janzé F 101 B4
Jarabá SK 99 C3
Jaraczewo PL 76 C2
Jarafuel E 159 B2
Jaraicejo E 156 A2
Jaraíz de la Vera
  E 150 B2
Jarak SRB 127 C1
Jarandilla de la Vera
  E 150 B2
Jaray E 152 A1
Järbo S 50 B3
Jard-sur-Mer F 114 B2
Jaren N 48 B2
Jargeau F 103 B4
Jarkovac SRB 126 B2
Järlåsa S 51 C4
Jarmen D 66 C2
Järna S 57 A3
Jarnac F 115 C3
Järnäs S 200 C5
Järnforsen S 62 A3
Jarny F 92 B1
Jarocin PL 76 C2
Jaroměř CZ 85 B3
Jaroměřice nad
  Rokytnou CZ 97 B3
Jaroslav CZ 97 A4
Jaroslavice CZ 97 C4
Jarosław PL 12 C5
Jarošov nad Nežarkou
  CZ 96 B3
Järpås S 55 B3
Järpen S 199 B10
Jarrow GB 37 B5
Järso FIN 51 B6
Järvenpää FIN 8 B4
Jarvornik CZ 85 B4
Järvsö S 200 E2
Jarzé F 102 B1
Jaša Tomic SRB . . .126 B2
Jasenak HR 123 B4
Jasenica BIH 124 C2
Jasenice HR 137 A4
Jasenovac HR 124 B2
Jasenovo SRB. 127 C3
Jasień PL. 84 A3
Jasienica PL 84 A2
Jásło PL. 12 D4
Jásova SK 112 B2
Jasseron F. 118 A2
Jastarnia PL. 69 A3
Jastrebarsko HR . . .123 B4
Jastrowie PL 68 B1
Jastrzębia-Góra PL 68 A3
Jastrzębie Zdrój
  PL. 98 B2
Jászals-
  Lószentgyörgy
  H 113 B4
Jászapáti H 113 B4
Jászárokszállás
  H 113 B3
Jászberény H 113 B3
Jászdózsa H 113 B4
Jászfényszaru H . . .113 B3
Jászjákóhalma H . . .113 B4
Jászkarajenő H 113 B3
Jászladány H 113 B4
Jászszentlászló
  H 113 C3
Jásztelek H 113 B4
Játar E 163 B4
Jättendal S 200 E3
Jatznick D 74 A2
Jaun CH 106 C2
Jausiers F 132 A2
Jávea E 159 C4
Jävenitz D 73 B4
Javerlhac F 115 C4
Javier E. 144 B2
Javorani BIH 124 C3
Javorina SK 99 B4
Javron F. 89 B3
Jawor PL 85 A4
Jaworzno PL 86 B3
Jaworzyna Śl. PL . . .85 B4
Jayena E 163 B4
Jažow PL 84 A2
Jebel RO 126 B3
Jebjerg DK 58 B2
Jedburgh GB. 35 C5
Jedlinsk PL 87 A5
Jedlnia PL 87 A5

Jedlnia Letnisko
  PL 87 A5
Jednorożec PL 77 A6
Jedovnice CZ 97 B4
Jędrychow PL. 69 B4
Jędrzejów PL. 87 B4
Jedwabno PL. 77 A5
Jeesiö FIN 197 B9
Jegłownik PL. 69 A4
Jegun F 129 C3
Jēkabpils LV 8 D4
Jektevik N 46 C2
Jektvik N 195 D4
Jelcz-Laskowice
  PL. 85 A5
Jelenec SK. 98 C2
Jelenia Góra PL 85 B3
Jelgava LV 8 D3
Jelka SK. 111 A4
Jelling DK 59 C2
Jels DK. 59 C2
Jelsa
  HR 138 B2
  N 52 A2
Jelšava SK. 99 C4
Jemgum D 71 A4
Jemnice CZ 97 B3
Jena D 82 B3
Jenaz CH 107 C4
Jenbach A 108 B2
Jenikow PL 75 A4
Jennersdorf A 111 C3
Jenny S 62 A4
Jerchel D 73 B4
Jeres del Marquesado
  E 164 B1
Jerez de la Frontera
  E 162 B1
Jerez de los Caballeros
  E 155 C4
Jerica E 159 B3
Jerichow D 73 B5
Jerka PL 75 B5
Jermenovci SRB . . .126 B3
Jerslev DK 58 A3
Jerte E 150 B2
Jerup DK 58 A3
Jerxheim D 73 B3
Jerzmanowice PL . .87 B3
Jerzu I. 179 C3
Jerzwałd PL. 69 B4
Jesberg D 81 B5
Jesenice
  Středočeský CZ. . .83 B5
  Středočeský CZ. . .96 B2
  SLO 109 C5
Jesenik CZ 85 B5
Jesenké SK 99 C4
Jesi I. 136 B2
Jésolo I 122 B1
Jessen D 83 A4
Jessenitz D 73 A4
Jessheim N. 48 B3
Jessnitz D 83 A4
Jesteburg D 72 A2
Jestrebí CZ 84 B2
Jesup E 18 B2
Jeumont F 79 B4
Jever D 71 A4
Jevičko CZ 97 B4
Jevišovice CZ 97 C3
Jevnaker N 48 B2
Jezerane HR 123 B4
Jezero
  BIH. 138 A3
  HR 123 B4
Jeżew PL 87 A3
Jezów PL. 87 A4
Jičín CZ 84 B3
Jičíneves CZ 84 B3
Jihlava CZ 97 B3
Jijona E 159 C3
Jilemnice CZ 84 B3
Jilové CZ 84 B2
Jílové u Prahy CZ. . .96 B2
Jimbolia RO. 126 B2
Jimena E 163 A4
Jimena de la Frontera
  E 162 B2
Jimera de Libar E . .162 B2
Jimramov CZ. 97 B4
Jince CZ. 96 B1
Jindřichovice CZ. . . .83 B4
Jindřichův Hradec
  CZ 96 B3
Jirkov CZ 83 B5
Jistebnice CZ 96 B2
Joachimsthal D 74 B2
João da Loura P . . .154 C2
Jobbágyi H 112 B3
Jochberg A 109 B3
Jockfall S 196 C5
Jódar E 163 A4
Jodoigne B 79 B4
Joensuu FIN 9 A6
Joesjö S 195 E5
Joeuf F 92 B1
Jõgeva EST 8 C5
Johanngeorgenstadt
  D 83 B4
Johannishus S 63 B3
Johanniskirchen D 95 C4
Johansfors S 63 B3
John o'Groats GB . .32 C3
Johnshaven GB 35 B5
Johnstone GB. 34 C3
Johnstown IRL 30 B1
Jõhvi EST. 8 C5
Joigny F 104 B2
Joinville F 91 C5
Jokkmokk S. 196 C2
Jöllenbeck D 72 B1
Jomala FIN 51 B6
Jonava LT 13 A6
Jonchery-sur-Vesle
  F. 91 B3
Jondal N 46 B3
Jondalen N 53 A5
Joniškis LT. 8 D4
Jönköping S 62 A2
Jonkowo PL. 69 B5

Jønnbu N 53 A5
Jonsberg S 56 B2
Jonsered S. 60 B2
Jonstorp S. 61 C2
Jonzac F 114 C3
Jorba E 147 C2
Jordanów PL. 99 B3
Jordanowo PL 75 B4
Jordanów Śląski
  PL. 85 B4
Jordbro S. 57 A4
Jordbrua N 195 D5
Jördenstorf D 66 C1
Jordet N. 49 A4
Jordøse DK 59 C3
Jork D 72 A2
Jörlanda S 60 B1
Jörmlien S 199 A10
Jormvattnet S 199 A11
Jörn S 200 A6
Jørpeland N 52 A2
Jorquera E 158 B2
Jošan HR 123 C4
Jošavka BIH 124 C3
Josipdol HR 123 B4
Josipovac HR 125 B4
Jössefors S. 54 A3
Josselin F 101 B3
Jøssund N. 199 A7
Jostedal N 47 A4
Jósvafő H 99 C4
Jou P 148 A2
Jouarre F 90 C3
Joué-lès-Tours F . . .102 B2
Joué-sur-Erdre F . .101 B4
Jouy F. 90 C1
Jouy-le-Châtel F . . .90 C3
Jouy-le-Potier F . . .103 B3
Joyeuse F 131 A3
Joze F 116 B3
Juankoski FIN 9 A6
Juan-les-Pins F . . .132 B3
Jübek D 64 B2
Jubera E 144 B1
Jubrique F 162 B2
Jüchsen D 82 B2
Judaberg N 52 A1
Judenburg A 110 B1
Juelsminde DK 59 C3
Jugon-les-Lacs F .101 A3
Juillac F 129 A4
Juillan F 145 A4
Juist D 71 A4
Jukkasjärvi S 196 B3
Jule N. 199 A10
Julianadorp NL 70 B1
Juliantown IRL 30 A2
Jülich D 80 B2
Jullouville F 88 B2
Jumeaux F 117 B3
Jumièges F 89 A4
Jumilhac-le-Grand
  F. 115 C5
Jumilla E 159 C2
Jumisko FIN 197 C11
Juncosa E 153 A4
Juneda E 147 C1
Jung S 55 B4
Jungingen D 93 C5
Junglingster L 92 B2
Juniville F 91 B4
Junosuando S 196 B5
Junqueira P 149 A2
Junsele S 200 C2
Juoksengi S 196 C6
Juoksenki FIN 196 C6
Juprelle B 80 B1
Jurata PL 69 A3
Jurbarkas LT 12 A5
Jurjevo HR 123 C3
Jūrmala LV. 8 D3
Jurmu FIN 197 D10
Jursla S 56 B2
Jussac F 116 C2
Jussey F 105 B4
Jussy F 90 B3
Juta H 112 C2
Jüterbog D 74 C2
Juuka FIN 3 E11
Juuma FIN 197 C12
Juvigny-le-Terte F . .88 B2
Juvigny-sous-Andaine
  F. 89 B3
Juzennecourt F 105 A3
Jyderup DK 61 D1
Jyrkänkoski FIN .197 C12
Jyväskylä FIN 8 A4

K

Kaamanen FIN . . .193 C11
Kaamasmukka
  FIN. 193 C10
Kaaresuvanto FIN 192 D6
Kaarssen D 73 A4
Kaatscheuvel NL. . . .79 A5
Kaba H 113 B5
Kåbdalis S 196 C3
Kačarevo SRB 127 C2
Kács H 113 B4
Kadan CZ 83 B5
Kadarkút H 125 A3
Kadınhanı TR. 189 A7
Kaduy RUS 9 C10
Kåfjord N 192 C7
Kåfjordbotn N 192 C4
Kågeröd S. 61 D3
Kahl D 93 A5
Kahla D 82 B3
Kainach bei Voitsberg
  A. 110 B2
Kaindorf A 110 B2
Kainulasjärvi S 196 C5

Kairala FIN 197 B10
Kaisepakte S 192 D3
Kaisersesch D. 80 B3
Kaiserslautern D. . . .93 B3
Kaisheim D 94 C2
Kajaani FIN 3 D10
Kajárpéc H. 111 B4
Kajdacs H 112 C2
Kakanj BIH 139 A4
Kakasd H 125 A4
Kaklik TR 189 B4
Kakolewo PL 85 A4
Kál H 113 B4
Kalajoki FIN 3 D8
Kalak N 193 B11
Kalamata GR 184 B3
Kalambaka GR 182 D3
Kalamria GR 182 C4
Kalandra GR 183 D5
Kälarne S 200 D2
Kalavrita GR 184 A3
Kalbe D 73 B4
Kalce SLO 123 B3
Káld H 111 B4
Kale
  Antalya TR. 189 C4
  Denizli TR 188 B3
Kalecik TR 23 A7
Kalefeld D 82 A2
Kalesija BIH 139 A4
Kalety PL 86 B2
Kalevala RUS 3 D12
Kalhovd N 47 B5
Kali HR 137 A4
Kalimnos GR. 188 C2
Kaliningrad RUS 69 A5
Kalinkavichy BY 13 B8
Kalinovac HR 124 A3
Kalinovik BIH. 139 B4
Kalinovo SK 99 C3
Kalirachi GR 183 C6
Kaliska
  Pomorskie PL 68 A3
  Pomorskie PL 68 B3
Kalisko PL 86 A3
Kalisz PL 86 A2
Kalisz Pomorski PL 75 A4
Kaljord N 194 B6
Kalkan TR 189 C4
Kalkar D 80 A2
Kalkım TR 186 C2
Kall
  D 80 B2
  S 199 B10
Källby S 55 B4
Kållered S 60 B2
Kållerstad S 60 B3
Kallinge S 63 B3
Kallmünz D 95 B3
Kallo FIN 196 B7
Kallsedet S 199 B9
Källvik S. 56 B3
Kalmar S 63 B4
Kalmthout B 79 A4
Kalná SK 112 A2
Kalocsa H 112 C2
Kalokhorio CY 181 B2
Kalo Nero GR 184 B2
Kaloni GR 186 C1
Káloz H 112 C2
Kals A 109 B3
Kalsdorf A 110 C2
Kaltbrunn CH 107 B4
Kaltenbach A 108 B2
Kaltenkirchen D 64 C2
Kaltennordheim D. . .82 B2
Kalundborg DK 61 D1
Kalush UA 13 D6
Kalv S 60 B3
Kalvåg N 198 D1
Kalvehave DK 65 A5
Kalwang A 110 B1
Kalwaria-Zebrzydowska
  PL. 99 B3
Kalyazin RUS 9 D10
Kam H 111 B3
Kaman TR 23 B7
Kamares CY 185 C5
Kambos CY 181 A1
Kamen D 81 A3
Kamenice CZ 97 B3
Kamenice nad Lipou
  CZ 96 B3
Kameničná SK 112 B2
Kamenný Most
  SK 112 B2
Kamenny Ujezd CZ 96 C2
Kamensko HR 138 B2
Kamenz D 84 A2
Kamičak BIH 124 C2
Kamień
  Pomorskie PL 75 A4
  PL 87 A4
Kamieniec Zabk PL 85 B4
Kamienka SK. 99 B4
Kamień Krajeński
  PL 76 A2
Kamienna Góra PL .85 B4
Kamień Pomorski
  PL 67 C3
Kamiros Skala
  GR 188 C2
Kamnik SLO 123 A3
Kampen NL 70 B2
Kampinos PL 77 B5
Kamp-Lintfort D 80 A2
Kamyanets-Podil's'kyy
  UA 13 D7
Kamyanka-Buz'ka
  UA 13 C6
Kamýk nad Vltavou
  CZ 96 B2
Kanal SLO 122 A2
Kanalia GR 182 D4
Kananaskis RUS . . .3 C13
Kandanos GR. 185 D4
Kandel D 93 B4
Kandern D 106 B2
Kandersteg CH 106 C2

Kandila GR 184 B3
Kandıra TR. 187 A5
Kandyty PL 69 A5
Kanfanar HR 122 B2
Kangasala FIN. 8 B4
Kangasjärvi FIN . . .196 B6
Kangos S 196 B5
Kangosjärvi FIN .196 B6
Kaniów PL 75 C3
Kanjiža SRB 126 A2
Kankaanpää FIN 8 B3
Kannus FIN 3 E8
Kanturk IRL 29 B3
Kapaklı TR. 186 A2
Kapellen
  B 110 B2
  B 79 A4
Kapellskär S 57 A5
Kapfenberg A. 110 B2
Kapfenstein A 110 C2
Kaplice CZ 96 C2
Kapljuh BIH 124 C2
Kápolna H 113 B4
Kápolnásnyék H . . .112 B2
Kaposfő H 125 A3
Kaposfüred H 125 A3
Kaposszekcsö H . . .125 A4
Kaposvár H 125 A3
Kapp N 48 B2
Kappel D 93 C3
Kappeln D 64 B2
Kappelshamn S. 57 C4
Kappl A 107 B5
Kappstad S 55 A4
Kaprun A 109 B3
Kaptol HR 125 B3
Kapuvár H 111 B4
Karaadilli TR 189 A5
Karabiğa TR 186 B2
Karabük TR 187 A7
Karaburun TR 186 D1
Karacabey TR 186 B3
Karacaköy TR 186 A3
Karacaören TR 189 A5
Karacasu TR 188 B3
Karácsond H 113 B4
Karád H 112 C1
Karahallı TR 189 A4
Karaisali TR. 23 C8
Karaman
  Balıkesir TR. 186 C3
  Karaman TR 23 C7
Karamanlı TR. 189 B4
Karamürsel TR 187 B4
Karan SRB 127 D1
Karancslapujtó H .113 A3
Karaova TR 188 B2
Karapınar TR 23 C7
Karasjok N 193 C9
Karasu TR 187 A5
Karataş
  Adana TR 23 C8
  Manisa TR 188 A3
Karatoprak TR 188 B2
Karavostasi CY 181 A1
Karben D 81 B4
Karbenning S 50 B3
Kårberg S 55 B5
Kårböle S. 199 D12
Karby
  D 64 B2
  DK 58 B1
Kårby S 57 A4
Karby S 57 A4
Karcag H 113 B4
Karczów PL. 86 B1
Karczowiska PL. 85 A4
Kardamena GR 188 C2
Kardamili GR 184 C3
Kardašova Řečice
  CZ 96 B2
Kardis S 196 C6
Karditsa GR 182 D3
Kärdla EST. 8 C3
Kardoskút H 113 C4
Kardzhali BG 183 B7
Karesuando S 192 D6
Kargı TR 23 A8
Kargopol RUS 9 B11
Kargowa PL 75 B4
Karigasniemi FIN .193 C9
Karise DK 65 A5
Karistos GR 185 A5
Karkkila FIN. 8 B4
Karlholmsbruk S . . .51 B4
Karlino PL 67 B4
Karlobag HR 137 A4
Karlovasi GR 188 B1
Karlovčic SRB 127 C2
Karlovo BG 17 D6
Karlovy Vary CZ . . .83 B4
Karłowice PL 86 B1
Karlsborg S 55 B5
Karlshamn S 63 B2
Karlshöfen D 72 A2
Karlshus N 54 A1
Karlskoga S 55 A5
Karlskrona S 63 B3
Karlsrud N 47 B5
Karlsruhe D 93 B4
Karlstad S 55 A4
Karlstadt D. 94 B1
Karlstetten A 110 A2
Karlstift A 96 C2
Karlstorp S 62 A3
Karmacs H 111 C4
Karmin PL 85 A5
Karmøy N 52 A1
Kärna S. 60 B1
Karnabrunn A 97 C4
Karnobat BG 17 D7
Karow D 73 A5
Karpacz PL 85 B3
Karperi GR 183 B5
Karpenisi GR 182 E3
Karpuzlu TR 188 B2
Kärra S 60 B2
Karrebaeksminde
  DK 65 A4
Kârsava LV 8 D5
Karsin PL 68 B2
Kårsta S 57 A4
Karstädt D 73 A4
Kartal TR 186 B4
Kartitsch A 109 C2
Kartuzy PL 68 A3
Karungi S 196 C7
Karunki FIN 196 C7
Karup DK 59 B2
Karviná CZ 98 B2
Kås DK 58 A2
Kaş TR 189 C5
Kasaba TR 189 C5
Kašava CZ 98 B1
Kåseberga S 66 A3
Kasejovice CZ 96 B1
Kasfjord N 194 B7
Kashin RUS 9 D10
Kašina HR 124 B2
Kasina-Wielka PL . .99 B4
Kaskinen FIN. 8 A2
Kašperské Hory
  CZ 96 B1
Kassandrino GR . . .183 C5
Kassel D 81 A5
Kassiopi GR 182 D1
Kastamonu TR 23 A7
Kastav HR 123 B3
Kasteli GR 185 D6
Kastellaun D 93 A3
Kastelli GR. 185 D6
Kaštel-Stari HR 138 B2
Kaštel Zegarski
  HR 138 A4
Kasterlee B 79 A4
Kastl D 95 B3
Kastlösa S 63 B4
Kastorf D 65 C3
Kastoria GR. 182 C3
Kastorio GR 184 B3
Kastraki GR 185 C5
Kastrosikia GR 182 D2
Kastsyukovichy
  BY 13 B11
Kaszaper H 113 C4
Katakolo GR 184 B2
Katapola GR 185 C6
Katastari GR 184 B1
Katerbow D 74 B1
Katerini GR 182 C4
Kathikas CY 181 B1
Kätkesuando S 196 A4
Katlenburg-Lindau
  D 82 A2
Kato Achaia GR . . .184 A2
Káto Pyrgos CY . . .181 A1
Katouna GR 182 E3
Katovice CZ 96 B1
Katowice PL. 86 B3
Katrineberg S 50 A3
Katrineholm S 56 B2
Kattarp S 61 C2
Kattavia GR 188 D2
Katthammarsvik S .57 C4
Kattilstorp S 55 B4
Katwijk NL 70 B1
Katymár H. 125 A4
Käty Wrocławskie
  PL 85 A4
Katzenelnbogen D .81 B3
Katzhütte D 82 B3
Kaub D 93 A3
Kaufbeuren D 108 B1
Kauhajoki FIN 8 A3
Kauhava FIN 8 A3
Kaukonen FIN 196 B7
Kauliranta FIN 196 C6
Kaulsdorf D 82 B3
Kaunas LT 13 A5
Kaunisvaara S 196 B6
Kaupanger N 47 A4
Kautokeino N 192 C7
Kautzen A 97 C3
Kavadarci MK 182 B4
Kavajë AL. 182 B1
Kavakköy TR. 186 B1
Kavaklı TR 186 A2
Kavaklıdere TR 188 B3
Kavala GR 183 C6
Kavarna BG 17 D8
Kävlinge S 61 D3
Kawcze PL 68 A1
Kaxås S 199 B10
Kaxholmen S 62 A2
Käylä FIN 197 C12
Kaymakçı TR 188 A3
Kaymaz TR 187 C6
Kaynarca TR 187 A5
Käyrämö FIN 197 C9
Kayseri TR 23 B8
Kaysersberg F 106 A2
Kazanlak BG 17 D6
Kazár H 113 A3
Kazimierza Wielka
  PL. 87 B4
Kazincbarcika H . . .113 A4
Kaźmierz PL. 75 B5
Kcynia PL. 76 A2
Kdyně CZ. 95 B5
Kea GR 185 B5
Keadew IRL 26 B2
Keady GB. 27 B4
Kecel H 112 C3
Keçiborlu TR 189 B5
Kecskemét H 113 C3
Kędainiai LT. 13 A5
Kędzierzyn-Koźle
  PL. 86 B2
Keel IRL 28 C1
Keenagh IRL 28 A4
Kefalos GR 188 C1
Kefenrod D 81 B5
Kefken TR. 187 A5
Keflavík IS 190 C2
Kegworth GB. 40 C2
Kehl D 93 C3
Kehrigk D 74 B2
Keighley GB 40 B2
Keila EST. 8 C4
Keillmore GB 34 C2

Keiss GB 32 C3
Keith GB 33 D4
Kelankylä FIN . . .197 D10
Kelberg D. 80 B2
Kelbra D. 82 A3
Kelč CZ 98 B1
Kelchsau A. 108 B3
Kelcyrë AL 182 C2
Keld GB 37 B4
Kelebia H. 126 A1
Kelekçi TR 188 B4
Kelemér H 99 C4
Keles TR 186 C4
Kelheim D. 95 C3
Kell D. 92 B2
Kellas GB. 32 D3
Kellinghusen D. . . .64 C2
Kelloselkä FIN. . .197 C11
Kells
  GB. 27 B4
  IRL 27 C4
Kelmis B 80 B2
Kelokedhara CY . . .181 B1
Kelottijärvi FIN . . .192 D6
Kelsall GB 38 A4
Kelso GB 35 C5
Kelsterbach D 93 A4
Keltneyburn GB . . .35 B3
Kelujärvi FIN . . .197 B10
Kemaliye TR 188 A2
Kemalpaşa TR 188 A2
Kematen A. 108 B2
Kemberg D 83 A4
Kemer
  Antalya TR. 189 C5
  Burdur TR 189 B5
  Muğla TR. 189 C4
Kemerkaya TR. 187 D6
Kemeten A. 111 B3
Kemi FIN 196 D7
Kemijärvi FIN. . . .197 C10
Keminmaa FIN. 196 D7
Kemnath D. 95 B3
Kempen D 80 A2
Kempsey GB 39 B4
Kempten D. 107 B5
Kemptthal CH 107 B3
Kendal GB. 37 B4
Kenderes H. 113 B4
Kengyel H. 113 B4
Kenilworth GB. 44 A2
Kenmare IRL 29 C2
Kenmore GB 35 B4
Kennacraig GB 34 C2
Kenyeri H 111 B4
Kenzingen D 106 A2
Kepez TR 186 B1
Kępice PL. 68 A1
Kępno PL. 86 A2
Kepsut TR 186 C3
Keramoti GR 183 C6
Keräntöjärvi S . . .196 B6
Keratea GR 185 B4
Kerava FIN. 8 B4
Kerecsend H 113 B4
Kerekegyhaza H . . .112 C3
Kerepestarcsa H. . .112 B3
Keri GR. 184 B1
Kérien F. 100 A2
Kerkafalva H 111 C3
Kerken D. 80 A2
Kerkrade NL. 80 B2
Kerkyra GR 182 D1
Kerlouan F. 100 A1
Kernascléden F. . . .100 A2
Kernhof A. 110 B2
Kerns CH. 106 C3
Kerpen D. 80 B2
Kerrysdale GB. 31 B3
Kerta H. 111 B4
Kerteminde DK 59 C3
Kerzers CH 106 C2
Kesgrave GB. 45 A5
Kesh GB. 26 B3
Keskin TR 23 B7
Kesselfall A. 109 B3
Keswick GB. 36 B3
Keszthely H. 111 C4
Kétegyháza H 113 C5
Kéthely H. 111 C4
Kętrzyn PL. 12 A4
Kettering GB. 44 A3
Kettlewell GB. 40 A1
Kęty PL. 99 B3
Ketzin D. 74 B1
Keula D. 82 A2
Keuruu FIN. 8 A4
Kevelaer D. 80 A2
Kevermes H. 113 C5
Kevi SRB. 126 B1
Keyingham GB. 41 B3
Keynsham GB. 43 A4
Kežmarok SK. 99 B4
Khimki RUS. 9 E10
Khisinev = Chişinău
  MD. 17 B8
Khmelnik UA. 13 D7
Khmelnytskyy UA. . .13 D7
Khodoriv UA. 13 D6
Kholm RUS. 9 D7
Khotyn UA. 13 D7
Khoyniki BY. 13 B8
Khust UA. 17 A5
Khvoynaya RUS 9 C9

Kiefersfelden D. . .108 B3
Kiel D. 64 B3
Kielce PL. 87 B4
Kiełczygłów PL. . . .86 A3
Kielder GB. 37 A4
Kiełpino PL. 68 A3
Kielpiny PL. 77 A4
Kierinki FIN. 197 B8
Kiernozia PL. 77 B4
Kierspe D. 81 A3
Kietrz PL. 86 B2
Kietz D. 74 B3
Kiev = Kyyiv UA. . .13 C9
Kiezmark PL. 69 A3
Kiffisia GR. 185 A4
Kifino Selo BIH. . .139 B4
Kihlanki
  FIN. 196 B6
  S. 196 B6
Kiistala FIN. 197 B8
Kije PL. 87 B4
Kijevo HR. 138 B2
Kikallen N. 46 B2
Kikinda SRB. 126 B2
Kil
  N. 53 B5
  Örebro S. 55 A6
  Värmland S. 55 A4
Kila S. 55 A3
Kilafors S. 50 A3
Kilbaha IRL. 29 B2
Kilbeggan IRL. 30 A1
Kilberry GB. 34 C2
Kilbirnie GB. 34 C3
Kilboghamn N. 195 D4
Kilbotn N. 194 B7
Kilb Rabenstein A .110 A2
Kilchattan GB. 34 C2
Kilchoan GB. 34 B1
Kilcock IRL. 30 A2
Kilconnell IRL. . . .28 A3
Kilcormac IRL. 28 A4
Kilcreggan GB. 34 C3
Kilcullen IRL. 30 A2
Kilcurry IRL. 27 B4
Kildare IRL. 30 A2
Kildinstroy RUS. . . .3 B13
Kildonan GB. 32 C3
Kildorrery IRL. . . .29 B3
Kilegrend N. 53 A4
Kilen N. 53 A4
Kilgarvan IRL. 29 C2
Kiliya UA. 17 C8
Kilkee IRL. 29 B2
Kilkeel GB. 27 B4
Kilkelly IRL. 26 C2
Kilkenny IRL. 30 B1
Kilkieran IRL. 28 A2
Kilkinlea IRL. 29 B2
Kilkis GR. 182 B4
Killadysert IRL. . . .29 B2
Killala IRL. 26 B1
Killaloe IRL. 28 B3
Killarney IRL. 29 B2
Killashandra IRL. . .27 B3
Killashee IRL. 28 A4
Killearn GB. 34 B3
Killeberg S. 61 C4
Killeigh IRL. 30 A1
Killenaule IRL. . . .29 B4
Killimor IRL. 28 A3
Killin GB. 34 B3
Killinaboy IRL. . . .28 B2
Killinge S. 196 B3
Killinick IRL. 30 B2
Killorglin IRL. . . .29 B2
Killucan IRL. 30 A1
Killybegs IRL. 26 B2
Killyleagh GB. 27 B5
Kilmacrenan IRL. . . .26 A3
Kilmacthomas IRL. . .30 B1
Kilmaine IRL. 28 A2
Kilmallock IRL. . . .29 B3
Kilmarnock GB. 36 A2
Kilmartin GB. 34 B2
Kilmaurs GB. 36 A2
Kilmeadan IRL. 30 B1
Kilmeedy IRL. 29 B3
Kilmelford GB. 34 B2
Kilmore Quay IRL. . .30 B2
Kilmuir GB. 32 D2
Kilmurry IRL. 27 C3
Kilninver GB. 34 B2
Kilpisjärvi FIN. . .192 C4
Kilrea GB. 27 B4
Kilrush IRL. 29 B2
Kilsmo S. 56 A1
Kilsyth GB. 35 C3
Kiltoom IRL. 28 A3
Kilwinning GB. 36 A2
Kimasozero RUS. 3 D12
Kimi GR. 185 A5
Kimolos GR. 185 C5
Kimovsk RUS. 9 E10
Kimratshofen D. . . .107 B5
Kimry RUS. 9 D10
Kimstad S. 56 B1
Kinbrace GB. 32 C3
Kincardine GB. 35 B4
Kincraig GB. 32 D3
Kindberg A. 110 B2
Kindelbruck D. 82 A3
Kingarrow IRL. 26 B2
Kingisepp RUS. 9 C6
Kingsbridge GB. . . .43 B3
Kingsclere GB. 44 B2
Kingscourt IRL. . . .27 C4
King's Lynn GB. . . .41 C4
Kingsteignton GB. . .43 B3
Kingston
  Greater London
    GB. 44 B3
  Moray GB 32 D3

Kingussie GB 32 D2
Kınık
  Antalya TR. 188 C4
  İzmir TR. 186 C2
Kinloch
  Highland GB. 31 B2
  Highland GB. 32 C2
Kinlochbervie GB. . .32 C1
Kinlochewe GB. 32 D1
Kinlochleven GB. . . .34 B3
Kinlochmoidart GB .34 B2
Kinloch Rannoch
  GB. 35 B3
Kinloss GB. 32 D3
Kinlough IRL. 26 B2
Kinn N. 48 B2
Kinna S. 60 B2
Kinnared S. 60 B3
Kinnarp S. 55 B4
Kinnegad IRL. 30 A1
Kinne-Kleva S. 55 B4
Kinnitty IRL. 28 A4
Kinrooi B. 80 A1
Kinross GB. 35 B4
Kinsale IRL. 29 C3
Kinsarvik N. 46 B3
Kintarvie GB. 31 A2
Kintore GB. 33 D4
Kinvarra IRL. 28 A3
Kioni GR. 184 A1
Kiparissia GR 184 B2
Kipfenburg D. 95 C3
Kiraz TR. 188 B3
Kirazlı TR. 186 B1
Kirberg D. 81 B4
Kirchbach in
  Steiermark A. . . .110 C2
Kirchberg
  CH 106 B2
  Baden-Württemberg
    D. 94 B1
  Rheinland-Pfalz D .93 B3
Kirchberg am Wechsel
  A. 110 B2
Kirchberg an der
  Pielach A. 110 A2
Kirchberg in Tirol
  A. 109 B3
Kirchbichl A. 108 B3
Kirchdorf
  Bayern D. 96 C1
  Mecklenburg-
    Vorpommern D. . . .65 C4
  Niedersachsen D. . .72 B1
Kirchdorf an der Krems
  A. 109 B5
Kirchdorf in Tirol
  A. 109 B3
Kirchenlamitz D. . . .83 B3
Kirchenthumbach
  D. 95 B3
Kirchhain D. 81 B4
Kirchheim
  Baden-Württemberg
    D. 94 C1
  Bayern D. 108 A1
  Hessen D. 81 B5
Kirchheimbolanden
  D. 93 B4
Kirchhundem D. 81 A4
Kirchlinteln D. . . .72 B2
Kirchschlag A. 111 B3
Kirchweidach D. . . .109 A3
Kirchzarten D. 106 B2
Kircubbin GB. 27 B5
Kireç TR. 186 C3
Kırıkkale TR. 23 B7
Kirillov RUS. 9 C11
Kirishi RUS. 9 C8
Kırka TR. 187 C5
Kırkağaç TR. 186 C2
Kirkbean GB. 36 B3
Kirkbride GB. 36 B3
Kirkby GB. 38 A4
Kirkby Lonsdale
  GB. 37 B4
Kirkby Malzeard
  GB. 40 A2
Kirkbymoorside
  GB. 37 B6
Kirkby Stephen GB .37 B4
Kirkcaldy GB. 35 B4
Kirkcolm GB. 36 B1
Kirkconnel GB. 36 A2
Kirkcowan GB. 36 B2
Kirkcudbright GB. . .36 B2
Kirkehamn N. 52 B2
Kirke Hyllinge DK . .61 D1
Kirkenær N. 49 B4
Kirkenes N. 193 C14
Kirkham GB. 38 A4
Kirkintilloch GB. . .35 C3
Kirkjubæjarklaustur
  IS. 191 D7
Kirkkonummi FIN. . . .8 B4
Kırklareli TR. . . .186 A2
Kirkmichael GB. 35 B4
Kirkoswald GB. 36 A2
Kirkpatrick Fleming
  GB. 36 A3
Kirkton of Glenisla
  GB. 35 B4
Kirkwall GB. 33 C4
Kirkwhelpington
  GB. 37 A5
Kirn D. 93 B3
Kirovsk RUS. 3 C13
Kirriemuir GB. 35 B5
Kırşehir TR. 23 B8
Kirton GB. 41 C3
Kirton in Lindsey
  GB. 40 B3
Kirtorf D. 81 B5
Kiruna S. 196 B3
Kisa S. 62 A3
Kisač SRB 126 B1
Kisbér H. 112 B2
Kiseljak BIH. 139 B4

Kisielice PL. 69 B4
Kisköre H. 113 B4
Kiskőrös H. 112 C3
Kiskunfélegyháza
  H. 113 C3
Kiskunhalas H. . . .112 C3
Kiskunlacháza H. . .112 B2
Kiskunmajsa H 113 C3
Kisláng H. 112 C2
Kisslegg D. 107 B4
Kissolt H. 112 C3
Kissónerga CY. 181 B1
Kist D. 94 B1
Kistanje HR. 138 B1
Kistelek H. 113 C3
Kisterenye H. 113 A3
Kisújszállás H. . . .113 B4
Kisvárda H. 16 A5
Kisvejke H. 112 C2
Kiszkowo PL. 76 B2
Kiszombor H. 126 A2
Kitee FIN. 9 A7
Kithnos GR. 185 B5
Kiti CY. 181 B2
Kitkiöjärvi S. . . .196 B6
Kitkiöjoki S. 196 B6
Kittelfjäll S. . . .195 E6
Kittendorf D. 74 A1
Kittilä FIN. 196 B7
Kittlitz D. 84 A2
Kittsee A. 111 A4
Kitzbühel A. 109 B3
Kitzingen D. 94 B2
Kiuruvesi FIN. 3 E10
Kivertsi UA. 13 C6
Kividhes CY. 181 B1
Kivik S. 63 C2
Kivotos GR. 182 C3
Kıyıköy TR. 186 A3
Kızılcabölük TR. . .188 B4
Kızılcadağ TR. 189 B4
Kızılcahamam TR . . .23 A7
Kızılırmak TR. 23 A7
Kızılkaya TR. 189 B5
Kızılkuyu TR. 187 D6
Kızılören
  Afyon TR. 189 A5
  Konya TR. 189 B7
Kjeldebotn N. 194 B7
Kjellerup DK. 59 B2
Kjellmyra N. 49 B4
Kjøllefjord N. . . .193 B11
Kjøpmannskjaer N. . .54 A1
Kjøpsvik N. 194 B7
Kl'ačno SK. 98 C2
Kladanj BIH. 139 A4
Kläden D. 73 B4
Klädesholmen S. . . .60 B1
Kladnice HR. 138 B2
Kladno CZ. 84 B2
Kladruby CZ. 95 B4
Klagenfurt A. 110 C1
Klågerup S. 61 D3
Klagstorp S. 66 A2
Klaipėda LT. 8 E2
Klaistow D. 74 B1
Klaksvik FO. 4 A3
Klana HR. 123 B3
Klanac HR. 123 C4
Klanjec HR. 123 A4
Klardorf D. 95 B4
Klarup DK. 58 A3
Klašnice BIH. 124 C3
Klässbol S. 55 A3
Klášterec nad Ohří
  CZ. 83 B5
Kláštor pod Znievom
  SK. 98 C2
Klatovy CZ. 96 B1
Klaus an der
  Pyhrnbahn A. 110 B1
Klazienaveen NL. . . .71 B3
Klecko D. 76 B2
Kleczew PL. 76 B3
Klein Plasten D. . . .74 A1
Klein Sankt Paul
  A. 110 C1
Kleinsölk A. 109 B4
Kleinzell A. 110 B2
Klejtrup DK. 58 B2
Klek SRB. 126 B2
Klemensker DK. 67 A3
Klenak SRB. 127 C1
Klenci pod Cerchovem
  CZ. 95 B4
Klenica PL. 75 C4
Klenje SRB. 127 C1
Klenoec MK. 182 B2
Klenovec SK. 99 C3
Klenovica HR. 123 B3
Klenovnik HR. 124 A2
Kleppe N. 52 B1
Kleppestø N. 46 B2
Kleptow D. 74 A2
Kleszewo PL. 77 B6
Kleve D. 80 A2
Klevshult S. 60 B4
Klewki PL. 77 A5
Kličevac SRB. 127 C3
Klietz D. 73 B5
Klikuszowa PL. 99 B3
Klimkovice CZ. 98 B2
Klimontów PL. 87 B5
Klimovichi BY. 13 B9
Klimpfjäll S. 195 E5
Klin RUS. 9 D10
Klinča Sela HR. . . .123 B4
Klingenbach A. 111 B3
Klingenberg D. 93 B5
Klingenmunster D. . .93 B4
Klingenthal D. 83 B4
Klinken D. 73 A4
Klintehamn S. 57 C4
Kliny PL. 77 A5
Kliplev DK. 64 B2
Klippan S. 61 C3
Klis HR. 138 B2
Klitmøller DK. 58 A1
Klitten D. 84 A2

Klixbüll D. 64 B1
Kljajićevo SRB. . . .126 B1
Ključ BIH. 138 A2
Klobouky CZ. 97 C4
Klobuck PL. 86 B2
Klockestrand S. . . .200 D3
Klodawa
  Lubuskie PL. 75 B4
  Wielkopolskie PL. .76 B3
Kłodzko PL. 85 B4
Kløfta N. 48 B3
Klokkarvik N. 46 B2
Klokkerholm DK. . . .58 A3
Klokočov SK. 98 B2
Kłomnice PL. 86 B3
Klonowa PL. 86 A2
Kloosterzande NL. . .79 A4
Klopot PL. 74 B3
Klos AL. 182 B2
Kloštar Ivanić HR .124 B2
Kloster
  D. 66 B2
  DK. 59 B1
Klösterle A. 107 B5
Klostermansfeld D .82 A3
Klosterneuburg A .97 C4
Klosters CH. 107 C4
Kloten CH. 107 B3
Klötze D. 73 B4
Klöverträsk S. . . .196 D4
Klövsjö S. 199 C11
Kluczbork PL. 86 B2
Kluczewo PL. 75 A5
Kluisbergen B. 79 B3
Klundert NL. 79 A4
Klutz D. 65 C4
Klwów PL. 87 A4
Klyetsk BY. 13 B7
Knaben N. 52 B2
Knaften S. 200 B4
Knapstad N. 54 A2
Knäred S. 61 C3
Knaresborough GB 40 A2
Knarvik N. 46 B2
Knebel DK. 59 B3
Knebworth GB. 44 B3
Knesebeck D. 73 B3
Knesselare B. 78 A3
Knežak SLO. 123 B3
Kneževi Vinogradi
  HR. 125 B4
Kneževo HR. 125 B4
Knežica BIH. 124 B2
Knić SRB. 127 D2
Knighton GB. 39 B3
Knin HR. 138 A2
Knislinge S. 61 C4
Knittelfeld A. 110 B1
Knivsta S. 57 A3
Knock IRL. 28 A3
Knocktopher IRL. . . .30 B1
Knokke-Heist B. . . .78 A3
Knowle GB. 44 A2
Knurów PL. 86 B2
Knutby S. 51 C5
Knutsford GB. 38 A4
Kobarid SLO. 122 A2
København =
  Copenhagen DK. .61 D2
Kobenz A. 110 B1
Kobersdorf A. 111 B3
Kobiernice PL. 99 B3
Kobierzyce PL. 85 B4
Kobilje SLO. 111 C3
Kobiór PL. 86 B2
Koblenz
  CH. 106 B3
  D. 81 B3
Kobryn BY. 13 B6
Kobylanka PL. 75 A3
Kobylin PL. 85 A5
Kobylniki PL. 77 B5
Kocaali TR. 187 A5
Kocaaliler TR. 189 B5
Kocaeli = İzmit
  TR. 187 B4
Kočani MK. 182 B4
Koçarlı TR. 188 B2
Koceljevo SRB. . . .127 C1
Kočerin BIH. 138 B3
Kočevje SLO. 123 B3
Kočevska Reka
  SLO. 123 B3
Kochel am see D. . .108 B2
Kocs H. 112 B2
Kocsér H. 113 B3
Kocsola H. 112 C2
Koczala PL. 68 B2
Kodal N. 53 A6
Kode S. 60 B1
Kodersdorf D. 84 A2
Kodrab PL. 86 A3
Koekelare B. 78 A2
Kofçaz TR. 186 A2
Köflach A. 110 B2
Køge DK. 61 D2
Kohlberg D. 95 B4
Kohtla-Järve EST. . . .8 C5
Köinge S. 60 B2
Kojetin CZ. 98 B1
Kökar FIN. 51 C7
Kokava SK. 99 C3
Kokkari GR. 188 B1
Kokkinotrimithia .181 A2
Kokkola FIN. 3 E8
Kokori BIH. 124 C3
Kokoski PL. 69 A3
Koksijde B. 78 A2
Kola
  BIH. 124 C3
  RUS. 3 B13
Köla S. 54 A3
Kołacin PL. 87 A3
Kolari FIN. 196 B6
Kolárovo SK. 112 B1
Kolašin MNE. 16 D3
Kolbäck S. 56 A2
Kolbeinsstaðir IS .190 C3
Kolbermoor D. 108 B3
Kolbnitz A. 109 C4
Kolbotn N. 54 A1

Kolbu N. 48 B2
Kolby Kås DK. 59 C3
Kolczewo PL. 67 C3
Kolczyglowy PL. . . .68 A2
Kolding DK. 59 C2
Kölesd H. 112 C2
Kolgrov N. 46 A1
Kolin CZ. 97 A3
Kolind DK. 59 B3
Kolinec CZ. 96 B1
Koljane HR. 138 B2
Kølkær DK. 59 B2
Kölleda D. 82 A3
Kollum NL. 70 A3
Köln = Cologne D. .80 B2
Koło PL. 76 B3
Kołobrzeg PL. 67 B4
Kolochau D. 83 A5
Kolomyya UA. 13 D6
Kolonowskie PL. . . .86 B2
Kolovec CZ. 95 B5
Kolpino RUS. 9 C7
Kolrep D. 73 A5
Kölsillre S. 199 C12
Kolsko PL. 75 C4
Kolsva S. 56 A1
Kolta SK. 112 A2
Koluničc BIH. 138 A2
Koluszki PL. 87 A3
Kolut SRB. 125 B4
Kolvereid N. 199 A8
Kølvrå DK. 59 B2
Komadi H. 113 B5
Komagvær N. 193 B14
Komarica BIH. 125 C3
Komárno SK. 112 B2
Komárom H. 112 B2
Komatou Yialou
  CY. 181 A3
Komboti GR. 182 D3
Komen SLO. 122 B2
Komin HR. 138 B3
Komiža HR. 138 B2
Komjáti H. 99 C4
Komjatice SK. 112 A2
Komló H. 125 A4
Kömlö H. 113 B4
Komoča SK. 112 B2
Komorniki PL. 75 B5
Komorzno PL. 86 A2
Komotini GR. 183 B7
Konak SRB. 126 B2
Konakovo RUS. 9 D10
Konarzyny PL. 68 B2
Kondias GR. 183 D7
Kondopaga RUS. 9 A9
Kondorfa H. 111 C3
Kondoros H. 113 C4
Konevo RUS. 9 A11
Køng DK. 65 A4
Konga S. 63 B3
Köngäs FIN. 196 B7
Kongerslev DK. 58 B3
Kongsberg N. 53 A5
Kongshamn N. 53 B4
Kongsmark DK. 64 A1
Kongsmoen N. 199 A9
Kongsvik N. 194 B7
Kongsvinger N. 48 B3
Konice CZ. 97 B4
Konie PL. 77 C5
Koniecpol PL. 86 B3
Königsberg D. 82 B2
Königsbronn D. 94 C2
Königsbrück D. 84 A1
Königsbrunn D. 94 C2
Königsdorf D. 108 B2
Königsee D. 82 B3
Königshorst D. 74 B1
Königslutter D. . . .73 B3
Königssee D. 109 B3
Königstein
  Hessen D. 81 B4
  Sachsen D. 84 B2
Königstetten A. . . .97 C4
Königswartha D. . . .84 A2
Konigswiesen A. . . .96 C2
Königswinter D. . . .80 B3
Königs Wusterhausen
  D. 74 B2
Konin PL. 76 B3
Konispol AL. 182 D2
Konitsa GR. 182 C2
Köniz CH. 106 C2
Konjevići BIH. 139 A5
Konjevrate HR. 138 B2
Konjic BIH. 139 B3
Konjščina HR. 124 A2
Könnern D. 83 A3
Konnerud N. 53 A6
Konopiska PL. 86 B2
Konotop PL. 75 C4
Końskie PL. 87 A4
Konsmo N. 52 B3
Konstancin-Jeziorna
  PL. 77 B6
Konstantynów Łódzki
  PL. 86 A3
Konstanz D. 107 B4
Kontich B. 79 A4
Kontiolahti FIN. . . .9 A6
Konya TR. 189 B7
Konz D. 92 B2
Kópasker IS. 191 A9
Kópavogur IS. 190 C4
Kopčany SK. 98 C1
Koper SLO. 122 B2
Kopervik N. 52 A1
Kópháza H. 111 B3
Kopice PL. 85 B5
Köping S. 56 A1
Köpingebro S. 66 A2
Köpingsvik S. 62 B4
Köpmanholmen
  S. 200 C4
Koppang N. 48 A3
Koppangen N. 192 C4
Kopparberg S. 50 C1

Koppelo FIN 193 D11
Koppom S. 54 A3
Koprivlen BG. 183 B5
Koprivna BIH. 125 C4
Koprivnica HR. 124 A2
Kopřivnice CZ. 98 B2
Köprübaşı TR. 186 D3
Koprzywnica PL. . . .87 B5
Kopstal L. 92 B2
Kopychyntsi UA. . . .13 D6
Kopytkowo PL. 69 B3
Korbach D. 81 A4
Körbecke D. 81 A4
Korçë AL. 182 C2
Korčula HR. 138 C3
Korczyców PL. 75 B3
Korenita SRB. 127 C1
Korets UA. 13 C7
Korfantów PL. 85 B5
Körfez TR. 187 B4
Korgen N. 195 D4
Korinth DK. 64 A3
Korinthos = Corinth
  GR. 184 B3
Korita
  BIH. 138 A2
  HR. 139 C3
Korithi GR. 184 B1
Korkuteli TR. 189 B5
Körmend H. 111 B3
Korne PL. 68 A2
Korneuburg A. 97 C4
Kornevo RUS. 69 A5
Kórnik PL. 76 B2
Kornsjø N. 54 B2
Környe H. 112 B2
Koromačno HR. 123 C3
Koroni GR. 184 C2
Koronos GR. 185 B6
Koronowo PL. 76 A2
Körösladány H. . . .113 C5
Köröstarcsa H. . . .113 C5
Korosten UA. 13 C8
Korostyshev UA. . . .13 C8
Korpikå S. 196 D6
Korpikylä FIN. . . .196 C6
Korpilombolo S. . . .196 C6
Korsberga
  Jönköping S. 62 A3
  Skaraborg S. 55 B5
Korshavn N. 54 A1
Korskrogen S. 200 E1
Korsnäs S. 50 B2
Korsør DK. 65 A4
Korsun
  Shevchenkovskiy
    UA. 13 D9
Korträsk S. 196 D3
Kortrijk B. 78 B3
Korucu TR. 186 C2
Korycany CZ. 98 B1
Korzeńsko PL. 85 A4
Korzybie PL. 68 A1
Kos GR. 188 C2
Kosakowo PL. 69 A3
Kosanica MNE. 139 B5
Kösching D. 95 C3
Kościan PL. 75 B5
Kościelec PL. 76 B3
Kościerzyna PL. . . .68 A2
Koserow D. 66 B2
Košetice CZ. 97 B3
Košice SK. 12 D4
Kosjerić SRB. 127 D1
Koška HR. 125 B4
Koskullskulle S. . .196 B3
Kosovska Mitrovica
  KOS. 16 D4
Kosta S. 62 B3
Kostajnica HR. 124 B2
Kostajnik SRB. . . .127 C1
Kostanjevica SLO 123 B4
Kostelec nad Černými
  Lesy CZ. 96 B2
Kostelec na Hané
  CZ. 97 B5
Kostice CZ. 84 B1
Kostkowo PL. 68 A3
Kostojevići SRB. . .127 C1
Kostolac SRB. 127 C3
Kostomłoty PL. 85 A4
Kostopil UA. 13 C7
Kostów PL. 86 A2
Kostrzyn
  Lubuskie PL. 74 B3
  Wielkopolskie PL. .76 B2
Koszalin PL. 67 B5
Koszęcin PL. 86 B2
Köszeg H. 111 B3
Koszwaly PL. 69 A3
Koszyce PL. 87 B4
Kot SLO. 123 B4
Kotala FIN. 197 B11
Kötelek H. 113 B4
Köthen D. 83 A3
Kotka FIN. 8 B5
Kotomierz PL. 76 A3
Kotor MNE. 16 D3
Kotoriba HR. 124 A2
Kotorsko BIH. 125 C4
Kotor Varoš BIH. . .124 C3
Kotronas GR. 184 C3
Kötschach D. 109 C3
Kötzting D. 95 B4
Koudum NL. 70 B2
Kout na Šumave
  CZ. 95 B5
Kovačevac SRB. . . .127 C2
Kovačica SRB. 126 B2
Kovdor RUS. 197 B13
Kovel' UA. 13 C6
Kovilj SRB. 126 B2
Kovin SRB. 127 C2
Kowal PL. 77 B4

Kowalewo Pomorskie
PL. 69 B3
Kowalów PL. 75 B3
Kowary PL. 85 B3
Köyceğiz TR 188 C3
Kozani GR 182 C3
Kozarac
BIH. 124 C2
HR. 124 B1
Kozárovce SK 98 C2
Kozelets UA. 13 C9
Kozica HR 138 B3
Koziegłowy PL. 86 B3
Kozienice PL. 87 A5
Kozina SLO 122 B2
Kozlu TR 187 A6
Kozluk BIH. 139 A5
Koźmin PL. 85 A5
Koźminek PL. 86 A2
Kozolupy CZ. 96 B1
Kožuchów PL 84 A3
Kožuhe BIH. 125 C4
Kozyatyn UA. 13 D8
Kozyürük TR 186 A1
Kräckelbräken S . .49 A6
Krackow D 74 A3
Kraddsele S. 195 E7
Krąg PL 68 A1
Kragenæs DK 65 B4
Kragerø N 53 B5
Krągi PL 68 B1
Kragujevac SRB . .127 C2
Kraiburg D 109 A3
Krajenka PL. 68 B1
Krajišnik SRB 126 B2
Krajková CZ. 83 B4
Krajné SK 98 C1
Krajnik Dolny PL. . . .74 A3
Krakača BIH. 124 B1
Kräklingbo S 57 C4
Kraków = Cracow
PL. 99 A3
Krakow am See D . .73 A5
Králíky CZ. 85 B4
Kraljevica HR 123 B3
Kraljevo SRB. 16 C4
Kral'ovany SK 99 B3
Kraljevo SRB 16 C4
Kral'ov Brod SK . . .111 A4
Kralovice CZ. 96 B1
Kralupy nad Vltavou
CZ. 84 B2
Králův Dvůr CZ. 96 B2
Kramfors S 200 D3
Kramsach A. 108 B2
Kramsk PL 76 B3
Kråmvik N 53 A4
Kranenburg D 80 A2
Krania GR 182 D3
Krania Elasonas
GR. 182 D4
Kranichfeld D 82 B3
Kranidi GR 184 B4
Kranj SLO 123 A3
Kranjska Gora
SLO 109 C4
Krapanj HR 138 B1
Krapina HR 124 A1
Krapje HR 124 B2
Krapkowice PL 86 B1
Kraselov CZ. 96 B1
Krašić HR 123 B4
Kråslava LV. 8 E5
Kraslice CZ. 83 B4
Krasna PL 87 A4
Krasna Lipa CZ. 84 B2
Krasne PL 77 B5
Kraśnik PL. 12 C5
Krašnja SLO 123 A3
Krásno SK 98 B2
Krásnohorské
Podhradie SK . . .99 C4
Krasno Polje HR . .123 C4
Krasnozavodsk
RUS. 9 D11
Krasnystaw PL. 13 C5
Krasnyy RUS. 13 A9
Krasnyy Kholm
RUS. 9 C10
Krasocin PL. 87 B4
Kraszewice PL. 86 A2
Kraszkowice PL. 86 A2
Kratigos GR. 186 C1
Kratovo MK 182 A4
Kraubath A. 110 B1
Krausnick D. 74 B2
Krautheim D 94 B1
Kravaře CZ. 84 B2
Kraváře CZ. 98 B2
Kravarsko HR 124 B2
Kraznějov CZ. 96 B1
Krčedin SRB 126 B2
Kŭrdzhali BG. 183 B7
Krefeld D. 80 A2
Kregme DK 61 D2
Krembz D. 73 A4
Kremenets UA. 13 C6
Kremmen D 74 B2
Kremna SRB 127 D1
Kremnica SK 98 C2
Krempe D. 64 C2
Krems A 97 C3
Kremsbrücke A 109 C4
Kremsmünster A. . .110 A1
Křemže CZ. 96 C2
Křenov CZ. 97 B4
Krepa PL 76 C3
Krępa Krajeńska
PL. 75 A5
Krepsko PL 68 B1
Kreševo BIH 139 B4
Kressbronn D 107 B4
Krestena GR 184 B2
Kretinga LT. 8 E2
Krettsy RUS. 9 C8
Kreuth D 108 B2
Kreuzau D 80 B2

Kreuzlingen CH. . . .107 B4
Kreuztal D 81 B3
Krewelin D 74 B2
Krezluk BIH. 138 A3
Krichem BG. 183 A6
Krieglach A 110 B2
Kriegsfeld D 93 B3
Kriens CH 106 B3
Krimml A 108 B3
Krimpen aan de IJssel
NL. 79 A4
Křinec CZ. 84 B3
Kristdala S. 62 A4
Kristiansand N 53 B4
Kristianstad S. 61 C4
Kristiansund N 198 B4
Kristiinankaupunki
FIN. 8 A2
Kristinefors S 49 B4
Kristinehamn S. 55 A5
Kriváň SK. 99 C3
Kriva Palanka MK .182 A4
Křivoklát CZ. 96 A1
Križ HR. 124 B2
Križanov CZ. 97 B4
Križevci HR 124 A2
Krk HR 123 B3
Krka SLO 123 B3
Krnjača SRB 127 C2
Krnjak HR 123 B4
Krnjeuša BIH 124 C2
Krnjevo SRB 127 C3
Krnov CZ. 98 A1
Krobia PL. 85 A4
Kroczyce PL. 86 B3
Krøderen N 48 B1
Krokek S 56 B2
Krokom S 199 B11
Krokowa PL. 68 A3
Krokstad-elva N 53 A5
Kromeříž CZ. 98 B1
Krommenie NL 70 B1
Krompachy SK 99 C4
Kronach D. 82 B3
Kronshagen D 64 B3
Kronshtadt RUS. 9 C6
Kröpelin D 65 B4
Kropp D 64 B2
Kroppenstedt D. 73 C4
Kropstädt D 74 C1
Krościenko nad
Dunajcem PL. . . .99 B4
Kröslin D 66 B2
Krośnice PL. 85 A5
Krośniewice PL. 77 B4
Krosno PL. 12 D4
Krosno Odrzańskie
PL. 75 B4
Krostitz D 83 A4
Krotoszyn PL. 85 A5
Krottendorf A. 110 B2
Krouna CZ. 97 B4
Krowiarki PL. 86 B2
Krrabë AL 182 B1
Kršan HR 123 B3
Krško SLO. 123 B4
Krstac MNE 139 C4
Krstur SRB 126 A2
Křtiny CZ. 97 B4
Kruft D 80 B3
Kruishoutem B 79 B3
Krujë AL 182 B1
Krulyewshchyna
BY. 13 A7
Krumbach
A. 111 B3
D 94 C2
Krumovgrad BG . . .183 B7
Krün D 108 B2
Krupá CZ. 84 B1
Krupa na Vrbasu
BIH. 124 C3
Krupanj SRB 127 C1
Krupina SK 99 C3
Krupka CZ. 84 B1
Krupki BY. 13 A8
Kruså DK 64 B2
Krušćica BIH 139 A3
Kruševac SRB. 16 D4
Kruševo MK. 182 B3
Kruszwica PL. 76 B3
Kruszyn PL. 77 B4
Krychaw BY. 13 B9
Krynica PL. 99 B4
Krynica Morska PL .69 A4
Krzcin PL. 75 A4
Krzelów PL. 85 A4
Krzepice PL. 86 B2
Krzepielów PL. 85 A4
Krzeszowice PL. 86 B3
Krzeszyce PL. 75 B4
Krzynowlaga Mała
PL. 77 A5
Krzywiń PL. 75 C5
Krzyżanowice PL. . . .98 B2
Krzyż Wielkopolski
PL. 75 B5
Ksiaz Wielkopolski
PL. 87 B4
Książ Wielkopolski
PL. 76 B2
Ktębowiec PL. 75 A5
Kübekháza H 126 A2
Küblis CH. 107 C4
Kuchary PL. 86 A1
Kuchl A. 109 B4
Kucice PL 77 B5
Kuciste HR 138 C3
Kuçovë AL 182 C1
Küçükbahçe TR . . .188 A1
Küçükköy TR. 186 C1
Küçükkuyu TR. 186 C1
Kucura SRB. 126 B1
Kuczbork-Osada
PL. 77 A5
Kudowa-Zdrój PL. . .85 B4

Kufstein A 108 B3
Kuggeboda S 63 B3
Kühbach D. 95 C3
Kuhmo FIN 3 D11
Kuhmoinen FIN. 8 B4
Kuhnsdorf A 110 C1
Kuhstedt D. 72 A1
Kuinre NL. 70 B2
Kuivaniemi FIN 197 D8
Kuivastu EST. 8 C3
Kukës AL 182 A2
Kuklin PL 77 A5
Kukljica HR 137 A4
Kukujevci SRB 127 B1
Kula
Srbija SRB 127 C3
Vojvodina SRB. . .126 B1
TR. 188 A3
Kuldīga LV. 8 D2
Kulen Vakuf BIH . .124 C2
Kulina BIH 125 C4
Kullstedt D 82 A2
Kulmain D 95 B3
Kulmbach D. 82 B3
Kuloharju FIN. 197 D11
Kulu TR 23 B7
Kumachevo RUS. . . .69 A5
Kumafşarı TR 189 B4
Kumane SRB. 126 B2
Kumanovo MK. 182 A3
Kumbağ TR 186 B2
Kumdanlı TR 189 A5
Kumkale TR 186 C1
Kumla S 56 A1
Kumlakyrkby S 56 B2
Kumlinge FIN. 51 B7
Kumluca TR. 189 C5
Kumrovec HR 123 A4
Kunadacs H 112 C3
Kunágota H 113 C5
Kunbaja H 126 A1
Kunda EST. 8 C5
Kundl A. 108 B2
Kunes N. 193 B10
Kunfehértó H. 126 A1
Kungälv S 60 B1
Kungsängen S 57 A3
Kungsäter S 60 B2
Kungsbacka S. 60 B2
Kungsgården S 50 B3
Kungshamn S 54 B2
Kungs-Husby S. 56 A3
Kungsör S 56 A2
Kunhegyes H 113 B4
Kunmadaras H 113 B4
Kunovice CZ. 98 B1
Kunów PL. 87 B5
Kunowo
Wielkopolskie PL .76 C2
Zachodnio-Pomorskie
PL. 74 A3
Kunštát CZ. 97 B4
Kunszállás H 113 C3
Kunszentmárton
H. 113 C4
Kunszentmiklós
H. 112 B3
Kunžak CZ. 97 B3
Künzelsau D 94 B1
Kuolayarvi RUS. . . .197 C12
Kuolio FIN. 197 D11
Kuopio FIN 8 A5
Kuosku FIN 197 B11
Kup
H 111 B4
PL. 86 B1
Kupferzell D. 94 B1
Kupinec HR 123 B4
Kupinečki Kraljevac
HR. 124 B1
Kupinovo SRB. 127 C2
Kupirovo HR 138 A2
Kupjak HR 123 B3
Kuppenheim D 93 C4
Kupres BIH 138 B3
Küps D. 82 B3
Kurd H. 112 C2
Küre TR 23 A7
Kurikka FIN 8 A3
Kuřim CZ. 97 B4
Kurivody CZ. 84 B2
Kurki PL. 77 A5
Kurort Oberwiesenthal
D. 83 B4
Kurort Schmalkalden
D. 82 B2
Kurort Stolberg D. . .82 A2
Kurort Wippra D. . . .82 A3
Kurów PL. 12 C5
Kurowice PL. 86 A3
Kurravaara S. 196 B3
Kursu FIN. 197 C11
Kurşunlu
Bursa TR 187 B4
Çankırı TR 23 A7
Kurtakko FIN. 196 B7
Kürten D. 80 A3
Kurucaşile TR 187 A7
Kurzelów PL. 87 B3
Kurvinen FIN. 197 D12
Kusadak SRB 127 C2
Kuşadası TR 188 B2
Kusel D 93 B3
Kusey D. 73 B4
Küsnacht CH 106 B3
Kütahya TR 187 C4
Kutenholz D. 72 A2
Kutina HR 124 B2
Kutjevo HR 125 B3
Kutná Hora CZ. 97 B3
Kutno PL 77 B4
Kuttara FIN 193 D10
Kúty SK 98 C1
Kuzelów PL. 87 B3
Kúty SK 98 C1
Kuusankoski FIN 8 B5
Kuyucak TR. 188 B3

Kuzmin SRB 127 B1
Kuźnia Raciborska
PL. 86 B2
Kuźnica Czarnkowska
PL. 75 B5
Kuźnica Żelichowska
PL. 75 B5
Kvåle N 52 B3
Kvaløysletta N. 192 C2
Kvalsund N 192 B7
Kvam
Nord-Trøndelag
N. 199 A8
Oppland N 198 D6
Kvamsøy N 46 A3
Kvænangsbotn N .192 C6
Kvanndal N 46 B3
Kvänum S 55 B4
Kværndrup DK 59 C3
Kvås N 52 B3
Kvasice CZ. 98 B1
Kvelde N 53 A5
Kvenna N. 198 C5
Kvernaland N 52 B1
Kvernes N 198 B4
Kvibille S 60 C2
Kvicksund S. 56 A2
Kvidinge S 61 C3
Kvikkjokk S 195 D8
Kvikne
Hedmark N 199 C7
Oppland N 47 A6
Kvilda CZ. 96 B1
Kville S 54 B2
Kvillsfors S 62 A3
Kvinesdal N 52 B2
Kvinnherad N 46 C3
Kvissel DK 58 A3
Kvissleby S 200 D3
Kviteseid N 53 A4
Kvitsøy N. 52 A1
Kwakowo PL 68 A2
Kwidzyn PL. 69 B3
Kwilcz PL. 75 B5
Kyjov CZ. 98 C1
Kyleakin GB. 31 B3
Kyle of Lochalsh
GB 31 B3
Kylerhea GB 31 B3
Kylestrome GB 32 C1
Kyllburg D 92 A2
Kyllini GR. 184 B2
Kynšperk nad Ohří
CZ. 83 B4
Kyperounda CY. . . .181 B1
Kyrenia CY. 181 A2
Kyritz D 73 B5
Kyrkesund S 60 A1
Kyrkhult S 63 B2
Kyrksæterøra N. . . .198 B6
Kythira GR 184 C3
Kythréa CY 181 A2
Kyyiv = Kiev UA. . . .13 C9
Kyustendil BG. 16 D5
Kyyjärvi FIN. 8 A4

L

Laa an der Thaya A .97 C4
La Adrada E. 150 B3
Laage D. 65 C5
La Alameda E. 157 A4
La Alberca E 149 B3
La Alberca de Záncara
E 158 B1
La Albergueria de
Argañán E. 149 B3
La Albuera E 155 C4
La Aldea del Portillo del
Busto E 143 B3
La Algaba E 162 A1
La Aliseda de Tormes
E 150 B2
La Almarcha E. 158 B1
La Almolda E 153 A3
La Almunia de Doña
Godina E. 152 A2
Laanila FIN 193 D11
La Antillas E 161 B2
La Arena E 141 A4
La Aulaga E 161 B3
La Balme-de-Sillingy
F. 118 B3
La Bañeza E. 141 B5
La Barca de la Florida
E 162 B2
La Barre-de-Monts
F. 114 B1
La Barre-en-Ouche
F. 89 B4
La Barrosa E 162 B1
La Barthe-de-Neste
F. 145 A4
La Bassée F 78 B2
La Bastide-de-Sérou
F. 146 A2
La Bastide-des-
Jourdans F 132 B1
Labastide-Murat F .129 B4
La Bastide-Puylaurent
F. 117 C2
Labastide-Rouairoux
F. 130 B1
Labastide-St Pierre
F. 129 C4
La Bathie F. 118 B3
La Baule-Escoublac
F. 101 B3
La Bazoche-Gouet
F. 102 A2
La Bégude-de-Mazenc
F. 131 A3
Labenne F 128 C1
La Bernerie-en-Retz
F. 114 A1
Labin HR 123 B3

Kuźmin SRB 127 B1
La Bisbal d'Empordà
E 147 C4
Łabiszyn PL. 76 B2
Lablachère F 131 A3
Lábod H. 124 A3
Laboe D 64 B3
La Boissière F 89 A4
Labouheyre F 128 B2
La Bourboule F 116 B2
La Bóveda de Toro
E 150 A2
La Brède F 128 B2
La Bresse F. 106 A1
La Bridoire F. 118 B2
La Brillanne F 132 B1
Labrit F 128 B2
Labros E 152 A2
La Bruffière F 114 A2
Labruguière F 130 B1
Labrujo P. 148 A1
L'Absie F 114 B3
La Bussière F 103 B4
Laç AL 182 B1
Lacalahorra E 164 B1
La Caillère F 114 B3
Lacanau F 128 B1
Lacanau-Océan F . .128 A1
Lacanche F 104 B3
La Canourgue F 130 A2
La Capelle F 91 B3
Lacapelle-Marival
F. 129 B4
Láčarak SRB 127 B1
La Cardanchosa
E 156 B2
La Caridad E 141 A4
La Carlota E 162 A3
La Carolina E 157 B4
Lacaune F 130 B1
La Cava E 153 B4
La Cavalerie F 130 A2
Laceby GB. 41 B3
Lacedónia I 172 A1
La Celle-en-Moravan
CZ. 83 B4
La Celle-St Avant
F. 102 B2
La Cerca E 143 B3
Láces I 108 C1
La Chaise-Dieu F. . .117 B3
La Chaize-Giraud
F. 114 B2
La Chaize-le-Vicomte
F. 114 B2
La Chambre F 118 B3
Lachania GR 188 D2
La Chapelaude F . . .116 A2
La Chapelle-d'Angillon
F. 103 B4
La Chapelle-en-
Aalgaudémar F. .118 C3
La Chapelle-en-Vercors
F. 118 C2
La Chapelle-Glain
F. 101 B4
La Chapelle-la-Reine
F. 90 C2
La Chapelle-Laurent
F. 116 B3
La Chapelle-St Luc
F. 91 C4
La Chapelle-sur-Erdre
F. 101 B4
La Chapelle-
Vicomtesse F. . . .103 B3
La Charce F 132 A1
La Charité-sur-Loire
F. 104 B2
La Chartre-sur-le-Loir
F. 102 B2
La Châtaigneraie
F. 114 B3
La Châtre F 103 C3
La Chaussée-sur-
Marne F 91 C4
La Chaux-de-Fonds
CH 106 B1
Lachen CH. 107 B3
Lachendorf D 72 B3
La Cheppe F 91 B4
La Chèze F. 101 A3
Lachowice PL. 99 B3
La Ciotat F. 132 B1
Łąck PL 77 B4
La Clayette F 117 A4
Lacock GB. 43 A4
La Codosera E 155 B3
La Concha E 143 A3
La Condamine-
Châtelard F 132 A2
Láconi I 179 C3
La Contienda E 161 A3
La Coquille F 115 C4
La Coronada E 156 B2
La Côte-St André
F. 118 B2
La Cotinière F 114 C2
Lacq F 145 A3
La Crau F 132 B2
La Croix F 102 B2
Lacroix-Barrez F . . .116 C2
Lacroix-St Ouen F . .90 B2
Lacroix-sur-Meuse
F. 92 C1
La Croix-Valmer F .132 B2
La Cumbre E 156 A2

Łącznik PL. 86 B1
Lad H 125 A3
Ladbergen D 71 B4
Lądek-Zdrój PL 85 B4
Ladelund D 64 B2
Ladendorf A. 97 C4
Ladignac-le-Long
F. 115 C5
Ladíspoli I 168 B2
Ladoeiro P. 155 B3
Ladon F. 103 B4
La Douze F. 129 A3
Ladushkin RUS. 69 A5
Ladybank GB. 35 B4
Laer D 71 B4
La Espina E 141 A4
La Estrella E 156 A2
La Farga de Moles
E 146 B2
La Fatarella E 153 A4
La Felipa E 158 B2
La Fère F 90 B3
La Ferrière
Indre-et-Loire F .102 B2
Vendée F 114 B2
La Ferrière-en-
Parthenay F 115 B3
La Ferté-Alais F 90 C2
La Ferté-Bernard
F. 102 A2
La Ferté-Frênel F. . .89 B4
La Ferté-Gaucher
F. 90 C3
La Ferté-Imbault
F. 103 B3
La Ferté-Macé F 89 B3
La Ferté-Milon F 90 B3
La Ferté-sous-Jouarre
F. 90 C3
La Ferté-St-Aubin
F. 103 B3
La Ferté-St-Cyr F. . .103 B3
La Ferté-Vidame F .89 B4
La Ferté Villeneuil
F. 103 B3
La Feuillie F 90 B1
Lafkos GR 183 D5
La Flèche F 102 B1
La Flotte F 114 B2
Lafnitz A 111 B3
Laceby GB. 41 B3
La Font de la Figuera
E 159 C3
La Fouillade F 130 A1
Lafrançaise F 129 B4
La Fregeneda E 149 B3
La Fresneda E 153 B4
La Fuencubierta E .162 A3
La Fuente de San
Esteban E 149 B3
La Fulioala E 147 C2
La Gacilly F 101 B3
La Galera E 153 B4
Lagan S 60 C3
Laganadi I 175 C1
Lagarde F 146 A2
La Garde-Freinet
F. 132 B2
Lagares
Coimbra P. 148 B2
Porto P. 148 A1
Lagaro I 135 A4
La Garnache F 114 B2
La Garriga E 147 C3
La Garrovilla E 155 C4
Lagartera E 150 C2
La Gaubretière F . . .114 B2
Lagbol S 51 B5
Lage
D 72 C1
Lägerdorf D 64 C2
Lagg GB. 34 C2
Laggan GB. 32 D2
Laggartorp S 55 A5
Łagiewniki PL. 85 B4
La Gineta E 158 B1
Láglio I 120 B2
Lagnieu F. 118 B2
Lagny-sur-Marne F .90 C2
Lago
Calabria I 175 B2
Veneto I 121 B5
Lagôa P. 160 B1
Lagoaça P. 149 A3
Lagonegro I 174 A1
Lagos
GR 183 B7
P 160 B1
Lagosanto I 121 C5
Łagów
Lubuskie PL. 75 B4
Świętokrzyskie PL .87 B5
La Granada E
Alicante E 159 C4
Lleida E 153 A4
La Grand-Combe
F. 131 A3
La Grande-Croix
F. 117 B4
La Grande-Motte
F. 131 B3
La Granja d'Escarp
E 153 A4
La Granjuela E 156 B2
Lagrasse F 146 A3
La Grave F 118 B3
La Gravelle F 101 A4
La Guardia E 151 C4
La Guardia de Jaén
E 163 A4
Laguarres E 145 B4
Laguenne F 116 B1
La Guerche-de-
Bretagne F 101 B4
La Guerche-sur-
l'Aubois F. 104 C1
La Guérinière F 114 B1
Laguiole F 116 C2
Laguna de Duera
E 150 A3

Laguna del
Marquesado E .152 B2
Laguna de Negrillos
E 142 B1
Lagundo I 108 C2
Laguilla E 149 B3
La Haba E 156 B2
Laharie F 128 B2
La Haye-du-Puits F .88 A2
La Haye-Pesnel F . . .88 B2
Lahden D. 71 B4
La Herlière F 78 B2
La Hermida E 142 A2
La Herrera E 158 C1
Laheycourt F. 91 C1
La Higuera E 158 C2
La Hiniesta E 149 A4
Lahnstein D. 81 B3
Laholm S. 61 C2
La Horcajada E 150 B2
La Horra E 143 C3
Lahr D 93 C3
La Hulpe B 79 B4
La Hutte F 89 B4
Laichingen D. 94 C1
L'Aigle F 89 B4
La Iglesuela E 150 B3
La Iglesuela del Cid
E 153 B3
Laignes F 104 B3
Laiguéglia I 133 B3
L'Aiguillon-sur-Mer
F. 114 B2
Laimbach am Ostrong
A. 97 C3
Laina E 152 A1
Lainio S 196 B5
Lairg GB. 32 C2
La Iruela E 164 B2
Laissac F 130 A1
Laisvall S 195 D7
Láives I 121 A4
La Javie F 132 A2
Lajkovac SRB 127 C2
La Jonchère-St
Maurice F 116 A1
La Jonquera E 146 B3
Lajoskomárom H .112 C2
Lajosmizse H 112 B3
Lak H 99 C4
Lakenheath GB 45 A4
Laki BG. 183 B6
Lakitelek H. 113 C4
Lakki GR 185 D7
Lakolk DK 64 A1
Łąkorz PL. 69 B4
Lakšárska Nová Ves
SK 98 C1
Lakselv N. 193 B9
Laksfors N 195 E4
Laktaši BIH 124 C3
La Lantejuela E 162 A3
Lalapaşa TR. 186 A1
L'Albagès E 153 A4
Lalbenque F 129 B4
L'Alcúdia E 159 B3
L'Aldea E 153 B4
Lalín E 140 B2
Lalinde F 129 B3
La Línea de la
Concepción E . .162 B2
Lalizolle F 116 A3
La Llacuna E 147 C2
Lalley F 118 C2
Lalling D 95 C5
Lalm N. 198 D6
La Meilleraye-de-
Bretagne F 101 B4
La Ménitré F 102 B1
L'Ametlla de Mar
E 153 B4
Lamia GR. 182 E4
Lammhult S 62 A2
La Mojonera E 164 C2
La Mole F 132 B2

Laguna del
Marquesado E .152 B2
Laguna de Negrillos
E 142 B1
Lagundo I 108 C2
Laguilla E 149 B3
La Haba E 156 B2
Laharie F 128 B2
La Haye-du-Puits F .88 A2
La Haye-Pesnel F . . .88 B2
Lahden D. 71 B4
La Herlière F 78 B2
La Hermida E 142 A2
La Herrera E 158 C1
Laheycourt F. 91 C1
La Higuera E 158 C2
La Hiniesta E 149 A4
Lahnstein D. 81 B3
Laholm S. 61 C2
La Horcajada E 150 B2
La Horra E 143 C3
Lahr D 93 C3
La Hulpe B 79 B4
La Hutte F 89 B4
Laichingen D. 94 C1
L'Aigle F 89 B4
La Iglesuela E 150 B3
La Iglesuela del Cid
E 153 B3
Laignes F 104 B3
Laiguéglia I 133 B3
L'Aiguillon-sur-Mer
F. 114 B2
Laimbach am Ostrong
A. 97 C3
Laina E 152 A1
Lainio S 196 B5
Lairg GB. 32 C2
La Iruela E 164 B2
Laissac F 130 A1
Laisvall S 195 D7
Láives I 121 A4
La Javie F 132 A2
Lajkovac SRB 127 C2
La Jonchère-St
Maurice F 116 A1
La Jonquera E 146 B3
Lajoskomárom H .112 C2
Lajosmizse H 112 B3
Lak H 99 C4
Lakenheath GB 45 A4
Laki BG. 183 B6
Lakitelek H. 113 C4
Lakki GR 185 D7
Lakolk DK 64 A1
Łąkorz PL. 69 B4
Lakšárska Nová Ves
SK 98 C1
Lakselv N. 193 B9
Laksfors N 195 E4
Laktaši BIH 124 C3
La Lantejuela E 162 A3
Lalapaşa TR. 186 A1
L'Albagès E 153 A4
Lalbenque F 129 B4
L'Alcúdia E 159 B3
L'Aldea E 153 B4
Lalín E 140 B2
Lalinde F 129 B3
La Línea de la
Concepción E . .162 B2
Lalizolle F 116 A3
La Llacuna E 147 C2
Lalley F 118 C2
Lalling D 95 C5
Lalm N. 198 D6
La Londe-les-Maures
F. 132 B2
La Loupe F 89 B5
La Louvière B 79 B4
L'Alpe-d'Huez F. . . .118 B3
La Luisiana E 162 A2
Laluque F 128 C1
Lam D 95 B5
La Machine F 104 C2
la Maddalena I 178 A3
Lama dei Peligni I . .169 A4
Lamadrid E 142 A2
Lamagistère F 129 B3
La Mailleraye-sur-Seine
F. 89 A4
La Malène F 130 A2
Lama Mocogno I . .135 A3
La Mamola E 163 B4
La Manresana dels
Prats E 147 C2
Lamarche F 105 A4
Lamarche-sur-Saône
F. 105 B4
Lamargelle F 105 B3
Lamarosa P 154 B2
Lamarque F 128 A2
Lamas P 148 B1
La Masadera E 145 C3
Lamas de Moaro
P 140 B2
Lamastre F 117 C4
La Mata E 150 C2
La Mata de Ledesma
E 149 A4
La Mata de
Monteagudo E .142 B1
Lambach A. 109 A4
Lamballe F. 101 A3
Lamberhurst GB 45 B4
Lambesc F 131 B4
Lambia GR. 184 B2
Lambley GB 37 B4
Lambourn GB 44 B2
La Meilleraye-de-
Bretagne F 101 B4
La Ménitré F 102 B1
L'Ametlla de Mar
E 153 B4
Lamia GR. 182 E4
Lammhult S 62 A2
La Mojonera E 164 C2
La Mole F 132 B2

La Molina E 147 B2
La Monnerie-le-Montel
F. 117 B3
La Morera E 155 C4
La Mothe-Achard
F. 114 B2
Lamothe-Cassel F 129 B4
Lamothe-Montravel
F. 128 B3
La Mothe-St Héray
F. 115 B3
Lamotte-Beuvron
F. 103 B4
La Motte-Chalançon
F. 131 A4
La Motte-du-Caire
F. 132 A2
La Motte-Servolex
F. 118 B2
Lampertheim D . .93 B4
Lampeter GB 39 B2
L'Ampolla E 153 B4
Lamprechtshausen
A. 109 B3
Lamsfeld D 74 C3
Lamspringe D . . .72 C3
Lamstedt D 72 A2
La Mudarra E . . .142 C2
La Muela E 152 A2
La Mure F. 118 C2
Lamure-sur-Azergues
F. 117 A4
Lana I 108 C2
Lanaja E 145 C3
Lanarce F. 117 C3
Lanark GB 36 A3
La Nava E 161 B3
La Nava de Ricomalillo
E. 156 A3
La Nava de Santiago
E 155 B4
Lancaster GB 37 B4
Lanchester GB . . .37 B5
Lanciano I 169 A4
Lancing GB 44 C3
Lançon-Provence
F 131 B4
Lancova Vas SLO .124 C1
Landau
Bayern D 95 C4
Rheinland-Pfalz D .93 B4
Landeck A 108 B1
Landen B 79 B5
Landerneau F 100 A1
Landeryd S 60 B3
Landesbergen D . .72 B2
Landete F 158 B2
Landévant F 100 B2
Landévennec F . . .100 A1
Landeyjahöfn 190 D5
Landivy F. 88 B2
Landl A 108 B3
Landön S 199 B11
Landos F 117 C3
Landouzy-le-Ville F .91 B4
Landquart CH . . .107 C4
Landrecies F 91 A3
Landreville F 104 A3
Landriano I 120 B2
Landsberg D 108 A1
Lands-berg D 83 A4
Landsbro S 62 A2
Landscheid D 92 B2
Landshut D 95 C4
Landskrona S 61 D2
Landstuhl D 93 B3
Lanesborough IRL .28 A4
Lanester F 100 B2
Lanestosa E 143 A3
La Neuve-Lyre F . .89 B4
La Neuveville CH. .106 B2
Langå DK 59 B2
Langada GR 185 A7
Langadas GR . . .183 C5
Langa de Duero E .151 A4
Langadia GR 184 B3
Langangen N 53 A5
Langared S 60 A2
Långaröd S 61 D3
Långaryd S 60 B3
Långås S 60 C2
Långasjö S 63 B3
Langau A 97 C3
Langeac F 117 B3
Langeais F 102 B2
Langedijk NL 70 B1
Langeln D 73 C3
Langelsheim D . . .72 C3
Langemark-Poelkapelle
B 78 B2
Langen
Hessen D 93 B4
Niedersachsen D. .72 A1
Langenau D 94 C2
Langenberg D 81 A4
Langenbruck CH. .106 B2
Langenburg D 94 B1
Langeneß D 64 B1
Langenfeld A 108 B1
Langenfeld D 80 A2
Langenhorn D 64 B1
Langenlois A 97 C3
Langenlonsheim D .93 B3
Langennaudorf D . .83 A5
Langenneufnach D .94 C2
Langenthal CH . . .106 B2
Langenzenn D 94 B2
Langeoog D 71 A4
Langeskov DK 59 C3
Langesund N 53 A5
Langewiesen D . . .82 B2
Långflon S 49 A4
Langförden D 71 B5
Langhagen D 73 A5
Länghem S 60 B3
Langhirano I 120 C3
Langholm GB 36 A4
Langholt IS 191 D7
Långlöt S 62 B4
Langnau CH 106 C2

Langø DK. 65 B4
Langogne F 117 C3
Langon F 128 B2
Langquaid D 95 C4
Långrådna S 56 B2
Langreo E 142 A1
Langres F 105 B4
Långsele S 200 C3
Långserud S 54 A3
Langset N 48 B3
Långshyttan S 50 B3
Långträsk S 196 D3
Långvik S 57 A4
Langwarden D. 71 A5
Langwathby GB . . .37 B4
Langwedel D 72 B2
Langwies CH. 107 C4
Lanheses P 148 A1
Lanięta PL 77 B4
Lanildut F 100 A1
Lanjarón E 163 B4
Lanmeur F 100 A2
Lanna
Jönköping S. 60 B3
Örebro S 55 A5
Lännäholm S 51 C4
Lannavaara S 196 A4
Lannéanou F 100 A2
Lannemezan F . . .145 A4
Lanneuville-sur-Meuse
F. 91 B5
Lannilis F 100 A1
Lannion F 100 A2
La Nocle-Maulaix
F. 104 C2
Lanouaille F 115 C5
Lansjärv S 196 C5
Lanškroun CZ 97 B4
Lanta F 129 C4
Lantadilla E 142 B2
Lanton F 128 B1
Lantosque F 133 B3
La Nuez de Arriba
E 143 B3
Lanusei I 179 C3
Lanúvio I 168 B2
Lanvollon F 100 A3
Lánycsók H 125 A4
Lanz D 73 A4
Lanza E 140 A2
Lanzada E 140 B2
Lanzahita E 150 B3
Lanžhot CZ 97 C4
Lanzo Torinese I .119 B4
Laole SRB 127 C3
Laons F 89 B5
La Paca E 164 B3
La Pacaudière F .117 A3
Lapalisse F 117 A3
La Palma d'Ebre
F. 153 A4
La Palma del Condado
E 161 B3
La Palme F 146 B4
La Palmyre F 114 C2
La Parra E 155 C4
Łapczyna Wola PL. .87 B3
La Pedraja de Portillo
E 150 A3
La Peraleja E 152 B1
La Petit-Pierre F . .93 C3
Lapeyrade F 128 B2
Lapeyrouse F 116 A2
Lapford GB 42 B3
La Pinilla E 165 B3
Lapithos CY 181 A2
La Plagne F 118 B3
La Plaza E 141 A4
Laplume F 129 B3
La Pobla de Lillet
E 147 B2
La Pobla de Vallbona
E 159 B3
La Pobla Llarga E .159 B3
La Pola de Gordón
E 142 B1
la Porta F 180 A2
La Pouèze F 102 B1
Lapoutroie F 106 A2
La Póveda de Soria
E 143 B4
Lapovo SRB 127 C3
Läppe S 56 A1
Lappeenranta FIN . .8 B6
Lappoluobbal N . .192 C7
Lappträsk S 196 C6
La Preste F 146 B3
La Primaube F . . .130 A1
Lapseki TR. 186 B1
Lapua FIN 8 A3
La Puebla de Almoradi
E 165 A4
La Puebla de Cazalla
E 162 A2
La Puebla de los
Infantes E 162 A2
La Puebla del Río
E 162 A1
La Puebla de
Montalbán E . .150 C3
La Puebla de Roda
E 145 B4
La Puebla de Valdavia
E 142 B2
La Puebla de Valverde
E 152 B3
La Pueblanueva E 150 C3
La Puerta de Segura
E 164 A2
La Punt CH 107 C4
L'Àquila E 169 A3
La Quintana E . . .162 A3
La Quintera E . . .162 A2

La Rábita
Granada E 164 C1
Jaén E 163 A3
Laracha E 140 A2
Laragh IRL 30 A2
La Rambla E 163 A3
l'Arboç E 147 C2
L'Arbresle F 117 B4
Lärbro S 57 C4
Larceveau F 144 A2
Larche
Alpes-de-Haute-
Provence F . . .132 A2
Corrèze F 129 A4
Lårdal N 53 A4
Lærdalsøyri N 47 A4
Lardosa P 155 B3
La Reale I 178 A2
Laredo E 143 A3
La Redondela E . .161 B2
La Réole F 128 B2
Largentière F 131 A3
L'Argentière-la-Bessée
F. 118 C3
Largs GB 34 C3
Lari I 134 B3
La Riera E 141 A4
La Riera de Gaià
E 147 C2
La Rinconada E . .162 A1
Lariño E 140 B1
Larino I 170 B2
Larisa GR. 182 D4
La Rivière-Thibouville
F. 89 A4
Larkhall GB 36 A3
Larkollen N 54 A1
Larmor-Plage F . .100 B2
Larnaca CY 181 B2
Larne GB 27 B5
La Robla E 142 B1
La Roche CH 106 C2
La Rochebeaucourt-
Argentine F . . .115 C4
La Roche-Bernard
F. 101 B3
La Roche-Canillac
F. 116 B1
La Roche-Chalais
F. 128 A3
La Roche Derrien
F. 100 A2
La Roche-des-Arnauds
F. 132 A1
La Roche-en-Ardenne
B 80 B1
La Roche-en-Brénil
F. 104 B3
La Rochefoucauld
F. 115 C4
La Roche-Guyon F .90 B1
La Rochelle F 114 B2
La Roche-Posay F 115 B4
La Roche-sur-Foron
F. 118 A3
La Roche-sur-Yon
F. 114 B2
Larochette L 92 B2
La Rochette F 131 A4
La Roda
Albacete E 158 B1
Oviedo E 141 A4
La Roda de Andalucía
E 162 A3
Laroquebrou F . . .116 C2
La Roquebrussanne
F. 132 B1
Laroque d'Olmes
F. 146 B2
La Roque-Gageac
F. 129 B4
La Roque-Ste
Marguerite F . .130 A2
Laroque-Timbaut
F. 129 B3
Larouco E 141 B3
Larraga E 144 B2
Larrau F 144 A3
Larrazet F 129 C4
Larsnes N 198 C2
La Rubia E 143 C4
Laruns F 145 A3
Larva E 164 B1
Larvik N 53 A6
La Sagrada E 149 B3
La Salceda E 151 A4
Lasalle F 131 A2
La Salle F 118 C3
la Salute di Livenza
I 122 B1
La Salvetat-Peyralés
F. 130 A1
La Salvetat-sur-Agout
F. 130 B1
Las Arenas E 142 A2
La Sarraz CH 105 C5
Lasarte E 144 A1
Låsby DK 59 B2
Las Cabezadas E .151 A4
Las Cabezas de San
Juan E 162 B2
Las Correderas E .157 B4
Las Cuevas de Cañart
E 153 B3
La Seca E 150 A2
La Selva del Camp
E 147 C2
La Senia E 153 B4
La Serra E 147 C2
La Seu d'Urgell E .146 B2
La Seyne-sur-Mer
F. 132 B1
Las Gabias E 163 A4
Las Herencias E . .150 C3
Las Herrerías E . .161 B2
Łasin PL 69 B4

Lask PL 86 A3
Laska PL 68 B2
Łaskarzow PL 87 A5
Laško SLO 123 A4
Laskowice PL 76 A3
Las Labores E . . .157 A4
Las Mesas E 158 B1
Las Minas E 164 A3
Las Navas E 163 A3
Las Navas de la
Concepción E . .156 C2
Las Navas del Marqués
E 150 B3
Las Navillas E . . .157 A3
Las Negras E 164 C3
La Solana E 157 B4
La Souterraine F .116 A1
Las Pajanosas E .161 B3
Laspaúles E 145 B4
Las Pedroñas E . .158 B1
La Spézia I 134 A2
Las Planes d'Hostoles
E 147 B3
Laspuña E 145 B4
Las Rozas
Cantabria E . . .142 B2
Madrid E 151 B4
Lassan D 66 C2
Lassay-les-Châteaux
F. 89 B3
Lasseube F 145 A3
Lassigny F 90 B2
La Storta I 168 B2
Lastovo HR 138 C2
Lastras de Cuéllar
E 151 A3
Lästringe S 56 B3
Lastrup D 71 B4
Las Uces E 149 A3
La Suze-sur-Sarthe
F. 102 B2
Las Veguillas E . .149 B4
Las Ventas con Peña
Aguilera E 157 A3
Las Ventas de San
Julián E 150 B2
Las Villes E 153 B4
Latasa E 144 B2
Látera I 168 A1
Laterza I 171 C4
La Teste F 128 B1
Lathen D 71 B4
Latheron GB 32 C3
La Thuile I 119 B3
Latiano I 173 B3
Latina I 169 B2
Latisana I 122 B2
Látky SK 99 C3
La Toba E 152 B2
La Toledana E . . .157 A3
La Torre de Cabdella
E 146 B1
La Torre de Esteban
Hambrán E 151 B3
La Torre del l'Espanyol
E 153 A4
La Torresaviñán
E 152 B1
La Tour d'Aigues
F. 132 B1
La Tour de Peilz
CH 106 C1
La Tour-du-Pin F .118 B2
La Tranche-sur-Mer
F. 114 B2
La Tremblade F . .114 C2
La Trimouille F . . .115 B5
La Trinité F 100 B2
La Trinité-Porhoët
F. 101 A3
Latrónico I 174 A2
Latronquière F . . .116 C2
Latterbach CH . . .106 C2
La Turballe F 101 B3
Laubach D 81 B4
Laucha D 83 A3
Lauchhammer D . .84 A1
Lauchheim D 94 C2
Lauda-Königshofen
D 94 B1
Laudal N 52 B3
Lauder GB 35 C5
Lauenau D 72 B2
Lauenburg D 73 A3
Lauf D 95 B3
Laufach D 94 A1
Laufen
CH 106 B2
D 109 B3
Lauffen D 93 B5
Laugar IS 191 B8
Laugarás IS 190 C5
Laugarbakki IS . . .190 B5
Laugarvatn IS . . .190 C5
Laugharne GB 39 C2
Lauingen D 94 C2
Laujar de Andarax
E 164 C2
Laukaa FIN 8 A4
Lauker S 196 D2
Laukvik N 194 C5
La Uña E 142 A1
La Unión E 165 B4
Launois-sur-Vence
F. 91 B4
Laupheim D 94 C1
Lauragh IRL 29 C2
Laureana di Borrello
I 175 C2
Laurencekirk GB. .35 B5
Laurencetown IRL. .28 A3
Laurenzana I 172 B1
Lauria I 174 A1
Laurière F 116 A1
Laurieston GB 36 B2
Laurino I 172 B1
Lausanne CH. . . .106 C1
Laussonne F 117 C4

Lauta D 84 A2
Lautenthal D 82 A2
Lauterach A 107 B4
Lauterbach D. 81 B5
Lauterbrunnen
CH 106 C2
Lauterecken D. . . .93 B3
Lauterhofen D 95 B3
Lautrec F 130 B1
Lauvsnes N 199 A7
Lauvvlk N 52 B2
Lauzerte F 129 B4
Lauzès F 129 B4
Lauzun F 129 B3
Lavagna I 134 A2
Laval F 102 A1
La Vall d'Uixó E . .159 B3
Lavamünd A 110 C1
Lavara GR 186 A1
Lavardac F 129 B3
Lavaris P 148 B1
Lavarone I 121 B4
Lavau F 104 B2
Lavaur F 129 C4
La Vecilla de Curueño
E 142 B1
La Vega
Asturias E 141 A5
Asturias E 142 A1
Cantabria E . . .142 A2
Lavelanet F 146 B2
La Velilla E 151 A4
La Velles E 150 A2
Lavello I 172 A1
Lavelsloh D 72 B1
Lavenham GB 45 A4
Laveno I 120 B1
La Ventosa E 152 B1
La Victoria E 162 A3
La Vid E 151 A4
Lavik N 46 A2
La Vilavella E 159 B3
La Vilella Baixa E .147 C1
La Villa de Don
Fadrique E 157 A4
Lavilledieu F 131 A3
La Villedieu F 115 B3
La Ville Dieu-du-Temple
F. 129 B4
Lavinio-Lido di Enea
I 168 B2
Lav is I 121 B4
Lavit F 129 C3
Lavoncourt F 105 B4
Lavos P 148 B1
La Voulte-sur-Rhône
F. 117 C4
Lavoûte-Chilhac
F. 117 B3
Lavre P 154 C1
Lavrio GR 185 B5
La Wantzenau F . .93 C3
Lawers GB 35 B3
Ławy PL 75 B3
Laxå S 55 B5
Laxamýri IS 191 B8
Laxe E 140 A2
Laxey GB 36 B2
Laxford Bridge GB .32 C1
Laxhall S 55 B4
Laxsjö S 199 B11
Laxtjarn S 49 B6
Laxvik S 61 C2
Laxviken S 199 B11
La Yesa E 159 B3
Laza E 141 B3
Laza F 144 A1
Lazarevac SRB . .127 C2
Lazarevo SRB . . .126 B2
Lazise I 121 B3
Łaziska Grn. PL. . .86 B2
Lazkao E 144 A1
Lázně Bělohrad
CZ 84 B3
Lázně Bohdaneč
CZ 97 A3
Lázně Kynžvart CZ 95 A4
Lazonby GB 37 B4
La Zubia E 163 A4
Łazy PL 67 B5
Lazzaro I 175 D1
Lea GB 40 B3
Leadburn GB 35 C4
Leadhills GB 36 A3
Leap IRL 29 C2
Leatherhead GB . .44 B3
Łeba PL 68 A2
Lebach D 92 B2
Le Barp F 128 B2
Le Bar-sur-Loup F 132 B2
Le Béage F 117 C4
Le Beausset F . . .132 B1
Lebekke B 79 A4
Lébény H 111 B4
Le Bessat F 117 B4
Le Blanc F 115 B5
Le Bleymard F . . .130 A2
Łebno PL 68 A3
Leboreiro E 140 B3
Le Boullay-Mivoye
F. 90 C1
Le Boulou F 146 B3
Le Bourg-d'Oisans
F. 118 B3
Le Bourget-du-Lac
F. 118 B2
Le Bourgneuf-la-Forêt
F. 101 A5
Le Bousquet d'Orb
F. 130 B2
Le Brassus CH . .105 C5
Le Breuil F 117 A3
Le Breuil-en-Auge
F. 89 A4
Lebring A 110 C2

Le Brusquet F . . .132 A2
Le Bry CH 106 C2
Le Bugue F 129 B3
Le Buisson F 129 B3
Lebus D 74 B3
Lebusa D 83 A5
Le Caloy F 128 C2
Le Cap d'Agde F .130 B2
Le Cateau Cambrésis
F. 91 A3
Le Caylar F 130 B2
Le Cayrol F 116 C2
Lecce I 173 B4
Lecco I 120 B2
Lécera E 153 A3
Lećevica HR 138 B2
Lech A 107 B5
Le Chambon-
Feugerolles F . .117 B4
Le Chambon-sur-
Lignon F 117 B4
Le Château d'Oléron
F. 114 C2
Le Châtelard F . . .118 B3
Le Châtelet F 103 C4
Le Chatelet-en-Brie
F. 90 C2
Lechbruck D 108 B1
Le Chesne F 91 B4
Le Cheylard F . . .117 C4
Lechlade GB 44 B2
Lechovice CZ 97 C4
Leciñena E 145 C3
Leck D 64 B1
Le Collet-de-Deze
F. 131 A2
Le Conquet F 100 A1
Le Creusot F 104 C3
Le Croisic F 101 B3
Le Crotoy F 78 B1
Lectoure F 129 C3
Łęczyca
Łódzkie PL 77 B4
Zachodnio-Pomorskie
PL 75 A4
Ledaña E 158 B2
Ledbury GB 39 B4
Lede B 79 B3
Ledeč nad Sázavou
CZ 97 B3
Ledenice CZ 96 C2
Ledesma E 149 A3
Lédignan F 131 B3
Lédigos E 142 B2
Ledmore GB 32 C2
Lednice CZ 97 C4
Lednicke-Rovné
SK 98 B2
Le Donjon F 117 A3
Le Dorat F 115 B5
Lędyczek PL 68 B1
Lędziny PL 86 B3
Leeds GB 40 B2
Leek
GB 40 B1
NL 71 A3
Leenaun IRL 28 A2
Leens NL 71 A3
Leer D 71 A4
Leerdam NL 79 A5
Leerhafe D 71 A4
Leese D 72 B2
Leeuwarden NL . . .70 A2
Leezen D 64 C3
Le Faou F 100 A1
Le Faoüet F 100 A2
Lefka CY 181 A1
Lefkada GR 182 E2
Lefkimis GR 182 D2
Lefkoniko CY 181 A2
Le Folgoet F 100 A1
Le Fossat F 146 A2
Le Fousseret F . .146 A2
Le Fugeret F 132 A2
Leganés E 151 B4
Legau D 107 B5
Le Gault-Soigny F .91 C3
Legbąd PL 68 B2
Legé F 114 B2
Lège-Cap-Ferret
F. 128 B1
Legionowo PL 77 B5
Léglise B 92 B1
Legnago I 121 B4
Legnano I 120 B1
Legnaro I 121 B4
Legnica PL 85 A4
Łęgowo PL 69 A3
Legrad HR 124 A2
Le Grand-Bornand
F. 118 B3
Le-Grand-Bourg F 116 A1
Le Grand-Lucé F .102 B2
Le Grand-Pressigny
F. 102 C2
Le Grand-Quevilly
F. 89 A5
Le Grau-du-Roi F .131 B3
Léguevin F 129 C4
Leguitiano E 143 A4
Le Havre F 89 A4
Lehesten D 82 B3
Lehnice SK 111 A4
Lehnin D 74 B1
Le Hohwald F 93 C3
Le Houga F 128 C2
Lehrberg D 94 B2
Lehre D 73 B3
Lehrte D 72 B2
Lehsen D 73 A4
Leibnitz A 110 C2
Leicester GB 40 C2
Leiden NL 70 B1
Leidschendam NL. .70 B1
Leigh GB 38 A4
Leighlinbridge IRL .30 B2

Leighton Buzzard
GB 44 B3
Leignon B 79 B5
Leikanger N 198 C2
Leimen D 93 B4
Leinefelde D 82 A2
Leinesfjord N 194 C6
Leintwardine GB . . .39 B4
Leipojärvi S 196 B4
Leipzig D 83 A4
Leira
Nordland N 195 D4
Oppland N 47 B6
Leirámoen N 195 D5
Leiria P 154 B2
Leirvassbu N 47 A5
Leirvik
Hordaland N . . .52 A1
Sogn og Fjordane
N 46 A2
Leisach A 109 C3
Leisnig D 83 A4
Leiston GB 45 A5
Leitholm GB 35 C5
Leitrim IRL 26 C2
Leitza E 144 A2
Leitzkau D 73 B4
Lejkowo PL 68 A1
Łękawa PL 86 A3
Łękawica PL 99 B3
Lekeitio E 143 A4
Lekenik HR 124 B2
Lekeryd S 62 A2
Leknes N 194 B4
Łęknica PL 84 A2
Leksand S 50 B1
Leksvik N 199 B7
Lekunberri E 144 A2
Lekvattnet S 49 B4
Le Lardin-St Lazare
F. 129 A4
Le Lauzet-Ubaye
F. 132 A2
Le Lavandou F . .132 B2
Le Lion-d'Angers
F. 102 B1
Lelkowo PL 69 A5
Le Locle CH 106 C1
Le Loroux-Bottereau
F. 101 B4
Le Louroux-Béconnais
F. 101 B5
Lelów PL 86 B3
Le Luc F 132 B2
Le Lude F 102 B2
Lelystad NL 70 B2
Lem
Ringkøbing DK . .59 B1
Viborg Amt. DK . .58 B1
Le Malzieu-Ville F .116 C3
Le Mans F 102 A2
Le Mas-d'Azil F . .146 A2
Le Massegros F . .130 A2
Le Mayet-de-Montagne
F. 117 A3
Lembach F 93 B3
Lemberg F 93 B3
Lembèye F 145 A3
Lemelerveld NL. . . .71 B3
Le Mêle-sur-Sarthe
F. 89 B4
Le Ménil F 105 A5
Le Merlerault F . . .89 B4
Le Mesnil-sur-Oger
F. 91 C4
Lemförde D 71 B5
Lemgo D 72 B1
Le Miroir F 105 C4
Lemland FIN 51 B7
Lemmer NL 70 B2
Le Molay-Littry F . .88 A3
Le Monastier-sur-
Gazeille F 117 C3
Le Monêtier-les-Bains
F. 118 C3
Le Mont-Dore F . .116 B2
Le Montet F 116 A3
Le Mont-St Michel
F. 88 B2
Lempdes F 116 B3
Le Muret F 128 B2
Le Muy F 132 B2
Lemvig DK 58 B1
Lemwerder D 72 A1
Lena N 48 B2
Lenart SLO 110 C2
Lenartovce SK . . .99 C4
Lenauheim RO . . .126 B2
Lencloitre F 102 C2
Lend A 109 B4
Lendalfoot GB 36 A2
Lendava SLO 111 C3
Lendery RUS 3 E12
Lendinara I 121 B4
Lendorf A 109 C4
Lendum DK 58 A3
Le Neubourg F . . .89 A4
Lengefeld D 83 B5
Lengerich
Niedersachsen D. .71 B4
Nordrhein-Westfalen
D. 71 B4
Lenggries D 108 B2
Lengyeltóti H 111 C4
Lenhovda S 62 B3
Lenk CH 106 C2
Lennartsfors S . . .54 A2
Lennestadt D 81 A4
Lennoxtown GB . . .35 C3
Leno I 120 B3
Lénola I 169 B3
Le Nouvion-en-
Thiérache F 91 A3
Lens
B 79 B3

Lens continued
F. 78 B2
Lensahn D 65 B3
Lens Lestang F . . .117 B5
Lensvik N. 198 B6
Lentellais E 141 B3
Lentföhrden D 64 C2
Lenti H 111 C3
Lentini I 177 B3
Lenungshammar S . .54 A3
Lenzburg CH 106 B3
Lenzen D 73 A4
Lenzerheide CH . . .107 C4
Leoben A 110 B2
Leogang A 109 B3
Leominster GB 39 B4
León E 142 B1
Léon F 128 C1
Leonberg D 93 C5
Léoncel F 118 C2
Leonding A 96 C2
Leonessa I 169 A2
Leonforte I 177 B3
Leonidio GR 184 B3
Leopoldsburg B 79 A5
Leopoldsdorf im
Marchfeld A 111 A3
Leopoldshagen D . . .74 A2
Leova MD. 17 B8
Le Palais F 100 B2
Le Parcq F 78 B2
Lepe E 161 B2
Le Péage-de-
Roussillon F 117 B4
Le Pellerin F 101 B4
Lepenou GR 182 E3
Le Perthus F 146 B3
Le Pertuis F 117 B4
Le Petit-Bornand
F. 118 B3
Lephin F 31 B2
L'Épine F 132 A1
Le Poët F 132 A1
Lepoglava HR 124 A2
Le Poirè-sur-Vie F .114 B2
Le Pont CH 105 C5
Le Pont-de-Montvert
F. 130 A2
Le Porge F 128 B1
Le Porge-Océan F .128 B1
Le Portel F 78 B1
Le Pouldu F 100 B2
Le Pouliguen F 101 B3
Leppäjärvi FIN. . . .192 D7
Leppävirta FIN. 8 A5
Leppin D 73 B4
le Prese I 120 A3
Lepsény H 112 C2
Le Puy-en-Velay F .117 B3
Le Puy-Ste Réparade
F. 131 B4
Le Quesnoy F 79 B3
Léquile I 173 B4
Le Rayol F 132 B2
Lercara Friddi I . . .176 B2
Lerdal S 54 B2
Leré F 103 B4
Lérici I 134 A2
Lerin E 144 B2
Lerma E 143 B3
Lerm-et-Musset F .128 B2
Lermoos A 108 B1
Le Roeulx B 79 B4
Le Rouget F 116 C2
Lérouville F 92 C1
Le Rozier F 130 A2
Lerum S 60 B2
Le Russey F 106 B1
Lervik N 54 A1
Lerwick GB 33 A5
Lés E 145 B4
Les Abrets F 118 B2
Les Aix-d'Angillon
F. 103 B4
Lesaka E 144 A2
Les Ancizes-Comps
F. 116 B2
Les Andelys F 90 B1
Les Arcs
Savoie F 119 B3
Var F 132 B2
Les-Aubiers F 102 C1
Les Baux-de-Provence
F. 131 B3
Les Bézards F 103 B4
Les Bois CH 106 B1
Les Bordes F 103 B4
Les Borges Blanques
E 147 C1
Les Borges del Camp
E 147 C2
Les Brunettes F . . .104 C2
Lesbury GB 37 A5
Les Cabannes F . . .146 B2
L'Escala E 147 B4
Lescar F 145 A3
L'Escarène F 133 B3
Lesce SLO 123 A3
Lescheraines F . . .118 B3
Lesconil F 100 B1
Les Contamines-
Montjoie F 118 B3
les Coves de Vinroma
E 153 B4
Les Déserts F 118 B2
Les Deux-Alpes F .118 B3
Les Diablerets CH 119 A4
Lesdins F 90 B3
Les Echelles F 118 B2
Le Sel-de-Bretagne
F. 101 B4
Le Sentier CH 105 C5
Les Escaldes
AND. 146 B2
Les Essarts F 114 B2
Les Estables F 117 C4

Les Eyzies-de-Tayac
F. 129 B4
Les Gets F 118 A3
Les Grandes-Ventes
F. 89 A5
Les Haudères CH . .119 A4
Les Herbiers F 114 B2
Les Hôpitaux-Neufs
F. 105 C5
Lesično SLO 123 A4
Lésina I 171 B3
Lesjaskog N 198 C5
Lesjöfors S 49 C6
Leskova Dolina
SLO 123 B3
Leskovec
CZ. 98 B1
SLO 123 B4
Leskovice CZ 97 B3
Leskovik AL. 182 C2
Leslie GB 35 B4
Les Lucs-sur-Boulogne
F. 114 B2
Les Mages F 131 A3
Les Mazures F 91 B4
Les Mées F 132 A1
Lesmont F 91 C4
Les Mureaux F 90 C1
Lesna PL 84 A3
Lešnica PL 100 A1
Lešnica D 86 B2
Lešnica SRB 127 C1
Leśniów Wielkopolski
PL. 75 C4
Lesnoye RUS 9 C9
Les Omergues F . . .132 A1
Les Ormes-sur-Voulzie
F. 90 C3
Les Orres F 132 A2
Le Souquet F 128 C1
Lesparre-Médoc
F. 128 A2
l'Espérance F 91 B3
l'Esperou F 130 A2
Les Pieux F 88 A2
Lesponne F 145 A4
Les Ponts-de-Cé
F. 102 B1
Les Ponts-de-Martel
CH 106 C1
Les Praz F 119 B3
L'Espunyola E 147 B2
Les Riceys F 104 B3
Les Roches F 117 B4
Les Rosaires F 101 A3
Les Rosiers F 102 B1
Les Rousses F 105 C5
Les Sables-d'Olonne
F. 114 B2
Lessach A 109 B4
Lessay F 88 A2
Lessebo S 62 B3
Les Settons F 104 B3
Lessines B 79 B3
L'Estany E 147 C3
Les Ternes F 116 B2
Lesterps F 115 B4
Les Thilliers en-Vexin
F. 90 B1
Les Touches F 101 B4
Les Trois Moûtiers
F. 102 B2
Les Vans F 131 A3
Les Verrières CH . .105 C5
Les Vignes F 130 A2
Leswalt GB 36 B1
Leszno
Mazowieckie PL. . .77 B5
Wielkopolskie PL. .85 A4
Leszno Górne PL . . .84 A3
Letchworth GB 44 B3
Le Teil F 131 A3
Le Teilleul F 88 B3
Le Temple-de-Bretagne
F. 101 B4
Letenye H 111 C3
Le Theil F 89 B4
Le Thillot F 106 B1
Letino I 170 B2
Letohrad CZ 97 A4
Le Touquet-Paris-Plage
F. 78 B1
Le Touvet F 118 B2
Letovice CZ. 97 B4
Le Translay F 90 B1
Le Tréport F 90 A1
Letschin D 74 B3
Letterfrack IRL. 28 A2
Letterkenny IRL. . . .26 B3
Lettermacaward
IRL. 26 B2
Lettoch GB 32 D3
Letton GB 39 B4
Letux E 153 A3
Letzlingen D 73 B4
Leucate F 146 B4
Leuchars GB 35 B5
Leuglay F 105 B3
Leuk CH 119 A4
Leukerbad CH 119 A4
Leumrabhagh GB . . .31 A2
Leuna D 83 A4
Leusden NL 70 B2
Leutenberg D 82 B3
Leuterschach D . . .108 B1
Leutershausen D . . .94 B2
Leutkirch D 107 B5
Leuven B 79 B4
Leuze-en-Hainaut
B 79 B3
Le Val F 132 B2
Le Val-André F . . .101 A3
Le Val-d'Ajol F . . .105 B5
Levan AL 182 C1
Levanger N 199 B8
Levanjska Varoš
HR 125 B4
Lévanto I 134 A2

Levaré F. 88 B3
Levata I 120 B3
Leveld N. 47 B5
Leven
East Yorkshire
GB. 41 B3
Fife GB 35 B5
Leverano I 173 B3
Le Verdon-sur-Mer
F. 114 C2
Leverkusen D 80 A2
Levern D 72 B1
Le Vernet F 132 A2
Levet F 103 C4
Levice SK. 112 A2
Lévico Terme I 121 A4
Levie F 180 B2
Levier F 105 C5
Le Vigan F 130 B2
Lévignen F 90 B2
le Ville I 135 B5
Levinovac HR 124 B3
Levoča SK 99 B4
Levroux F 103 C3
Lewes GB 45 C4
Lewin Brzeski PL . . .85 B5
Lewisham GB 44 B3
Leyburn GB 37 B5
Leyland GB 38 A4
Leysdown-on-Sea
GB 45 B4
Leysin CH 119 A4
Lezajsk PL 12 C5
Lézardrieux F 100 A2
Lézat-sur-Léze F . .146 A2
Lezay F 115 B3
Lezhë AL 182 B1
Lezignan-Corbières
F. 130 B1
Lezignan-la-Cèbe
F. 130 B2
Ležimir SRB 126 B1
Lézinnes F 104 B3
Lezoux F 117 B3
Lezuza E 158 C1
Lhenice CZ 96 C2
Lherm F 146 A2
Lhommaizé F 115 B4
L'Hospitalet F 146 B2
L'Hospitalet de l'Infant
E 147 D1
L'Hospitalet de
Llobregat E 147 C3
L'Hospitalet-du-Larzac
F. 130 B2
Lhuître F 91 C4
Liancourt F 90 B2
Liart F 91 B4
Liatorp S 63 B2
Liatrie GB 32 D2
Libáň CZ 84 B3
Libceves CZ 84 B1
Liběchov CZ 84 B2
Liber E 141 B3
Liberec CZ 84 B2
Libiąż PL 86 B3
Libina CZ 98 B1
Libochovice CZ. 84 B2
Libohovë AL. 182 C2
Libourne F 128 B2
Libramont B. 92 B1
Librazhd AL. 182 B2
Librilla E 165 B3
Libros E 152 B2
Licata I 176 B2
Licciana Nardi I . . .134 A3
Licenza I 169 A2
Liceros E 151 A4
Lich D 81 B4
Lichères-près-
Aigremont F 104 B2
Lichfield GB. 40 C2
Lichtenau
A. 97 C3
D 81 A4
Lichtenberg D. 83 B3
Lichtenfels D. 82 B3
Lichtensteig CH . . .107 B4
Lichtenstein D 83 B4
Lichtenvoorde NL. . .71 C3
Lichtervelde B 78 A3
Lička Jesenica
HR 123 B4
Lickershamn S 57 C4
Lički Osik HR. 123 C4
Ličko Lešče HR . . .123 C4
Licodía Eubéa I . . .177 B3
Licques F 78 B1
Lida BY. 13 B6
Lidar N. 47 A6
Lidečko CZ 98 B2
Lidhult S 60 C3
Lidköping S 55 B4
Lido I 122 B1
Lido Azzurro I 173 B3
Lido degli Estensi
I 122 C1
Lido degli Scacchi
I 122 C1
Lido della Nazioni
I 122 C1
Lido di Camaiore I .134 B3
Lido di Casalbordino
I 169 A4
Lido di Castél Fusano
I 168 B2
Lido di Cincinnato
I 168 B2
Lido di Classe I . . .135 A5
Lido di Fermo I . . .136 B2
Lido di Fondi I 169 B3
Lido di Jésolo I . . .122 B1
Lido di Lícola I 170 C2
Lido di Metaponto
I 174 A2
Lido di Óstia I 168 B2
Lido di Policoro I . .174 A2
Lido di Pomposa I .122 C1

Lido di Savio I 135 A5
Lido di Scanzano
I 174 A2
Lido di Siponto I . .171 B3
Lido di Squillace I .175 C2
Lido di Volano I . . .122 C1
Lido Riccio I 169 A4
Lido Silvana I 173 B3
Lidzbark PL 77 A4
Lidzbark Warmiński
PL. 69 A5
Liebenau
A. 96 C2
D 72 B2
Liebenwalde D 74 B2
Lieberose D. 74 C3
Liebling RO 126 B3
Lieboch A. 110 C2
Liège B. 80 B1
Lieksa FIN 3 E12
Lienen D 71 B4
Lienz A 109 C3
Liepāja LV 8 D2
Lier B 79 A4
Lierbyen N. 54 A1
Liernais F 104 B3
Liesing A 109 C3
Liestal CH 106 B2
Liétor E 158 C2
Lieurac F 146 B2
Lieurey F. 89 A4
Liévin F 78 B2
Liezen A 110 B1
Liffol-le-Grand F . . .92 C1
Lifford IRL 27 B3
Liffré F 101 A4
Ligardes F 129 B3
Lignano Sabbiadoro
I 122 B2
Ligne F 101 B4
Lignières F 103 C4
Ligny-en-Barrois F . .92 C1
Ligny-le-Châtel F .104 B2
Ligoła Polska PL. . .85 A5
Ligourió GR 184 B3
Ligowo PL 77 B4
Ligueil F 102 B2
Likavka SK 99 B3
Likenäs S 49 B5
Likhoslavl RUS 9 D9
Lild Strand DK. 58 A1
L'Île-Bouchard F . .102 B2
L'Île-Rousse F 180 A1
Lilienfeld A. 110 A2
Lilienthal D 72 A1
Lilla Edet S 54 B3
Lilla Tjärby S 61 C3
Lille
B 79 A4
F. 78 B3
Lillebonne F 89 A4
Lillehammer N 48 A2
Lillerød DK. 61 D2
Lillers F 78 B2
Lillesand N 53 B4
Lillestrøm N 48 C3
Lillhärdal S 199 D11
Lillkyrka S 56 A3
Lillo E 157 A4
Lillögda S 200 B3
Lillpite S 196 D4
Lima S 49 B5
Limanowa PL. 99 B4
Limassol CY 181 B2
Limavady GB. 27 A4
Limbach-Oberfrohna
D 83 B4
Limburg B 80 B1
Limburg D 81 B4
Lime DK. 58 B3
Limedsforsen S. 49 B5
Limenaria GR 183 C6
Limenas Chersonisou
GR 185 D6
Limerick IRL 29 B3
Limes I 121 B3
Limésy F 89 A4
Limmared S 60 B3
Limni GR 183 E5
Limoges F 115 C5
Limogne-en-Quercy
F. 129 B4
Limoise F 104 C2
Limone Piemonte
I 133 A3
Limone sul Garda
I 121 B3
Limons F 117 B3
Limours F 90 C2
Limoux F 146 A3
Linares E 157 B4
Linares de Mora E .153 B3
Linares de Riofrio
E 149 B4
Linaria GR 183 E6
Linas de Broto E . .145 B3
Lincoln GB 40 B3
Lindås DK 59 B1
Lindau D 107 B4
Lindberget N 48 A3
Lindé DK 65 B3
Lindelse DK 65 B3
Lindenberg D 74 B3
Lindenberg im Allgäu
D 107 B4
Lindern D 71 B4
Linderöd S 61 D3
Lindesberg S 56 A1
Lindesnäs S 50 B1
Lindesnes N 52 B3
Lindholmen S 57 A4
Lindknud DK. 59 C2
Lindö S 56 B2
Lindome S 60 B2
Lindos GR 188 C3
Lindoso P 148 A1

Lindow D 74 B1
Lindsdal S 62 B4
Lindshammar S. 62 A3
Lindstedt D 73 B4
Lindved DK 59 C2
Lingbo S 50 A3
Lingen D 71 B4
Linghed S 50 B2
Linghem S 56 B1
Linguaglossa I 177 B4
Linia PL 68 A2
Linie PL 74 A3
Liniewo PL 68 A3
Linkenheim D 93 B4
Linköping S 56 B1
Linksness GB 33 C3
Linlithgow GB 35 C4
Linneryd S 63 B3
Linnes Hammarby
S 51 C4
Linnich D 80 B2
Linsell S 199 C10
Linslade GB 44 B3
Linthal CH 107 C4
Linyola E 147 C1
Linz
A. 96 C2
D 80 B3
Liomseter N. 47 A6
Lionárisso CY 181 A3
Lioni I 172 B1
Lion-sur-Mer F 89 A3
Lipany SK 99 B4
Lipar SRB 126 B1
Liparí I 177 A3
Lipcani MD 17 A7
Liperi FIN. 9 A6
Liphook GB 44 B3
Lipiany PL 75 A3
Lipik HR 124 B3
Lipka PL 68 B2
Lipki Wielkie PL. . . .75 B4
Lipnica PL 68 B2
Lipnica Murowana
PL. 99 B4
Lipnik PL 87 B5
Lipník nad Bečvou
CZ. 98 B1
Lipno
Kujawsko-Pomorskie
PL. 77 B4
Łódzkie PL. 86 A2
Liposthey F 128 B2
Lipovac HR 125 B5
Lipovec CZ 97 B4
Lipovets UA 13 D8
Lipovljani HR 124 B2
Lipowiec PL 77 A6
Lipowina PL 69 A4
Lippborg D. 81 A4
Lippó H 125 B4
Lippoldsberg D 81 A5
Lippstadt D 81 A4
Lipsko PL 87 A5
Liptál CZ 98 B1
Liptovská-Lúžna
SK 99 C3
Liptovská Osada
SK 99 C3
Liptovská-Teplička
SK 99 C4
Liptovský Hrádok
SK 99 B3
Liptovský Milkuláš
SK 99 B3
Lipusz PL 68 A2
Lipůvka CZ 97 B4
Liré F 101 B4
Lisac BIH 139 A3
Lisbellaw GB 27 B3
Lisboa = Lisbon P 154 C1
Lisbon = Lisboa P 154 C1
Lisburn GB 27 B4
Liscannor IRL 28 B2
Lisdoonvarna IRL . .28 A2
Lisewo PL 69 B3
Lisia Góra PL. 87 B5
Lisięcice PL 86 B1
Lisieux F 89 A4
Lisjö S 56 A2
Liskeard GB 42 B2
L'Isle CH 105 C5
L'Isle-Adam F 90 B2
L'Isle-de-Noé F . . .129 C3
L'Isle-en-Dodon F 145 A4
L'Isle-Jourdain
Gers F 129 C4
Vienne F 115 B4
L'Isle-sur-la-Sorgue
F. 131 B4
L'Isle-sur-le-Doubs
F. 105 B5
L'Isle-sur-Serein
F. 104 B3
Lismore IRL 29 B4
Lisnaskea GB 27 B3
Lišov CZ 96 B2
Lisów
Lubuskie PL 74 B3
Śląskie PL 86 B2
Lisse NL 70 B1
Lissycasey IRL 28 B2
List D 64 A1
Listerby S 63 B3
Listowel IRL 29 B2
Listrac-Médoc F . . .128 A2
Liszki PL 99 A3
Liszkowo PL 76 A2
Lit S 199 B11
Litava SK 99 C3
Litcham GB 41 C4
Litava SK 99 C3
Lit-et-Mixe F 128 B1
Litija SLO 123 A3
Litke H 112 A3
Litlabø N 52 A1
Litochoro GR 182 C4
Litoměřice CZ 84 B2
Litomyšl CZ 97 B4

Litovel CZ 98 B1
Litschau A 96 C3
Littlehampton GB . .44 C3
Littleport GB 45 A4
Littleton IRL. 29 B4
Little Walsingham
GB 41 C4
Litvinov CZ 83 B5
Livadero GR 182 C3
Livadhia CY 181 B2
Livádi GR. 182 C3
Livadia GR 184 A3
Livarot F 89 B4
Liverá CY 181 A1
Livernon F 129 B4
Liverovici MNE . . .139 C5
Liverpool GB 38 A4
Livigno I 107 C5
Livingston GB 35 C4
Livno BIH 138 B2
Livold SLO 123 B3
Livorno I 134 B3
Livorno Ferraris I . .119 B5
Livron-sur-Drôme
F. 117 C4
Livry-Louvercy F. . . .91 B4
Lixheim F 92 C3
Lixouri GR 184 A1
Lizard GB 42 C1
Lizy-sur-Ourcq F . . .90 B3
Lizzano I 173 B3
Lizzano in Belvedere
I 135 A3
Ljig SRB 127 C2
Ljørdalen N 49 A4
Ljosland N 52 B3
Ljubija BIH 124 C2
Ljubinje BIH 139 C4
Ljubiški BIH 138 B3
Ljugarn S 57 C4
Ljung S 60 B3
Ljunga S 56 B2
Ljungaverk S 200 D2
Ljungby S 60 C3
Ljungbyhed S 61 C3
Ljungbyholm S 63 B4
Ljungdalen S 199 C9
Ljungsarp S 60 B3
Ljungsbro S 56 B1
Ljungskile S 54 B2
Ljusdal S 200 E2
Ljusfallshammar S .56 B1
Ljusne S 51 A4
Ljusterö S 57 A4
Ljutomer SLO 111 C3
Lŭki BG 183 B6
Lladurs E 147 B2
Llafranc E 147 C4
Llagostera E 147 C3
Llanaelhaiarn GB . .38 B2
Llanarth GB 39 B2
Llanarthney GB 39 C2
Llanbedr GB 38 B2
Llanbedrog GB 38 B2
Llanberis GB 38 A2
Llanbister GB 39 B3
Llanbrynmair GB. . .39 B3
Llançà E 146 B4
Llandeilo GB 39 C3
Llandissilio GB 39 C2
Llandovery GB 39 C3
Llandrillo GB 38 B3
Llandrindod Wells
GB 39 B3
Llandudec F 100 A1
Llandudno GB 38 A3
Llandysul GB. 39 B2
Llanelli GB 39 C2
Llanerchymedd GB .38 A2
Llanes E 142 A2
Llanfair Caereinion
GB 38 B3
Llanfairfechan GB. .38 A3
Llanfyllin GB 38 B3
Llangadog GB 39 C3
Llangefni GB 38 A2
Llangollen GB 38 B3
Llangranog GB 39 B2
Llangurig GB 39 B3
Llanidloes GB 39 B3
Llanilar GB 39 B2
Llanrhystud GB 39 B2
Llanrwst GB 38 A3
Llansannan GB 38 A3
Llansawel GB 39 B2
Llanstephan GB . . .39 C2
Llanteno E 143 A3
Llanthony GB 39 C3
Llantrisant GB 39 C3
Llantwit-Major GB. .39 C3
Llanuwchllyn GB . .38 B3
Llanwddyn GB 38 B3
Llanwrda GB 39 C3
Llanwrtyd Wells
GB 39 B3
Llanybydder GB . . .39 B2
Llanymynech GB . .38 B3
Llavorsi E 146 B2
Lleida E 153 A4
Llera E 156 B1
Llerena E 156 B1
Lles E 146 B2
Llessui E 146 B2
Llinars E 147 B2
Lliria E 159 B3
Llivia E 146 B2
Llodio E 143 A4
Lloret de Mar E . . .147 C3
Llosa de Ranes E . .159 B3
Lloseta E 167 B2
Llucena del Cid E .153 B3
Llucmajor E 167 B2
Llutxent E 159 C3
Llwyngwril GB 38 B2
Llysawen GB 39 B3

Lniano PL 76 A3
Loanhead GB 35 C4
Loano I 133 A4
Loarre E 145 B3
Löbau D 84 A2
Löbejün D 83 A3
Löberöd S 61 D3
Lobez PL 75 A4
Löbnitz D 66 B1
Lobón E 155 C4
Loburg D 73 B5
Łobżenica PL 76 A2
Locana I 119 B4
Locarno CH 120 A1
Loccum D 72 B2
Loče SLO 123 A4
Lochailort GB 34 B2
Lochaline GB 34 B2
Lochans GB 36 B1
Locharbriggs GB . . .36 A3
Lochau A 107 B4
Loch Baghasdail
GB 31 B1
Lochcarron GB 31 B3
Lochearnhead GB . .34 B3
Lochem NL 71 B3
Loches F 102 B2
Lochgelly GB 35 B4
Lochgilphead GB . .34 B2
Lochgoilhead GB . .34 B3
Lochinver GB 32 C1
Loch nam Madadh
GB 31 B1
Lochranza GB 34 C2
Ločika SRB 127 C3
Lockenhaus A 111 B3
Lockerbie GB 36 A3
Löcknitz D. 74 A3
Locmaria F 100 B2
Locmariaquer F . . .100 B2
Locminé F. 100 B3
Locorotondo I 173 B3
Locquirec F 100 A2
Locri I 175 C2
Locronan F 100 A1
Loctudy F 100 B1
Lodares de Osma
E 151 A4
Lodé I 178 B3
Lodève F 130 B2
Lodi I 120 B2
Løding N 194 C6
Lødingen N 194 B6
Lodosa E 144 B1
Lödöse S 54 B3
Łódź PL 86 A3
Loeches E 151 B4
Løfallstrand N 46 B3
Lofer A 109 B3
Lofsdalen S 199 C10
Loftahammar S 62 A4
Lofthus N. 46 B3
Loftus GB 37 B6
Loga N 52 B3
Logatec SLO 123 B3
Lograto I 120 B3
Logroño E 143 B4
Logrosán E 156 A2
Løgstør DK 58 B2
Løgumgårde DK . . .64 C1
Løgumkloster DK . .64 C1
Lohals DK 65 A3
Lohiniva FIN 197 B8
Lohja FIN 8 B4
Löhlbach D 81 A4
Lohmen
Mecklenburg-
Vorpommern D . .65 C5
Sachsen D. 84 B2
Löhnberg D 81 B4
Lohne D 71 B5
Löhne D 72 B1
Lohr D 94 B1
Lohra D 81 B4
Lohsa D 84 A2
Loiano I 135 A4
Loimaa FIN 8 B3
Lóiri I 178 B3
Loivos I 148 A2
Loivos do Monte
P 148 A2
Loja E 163 A3
Lojanice SRB 127 C1
Lojsta S 57 C4
Løjt Kirkeby DK 64 A2
Lok SK 112 A2
Lokca SK 99 B3
Løken N 54 A2
Lokeren B 79 A4
Loket CZ 83 B4
Lokka FIN 197 B10
Løkken
DK 58 A2
N 198 B6
Loknya RUS 9 D7
Lökosháza H 113 C5
Lokve SRB 126 B3
Lollar D 81 B4
L'Olleria E 159 C3
Lölling-Graben A . .110 C1
Lom
BG 17 D5
N 198 D5
SK 99 C3
Lombez F 146 A1
Lomello I 120 B1
Łomianki PL. 77 B5
Lomma S 61 D2
Lommaryd S 62 A2
Lommatzsch D 83 A5
Lommel B 79 A4
Lommersum D 80 B2
Lomnice CZ. 97 B4
Lomnice nad Lužnicí
CZ. 96 B2
Lomnice-nad Popelkou
CZ. 84 B3

Lompolo FIN 196 A7
Łomza PL.........12 B5
Lönashult S......63 B2
Lønborg DK.......59 C1
Londerzeel B......79 A4
Londinières F.....89 A5
London GB.......44 B3
Lonevåg N........46 B2
Longa GR.......184 C2
Longare I........121 B4
Longares E.......152 A2
Longarone I......122 A1
Longastrino I.....135 A5
Long Bennington
GB.............40 C3
Longbenton GB....37 A5
Longchamp-sur-Aujon
F..............105 A3
Longchaumois F..118 A2
Long Eaton GB....40 C2
Longeau F.......105 B4
Longecourt-en-Plaine
F..............105 B4
Longeville-les-St Avold
F...............92 B2
Longeville-sur-Mer
F..............114 B2
Longford IRL......28 A4
Longframlington
GB..............37 A5
Longhope GB.....33 C3
Longhorsley GB...37 A5
Longhoughton GB .37 A5
Longi I..........177 A3
Long Melford GB...45 A4
Longny-au-Perche
F...............89 B4
Longobucco I....174 B2
Long Preston GB ..40 A1
Longré F........115 B3
Longridge GB.....38 A4
Longroiva P......149 B2
Long Sutton GB ...41 C4
Longtown
Cumbria GB......36 A4
Herefordshire GB. 39 C4
Longueau F.......90 B2
Longué-Jumelles
F..............102 B1
Longuyon F.......92 B1
Longvic F........105 B4
Longvilly B.......92 A1
Longwy F.........92 B1
Lonigo I..........121 B4
Löningen D.......71 B4
Lonja HR........124 B2
Lönneberga S.....62 A3
Lönsboda S......63 B2
Lønset N........198 C6
Lons-le-Saunier F 105 C4
Lønstrup DK.......58 A2
Looe GB..........42 B2
Loone-Plage F.....78 A2
Loon op Zand NL...79 A5
Loosdorf A.......110 A2
Lo Pagán E......165 B4
Lopar HR........123 C3
Lopare BIH.......125 C4
Lopera E........157 C3
Lopigna F.......180 A1
Loppersum NL.....71 A3
Łopuszna PL.......99 B4
Łopuszno PL......87 B4
Lor F............91 B4
Lora N..........198 C5
Lora de Estepa E..162 A3
Lora del Río E....162 A2
Loranca del Campo
E..............151 B5
Lorbé...........140 A2
Lörby S..........63 B2
Lorca E.........164 B3
Lorch D..........93 A3
Lørenfallet N.....48 B3
Lørenskog N......48 C2
Loreo I..........122 B1
Loreto I.........136 B2
Lorgues F.......132 B2
Lorica I........174 B2
Lorient F.......100 B2
Lorignac F......114 C3
Lörinci H.......112 B3
Loriol-sur-Drôme
F..............117 C4
Lormes F........104 B2
Loro Ciuffenna I..135 B4
Lorqui E........165 A3
Lörrach D.......106 B2
Lorrez-le-Bocage
F..............103 A4
Lorris F.........103 B4
Lorup D..........71 B4
Loś PL...........77 C5
Los S..........199 D12
Losacino E......149 A3
Los Alcázares E..165 B4
Los Arcos E......144 B1
Losar de la Vera E 150 B2
Los Barios de Luna
E..............141 B5
Los Barrios E....162 B2
Los Caños de Meca
E..............162 B1
Los Cerricos E....164 B2
Los Corrales E....162 A3
Los Corrales de Buelna
E..............142 A2
Los Dolores E....165 B3
Losenstein A.....110 B1
Los Gallardos E...164 B3
Losheim
Nordrhein-Westfalen
D...............80 B2
Saarland D.......92 B2
Los Hinojosos E..158 B1
Los Isidros E.....159 B2
Los Molinos E....151 B3
Los Morales E....162 A2
Los Navalmorales
E..............156 A3
Los Navalucillos
E..............156 A3
Losne F.........105 B4
Los Nietos E.....165 B4
Løsning DK.......59 C2
Los Palacios y
Villafranca E....162 A2
Los Pozuelos de
Calatrava E.....157 B3
Los Rábanos E...143 C4
Los Santos E.....149 B4
Los Santos de la
Humosa E.......151 B4
Los Santos de
Maimona E.....155 C4
Lossburg D.......93 C4
Losse F.........128 B2
Losser NL........71 B4
Lossiemouth GB..32 D3
Lössnitz D........83 B4
Loštice CZ........97 B4
Los Tijos E.......142 A2
Lostwithiel GB....42 B2
Los Villares E....163 A4
Los Yébenes E...157 A4
Løten N..........48 B3
Lotorp S..........56 B1
Lottefors S........50 A3
Löttorp S.........62 A5
Lotyń PL..........68 B1
Lotzorai I........179 C3
Louargat F.......100 A2
Loudéac F.......101 A3
Loudun F........102 B2
Loué F..........102 B1
Loughborough GB .40 C2
Loughbrickland GB 27 B4
Loughrea IRL......28 A3
Louhans F.......105 C4
Louisburgh IRL....28 A2
Loukhi RUS.......3 C13
Loulay F.........114 B3
Loulé P.........160 B1
Louny CZ.........84 B1
Lourdes F.......145 A3
Lourenzá E......141 A3
Loures P........154 C1
Loures-Barousse
F..............145 A4
Louriçal P.......154 A2
Lourinhã P.......154 B1
Lourmarin F.....131 B4
Loury F.........103 B4
Lousa
Bragança P......149 A2
Castelo Branco P 155 B3
Lousã P.........148 B1
Lousa P.........154 C1
Lousada
E..............140 B3
P..............148 A1
Louth GB.........41 B3
Loutra Edipsou
GR.............183 E5
Loutraki GR......184 B3
Loutropoli Thermis
GR.............186 C1
Louverné F......102 A1
Louvie-Juzon F...145 A3
Louviers F........89 A5
Louvigné-du-Désert
F...............88 B2
Louvois F.........91 B4
Lova I...........121 B5
Lovasberény H...112 B2
Lövåsen S........49 C5
Lovászpatona H..111 B4
Lövberga S......200 C1
Lovech BG........17 D6
Lövenich D.......80 A2
Lóvere I.........120 B3
Lövestad S........61 D3
Loviisa FIN.........8 B5
Lovikka S........196 B5
Lovinobaňa SK....99 C3
Loviste HR.......138 B3
Lovke HR........123 B3
Lovnäs S.........49 A5
Lövö H..........111 B3
Lovosice CZ......84 B2
Lovozero RUS.....3 C14
Lovran HR.......123 B3
Lovreć HR.......138 B2
Lovrenc na Pohorju
SLO............110 C2
Lovrin RO.......126 B2
Lövstabruk S.....51 B4
Löwenberg D.....74 B2
Löwenstein D.....94 B1
Lowestoft GB.....41 C5
Lowick GB........37 A5
Łowicz PL........77 B4
Loxstedt D........72 A1
Loyew BY.........13 C9
Lož SLO.........123 B3
Loza CZ..........96 B1
Łozina PL.........85 A5
Loznica SRB......127 C1
Lozničko Polje
SRB............127 C1
Lozorno SK......111 A4
Lozovik SRB......127 C3
Lozoya E........151 B4
Lozoyuela E......151 B4
Lozzo di Cadore I .109 C3
Luanco E........141 A5
Luarca E........141 A4
Lubaczów PL......13 C5
Lubań PL.........84 A3
Lubanie PL.......76 B3
Lubanów PL......86 A3
Lubars D.........73 B5
Lubasz PL........75 B5
Lubawa PL........69 B4
Lubawka PL......85 B4
Lübbecke D.......72 B1
Lübben D.........74 C2
Lübbenau D.......84 A1
Lubczyna PL......74 A3
Lübeck D.........65 C3
Lubenec CZ........83 B5
Lubersac F.......115 C5
Lübesse D........73 A4
Lubia E..........152 A1
Lubian E.........141 B4
Lubiatowo PL.....75 A4
Lubichowo PL.....69 B3
Lubicz Dolny PL ...76 A3
Lubień PL........99 B3
Lubienia PL.......87 A5
Lubień Kujawski
PL..............77 B4
Lubieszewo PL....75 A4
Lubin
Dolnośląskie PL...85 A4
Zachodnio-Pomorskie
PL..............67 C3
Lublin PL.........12 C5
Lubliniec PL......86 B2
Lubmin D.........66 B2
Lubniewice PL....75 B4
Lubochnia PL.....87 A4
Lubomierz
Dolnośląskie PL...84 A3
Małopolskie PL...99 B4
Lubomino PL......69 A5
Luboń PL.........76 B1
L'ubotín SK.......99 B4
Lubowidz PL......77 A4
Łubowo
Wielkopolskie PL..76 B2
Zachodnio-Pomorskie
PL..............68 B1
Lubraniec PL......76 B3
Lubrin E.........164 B2
Lubrza PL........85 B5
Lubsko PL........84 A2
Lübtheen D.......73 A4
Lubuczewo PL.....68 A2
Luby CZ..........83 B4
Lübz D...........73 A5
Luc F...........117 C3
Lucainena de las
Torres E........164 B2
Lucan IRL........30 A2
Lučani SRB......127 D2
Lúcar E..........164 B2
Luçay-le-Mâle F...103 B3
Lucca I..........134 B3
Lucciana F.......180 A2
Lucé F...........90 C1
Luče SLO........123 A3
Lucena
Córdoba E......163 A3
Huelva E........161 B3
Lucenay-les-Aix F 104 C2
Lucenay-l'Evéque
F..............104 B3
Luc-en-Diois F...118 C2
Lučenec SK.......99 C3
Luceni E.........144 C2
Lucens CH.......106 C1
Lucera I.........171 B3
Luceram F.......133 B3
Lüchow D........73 B4
Luciana E.......157 B3
Lucignano I......135 B4
Lucija SLO.......122 B2
Lucka D..........83 A4
Luckau D.........84 A1
Luckenwalde D....74 B2
Lückstedt D.......73 B4
Luco dei Marsi I..169 B3
Luçon F.........114 B2
Luc-sur-Mer F.....89 A3
Ludanice SK......98 C2
Ludbreg HR......124 A2
Lüdenscheid D....81 A3
Lüderitz D........73 B4
Lüdersdorf D......65 C3
Ludgershall GB....44 B2
Ludgo S..........56 B3
Lüdinghausen D...80 A3
Ludlow GB........39 B4
Ludomy PL.......75 B5
Ludvika S.........50 B2
Ludweiler Warndt
D...............92 B2
Ludwigsburg D....94 C1
Ludwigsfelde D....74 B2
Ludwigshafen D...93 B4
Ludwigslust D.....73 A4
Ludwigsstadt D....82 B3
Ludza LV..........8 D5
Luesia E.........144 B2
Luftkurort Arendsee
D...............73 B4
Lug
BIH............139 C4
HR.............125 B4
Luga RUS..........9 C6
Lugagnano Val d'Arda
I...............120 C2
Lugano CH......120 A1
Lugau D..........83 B4
Lugnas S.........55 B4
Lúgnola I........168 A2
Lugny F.........105 C3
Lugo
E..............140 A3
I...............135 A4
Lugoj RO..........16 C4
Lugones E.......141 A5
Lugros E........163 A4
Luhačovice CZ....98 B1
Luhe D...........95 B4
Luino I..........120 B1
Luintra E........140 B3
Lújar E..........163 B4
Luka nad Jihlavou
CZ..............97 B3
Lukavac BIH......125 C4
Lukavika BIH.....125 C4
Lukovë AL.......182 D1
Lukovica SLO.....123 A3
Lukovit BG........17 D6
Lukovo HR.......123 C3
Lukovo Šugorje
HR.............137 A4
Łuków PL.........12 C5
Łukowice Brzeskie
PL..............85 B5
Luksefjell N.......53 A5
Łukta PL..........69 B5
Lula I............178 B3
Luleå S..........196 D5
Lüleburgaz TR....186 A2
Lumbarda HR.....138 C3
Lumbier E........144 B2
Lumbrales E......149 B3
Lumbreras E......143 B4
Lumbres F........78 B2
Lummelunda S....57 C4
Lummen B........79 B5
Lumparland FIN ...51 B7
Lumpiaque E.....152 A2
Lumsås DK........61 D1
Lumsden GB......33 D4
Lumsheden S.....50 B3
Lun HR..........123 C3
Luna E..........144 B3
Lunamatrona I....179 C2
Lunano I.........136 B1
Lunas F.........130 B2
Lund
N..............199 A8
Skåne S.........61 D3
Västra Götaland
S...............54 A3
Lundamo N......199 B7
Lunde
DK..............59 C1
Sogn og Fjordane
N...............46 A3
Sogn og Fjordane
N...............46 A3
Telemark N......53 A5
S..............200 D3
Lundebyvollen N...49 B4
Lunden D.........64 B2
Lunderseter N.....49 B4
Lunderskov DK....59 C2
Lundsberg S......55 A5
Lüneburg D.......72 A3
Lunel F..........131 B3
Lünen D..........81 A3
Lunéville F.......92 C2
Lungern CH......106 C3
Lungro I.........174 B2
Luninyets BY......13 B7
Lünne D..........71 B4
Lunner N.........48 B2
Lunteren NL.......70 B2
Lunz am See A....110 B2
Luogosanto I.....178 A3
Łupawa PL........68 A2
Lupión E........157 B4
Lupoglav HR.....123 B3
Luppa D..........83 A4
Luque E.........163 A3
Lurago d'Erba I...120 B2
Lúras I..........178 B3
Lurcy-Lévis F....104 C1
Lure F...........105 B5
Lurgan GB........27 B4
Luri F...........180 A2
Lury-sur-Arnon F .103 B4
Lušci Palanka BIH 124 C2
Lusévera I.......122 A2
Lushnjë AL.......182 C1
Lusignan F.......115 B4
Lusigny-sur-Barse
F..............104 A3
Lusnić BIH.......138 B2
Luso P..........148 B1
Lusówko PL.......75 B5
Luspebryggan S..196 B2
Luss GB..........34 B3
Lussac F........128 B2
Lussac-les-Châteaux
F..............115 B4
Lussac-les-Eglises
F..............115 B5
Lussan F........131 A3
Lüssow D.........65 C5
Lustenau A.......107 B4
Luštěnice CZ......84 B2
Luster N..........47 A4
Lutago I.........108 C2
Lutherstadt Wittenberg
D...............83 A4
Lütjenburg D......65 B3
Lutnes N.........49 A4
Lutocin PL........77 B4
Lutomiersk PL.....86 A3
Luton GB.........44 B3
Lutry CH........106 C1
Lutsk UA.........13 C6
Lutter am Barenberge
D...............72 C3
Lutterworth GB....40 C2
Lututów PL.......86 A2
Lützen D.........83 A4
Lutzow D.........73 A4
Luusua FIN......197 C10
Luvos S..........196 C1
Luxembourg L.....92 B2
Luxeuil-les-Bains
F..............105 B5
Luxey F.........128 B2
Luz
Évora P........155 C3
Faro P.........160 B1
Faro P.........160 B2
Luzarches F.......90 B2
Luže CZ..........97 B4
Luzech F........129 B4
Luzern CH.......106 B3
Luzino PL.........68 A3
Luz-St Sauveur F .145 B3
Luzy F..........104 C2
Luzzi I..........174 B2
L'viv UA..........13 D6
Lwówek PL........75 B5
Lwówek Śląski PL..84 A3
Lyakhavichy BY....13 B7
Lybster GB........32 C3
Lychen D.........74 A2
Lychkova RUS......9 D8
Lyckeby S.........63 B3
Lycksele S.......200 B4
Lydd GB..........45 C4
Lydford GB.......42 B2
Lydney GB........39 C4
Lyepyel BY........13 A8
Lygna N..........48 B2
Lykkja N..........47 B5
Lykling N.........52 A1
Lyme Regis GB....43 B4
Lymington GB.....44 C2
Lympne GB.......45 B5
Lyndhurst GB.....44 C2
Lyneham GB......43 A5
Lyness GB........33 C3
Lyngdal
Buskerud N......47 C6
Vest-Agder N.....52 B3
Lyngør N.........53 B5
Lyngsa DK........58 A3
Lyngseidet N.....192 C4
Lyngsnes N......199 A8
Lynmouth GB.....42 A3
Lynton GB........42 A3
Lyntupy BY........13 A7
Lyon F..........117 B4
Lyons-la-Forêt F...90 B1
Lyozna BY........13 A9
Lyrestad S........55 B5
Lysánad Labem
CZ..............84 B2
Lysápod Makytou
SK..............98 B2
Lysebotn N.......52 A2
Lysekil S.........54 B2
Lysice CZ.........97 B4
Lysomice PL......76 A3
Lysøysund N......198 B6
Lyss CH.........106 B2
Lystrup DK........59 B3
Lysvik S..........49 B5
Łyszkowice PL....77 C4
Lytham St Anne's
GB..............38 A3
Lyuban RUS........9 C7
Lyubertsy RUS....9 E10
Lyubimets BG.....183 B8
Lyuboml' UA......13 C6
Lyubytino RUS.....9 C8

M

Maaninkavaara
FIN............197 C11
Maarheeze NL.....80 A1
Maaseik B........80 A1
Maastricht NL.....80 B1
Mablethorpe GB...41 B4
Mably F.........117 A4
Macael E........164 B2
Maçanet de Cabrenys
E..............146 B3
Mação P.........154 B2
Macau F.........128 A2
Maccagno-Agra I..120 A1
Maccarese I......168 B2
Macchiagódena I..170 B2
Macclesfield GB...40 B1
Macduff GB.......33 D4
Maceda E........140 B3
Macedo de Cavaleiros
P..............149 A3
Maceira
Guarda P.......148 B2
Leiria P........154 B2
Macelj HR.......124 A1
Macerata I.......136 B2
Macerata Féltria I .136 B1
Machault F.......91 B4
Machecoul F.....114 B2
Mchowo PL.......77 A5
Machrihanish GB..34 C2
Machynlleth GB....39 B3
Macieira P.......148 A1
Maciejowice PL....87 A5
Macinaggio F.....180 A2
Mackenrode D.....82 A2
Mačkovci SLO....111 C3
Macomer I.......178 B2
Macon B..........91 A4
Mâcon F.........117 A4
Macotera E.......150 B2
Macroom IRL.......29 C3
Macugnaga I......119 B4
Madan BG........183 B6
Madängsholm S....55 B4
Madaras H.......126 A1
Maddaloni I......170 B2
Made NL..........79 A4
Madeley GB.......38 B4
Maderuelo E......151 A4
Madetkoski FIN...197 B9
Madley GB........39 B4
Madocsa H.......112 C2
Madona LV..........8 D5
Madonna di Campiglio
I...............121 A3
Madrid E........151 B4
Madridejos E.....157 A4
Madrigal de las Altas
Torres E........150 A2
Madrigal de la Vera
E..............150 B2
Madrigalejo E....156 A2
Madrigalejo de Monte
E..............143 B3
Madriguera E.....151 A4
Madrigueras E....158 B2
Madroñera E.....156 A2
Maël-Carhaix F...100 A2
Maella E.........153 A4
Maello E.........150 B3
Maesteg GB.......39 C3
Mafra P.........154 C1
Magacela E.......156 B2
Magallon E.......144 C2
Magaluf E........166 B2
Magán E.........151 C4
Magaña E........144 C1
Magasa I.........121 B3
Magaz E.........142 C2
Magdeburg D......73 B4
Magenta I........120 B1
Magescq F.......128 C1
Maghera GB.......27 B4
Magherafelt GB....27 B4
Maghull GB.......38 A4
Magilligan GB.....27 A4
Magione I........135 B5
Magioto P........154 C1
Maglaj BIH.......125 C4
Maglehem S.......63 C2
Magliano de'Marsi
I...............169 A3
Magliano in Toscana
I...............168 A1
Magliano Sabina I 168 A2
Maglić SRB.......126 B1
Máglie I.........173 B4
Maglód H........112 B3
Magnac-Bourg F ..115 C5
Magnac-Laval F...115 B5
Magnieres F.......92 C2
Magnor N.........49 C4
Magnuszew PL.....87 A5
Magny-Cours F ...104 C2
Magny-en-Vexin F..90 B1
Mágocs H........125 A4
Maguilla E.......156 B2
Maguiresbridge GB 27 B3
Magyarbóly H....125 B4
Magyarkeszi H....112 C2
Magyarszék H....125 A4
Mahide E........141 C4
Mahilyow BY......13 B9
Mahmudiye TR....187 C5
Mahora E........158 B2
Mahovo HR.......124 B2
Mähring D........95 B4
Maia
E..............144 A2
P..............148 A1
Maiaelrayo E.....151 A4
Maials E........153 A4
Maîche F........106 B1
Máida I.........175 C2
Maiden Bradley GB 43 A4
Maidenhead GB....44 B3
Maiden Newton GB 43 B4
Maidstone GB.....45 B4
Maienfeld CH.....107 B4
Maignelay Montigny
F...............90 B2
Maijanen FIN.....197 B8
Maillezais F......114 B3
Mailly-le-Camp F ..91 C4
Mailly-le-Château
F..............104 B2
Mainar E........152 A2
Mainbernheim D ...94 B2
Mainburg D.......95 C3
Mainhardt D.......94 B1
Maintal D.........81 B4
Maintenon F......90 C1
Mainvilliers F.....90 C1
Mainz D..........93 A4
Maiorca P.......148 B1
Mairena de Aljarafe
E..............162 A1
Mairena del Alcor
E..............162 A2
Maisach D.......108 A2
Maishofen A.....109 B3
Maison-Rouge F ...90 C3
Maissau A........97 C3
Maisse F..........90 C2
Maizières-lès-Vic F 92 C2
Maja HR.........124 B2
Majadahonda E...151 B4
Majadas E.......150 C2
Majavatn N......195 E4
Majs H..........125 A4
Majšperk SLO....123 A4
Makarska HR.....138 B3
Makkum NL.......70 A2
Maklár H........113 B4
Makó H..........126 A2
Makoszyce PL.....85 B5
Makov SK.........98 B2
Mąkowarsko PL....76 A2
Maków Mazowiecki
PL..............77 B6
Maków Podhalański
PL..............99 B3
Makrakomi GR....182 E4
Maksniemi FIN....196 D7
Malá S..........195 E9
Mala Bosna SRB..126 A1
Malacky SK.......97 C5
Maladzyechna BY ..13 A7
Málaga E........163 B3
Malagón E.......157 A4
Malaguilla E.....151 B4
Malahide IRL......30 A2
Mala Kladuša BIH 124 B1
Mala Krsna SRB ..127 C3
Malalbergo I.....121 C4
Malá Lehota SK....98 C2
Malanów PL.......76 C3
Mala Pijace SRB ..126 A1
Mala Subotica HR 124 A2
Malaucène F.....131 A4
Malaunay F.......89 A5
Malaya Vishera RUS 9 C8
Malborghetto I....109 C4
Malbork PL........69 A4
Malborn D.........92 B2
Malbuisson F.....105 C5
Malcésine I......121 B3
Malchin D.........74 A1
Malching D........96 C1
Malchow D........73 A5
Malcocinado E....156 B2
Malczyce PL......85 A4
Maldegem B......79 A3
Maldon GB........45 B4
Małdyty PL........69 B4
Malè I..........121 A3
Malemort F......129 A4
Malente D........65 B3
Målerås S.........62 B3
Males GR........185 D6
Malesherbes F.....90 C2
Malesina GR.....183 E5
Malestroit F......101 B3
Maletto I........177 B3
Malexander S.....56 B1
Malgrat de Mar E ..147 C3
Malhadas P......149 A3
Malia
CY.............181 B1
GR.............185 D6
Malicorne-sur-Sarthe
F..............102 B1
Malijai F........132 A2
Malildjoš SRB....126 B1
Målilla S..........62 A3
Mali Lošinj HR....137 A3
Malin IRL.........27 A3
Málinec SK.......99 C3
Målingsbo S.......50 C2
Maliniec PL.......76 B3
Malinska HR.....123 B3
Maliq AL........182 C2
Maljevac HR.....123 B4
Malkara TR......186 B1
Małki PL..........69 B4
Malko Tarnovo BG .17 D7
Mallaig GB........34 A2
Mallaranny IRL....28 A2
Mallemort F......131 B4
Mallén E.........144 C2
Malléon F........146 A2
Mallersdorf-Pfaffenberg
D...............95 C4
Málles Venosta I ..108 C1
Malling DK........59 B3
Mallnitz A.......109 C4
Mallow IRL........29 B3
Mallwyd GB.......38 B3
Malm N..........199 A8
Malmbäck S.......62 A2
Malmberget S....196 B3
Malmby S.........56 A3
Malmédy B........80 B2
Malmesbury GB...43 A4
Malmköping S.....56 A2
Malmö S..........61 D3
Malmon S.........54 B2
Malmslätt S.......56 B1
Malnate I........120 B1
Malo I...........121 B4
Małogoszcz PL.....87 B4
Maloja CH.......120 A2
Małomice PL.......84 A3
Måløy N.........198 D2
Malpartida E.....155 B4
Malpartida de la Serena
E..............156 B2
Malpartida de Plasencia
E..............150 C1
Malpas
E..............145 B4
GB..............38 A4
Malpica P.......155 B3
Malpica de Bergantiños
E..............140 A2
Malpica de Tajo E .150 C3
Malsch D.........93 C4
Malšice CZ........96 B2
Malta A..........109 C4
Maltat F.........104 C2
Maltby GB........40 B2
Malung S.........49 B5
Malungsfors S.....49 B5
Maluszów PL......75 B4
Maluszyn PL......87 B3
Malva E.........142 C1
Malvaglia CH.....120 A1
Malveira P.......154 C1
Malvik N.........199 B7
Malyn UA..........13 C8
Mamarrosa P.....148 B1
Mamer L..........92 B2
Mamers F.........89 B4
Mamirolle F......105 B5
Mammendorf D....108 A2
Mámmola I.......175 C2
Mamoiada I......178 B3
Mamonovo RUS....69 A4
Mamuras AL......182 B1
Maňa SK.........112 A2
Manacor E.......167 B3
Manavgat TR.....189 C6
Mancera de Abajo
E..............150 B2
Mancha Real E ...163 A4
Manchester GB....40 B1
Manching D.......95 C3
Manchita E.......156 B1
Manciano I.......168 A1
Manciet F........128 C3
Mandal N.........52 B3
Mandanici I......177 A4
Mándas I........179 C3
Mandatoriccio I...174 B2
Mandayona E 151 B5
Mandelieu-la-Napoule
F..............132 B2
Mandello del Lário
I...............120 B2
Mandelsloh D.....72 B2
Manderfeld B......80 B2
Manderscheid D...80 B2
Mandino Selo BIH 138 B3
Mandoudi GR.....183 E5
Mandra GR.......185 A4
Mandraki GR.....188 C2
Mandúria I.......173 B3
Mane
Alpes-de-Haute-
Provence F.....132 B1
Haute-Garonne F 145 A4
Manérbio I.......120 B3
Mañeru E........144 B2
Manetin CZ........96 B1
Manfredónia I....171 B3

Mangalia RO 17 D8
Manganeses de la Lampreana E . . 149 A4
Manganeses de la Polvorosa E . . 141 B5
Mangen N 48 C3
Manger N 46 B2
Mangiennes F . . .92 B1
Mangotsfield GB . .43 A4
Manguarde P . . . 148 B2
Maniago I 122 A1
Manilva E 162 B2
Manisa TR 186 D2
Manises E 159 B3
Mank A 110 A2
Månkarbo S 51 B4
Manlleu E 147 C3
Manna DK 58 A2
Männedorf CH . . 107 B3
Mannersdorf am Leithagebirge A . 111 B3
Mannheim D 93 B4
Manningtree GB . .45 B5
Manoppello I . . . 169 A4
Manorbier GB 39 C2
Manorhamilton IRL 26 B2
Manosque F 132 B1
Manowo PL 67 B5
Manresa E 147 C2
Månsarp S 62 A2
Månsåsen S 199 B11
Manschnow D 74 B3
Mansfeld D 82 A3
Mansfield GB 40 B2
Mansilla de Burgos E . . 143 B3
Mansilla de las Mulas E . . 142 B1
Manskog S 55 A3
Mansle F 115 C4
Manso F 180 A1
Manteigas P 148 B2
Mantel D 95 B4
Mantes-la-Jolie F . .90 C1
Mantes-la-Ville F . .90 C1
Manthelan F 102 B2
Mantorp S 56 B1
Mántova I 121 B3
Mänttä FIN 8 A4
Mäntyjärvi FIN . . 197 C10
Manuel E 159 B3
Manyas TR 186 B2
Manzanal de Arriba E . . 141 B4
Manzanares E . . . 157 A4
Manzanares el Real E . . 151 B4
Manzaneda
  León E 141 B4
  Orense E 141 B3
Manzanedo E . . . 143 B3
Manzaneque E . . . 157 A4
Manzanera E . . . 153 B3
Manzanilla E . . . 161 B3
Manzat F 116 B2
Manziana I 168 A2
Manziat F 117 A4
Maó E 167 B4
Maoča BIH 125 C4
Maqueda E 150 B3
Mara E 152 A2
Maramaraereğlisi TR . . 186 B2
Maraña E 142 A1
Maranchón E . . . 152 A1
Maranello I 135 A3
Marano I 170 C2
Marano Lagunare I . . 122 B2
Marans F 114 B2
Maratea I 174 B1
Marateca P 154 C2
Marathokambos GR . . 188 B1
Marathonas GR . . 185 A4
Marathóvouno CY . . 181 A2
Marazion GB 42 B1
Marbach
  Baden-Württemberg D . . .94 C1
  Hessen D 82 B1
  F 92 C2
Marbäck S 60 B3
Mårbacka S 55 A4
Marbella E 162 B3
Marboz F 118 A2
Marburg D 81 B4
Marcali H 111 C4
Marčana HR 122 C2
Marcaria I 121 B3
Marcelová SK . . . 112 B2
Marcenat F 116 B2
March GB 41 C4
Marchamalo E . . . 151 B4
Marchaux F 105 B5
Marche-en-Famenne B . . .79 B5
Marchegg A 111 A3
Marchena E 162 A2
Marchenoir F . . . 103 B3
Marcheprime F . . 128 B2
Marciac F 128 C3
Marciana Marina I 134 C2
Marcianise I 170 B2
Marcigny F 117 A4
Marcilla E 144 B2
Marcillac-la-Croisille F . . 116 B2
Marcillac-Vallon F 130 A1
Marcillat-en-Combraille F . . 116 A2
Marcille-sur-Seine F . . .91 C3
Marcilloles F 118 B2
Marcilly-le-Hayer F .91 C3

Marcinkowice PL . .75 A5
Marciszów PL 85 B4
Marck F 78 B1
Marckolsheim F . . 106 A2
Marco de Canevezes P . . 148 A1
Mårdsele S 200 B5
Mårdsjö S 200 C1
Mareham le Fen GB . . .41 B3
Marek S 62 A3
Marennes F 114 C2
Maresquel F 78 B1
Mareuil F 115 C4
Mareuil-en-Brie F . .91 C3
Mareuil-sur-Arnon F . . 103 C4
Mareuil-sur-Lay F . 114 B2
Mareuil-sur-Ourcq F . . .90 B3
Margam GB 39 C3
Margariti GR 182 D2
Margate GB 45 B5
Margaux F 128 A2
Margerie-Hancourt F . . .91 C4
Margès F 117 B5
Margherita di Savóia I . . 171 B4
Margita SRB 126 B3
Margone I 119 B4
Margonin PL 76 B2
Marguerittes F . . . 131 B3
Margut F 91 B5
Maria E 164 B2
Maria DK 58 B2
Mariana E 152 B1
Maria Neustift A . . 110 B1
Mariannelund S . . .62 A3
Marianópoli I 176 B2
Mariánské Lázně CZ . . .95 B4
Mariapfarr A 109 B4
Maria Saal A 110 C1
Mariazell A 110 B2
Maribo DK 65 B4
Maribor SLO 110 C2
Marieberg S 56 A1
Mariefred S 56 A3
Mariehamn FIN . . .51 B6
Marieholm S 61 D3
Mariembourg B . . .91 A4
Marienbaum D 80 A2
Marienberg D 83 B5
Marienheide D 81 A3
Mariental D 73 B3
Mariestad S 55 B4
Marieux F 90 A2
Marigliano I 170 C2
Marignane F 131 B4
Marigny
  Jura F 105 C4
  Manche F 88 A2
Marigny-le-Châtel F . . .91 C3
Marija Bistrica HR 124 A2
Marijampolė LT . . .13 A5
Marín E 140 B2
Marina HR 138 B2
Marina del Cantone I . . 170 C2
Marina di Acquappesa I . . 174 B1
Marina di Alberese I . . 168 A1
Marina di Amendolara I . . 174 B2
Marina di Árbus I . 179 C2
Marina di Campo I 134 C3
Marina di Carrara I . . 134 A3
Marina di Castagneto-Donorático I . . 134 B3
Marina di Cécina I 134 B3
Marina di Gáiro I . 179 C3
Marina di Ginosa I 173 B2
Marina di Gioiosa Iónica I . . 175 C2
Marina di Grosseto I . . 135 C3
Marina di Léuca I . 173 C4
Marina di Massa I . 134 A3
Marina di Nováglie I . . 173 C4
Marina di Pisa I . . 134 B3
Marina di Ragusa I . . 177 C3
Marina di Ravenna I . . 135 A5
Marina di Torre Grande I . . 179 C2
Marinaleda E 162 A3
Marina Romea I . . 135 A5
Marine de Sisco F 180 A2
Marinella I 176 B1
Marinella di Sarzana I . . 134 A3
Marineo I 176 B2
Marines F 90 B1
Maringues F 116 B3
Marinha das Ondas P . . 148 B1
Marinha Grande P 154 B2
Marinhas P 148 A1
Marino I 168 B2
Marjaliza E 157 A4
Markabygd N 199 B8
Markaryd S 61 C3
Markdorf D 107 B4
Markelo NL 71 B3
Market Deeping GB 41 C3
Market Drayton GB 38 B4
Market Harborough GB . . .40 C3
Markethill GB 27 B4
Market Rasen GB . .40 B3
Market Warsop GB .40 B2
Market Weighton GB . . .40 B3
Markgröningen D . .93 C5

Markhausen D 71 B4
Marki PL 77 B6
Markina-Xemein E 143 A4
Markinch GB 35 B4
Märkische Buchholz D . . .74 B2
Markitta S 196 B4
Markkleeberg D . . .83 A4
Marklohe D 72 B2
Marknesse NL 70 B2
Markneukirchen D .83 B4
Markopoulo GR . . 185 B4
Markovac
  Srbija SRB . . . 127 C3
  Vojvodina SRB . 126 B3
Markowice PL 86 B2
Markranstädt D . . .83 A4
Marksuhl D 82 B2
Markt Allhau A . . . 111 B3
Markt Bibart D 94 B2
Marktbreit D 94 B2
Markt Erlbach D . . .94 B2
Markt-heidenfeld D 94 B1
Markt Indersdorf D 95 C3
Marktl D 95 C4
Marktleuthen D . . .83 B3
Marktoberdorf D . 108 B1
Marktredwitz D . . .95 A4
Markt Rettenbach D . . 108 B1
Markt Schwaben D . . 108 A2
Markt-Übelbach A 110 B2
Markusica HR . . . 125 B4
Markušovce SK . . .99 C4
Marl D 80 A3
Marlborough
  Devon GB 42 B3
  Wiltshire GB 44 B2
Marle F 91 B3
Marlieux F 117 A5
Marlow
  D 66 B1
  GB 44 B3
Marma S 51 B4
Marmagne F 104 C3
Marmande F 128 B3
Marmara TR 186 B2
Marmaris TR 188 C3
Marmelete I 160 B1
Marmolejo E 157 B3
Marmoutier F 93 C3
Marnay F 105 B4
Marne D 64 C2
Marnheim D 93 B4
Marnitz D 73 A4
Maroldsweisach D .82 B2
Marolles-les-Braults F . . .89 B4
Maromme F 89 A5
Marone I 120 B3
Maronia GR 183 C7
Maroslele H 126 A2
Maróstica I 121 B4
Marotta I 136 B2
Marpisa GR 185 B6
Marquion F 78 B3
Marquise F 78 B1
Marradi I 135 A4
Marrasjärvi FIN . . 197 C8
Marraskoski FIN . . 197 C8
Marratxi E 166 B2
Marrúbiu I 179 C2
Marrum NL 70 A2
Marrupe E 150 B3
Marsac F 129 C5
Marsac-en-Livradois F . . 117 B3
Marságlia I 120 C2
Marsala I 176 B1
Marsberg D 81 A4
Marsciano I 135 C5
Marseillan F 130 B2
Marseille = Marseilles F . . 131 B4
Marseille en Beauvaisis F . . .90 B1
Marseilles = Marseille F . . 131 B4
Mársico Nuovo I . . 172 B1
Marske-by-the-Sea GB . . .37 B5
Mars-la-Tours F . . .92 B1
Marsliden S 195 E6
Marson F 91 C4
Märsta S 57 A3
Marstal DK 65 B3
Marstrand S 60 B1
Marta I 168 A1
Martano I 173 B4
Martel F 129 B4
Martelange B 92 B1
Martfeld D 72 B2
Martfű H 113 B4
Martham GB 41 C5
Marthon F 115 C4
Martiago E 149 B3
Martigné-Briand F 102 B1
Martigné-Ferchaud F . . 101 B4
Martigny CH 119 A4
Martigny-les-Bains F . . 105 A4
Martigues F 131 B4
Martim-Longo P . . 160 B2
Martin SK 98 B2
Martina CH 108 C1
Martina Franca I . . 173 B3
Martinamor E . . . 150 B2
Martín de la Jara E . . 162 A3
Martinengo I 120 B2
Martín Muñoz de las Posadas E . . . 150 A3
Martinsberg A 97 C3
Martinšćica HR . . 123 C3
Martinshöhe D 93 B3
Martinsicuro I . . . 136 C2

Martinszell D . . . 107 B5
Mártis I 178 B2
Martofte DK 59 C3
Martonvásár H . . . 112 B2
Martorell E 147 C2
Martos E 163 A4
Martres Tolosane F . . 146 A1
Martti FIN 197 B11
Marugán E 150 B3
Marúggio I 173 B3
Marvão P 155 B3
Marvejols F 130 A2
Marville F 92 B1
Marwald PL 77 A4
Marykirk GB 35 B5
Marypark GB 32 D3
Maryport GB 36 B3
Marytavy GB 42 B2
Marzabotto I 135 A4
Marzahna D 74 C1
Marzahne D 73 B5
Marzamemi I 177 C4
Marzocca I 136 B2
Masa E 143 B3
Mas-Cabardès F . 146 A3
Máscali I 177 B4
Mascaraque E . . . 157 A4
Mascarenhas P . . 149 A2
Mascioni I 169 A3
Mas de Barberáns E . . 153 B4
Mas de las Matas E . . 153 B3
Masegoso E 158 C1
Masegoso de Tajuña E . . 151 B5
Masera I 119 A5
Masevaux F 106 B1
Masfjorden N 46 B2
Masham GB 37 B5
Masi N 192 C7
Maside E 140 B2
Maslacq F 144 A3
Maslinica HR 138 B2
Maşloc RO 126 B3
Maslovare BIH . . . 138 A3
Masone I 133 A4
Massa I 134 A3
Massa Fiscáglia I . 121 C5
Massafra I 173 B3
Massa Lombarda I . . 135 A4
Massa Lubrense I . 170 C2
Massamagrell E . . 159 B3
Massa Marittima I . 135 B3
Massa Martana I . 136 C1
Massanassa E . . . 159 B3
Massarosa I 134 B3
Massat F 146 B2
Massay F 103 B3
Massbach D 82 B2
Masseret F 116 B1
Masseube F 145 A4
Massiac F 116 B3
Massignac F 115 C4
Massing D 95 C4
Massmechelen B . .80 B1
Masterud N 49 B4
Mästocka S 61 C3
Masty BY 13 B6
Masúa I 179 C2
Masueco E 149 A3
Masugnsbyn S . . . 196 B5
Mašun SLO 123 B3
Maszewo
  Lubuskie PL 75 B3
  Zachodnio-Pomorskie PL 75 A4
Mata de Alcántara E . . 155 B4
Matala GR 185 E5
Matalebreras E . . 144 C1
Matallana de Torio E . . 142 B1
Matamala E 151 A5
Mataporquera E . . 142 B2
Matapozuelos E . . 150 A3
Mataró E 147 C3
Matarocco I 176 B1
Matélica I 136 B2
Matera I 172 B2
Mátészalka H 16 B5
Matet E 159 B3
Matfors S 200 D3
Matha F 115 C3
Mathay F 106 B1
Matignon F 101 A3
Matilla de los Caños del Rio E . . . 149 B4
Matlock GB 40 B2
Matosinhos P . . . 148 A1
Matour F 117 A4
Mátraföldréd H . . 113 B3
Mátraterenye H . . 113 A3
Matre
  Hordaland N 46 B2
  Hordaland N 52 A1
Matrei am Brenner A . . 108 B2
Matrei in Osttirol A . . 109 B3
Matrice I 170 B2
Matsdal S 195 E6
Mattarello I 121 A4
Mattersburg A . . . 111 B3
Mattighofen A . . . 109 A4
Mattinata I 171 B4
Mattos P 154 B2
Mattsee A 109 B4
Måttsund S 196 D5
Matulji HR 123 B3
Maubert-Fontaine F . . .91 B4
Maubeuge F 79 B4
Maubourguet F . . 145 A4
Mauchline GB 36 A2
Maud GB 33 D4
Mauer-kirchen A . 109 A4

Mauern D 95 C3
Mauguio F 131 B3
Maulbronn D 93 C4
Maule F 90 C1
Mauléon F 114 B3
Mauléon-Barousse F . . 145 B4
Mauléon-Licharre F . . 144 A3
Maulévrier F 114 A3
Maum IRL 28 A2
Maurach A 108 B2
Maure-de-Bretagne F . . 101 B4
Maureilhan F 130 B2
Mäureni RO 126 B3
Mauriac F 116 B2
Mauron F 101 A3
Maurs F 116 C2
Maury F 146 B3
Maussane-les-Alpilles F . . 131 B3
Mautern A 97 C3
Mauterndorf A . . . 109 B4
Mautern im Steiermark A . . 110 B1
Mauthausen A . . . 110 A1
Mauthen A 109 C3
Mauvezin F 129 C3
Mauzé-sur-le-Mignon F . . 114 B3
Maxent F 101 B3
Maxey-sur-Vaise F .92 C1
Maxial P 154 B1
Maxieira P 154 B2
Maxwellheugh GB .35 C5
Mayalde E 149 A4
Maybole GB 36 A2
Mayen D 80 B3
Mayenne F 88 B3
Mayet F 102 B2
Mayorga E 142 B1
Mayres F 117 C4
Mayrhofen A 108 B2
Mazagón E 161 B3
Mazaleón E 153 A4
Mazamet F 130 B1
Mazan F 131 A4
Mazara del Vallo I . 176 B1
Mazarambroz E . . 157 A3
Mazarete E 152 B1
Mazaricos E 140 B2
Mazarrón E 165 B3
Mažeikiai LT 8 D3
Mazères F 146 A2
Mazères-sur-Salat F . . 145 A4
Mazières-en-Gâtine F . . 115 B3
Mazin HR 138 A1
Mazuelo E 143 B3
Mazyr BY 13 B8
Mazzarino I 177 B3
Mazzarrà Sant'Andrea I . . 177 A4
Mazzo di Valtellina I . . 120 A3
Mdzewo PL 77 B5
Mealabost GB 31 A2
Mealhada P 148 B1
Méan B 79 B5
Meana Sardo I . . . 179 C3
Meaulne F 103 C4
Meaux F 90 C2
Mebonden N 199 B8
Mecerreyes E . . . 143 B3
Mechelen B 79 A4
Mechernich D 80 B2
Mechnica PL 86 B2
Mechowo PL 67 C4
Mechterstädt D . . .82 B2
Mecidiye TR 186 B1
Mecikal PL 68 B2
Mecina-Bombarón E . . 164 C1
Mecitözü TR 23 A8
Meckenbeuren D . 107 B4
Meckenheim
  Rheinland-Pfalz D . . .80 B3
  Rheinland-Pfalz D 93 B4
Meckesheim D 93 B4
Mecseknádasd H . 125 A4
Meda
  I 120 B2
  P 149 B2
Medak HR 137 A4
Mede I 120 B1
Medebach D 81 A4
Medelim P 155 B3
Medemblik NL 70 B2
Medena Selista BIH . . 138 A2
Medesano I 120 C3
Medevi S 55 B5
Medgidia RO 17 C8
Medgyesháza H . . 113 C5
Medhamn S 55 A4
Mediaş RO 17 B6
Medicina I 135 A4
Medinaceli E 152 A1
Medina del Campo E . . 150 A3
Medina de Pomar E . . 143 B3
Medina de Ríoseco E . . 142 C1
Medina Sidonia E . 162 B2
Medinilla E 150 B2
Medja SRB 126 B2
Medjedja BIH . . . 139 B5
Medulin HR 122 C2
Meduno I 122 A1
Medveda SRB . . . 127 C3
Medvedov SK . . . 111 B4
Medvezhyegorsk RUS 9 A9
Medvide HR 137 A4

Medvode SLO . . . 123 A3
Medzev SK 99 C4
Medžitlija MK 182 C3
Meerane D 83 B4
Meerle B 79 A4
Meersburg D 107 B4
Meeuwen B 79 A5
Megala Horio GR . 188 C2
Megalopoli GR . . . 184 B3
Mégara GR 185 A4
Megève F 118 B3
Meggenhofen A . . 109 A4
Megra RUS 9 B10
Megyaszó H 113 A5
Mehamn N 193 A11
Mehedeby S 51 B4
Méhkerék H 113 C5
Mehun-sur-Yèvre F . . 103 B4
Meigle GB 35 B4
Meijel NL 80 A1
Meilen CH 107 B3
Meilhan F 128 C2
Meimôa P 149 B2
Meina I 119 B5
Meine D 73 B3
Meinersen D 72 B3
Meinerzhagen D . . .81 A3
Meiningen D 82 B2
Meira E 141 A3
Meiringen CH . . . 106 C3
Meisenheim D 93 B3
Meissen D 83 A5
Meitingen D 94 C2
Meix-devant-Virton B . . .92 B1
Męka PL 86 A2
Meka Gruda BIH . 139 B4
Mel I 121 A5
Melbu N 194 B5
Melč CZ 98 B1
Meldal N 198 B6
Méldola I 135 A5
Meldorf D 64 B2
Melegnano I 120 B2
Melenci SRB 126 B2
Melendugno I . . . 173 B4
Melfi I 172 B1
Melfjordbotn N . . 195 D4
Melgaço P 140 B2
Melgar de Arriba E . . 142 B1
Melgar de Fernamental E . . 142 B2
Melgar de Yuso E . 142 B2
Melhus N 199 B7
Meliana E 159 B3
Melide
  CH 120 B1
  E 140 B2
Melides P 160 A1
Meligales GR . . . 184 B2
Melilli I 177 B4
Melinovac HR . . . 124 C1
Melisenda I 179 C3
Melisey F 105 B5
Mélito di Porto Salvo I . . 175 D1
Melk A 110 A2
Melksham GB 43 A4
Mellakoski FIN . . . 196 C7
Mellanström S . . . 195 E9
Mellbystrand S . . .61 C2
Melle
  B 79 A3
  D 71 B5
  F 115 B3
Mellendorf D 72 B2
Mellerud S 54 B3
Mellieha M 175 C3
Mellösa S 56 A2
Mellrichstadt D . . .82 B2
Mělnické Vtelno CZ . . .84 B2
Mělník CZ 84 B2
Melón E 140 B2
Melrose GB 35 C5
Mels CH 107 B4
Melsungen D 82 A1
Meltaus FIN 197 C8
Meltham GB 40 B2
Melton Mowbray GB . . .40 C3
Meltosjärvi FIN . . 196 C7
Melun F 90 C2
Melvaig GB 31 B3
Melvich GB 32 C3
Mélykút H 126 A1
Melzo I 120 B2
Memaliaj AL 182 C1
Membrilla E 157 B4
Membrio E 155 B3
Memer F 129 B4
Memmelsdorf D . . .94 B2
Memmingen D . . . 107 B5
Memoria P 154 B2
Menággio I 120 A2
Menai Bridge GB . .38 A2
Menasalbas E . . . 157 A3
Menat F 116 A2
Mendavia E 144 B1
Mendaza E 144 B1
Mende F 130 A2
Menden D 81 A3
Menderes TR . . . 188 A2
Mendig D 80 B3
Mendiga P 154 B2
Mendrisio CH . . . 120 B1
Ménéac F 101 A3
Menemen TR . . . 188 A2
Menen B 78 B3
Menesjärvi FIN . . 193 D10
Menetou-Salon F . 103 B4
Menfi I 176 B1
Menfőcsanak H . . 111 B4
Mengamuñoz E . . 150 B3
Mengen
  D 107 A4
  TR 187 B7
Mengeš SLO 123 A3

Mengibar E . . . . . 157 C
Mengkofen D . . . . .95 C
Menou F . . . . 104 B
Mens F . . . . 118 C
Menslage D . . . . .71 B
Mensträsk S . . . . 200 A
Mentana I . . . . . 168 A
Menton F . . . . . . 133 B
Méntrida E . . . . . 151 B
Méobecq F . . . . . 115 B
Méounes-les-Montrieux F . . 132 B
Meppel NL . . . . . .70 B
Meppen D . . . . . .71 B
Mequinenza E . . . 153 A
Mer F . . . . 103 B
Mera
  Coruña E . . . . 140 A
  Coruña E . . . . 140 A
Meråker N . . . . . 199 B
Merano I . . . . . . 108 C
Merate I . . . . . . 120 B
Mercadillo E . . . . 143 A
Mercatale I . . . . . 135 B
Mercatino Conca I 136 B
Mercato San Severino I . . 170 C
Mercato Saraceno I . . 135 B
Merching D . . . . . 108 A
Merchtem B . . . . .79 B
Merdrignac F . . . . 101 A
Merdžanići BIH . . 139 B
Meré E . . . . 142 A
Mere GB . . . . . . .43 A
Méréville F . . . . . .90 C
Merfeld D . . . . . . .80 A
Méribel F . . . . . . 118 B
Méribel Motraret F . . 118 B
Meriç TR . . . . . . 186 A
Mérida E . . . . . . 155 C
Mérignac F . . . . . 128 B
Měřín CZ . . . . . . .97 B
Mering D . . . . . . .94 C
Merkendorf D . . . .94 B
Merklín CZ . . . . . .96 B
Merksplas B . . . . .79 A
Merlánna S . . . . . .56 A
Merlimont Plage F .78 B
Mern DK . . . . . . .65 A
Mernye H . . . . . . 111 C
Mersch L . . . . . . .92 B
Merseburg D . . . . .83 A
Mers-les-Bains F . .90 A
Merthyr Tydfil GB .39 C
Mertingen D . . . . .94 C
Mértola P . . . . . . 160 B
Méru F . . . . .90 B
Merufe P . . . . . . 140 B
Mervans F . . . . . 105 C
Merville F . . . . . . .78 B
Méry-sur-Seine F . .91 C
Merzen D . . . . . . .71 B
Merzifon TR . . . . .23 A
Merzig D . . . . . . .92 B
Mesagne I . . . . . 173 B
Mesão Frio P . . . 148 A
Mesas de Ibor E . 156 A
Meschede D . . . . .81 A
Meschers-sur-Gironde F . . 114 C
Meslay-du-Maine F . . 102 B
Mesna N . . . . . . .48 A
Mesnalien N . . . . .48 A
Mesocco CH . . . . 120 A
Mésola I . . . . . . 122 C
Mesologi GR . . . . 184 A
Mesopotamo GR . 182 D
Mesoraca I . . . . . 175 B
Messac F . . . . . . 101 B
Messancy B . . . . .92 B
Messdorf D . . . . . .73 B
Messei F . . . . . . .88 B
Messejana P . . . . 160 B
Messelt N . . . . . . .48 A
Messina I . . . . . . 177 A
Messingen D . . . . .71 B
Messini GR . . . . . 184 B
Messkirch D . . . . 107 B
Messlingen S . . . 199 C
Messstetten D . . . 107 A
Mesta GR . . . . . . 185 A
Mestanza E . . . . 157 B
Městec Králové CZ 84 B
Mestlin D . . . . . . .73 A
Město Albrechtice CZ . . .85 B
Město Libavá CZ . .98 B
Město Touškov CZ .96 B
Mestre I . . . . 122 B
Mesvres F . . . . . 104 C
Mesztegnyő H . . . 111 C
Meta I . . . . 170 C
Metajna HR . . . . 137 A
Metelen D . . . . . . .71 B
Methana GR . . . . 185 B
Methlick GB . . . . .33 D
Methven GB . . . . .35 B
Methwold GB . . . .41 C
Metković HR . . . . 139 B
Metlika SLO . . . . 123 B
Metnitz A . . . . . . 110 C
Metsäkylä FIN . . . 197 D1
Metslawier NL . . . .70 A
Metsovo GR . . . . 182 D
Metten D . . . . . . .95 C
Mettendorf D . . . . .92 B
Mettet B . . . . . . .79 B
Mettingen D . . . . .71 B
Mettlach D . . . . . .92 B
Mettlen CH . . . . . 106 C
Mettmann D . . . . .80 A
Metz F . . . . .92 B
Metzervisse F . . . .92 B
Metzingen D . . . . .94 C
Meulan F . . . . . . .90 C
Meung-sur-Loire F . . 103 B

Meuselwitz D 83 A4
Meuzac F 115 C5
Mevagissey GB 42 B2
Mexborough GB 40 B2
Meximieux F 118 B2
Mey GB 32 C3
Meyenburg D 73 A5
Meyerhöfen D 71 B5
Meylan F 118 B2
Meymac F 116 B2
Meyrargues F 132 B1
Meyrueis F 130 A2
Meyssac F 129 A4
Meysse F 117 C4
Meyzieu F 117 B4
Mèze F 130 B2
Mézériat F 117 A5
Mežica SLO 110 C1
Mézidon-Canon F 89 A3
Mézières-en-Brenne F 115 B5
Mézières-sur-Issoire F 115 B4
Mézilhac F 117 C4
Mézilles F 104 B2
Mézin F 128 B3
Mezőberény H 113 C5
Mezőcsát H 113 B4
Mezőfalva H 112 C2
Mezőhegyes H 126 A2
Mezőkeresztes H 113 B4
Mezőkomárom H 112 C2
Mezőkovácsháza H 113 C4
Mezőkövesd H 113 B4
Mezőörs H 111 B4
Mézos F 128 B1
Mezőszilas H 112 C2
Mezőtúr H 113 B4
Mezquita de Jarque E 153 B3
Mezzano
Emilia Romagna I 135 A5
Trentino Alto Adige I 121 A4
Mezzojuso I 176 B2
Mezzoldo I 120 B2
Mezzolombardo I 121 A4
Mgarr M 175 C3
Miajadas E 156 A2
Miały PL 75 B5
Mianowice PL 68 A2
Miasteczko Krajeńskie PL 76 A2
Miasteczko Sł. PL 86 B2
Miastko PL 68 A1
Michalovce SK 12 D4
Michałowice PL 87 B3
Michelau D 94 B2
Michelbach D 94 B2
Micheldorf A 110 B1
Michelhausen A 110 A2
Michelsneukirchen D 95 B4
Michelstadt D 93 B5
Michendorf D 74 B2
Mickleover GB 40 C2
Midbea GB 33 B4
Middelburg NL 79 A3
Middelfart DK 59 C2
Middelharnis NL 79 A4
Middelkerke B 78 A2
Middelstum NL 71 A3
Middlesbrough GB 37 B5
Middleton Cheney GB 44 A2
Middleton-in-Teesdale GB 37 B4
Middletown GB 27 B4
Middlewich GB 38 A4
Middlezoy GB 43 A4
Midhurst GB 44 C3
Midleton IRL 29 C3
Midlum D 64 C1
Midsomer Norton GB 43 A4
Midtgulen N 198 D2
Midtskogberget N 49 A4
Midwolda NL 71 A4
Mid Yell GB 33 A5
Miechów PL 87 B4
Miedes de Aragón E 152 A2
Miedes de Atienza E 151 A4
Międzybodzie Bielskie PL 99 B3
Międzybórz PL 85 A5
Międzychód PL 75 B4
Międzylesie PL 85 B4
Międzyrzec Podlaski PL 12 C5
Międzyrzecz PL 75 B4
Międzywodzie PL 67 B3
Międzyzdroje PL 67 C3
Miejska Górka PL 85 A4
Miélan F 145 A4
Mielec PL 87 B5
Mielęcin PL 75 A3
Mielno
Warmińsko-Mazurskie PL 77 A5
Zachodnio-Pomorskie PL 67 B5
Miengo E 143 A3
Mieraslompolo FIN 193 C11
Miercurea Ciuc RO 17 B6
Mieres
Asturias E 141 A5
Girona E 147 B3
Mieroszów PL 85 B4
Mierzyn PL 86 A3
Miesau D 93 B3
Miesbach D 108 B2
Mieścisko PL 76 B2
Mieste D 73 B4
Miesterhorst D 73 B4
Mieszków PL 76 B2
Mieszkowice PL 74 B3
Mietków PL 85 B4
Migennes F 104 B2
Miggiano I 173 C4
Migliánico I 169 A4
Migliarino I 121 C4
Migliónico I 172 B2
Mignano Monte Lungo I 169 B3
Migné F 115 B5
Miguel Esteban E 157 A4
Miguelturra E 157 B4
Mihajlovac SRB 127 C2
Miháld H 111 C4
Mihalgazi TR 187 B5
Mihalıççık TR 187 C6
Mihályi H 111 B4
Mihla D 82 A2
Mihohnić HR 123 B3
Miholjsko HR 123 B4
Mihovljan HR 124 A1
Mijares E 150 B3
Mijas E 163 B3
Mike H 124 A3
Mikines GR 184 B3
Mikkeli FIN 8 B5
Mikkelvik N 192 B3
Mikleuš HR 125 B3
Mikołajki Pomorskie PL 69 B4
Mikolów PL 86 B2
Mikonos GR 185 B6
Mikorzyn PL 86 A2
Mikro Derio GR 183 B8
Mikstat PL 86 A1
Mikulášovice CZ 84 B2
Mikulov CZ 97 C4
Mikulovice CZ 85 B5
Milagro E 144 B2
Miłakowo PL 69 A5
Milan = Milano I 120 B2
Miland N 47 C5
Milano = Milan I 120 B2
Milano Marittima I 135 A5
Milas TR 188 B2
Milazzo I 177 A4
Mildenhall GB 45 A4
Milejewo PL 69 A4
Milelín CZ 85 B3
Miletić SRB 125 B5
Miletićevo SRB 126 B3
Mileto I 175 C2
Milevsko CZ 96 B2
Milford IRL 26 A3
Milford Haven GB 39 C1
Milford on Sea GB 44 C2
Milhão P 149 A3
Milići BIH 139 A5
Miličin CZ 96 B2
Milicz PL 85 A5
Milín CZ 96 B2
Militello in Val di Catánia I 177 B3
Miljevina BIH 139 B4
Milkowice PL 85 A4
Millançay F 103 B3
Millares E 159 B3
Millas F 146 B3
Millau F 130 A2
Millesimo I 133 A4
Millevaches F 116 B2
Millom GB 36 B3
Millport GB 34 C3
Millstatt A 109 C4
Millstreet
Cork IRL 29 B2
Waterford IRL 29 B4
Milltown
Galway IRL 28 A3
Kerry IRL 29 B1
Milltown Malbay IRL 28 B2
Milly-la-Forêt F 90 C2
Milmarcos E 152 A2
Milmersdorf D 74 A2
Milna HR 138 B2
Milnthorpe GB 37 B4
Miłogórze PL 69 A5
Miłomłyn PL 69 B4
Milos GR 185 C5
Miloševo SRB 127 C3
Miłosław PL 76 B2
Milot AL 182 B1
Milówka PL 99 B3
Miltach D 95 B4
Miltenberg D 94 B1
Milton Keynes GB 44 A3
Miltzow D 66 B2
Milverton GB 43 A3
Milzyn PL 76 B3
Mimice HR 138 B2
Mimizan F 128 B1
Mimizan-Plage F 128 B1
Mimoň CZ 84 B2
Mina de Juliana P 160 B1
Mina de São Domingos P 160 B2
Minas de Riotinto E 161 B3
Minateda E 158 C2
Minaya E 158 B1
Minde P 154 B2
Mindelheim D 108 A1
Mindelstetten D 95 C3
Minden D 72 B1
Mindszent H 113 C4
Minehead GB 43 A3
Mineo I 177 B3
Minerbe I 121 B4
Minérbio I 121 C4
Minervino Murge I 171 B4
Minglanilla E 158 B2
Mingorria E 150 B3
Minnesund N 48 B3
Miño E 140 A2
Miño de San Esteban E 151 A4
Minsen D 71 A4
Minsk BY 13 B7
Mińsk Mazowiecki PL 12 B4
Minsterley GB 39 B4
Mintlaw GB 33 D4
Minturno I 169 B3
Mionica
BIH 125 C4
SRB 127 C2
Mios F 128 B2
Mira
E 158 B2
I 121 B5
P 148 B1
Mirabel E 155 B4
Mirabel-aux-Baronnies F 131 A4
Mirabella Eclano I 170 B3
Mirabella Imbáccari I 177 B3
Mirabello I 121 C4
Miradoux F 129 B3
Miraflores de la Sierra E 151 B4
Miralrio E 151 B5
Miramar P 148 A1
Miramare I 136 A1
Miramas F 131 B3
Mirambeau F 114 C3
Miramont-de-Guyenne F 129 B3
Miranda de Arga E 144 B2
Miranda de Ebro E 143 B4
Miranda do Corvo P 148 B1
Miranda do Douro P 149 A3
Mirande F 129 C3
Mirandela P 149 A2
Mirandilla E 155 C4
Mirándola I 121 C4
Miranje HR 137 A4
Mirano I 121 B5
Miras AL 182 C2
Miravet E 153 A4
Miré F 102 B1
Mirebeau F 102 C2
Mirebeau-sur-Bèze F 105 B4
Mirecourt F 105 A5
Mirepoix F 146 A2
Mires GR 185 D5
Miribel F 117 B4
Miričina BIH 125 C4
Mirina GR 183 D7
Mirna SLO 123 B4
Miroslav CZ 97 C4
Mirosławice PL 85 B4
Mirosławiec PL 75 A5
Mirošov CZ 96 B1
Mirotice CZ 96 B2
Mirovice CZ 96 B2
Mirow D 74 A1
Mirsk PL 84 B3
Mirzec PL 87 A5
Misi FIN 197 C9
Misilmeri I 176 A2
Miske H 112 C3
Miskolc H 113 A4
Mislinja SLO 110 C2
Missanello I 174 A2
Missillac F 101 B3
Mistelbach
A 97 C4
D 95 B3
Misten N 194 C5
Misterbianco I 177 B4
Misterhult S 62 A4
Mistretta I 177 B3
Misurina I 109 C3
Mitchelstown IRL 29 B3
Mithimna GR 186 C1
Mithoni GR 184 C2
Mitilini GR 186 C1
Mitilinii GR 188 B1
Mittelberg
Tirol A 108 C1
Vorarlberg A 107 B5
Mittenwald D 108 B2
Mittenwalde D 74 B2
Mitterback A 110 B2
Mitterdorf im Mürztal A 110 B2
Mitter-Kleinarl A 109 B4
Mittersheim F 92 C2
Mittersill A 109 B3
Mitterskirchen D 95 C4
Mitterteich D 95 B4
Mitton F 128 B2
Mittweida D 83 B4
Mitwitz D 82 B3
Mizhhir'ya UA 13 D5
Mjällby S 63 B2
Mjåvatn N 53 B4
Mjöbäck S 60 B2
Mjölby S 56 B1
Mjølfjell N 46 B3
Mjøndalen N 53 A6
Mjørlund N 48 B2
Mladá Boleslav CZ 84 B2
Mladá Vožice CZ 96 B2
Mladé Buky CZ 85 B3
Mladenovac SRB 127 C2
Mladenovo SRB 126 B1
Mladikovine BIH 139 A3
Mława PL 77 A5
Mlinište BIH 138 A2
Młodzieszyn PL 77 B5
Młogoszyn PL 77 B4
Młynary PL 69 A4
Mnichóvice CZ 96 B2
Mnichovo Hradiště CZ 84 B2
Mniów PL 87 A4
Mnisek nad Hnilcom SK 99 C4
Mníšek pod Brdy CZ 96 B2
Mniszek PL 87 A4
Mniszków PL 87 A4
Mo
Hedmark N 48 B3
Hordaland N 46 B2
Møre og Romsdal N 198 C5
Telemark N 53 A3
Gävleborg S 51 A3
Västra Götaland S 54 B2
Moaña E 140 B2
Moate IRL 28 A4
Mocejón E 151 C4
Močenok SK 111 A4
Mochales E 152 A1
Mochowo PL 77 B4
Mochy PL 75 B5
Mockern D 73 B4
Mockfjärd S 50 B1
Möckmühl D 94 B1
Mockrehna D 83 A4
Moclin E 163 A4
Mocsa H 112 B2
Möcsény H 125 A4
Modane F 118 B3
Modbury GB 42 B3
Módena I 121 C3
Módica I 177 C3
Modigliana I 135 A4
Modlin PL 77 B5
Mödling A 111 A3
Modliszewice PL 87 A4
Modliszewko PL 76 B2
Modogno I 171 B4
Modra SK 98 C1
Modran BIH 125 C3
Modriča BIH 125 C4
Möðrudalur IS 191 B10
Modrý Kamen SK 99 C3
Moëlan-sur-Mer F 100 B2
Moelfre GB 38 A2
Moelv N 48 B2
Moen N 194 A9
Moena I 121 A4
Moerbeke B 79 A3
Moers D 80 A2
Móes P 148 B2
Moffat GB 36 A3
Mogadouro P 149 A3
Mogata S 56 B2
Móggio Udinese I 122 A2
Mogielnica PL 87 A4
Mogilany PL 99 B3
Mogilno PL 76 B2
Mogliano I 136 B2
Mogliano Véneto I 122 B1
Mogor E 140 B2
Mógoro I 179 C2
Moguer E 161 B3
Mohács H 125 B4
Moheda S 62 A2
Mohedas E 149 B3
Mohedas de la Jara E 156 A2
Mohelnice CZ 97 B4
Mohill IRL 26 C3
Möhlin CH 106 B2
Moholm S 55 B5
Mohorn D 83 A5
Mohyliv-Podil's'kyy UA 13 D7
Moi N 52 B2
Moià E 147 C3
Móie I 136 B2
Moimenta da Beira P 148 B2
Mo i Rana N 195 D5
Moirans F 118 B2
Moirans-en-Montagne F 118 A2
Moisaküla EST 8 C4
Moisdon-la-Rivière F 101 B4
Moissac F 129 B4
Moita
Coimbra P 148 B1
Guarda P 149 B2
Santarém P 154 B2
Setúbal P 154 C1
Moita dos Ferreiros P 154 B1
Moixent E 159 C3
Mojacar E 164 B3
Mojados E 150 A3
Mojmírovce SK 112 A2
Mojtin SK 98 C2
Möklinta S 50 B3
Mokošica HR 139 C4
Mokronog SLO 123 B4
Mokro Polje HR 138 A2
Mokrzyska PL 99 A4
Møkster N 46 B2
Mol
B 79 A5
SRB 126 B2
Mola di Bari I 173 A3
Molai GR 184 C3
Molare I 133 A4
Molaretto I 119 B4
Molas F 145 A4
Molassano I 134 A1
Molbergen D 71 B4
Mold GB 38 A3
Molde N 198 C4
Møldrup DK 58 B2
Moledo do Minho P 148 A1
Molfetta I 171 B4
Molfsee D 64 B3
Moliden S 200 C4
Molières F 129 B4
Molina de Aragón E 152 B2
Molina de Segura E 165 A3
Molinar E 143 A3
Molinaseca E 141 B4
Molinella I 121 C4
Molinet F 104 C2
Molinicos E 158 C1
Molini di Tures I 108 C2
Molinos de Duero E 143 C4
Molins de Rei E 147 C3
Moliterno I 174 A1
Molkom S 55 A4
Möllbrücke A 109 C4
Mölle S 61 C2
Molledo E 142 A2
Möllenbeck D 74 A2
Mollerussa E 147 C1
Mollet de Perelada E 146 B3
Mollina E 163 A3
Mölln D 73 A3
Molló E 146 B3
Mollösund S 54 B2
Mölltorp S 55 B5
Mölnbo S 56 A3
Mölndal S 60 B2
Mölnlycke S 60 B2
Molompize F 116 B3
Moloy F 105 B3
Molsheim F 93 C3
Moltzow D 73 A5
Molve HR 124 A3
Molveno I 121 A3
Molvizar E 163 B4
Molzbichl A 109 C4
Mombaróccio I 136 B1
Mombeltrán E 150 B2
Mombris D 93 A5
Mombuey E 141 B4
Momchilgrad BG 183 B7
Mommark DK 64 B3
Momo I 119 B5
Monaghan IRL 27 B4
Monar Lodge GB 32 D2
Monasterace Marina I 175 C2
Monasterevin IRL 30 A1
Monasterio de Rodilla E 143 B3
Monastir I 179 C3
Monbahus F 129 B3
Monbazillac F 129 B3
Moncada E 159 B3
Moncalieri I 119 B4
Moncalvo I 119 B5
Monção P 140 B2
Moncarapacho P 160 B2
Moncel-sur-Seille F 92 C2
Monchegorsk RUS 3 C13
Mönchengladbach = Munchen-Gladbach D 80 A2
Mónchio della Corti I 134 A3
Monchique P 160 B1
Monclar-de-Quercy F 129 C4
Moncofa E 159 B3
Moncontour F 101 A3
Moncoutant F 114 B3
Monda E 162 B3
Mondariz E 140 B2
Mondavio I 136 B1
Mondéjar E 151 B4
Mondello I 176 A2
Mondim de Basto P 148 A2
Mondolfo I 136 B2
Mondoñedo E 141 A3
Mondorf-les-Bains L 92 B2
Mondoubleau F 102 B2
Mondovì I 133 A3
Mondragon F 131 A3
Mondragone I 170 B1
Mondsee A 109 B4
Monéglia I 134 A2
Monegrillo E 153 A3
Monein F 145 A3
Monemvasia GR 184 C4
Mónesi I 133 A3
Monesiglio I 133 A4
Monesterio E 161 A3
Monestier-de-Clermont F 118 C2
Monestiés F 130 A1
Monéteau F 104 B2
Moneygall IRL 28 B4
Moneymore GB 27 B4
Monfalcone I 122 B2
Monfero E 140 A2
Monflanquin F 129 B3
Monflorite E 145 B3
Monforte P 155 B3
Monforte da Beira
E 155 B3
P 155 B3
Monforte d'Alba I 133 A3
Monforte del Cid E 165 A4
Monforte de Lemos E 140 B3
Monforte de Moyuela E 152 A2
Monghidoro I 135 A4
Mongiana I 175 C2
Monguelfo I 108 C3
Monheim D 94 C2
Moniaive GB 36 A3
Monifieth GB 35 B5
Monikie GB 35 B5
Monistrol-d'Allier F 117 C3
Monistrol de Montserrat E 147 C2
Monistrol-sur-Loire F 117 B4
Mönkebude D 74 A2
Monkton GB 36 A2
Monmouth GB 39 C4
Monnaie F 102 B2
Monnerville F 90 C2
Monnickendam NL 70 B2
Monolithos GR 188 C2
Monópoli I 173 B3
Monor H 112 B3
Monóvar E 159 C3
Monpazier F 129 B3
Monreal
D 80 B3
E 144 B2
Monreal del Campo E 152 B2
Monreale I 176 A2
Monroy E 155 B4
Monroyo E 153 B3
Mons B 79 B3
Monsaraz P 155 C3
Monschau D 80 B2
Monségur F 128 B3
Monsélice I 121 B4
Mønshaug N 46 B3
Monster NL 70 B1
Mönsterås S 62 A4
Monsummano Terme I 135 B3
Montabaur D 81 B3
Montafia I 119 C5
Montagnac F 130 B2
Montagnana I 121 B4
Montaigu F 114 B2
Montaigu-de-Quercy F 129 B4
Montaiguët-en-Forez F 117 A3
Montaigut F 116 A2
Montaigut-sur-Save F 129 C4
Montainville F 90 C1
Montalbán E 153 B3
Montalbán de Córdoba E 163 A3
Montalbano Elicona I 177 A4
Montalbano Iónico I 174 A2
Montalbo E 158 B1
Montalcino I 135 B4
Montaldo di Cósola I 120 C2
Montalegre P 148 A2
Montalieu-Vercieu F 118 B2
Montalivet-les-Bains F 114 C2
Montallegro I 176 B2
Montalto delle Marche I 136 C2
Montalto di Castro I 168 A1
Montalto Pavese I 120 C2
Montalto Uffugo I 174 B2
Montalvão P 155 B3
Montamarta E 149 A4
Montana BG 17 D5
Montana-Vermala CH 119 A4
Montánchez E 156 A1
Montanejos E 153 B3
Montano Antilia I 172 B1
Montans F 129 C4
Montargil P 154 B2
Montargis F 103 B4
Montastruc-la-Conseillère F 129 C4
Montauban F 129 B4
Montauban-de-Bretagne F 101 A3
Montbard F 104 B3
Montbarrey F 105 B4
Montbazens F 130 A1
Montbazon F 102 B2
Montbéliard F 106 B1
Montbenoit F 105 C5
Montbeugny F 104 C2
Montblanc E 147 C2
Montbozon F 105 B5
Montbrison F 117 B4
Montbron F 115 C4
Montbrun-les-Bains F 131 A4
Montceau-les-Mines F 104 C3
Montcenis F 104 C3
Montchanin F 104 C3
Montcornet F 91 B4
Montcuq F 129 B4
Montdardier F 130 B2
Mont-de-Marsan F 128 C2
Montdidier F 90 B2
Monteagudo E 165 A3
Monteagudo de las Vicarias E 152 A1
Montealegre E 142 C2
Montealegre del Castillo E 159 C2
Montebello Iónico I 175 D1
Montebello Vicentino I 121 B4
Montebelluna I 121 B5
Montebourg F 88 A2
Montebruno I 134 A2
Monte-Carlo MC 133 B3
Montecarotto I 136 B2
Montecassiano I 136 B2
Montecastrilli I 168 A2
Montecatini Terme I 135 B3
Montécchio I 136 B1
Montécchio Emilia I 121 C3
Montécchio Maggiore I 121 B4
Montech F 129 C4
Montechiaro d'Asti I 119 B5
Monte Clara P 155 B3
Monte Clérigo P 160 B1
Montecórice I 170 C2
Montecorvino Rovella I 170 C2
Monte da Pedra P 155 B3
Monte de Goula P 155 B3
Montederramo E 141 B3
Montedoro I 176 B2
Monte do Trigo P 155 C3
Montefalco I 136 C1
Montefalcone di Val Fortore I 170 B3
Montefalcone nel Sánnio I 170 B2
Montefano I 136 B2
Montefiascone I 168 A2
Montefiorino I 134 A3
Montefortino I 136 C2
Montefranco I 168 A2
Montefrio E 163 A4
Montegiordano Marina I 174 A2
Montegiórgio I 136 B2
Monte Gordo P 160 B2
Montegranaro I 136 B2
Montehermoso E 149 B3
Montejicar E 163 A4
Montejo de la Sierra E 151 A4
Montejo de Tiermes E 151 A4
Monte Juntos P 155 C3
Montel-de-Gelat F 116 B2
Monteleone di Púglia I 171 B3
Monteleone di Spoleto I 169 A2
Monteleone d'Orvieto I 135 C5
Montelepre I 176 A2
Montelibretti I 168 A2
Montelier F 117 C5
Montélimar F 131 A3
Montella
E 146 B2
I 170 C3
Montellano E 162 A2
Montelupo Fiorentino I 135 B4
Montemaggiore Belsito I 176 B2
Montemagno I 119 C5
Montemayor E 163 A3
Montemayor de Pinilla E 150 A3
Montemésola I 173 B3
Montemilleto I 170 B2
Montemilone I 172 A1
Montemolin E 161 A3
Montemónaco I 136 C2
Montemor-o-Novo P 154 C2
Montemor-o-Velho P 148 B1
Montemurro I 174 A1
Montendre F 128 A2
Montenegro de Cameros E 143 B4
Montenero di Bisáccia I 170 B2
Monteneuf F 101 B3
Monteparano I 173 B3
Montepescali I 135 C4
Montepiano I 135 A4
Monte Porzio I 136 B2
Montepulciano I 135 B4
Monte Real P 154 B2
Montereale I 169 A3
Montereale Valcellina I 122 A1
Montereau-Faut-Yonne F 90 C2
Monte Redondo P 154 B2
Monterénzio I 135 A4
Monte Romano I 168 A1
Monteroni d'Arbia I 135 B4
Monteroni di Lecce I 173 B4
Monterosso al Mare I 134 A2
Monterosso Almo I 177 B3
Monterosso Grana I 133 A3
Monterotondo I 168 A2
Monterotondo Maríttimo I 135 B3
Monterrey E 141 C3
Monterroso E 140 B3
Monterrubio de la Serena E 156 B2
Monterubbiano I 136 B2
Montesa E 159 C3
Montesalgueiro E 140 A2
Monte San Giovanni Campano I 169 B3
Montesano sulla Marcellana I 174 A1
Monte San Savino I 135 B4
Monte Sant'Ángelo I 171 B3
Montesárchio I 170 B2
Montescaglioso I 171 C4
Montesclaros E 150 B3
Montesilvano I 169 A4
Montespértoli I 135 B4
Montesquieu-Volvestre F 146 A2
Montesquiou F 129 C3
Montestruc-sur-Gers F 129 C3
Montes Velhos P 160 B1
Montevarchi I 135 B4
Montéveglio I 135 A4
Monte Vilar P 154 B1
Montfaucon F 101 B4
Montfaucon-d'Argonne F 91 B5
Montfaucon-en-Velay F 117 B4
Montferrat
Isère F 118 B2
Var F 132 B2

Montfort-en-Chalosse
F.........128 C2
Montfort-l'Amaury
F.........90 C1
Montfort-le-Gesnois
F.........102 A2
Montfort-sur-Meu
F.........101 A4
Montfort-sur-Risle
F.........89 A4
Montgai E......147 C1
Montgaillard F...145 A4
Montgenèvre F...118 C3
Montgiscard F...146 A2
Montgomery GB...39 B3
Montguyon F....128 A2
Monthermé F....91 B4
Monthey CH....119 A3
Monthois F.....91 B4
Monthureux-sur-Saône
F.........105 A4
Monti I.......178 B3
Monticelli d'Ongina
I.........120 B2
Montichiari I....120 B3
Monticiano I....135 B4
Montiel E......158 C1
Montier-en-Der F..91 C4
Montieri I......135 B4
Montiglio I.....119 B5
Montignac F....129 A4
Montigny-le-Roi F 105 B4
Montigny-lès-Metz
F.........92 B2
Montigny-sur-Aube
F.........105 B3
Montijo
E.........155 C4
P.........154 C2
Montilla E......163 A3
Montillana E....163 A4
Montilly F......104 C2
Montivilliers F...89 A4
Montjaux F.....130 A1
Montjean-sur-Loire
F.........102 B1
Montlhéry F....90 C2
Montlieu-la-Garde
F.........128 A2
Mont-Louis F...146 B3
Montlouis-sur-Loire
F.........102 B2
Montluçon F....116 A2
Montluel F.....117 B5
Montmarault F...116 A2
Montmartin-sur-Mer
F.........88 B2
Montmédy F....92 B1
Montmélian F...118 B3
Montmeyan F...132 B2
Montmeyran F...117 C4
Montmirail
Marne F....91 C3
Sarthe F....102 A2
Montmiral F....118 B2
Montmirat F....131 B3
Montmirey-le-Château
F.........105 B4
Montmoreau-St Cybard
F.........115 C4
Montmorency F...90 C2
Montmorillon F..115 B4
Montmort-Lucy F..91 C3
Montoir-de-Bretagne
F.........101 B3
Montoire-sur-le-Loir
F.........102 B2
Montoito P.....155 C3
Montolieu F....146 A3
Montório al Vomano
I.........169 A3
Montoro E......157 B3
Montpellier F...131 B2
Montpezat-de-Quercy
F.........129 B4
Montpezat-sous-
Bouzon F....117 C4
Montpon-Ménestérol
F.........128 A3
Montpont-en-Bresse
F.........105 C4
Montréal
Aude F.....146 A3
Gers F.....128 C2
Montredon-
Labessonnié F..130 B1
Montréjeau F...145 A4
Montrésor F....103 B3
Montresta I.....178 B2
Montret F......105 C4
Montreuil
Pas de Calais F..78 B1
Seine St Denis F..90 C2
Montreuil-aux-Lions
F.........90 B3
Montreuil-Bellay F 102 B1
Montreux CH....106 C1
Montrevault F...101 B4
Montrevel-en-Bresse
F.........118 A2
Montrichard F...103 B3
Montricoux F...129 B4
Mont-roig del Camp
E.........147 C1
Montrond-les-Bains
F.........117 B4
Montroy F.....159 B3
Montsalvy F....116 C2
Montsauche-les-
Settons F....104 B3
Montseny E....147 C3
Montsoreau F...102 B2
Monts-sur-Guesnes
F.........102 C2

Mont-St Aignan F..89 A5
Mont-St Vincent F 104 C3
Montsûrs F.....102 A1
Montuenga E....150 A3
Montuïri E......167 B3
Monturque E....163 A3
Monza I.......120 B2
Monzón E......145 C4
Monzón de Campos
E.........142 B2
Moorbad Lobenstein
D.........83 B3
Moordorf D.....71 A4
Moorslede B....78 B3
Moos D.......107 B3
Moosburg D....95 C3
Moosburg im Kärnten
A.........110 C1
Mór H........112 B2
Mora E.......157 A4
Mora P.......154 C2
Mora S.......50 A1
Moraby S......50 B2
Mòra d'Ebre E...153 A4
Mora de Rubielos
E.........153 B3
Moradillo de Roa
E.........151 A4
Morąg PL......69 B4
Mórahalom H....126 A1
Moraime F.....140 A1
Morais P......149 A3
Mòra la Nova E..153 A4
Moral de Calatrava
E.........157 B4
Moraleda de Zafayona
E.........163 A4
Moraleja E.....149 B3
Moraleja del Vino
E.........150 A2
Morales del Vino
E.........150 A2
Morales de Toro E 150 A2
Morales de Valverde
E.........141 C5
Moralina E.....149 A3
Morano Cálabro I 174 B2
Mörarp S......61 C2
Morasverdes E..149 B3
Morata de Jalón
E.........152 A2
Morata de Jiloca
E.........152 A2
Morata de Tajuña
E.........151 B4
Moratalla E....164 A3
Moravče SLO....123 A3
Moravec CZ....97 B4
Moraviţa RO....126 B3
Moravská Třebová
CZ........97 B4
Moravské Budějovice
CZ........97 B3
Moravské Lieskové
SK........98 C1
Moravske Toplice
SLO.......111 C3
Moravský-Beroun
CZ........98 B1
Moravský Krumlov
CZ........97 B4
Moravský Svätý Ján
SK........98 C1
Morawica PL....87 B4
Morawin PL.....86 A2
Morbach D.....92 B3
Morbegno I.....120 A2
Morbier F......105 C5
Mörbisch am See
A.........111 B3
Mörbylånga S...63 B4
Morcenx F.....128 B2
Morciano di Romagna
I.........136 B1
Morcone I......170 B2
Morcuera E....151 A4
Mordelles F....101 A4
Mordoğan TR...188 A1
Moréac F......100 B3
Morebattle GB...35 C5
Morecambe GB...36 B4
Moreda
Granada E...163 A4
Oviedo E....142 A1
Morée F.......103 B3
Moreles de Rey E 141 B5
Morella E......153 B3
Moreruela de los
Infanzones E..149 A4
Mores I.......178 B2
Móres I.......178 B2
Morestel F.....118 B2
Moretonhampstead
GB........43 B3
Moreton-in-Marsh
GB........44 B2
Moret-sur-Loing F..90 C2
Moretta I......119 C4
Moreuil F......90 B2
Morez F.......105 C5
Mörfelden D....93 B4
Morgat F......100 A1
Morges CH.....105 C5
Morgex I......119 B4
Morgongåva S..51 C3
Morhange F....92 C2
Morhet B......92 B1
Mori I........121 B3
Morialmé B....79 B4
Moriani Plage F..180 A2
Mórichida H....111 B4
Moriles E......163 A3
Morille E......150 B2
Moringen D....82 A1
Morjärv S......196 C5
Morkarla S.....51 B4
Mørke DK......59 B3
Mørkøv DK.....61 D1

Morkovice-Slížany
CZ........98 B1
Morlaàs F.....145 A3
Morlaix F......100 A2
Morley F......91 C5
Mörlunda S....62 A3
Mormanno I....174 B1
Mormant F.....90 C2
Mornant F.....117 B4
Mornay-Berry F..103 B4
Morón de Almazán
E.........152 A1
Morón de la Frontera
E.........162 A2
Morovič SRB....125 B5
Morozzo I......133 A3
Morpeth GB....37 A5
Morphou CY....181 A1
Morsbach D....81 B3
Mörsch D......93 C4
Morsum D......64 B1
Mørsvikbotn N..194 C6
Mortagne-au-Perche
F.........89 B4
Mortagne-sur-Gironde
F.........114 C3
Mortagne-sur-Sèvre
F.........114 B3
Mortágua P....148 B1
Mortain F......88 B3
Mortara I......120 B1
Morteau F.....105 B5
Mortegliano I...122 B2
Mortelle I......177 A4
Mortemart F....115 B4
Mortimer's Cross
GB........39 B4
Mortrée F......89 B4
Mörtschach A...109 C3
Mortsel B......79 A4
Morud DK......59 C3
Morwenstow GB..42 B2
Moryń PL......74 B3
Morzeszczyn PL..69 B3
Morzewo PL....69 B4
Morzine F......118 A3
Mosbach D....93 B5
Mosbjerg DK...58 A3
Mosby N.......53 B3
Mosca I.......149 A3
Moscavide P....154 C1
Moščenica HR...124 B2
Moščenička Draga
HR........123 B3
Mosciano Sant'Ángelo
I.........136 C2
Mościsko PL....85 B4
Moscow = Moskva
RUS.......9 E10
Mosina PL.....75 B5
Mosjøen N....195 E4
Moskog N......46 A3
Moskorzew PL..87 B3
Moskosel S....196 D2
Moskuvarra FIN..197 B9
Moskva = Moscow
RUS.......9 E10
Moslavina Podravska
HR........125 B3
Moşniţa Nouă RO 126 B3
Moso in Passíria I 108 C2
Mosonmagyaróvár
H.........111 B4
Mošorin SRB....126 B2
Mošovce SK....98 C2
Mosqueruela E..153 B3
Moss N.......54 A1
Mossfellsbær IS..190 C4
Mössingen D...93 C5
Møsstrand N...47 C5
Most CZ.......83 B5
Mosta M......175 C3
Mostar BIH.....139 B3
Mosterhamn N..52 A1
Mostki PL......75 B4
Most na Soči SLO 122 A2
Móstoles E.....151 B4
Mostová SK....111 A4
Mostowo PL....68 A1
Mostuéjouls F...130 A2
Mosty PL......75 A3
Mostys'ka UA...13 D5
Mosvik N......199 B7
Mota del Cuervo
E.........158 B1
Mota del Marqués
E.........150 A2
Motala S......55 B6
Motherwell GB...35 C4
Möthlow D.....74 B1
Motilla del Palancar
E.........158 B2
Motnik SLO....123 A3
Motovun HR....122 B2
Motril E.......163 B4
Motta I.......121 B4
Motta di Livenza I 122 B1
Motta Montecorvino
I.........170 B3
Motta Visconti I..120 B1
Mottisfont GB...44 B2
Móttola I......173 B3
Mou DK.......58 B3
Mouchard F....105 C4
Moudon CH....106 C1
Moudros GR....183 D7
Mougins F......132 B2
Mouilleron-en-Pareds
F.........114 B3
Mouliherne F...102 B2
Moulin F......133 A3
Moulins F......104 C2
Moulins-Engilbert
F.........104 C2
Moulins-la-Marche
F.........89 B4
Moulismes F...115 B4

Moult F.......89 A3
Mountain Ash GB..39 C3
Mountbellew IRL..28 A3
Mountfield GB...27 B4
Mountmellick IRL..30 A1
Mountrath IRL...30 A1
Mountsorrel GB..40 C2
Moura P......160 A2
Mourenx F.....145 A3
Mouriés F......131 B3
Mourmelon-le-Grand
F.........91 B4
Mouronho P....148 B1
Mourujärvi FIN..197 C11
Mouscron B....78 B3
Mousehole GB..42 B1
Moussac F.....131 B3
Moussey F.....92 C2
Mousteru F....100 A2
Moustey F.....128 B2
Moustiers-Ste Marie
F.........132 B2
Mouthe F......105 C5
Mouthier-Haute-Pierre
F.........105 B5
Mouthoumet F..146 B3
Moutier CH....106 B2
Moûtiers F.....118 B3
Moutiers-les-Mauxfaits
F.........114 B2
Mouy F.......90 B2
Mouzaki GR....182 D3
Mouzon F.....91 B5
Moy
Highland GB..32 D2
Tyrone GB...27 B4
Moycullen IRL...28 A2
Moyenmoutier F..92 C2
Moyenvic F....92 C2
Moylough IRL...28 A3
Mózar E.......141 C5
Mozhaysk RUS..9 E10
Mozirje SLO....123 A3
Mözs H.......112 C2
Mozzanica I....120 B2
Mramorak SRB..127 C2
Mrčajevci SRB...127 D2
Mrkonjić Grad BIH 138 A3
Mrkopalj HR....123 B3
Mrocza PL.....76 A2
Mroczeń PL....86 A1
Mroczno PL....69 B4
Mrzezyno PL....67 B4
Mšec CZ.......84 B1
Mšeno CZ.....84 B2
Mstów PL......86 B3
Mstislaw BY....13 A9
Mszana Dolna PL..99 B4
Mszczonów PL..77 C5
Muć HR.......138 B2
Múccia I.......136 B2
Much D.......80 B3
Mücheln D.....83 A3
Much Marcle GB..39 C4
Muchów PL....85 A4
Much Wenlock GB..39 B4
Mucientes E....142 C2
Muckross IRL...29 B2
Mucur TR......23 B8
Muda P.......160 B1
Mudanya TR....186 B3
Mudau D......93 B5
Müden D......72 B3
Mudersbach D..81 B3
Mudurnu TR....187 B6
Muel E.......152 A2
Muelas del Pan E 149 A4
Muess D.......73 A4
Muff IRL......27 A3
Mugardos E....140 A2
Muge F.......154 B2
Mügeln
Sachsen D...83 A5
Sachsen-Anhalt D 83 A5
Múggia I......122 B2
Mugnano I.....135 B5
Mugron F......128 C2
Mugueimes E...140 C3
Muhi H.......113 B4
Mühlacker D....93 C4
Mühlbach am
Hochkönig A..109 B4
Mühlberg
Brandenburg D..83 A5
Thüringen D...82 B2
Mühldorf
A.........109 C4
D.........95 C4
Muhleberg CH...106 C2
Mühleim D.....107 A3
Muhlen-Eichsen D 65 C4
Mühlhausen
Bayern D....94 B2
Thüringen D...82 A2
Mühltroff D.....83 B3
Muhos FIN.....3 D10
Muhr A.......109 B4
Muine Bheag IRL..30 B2
Muirkirk GB....36 A2
Muir of Ord GB..32 D2
Muirteira P....154 B1
Mukacheve UA..12 D5
Muker GB......37 B4
Mula E.......165 A3
Muğla TR......188 B3
Mulben GB.....32 D3
Mulegns CH....107 C4
Mulhacén E....163 B4
Mülheim D.....80 A2
Mulhouse F....106 B2
Muljava SLO....123 B3
Mullanys Cross IRL 26 B2
Müllheim D.....106 B2
Mullhyttan S....55 A5
Mullinavat IRL...30 B1
Mullingar IRL...30 A1
Mullion GB.....42 B1

Müllrose D.....74 B3
Mullsjö S......60 B3
Mulseryd S....60 B3
Munaðarnes IS..190 A4
Munana E......150 B2
Muñás E......141 A4
Münchberg D...83 B3
Müncheberg D..74 B3
München = Munich
D.........108 A2
Munchen-Gladbach =
Mönchengladbach
D.........80 A2
Münchhausen D..81 B4
Mundaka E.....143 A4
Münden D......82 A1
Munderfing A...109 A4
Munderkingen D 107 A4
Mundesley GB..41 C5
Munera E......158 B1
Mungia E......143 A4
Munich = München
D.........108 A2
Muñico E......150 B2
Muniesa E.....153 A3
Munka-Ljungby S 61 C2
Munkebo DK...59 C3
Munkedal S....54 B2
Munkflohögen S 199 B11
Munkfors S....49 C5
Munktorp S....56 A2
Münnerstadt D..82 B2
Muñopepe E...150 B3
Muñotello E....150 B2
Münsingen
CH........106 C2
D.........94 C1
Munsö S......57 A3
Münster
CH........106 C2
Hessen D....93 B4
Munster D.....72 B3
Münster D.....71 C4
Munster F......106 A2
Muntibar E.....143 A4
Münzkirchen A..96 C1
Muodoslompolo S 196 B6
Muonio FIN....196 B6
Muotathal CH...107 C3
Muradiye TR....186 D2
Murakeresztúr H 124 A2
Murán SK......99 C4
Murano I......122 B1
Muras E.......140 A3
Murat F.......116 B2
Muratlı TR......186 A2
Murato F......180 A2
Murat-sur-Vèbre
F.........130 B1
Murau A.......109 B5
Muravera I.....179 C3
Murazzano I....133 A4
Murça P......148 A2
Murchante E....144 B2
Murchin D.....66 C2
Murcia E.......165 B3
Murczyn PL....76 B2
Mur-de-Barrez F 116 C2
Mur-de-Bretagne
F.........100 A2
Mur-de-Sologne F 103 B3
Mureck A......110 C2
Mürefte TR.....186 B2
Muret F.......146 A2
Murg CH......107 B4
Murguia E.....143 B4
Muri CH.......106 B3
Murias de Paredes
E.........141 B4
Muriedas E....143 A3
Muriel Viejo E...143 C4
Murillo de Rio Leza
E.........143 B4
Murillo el Fruto E 144 B2
Murjek S......196 C3
Murlaggan GB..34 B2
Murmansk RUS..3 B13
Murmashi RUS..3 B13
Murnau D......108 B2
Muro
E.........167 B3
F.........180 A1
Muro de Alcoy E 159 C3
Muro Lucano I..172 B1
Muron F......114 B3
Muros E.......140 B1
Muros de Nalón E 141 A4
Murowana Goślina
PL........76 B2
Mürren CH.....106 C2
Murrhardt D....94 C1
Murska Sobota
SLO.......111 C3
Mursko Središče
HR........111 C3
Murtas E......164 C1
Murten CH....106 C2
Murter HR.....137 B4
Murtiçi TR.....189 C6
Murtosa P.....148 B1
Murtovaara FIN..197 D12
Murvica HR....137 A4
Murviel-lès-Béziers
F.........130 B2
Mürzsteg A....110 B2
Murzynowo PL..75 B4
Mürzzuschlag A..110 B2
Musculdy F....144 A3
Muskö S......57 A4
Mušov CZ.....97 C4
Musselburgh GB..35 C4
Musselkanaal NL..71 B4
Mussidan F....129 A3
Mussomeli I....176 B2
Musson B......92 B1
Mussy-sur-Seine
F.........104 B3
Mustafakemalpaşa
TR........186 B3

Muszaki PL.....77 A5
Muszyna PL....99 B4
Mut TR.......23 C7
Muta SLO......110 C2
Muthill GB.....35 B4
Mutné SK......99 B3
Mutriku E......143 A4
Muttalip TR....187 C5
Mutterbergalm A 108 B2
Muurola FIN....197 C8
Muxía E.......140 A1
Muxika E......143 A4
Muxilka-Ugarte E 143 A4
Muzillac F.....101 B3
Mužla SK......112 B2
Muzzano del Turgnano
I.........122 B2
Mybster GB....32 C3
Myckelgensjö S..200 C3
Myennes F.....104 B1
Myjava SK.....98 C1
Myking N......46 B2
Mykland N.....53 B4
Myra N.......53 B5
Myrdal N......46 B4
Myre
Nordland N..194 A6
Nordland N..194 B6
Myresjö S.....62 A2
Mýrdalsjökull IS 190 D5
Myronivka UA..13 D9
Myrtou CY.....181 A2
Mysłakowice PL..85 B3
Myślenice PL...99 B3
Myślibórz PL....75 B3
Mysłowice PL...86 B3
Myszków PL....86 B3
Mytishchi RUS...9 E10
Mýtna S.......99 C3
Mýtne Ludany SK 112 A2
Mýto CZ.......96 B1

N

Nå N........46 B3
Naaldwijk NL....79 A4
Naantali FIN....8 B2
Naas IRL......30 A2
Nabais P......148 B2
Nabbelund S...62 A5
Nabburg D.....95 B4
Načeradec CZ...96 B2
Náchod CZ....85 B4
Nacław PL.....68 A1
Nadarzyce PL...75 A5
Nadarzyn PL...77 B5
Nádasd H.....111 C3
Nádlac RO.....126 A2
Nádudvar H....113 B5
Nadvirna UA...13 D6
Näfels CH......107 B4
Nafpaktos GR...184 A2
Nafplio GR.....184 B3
Nagel D.......95 B3
Nagele NL.....70 B2
Naggen S......200 D2
Nağloice PL....87 B4
Nagold D......93 C4
Nagore E......144 B2
Nagyatád H....124 A3
Nagybajom H..124 A3
Nagybaracska H 125 A4
Nagybátony H..113 B3
Nagyberény H..112 C2
Nagybörzsöny H..112 B2
Nagycenk H....111 B3
Nagycserkesz H 113 B5
Nagydorog H...112 C2
Nagyfüged H...113 B4
Nagyhersány H..125 B4
Nagyigmánd H..112 B2
Nagyiván H....113 B4
Nagykanizsa H..111 C3
Nagykáta H....113 B3
Nagykonyi H...112 C2
Nagykőrös H...113 B3
Nagykörü H....113 B4
Nagylóc H.....112 A3
Nagymágocs H..113 C4
Nagymányok H..125 A4
Nagymaros H...112 B2
Nagyoroszi H...112 A3
Nagyrábé H....113 B5
Nagyréde H....113 B3
Nagyszékely H..112 C2
Nagyszénás H..113 C4
Nagyszokoly H..112 C2
Nagytőke H....113 C4
Nagyvázsony H..111 C4
Nagyvenyim H..112 C2
Naharros E.....152 B1
Nahe D.......64 C3
Naila D.......83 B3
Nailloux F.....146 A2
Nailsworth GB..43 A4
Naintré F......115 B4
Nairn GB......32 D3
Najac F.......129 B4
Nájera E......143 B4
Nak H........112 C2
Nakksjø N.....53 A5
Nakło nad Notecią
PL........76 A2
Nakskov DK....65 B4
Nalda E.......143 B4
Nälden S......199 B11
Nálepkovo SK..99 C4
Nalliers F......114 B2
Nallıhan TR....187 B6
Nalzen F......146 B2
Nalžouské Hory
CZ........96 B1

Namysłów PL....86 A1
Nançay F......103 B4
Nanclares de la Oca
E.........143 B4
Nancy F.......92 C2
Nangis F......90 C3
Nannestad N...48 B3
Nant F.......130 A2
Nanterre F.....90 C2
Nantes F......101 B4
Nanteuil-le-Haudouin
F.........90 B2
Nantiat F......115 B5
Nantua F......118 A2
Nantwich GB...38 A4
Naoussa
Cyclades GR..185 B6
Imathia GR...182 C4
Napajedla C....98 B1
Napiwoda PL...77 A5
Naples = Nápoli I 170 C2
Nápoli = Naples I 170 C2
Nar S........57 C4
Nara N.......46 A1
Naraval E......141 A4
Narberth GB....39 C2
Nærbø N......52 B1
Narbonne F....130 B1
Narbonne-Plage F 130 B2
Narbuvollen N..199 C8
Narcao I......179 C2
Nardò I.......173 B4
Narkaus FIN....197 C9
Narken S......196 C5
Narmo N......48 B3
Narni I.......168 A2
Naro I........176 B2
Naro Fominsk RUS 9 E10
Narón E.......140 A2
Narros del Castillo
E.........150 B2
Narta HR......124 B2
Naruszewo PL..77 B5
Narva EST......8 C6
Narvik N......194 B8
Narzole I......133 A3
Näs FIN.......51 B7
Nås S........50 B1
Näs S........57 C4
Näsåker S.....200 C2
Näsaud RO.....17 B6
Nasavrky CZ....97 B3
Nasbinals F....116 C3
Næsbjerg DK...59 C1
Näshull S......62 A3
Našice HR.....125 B4
Nasielsk PL....77 B5
Naso I........177 A3
Nassau D......81 B3
Nassenfels D...95 C3
Nassenheide D..74 B2
Nassereith A....108 B1
Nässjö S......62 A2
Nastätten D....81 B3
Næstved DK....65 A4
Näsum S......63 B2
Näsviken S.....199 B12
Natalinci SRB...127 C2
Naters CH.....119 A5
Nater-Stetten D..108 A2
Nattavaara S...196 C3
Natters A......108 B2
Nattheim D....94 C2
Nättraby S.....63 B3
Naturno I......108 C1
Naucelle F.....130 A1
Nauders A.....108 C1
Nauen D......74 B1
Naul IRL......30 A2
Naumburg D...83 A3
Naundorf D....83 B4
Naunhof D.....83 A4
Naustdal N....46 A2
Nautijaur S....196 C2
Nautsi RUS....193 D13
Nava E.......142 A1
Navacerrada E..151 B3
Navaconcejo E..149 B4
Nava de Arévalo
E.........150 B3
Nava de la Asunción
E.........150 A3
Nava del Rey E..150 A2
Navafría E.....151 A4
Navahermosa E..157 A3
Navahrudak BY..13 B6
Naval E.......145 B4
Navalacruz E...150 B3
Navalcán E....150 B2
Navalcarnero E..151 B3
Navaleno E.....143 C3
Navalmanzano E 151 A3
Navalmoral E...150 B3
Navalmoral de la Mata
E.........150 C2
Navalón E.....159 C3
Navalonguilla E..150 B2
Navalperal de Pinares
E.........150 B3
Navalpino E....157 A3
Navaltalgordo E 150 B3
Navaltoril E....156 A3
Navaluenga E..150 B3
Navalvillar de Pela
E.........156 A2
Navan IRL.....30 A2
Navapolatsk BY..13 A8
Navarclés E....147 C2
Navarredonda de
Gredos E...150 B2
Navarrenx F....144 A3
Navarrés E.....159 B3
Navarrete E....143 B4
Navarrevisca E..150 B3
Navás E.......147 C2
Navascués E...144 B3
Navas del Madroño
E.........155 B4

Navas del Rey E . .151 B3
Navas del Sepillar
  E 163 A3
Navas de Oro E . .150 A3
Navas de San Juan
  E 157 B4
Navasfrias E . . . 149 B3
Nave I. 120 B3
Nave de Haver P . 149 B3
Nävekvarn S 56 B2
Navelli I. 169 A3
Navenby GB 40 B3
Naverstad S. 54 B2
Navés E 147 C2
Navezuelas E . . .156 A2
Navia E. 141 A4
Navia de Suarna
  E 141 B4
Navilly F 105 C4
Năvodari RO 17 C8
Nawja F 145 A3
Nazaré P. 154 B1
Nazarje SLO. . . .123 A3
Nazilli TR 188 B3
Nazza D 82 A2
Nea Anchialos
  GR. 182 D4
Nea Epidavros
  GR. 184 B4
Nea Flippias GR .182 D2
Nea Kalikratia GR 183 C5
Nea Makri GR . . .185 A4
Nea Moudania GR 183 C5
Neap GB. 33 A5
Nea Peramos GR. 183 C6
Neapoli
  Kozani GR . . . 182 C3
  Kriti GR 185 D6
  Lakonia GR . . .184 C4
Nea Stira GR . . . 185 A5
Neath GB 39 C3
Nea Visa GR . . . 186 A1
Nea Zichni GR. . .183 B5
Nebljusi HR 124 C1
Neblo SLO 122 A2
Nebolchy RUS. . . .9 C8
Nebra D 82 A3
Nechanice CZ . . .84 B3
Neckargemünd D .93 B4
Neckarsulm D . . .94 B1
Neda E 140 A2
Nedde SK 112 A1
Nedelišće HR. . . 124 A2
Nederweert NL. . .80 A1
Nedreberg N 48 B3
Nedre Gärdsjö S . 50 B2
Nedre Soppero S . 196 A4
Nedstrand N 52 A1
Nedvědice CZ . . .97 B4
Nędza PL 86 B2
Neede NL. 71 B3
Needham Market
  GB 45 A5
Needingworth GB .44 A3
Neermoor D 71 A4
Neeroeteren B . . .80 A1
Neerpelt B 79 A5
Neesen D 72 B1
Neetze D 73 A3
Nefyn GB 38 B2
Negotin SRB 16 C5
Negotino MK 182 B4
Negrar I 121 B3
Negredo E 151 A4
Negreira E 140 B2
Nègrepelisse F . . 129 B4
Negru Vodă RO . . 17 D8
Negueira de Muñiz
  E 141 A4
Neheim D 81 A3
Neila E 143 B4
Neive I 119 C5
Nejdek CZ 83 B4
Nekla PL 76 B2
Neksø DK 67 A4
Nelas P 148 B2
Nelaug N 53 B4
Nelidovo RUS 9 D8
Nelim FIN 193 D12
Nellingen D 94 C1
Nelson GB 40 B1
Neman RUS 12 A5
Nemea GR 184 B3
Nemesgörzsöny
  H 111 B4
Nemeskér 111 B3
Nemesszalók H . . 111 B4
Nemesnádudvar
  H 125 A5
Németkér H 112 C2
Nemours F 103 A4
Nemška Loka
  SLO. 123 B4
Nemšová SK 98 C2
Nenagh IRL 28 B3
Nenince SK 112 A3
Nenita GR 185 A7
Nenzing A 107 B4
Neochori GR. . . .182 D3
Neo Chori GR . . .184 A2
Neo Petritsi GR. . 183 B5
Nepi I 168 A2
Nepomuk CZ 96 B1
Nérac F 129 B3
Neratovice CZ . . .84 B2
Nerchau D 83 A4
Néré F 115 C3
Neresheim D 94 C2
Nereto I 136 C2
Nerezine HR 123 C3
Nerežišća HR. . . 138 B2
Neringa LT 12 A4
Néris-les Bains F .116 A2
Nerito I 169 A3
Nerja E 163 B4
Néronde F 117 B4
Nérondes F 103 C4

Nerpio E. 164 A2
Nersingen D 94 C2
Nerva E 161 B3
Nervesa della Battáglia
  I 121 B5
Nervi I. 134 A2
Nes
  Buskerud N . . .48 B1
  Hedmark N . . .48 B2
  NL 70 A2
  Sogn og Fjordane
  N 46 A3
  Sør-Trøndelag N . 198 B6
Nesbyen N 47 B6
Neset N 199 D7
Nesflaten N 52 A2
Nesjahverfi IS . . .191 C10
Neskaupstaður
  IS 191 B12
Nesland N 53 A3
Neslandsvatn N . .53 B5
Nesle F. 90 B2
Nesna N 195 D4
Nesoddtangen N . .48 C2
Nesovice CZ. . . .98 B1
Nesselwang D . . .108 B1
Nesslau CH 107 B4
Nessmersiel D . . .71 A4
Nesso I 120 B2
Nesterov UA 13 C5
Nestorio GR. . . .182 C3
Nesttun N 46 B2
Nesvady SK 112 B2
Nesvatnstemmen
  N 53 B4
Nether Stowey GB .43 A3
Netland N 52 B2
Netolice CZ 96 B2
Netphen D 81 B4
Netstal CH 107 B4
Nettancourt F . . .91 C4
Nettetal D 80 A2
Nettlingen D 72 B3
Nettuno I 168 B2
Neubeckum D . . .81 A4
Neubrandenburg D 74 A2
Neubruchhausen D 72 B1
Neubukow D 65 B4
Neuburg D 94 C3
Neuchâtel CH . . .106 C1
Neu Darchau D . . .73 A3
Neudau A 111 B3
Neudietendorf D . .82 B2
Neudorf D 93 B4
Neuenbürg D 93 C4
Neuenburg D 71 A4
Neuenburg D 71 A4
Neuendorf D 66 B2
Neuenhagen D . . .74 B2
Neuenhaus D 71 B3
Neuenkirchen
  Niedersachsen D . 71 B5
  Niedersachsen D . 72 A1
  Nordrhein-Westfalen
  D 71 B4
  Nordrhein-Westfalen
  D 81 B3
Neuenrade D 81 A3
Neuenwalde D . . .64 C1
Neuerburg D 92 A2
Neufahrn
  Bayern D . . . 95 C3
  Bayern D . . . 95 C4
Neuf-Brisach F . .106 A2
Neufchâteau
  B 92 B1
  F 92 C1
Neufchâtel-en-Bray
  F 90 B1
Neufchâtel-sur-Aisne
  F 91 B4
Neuflize F 91 B4
Neugersdorf D . . .84 B2
Neuhardenberg D .74 B3
Neuharlingersiel D .71 A4
Neuhaus
  Bayern D . . . 95 B3
  Bayern D . . . 96 C1
  Niedersachsen D . 64 C2
  Niedersachsen D . 73 A3
  Niedersachsen D . 81 A5
Neuhaus a Rennweg
  D 82 B3
Neuhausen
  CH 107 B3
  D 83 B6
Neuhausen ob Eck
  D 107 B3
Neuhof
  Bayern D 94 B2
  Hessen D 82 B1
Neuhofen an der Krems
  A 110 A1
Neuillé-Pont-Pierre
  F 102 B2
Neuilly-en-Thelle F .90 B2
Neuilly-le-Réal F .104 C2
Neuilly-l'Évêque
  F 105 B4
Neuilly-St Front F .90 B3
Neu-Isenburg D . .93 A4
Neukalen D 66 C1
Neu Kaliss D 73 A4
Neukirch D 84 A2
Neukirchen
  A 109 A3
  Hessen D 81 B5
  Schleswig-Holstein
  D 64 B1
Neukirchen am
  Grossvenediger
  A 109 B3
Neukirchen bei Heiligen
  Blut D 95 B4
Neukloster D 65 C4
Neulengbach A . . 110 A2
Neulise F 117 B4
Neu Lübbenau D . .74 B2
Neum BIH. 139 C3
Neumagen D 92 B2

Neumarkt D 95 B3
Neumarkt am Wallersee
  A 109 B4
Neumarkt im
  Hausruckkreis A 109 A4
Neumarkt im Mühlkreis
  A 96 C2
Neumarkt im
  Steiermark A . . 110 B1
Neumarkt Sankt Veit
  D 95 C4
Neumünster D . . .64 B2
Neunburg vorm Wald
  D 95 B4
Neung-sur-Beuvron
  F 103 B3
Neunkirch
  Luzern CH . . . 106 B3
  Schaffhausen CH 107 B3
Neunkirchen
  A 111 B3
  Nordrhein-Westfalen
  D 80 B3
  Saarland D. . . .92 B3
Neunkirchen am Brand
  D 94 B3
Neuötting D 95 C4
Neupetershain D . .84 A2
Neuravensburg D .107 B4
Neureut D 93 B4
Neuruppin D 74 B1
Neusäss D 94 C2
Neusiedl A 111 B3
Neuss D 80 A2
Neussargues-Moissac
  F 116 B2
Neustadt
  Bayern D 94 B2
  Bayern D 95 B4
  Bayern D 95 C3
  Brandenburg D . 73 B5
  Hessen D 81 B5
  Niedersachsen D . 72 B2
  Rheinland-Pfalz D .93 B4
  Sachsen D 84 A2
  Schleswig-Holstein
  D 65 B3
  Thüringen D . . .82 B3
  Thüringen D . . .83 B3
Neustadt-Glewe D .73 A4
Neustift im Stubaital
  A 108 B2
Neustrelitz D 74 A2
Neutal A 111 B3
Neutrebbin D 74 B3
Neu-Ulm D 94 C2
Neuves-Maisons F .92 C2
Neuvic
  Corrèze F 116 B2
  Dordogne F . . .129 A3
Neuville-aux-Bois
  F 103 A4
Neuville-de-Poitou
  F 115 B4
Neuville-les-Dames
  F 117 A5
Neuville-sur-Saône
  F 117 B4
Neuvy-le-Roi F . . 102 B2
Neuvy-Santour F . 104 A2
Neuvy-St Sépulchre
  F 103 C3
Neuvy-sur-Barangeon
  F 103 B4
Neuwied D 80 B3
Neuzelle D 74 B3
Névache F 118 B3
Neveklov CZ 96 B2
Nevel RUS 9 D6
Neverfjord N 192 B7
Nevers F 104 C2
Nevesinje BIH . . .139 B4
Névez F 100 B2
Nevlunghavn N . . .53 B5
Nevşehir TR. 23 B8
New Abbey GB . . .36 B3
New Aberdour GB .33 D4
New Alresford GB .44 B2
Newark-on-Trent
  GB 40 B3
Newbiggin-by-the-Sea
  GB 37 A5
Newbliss IRL 27 B3
Newborough GB . .38 A2
Newbridge IRL . . .30 A2
Newbridge on Wye
  GB 39 B3
Newburgh
  Aberdeenshire
  GB. 33 D4
  Fife GB 35 B4
Newbury GB 44 B2
Newby Bridge GB .36 B4
Newcastle GB . . .27 B5
Newcastle Emlyn
  GB 39 B2
Newcastleton GB . .37 A4
Newcastle-under-Lyme
  GB 40 B1
Newcastle upon Tyne
  GB 37 B5
Newcastle West
  IRL 29 B2
Newchurch GB . . .39 B3
New Costessey GB 41 C5
New Cumnock GB .36 A2
New Deer GB 33 D4
New Galloway GB .36 A2
Newham GB 45 B4
Newhaven GB . . .45 C4
Newinn IRL 29 B4
Newlyn GB 42 B1
Newmachar GB . .33 D4
Newmarket
  Suffolk GB 45 A4
  Western Isles GB. 31 A1
  IRL 29 B2
Newmarket-on-Fergus
  IRL 28 B3

New Mills GB 40 B2
New Milton GB. . .44 C2
New Pitsligo GB . .33 D4
Newport
  Isle of Wight GB. .44 C2
  Newport GB 39 C4
  Pembrokeshire GB 39 B2
  Telford & Wrekin
  GB. 38 B4
  Mayo IRL 28 A2
  Tipperary IRL. . .29 B3
Newport-on-Tay
  GB 35 B5
Newport Pagnell
  GB 44 A3
Newquay GB 42 B1
New Quay GB . . .39 B2
New Radnor GB. . .39 B3
New Romney GB . .45 C4
New Ross IRL 30 B2
Newry GB. 27 B4
New Scone GB . . .35 B4
Newton Abbot GB .43 B3
Newton Arlosh GB .36 B3
Newton Aycliffe GB 37 B5
Newton Ferrers GB 42 B2
Newtonhill GB . . .33 D4
Newtonmore GB . .32 D2
Newton Stewart GB 36 B2
Newtown
  Herefordshire
  GB. 39 B4
  Powys GB 39 B3
Newtownabbey GB .27 B5
Newtownards GB . .27 B5
Newtownbutler GB .27 B3
Newtown Cunningham
  IRL 27 B3
Newtownhamilton
  GB 27 B4
Newtownmountkennedy
  IRL 30 A2
Newtown St Boswells
  GB 35 C5
Newtown Sands
  IRL 29 B2
Newtownstewart
  GB 27 B3
Nexon F 115 C5
Neyland GB 39 C2
Nibbiano I. 120 C2
Nibe DK 58 B2
Nicastro I 175 C2
Niccone I 135 B5
Nice F 133 B3
Nickelsdorf A . . . 111 B4
Nicolosi I 177 B4
Nicosia
  CY 181 A2
  I 177 B3
Nicótera I 175 C1
Nidda D 81 B5
Nideggen D. 80 B2
Niderviller F 92 C3
Nidzica PL 77 A5
Niebla E 161 B3
Nieborów PL 77 B5
Niebüll D 64 B1
Niechanowo PL . . .76 B2
Niechorze PL 67 B3
Niedalino PL 67 B5
Niederaula D 82 B1
Niederbipp CH. . .106 B2
Niederbronn-les-Bains
  F 93 C3
Niederfischbach D .81 B3
Niedergörsdorf D .74 C1
Niederkrüchten D .80 A2
Niederndorf A . . .108 B3
Nieder-Olm D 93 B4
Niedersachswerfen
  D 82 A2
Niederstetten D . . .94 B1
Niederurnen CH . .107 B4
Niederwölz A . . . 110 B1
Niedoradz PL 85 A3
Niedzica PL 99 B4
Niegosławice PL . .85 A3
Nieheim D 81 A5
Niemcza PL 85 B4
Niemegk D 74 B1
Niemisel S 196 C5
Niemodlin PL 85 B5
Nienburg
  Niedersachsen D . 72 B2
  Sachsen-Anhalt D .83 A3
Niepołomice PL . . .99 A4
Nierstein D 93 B4
Niesky D 84 A2
Niestronno PL . . .76 B2
Nieświń PL 87 A4
Nieszawa PL 76 B3
Nieul-le-Dolent F .114 B2
Nieul-sur-Mer F . .114 B2
Nieuw-Amsterdam
  NL 71 B3
Nieuw-Buinen NL .71 B3
Nieuwegein NL . . .70 B2
Nieuwe Niedorp NL 70 B1
Nieuwe-Pekela NL .71 A3
Nieuwerkerken B . .79 B5
Nieuwe-schans NL .71 A4
Nieuwolda NL 71 A3
Nieuwpoort B 78 A2
Nieuw-Weerdinge
  NL 71 B3
Nigrita GR. 183 C5
Nigüelas E 163 B4
Nijar E 164 C2
Nijemci HR 125 B5
Nijkerk NL 70 B2
Nijlen B 79 A4
Nijmegen NL 80 A1
Nijverdal NL 71 B3
Nikel RUS 193 C14
Nikinci SRB. 127 C1
Nikiti GR 183 C5
Nikitsch A. 111 B3
Nikkaluokta S . . .196 B2
Nikla H 111 C4
Niklasdorf A. . . . 110 B2

Nikšić MNE 139 C4
Nilivaara S 196 B4
Nîmes F 131 B3
Nimis I 122 A2
Nimtofte DK. 58 B3
Nin HR 137 A4
Nindorf D 64 B2
Ninemilehouse IRL .30 B1
Ninove B 79 B4
Niort F 114 B3
Niš SRB 16 D4
Nisa P 155 B3
Niscemi I 177 B3
Niškala FIN 197 D10
Nissafors S 60 B3
Nissan-lez-Ensérune
  F. 130 B2
Nissedal N 53 A4
Nissumby DK 58 B1
Nisterud N 53 A5
Niton GB 44 C2
Nitra SK 98 C2
Nitrianske-Pravno
  SK. 98 C2
Nitrianske Rudno
  SK 98 C2
Nitry F 104 B2
Nittedal N 48 B2
Nittenau D 95 B4
Nittendorf D 95 B3
Nivala FIN 3 E9
Nivelles B 79 B4
Nivnice CZ 98 C1
Nižná SK 99 B3
Nižná Boca SK. . .99 C3
Nižné Repaše SK .99 B4
Nizza Monferrato I 119 C5
Njarðvík IS 190 D3
Njegoševo SRB . .126 B1
Njivice HR 123 B3
Njurundabommen
  S 200 D3
Njutånger S 200 D3
Noailles F 90 B2
Noain E 144 B2
Noale I 121 B5
Noalejo E 163 A4
Noblejas E 151 C4
Noceda E 141 B4
Nocera Inferiore I .170 C2
Nocera Terinese I .175 B2
Nocera Umbra I . .136 B1
Noceto I 120 C3
Noci I 173 B3
Nociglia I 173 B4
Nodeland N 53 B3
Nödinge S 60 B2
Nods F 105 B5
Noé F 146 A2
Noépoli I 174 A2
Noeux-les-Mines F .78 B2
Noez E 157 A3
Nogales E 155 C4
Nogara I. 121 B4
Nogarejas E 141 B4
Nogaro F 128 C2
Nogent F 105 A4
Nogent l'Artaud F .90 C3
Nogent-le-Roi F . .90 C1
Nogent-le-Rotrou F 89 B4
Nogent-sur-Seine
  F. 91 C3
Nogent-sur-Vernisson
  F 103 B4
Nogersund S 63 B2
Noguera E 152 B2
Nogueres F 145 A3
Nohfelden D 92 B3
Nohn D 80 B2
Noia E 140 B2
Noicáttaro I 173 A2
Noirétable F 117 B3
Noirmoutier-en-l'Île
  F 114 A1
Noja E 143 A3
Nojewo PL. 75 B5
Nokia FIN 8 B3
Nol S 60 B2
Nola I 170 C2
Nolay F 104 C3
Noli I 133 A4
Nolnyra S 51 B4
Nombela E 150 B3
Nomeny F 92 C2
Nomexy F 92 C2
Nonancourt F 89 B5
Nonant-le-Pin F . .89 B4
Nonántola I 121 C4
Nonaspe E 153 A4
None I 119 C4
Nontron F 115 C4
Nonza F 180 A2
Noordhorn NL 71 A3
Noordwijk NL. . . .70 B1
Noordwijkerhout
  NL 70 B1
Noordwolde NL . . .70 B3
Noppikoski S. 50 A1
Nora S 55 A6
Nørager DK 58 B2
Norberg S 50 B2
Norboda S 51 B5
Nórcia I 136 C2
Nord S 200 B4
Nordager N 53 A5
Nordanås S 200 B4
Nordausques F . . .78 B2
Nordborg DK 64 A2
Nordby
  Aarhus Amt. DK. .59 C3
  Ribe Amt. DK . . .59 C1
Norddeich D 71 A4
Norden D 71 A4
Nordenham D 72 A1
Norderhov N 48 B2
Norderney D 71 A4
Norderstapel D . . .64 B2
Norderstedt D 64 C3
Nordfjord N 193 B14
Nordfjordeid N . .198 D3

Nordfold N 194 C6
Nordhalben D 82 B3
Nordhausen D . . .82 A2
Nordheim vor der Rhön
  D 82 B2
Nordholz D 64 C1
Nordhorn D 71 B4
Nordingrå S. 200 D4
Nordkjosbotn N. . .192 C3
Nordli N 199 A10
Nordmaling S 200 C5
Nordmark S 49 C6
Nordmela N 194 A6
Nord-Odal N 48 B3
Nordre Osen N . . .48 A3
Nordsinni N 48 B1
Nørdstedalsseter
  N 198 D4
Nordstemmen D . .72 B2
Nordvågen N 193 B10
Nordwalde D 71 B4
Noreña E. 142 A1
Noresund N 48 B1
Norg NL 71 A3
Norheimsund N . . .46 B3
Norie S 63 B2
Norma I 169 B2
Nornäs S 49 A5
Norråker S 200 B1
Norrahammar S . .62 A2
Norråker S 200 B1
Norrala S 51 A3
Norra Vi S 62 A3
Nørre Aaby DK . . .59 C2
Nørre Alslev DK . .65 B4
Nørre Lyndelse DK .59 C3
Nørre Nebel DK . .59 C1
Norrent-Fontes F . .78 B2
Nørre Snede DK . .59 C2
Nørresundby DK . .58 A2
Nørre Vorupør DK .58 B1
Norrfjärden S . . .196 D4
Norrhed S 196 C3
Norrhult Klavreström
  S 62 A3
Norrköping S 56 B2
Norrskedika S 51 B5
Norrsundet S 51 B4
Norrtälje S 57 A4
Nors DK 58 A1
Norsbron S 55 A4
Norsholm S 56 B1
Norsjö S 200 B5
Nörten-Hardenberg
  D 82 A1
Northallerton GB. . .37 B5
Northampton GB. . .44 A3
North Berwick GB . .35 B5
North Charlton GB .37 A5
Northeim D 82 A1
Northfleet GB 45 B4
North Frodingham
  GB 40 B3
North Kessock GB .32 D2
Northleach GB . . .44 B2
North Molton GB . .42 A3
North Petherton
  GB 43 A3
Northpunds GB . . .33 B5
North Somercotes
  GB 41 B4
North Tawton GB . .42 B3
North Thoresby GB .41 B3
North Walsham GB 41 C5
Northwich GB 38 A4
Norton GB 40 A3
Nortorf D 64 B2
Nort-sur-Erdre F . .101 B4
Nörvenich D 80 B2
Norwich GB 41 C5
Norwick GB 33 A6
Nøsen N 47 B5
Nossa Senhora do
  Cabo P 154 C1
Nossebro S 55 B3
Nössemark S 54 A2
Nossen D 83 A5
Notaresco I 169 A3
Noto I 177 C4
Notodden N 53 A5
Nottingham GB . . .40 C2
Nottuln D 71 C4
Nouan-le-Fuzelier
  F 103 B4
Nouans-les-Fontaines
  F 103 B3
Nougaroulet F . . .129 C3
Nouvion F 78 B1
Nouzonville F 91 B4
Nova H 111 C3
Nová Baňa SK . . .98 C2
Nová Bystrica SK .99 B3
Nová Bystřice CZ .97 B3
Nova Crnja SRB . .126 B2
Novafeltria I 135 B5
Nova Gorica SLO .122 B2
Nova Gradiška
  HR 124 B3
Nováky SK 98 C2
Novalaise F 118 B2
Novales E 145 B3
Nova Levante I . . .108 C2
Nováljka HR 137 A4
Nova Pazova SRB 127 C2
Nová Pec CZ 96 C1
Novara I 120 B1
Novara di Sicília I .177 A4
Nova Siri I 174 A2
Novate Mezzola I . 120 A2
Nova Topola BIH . 125 B3
Nové Hrady CZ . . .96 C2
Novelda E 165 A4
Novellara I 121 C3
Nové Město SK . . .98 C1
Nové Město nad Metují
  CZ 85 B4

Nové Město na Moravě
  CZ 97 B4
Nové Město pod
  Smrkem CZ. . . .84 B3
Nové Mitrovice CZ .96 B1
Noventa di Piave I 122 B1
Noventa Vicentina
  I 121 B4
Novés E 151 B3
Noves F 131 B3
Nové Sady SK . . .98 C1
Novés de Segre E 147 B2
Nové Strašeci CZ .84 B1
Nové Zámky SK. . 112 B2
Novgorod RUS 9 C7
Novi Bečej SRB . .126 B2
Novi di Módena I . 121 C3
Novigrad
  Istarska HR . . .122 B2
  Zadarsko-Kninska
  HR. 137 A4
Novigrad Podravski
  HR 124 A2
Novi Kneževac
  SRB 126 A2
Novi Lígure I 120 C1
Noville B 92 A1
Novi Marof HR . . .124 A2
Novion-Porcien F . .91 B4
Novi Pazar
  BG 17 D7
  SRB 16 D4
Novi Sad SRB . . .126 B1
Novi Slankamen
  SRB 126 B2
Novi Travnik BIH . 139 A3
Novi Vinodolski
  HR 123 B3
Novohrad-Volynskyy
  UA 13 C7
Novo Mesto SLO . 123 B4
Novo Miloševo
  SRB 126 B2
Novozhyvotiv RUS . .9 D6
Novo Selo BIH. . .125 B3
Novoselytsya UA. .17 A7
Novosokolniki RUS .9 D6
Novoveská Huta
  SK 99 C4
Novovolynsk UA . .13 C6
Novska HR. 124 B2
Nový Bor CZ 84 B2
Nový Bydžov CZ . .84 B3
Nový-Chevrières F .91 B4
Novy Dwór Mazowiecki
  PL. 77 B5
Nový-Hrozenkov
  CZ 98 B2
Nový Jičín CZ 98 B2
Nový Knin CZ 96 B2
Nowa Cerekwia PL .86 B1
Nowa Dęba PL. . . .87 B5
Nowa Karczma PL. 68 A3
Nowa Kościoł PL . .85 A3
Nowa Ruda PL . . .85 B4
Nowa Słupia PL. . .87 B5
Nowa Sól PL 85 A3
Nowa Wieś PL . . .69 B4
Nowa-Wieś Wielka
  PL. 76 B3
Nowe PL. 69 B3
Nowe Brzesko PL .87 B4
Nowe Grudze PL. .77 B4
Nowe Kiejkuty PL .77 A6
Nowe Miasteczko
  PL. 85 A3
Nowe Miasto
  Mazowieckie PL. .77 B5
  Mazowieckie PL. .87 A4
Nowe Miasto
  Lubawskie PL. . .69 B4
Nowe Miasto nad Wartą
  PL. 76 B2
Nowe Skalmierzyce
  PL. 86 A2
Nowe Warpno PL. .74 A3
Nowica PL 69 A4
Nowogard PL 75 A4
Nowogród Bobrzanski
  PL. 84 A3
Nowogrodziec PL . .84 A3
Nowosolna PL. . . .86 A3
Nowy Dwór Gdański
  PL. 69 A4
Nowy Korczyn PL . .87 B4
Nowy Sącz PL . . .99 B4
Nowy Staw PL . . .69 A4
Nowy Targ PL . . .99 B4
Nowy Tomyśl PL . .75 B5
Nowy Wiśnicz PL. .99 B4
Noyal-Pontivy F . .100 A3
Noyant F 102 B2
Noyelles-sur-Mer F 78 B1
Noyen-sur-Sarthe
  F 102 B1
Noyers F 104 B2
Noyers-sur-Cher
  F 103 B3
Noyers-sur-Jabron
  F 132 A1
Noyon F 90 B2
Nozay F 101 B4
Nuaillé F 102 B1
Nuaillé-d'Aunis F .114 B3
Nuars F 104 B2
Nubledo E 141 A5
Nueno E 145 B3
Nuestra Señora Sa
  Verge des Pilar
  E 166 C1
Nueva E 142 A2
Nueva Carteya E . 163 A3
Nuevalos E 152 A2
Nuits F 104 B3
Nuits-St Georges
  F 105 B3

Nule I 178 B3
Nules E 159 B3
Nulvi I 178 B2
Numana I 136 B2
Numansdorp NL . . .79 A4
Nümbrecht D 81 B3
Nunchritz D 83 A5
Nuneaton GB 40 C2
Nunnanen FIN 196 A7
Nunspeet NL 70 B2
Nuñomoral E 149 B3
Nuorgam FIN 193 B11
Núoro I 178 B3
Nurallao I 179 C3
Nuremberg = Nürnberg
  D 94 B3
Nurmes FIN 3 E11
Nürnberg = Nuremberg
  D 94 B3
Nurri I 179 C3
Nürtingen D 94 C1
Nus I 119 B4
Nusnäs S 50 B1
Nusplingen D 107 A3
Nuštar HR 125 B4
Nuupas FIN 197 C9
Nyåker S 200 C5
Nyáregyháza H 112 B3
Nyarlörinc H 113 C3
Nyasvizh BY 13 B7
Nybble S 55 A5
Nybergsund N 49 A4
Nybøl DK 64 B2
Nyborg
  DK 59 C3
  S 196 D6
Nybro S 62 B3
Nybster GB 32 C3
Nyby DK 65 B5
Nye S 62 A3
Nyékládháza H 113 B4
Nyergesujfalu H . . .112 B2
Nyhammar S 50 B1
Nyhyttan S 55 A5
Nyirád H 111 B4
Nyírbátor H 16 B5
Nyíregyháza H 16 B4
Nyker DK 67 A3
Nykil S 56 B1
Nykirke N 48 B2
Nykøbing
  Falster DK 65 B4
  Vestsjællands Amt.
  DK 61 D1
Nykøbing Mors DK .58 B1
Nyköping S 56 B3
Nykroppa S 55 A5
Nykvarn S 56 A3
Nykyrke S 55 B5
Nyland S 200 C3
Nylars DK 67 A3
Nymburk CZ 84 B3
Nynäshamn S 57 B3
Nyon CH 118 A3
Nyons F 131 A4
Nýřany CZ 96 B1
Nýrsko CZ 95 B5
Nyrud N 193 C13
Nysa PL 85 B5
Nysäter S 55 A3
Nyseter N 198 C5
Nyskoga S 49 B4
Nysted DK 65 B4
Nystrand N 53 A5
Nyúl H 111 B4
Nyvoll N 192 B7

O

Oadby GB 40 C2
Oakengates GB 38 B4
Oakham GB 40 C3
Oanes N 52 B2
Obalj BIH 139 B4
Oban GB 34 B2
O Barco E 141 B4
Obbola S 200 C6
Obdach A 110 B1
Obejo E 156 B3
Oberammergau D .108 B2
Oberasbach D 94 B2
Oberau D 108 B2
Oberaudorf D 108 B3
Oberbruck F 106 B1
Oberdiessbach
  CH 106 C2
Oberdorf CH 106 B2
Oberdrauburg A . . .109 C3
Oberelsbach D 82 B2
Obere Stanz A 110 B2
Ober Grafendorf
  A 110 A2
Obergünzburg D . . .108 B1
Obergurgl A 108 C2
Oberhausen D 80 A2
Oberhof D 82 B2
Oberkirch D 93 C4
Oberkirchen D 81 A4
Oberkochen D 94 C2
Obermassfeld-
  Grimmenthal D . . .82 B2
Ober-Morlen D 81 B4
Obermünchen D 95 C3
Obernai F 93 C3
Obernberg A 96 C1
Obernburg D 93 B5
Oberndorf D 93 C4
Oberndorf bei Salzburg
  A 109 B3
Obernkirchen D 72 B2
Obernort A 110 B2
Oberpullendorf A . .111 B3
Oberriet CH 107 B4
Oberröblingen D . . .82 A3
Oberrot D 94 B1

Oberstaufen D 107 B5
Oberstdorf D 107 B5
Obertauern A 109 B4
Obertilliach A 109 C3
Obertraubling D 95 C4
Obertraun A 109 B4
Obertrubach D 95 B3
Obertrum A 109 B4
Oberursel D 81 B4
Obervellach A 109 C4
Oberviechtach D 95 B4
Oberwart A 111 B3
Oberwesel D 93 A3
Oberwinter D 80 B3
Oberwölzstadt A . .110 B1
Oberzell D 96 C1
Obice PL 87 B4
Óbidos P 154 B1
Obing D 109 B3
Objat F 129 A4
Objazda PL 68 A2
Öblarn A 109 B5
Obninsk RUS 9 E10
O Bolo E 141 B3
Oborniki PL 75 B5
Oborniki Śląskie
  PL 85 A4
Obornjača SRB 126 B1
Obrenovac SRB 127 C2
Obrež SRB 127 C1
Obrigheim D 93 B5
Obrov SLO 123 B3
Obrovac
  HR 137 A4
  SRB 126 B1
Obrovac Sinjski
  HR 138 B2
Obruk TR 23 B7
Obrzycko PL 75 B5
Obudovac BIH 125 C4
Ocaña E 151 C4
O Carballiño E 140 B2
Occhiobello I 121 C4
Occimiano I 119 B5
Očevlja BIH 139 A4
Ochagavía E 144 B2
Ochiltree GB 36 A2
Ochla PL 84 A3
Ochotnica-Dolna
  PL 99 B4
Ochotnica-Górna
  PL 99 B4
Ochsenfurt D 94 B2
Ochsenhausen D . .107 A4
Ochtendung D 80 B3
Ochtrup D 71 B4
Ocieka PL 87 B5
Ockelbo S 50 B3
Öckerö S 60 B1
Ocnita MD 17 A7
O Corgo E 141 B3
Očová SK 99 C3
Ócsa H 112 B3
Ócseny H 125 A4
Ócsöd H 113 C4
Octeville F 88 A2
Ocypel PL 69 B3
Ödåkra S 61 C2
Odby DK 58 B1
Odda N 46 B3
Odder DK 59 C3
Ödeborg S 54 B2
Odeceixe P 160 B1
Odechów PL 87 A5
Odeleite P 160 B2
Odemira P 160 B1
Ödemiş TR 188 A2
Odensbacken S 56 A1
Odense DK 59 C3
Odensjö
  Jönköping S 62 A2
  Kronoberg S 60 C3
Oderberg D 74 B3
Oderzo I 122 B1
Odesa = Odessa
  UA 17 B9
Ödeshög S 55 B5
Odessa = Odesa
  UA 17 B9
Odiáxere P 160 B1
Odie GB 33 B4
Odiham GB 44 B3
Odilo Peak PL 86 B2
Odivelas P 160 A1
Odolanów PL 85 A5
Odón E 152 B2
Odorheiu Secuiesc
  RO 17 B6
Odrowaz PL 87 A4
Odry CZ 98 B1
Odrzywół PL 87 A4
Ødsted DK 59 C2
Odžaci SRB 126 B1
Odžak BIH 125 B4
Oebisfelde D 73 B3
Oederan D 83 B5
Oeding D 71 B3
Oegstgeest NL 70 B1
Oelde D 81 A4
Oelsnitz D 83 B4
Oer-Erkenschwick
  D 80 A3
Oerlinghausen D . . .72 C1
Oettingen D 94 C2
Oetz A 108 B1
Oeventrop D 81 A4
Offanengo I 120 B2
Offenbach D 81 B4
Offenburg D 93 C3
Offida I 136 C2
Offranville F 89 A5
Ofte N 53 A4
Ofterschwang D . . .107 B5
Oggiono I 120 B2
Ogihares E 163 A4
Ogliastro Cilento I .170 C3
Ogliastro Marina I .170 C2
Ogmore-by-Sea GB 39 C3
Ogna N 52 B1

Ogre LV 8 D4
Ogrodzieniec PL . . .86 B3
Oguchi HR 123 B4
Ögur IS 190 A3
Ohanes E 164 B2
Ohey B 79 B5
Ohlstadt D 108 B2
Ohrdruf D 82 B2
Ohrid MK 182 B2
Öhringen D 94 B1
Oia E 140 B2
Oiã P 148 B1
Oiartzun E 144 A2
Oijärvi FIN 197 D8
Oilgate IRL 30 B2
Oimbra E 148 A2
Oiselay-et-Grachoux
  F 105 B4
Oisemont F 90 B1
Oisterwijk NL 79 A5
Öja S 57 C4
Öjebyn S 49 B5
Ojén E 162 B3
Ojrzeń PL 77 B5
Ojuelos Altos E . . .156 B2
Okalewo PL 77 A4
Okány H 113 C5
Okehampton GB . . .42 B2
Oklaj HR 138 B2
Øksneshamn N . . .194 B6
Okoč SK 111 B4
Okoličné SK 99 B3
Okonek PL 68 B1
Okonin PL 69 B3
Okříšky CZ 97 B3
Oksa PL 87 B4
Øksfjord N 192 B6
Øksna N 48 B3
Okučani HR 124 B3
Okulovka RUS 9 C8
Ólafsfjörður IS 191 A7
Ólafsvík IS 190 C2
Ölagnö S 57 A4
Olague E 144 B2
Öland S 63 B4
Olargues F 130 B1
Oława PL 85 B5
Olazagutía E 144 B1
Olbernhau D 83 B5
Ólbia I 178 B3
Olching D 108 A2
Oldbury GB 43 A4
Old Deer GB 33 D4
Oldcastle IRL 27 C3
Old Deer GB 33 D4
Oldeberkoop NL . . .70 B3
Oldeboorn NL 70 A2
Olden N 198 D3
Oldenbrok D 71 A5
Oldenburg
  Niedersachsen D .71 A5
  Schleswig-Holstein
  D 65 B3
Oldenzaal NL 71 B3
Olderdalen N 192 C4
Olderfjord N 193 B9
Oldersum D 71 A4
Oldervik N 192 C2
Oldham GB 40 B1
Oldisleben D 82 A3
Oldmeldrum GB . . .33 D4
Olea E 142 B2
Oleby S 49 B5
Olechów PL 87 A5
Oléggio I 120 B1
Oleiros
  Coruña E 140 A2
  Coruña E 140 B1
  P 154 B2
Oleksandriya UA . . .13 C7
Olen B 79 A4
Ølen N 52 A1
Olenegorsk RUS . . .3 B13
Olenino RUS 9 D8
Olesa de Montserrat
  E 147 C2
Oleśnica PL 85 A5
Oleśnice CZ 97 B4
Olesno PL 86 B2
Oletta F 180 A2
Olette F 146 B3
Olevsk UA 13 C7
Olfen D 80 A3
Olgiate Comasco
  I 120 B1
Olginate I 120 B2
Ølgod DK 59 C1
Olgrinmore GB 32 C3
Olhão P 160 B2
Olhava FIN 197 D8
Olhavo P 154 B1
Olias del Rey E 151 C4
Oliena I 178 B3
Oliete E 153 B3
Olimbos GR 188 D2
Olite E 144 B2
Oliva E 159 C3
Oliva de la Frontera
  E 155 C4
Oliva de Mérida E .156 B1
Oliva de Plasencia
  E 149 B3
Olivadi I 175 C2
Olival P 154 B2
Olivar E 163 B4
Olivares E 161 B3
Olivares de Duero
  E 142 C2
Olivares de Júcar
  E 158 B1
Oliveira de Azeméis
  P 148 B1
Oliveira de Frades
  P 148 B1
Oliveira do Conde
  P 148 B2

Oliveira do Douro
  P 148 A1
Oliveira do Hospital
  P 148 B2
Olivenza E 155 C3
Olivet F 103 B3
Olivone CH 107 C3
Öljehult S 63 B3
Ollerton GB 40 B2
Ollerup DK 65 A3
Olliergues F 117 B3
Olmeda del Rey E .158 B2
Olmedilla de Alarcón
  E 158 B1
Olmedillo de Roa
  E 143 C3
Olmedo
  E 150 A3
  I 178 B2
Olmeto F 180 B1
Olmillos de Castro
  E 149 A3
Olmos de Ojeda E .142 B2
Olney GB 44 A3
Ołobok PL 86 A2
Olocau del Rey E .153 B3
Olofström S 63 B2
Olomouc CZ 98 B1
Olonets RUS 9 B8
Olonne-sur-Mer F .114 B2
Olonzac F 130 B1
Oloron-Ste Marie
  F 145 A3
Olost E 147 C3
Olot E 147 B3
Olovo BIH 139 A4
Olpe D 81 A3
Olsberg D 81 A4
Olsene B 79 B3
Olserud S 55 A4
Olshammar S 55 B5
Olshanka UA 13 D9
Olszanica PL 85 A3
Olsztyn
  Śląskie PL 86 B3
  Warmińsko-Mazurskie
  PL 69 B5
Olsztynek PL 77 A5
Olszyna PL 84 A3
Olszyny PL 77 A6
Oltedal N 52 B2
Olten CH 106 B2
Olteniţa RO 17 C7
Olula del Rio E 164 B2
Ølve N 46 B2
Olvega E 144 C2
Olvera E 162 B2
Olzai I 178 B3
Omagh GB 27 B3
Omalos GR 185 D4
Omans I 119 B5
Omiš HR 138 B2
Omišalj HR 123 B3
Ommen NL 71 B3
Omodhos CY 181 B1
Omoljica SRB 127 C2
On B 79 B5
Oña E 143 B3
Onano I 168 A1
O Näsberg S 49 B5
Onda E 159 B3
Ondara E 159 C4
Ondarroa E 143 A4
Onesse-et-Laharie
  F 128 B1
Oneşti RO 17 B7
Onhaye B 79 B4
Onich GB 34 B2
Onil E 159 C3
Onis E 142 A2
Önnestad S 61 C4
Onsala S 60 B2
Ontinyent E 159 C3
Ontur E 158 C2
Onzain F 103 B3
Onzonilla E 142 B1
Oostburg NL 79 A3
Oostende B 78 A2
Oosterend NL 70 A2
Oosterhout NL 79 A4
Oosterwolde NL . . .71 B3
Oosterzele B 79 B3
Oosthuizen NL 70 B2
Oostkamp B 78 A3
Oostmalle B 79 A4
Oost-Vlieland NL . . .70 A2
Oostvoorne NL 79 A4
Ootmarsum NL 71 B3
Opalenica PL 75 B5
O Páramo E 140 B3
Opařany CZ 96 B2
Opatija HR 123 B3
Opatów
  Śląskie PL 86 B2
  Świętokrzyskie PL 87 B5
  Wielkopolskie PL .86 A2
Opatówek PL 86 A2
Opatowiec PL 87 B4
Opava CZ 98 B1
Oped Pedrouzo E .140 B2
Opeinde NL 70 A3
Oper Thalkirchdorf
  D 107 B5
Opglabbeek B 80 A1
Opicina I 122 B2
O Pino E 140 B2
O Porriño E 140 B2
Opole PL 86 B1
Oporów PL 77 B4
Oppach D 84 A2

Oppdal N 198 C6
Oppeby
  Östergötland S . .56 B1
  Södermanland S .56 B2
Oppedal N 46 A2
Oppegård N 54 A1
Oppenau D 93 C4
Oppenberg A 110 B1
Oppenheim D 93 B4
Oppido Lucano I . .172 B1
Óppido Mamertina
  I 175 C1
Opponitz A 110 B1
Oppstad N 48 B3
Oprtalj HR 122 B2
Opsaheden S 49 B5
Opuzen HR 138 B3
Ora
  CY 181 B2
  I 121 A4
Orada P 155 C3
Oradea RO 16 B4
Oradour-sur-Glane
  F 115 C5
Oradour-sur-Vayres
  F 115 C4
Oragonja SLO 122 B2
Orah BIH 139 C4
Orahova BIH 138 A3
Orahovica HR 125 B3
Orahovo BIH 124 B3
Oraison F 132 B1
Orajärvi FIN 196 C7
Orange F 131 A3
Orani I 178 B3
Oranienbaum D 83 A4
Oranienburg D 74 B2
Oranmore IRL 28 A3
Orašac SRB 127 C2
Orašje BIH 125 B4
Oravská Lesná SK .99 B3
Oravská Polhora
  SK 99 B3
Oravské Veselé SK .99 B3
Oravsky-Podzámok
  SK 99 B3
Orba E 159 C3
Orbacém P 148 A1
Orbais F 91 C3
Ørbæk DK 59 C3
Orbassano I 119 B4
Orbe CH 105 C5
Orbec F 89 A4
Orbetello I 168 A1
Orbetello Scalo I . .168 A1
Orbigny F 103 B3
Ørby DK 59 B3
Orce E 164 B2
Orcera E 164 A2
Orchamps-Vennes
  F 105 B5
Orches F 102 C2
Orchete E 159 C3
Orchies F 78 B3
Orchowo PL 76 B3
Orcières F 118 C3
Ordes E 140 A2
Ordhead GB 33 D4
Ordino AND 146 B2
Ordizia E 144 A1
Orduña E 143 B4
Ore S 50 A2
Orea E 152 B2
Orebić HR 138 C3
Örebro S 56 A1
Öregcsertő H 112 C3
Öregrund S 51 B5
Os
  Hedmark N 48 B3
  Hedmark N 199 C8
Osann-Monzel D . . .92 B2
Osbruk S 62 A2
Øsby DK 59 C3
Osby S 61 C3
Oščadnica SK 98 B2
Oschatz D 83 A5
Oschersleben D 73 B4
Óschiri I 178 B3
Osciłowo PL 77 B5
Osdorf D 64 B2
Osečina SRB 127 C1
Osečná CZ 84 B1
Oseja de Sajambre
  E 142 A1
Osek CZ 84 B1
Osen N 199 A7
Osera de Ebro E . .153 A3
Osidda I 178 B3
Osie PL 69 B3
Osieciny
  Pomorskie PL . . .68 B3
  Wielkopolskie PL 75 C5
Osieczno PL 75 A4
Osiek
  Kujawsko-Pomorskie
  PL 76 B3
  Kujawsko-Pomorskie
  PL 77 A4
  Pomorskie PL . . .69 B3
  Świętokrzyskie PL 87 B5
Osiek nad Notecią
  PL 76 A2
Osielsko PL 76 A3
Osijek HR 125 B4
Osilnica SLO 123 B3
Ósilo I 178 B2
Ósimo I 136 B2
Osina PL 75 A3
Osintorf BY 13 A9
Osipaonica SRB . . .127 C3
Osjaków PL 86 A2
Oskamull GB 34 B1
Oskarshamn S 62 A4
Oskarström S 60 C2
Oslany SK 98 C2
Oslavany CZ 97 B4
Ošlje HR 139 C4
Oslo N 48 C2
Øsløs DK 58 A1

Ornans F 105 B5
Ornäs S 50 B2
Ørnes N 195 D4
Orneta PL 69 A5
Ørnhøj DK 59 B1
Ornö S 57 A4
Örnsköldsvik S . . .200 C4
Orolik HR 125 B4
Orom SRB 126 B1
Oron-la-Ville CH . .106 C1
Oronsko PL 87 A4
Oropa I 119 B4
Oropesa
  Castellón de la Plana
  E 153 B4
  Toledo E 150 C2
O Rosal E 140 C2
Orosei I 178 B3
Orosháza H 113 C4
Oroslavje HR 124 B1
Oroszlány H 112 B2
Oroszlo H 125 A4
Orotelli I 178 B3
Orozko E 143 A4
Orphir GB 33 C3
Orpington GB 45 B4
Orreaga-Roncesvalles
  E 144 A2
Orrefors S 62 B3
Orrviken S 199 B11
Orsa S 50 A1
Orsara di Púglia I .171 B3
Orsay F 90 C2
Orscholz D 92 B2
Orsennes F 103 C3
Orserum S 55 B5
Orsha BY 13 A9
Orsières CH 119 A4
Örsjö S 63 B3
Ørslev DK 65 A4
Örslösa S 55 B3
Orsogna I 169 A4
Orsomarso I 174 B1
Orşova RO 16 C5
Ørsta N 198 C3
Orsундsbro S 56 A3
Ortaca TR 188 C3
Ortakent TR 188 B2
Ortaklar TR 188 B2
Ortaköy TR 23 B8
Orta Nova I 171 B3
Orte I 168 A2
Ortenburg D 96 C1
Orth A 111 A3
Orthez F 128 C2
Ortigueira E 140 A3
Ortilla E 145 B3
Ortisei I 108 C2
Ortnevik N 46 A3
Orton GB 37 B4
Ortona I 169 A4
Ortrand D 84 A1
Orubica HR 124 B3
Orune I 178 B3
Orusco E 151 B4
Orvalho P 155 A3
Orvault F 101 B4
Ørvella N 53 A5
Orvieto I 168 A2
Orvínio I 169 A2
Oryahovo BG 17 D5
Orzesze PL 86 B2
Orzinuovi I 120 B2
Orzivécchi I 120 B2
Orzyny PL 77 A6

Osmancık TR 23 A8
Osmaneli TR 187 B4
Ösmo S 57 B3
Osmolin PL 77 B4
Osnabrück D 71 B5
Ośno Lubuskie PL .75 B3
Osoblaha CZ 85 B5
Osor HR 123 C3
Osorno E 142 B2
Øsoyra N 46 A2
Øspakseyri IS 190 B4
Os Peares E 140 B3
Ospedaletti I 133 B3
Ospitaletto I 120 B3
Oss NL 80 A1
Ossa de Montiel E .158 C1
Ossi I 178 B2
Ossjøen N 47 B3
Ossun F 145 A3
Ostanå S 61 C4
Ostanvik S 50 A2
Ostashkov RUS 9 D8
Östavall S 200 D1
Østbevern D 71 B4
Østborg N 199 A10
Østby N 49 A4
Østed DK 61 D1
Ostenfeld D 64 B2
Oster UA 13 C9
Øster Assels DK . . .58 B1
Osterburg D 73 B4
Osterburken D 94 B1
Øster Bjerregrav DK 58 B2
Østerbybruk S 51 B4
Østerbyhavn DK . . .58 A4
Østerbymo S 62 A3
Ostercappeln D 71 B5
Österfärnebo S 51 B3
Osterfeld D 83 A3
Österforse S 200 C3
Osterhever D 64 B1
Osterhofen D 95 C5
Osterholz-Scharmbeck
  D 72 A1
Øster Hornum DK . .58 B2
Øster Hurup DK . . .58 B3
Østerild DK 58 A1
Øster Jølby DK 58 B1
Österlövsta S 51 B4
Øster-marie DK 67 A4
Ostermiething A . . .109 A3
Osterode am Harz
  D 82 A2
Ostersiel D 64 B1
Östersund S 199 B11
Øster Tørslev DK . .58 B3
Österväla S 51 B4
Östervallskog S 54 A2
Östervrå DK 58 A3
Osterwieck D 73 C3
Osterzell D 108 B1
Ostffyasszonyfa
  H 111 B4
Östfora S 51 C4
Östhammar S 51 B5
Ostheim F 106 A2
Ostheim vor der Rhön
  D 82 B2
Osthofen D 93 B4
Ostiano I 120 B3
Ostíglia I 121 B4
Ostiz E 144 B2
Östmark S 49 B4
Östnor S 50 A1
Ostojićevo SRB . . .126 B2
Ostra I 136 B2
Östra Amtervik S . . .55 A4
Östraby S 61 D3
Ostrach D 107 B4
Östra Husby S 56 B2
Östra Ljungby S . . .61 C3
Östra Ryd S 56 B2
Ostrau D 83 A5
Ostrava CZ 98 B2
Østre Halsen N 53 A6
Ostrhauderfehn D . .71 A4
Ostritz D 84 A2
Ostróda PL 69 B4
Ostroh UA 13 C7
Ostrołęka PL 12 B4
Ostropole PL 68 B1
Ostroróg PL 75 B5
Ostrošovac BIH 124 C1
Ostrov
  CZ 83 B4
  RUS 8 D6
Ostrov nad Oslavou
  CZ 97 B3
Ostrówek PL 86 A2
Ostrowiec PL 68 A1
Ostrowiec-
  Świętokrzyski PL .87 B5
Ostrowite PL 77 A4
Ostrów Mazowiecka
  PL 12 B4
Ostrowo PL 76 B3
Ostrów Wielkopolski
  PL 86 A1
Ostrožac BIH 139 B3
Ostrzeszów PL 86 A1
Ostseebad
  Kühlungsborn D .65 B4
Ostuni I 173 B3
Osuna E 162 A2
Osvětimany CZ 98 B1
Oswestry GB 38 B3
Oświęcim PL 86 B3
Osztopán H 111 C4
Oteiza E 144 B2
Otelec RO 126 B2
Oteo E 143 A3
Oterbekk N 54 A1
Oter de Herreros
  E 151 B3
Otero de O Bodas
  E 141 C4
Othem S 57 C4
Otley GB 40 B2
Otmuchów PL 85 B5
Otočac HR 123 C4

tok
Splitsko-Dalmatinska
HR. 138 B2
Vukovarsko-Srijemska
HR. 125 B4
oka BIH 124 C2
tranto I. 173 B4
trić HR 138 A2
tricoli I. 168 A2
trokovice CZ 98 B1
tta N. 198 D6
ttana I 178 B3
ttaviano I. 170 C2
ttenby S. 63 B4
ttendorf-Okrilla D 84 A1
ttenhöfen D. 93 C4
ttenschlag A 97 C3
tterbach D. 93 B3
tterbäcken S. 55 B5
tterberg D 93 B3
tterburn GB 37 A4
tter Ferry GB 34 B2
tterndorf D 64 C1
ttersburg D 72 A2
ttersweier D 93 C4
tterup DK 59 C3
ttery St Mary GB. .43 B3
ttignies S. 79 B4
ttmarsheim F 106 B2
ttobeuren D. 107 B5
ttömös H. 126 A1
ttone I 120 C2
ttsjö S 199 B10
ttweiler D. 92 B3
tvöskónyi H 124 A3
twock PL. 12 B4
uanne F. 104 B2
uarville F. 90 C1
ucques F. 103 B3
ud-Beijerland NL .79 A4
udemirdum NL 70 B2
udenaarde B 79 B3
udenbosch NL 79 A4
udenburg B. 78 A3
ude-Pekela NL 71 A4
ude-Tonge NL 79 A4
udewater NL 70 B1
ud Gastel NL. 79 A4
udon F. 101 B4
ue DK. 58 C2
ughterard IRL 28 A2
uguela P 155 B3
uistreham F 89 A3
ulainen FIN 3 D9
ulchy-le-Château
. . . . .91 B3
ullins F 117 B4
ulmes F 114 B3
ulton GB 41 C5
ulton Broad GB. . .41 C5
ulu FIN. 3 D9
ulx I 119 B3
undle GB. 40 C3
uranopoli GR 183 C6
urém P. 154 B2
urense E 140 B3
urique P. 160 B1
urol E. 140 A3
uroux-en-Morvan
. . . . .104 B2
usdale GB 32 C3
ust F 146 B2
utakoski FIN 193 C10
uteiro P. 154 B2
uteiro de Rei E . .140 A3
utes E. 140 B2
utokumpu FIN. . . .9 A6
utreau F. 78 B1
utwell GB 41 C4
uzouer-le-Marché
. . . . .103 B3
uzouer-sur-Loire
. . . . .103 B4
vada I. 133 A4
var F 148 B1
velgönne D 72 A1
verath D 80 B3
verbygd N. 192 D3
verdinkel NL 71 B4
verenhörna S 56 A3
verhalla N. 199 A8
verijse B 79 B4
ver-jerstal DK 59 C2
verlade DK 58 B2
verlida S 60 B2
verö FIN 51 B7
verpelt B 79 A5
verton GB 38 B4
vertornea S. 196 C6
verum S. 62 A4
vidiopol UA. 17 B9
viedo E 141 A5
viglio I 119 C5
vindoli I 169 A3
vodda I 178 B3
vre Ardal N. 47 A4
vrebygd N. 52 B2
vre Rendal N. . . .199 D8
vre Sirdal N. 52 B2
vre Soppero S. . . .196 A4
vre Ullerud S. 55 A4
vruch UA .13 C8
vtrup DK 59 C1
vinska PL. 76 B1
xaback S. 60 B2
xberg S 49 A6
xelösund S 56 B3
xford GB 44 B2
xie S 61 D3
xenholme GB 37 B4
xford GB 44 B2
xie S 61 D3
xilithos GR 185 A5
xted GB. 45 B4
yaca TR. 187 C7
ye N. 47 A5
yenkilen N. 54 A1
yer N 48 A2

Øyeren N 49 B4
Oyfiell N 53 A4
Øygärdslia N 53 B4
Oykel Bridge GB . .32 D2
Øymark N. 54 A2
Øyslebø N 52 B3
Øystese N 46 B3
Oyten D 72 A2
Øyuvsbu N. 52 A3
Ozaeta E 143 B4
Ozalj HR. 123 B4
Ożarów PL. 87 B5
Ożarów Maz PL. . . .77 B5
Ożbalt SLO 110 C2
Ozd H. 113 A4
Ożd'any SK 99 C3
Ozieri I. 178 B3
Ozimek PL. 86 B2
Ozimica BIH. 139 A4
Ozora H. 112 C2
Ozorków PL 77 C4
Ozzano Monferrato
I. 119 B5

P

Paakkola FIN. 196 D7
Paal B. 79 A5
Pabianice PL. 86 A3
Pacanów PL. 87 B5
Paceco I 176 B1
Pachino I 177 C4
Pačir SRB 126 B1
Pack A 110 B2
Paços de Ferreira
P 148 A1
Pacov CZ 96 B3
Pacsa H. 111 C4
Pacy-sur-Eure F . .89 A5
Paczków PL. 85 B5
Padany RUS. 3 E13
Padborg DK. 64 B2
Padej SRB 126 B2
Padene HR. 138 A2
Paderborn D 81 A4
Paderne P 160 B1
Padiham GB 40 B1
Padina SRB 126 B2
Padinska Skela
SRB. 127 C2
Padornelo P. 148 A1
Pádova I 121 B4
Padragkút H 111 B4
Padria I 178 B2
Padrón E 140 B2
Padru I 178 B3
Padstow GB. 42 B2
Padul E 163 A4
Padula I 172 B1
Paduli I. 170 B2
Paesana I 119 C4
Paese I 121 B5
Pag HR. 137 A4
Pagani I 170 C2
Pagánica I 169 A3
Pagánico I 135 C4
Pagl ieta I 169 A4
Pagny-sur-Moselle
F. 92 C2
Páhi H 112 C3
Pahkakumpu
FIN. 197 C11
Pahl D 108 B2
Paide EST 8 C4
Paignton GB 43 B3
Pailhès F 146 A2
Paimboeuf F 101 B3
Paimpol F 100 A2
Paimpont F 101 A3
Painswick GB 43 A4
Painten D 95 C3
Paisley GB 34 C3
Pajala S. 196 B6
Pajares E. 141 A5
Pajares de los Oteros
E 142 B1
Pajęczno PL. 86 A2
Páka H. 111 C3
Pakość PL 76 B3
Pakosławice PL. . .85 B5
Pakoštane HR. . . .137 B4
Pakrac HR 124 B3
Paks H. 112 C2
Palacios de la Sierra
E 143 C3
Palaciòs de la
Valduerna E 141 B5
Palacios del Sil E .141 B4
Palacios de Sanabria
E 141 B4
Palaciosrubios E. .150 A2
Palafrugell E 147 C4
Palagiano I. 173 B3
Palagonía I. 177 B3
Palaiseau F 90 C2
Palamas GR. 182 D4
Palamòs E 147 C4
Pålänge S 196 D5
Palanga LT. 8 E2
Palanzano I. 134 A3
Palárikovo SK 112 A2
Palas de Rei E . . .140 B3
Palata I 170 B2
Palau I 178 A3
Palavas-les-Flots
F 131 B2
Palazuelos de la Sierra
E 143 B3
Palazzo Adriano I .176 B2
Palazzo del Pero I 135 B4
Palazzolo Acréide
I 177 B3
Palazzolo sull Oglio
I. 120 B2

Palazzo San Gervásio
I. 172 B1
Palazzuolo sul Senio
I. 135 A4
Paldiski EST 8 C4
Pale BIH 139 B4
Palekastro GR. . . .185 D7
Palena I 169 B4
Palencia E 142 B2
Palenciana E 163 A3
Paleochora GR . . .185 D4
Paleometokho CY 181 A2
Palermo I 176 A2
Paleros GR 182 E2
Palestrina I 169 B2
Pálfa H 112 C2
Palfau A 110 B1
Palhaça P. 148 B1
Palheiros da Tocha
P 148 B1
Palheiros de Quiaios
P 148 B1
Paliaopoli GR 185 B5
Palić SRB. 126 A1
Palidoro I 168 B2
Palinuro I 172 B1
Paliouri GR 183 D5
Paliseul B. 91 B5
Pallanza I 119 B5
Pallares E 161 A3
Palau-de-Monegros
E 153 A3
Pallas Green IRL .29 B3
Pallerols E 146 B2
Palling D 109 A3
Palluau F 114 B2
Palma P 154 C2
Palma Campánia
I. 170 C2
Palma del Río E . .162 A2
Palma de Mallorca
E 166 B2
Palma di Montechiaro
I. 176 B2
Palmádula I 178 B2
Palmanova I. 122 B2
Palma Nova E 166 B2
Palmela P 154 C2
Palmerola E 147 B3
Palmi I 175 C1
Pälmonostora H . .113 C3
Palo del Colle I . . .171 B4
Palojärvi FIN 192 D7
Palojoensuu FIN .196 A6
Palomares E 164 B3
Palomares del Campo
E 158 B1
Palomas E 156 B1
Palombara Sabina
I. 168 A2
Palos de la Frontera
E 161 B3
Palotaboszok H . .125 A4
Palotás H. 112 B3
Pals E. 147 C4
Pålsboda S. 56 A1
Paluzza I 109 C4
Pamhagen A 111 B3
Pamiers F 146 A2
Pamiętowo PL. 76 A2
Pampaneira E 163 B4
Pamparato I 133 A3
Pampilhosa
Aveiro P. 148 B1
Coimbra P 148 B2
Pampliega E 143 B3
Pamplona E 144 B2
Pampow D 73 A4
Pamukçu TR 186 C2
Pamukkale TR . . .188 B4
Pamukova TR 187 B5
Panage East IRL .30 B2
Pancalieri I. 119 C4
Pančevo SRB 127 C2
Pancey F 91 C5
Pancorvo E 143 B3
Pancrudo E 152 B2
Pandino I. 120 B2
Pandrup DK. 58 A2
Panensky-Týnec
CZ 84 B1
Panes E 142 A2
Panevėžys LT 8 E4
Pangbourne GB . . .44 B2
Panissières F 117 B4
Panki PL. 86 B2
Pannes F 103 A4
Panningen NL. 80 A1
Pannonhalma H . .111 B4
Pano Lefkara CY .181 B2
Pano Panayia CY .181 B1
Panormos GR 185 B6
Panschwitz-Kuckau
D. 84 A2
Pansdorf D 65 C3
Pantano de Cijara
E 156 A3
Panticosa E 145 B3
Pantín E. 140 A2
Pantoja E 151 B4
Pantón E 140 B3
Panxon E 140 B2
Páola I 174 B2
Paola M 175 C3
Papasídero I 174 B1
Pápateszér H 111 B4
Papenburg D 71 A4
Paphos CY. 181 B1
Paprotnia PL. 77 B5
Parábita I 173 B4
Paracín SRB 127 D3
Parád H 113 B4
Parada
Bragança P 149 A3
Viseu P 148 B1
Paradas E 162 A2
Paradela E 140 B3

Parades de Rubiales
E 150 A2
Paradinas de San Juan
E 150 B2
Paradiso di Cevadale
I. 108 C1
Paradyż PL. 87 A4
Parainen FIN 8 B3
Parakhino Paddubye
RUS. 9 C8
Parakka S. 196 B4
Paralimni CY 181 A2
Parallo Astros GR 184 B3
Paramé F. 88 B2
Páramo E 141 A4
Páramo del Sil E .141 B4
Parandaça P 148 A2
Paravadella E 141 A3
Paray-le-Monial F .104 C3
Parceiros P 154 B2
Parcey F 105 B4
Parchim D 73 A4
Parciaki PL. 77 A6
Parcice PL. 86 A2
Pardilla E 151 A4
Pardubice CZ 97 A3
Paredes
E 151 B5
P 148 A1
Paredes de Coura
P 140 C2
Paredes de Nava
E 142 B2
Paredes de Siguenza
E 151 A5
Pareja E 151 B5
Parennes F 102 A1
Parenti I 175 B2
Parentis-en-Born
F 128 B1
Parey D 73 B4
Parfino RUS. 9 D7
Parga GR 182 D2
Pargny-sur-Saulx F 91 C4
Pari-Gagné F 117 A4
Parigné-l'Évêque
F 102 B2
Parikkala FIN. 9 B6
Paris F 90 C2
Parisot F 129 B4
Parkalompolo S . .196 B5
Parkano FIN. 8 A3
Parknasilla IRL . . .29 C2
Parla E 151 B4
Parlavá E 147 B4
Parma I. 120 C3
Parndorf A 111 B3
Párnica SK. 99 B3
Parnu EST 8 C4
Parolis E 164 A2
Paros GR 185 B6
Parrillas E 150 B2
Parsberg D 95 B3
Parstein D 74 B3
Partakko FIN 193 C11
Partanna I. 176 B1
Parthenay F 102 C1
Partinico I 176 A2
Partizani SRB 127 C2
Partizánske SK 98 C2
Partney GB 41 B4
Påryd S 63 B3
Parzymiechy PL. . .86 A2
Paşcani RO 17 B7
Pasewalk D 74 A2
Pašina Voda MNE .139 B5
Påskallavik S. 62 A4
Pasłęk PL. 69 A4
Passage East IRL .30 B2
Passais F. 88 B3
Passau D. 96 C1
Passegnano sul
Trasimeno I. . . .135 B5
Passignano sul
Trasimeno I. . . .135 B5
Passo di Tréia I . .136 B2
Passopisciaro I . . .177 B4
Passow D. 74 A3
Passy F 118 B3
Pasucy BY 13 A7
Pástena I 170 B2
Pastrana E 151 B5
Pastrengo I 121 B3
Pasym PL. 77 A5
Pászto H 113 B3
Pata SK 98 C1
Patay F. 103 A3
Pateley Bridge GB. 40 A2
Paterek PL. 76 A2
Paterna E 159 B3
Paterna del Campo
E 161 B3
Paterna del Madera
E 158 C1
Paterna de Rivera
E 162 B2
Paternion A 109 C4
Paternò I 177 B3
Paternópoli I 170 C3
Patersdorf D 95 B4
Paterswolde NL. . .71 A3
Patitiri GR 183 D5
Patmos GR 188 B1
Patna GB 36 A2
Patnow PL. 76 B3
Patoniva FIN 193 C11
Patopirtti FIN 197 B12
Patos AL. 182 C1
Patra = Patras GR 184 A2
Patras = Patra GR 184 A2
Patreksfjördur IS. .190 B2
Patrickswell IRL . .29 B3
Patrimonio F 180 A2
Patrington GB 41 B4
Pattada I 178 B3
Pattensen
Niedersachsen D. 72 A3
Niedersachsen D. .72 B1

Patterdale GB 36 B4
Patti I 177 A3
Paty H 112 B2
Pau F. 145 A3
Pauillac F. 128 A2
Paularo I 109 C4
Paulhaguet F 117 B3
Paulhan F 130 B2
Paulilátino I 178 B2
Paulistrom S 62 A3
Paullo I. 120 B2
Paulstown IRL 30 B1
Pausa D. 83 B3
Pauträsk S 200 B3
Pavia
I 120 B2
P 154 C2
Pavias E. 159 B3
Pavilly F 89 A4
Pāvilosta LV. 8 D2
Pavullo nel Frignano
I. 135 A3
Pawlowice PL. 86 A1
Pawlowice PL. 98 B2
Paxi GR 182 D2
Payallar TR 189 C6
Payerne CH. 106 C1
Paymogo E. 161 B2
Payrac F. 129 B4
Pazardzhik BG. . . .183 A6
Pazaryeri TR 187 B4
Pazin HR 122 B2
Paziols F 146 B3
Pčelić HR. 124 B3
Peal de Becerro E 164 B1
Peasmarsh GB. . . .45 C4
Peć KOS. 16 D4
Péccioli I 135 B3
Pécel H. 112 B3
Pechao P. 160 B2
Pechenga RUS. 3 B12
Pechenizhyn UA . .13 D6
Pecica RO 126 A3
Pećinci SRB. 127 C1
Pecka SRB. 127 C1
Peckelsheim D 81 A5
Pečory RUS. 8 D5
Pécs H 125 A4
Pécsvárad H 125 A4
Peداvena I 121 A4
Pedaça I 121 B4
Pedersker DK 67 A3
Pedersöre FIN . . .3 E9
Pédima BIH 121 B4
Pedola I. 121 B4
Pedrafita E 141 B3
Pedrajas de San
Esteban E 150 A3
Pedralba E. 159 B3
Pedralba de la Praderia
E 141 B4
Pedraza E 151 A4
Pedreguer E 159 C4
Pedrera E. 162 A3
Pedro Abad E 157 C3
Pedro Bernardo E 150 B3
Pedroche E 156 B3
Pedrógao P 149 B2
Pedrógão P 154 B2
Pedrógão Grande
P 154 B2
Pedrola E 144 C2
Pedro-Martinez E .164 B1
Pedro Muñoz E . . .158 B1
Pedrosa del Rey
E 150 A2
Pedrosa del Rio Urbel
E 143 B3
Pedrosa de Tobalina
E 143 B3
Pedrosillo de los Aires
E 150 B2
Pedrosillo el Ralo
E 150 A2
Pedzewo PL. 76 A3
Peebles GB. 35 C4
Peel GB. 36 B2
Peenemünde D . . .66 B2
Peer B 79 A5
Pega P 149 B2
Pegalajar E 163 A4
Pegau D. 83 A4
Peggau A 110 B2
Pegli I 133 A4
Pegnitz D 95 B3
Pego E 159 C3
Pegões-Estação
P 154 C2
Pegões Velhos P. .154 C2
Pegow PL. 85 A4
Pegswood GB 37 A5
Peguera E 166 B2
Pehlivanköy TR . .186 A1
Pehrliwanköy TR . .186 A1
Peine D 72 B3
Peisey-Nancroix F 118 B3
Peissenberg D. . . .108 B2
Peiting D. 108 B1
Peitz D 84 A2
Péjo I 121 A3
Pelagićevo BIH . . .125 C4
Pelahustán E. 150 B3
Pełczyce PL. 75 A4
Pelhřimov CZ 97 B3
Pélissanne F 131 B4
Pelkosenniemi
FIN. 197 B10
Pellegrino Parmense
I. 120 C2
Pellegrue F 128 B3
Pellérd H 125 A4
Pellevoisin F 103 C3
Pellizzano I 121 A3
Pello
FIN. 196 C7
S. 196 C6
Peloche E 156 A2
Pelplin PL. 69 B3
Perlez SRB. 126 B2
Pelussin F 117 B4

Pély H. 113 B4
Pembroke GB 39 C2
Pembroke Dock
GB. 39 C2
Peñacerrada E. . . .143 B4
Penacova P 148 B1
Peña de Cabra E .149 B4
Peñafiel E 151 A3
Penafiel P. 148 A1
Peñaflor E. 162 A2
Peñalba de Santiago
E 141 B4
Peñalsordo E. 156 B2
Penalva do Castelo
P 148 B2
Penamacôr P 149 B2
Peñaparda E 149 B3
Peñaranda de
Bracamonte E. .150 B2
Peñaranda de Duero
E 143 C3
Peñarroya de Tastavins
E 153 B4
Peñarroya-
Pueblonuevo E. .156 B2
Peñarrubia E 141 B3
Peñascosa E 158 C1
Peñas de San Pedro
E 158 C2
Peñausende E 149 A4
Penc H 112 B3
Pencoed GB 39 C3
Pendeen GB 42 B1
Pendine GB 39 C2
Pendueles E 142 A2
Penedono P. 148 B2
Penela P. 154 A2
Pénestin F 101 B3
Penhas Juntas P. .149 A2
Peniche P. 154 B1
Penicuik GB 35 C4
Penig D 83 B4
Penilhos P 160 B2
Peñíscola E 153 B4
Penistone GB 40 B2
Penkridge GB 40 C1
Penkun D. 74 A3
Penmarch F 100 B1
Pennabilli I 135 B5
Penne I 169 A3
Penne-d'Agenais
F. 129 B3
Pennes I 108 C2
Pennyghael GB. . . .34 B1
Penpont GB. 36 A3
Penrhyndeudraeth
GB. 38 B2
Penrith GB 37 B4
Penryn GB. 42 B1
Pentraeth GB. 38 A2
Penybontfawr GB .38 B3
Penygroes
Carmarthenshire
GB. 39 C2
Gwynedd GB . . .38 A2
Penzance GB. 42 B1
Penzberg D 108 B2
Penzlin D 74 A2
Pepinster B 80 B1
Peqin AL. 182 B1
Pera Boa P 148 B2
Perachora GR 184 A3
Perafita P. 148 A1
Peraleda de la Mata
E 150 C2
Peraleda del Zaucejo
E 156 B2
Peraleda de San
Román E 156 A2
Perales de Alfambra
E 152 B2
Perales del Puerto
E 149 B3
Perales de Tajuña
E 151 B4
Peralta E 144 B2
Peralta de la Sal E 145 C4
Peralva P. 160 B2
Peralveche E 152 B1
Perama GR 185 D5
Peranka FIN 197 D12
Perbál H. 112 B2
Perchtoldsdorf A. .111 A3
Percy F. 88 B2
Perdasdefogu I . . .179 C3
Perdiguera E 145 C3
Peredo P 149 A3
Peregu Mare RO. .126 A2
Pereira
Faro P 160 B2
Guarda P 149 B2
Santarém P 154 B2
Pereiro de Aguiar
E 140 B3
Perelada E 147 B4
Perelejos de las
Truchas E 152 B2
Pereña E 149 A3
Pereruela E 149 A4
Pérfugas I 178 B2
Perg A. 110 A1
Pérgine Valsugana
I 121 A4
Pérgola I 136 B1
Pergusa I. 177 B3
Periam RO 126 A2
Periana E 163 B3
Périers F 88 A2
Périgueux F 129 A3
Perino I. 120 C2
Perjasica HR 123 B4
Perkáta I. 112 B2
Perković HR 138 B2
Perleberg D 73 A4
Perlez SRB 126 B2
Përmet AL. 182 C2

Pernarec CZ 95 B5
Pernek SK 98 C1
Pernes F 154 B2
Pernes-les-Fontaines
F. 131 A4
Pernik BG 17 D5
Pernink CZ. 83 B4
Pernitz A. 110 B2
Pernu FIN. 197 C10
Peroguarda P 160 A1
Pérols F 131 B2
Péronne F 90 B2
Péronnes S 79 B4
Pero Pinheiro P . .154 C1
Perorrubio E 151 A4
Perosa Argentina
I. 119 C4
Perozinho P. 148 A1
Perpignan F. 146 B3
Perranporth GB. . .42 B1
Perranzabuloe GB. .42 B1
Perrecy-les-Forges
F. 104 C3
Perrero I 119 C4
Perrignier F 118 A3
Perros-Guirec F . .100 A2
Persan F 90 B2
Persberg S. 55 A5
Persenbeug A 110 A2
Pershore GB 44 A1
Persön S. 196 D5
Perstorp S. 61 C3
Perth GB 35 B4
Pertisau A 108 B2
Pertoča SLO 111 C3
Pertuis F 131 B4
Perućac SRB 127 D1
Perúgia I 136 B1
Perušić HR 123 C4
Péruwelz B 79 B3
Pervomaysk UA. . .13 D9
Perwez B 79 B4
Pesadas de Burgos
E 143 B3
Pesaguero E 142 A2
Pésaro I 136 B1
Pescantina I 121 B3
Pescara I 169 A4
Pescasséroli I 169 B3
Peschici I. 171 B4
Peschiera del Garda
I 121 B3
Péscia I 135 B3
Pescina I 169 A3
Pescocostanzo I. .169 B4
Pescopagano I . . .172 B1
Pesco Sannita I . .170 B2
Peshkopi AL. 182 B2
Peshtera BG 183 A6
Pesmes F 105 B4
Pesnica SLO 110 C2
Peso da Régua P. .148 A2
Pesquera de Duero
E 142 C2
Pessac F 128 B2
Pestovo RUS. 9 C9
Petäjäskoski FIN. .197 C8
Petalidi GR 184 C2
Pétange L. 92 B1
Petas GR 182 D3
Peteranec HR 124 A2
Peterborough GB . .41 C3
Petercolter GB. . . .33 D4
Peterhead GB 33 D5
Peterlee GB. 37 B5
Petersfield GB. . . .44 B3
Petershagen
Brandenburg D . .74 B2
Brandenburg D . .74 B3
Nordrhein-Westfalen
D. 72 B1
Petershausen D . . .95 C3
Peterswell IRL 28 A3
Pétervására H 113 A4
Petília Policastro I 175 B2
Petín E 141 B3
Pětipsy CZ. 83 B5
Petkus D 74 C2
Petlovac HR. 125 B4
Petlovača SRB . . .127 C1
Petöfiszállás H . . .113 C3
Petra E 167 B3
Petralia Sottana I. .177 B3
Petrčane HR 137 A4
Petrella Tifernina I 170 B2
Petrer E 159 C3
Petreto-Bicchisano
F. 180 B1
Petrich BG 183 B5
Petrijevci HR 125 B4
Petrinja HR 124 B2
Petrodvorets RUS. . .9 C6
Pétrola E 158 C2
Petronà I 175 B2
Petronell A 111 A3
Petroşani RO. 17 C5
Petrovac SRB 127 C3
Petrovaradin SRB 126 B1
Petrovice
BIH. 139 A4
CZ 84 B1
Petrovo RUS 69 A5
Petrozavodsk RUS . .9 B9
Pettenbach A. . . .109 B5
Pettigo IRL 26 B3
Petworth GB. 44 C3
Peuerbach A. 96 C1
Peuntenansa I . . .142 A2
Peurasuvanto FIN 197 B9
Pevensey Bay GB . .45 C4
Peveragno I. 133 A3
Pewsey GB 44 B2
Pewsum D. 71 A4
Peyrat-le-Château
F. 116 B1
Peyrehorade F. . . .128 C1

Peyriac-Minervois F 146 A3
Peyrins F 117 B5
Peyrissac F 116 B1
Peyrolles-en-Provence F 132 B1
Peyruis F 132 A1
Pézarches F 90 C2
Pézenas F 130 B2
Pezinok SK 111 A4
Pezuls F 129 B3
Pfaffenhausen D . 108 A1
Pfaffenhofen
  Bayern D 94 C2
  Bayern D 95 C3
Pfaffenhoffen F . . 93 C3
Pfäffikon CH . . . 107 B3
Pfarrkirchen D . . 95 C4
Pfeffenhausen D . 95 C3
Pfetterhouse F . . 106 B2
Pforzheim D 93 C4
Pfreimd D 95 B4
Pfronten D 108 B1
Pfullendorf D . . . 107 B4
Pfullingen D 94 C1
Pfunds A 108 C1
Pfungstadt D . . . 93 B4
Pfyn CH 107 B3
Phalsbourg F . . . 92 C3
Philippeville B . . . 79 B4
Philippsreut D . . . 96 C1
Philippsthal D . . . 82 B1
Piacenza I 120 B2
Piacenza d'Adige I 121 B4
Piádena I 120 B3
Piana F 180 A1
Piana Crixia I . . . 133 A4
Piana degli Albanesi I 176 B2
Piana di Monte Verna I 170 B2
Piancastagnáio I . 135 C4
Piandelagotti I . . 134 A3
Pianella
  Abruzzi I 169 A4
  Toscana I 135 B4
Pianello Val Tidone I 120 C2
Pianoro I 135 A4
Pians A 108 B1
Pías E 141 B4
Pias P 160 A2
Piaseczno PL . . . 77 B6
Piasek PL 74 B3
Piaski PL 69 A4
Piastów PL 77 B5
Piaszcyna PL . . . 68 A2
Piątek PL 77 B4
Piatra Neamţ RO . 17 B7
Piazza al Sérchio I 134 A3
Piazza Armerina I . 177 B3
Piazza Brembana I 120 B2
Piazze I 135 C4
Piazzola sul Brenta I 121 B4
Picassent E 159 B3
Piccione I 136 B1
Picerno I 172 B1
Picher D 73 A4
Pickering GB . . . 40 A3
Pico I 169 B3
Picón E 157 A3
Picquigny F 90 B2
Piechowice PL . . . 84 B3
Piecnik PL 75 A5
Piedicavallo I . . . 119 B4
Piedicroce F 180 A2
Piedimonte Etneo I 177 B4
Piedimonte Matese I 170 B2
Piedimulera I . . . 119 A5
Piedipaterno I . . . 136 C1
Piedrabuena E . . 157 A3
Piedraescrita E . . 156 A3
Piedrafita E 142 A1
Piedralaves E . . . 150 B3
Piedras Albas E . . 155 B4
Piedras Blancas E 141 A5
Piegaro I 135 C5
Piekary Śl. PL . . . 86 B2
Piekoszów PL . . . 87 B4
Pieksämäki FIN . . 8 A5
Pielenhofen D . . . 95 B3
Pielgrzymka PL . . 85 A3
Pieniężno PL . . . 69 A5
Pieńsk PL 84 A3
Pienza I 135 B4
Piera E 147 C2
Pieranie PL 76 B3
Pierowall GB . . . 33 B4
Pierre-Buffière F . 115 C5
Pierrecourt F . . . 105 B4
Pierre-de-Bresse F 105 C4
Pierrefeu-du-Var F 132 B2
Pierrefitte-Nestalas F 145 B3
Pierrefitte-sur-Aire F 92 C1
Pierrefonds F . . . 90 B2
Pierrefontaine-les-Varans F 105 B5
Pierrefort F 116 C2
Pierrelatte F 131 A3
Pierrepont
  Aisne F 91 B3
  Meurthe-et-Moselle F 92 B1
Piesendorf A . . . 109 B3
Pieštany SK 98 C1
Pieszkowo PL . . . 69 A5

Pieszyce PL 85 B4
Pietarsaari FIN . . 3 E8
Pietragalla I 172 B1
Pietra Ligure I . . . 133 A4
Pietralunga I 136 B1
Pietramelara I . . . 170 B2
Pietraperzia I . . . 177 B3
Pietrasanta I 134 B3
Pietravairano I . . . 170 B2
Pieve del Cáiro I . 120 B1
Pieve di Bono I . . 121 B3
Pieve di Cadore I . 122 A1
Pieve di Cento I . . 121 C4
Pieve di Soligo I . 121 B5
Pieve di Teco I . . 133 A3
Pievepélago I . . . 134 A3
Pieve Santo Stefano I 135 B5
Pieve Torina I . . . 136 B2
Piges GR 182 D3
Píglio I 169 B3
Pigna I 133 B3
Pignan F 130 B2
Pignataro Maggiore I 170 B2
Piittisjärvi FIN . . . 197 C9
Pijnacker NL 70 B1
Pikalevo RUS . . . 9 C9
Piła PL 75 A5
Pilar de la Horadada E 165 B4
Pilas E 161 B3
Pilastri I 121 C4
Piława Górna PL . 85 B4
Piławki PL 69 B4
Pilchowice PL . . . 86 B2
Pilea GR 183 C5
Pilgrimstad S . . . 199 C12
Pili
  Dodekanisa GR . 188 C2
  Trikala GR . . . 182 D3
Pilis H 112 B3
Pilisszántó H . . . 112 B2
Pilisvörösvár H . . 112 B2
Pilos GR 184 C2
Pilsting D 95 C4
Pilszcz PL 98 A1
Piltene LV 8 D2
Pilu RO 113 C5
Pina de Ebro E . . 153 A3
Piñar E 163 A4
Pınarbaşı TR . . . 186 C1
Pınarhisar TR . . . 186 A2
Pinas F 145 A4
Pincehely H 112 C2
Pinchbeck GB . . . 41 C3
Pińczów PL 87 B4
Pineda de la Sierra E 143 B3
Pineda de Mar E . 147 C3
Pinerella I 135 A5
Pinerolo I 119 C4
Pineta Grande I . . 170 C1
Pineto I 169 A4
Piney F 91 C4
Pinggau A 111 B3
Pinhal Novo P . . 154 C2
Pinhão P 148 A2
Pinheiro
  Aveiro P 148 A1
  Aveiro P 148 B1
Pinheiro Grande P 154 B2
Pinhel P 149 B2
Pinhoe GB 43 B3
Pinilla E 158 C2
Pinilla de Toro E . 150 A2
Pinkafeld A 111 B3
Pinneberg D 72 A2
Pinnow D 74 C3
Pino F 180 A2
Pino del Rio E . . 142 B2
Pino de Val E . . . 140 B2
Pinofranqueado E 149 B3
Pinols F 117 B3
Piñor E 140 B2
Pinos del Valle E . 163 B4
Pinoso E 159 C2
Pinos Puente E . . 163 A4
Pinsk BY 13 B7
Pintamo FIN . . . 197 D10
Pinto E 151 B4
Pinzano al Tagliamento I 122 A1
Pinzio P 149 B2
Pinzolo I 121 A3
Pióbbico I 136 B1
Piombino I 134 C3
Pionki PL 87 A5
Pionsat F 116 A2
Pióraco I 136 B1
Piornal E 150 B2
Piotrkowice PL . . 87 B4
Piotrków-Kujawski PL 76 B3
Piotrków Trybunalski PL 86 A3
Piotrowo PL 75 B5
Piove di Sacco I . 121 B5
Piovene I 121 B4
Piperskärr S . . . 62 A4
Pipriac F 101 B4
Piraeus = Pireas GR 185 B4
Piran SLO 122 B2
Pireas = Piraeus GR 185 B4
Piré-sur-Seiche F . 101 A4
Pirgi GR 185 A6
Pirgos
  Ilia GR 184 B2
  Kriti GR 185 D6
Piriac-sur-Mer F . 101 B3
Piringsdorf A . . . 111 B3
Pirmasens D . . . 93 B3
Pirna D 84 B1
Pirnmill GB 34 C2
Pirot SRB 16 D5

Pirovac HR 137 B4
Pirttivuopio S . . . 196 B2
Pisa I 134 B3
Pisany F 114 C3
Pisarovina HR . . . 124 B1
Pischelsdorf in der
  Steiermark A . . 110 B2
Pişchia RO 126 B3
Pisciotta I 172 B1
Pisek CZ 96 B2
Pisogne I 120 B3
Pissos F 128 B2
Pissouri CY 181 B1
Pisticci I 174 A2
Pistóia I 135 B3
Piteå S 196 D4
Pithiviers F 103 A4
Pitigliano I 168 A1
Pitkyaranta RUS . 9 B7
Pitlochry GB . . . 35 B4
Pitomača HR . . . 124 B3
Pitres E 163 B4
Pittentrail GB . . . 32 D2
Pitvaros H 126 A2
Pivka SLO 123 B3
Pivnice SRB 126 B1
Piwniczna PL . . . 99 B4
Pizarra E 163 B3
Pizzighettone I . . 120 B2
Pizzo I 175 C2
Pizzoli I 169 A3
Pizzolungo I 176 A1
Pjätteryd S 61 C4
Plabennec F 100 A1
Placencia E 143 A4
Plaffeien CH 106 C2
Plaisance
  Gers F 128 C3
  Haute-Garonne F 129 C4
  Tarn F 130 B1
Plaka GR 183 D7
Plan E 145 B4
Planá CZ 95 B4
Planánad Lužnici CZ 96 B2
Plaňany CZ 96 A3
Planchez F 104 B3
Plancoët F 101 A3
Plancy-l'Abbaye F 91 C3
Plan-de-Baix F . . 118 C2
Plandište SRB . . . 126 B3
Plan-d'Orgon F . . 131 B3
Plánice CZ 96 B1
Planina
  SLO 123 A4
  SLO 123 B3
Plankenfels D . . . 95 B3
Plasencia E 149 B3
Plasenzuela E . . . 156 A1
Plaški HR 123 B4
Plassen
  Buskerud N . . . 47 B4
  Hedmark N . . . 49 A4
Plášť'ovce SK . . . 112 A3
Plasy CZ 96 B1
Platamona Lido I . 178 B2
Platania I 175 B2
Platanos GR 185 D4
Plati I 175 C2
Platičevo SRB . . . 127 C1
Platja d'Aro E . . . 147 C4
Plattling D 95 C4
Plau D 73 A5
Plaue
  Brandenburg D . 73 B5
  Thüringen D . . 82 B2
Plauen D 83 B4
Plavecký Mikuláš SK 98 C1
Plavinas LV 8 D4
Plavna SRB 125 B5
Plavnica SK 99 B4
Plavno HR 138 A2
Pléaux F 116 B2
Pleine-Fougères F 88 B2
Pleinfeld D 94 B2
Pleinting D 95 C5
Plélan-le-Grand F 101 B3
Plémet F 101 A3
Pléneuf-Val-André F 101 A3
Plentzia E 143 A4
Plérin F 101 A3
Plessa D 83 A5
Plessé F 101 B4
Plestin-les-Grèves F 100 A2
Pleszew PL 76 C2
Pleternica HR . . . 125 B3
Plettenberg D . . . 81 A3
Pleubian F 100 A2
Pleumartin F . . . 115 B4
Pleumeur-Bodou F 100 A2
Pleurs F 91 C3
Pleven BG 17 D6
Plevnik-Drienové SK 98 B2
Pleyben F 100 A2
Pleyber-Christ F . 100 A2
Pliego E 165 B3
Pliešovce SK . . . 99 C3
Plitvička Jezera HR 123 C4
Plitvički Ljeskovac HR 123 C4
Ploaghe I 178 B2
Ploče HR 138 B3
Plochingen D . . . 94 C1
Plock PL 77 B4
Ploemeur F 100 B2
Ploërmel F 101 B3
Ploeuc-sur-Lié F . 101 A3
Plogastel St Germain F 100 B1
Plogoff F 100 A1
Ploiești RO 17 C7

Plomari GR 186 D1
Plombières-les-Bains F 105 B5
Plomin HR 123 B3
Plön D 65 B3
Plonéour-Lanvern F 100 B1
Płonia PL 74 A3
Płoniawy PL 77 B6
Płońsk PL 77 B5
Płoskinia PL 69 A4
Plössberg D 95 B4
Płoty PL 67 C4
Plouagat F 100 A2
Plouaret F 100 A2
Plouarzel F 100 A1
Plouay F 100 B2
Ploubalay F 101 A3
Ploubazlanec F . . 100 A2
Ploudalmézeau F . 100 A1
Ploudiry F 100 A1
Plouescat F 100 A1
Plouézec F 100 A2
Plougasnou F . . . 100 A2
Plougastel-Daoulas F 100 A1
Plougonven F . . . 100 A2
Plougonver F . . . 100 A2
Plougrescant F . . 100 A1
Plouguenast F . . 101 A3
Plouguerneau F . . 100 A1
Plouha F 100 A2
Plouhinec F 100 A1
Plouigneau F . . . 100 A2
Ploumanach F . . 100 A2
Plounévez-Quintin F 100 A2
Plouray F 100 A2
Plouzévédé F . . . 100 A1
Plovdiv BG 183 A6
Plozévet F 100 B1
Plumbridge GB . . 27 B3
Pluméliau F 100 B3
Plumlov CZ 97 B5
Plungė LT 8 E2
Pluty PL 69 A5
Pluvigner F 100 B3
Plužine
  BIH 139 B4
  MNE 139 B4
Plymouth GB . . . 42 B2
Plymstock GB . . . 42 B2
Płytnica PL 68 B1
Plyusa RUS 9 C6
Plzeň CZ 96 B1
Pniewy PL 75 B5
Pobes E 143 B4
Pobědovice CZ . . 95 B4
Pobiedziska PL . . 76 B2
Pobierowo PL . . . 67 B3
Pobla de Segur E . 145 B4
Pobladura del Valle E 142 B1
Pobla-Tornesa E . 153 B4
Pobra de Trives E 141 B3
Pobra do Brollón E 141 B3
Pobra do Caramiñal E 140 B2
Pobudje BIH . . . 139 A5
Počátky CZ 97 B3
Poceirão P 154 C2
Pöchlarn A 110 A2
Pociecha PL 87 A4
Pockau D 83 B5
Pocking D 96 C1
Pocklington GB . . 40 B3
Podbořany CZ . . . 83 B5
Podbrdo SLO . . . 122 A2
Podbrezová SK . . 99 C3
Podčetrtek SLO . . 123 A4
Poddębice PL . . . 76 C3
Poděbrady CZ . . . 84 B3
Podence P 149 A3
Podensac F 128 B2
Podenzano I 120 C2
Podersdorf am See A 111 B3
Podgaje PL 68 B1
Podgora HR 138 B3
Podgóra PL 87 A5
Podgorač HR . . . 125 B4
Podgorica MNE . . 16 D3
Podgorie AL 182 C2
Podgrad SLO . . . 123 B3
Podhájska SK . . . 112 A2
Podkova BG 183 B7
Podlapača HR . . . 123 C4
Podlejki PL 69 B5
Podlužany SK . . . 98 C2
Podnovlje BIH . . . 125 C4
Podolie SK 98 C1
Podolínec SK . . . 99 B4
Podolsk RUS . . . 9 E10
Podporozhy RUS . 9 B9
Podromanija BIH . 139 B4
Podturen HR . . . 111 C3
Podvín CZ 97 C4
Podwilk PL 99 B3
Poetto I 179 C3
Poggendorf D . . . 66 B2
Poggiardo I 173 B4
Poggibonsi I 135 B4
Póggio a Caiano I 135 B4
Poggio Imperiale I 171 B3
Póggio Mirteto I . 168 A2
Póggio Moiano I . 169 A2
Póggio Renatico I 121 C4
Póggio Rusco I . . 121 C4
Pöggstall A 110 A2
Pogny F 91 C4
Pogorzela PL . . . 85 A5
Pogorzelice PL . . 68 A2
Pogradec AL . . . 182 C2
Pogrodzie PL . . . 69 A4
Pohorelá SK 99 C4
Pohořelice CZ . . . 97 C4
Pohronská Polhora SK 99 C3

Poiares P 148 B1
Poio E 140 B2
Poirino I 119 C4
Poisson F 117 A4
Poissons F 91 C5
Poissy F 90 C2
Poitiers F 115 B4
Poix-de-Picardie F 90 B1
Poix-Terron F . . . 91 B4
Pokka FIN 197 A8
Pokój PL 86 B1
Pokupsko HR . . . 124 B1
Pol E 141 A3
Pola RUS 9 D7
Pola Charra GB . . 31 B1
Pola de Allande E 141 A4
Pola de Laviana E 142 A1
Pola de Lena E . . 141 A5
Pola de Siero E . . 142 A1
Pola de Somiedo E 141 A4
Polaincourt-et-Clairefontaine F 105 B5
Połajewo PL 75 B5
Polán E 151 C3
Polanica-Zdrój PL 85 B4
Połaniec PL 87 B5
Polanów PL 68 A1
Polati TR 187 C7
Polatsk BY 13 A8
Polch D 80 B3
Polcirkeln S 196 C4
Pólczno PL 68 A2
Połczyn-Zdrój PL . 67 C5
Polegate GB . . . 45 C4
Poleñino E 145 C3
Polesella I 121 C4
Polessk RUS . . . 12 A4
Polgár H 113 B5
Polgárdi H 112 B2
Polhov Gradec SLO 123 A3
Police PL 74 A3
Police nad Metují CZ 85 B4
Polichnitos GR . . 186 C1
Polička CZ 97 B4
Poličnik HR 137 A4
Policoro I 174 A2
Policzna PL 87 A5
Poligiros GR 183 C5
Polignano a Mare I 173 B3
Poligny F 105 C4
Polis CY 181 A1
Polistena I 175 C2
Polizzi Generosa I 176 B3
Poljana SRB 127 C3
Poljanak HR 123 C4
Poljčane SLO . . . 123 A4
Polje BIH 125 C3
Poljice
  BIH 138 A2
  BIH 139 A4
Polkowice PL . . . 85 A4
Polla I 172 B1
Pollas E 150 A2
Pöllau A 110 B2
Polleben D 82 A3
Pollença E 167 B3
Pollenfeld D 95 C3
Pollfoss N 198 D4
Póllica I 170 C3
Polminhac F 116 C2
Polná CZ 97 B3
Polna RUS 8 C6
Polne PL 75 A5
Polomka SK 99 C3
Polonne UA 13 C7
Polperro GB 42 B2
Polruan GB 42 B2
Pöls A 110 B1
Polska Cerekiew PL 86 B2
Poltár SK 99 C3
Põltsamaa EST . . 8 C4
Polyarny RUS . . . 3 B13
Polyarnyye Zori RUS 3 C13
Polzela SLO 123 A4
Pomarance I 135 B3
Pomarez F 128 C2
Pomárico I 172 B2
Pomáz H 112 B3
Pombal P 154 B2
Pomeroy GB . . . 27 B4
Pomézia I 168 B2
Pommard F 105 B3
Pommelsbrunn D . 95 B3
Pomonte I 134 C3
Pomorie BG 17 D7
Pompei I 170 C2
Pompey F 92 C2
Pomposa I 122 C1
Poncin F 118 A2
Pondorf D 95 C3
Ponferrada E . . . 141 B4
Poniec PL 85 A4
Ponikva SLO . . . 123 A4
Poniky SK 99 C3
Ponsacco I 134 B3
Pont I 119 B4
Poo E 142 A2
Poole GB 43 B5
Poolewe GB 31 B3
Poperinge B 78 B2
Poppel B 79 A5
Poppenhausen
  Bayern D 82 B2
  Hessen D 82 B1
Poppi I 135 B4
Poprad SK 99 B4
Popučke SRB . . . 127 C1
Pópulo P 148 A2
Populónia I 134 C3

Pörböly H 125 A4
Porcuna E 163 A3
Pordenone I 122 B1
Pordic F 100 A3
Poręba PL 86 B3
Poreč HR 122 B2
Pori FIN 8 B2
Porjus S 196 C2
Porkhov RUS . . . 9 D6
Porlezza I 120 A2
Porlock GB 43 A4
Pörnbach D 95 C3
Pornic F 101 B3
Pornichet F 101 B3
Porodin SRB . . . 127 C3
Poronin PL 99 B3
Poros
  Attiki GR 185 B4
  Kefalonia GR . . 184 A1
Poroszló H 113 B4
Porozina HR 123 B3
Porquerolles F . . 132 C2
Porrentruy CH . . 106 B2
Porreres E 167 B3
Porretta Terme I . 135 A4
Porsgrunn N 53 A5
Porspoder F 100 A1
Port-a-Binson F . . 91 B3
Portacloy IRL . . . 26 B1
Portadown GB . . 27 B4
Portaferry GB . . . 27 B5
Portaje E 155 B4
Portalegre P 155 B3
Portarlington IRL . 30 A1
Port Askaig GB . . 34 C1
Portavadie GB . . 34 C2
Portavogie GB . . 27 B5
Portbail F 88 A2
Port Bannatyne GB 34 C2
Port-Barcarès F . . 146 B3
Portbou E 146 B4
Port-Camargue F . 131 B3
Port Charlotte GB . 34 C1
Port d'Andratx E . 166 B2
Port-de-Bouc F . . 131 B3
Port-de-Lanne F . 128 C2
Port de Pollença E 167 B3
Port-des-Barques F 114 C2
Port de Sóller E . 166 B2
Portegrandi I . . . 122 B1
Portel P 155 C3
Portela P 148 B1
Port Ellen GB . . . 34 C1
Portelo P 141 C4
Portemouro E . . . 140 B2
Port-en-Bessin F . 88 A3
Port'Ercole I 168 A1
Port Erin GB . . . 36 B2
Portes-lès-Valence F 117 C4
Port Eynon GB . . 39 C2
Portezuelo E . . . 155 B4
Port Glasgow GB . 34 C3
Portglenone GB . . 27 B4
Porthcawl GB . . . 39 C3
Port Henderson GB 31 B3
Porthleven GB . . 42 B1
Porthmadog GB . . 38 B2
Porticcio F 180 B1
Portici I 170 C2
Portico di Romagna I 135 A4
Portilla de la Reina E 142 A2
Portillo E 150 A3
Portimao P 160 B1
Portinatx E 166 B1
Portinho da Arrabida P 154 C1
Port Isaac GB . . . 42 B2
Portishead GB . . 43 A4
Port-Joinville F . . 114 B1
Portknockie GB . . 33 D2
Port-la-Nouvelle F 130 B2
Portlaoise IRL . . . 30 A1
Portlethen GB . . . 33 D4
Port Logan GB . . 36 B2
Port Louis F 100 B2
Portmagne IRL . . 29 C1
Portmahomack GB 32 D3
Portman E 165 B4
Port Manech F . . 100 B2
Portnacroish GB . 34 B2
Portnahaven GB . 34 C1
Port Nan Giuran GB 31 A2
Port-Navalo F . . . 100 B3
Port Nis GB 31 A2
Porto
  F 180 A1
  P 148 A1
Porto-Alto P . . . 154 C2
Porto Azzurro I . . 134 C3
Portocannone I . . 170 B2
Porto Cerésio I . . 120 B1
Porto Cervo I . . . 178 A3
Porto Cesáreo I . 173 B3
Porto Colom E . . 167 B3
Porto Covo P . . . 160 B1
Porto Cristo E . . 167 B3
Porto d'Áscoli I . . 136 C2
Porto de Lagos P 160 B1
Porto de Mos P . . 154 B2
Porto de Rei P . . 154 C2
Porto do Son E . . 140 B2
Porto Empédocle I 176 B2
Portoferráio I . . . 134 C3
Portofino I 134 A2
Porto Garibaldi I . 122 C1
Portogruaro I . . . 122 B1
Portokhelion GR . 184 B4
Portomaggiore I . 121 C4
Portomarin E . . . 140 B3
Porton GB 44 B2
Portonovo E 140 B2

rtopalo di Capo
Passero I 177 C4
orto Petro E 167 B3
orto Pino I 179 D2
orto Potenza Picena
. . . . . . 136 B2
rter N 53 B5
orto Recanati I . 136 B2
orto San Giórgio
. . . . . . 136 B2
orto Sant'Elpídio
. . . . . . 136 B2
orto Santo Stéfano
. . . . . . 168 A1
rtoscuso I 179 C2
orto Tolle I . . . 122 C1
orto Tórres I . . 178 B2
orto-Vecchio F . 180 B2
rtovénere I 134 C2
rtpatrick GB . . . 36 B1
rtreath GB 42 B1
rtree GB 31 B2
rtroe IRL 28 B3
rtrush GB 27 A4
rt St Mary GB . . 36 B2
rtsall F 100 A1
rtsmouth GB . . . 44 C2
rtsoy GB 33 D4
rt-Ste Marie F . 129 B3
rtstewart GB . . . 27 A4
rt-St-Louis-du-
 Rhône F 131 B3
rt-sur-Saône F . 105 B5
rt Talbot GB 39 C3
rtugalete E . . . 143 A4
rtumna IRL 28 A3
rt-Vendres F . . 146 B4
rt William GB . . . 36 B2
rvoo FIN 8 B4
rzuna E 157 A3
osada
 Oviedo E 141 A5
 Oviedo E 142 A2
. . . . . . 178 B3
osada de Valdeón
E 142 A2
osadas E 162 A2
oschiavo CH . . 120 A3
osedarje HR . . . 123 B4
osedarje HR 197 C11
ositano I 170 C2
ossagno I 121 B4
osseck D 83 B4
ossesse F 91 C4
ossneck D 83 B3
osta I 169 A3
ostal I 108 C2
osta Piana I . . 172 A1
ostbauer-Heng D . 95 B3
osterholt NL . . . 80 A2
ostioma I 121 B5
ostira HR 138 B2
ostojna SLO . . 123 B3
ostoloprty CZ . . . 84 B1
ostomino PL 68 A1
osušje BIH 138 B3
otamos
 Attiki GR 184 C3
 Attiki GR 184 D4
otegowo PL 68 A2
otenza I 172 B1
otenza Picena I . 136 B2
otes E 142 A2
otigny F 89 B3
otočari BIH 127 C1
otoci
 BIH 138 A2
 BIH 139 B3
otony H 125 B3
otries E 159 C3
otsdam D 74 B2
otštát CZ 98 B1
ottenbrunn A . . . 110 A2
ottendorf A . . . 111 B3
ottenstein
 A 111 B3
. . . . . . 95 B3
otters Bar GB . . 44 B3
öttmes D 94 C3
öttsching A . . . 111 B3
otworów PL 87 A4
ouancé F 101 B4
ougues-les-Eaux
 . . . . . . 104 B2
ouilly-en-Auxois
 . . . . . . 104 B3
ouilly-sous Charlieu
 . . . . . . 117 A4
ouilly-sur-Loire
 . . . . . . 104 B1
oujol-sur-Orb F . 130 B2
oulaouen F 100 A2
oulton-le-Fylde
GB 38 A4
oundstock GB . . . 42 B2
ourcy F 91 B3
ourrain F 104 B2
oussu FIN 197 C12
ouyastruc F . . . 145 A4
ouy-de-Touges
 . . . . . . 146 A2
ouzauges F 114 B3
ova de Santa Iria
P 154 C1
ovažská Bystrica
SK 98 B2
ovedilla E 158 C1
ovenets RUS 9 A9
ovlja HR 138 B2
ovljana HR 137 A4
óvoa
 Beja P 161 A2
 Santarém P . . . 154 B2
ova de Lanhoso
P 148 A1
óvoa de Varzim
P 148 A1
óvoa e Meadas
P 155 B3
owidz PL 76 B2

Poyales del Hoyo
E 150 B2
Poynton GB 40 B1
Poyntz Pass GB . . 27 B4
Poysdorf A 97 C4
Poza de la Sal E . 143 B3
Pozaldez E 150 A3
Pozán de Vero E . 145 B3
Pozanti TR 23 C8
Požarevac SRB . 127 C3
Požega
 HR 125 B3
 SRB 127 D2
Poznań PL 76 B1
Pozo Alcón E . . . 164 B2
Pozoantiguo E . 150 A2
Pozoblanco E . 156 B3
Pozo Cañada E . 158 C2
Pozo de Guadalajara
E 151 B4
Pozo de la Serna
E 157 B4
Pozohondo E . . . 158 C2
Pozondón E 152 B2
Poźrzadło Wielkie
PL 75 A4
Pozuel del Campo
E 152 B2
Pozuelo de Alarcón
E 151 B4
Pozuelo de Calatrava
E 157 B4
Pozuelo del Páramo
E 142 B1
Pozuelo de Zarzón
E 149 B3
Pozzallo I 177 C3
Pozzomaggiore I . 178 B2
Pozzo San Nicola
I 178 B2
Pozzuoli I 170 C2
Pozzuolo I 135 B4
Prabuty PL 69 B4
Prača BIH 139 B4
Prachatice CZ . . . 96 B1
Prada E 141 B3
Pradelle F 118 C2
Pradelles F 117 C2
Prades
 E 147 C1
 F 146 B3
Pradła PL 86 B3
Prado
 E 142 A1
 P 148 A1
Prado del Rey E . 162 B2
Pradoluengo E . 143 B3
Pragelato I 119 B3
Pragersko SLO . 123 A4
Prägraten A . . . 109 B3
Prague = Praha CZ . 84 B2
Praha = Prague CZ . 84 B2
Prahecq F 115 B3
Praia I 154 B1
Práia a Mare I . . 174 B1
Praia da Rocha P . 160 B1
Praia da Viera P . 154 B2
Praia de Mira P . . 148 B1
Praiano I 170 C2
Pralboino I 120 B3
Pralognan-la-Vanoise
 F 118 B3
Pramanda GR . . 182 D3
Pranjani SRB . . 127 C2
Prapatnica HR . 138 B2
Præstø DK 65 A5
Praszka PL 86 A2
Prat F 146 A1
Prata I 135 B3
Prata di Pordenone
 I 122 B1
Pratau D 83 A4
Prat de Compte E . 153 B4
Pratdip E 147 C1
Pratella I 170 B2
Prato I 135 B4
Prátola Peligna I . 169 A3
Pratola Serra I . . 170 C2
Prats-de-Mollo-la-
 Preste F 146 B3
Prauthoy F 105 B4
Pravia E 141 A4
Praxmar A 108 B2
Prayssac F 129 B4
Prazzo I 132 A3
Prebold SLO . . 123 A4
Préchac F 128 B2
Précy-sur-Thil F . 104 B3
Predappio I 135 A4
Predazzo I 121 A4
Předin CZ 97 B3
Preding A 110 C2
Predjame SLO . . 123 B3
Predlitz A 109 B4
Predmeja SLO . 122 B3
Predoi I 108 B3
Pré-en-Pail F . . 89 B3
Prees GB 38 B4
Preetz D 64 B3
Préfailles F 101 B3
Pregarten A 96 C2
Pregrada HR . . 123 A4
Preignan F 129 C3
Preili LV 8 D5
Preitenegg A . . 110 C1
Prekaja BIH . . 138 A2
Preko HR 137 A4
Preljina SRB . . 127 D2
Prelog HR 124 A2
Prelošćica HR . 124 B2
Přelouč CZ 97 A3
Prem SLO 123 B3
Premantura HR . 122 C2
Prémery F 104 B2
Premià de Mar E . 147 C3
Premnitz D 73 B5
Prémont F 91 A3
Prenzlau D 74 A2
Preodac BIH . . 138 A2

Přerov CZ 98 B1
Prerow D 66 B1
Presencio E . . . 143 B3
Presicce I 173 C4
Presly F 103 B4
Prešov SK 12 D4
Pressac F 115 B4
Pressath D 95 B3
Pressbaum A . . . 111 A3
Prestatyn GB . . . 38 A3
Presteigne GB . . 39 B3
Přeštice CZ 96 B1
Preston
 Lancashire GB . . . 38 A4
 Scottish Borders
 GB 35 C5
Prestonpans GB . 35 C5
Prestwick GB . . . 36 A2
Prettin D 83 A4
Preturo I 169 A3
Pretzchendorf D . 83 B5
Pretzier D 73 B4
Pretzsch D 83 A4
Preuilly-sur-Claise
 F 115 B4
Prevalje SLO . . 110 C1
Prevenchères F . 131 A2
Préveranges F . . 116 A2
Preveza GR 182 E2
Prevršac HR . . 124 B2
Prezid HR 123 B3
Priaranza del Bierzo
E 141 B4
Priay F 118 A2
Pribeta SK 112 B2
Priboj
 BIH 125 C4
 SRB 16 D3
Příbor CZ 98 B2
Příbram CZ 96 B2
Pribylina SK 99 B3
Přibyslav CZ . . . 97 B3
Pričević SRB . . 127 C1
Pridjel BIH 125 C4
Priego E 152 B1
Priego de Córdoba
 E 163 A3
Priekule LV 8 D2
Prien D 109 B3
Prienai LT 13 A5
Prievidza SK . . . 98 C2
Prigradica HR . 138 C2
Prigrevica SRB . 125 B5
Prijeboj HR 123 C4
Prijedor BIH . . . 124 C2
Prijepolje SRB . . . 16 D3
Prilep MK 182 B3
Priluka BIH 138 B2
Primda CZ 95 B4
Primel-Trégastel
 F 100 A2
Primišlje HR . . 123 B4
Primorsk
 Kaliningrad RUS . . 69 A5
 Severo-Zapadnyy
 RUS 9 B6
Primošten HR . . 138 B1
Primstal D 92 B2
Princes Risborough
GB 44 B3
Princetown GB . . 42 B2
Principina a Mare
 . . . . . . 135 C4
Priolo Gargallo I . 177 B4
Prioro E 142 B2
Priozersk RUS . . . 9 B7
Prirechnyy RUS . 193 C14
Prisoje BIH 138 B3
Priština KOS . . . 16 D4
Pritzerbe D 73 B5
Pritzier D 73 A4
Pritzwalk D 73 A5
Privas F 117 C4
Priverno I 169 B3
Privlaka
 Vukovarsko-
 Srijemska HR . 125 B4
 Zadarska HR . . 137 A4
Prizna HR 123 C3
Prizren KOS . . . 16 D4
Prizzi I 176 B2
Prnjavor
 BIH 125 C3
 HR 124 B1
 SRB 127 C1
Proaza E 141 A4
Probstzella D . . . 82 B3
Probus GB 42 B2
Prócchio I 134 C3
Prochowice PL . . 85 A4
Prócida I 170 C2
Prodhromos CY . 181 B1
Prodo I 135 C5
Proença-a-Nova P . 154 B3
Proença-a-Velha
 P 155 A3
Profondeville B . . 79 B4
Prokuplje SRB . . . 16 D4
Propriano F 180 B1
Prosec CZ 97 B4
Prösen D 83 A5
Prosenjakovci
 SLO 111 C3
Prosotsani GR . . 183 B5
Prostějov CZ . . . 98 B1
Prószków PL 86 B1
Proszowice PL . . . 87 B4
Protić BIH 138 A2
Protivanov CZ . . . 97 B4
Protivín CZ 96 B2
Prötzel D 74 B2
Provins F 90 C3
Prozor BIH 139 B3
Prrenjas AL 182 B2
Prudhoe GB 37 B5
Prudnik PL 85 B5
Pruggern A 109 B4
Prügy H 113 A5
Prüm D 80 B2

Pruna E 162 B2
Prunelli-di-Fiumorbo
 F 180 A2
Prunetta I 135 A3
Pruniers F 103 C4
Prusice PL 85 A4
Pruské SK 98 B2
Pruszcze PL 76 A3
Pruszcz Gdański
 PL 69 A3
Pruszków PL 77 B5
Prutz A 108 B1
Pruzhany BY 13 B6
Pružina SK 98 B2
Půrvomay BG . . 183 A7
Prylek PL 75 B4
Przasnysz PL . . . 77 A5
Przechlewo PL . . . 68 B2
Przecław PL 87 B5
Przedbórz PL . . . 87 A3
Przedecz PL 76 B3
Przejęslaw PL . . . 84 A3
Przemków PL . . . 85 A3
Przemocze PL . . . 75 A3
Przemyśl PL 12 D5
Przerąb PL 87 A3
Przewodnik PL . . . 69 B3
Przewodowo Parcele
 PL 77 B5
Przeźmierowo PL . 75 B5
Przodkowo PL . . . 68 A3
Przybiernów PL . 75 A3
Przyborowice PL . 77 B5
Przybyszew PL . . . 87 A4
Przybyszów PL . . . 86 A3
Przyleg PL 75 B4
Przysucha PL . . . 87 A4
Przytoczna PL . . . 75 B4
Przytyk PL 87 A4
Przywidz PL 68 A3
Psachna GR 185 A4
Psara GR 185 A6
Psary PL 76 C3
Pskov RUS 8 D6
Pszczew PL 75 B4
Pszczółki PL 69 A3
Pszczyna PL 98 B2
Pszów PL 86 B2
Pteleos GR 182 D4
Ptolemaida GR . 182 C3
Ptuj SLO 124 A1
Ptusza PL 68 B1
Puch A 109 B4
Puchberg am
 Schneeberg A . . 110 B2
Puchevillers F . . . 90 A2
Puchheim D 108 A2
Púchov SK 98 B2
Pučišća HR 138 B2
Puck PL 69 A3
Puçol E 159 B3
Puconci SLO . . 111 C3
Pudasjärvi FIN . . 197 D10
Puderbach D 81 B3
Pudozh RUS 9 B10
Puebla de Albortón
 E 153 A3
Puebla de Alcocer
 E 156 B2
Puebla de Beleña
 E 151 B4
Puebla de Don
 Fadrique E . . 164 B2
Puebla de Don Rodrigo
 E 156 A3
Puebla de Guzmán
 E 161 B2
Puebla de la Calzada
 E 155 C4
Puebla de la Reina
 E 156 B1
Puebla de Lillo E . 142 A1
Puebla del Maestre
 E 161 A3
Puebla del Principe
 E 158 C1
Puebla de Obando
 E 155 B4
Puebla de Sanabria
 E 141 B4
Puebla de Sancho
 Pérez E 155 C4
Puente Almuhey
 E 142 B2
Puente de Domingo
 Flórez E 141 B4
Puente de Génave
 E 164 A2
Puente del Congosto
 E 150 B2
Puente de Montañana
 E 145 B4
Puente Duero E . 150 A3
Puente-Genil E . . 162 A3
Puente la Reina E . 144 B2
Puente la Reina de
 Jaca E 144 B3
Puentelarra E . . 143 B3
Puente Mayorga E . 162 B2
Puente Viesgo E . 143 A3
Puertas
 Asturias E . . . 142 A2
 Salamanca E . . 149 A3
Puerto de Mazarrón
 E 165 B3
Puerto de Santa Cruz
 E 156 A2
Puerto de San Vicente
 E 156 A2
Puerto-Lápice E . 157 A4
Puertollano E . . 157 B3
Puerto Lumbreras
 E 164 B3
Puerto Moral E . 161 B3
Puerto Real E . . 162 B1
Puerto Rey E . . 156 A2
Puerto Seguro E . 149 B3
Puerto Serrano E . 162 B2

Puget-Sur-Argens
 F 132 B2
Puget-Théniers F . 132 B2
Puget-ville F . . 132 B2
Pugnochiuso I . . 171 B4
Puigcerdà E . . 146 B2
Puigpunyent E . 166 B2
Puig Reig E . . 147 C2
Puillon F 128 C2
Puimichel F 132 B2
Puimoisson F . . 132 B2
Puiseaux F 103 A4
Puisieux F 90 A2
Puisserguier F . . 130 B2
Puivert F 146 B3
Pujols F 128 B2
Pukanec SK 98 C2
Pukavik S 63 B2
Pukë AL 182 A1
Pula
 HR 122 C2
 I 179 C2
Puławy PL 12 C4
Pulborough GB . . 44 C3
Pulfero I 122 A2
Pulgar E 157 A3
Pulheim D 80 A2
Pulkau A 97 C3
Pulpí E 164 B3
Pulsano I 173 B3
Pulsnitz D 84 A2
Pułtusk PL 77 B6
Pumpsaint GB . . . 39 B3
Punat HR 123 B3
Punta Marina I . . 135 A5
Punta Prima E . . 167 B4
Punta Sabbioni I . 122 B1
Puntas de Calnegre
 E 165 B3
Punta Umbria I . . 161 B3
Puoltikasvaara S . 196 B4
Puolanka FIN . . . 3 D10
Puoltsa S 196 B2
Puračić BIH 125 C4
Purbach am Neusiedler
 See A 111 B3
Purchena E 164 B2
Purfleet GB 45 B4
Purgstall A 110 A2
Purkersdorf A . . 111 A3
Purmerend NL . . . 70 B1
Purullena E 164 B1
Pushkin RUS 9 C7
Pushkino RUS . . . 9 D10
Püspökladány H . . 113 B5
Pusté Ulany SK . . 111 A4
Pustoshka RUS . . . 9 D6
Puszcza Mariańska
 PL 77 C5
Puszczykowo PL . 76 B1
Pusztamagyaród
 H 111 C3
Pusztamonostor
 H 113 B3
Pusztaszabolcs H . 112 B2
Pusztavám H . . . 112 B2
Putanges-Pont-Ecrepin
 F 89 B3
Putignano I 173 B3
Putlitz D 73 A5
Putnok H 99 C4
Putte B 79 A4
Puttelange-aux-Lacs
 F 92 B2
Putten NL 70 B2
Puttgarden D . . . 65 B4
Püttlingen D . . . 92 B2
Putzu Idu I 179 B2
Puy-Guillaume F . 117 B3
Puylaurens F . . 129 C4
Puy-l'Évêque F . 129 B4
Puymirol F 129 B3
Puyôo F 128 C2
Puyrolland F 114 B3
Pwllheli GB 38 B2
Pyetrikaw BY 13 B8
Pyhäjärvi FIN . . . 3 E9
Pyhäkylä FIN . . 197 D11
Pyla CY 181 A2
Pyla-sur-Mer F . . 128 B1
Pyrzyce PL 75 A3
Pysely CZ 96 B2
Pyskowice PL . . . 86 B2
Pytalovo RUS 8 D5
Pyzdry PL 76 B2

Q

Quakenbrück D . . 71 B4
Quargnento I . . . 119 C5
Quarré-les-Tombes
 F 104 B2
Quarteira P 160 B1
Quartu Sant'Élena
 I 179 C3
Quatre-Champs F . 91 B4
Quedlinburg D . . 82 A3
Queensferry
 Edinburgh GB . . 35 C4
 Flintshire GB . . 38 A3
Queige F 118 B3
Queipo E 161 B3
Queixans E 146 B2
Quel E 144 B1
Quelaines-St-Gault
 F 102 B1
Queljada P 148 A1
Quemada E 143 C3
Queralbs E 147 B3
Quercianella I . . 134 B3
Querfurt D 82 A3
Quérigut F 146 B3
Quero
 E 157 A4
 I 121 B4
Querqueville F . . 88 A2
Quesada E 164 B1

Questembert F . . 101 B3
Quettehou F . . . 88 A2
Quevauvillers F . . 90 B2
Quevy B 79 B4
Quiaios P 148 B1
Quiberon F . . . 100 B2
Quiberville F . . . 89 A4
Quickborn D 64 C2
Quiévrain B 79 B3
Quillan F 146 B3
Quillebeuf F 89 A4
Quimper F 100 A1
Quimperlé F 100 B2
Quincampoix F . . 89 A5
Quincoces de Yuso
 E 143 B3
Quincy F 103 B4
Quinéville F 88 A2
Quingey F 105 B4
Quinson F 132 B2
Quinssaines F . . 116 A2
Quinta-Grande P . 154 C2
Quintana de la Serena
 E 156 B2
Quintana del Castillo
 E 141 B4
Quintana del Marco
 E 141 B5
Quintana del Puente
 E 142 B2
Quintana-Martin
 Galindez E . . 143 B3
Quintanaortuño E . 143 B3
Quintanapalla E . 143 B3
Quintanar de la Orden
 E 157 A4
Quintanar de la Sierra
 E 143 C3
Quintanar del Rey
 E 158 B2
Quintanilla de la Mata
 E 143 C3
Quintanilla del Coco
 E 143 C3
Quintanilla de Onésimo
 E 150 A3
Quintanilla de Somoza
 E 141 B4
Quintas de Valdelucio
 E 142 B2
Quintela P 148 B2
Quintin F 100 A3
Quinto E 153 A3
Quinzano d'Oglio
 I 120 B3
Quiroga E 141 B3
Quismondo E . . 150 B3
Quissac F 131 B2
Quistello I 121 B3

R

Raab A 96 C1
Raabs an der Thaya
 A 97 C3
Raahe FIN 3 D9
Raajärvi FIN . . . 197 C9
Raalte NL 71 B3
Raamsdonksveer
 NL 79 A4
Raanujarvi FIN . . 196 C7
Raattama FIN . . . 196 A7
Rab HR 123 C3
Rábade E 140 A3
Rábafüzes H . . . 111 C3
Rábahidvég H . . 111 B3
Rabanales E . . . 149 A3
Rábapatona H . . 111 B4
Rabapordány H . . 111 B4
Rabastens F . . . 129 C4
Rabastens-de-Bigorre
 F 145 A4
Rabat = Victoria
 M 175 C3
Rabat M 175 C3
Rabča SK 99 B3
Rabe SRB 126 A2
Rabi CZ 96 B1
Rabino I 67 C4
Rabka PL 99 B3
Rabrovo SRB . . . 127 C3
Rača SRB 127 C3
Rácale I 173 C4
Racalmás H 112 B2
Racalmuto I 176 B2
Racconigi I 119 C4
Rače SLO 110 C2
Rachecourt-sur-Marne
 F 91 C4
Raciąż PL 77 B5
Racibórz PL 86 B2
Račinovci HR . . 125 C4
Ráckeve H 112 B2
Racławice PL . . . 87 B4
Racławice Śląskie
 PL 86 B1
Racot PL 75 B5
Råda
 Skaraborg S . . . 55 B4
 Värmland S . . . 49 B5
Radalj SRB 127 C1
Rădăuţi RO 17 B6
Radda in Chianti I . 135 B4
Raddusa I 177 B3
Radeberg D 84 A1
Radeburg D 84 A1
Radeče SLO 123 A4
Radekhiv UA . . . 13 C6
Radenci SLO . . . 111 C3
Radenthein A . . . 109 C4
Radevormwald D . 80 A3
Radičević I 135 C4
Radicófani I 135 C4
Radicóndoli I . . . 135 B4
Radišići BIH 138 B3
Radizel SLO . . . 110 C2
Radków PL 85 B4

Radlje ob Dravi
 SLO 110 C2
Radłów PL 87 B4
Radmer an der Stube
 A 110 B1
Radnejaur S 195 E9
Radnice CZ 96 B1
Radohova BIH . . 138 A3
Radojevo SRB . 126 B2
Radolfzell D . . . 107 B3
Radom PL 87 A5
Radomice PL . . . 77 B4
Radomin PL 77 A4
Radomsko PL . . . 86 A3
Radomyšl I 13 C8
Radomyśl Wielki
 PL 87 B5
Radošina SK . . . 98 C1
Radošovce SK . . . 98 C1
Radoszewice PL . . 86 A2
Radoszyce PL . . . 87 A4
Radotin CZ 96 B2
Radovets BG . . . 186 A1
Radoviš MK 182 B4
Radovljica SLO . 123 A3
Radowo Wielkie PL . 75 A4
Radstadt A 109 B4
Radstock GB 43 A4
Raduc HR 137 A4
Raduša MK 182 A3
Radviliškis LT . . . 8 E3
Radzanów
 Mazowieckie PL . . . 77 B5
 Mazowieckie PL . . . 87 A4
Radziejów PL . . . 76 B3
Radziejowice PL . 77 B5
Radzików PL . . . 75 B4
Radzovce SK . . . 113 A3
Radzyń Chełmiński
 PL 69 B3
Raeren B 80 B2
Raesfeld D 80 A2
Raffadali I 176 B2
Rafina GR 185 A4
Rafsbotn N 192 B7
Ragachow BY . . . 13 B9
Ragály H 99 C4
Rågeleje DK 61 C2
Raglan GB 39 C4
Ragnitz A 110 C2
Ragusa I 177 C3
Rahden D 72 B1
Råholt N 48 B3
Raiano I 169 A3
Raigada E 141 B3
Rain D 94 C2
Rainbach im Mühlkreis
 A 96 C2
Rainham GB 45 B4
Rairiz de Veiga E . 140 B3
Raisdorf D 64 B3
Raisio FIN 8 B3
Raiskio FIN . . . 197 D9
Raiva
 Aveiro P 148 A1
 Coimbra P . . . 148 B1
Raja-Jooseppi
 FIN 193 D12

Ramsgate GB 45 B5
Ramsjö S 200 D1
Ramstein-Meisenbach D 93 B3
Ramsund N 194 B7
Ramundberget S 199 C9
Ramvik S 200 D3
Ranalt A 108 B2
Rånäs S 51 C5
Rånåsfoss N 48 B3
Rance B 91 A4
Ránchio I 135 B5
Randaberg N 52 A1
Randalstown GB 27 B4
Randan F 117 A3
Randazzo I 177 B3
Rånddalen S 199 C10
Randegg A 110 A1
Randers DK 58 B3
Randijaur S 196 C2
Randin E 140 C3
Randsverk N 198 D6
Råneå S 196 D5
Rânes F 89 B3
Rångedala S 60 B3
Ranis D 82 B3
Rankweil A 107 B4
Rånnaväg S 60 B3
Ränneslöv S 61 C3
Rannoch Station GB 34 B3
Ranovac SRB 127 C3
Ransäter S 55 A4
Ransbach-Baumbach D 81 B3
Ransta S 56 A2
Ranttila FIN 193 C9
Ranua FIN 197 D9
Ranum DK 58 B2
Ranvalhal P 154 B1
Raon-l'Étape F 92 C2
Ráossi I 121 B4
Rapallo I 134 A2
Rapla EST 8 C4
Rapness GB 33 B4
Rapolano Terme I 135 B4
Rapolla I 172 B1
Raposa P 154 B2
Rapperswil CH 107 B3
Raša HR 123 B3
Rasal E 145 B3
Rascafria E 151 B4
Rasdorf D 82 B1
Raseiniai LT 13 A5
Rašica SLO 123 B3
Rasines E 143 A3
Rasquera E 153 A4
Rássina I 135 B4
Rastatt D 93 C4
Rastede D 71 A5
Rastenberg D 82 A3
Rastošnica BIH 125 C4
Rastovac MNE 139 C4
Rasueros E 150 A2
Rasy PL 86 A3
Raszków PL 86 A1
Rätan S 199 C11
Rateče SLO 109 C4
Ratekau D 65 C3
Ratež SLO 123 B4
Rathangan IRL 30 A2
Rathcoole IRL 30 A2
Rathcormack IRL 29 B3
Rathdrum IRL 30 B2
Rathebur D 74 A2
Rathenow D 73 B5
Rathfriland GB 27 B4
Rathkeale IRL 29 B3
Rathmelton IRL 27 A3
Rathmolyon IRL 30 A2
Rathmore IRL 29 B2
Rathmullan IRL 27 A3
Rathnew IRL 30 B2
Rathvilly IRL 30 B2
Ratibořské Hory CZ 96 B2
Ratingen D 80 A2
Ratková SK 99 C4
Ratkovo SRB 126 B1
Ratne UA 13 C6
Rattelsdorf D 94 A2
Ratten A 110 B2
Rattosjärvi FIN 196 C7
Rattray GB 35 B4
Rättvik S 50 B2
Ratvika N 199 B7
Ratzeburg D 65 C3
Rätzlingen D 73 B4
Raucourt-et-Flaba F 91 B4
Raudeberg N 198 D2
Raufarhöfn IS 191 A10
Raufoss N 48 B2
Rauhala FIN 196 B7
Rauland N 53 A4
Raulhac F 116 C2
Raulia N 195 E5
Rauma FIN 8 B2
Raundal N 46 B3
Raunds GB 44 A3
Rauris A 109 B4
Rautas S 196 B2
Rautavaara FIN 3 E11
Rauville-la-Bigot F 88 A2
Rauzan F 128 B2
Ravanusa I 176 B2
Rava-Rus'ka UA 13 C5
Ravča HR 138 B3
Ravels B 79 A4
Rävemåla S 63 B3
Ravenglass GB 36 B3
Ravenna I 135 A5
Ravensburg D 107 B4
Rävlanda S 60 B2
Ravna Gora HR 123 B3
Ravne na Koroškem SLO 110 C1
Ravnje SRB 127 C1
Ravno BIH 139 C3
Ravno Selo SRB 126 B1
Rawa Mazowiecka PL 87 A4
Rawicz PL 85 A4
Rawtenstall GB 40 B1
Rayleigh GB 45 B4
Ražana SRB 127 C1
Ražanac HR 137 A4
Razboj BIH 124 B3
Razes F 115 B5
Razgrad BG 17 D7
Razkrižie SLO 111 C3
Razlog BG 183 B5
Razo E 140 A2
Reading GB 44 B3
Réalmont F 130 B1
Rebais F 90 C3
Reboly RUS 3 E12
Rebordelo P 149 A2
Recanati I 136 B2
Recas E 151 B4
Recco I 134 A2
Recess IRL 28 A2
Recey-sur-Ource F 105 B3
Recezinhos P 148 A1
Rechnitz A 111 B3
Rechytsa BY 13 B9
Recke D 71 B4
Recklinghausen D 80 A3
Recoaro Terme I 121 B4
Recogne B 92 B1
Recoules-Prévinquières F 130 A1
Recsk H 113 B4
Recz PL 75 A4
Reda PL 69 A3
Redalen N 48 B2
Redange L 92 B1
Redcar GB 37 B5
Redditch GB 44 A2
Redefin D 73 A4
Redhill GB 44 B3
Redics H 111 C3
Redkino RUS 9 D10
Redland GB 33 B3
Redlin D 73 A5
Redon F 101 B3
Redondela E 140 B2
Redondo P 155 C3
Red Point GB 31 B3
Redruth GB 42 B1
Redzikowo PL 68 A2
Reepham GB 41 C5
Rees D 80 A2
Reeth GB 37 B5
Reetz D 73 A4
Reftele S 60 B3
Regalbuto I 177 B3
Regen D 95 C5
Regensburg D 95 B4
Regenstauf D 95 B4
Reggello I 135 B4
Réggio di Calábria I 175 C1
Reggiolo I 121 C3
Réggio nell'Emília I 121 C3
Reghin RO 17 B6
Régil E 144 A1
Regna S 56 B1
Regniéville F 92 C1
Regny F 117 B4
Rego da Leirosa P 154 A2
Regöly H 112 C2
Regueiro E 140 B2
Reguengo
Portalegre P 155 B3
Santarém P 154 B2
Reguengos de Monsaraz P 155 C3
Rehau D 83 B4
Rehburg D 72 B2
Rehden D 72 B1
Rehna D 65 C4
Reichelsheim D 93 B4
Reichelshofen D 94 B2
Reichenau A 110 B2
Reichenbach
Sachsen D 83 B4
Sachsen D 84 A2
Reichenfels A 110 B1
Reichensachsen D 82 A2
Reichertshofen D 95 C3
Reichshoffen F 93 C3
Reiden CH 106 B2
Reigada
E 141 A4
P 149 B3
Reigate GB 44 B3
Reillanne F 132 B1
Reillo E 158 B2
Reims F 91 B4
Reinach CH 106 B3
Reinbek D 72 A3
Reinberg D 66 B2
Reine N 194 C4
Reinfeld D 65 C3
Reinheim D 93 B4
Reinli N 47 B6
Reinosa E 142 A2
Reinstorf D 65 C4
Reinsvoll N 48 B2
Reisach A 109 C4
Reiss GB 32 C3
Reitan N 199 C8
Reit im Winkl D 109 B3
Rejmyre S 56 B1
Rekavice BIH 124 C3
Rekovac SRB 127 D3
Relleu E 159 C3
Rém H 125 A5
Remagen D 80 B3
Rémalard F 89 B4
Rembercourt-aux-Pots F 91 C5
Remedios P 154 B1
Remels D 71 A4
Remetea Mare RO 126 B3
Remich L 92 B2
Rémilly F 92 B2
Remiremont F 105 A5
Remolinos E 144 C2
Remoulins F 131 B3
Remscheid D 80 A3
Rémuzat F 131 A4
Rena N 48 A3
Renaison F 117 A3
Renazé F 101 B4
Renchen D 93 C4
Rencurel F 118 B2
Rende I 174 B2
Rendina GR 182 D3
Rendsburg D 64 B2
Renedo E 150 A3
Renens CH 105 C5
Renfrew GB 34 C3
Rengsjö S 50 A3
Reni UA 17 C8
Rennebu N 198 C6
Rennerod D 81 B4
Rennertshofen D 94 C3
Rennes F 101 A4
Rennes-les-Bains F 146 B3
Rennweg A 109 B4
Rens DK 64 B2
Rensjön S 196 A2
Rentería E 144 A2
Rentjärn S 200 A4
Répcelak H 111 B4
Repojoki FIN 193 D9
Repvåg N 193 B9
Requena E 159 B2
Réquista F 130 A1
Rerik D 65 B4
Resana I 121 B4
Resarö S 57 A4
Reschen = Résia I 108 C1
Resen MK 182 B3
Resende P 148 A2
Résia = Reschen I 108 C1
Reşiţa
RO 16 C4
RO 126 B3
Resko PL 67 C4
Resnik SRB 127 C2
Ressons-sur-Matz F 90 B2
Restábal E 163 B4
Resuttano I 177 B3
Retamal E 155 C4
Retford GB 40 B3
Rethel F 91 B4
Rethem D 72 B2
Rethimno GR 185 D5
Retie B 79 A5
Retiers F 101 B4
Retortillo E 149 B3
Retortillo de Soria E 151 A4
Retournac F 117 B4
Rétság H 112 B3
Rettenegg A 110 B2
Retuerta del Bullaque E 157 A3
Retz A 97 C3
Retzbach D 94 B1
Reuden D 73 B5
Reuilly F 103 B4
Reus E 147 C2
Reusel NL 79 A5
Reuterstadt Stavenhagen D 74 A1
Reuth D 95 B4
Reutlingen D 94 C1
Reutte A 108 B1
Reuver NL 80 A2
Revel F 146 A2
Revello I 119 C4
Revenga E 151 B3
Revest-du-Bion F 132 A1
Révfülöp H 111 C4
Revigny-sur-Ornain F 91 C4
Revin F 91 B4
Řevnice CZ 96 B2
Řevničov CZ 84 B1
Revo I 121 A4
Revsnes N 47 A4
Revúca SK 99 C4
Rewa PL 69 A3
Rewal PL 67 B4
Rexbo S 50 B2
Reyðarfjörður IS 191 B11
Reyero E 142 B1
Reykhólar IS 190 B3
Reykholt
Árnessýsla IS 190 C5
Borgarfjarðarsýsla IS 190 C4
Reykjahlið IS 191 B9
Reykjavík IS 190 C4
Rezé F 101 B4
Rēzekne LV 8 D5
Rezovo BG 17 E8
Rezzato I 120 B3
Rezzoáglio I 134 A2
Rhade D 72 A2
Rhaunen D 93 B3
Rhayader GB 39 B3
Rheda-Wiedenbrück D 81 A4
Rhede
Niedersachsen D 71 A4
Nordrhein-Westfalen D 80 A2
Rheinau D 93 C3
Rheinbach D 80 B2
Rheinberg D 80 A2
Rheine D 71 B4
Rheinfelden D 106 B2
Rheinsberg D 74 A1
Rhêmes-Notre-Dame I 119 B4
Rhenen NL 70 C2
Rhens D 81 B3
Rheydt D 80 A2
Rhiconich GB 32 C2
Rhinow D 73 B5
Rhiw GB 38 B2
Rho I 120 B2
Rhodes GR 188 C3
Rhondda GB 39 C3
Rhosllanerchrugog GB 38 A3
Rhosneigr GB 38 A2
Rhossili GB 39 C2
Rhubodach GB 34 C2
Rhuddlan GB 38 A3
Rhyl GB 38 A3
Rhynie GB 33 D4
Riala S 57 A4
Riallé F 101 B4
Riaño E 142 B1
Riano I 168 A2
Rians F 132 B1
Rianxo E 140 B2
Riaza E 151 A4
Riba E 143 A3
Ribadavia E 140 B2
Ribadeo E 141 A3
Riba de Saelices E 152 B1
Ribadesella E 142 A1
Ribaflecha E 143 B4
Ribaforada E 144 C2
Ribare SRB 127 C3
Riba-roja d'Ebre E 153 A4
Riba-Roja de Turia E 159 B3
Ribe DK 59 C1
Ribeauvillé F 106 A2
Ribécourt-Dreslincourt F 90 B2
Ribeira da Pena P 148 A2
Ribeira de Piquín E 141 A3
Ribemont F 91 B3
Ribera I 176 B2
Ribérac F 129 A3
Ribera de Cardós E 146 B2
Ribera del Fresno E 156 B1
Ribesalbes E 159 A3
Ribes de Freser E 147 B3
Ribiers F 132 A1
Ribnica
BIH 139 A4
SLO 123 B3
Ribnica na Potorju SLO 110 C2
Ribnik HR 123 B4
Rîbniţa MD 17 B8
Ribnitz-Damgarten D 66 B1
Ribolla I 135 C4
Říčany CZ 97 B4
Říčany CZ 96 B2
Riccia I 170 B2
Riccione I 136 A1
Ricco Del Golfo I 134 A2
Richebourg F 105 A4
Richelieu F 102 B2
Richisau CH 107 B3
Richmond
Greater London GB 44 B3
North Yorkshire GB 37 B5
Richtenberg D 66 B1
Richterswil CH 107 B3
Rickling D 64 B3
Rickmansworth GB 44 B3
Ricla E 152 A2
Riddarhyttan S 50 C2
Ridderkerk NL 79 A4
Riddes CH 119 A4
Ridjica SRB 125 B5
Riec-sur-Bélon F 100 B2
Ried A 109 A4
Riedenburg D 95 C3
Ried im Oberinntal A 108 B1
Riedlingen D 107 A4
Riedstadt D 93 B4
Riegersburg A 110 C2
Riego de la Vega E 141 B5
Riego del Camino E 149 A4
Riello E 141 B5
Riemst B 80 B1
Rienne B 91 B4
Riénsena E 142 A2
Riesa D 83 A5
Riese Pio X I 121 B4
Riesi I 177 B3
Riestedt D 82 A3
Rietberg D 81 A4
Rieti I 169 A2
Rietschen D 84 A2
Rieumes F 146 A2
Rieupeyroux F 130 A1
Rieux-Volvestre F 146 A2
Riez F 132 B2
Rīga LV 8 D4
Riggisberg CH 106 C2
Rignac F 130 A1
Rignano Gargánico I 171 B3
Rigolato I 109 C3
Rigside GB 36 A3
Rigutino I 135 B4
Riihimäki FIN 8 B4
Rijeka HR 123 B3
Rijen NL 79 A4
Rijkevorsel B 79 A4
Rijssen NL 71 B3
Rila BG 183 A5
Rilić BIH 138 B3
Rilievo I 176 B1
Rillé F 102 B2
Rillo de Gallo E 152 B2
Rimavská Baňa SK 99 C3
Rimavská Seč SK 99 C4
Rimavská Sobota SK 99 C4
Rimbo S 57 A4
Rimforsa S 56 B1
Rímini I 136 A1
Rîmnicu Sărat RO 17 C7
Rimogne F 91 B4
Rimpar D 94 B1
Rimske Toplice SLO 123 A4
Rincón de la Victoria E 163 B3
Rincón de Soto E 144 B2
Rindal N 198 B6
Rinde N 46 A3
Ringarum S 56 B2
Ringaskiddy IRL 29 C3
Ringe DK 59 C3
Ringebu N 48 A2
Ringkøbing DK 59 B1
Ringsaker N 48 B2
Ringsted DK 61 D1
Ringwood GB 44 C2
Rinkaby S 63 C2
Rinkabyholm S 63 B4
Rinlo E 141 A3
Rinn A 108 B2
Rinteln D 72 B2
Rio E 140 B3
Riobo E 140 B2
Riodeva E 152 B2
Rio do Coures P 154 B2
Rio Douro P 148 A2
Riofrio E 150 B3
Rio Frio P 154 C2
Riofrio de Aliste E 149 A3
Rio frio de Riaza E 151 A4
Riogordo E 163 B3
Rioja E 164 C2
Riola I 135 A4
Riola Sardo I 179 C2
Riolobos E 155 B4
Riom F 116 B3
Riomaggiore I 134 A2
Rio Maior P 154 B2
Rio Marina I 134 C3
Riom-ès-Montagnes F 116 B2
Rion-des-Landes F 128 C2
Rionegro del Puente E 141 B4
Rionero in Vúlture I 172 B1
Riopar E 158 C1
Riós E 141 C3
Rioseco E 142 A1
Rioseco de Tapia E 141 B5
Rio Tinto P 148 A1
Riotord F 117 B4
Riotorto E 141 A3
Rioz F 105 B5
Ripač BIH 124 C1
Ripacándida I 172 B1
Ripanj SRB 127 C2
Ripatransone I 136 C2
Ripley GB 40 B2
Ripoll E 147 B3
Ripon GB 40 A2
Riposto I 177 B4
Ripsa S 56 B2
Risan MNE 16 D3
Risbäck S 200 B1
Risca GB 39 C3
Rischenau D 81 A5
Riscle F 128 C2
Risebo S 56 B2
Risnes N 46 A2
Rišňovce SK 98 C1
Risør N 53 B5
Risøyhamn N 194 B6
Rissna S 199 B12
Ritsem S 194 C8
Ritterhude D 72 A1
Riutula FIN 193 D10
Riva del Garda I 121 B3
Riva Ligure I 133 B3
Rivanazzano I 120 C2
Rivarolo Canavese I 119 B4
Rivarolo Mantovano I 121 B3
Rive-de-Gier F 117 B4
Rivedoux-Plage F 114 B2
Rivello I 174 A1
Rivergaro I 120 C2
Rives F 118 B2
Rivesaltes F 146 B3
Rivignano I 122 B2
Rivne UA 13 C7
Rívoli I 119 B4
Rivolta d'Adda I 120 B2
Rixheim F 106 B2
Rixo S 54 B2
Riza GR 183 C5
Rizokarpaso CY 181 A3
Rjukan N 47 C5
Rø DK 67 A3
Rö S 57 A4
Roa
E 143 C3
N 48 B2
Roade GB 44 A3
Roager DK 59 C1
Roaldkvam N 52 A2
Roanne F 117 A4
Röbäck S 200 C6
Robakowo PL 69 B3
Róbbio I 120 B1
Röbel D 73 A5
Roberton GB 35 C5
Robertsfors S 200 B6
Robertville B 80 B2
Robin Hood's Bay GB 37 B6
Robleda E 149 B3
Robledillo de Trujillo E 156 A2
Robledo
Albacete E 158 C1
Orense E 141 B4
Robledo de Chavela E 151 B3
Robledo del Buey E 156 A3
Robledo del Mazo E 156 A3
Robledollano E 156 A2
Robles de la Valcueva E 142 B1
Robliza de Cojos E 149 B4
Robres E 145 C3
Robres del Castillo E 144 B1
Rocafort de Queralt E 147 C2
Rocamadour F 129 B4
Roccabernarda I 175 B2
Roccabianca I 120 B3
Roccadáspide I 172 B1
Rocca di Mezzo I 169 A3
Rocca di Papa I 168 B2
Roccagorga I 169 B3
Rocca Imperiale I 174 A2
Roccalbegna I 135 C4
Roccalumera I 177 B4
Roccamena I 176 B2
Roccamonfina I 170 B1
Roccanova I 174 A2
Roccapalumba I 176 B2
Roccapassa I 169 A3
Rocca Priora I 136 B2
Roccaraso I 169 B4
Rocca San Casciano I 135 A4
Roccasecca I 169 B3
Rocca Sinibalda I 169 A2
Roccastrada I 135 B4
Roccatederighi I 135 B4
Roccella Iónica I 175 C2
Rocchetta Sant'António I 172 A1
Rocester GB 40 C2
Rochdale GB 40 B1
Rochechouart F 115 C4
Rochefort
B 79 B5
F 114 C3
Rochefort-en-Terre F 101 B3
Rochefort-Montagne F 116 B2
Rochefort-sur-Nenon F 105 B4
Roche-lez-Beaupré F 105 B5
Rochemaure F 131 A3
Rocheservière F 114 B2
Rochester
Medway GB 45 B4
Northumberland GB 37 A4
Rochlitz D 83 A4
Rociana del Condado E 161 B3
Rockenhausen D 93 B3
Rockhammar S 56 A1
Rockneby S 62 B4
Ročko Polje HR 123 B3
Ročov CZ 84 B1
Rocroi F 91 B4
Rodach D 82 B2
Roda de Bara E 147 C2
Roda de Ter E 147 C3
Rodalben D 93 B3
Rødberg N 47 B5
Rødby DK 65 B4
Rødbyhavn DK 65 B4
Rødding
Sonderjyllands Amt. DK 59 C2
Viborg Amt. DK 58 B1
Rödeby S 63 B3
Rodeiro E 140 B3
Rødekro DK 64 A2
Roden NL 71 A3
Ródenas E 152 B2
Rodenkirchen D 72 A1
Rödental D 82 B3
Rödermark D 93 B4
Rodewisch D 83 B4
Rodez F 130 A1
Rodi Gargánico I 171 B3
Roding D 95 B4
Rödjebro S 51 B4
Rødkærsbro DK 59 B2
Rodolivas GR 183 C5
Rodoñá E 147 C2
Rødvig DK 65 A5
Roermond NL 80 A1
Roesbrugge B 78 B2
Roeschwoog F 93 C4
Roeselare B 78 B3
Roetgen D 80 B2
Roffiac F 116 B3
Röfors S 55 B5
Rofrano I 172 B1
Rogač HR 138 B2
Rogačica SRB 127 C1
Rogalinek PL 76 B1
Rogaška Slatina SLO 123 A4
Rogatec SLO 123 A4
Rogatica BIH 139 B5
Rogatyn UA 13 D6
Rogätz D 73 B4
Roggendorf D 65 C4
Roggiano Gravina I 174 B2
Roghadal GB 31 B2
Rogliano
F 180 A2
I 175 B2
Rognan N 195 C6
Rogne N 47 A6
Rognes F 131 B4
Rogny-les-7-Ecluses F 103 B
Rogowo PL 76 B
Rogoznica HR 138 B
Rogoźnica PL 85 A
Rogoźno PL 76 B
Rohan F 101 A
Röhlingen D 94 C
Rohožnik SK 98 C
Rohr D 82 B
Rohrbach A 96 C
Rohrbach-lès-Bitche F 92 B
Rohrberg D 73 B
Rohr im Gebirge A 110 B
Röhrnbach D 96 C
Roisel F 90 B
Roja LV 8 D
Rojales E 165 A
Röjeråsen S 50 B
Rojewo PL 76 B
Rokiciny PL 87 A
Rokietnica PL 75 B
Rokiškis LT 8 E
Rokitki PL 85 A
Rokycany CZ 96 B
Rolampont F 105 B
Rold DK 58 B
Røldal N 52 A
Rolde NL 71 B
Rolfs S 196 D
Rollag N 47 B
Rollán E 149 B
Rolle CH 105 C
Roma = Rome I 168 B
Roma S 57 C
Romagnano Sésia I 119 B
Romagné F 88 B
Romakloster S 57 C
Roman RO 17 B
Romana I 178 B
Romanèche-Thorins F 117 A
Romano di Lombardia I 120 B
Romanshorn CH 107 B
Romans-sur-Isère F 118 B
Rombas F 92 B
Rome = Roma I 168 B
Romeán E 141 B
Romenay F 105 C
Romeral E 157 A
Römerstein D 94 C
Rometta I 177 A
Romford GB 45 B
Romhány H 112 B
Römhild D 82 B
Romilly-sur-Seine F 91 C
Romont CH 106 C
Romorantin-Lanthenay F 103 B
Romrod D 81 B
Romsey GB 44 C
Rømskog N 54 A
Rønbjerg DK 58 B
Roncal E 144 B
Ronce-les-Bains F 114 C
Ronchamp F 106 B
Ronchi dei Legionari I 122 B
Ronciglione I 168 A
Ronco Canavese I 119 B
Ronco Scrivia I 120 C
Ronda E 162 B
Rønde DK 59 B
Rone S 57 C
Ronehamn S 57 C
Rong N 46 B
Rönnäng S 60 B
Rønne DK 67 A
Ronneburg D 83 B
Ronneby S 63 B
Rönneshytta S 55 B
Rönninge S 57 A
Rönnöfors S 199 B1
Rönö S 56 B
Ronov nad Doubravou CZ 97 B
Ronse B 79 B
Roosendaal NL 79 A
Roosky IRL 26 C
Ropczyce PL 87 B
Ropeid N 52 A
Ropinsalmi FIN 192 D
Ropuerelos del Páramo E 141 B
Roquebilière F 133 A
Roquebrun F 130 B
Roquecourbe F 130 B
Roquefort F 128 B
Roquemaure F 131 A
Roquesteron F 132 B
Roquetas de Mar E 164 C
Roquetes E 153 B
Roquevaire F 132 B
Røra N 199 B
Rörbäcksnäs S 49 A
Rørbæk DK 58 B
Rore BIH 138 A
Röro S 60 B
Røros N 199 C
Rorschach CH 107 B
Rørvig DK 61 D
Rørvik N 199 A
Rörvik S 62 A
Rosà I 121 B
Rosal de la Frontera E 161 B
Rosalina Mare I 122 B
Rosa Marina I 173 B
Rosans F 132 A
Rosário P 160 B
Rosarno I 175 C
Rosbach D 81 B

S

St Jean-de-Luz F . .144 A2
St Jean-de-Maurienne F 118 B3
St Jean-de-Monts F 114 B1
St Jean-d'Illac F . .128 B2
St Jean-du-Bruel F 130 A2
St Jean-du-Gard F 131 A2
St Jean-en-Royans F 118 B2
St Jean-la-Riviere F 133 B3
St Jean-Pied-de-Port F 132 A2
St Jean-Poutge F .129 C3
St Jeoire F 118 A3
St Joachim F 101 B3
St Johnstown IRL . .27 B3
St Jorioz F 118 B3
St Joris Winge B . .79 B4
St Jouin-de-Marnes F 102 C1
St Juéry F 130 B1
St Julien F 118 A2
St Julien-Chapteuil F 117 B4
St Julien-de-Vouvantes F 101 B4
St Julien-du-Sault F 104 A2
St Julien-du-Verdon F 132 B2
St Julien-en-Born F 128 B1
St Julien-en-Genevois F 118 A3
St Julien-l'Ars F .115 B4
St Julien la-Vêtre F 117 B3
St Julien-Mont-Denis F 118 B3
St Julien-sur-Reyssouze F . . .118 A2
St Junien F 115 C4
St Just
  F 131 A3
  GB 42 B1
St Just-en-Chaussée F 90 B2
St Just-en-Chevalet F 117 B3
St Justin F 128 C2
St Just-St Rambert F 117 B4
St Keverne GB. 42 B1
St Lary-Soulan F .145 B4
St Laurent-d'Aigouze F 131 B3
St Laurent-de-Chamousset F .117 B4
St Laurent-de-Condel F 89 A3
St Laurent-de-la-Cabrerisse F .146 A3
St Laurent-de-la-Salanque F 146 B3
St Laurent-des-Autels F 101 B4
St Laurent-du-Pont F 118 B2
St Laurent-en-Caux F 89 A4
St Laurent-en-Grandvaux F . . .105 C4
St Laurent-Médoc F 128 A2
St Laurent-sur-Gorre F 115 C4
St Laurent-sur-Mer F 88 A3
St Laurent-sur-Sèvre F 114 B3
St Leger B 92 B1
St Léger-de-Vignes F 104 C2
St Léger-sous-Beuvray F 104 C3
St Léger-sur-Dheune F 104 C3
St Léonard-de-Noblat F 116 B1
St Leonards GB. . . .45 C4
St Lô F 88 A2
St Lon-les-Mines F 128 C1
St Louis F 106 B2
St Loup F 117 A3
St Loup-de-la-Salle F 105 C3
St Loup-sur-Semouse F 105 B5
St Lunaire F 101 A3
St Lupicin F 118 A2
St Lyphard F 101 B3
St Lys F 146 A2
St Macaire F 128 B2
St Maclou F 89 A4
St Maixent-l'École F 115 B3
St Malo F 88 B1
St Mamet-la-Salvetat F 116 C2
St Mandrier-sur-Mer F 132 B1
St Marcel
  Drôme F 117 C4
  Saône-et-Loire F 105 C3
St Marcellin F . . .118 B2
St Marcellin sur Loire F 117 B4
St Marcet F 145 A4
St Mards-en-Othe F 104 A2
St Margaret's-at-Cliffe GB 45 B5

St Margaret's Hope GB 33 C4
St Mars-la-Jaille F 101 B4
St Martin-d'Ablois F 91 C3
St Martin-d'Auxigny F 103 B4
St Martin-de-Belleville F 118 B3
St Martin-de-Bossenay F 91 C3
St Martin-de-Crau F 131 B3
St Martin-de-Londres F 130 B2
St Martin-d'Entraunes F 132 A2
St Martin-de-Queyrières F . . .118 C3
St Martin-de-Ré F .114 B2
St Martin des Besaces F 88 A3
St Martin-d'Estreaux F 117 A3
St Martin-de-Valamas F 117 C4
St Martin-d'Hères F 118 B2
St Martin-du-Frêne F 118 A2
St Martin-en-Bresse F 105 C4
St Martin-en-Haut F 117 B4
St Martin-la-Méanne F 116 B1
St Martin-Osmonville F 90 B1
St Martin-sur-Ouanne F 104 B2
St Martin-Valmeroux F 116 B2
St Martin-Vésubie F 133 A3
St Martory F 145 A4
St Mary's GB 33 C4
St Mathieu F 115 C4
St Mathieu-de-Tréviers F 131 B2
St Maurice CH . . .119 A3
St Maurice-Navacelles F 130 B2
St Maurice-sur-Moselle F 106 B1
St Mawes GB. 42 B1
St Maximin-la-Ste Baume F 132 B1
St Méard-de-Gurçon F 128 B3
St Médard-de-Guizières F 128 A2
St Médard-en-Jalles F 128 B2
St Méen-le-Grand F 101 A3
St Menges F 91 B4
St Merløse DK 61 D1
St Mesto CZ. 85 B4
St M'Hervé F 101 A4
St Michel
  Aisne F 91 B4
  Gers F 145 A4
St Michel-Chef-Chef F 101 B3
St Michel-de-Castelnau F 128 B2
St Michel-de-Maurienne F 118 B3
St Michel-en-Grève F 100 A2
St Michel-enl'Herm F 114 B2
St Michel-Mont-Mercure F 114 B3
St Mihiel F 92 C1
St Monance GB 35 B5
St Montant F 131 A3
St Moritz CH 107 C4
St Nazaire F 101 B3
St Nazaire-en-Royans F 118 B2
St Nazaire-le-Désert F 131 A4
St Nectaire F 116 B2
St Neots GB. 44 A3
St Nicolas-de-Port F 92 C2
St Nicolas-de-Redon F 101 B3
St Nicolas-du-Pélem F 100 A2
St Niklaas B 79 A4
St Omer F 78 B2
St Pair-sur-Mer F . .88 B2
St Palais F 144 A2
St Palais-sur-Mer F 114 C2
St Pardoux-la-Rivière F 115 C4
St Paul-Cap-de-Joux F 129 C4
St Paul-de-Fenouillet F 146 B3
St Paul-de-Varax F 118 A2
St Paulien F 117 B3
St Paul-le-Jeune F 131 A3
St Paul-lès-Dax F .128 C1
St Paul-Trois-Châteaux F 131 A3
St Pé-de-Bigorre F 145 A3
St Pée-sur-Nivelle F 144 A2
St Péravy-la-Colombe F 103 B3
St Péray F 117 C4
St Père-en-Retz F .101 B3
St Peter Port GB . .88 A1

St Petersburg = Sankt-Peterburg RUS . . .9 C7
St Philbert-de-Grand-Lieu F 114 A2
St Pierre F 130 B1
St Pierre-d'Albigny F 118 B3
St Pierre-d'Allevard F 118 B3
St Pierre-de-Chartreuse F 118 B2
St Pierre-de-Chignac F 129 A3
St Pierre-de-la-Fage F 130 B2
St Pierre-d'Entremont F 118 B2
St Pierre-d'Oléron F 114 C2
St Pierre-Eglise F . .88 A2
St Pierre-en-Port F .89 A4
St Pierre-le-Moûtier F 104 C2
St Pierre Montlimart F 101 B4
St Pierre-Quiberon F 100 B2
St Pierre-sur-Dives F 89 A3
St Pierreville F . . .117 C4
St Pieters-Leeuw B 79 B4
St Plancard F 145 A4
St Poix F 101 B4
St Pol-de-Léon F . .100 A2
St Polgues F 117 B3
St Pol-sur-Ternoise F 78 B2
St Pons-de-Thomières F 130 B1
St Porchaire F . . .114 C3
St Pourçain-sur-Sioule F 116 A3
St Priest F 117 B4
St Privat F 116 B2
St Quay-Portrieux F 100 A3
St Quentin F 90 B3
St Quentin-la-Poterie F 131 A3
St Quentin-les-Anges F 102 B1
St Rambert-d'Albon F 117 B4
St Rambert-en-Bugey F 118 B2
St Raphaël F 132 B2
St Rémy-de-Provence F 131 B3
St Rémy-du-Val F . .89 B4
St Remy-en-Bouzemont F 91 C4
St Renan F 100 A1
St Révérien F 104 B2
St Riquier F 90 A1
St Romain-de-Colbosc F 89 A4
St Rome-de-Cernon F 130 A1
St Rome-de-Tarn F 130 A1
St Sadurní-d'Anoia E 147 C2
St Saëns F 89 A5
St Sampson GB. . . .88 A1
St Samson-la-Poterie F 90 B1
St Saturnin-de-Lenne F 130 A2
St Saturnin-lès-Apt F 131 B4
St Sauflieu F 90 B2
St Saulge F 104 B2
St Sauveur
  Finistère F 100 A2
  Haute-Saône F .105 B5
St Sauveur-de-Montagut F 117 C4
St Sauveur-en-Puisaye F 104 B2
St Sauveur-en-Rue F 117 B4
St Sauveur-Lendelin F 88 A2
St Sauveur-le-Vicomte F 88 A2
St Sauveur-sur-Tinée F 132 A3
St Savin
  Gironde F 128 A2
  Vienne F 115 B4
St Savinien F 114 C3
St Savournin F . . .131 B4
St Seine-l'Abbaye F 105 B3
St Sernin-sur-Rance F 130 B1
St Sevan-sur-Mer F 88 B1
St Sever F 128 C2
St Sever-Calvados F 88 B2
St Sorlin-d'Arves F 118 B3
St Soupplets F 90 B2
St Sulpice F 129 C4
St Sulpice-Laurière F 116 A2
St Sulpice-les-Feuilles F 115 B5
St Symphorien F . .128 B2
St Symphoriende-Lay F 117 B4
St Symphorien d'Ozon F 117 B4
St Symphoriensur-Coise F 117 B4
St Teath GB 42 B2
St Thégonnec F . .100 A2
St Thiébault F . . .105 A4
St Trivier-de-Courtes F 118 A2

St Trivier sur-Moignans F 117 A4
St Trojan-les-Bains F 114 C2
St Tropez F 132 B2
St Truiden B 79 B5
St Vaast-la-Hougue F 88 A2
St Valérien F 104 A2
St Valery-en-Caux F 89 A4
St Valéry-sur-Somme F 78 B1
St Vallier
  Drôme F 117 B4
  Saône-et-Loire F 104 C3
St Vallier-de-Thiey F 132 B2
St Varent F 102 C1
St Vaury F 116 A1
St Venant F 78 B2
St Véran F 119 C3
St Vincent I 119 B4
St Vincent-de-Tyrosse F 128 C1
St Vit F 105 B4
St Vith B 80 B2
St Vivien-de-Médoc F 114 C2
St Yan F 117 A4
St Ybars F 146 A2
St Yorre F 117 A3
St Yrieix-la-Perche F 115 C5
Saissac F 146 A3
Saja E 142 A2
Sajan SRB 126 B2
Šajkaš SRB 126 B2
Sajókaza H. 99 C4
Sajószentpéter H .113 A4
Sajóvámos H 113 A4
Sakarya TR 187 B5
Sakskøbing DK 65 B4
Sakule SRB 126 B2
Sala S. 50 C3
Šal'a SK 111 A4
Sala Baganza I . . .120 C3
Sala Consilina I . . .172 B1
Salakovac SRB . . .127 C3
Salamanca E 150 B2
Salamina GR 185 B4
Salandra I 172 B2
Salaparuta I 176 B1
Salar E 163 A3
Salardú E 145 B4
Salas E 141 A4
Salas de los Infantes E 143 B3
Salau F 146 B2
Salavaux CH 106 C2
Salbertrand I 119 B3
Salbohed S 50 C3
Salbris F 103 B4
Salbu N 46 A2
Salce E 141 B4
Salching D. 95 C4
Salcombe GB 43 B3
Saldaña E 142 B2
Saldus LV. 8 D3
Sale I 120 C1
Saleby S. 55 B4
Salem D 107 B4
Salemi I 176 B1
Salen
  Argyll & Bute GB .34 B2
  Highland GB . . .34 B2
  N 199 A8
Sälen S 49 A5
Salernes F 132 B2
Salerno I 170 C2
Salers F 116 B2
Salford GB. 40 B1
Salgótarján H 113 A3
Salgueiro P 155 B3
Salhus N 46 B2
Sali HR 137 B4
Sálica Salentino I .173 B3
Salientes E 141 B4
Salies-de-Béarn F .144 A3
Salies-du-Salat F .145 A4
Salignac-Eyvigues F 129 B4
Saligney-sur-Roudon F 104 C2
Salihli TR 188 A3
Salihorsk BY 13 B7
Salinas
  Alicante E 159 C3
  Huesca E 145 B4
Salinas de Medinaceli E 152 A1
Salinas de Pisuerga E 142 B2
Salindres F 131 A3
Saline di Volterra I 135 B3
Salins-les-Bains F 105 C4
Salir P 160 B1
Salisbury GB. 44 B2
Salla
  A. 110 B1
  FIN. 197 C11
Sallachy GB. 32 C2
Sallanches F 118 B3
Sallent E 147 C2
Sallent de Gállego E 145 B3
Salles F 128 B2
Salles-Curan F . . .130 A1
Salles-sur-l'Hers F 146 A2
Sallins IRL 30 A2
Sällsjö S. 199 B10
Salmerón E 152 B1
Salmiech F 130 A1
Salmivaara FIN .197 C11
Salmoral E 150 B2
Salo FIN 8 B3
Salò I 121 B3

Salobreña E 163 B4
Salon-de-Provence F 131 B4
Salonica = Thessaloniki GR 182 C4
Salonta RO 16 B4
Salorino E 155 B3
Salornay-sur-Guye F 104 C3
Salorno I 121 A4
Salou E 147 C2
Šalovci SLO 111 C3
Salsbruket N 199 A8
Salses-le-Chateau F 146 B3
Salsomaggiore Terme I 120 C2
Salt E 147 C3
Saltaire GB 40 B2
Saltara I 136 B1
Saltash GB. 42 B2
Saltburn-by-the-Sea GB 37 B6
Saltcoats GB 34 C3
Saltfleet GB 41 B4
Salto P 148 A2
Saltrød N 53 B4
Saltsjöbaden S . . .57 A4
Saltvik
  FIN. 51 B7
  S 62 A4
Saludécio I 136 B1
Salussola I 119 B5
Saluzzo I 119 C4
Salvacañete E . . .152 B2
Salvada P. 160 B2
Salvagnac F 129 C4
Salvaleon E 155 C4
Salvaterra de Magos P 154 B2
Salvaterra do Extremo P 155 B4
Salvatierra
  Avila E 143 B4
  Badajoz E 155 C4
Salvatierra de Santiago E 156 A1
Salviac F 129 B4
Salvÿ ... Salzburg A 109 B4
Salzgitter D 72 B3
Salzgitter Bad D . .72 B3
Salzhausen D 72 A3
Salzhemmendorf D 72 B2
Salzkotten D 81 A4
Salzmünde D 83 A3
Salzwedel D 73 B4
Samadet F 128 C2
Samandıra TR . . .186 B4
Samassi I 179 C2
Samatan F 146 A1
Sambiase I 175 C2
Sambir UA 13 D5
Samborowo PL . . .69 B4
Sambuca di Sicilia I 176 B2
Samedan CH 107 C4
Samer F 78 B1
Sami GR 184 A1
Šamlı TR 186 C2
Sammichele di Bari I 173 B2
Samnaun CH 107 C5
Samobor HR 123 B4
Samoëns F 118 A3
Samogneux F 92 B1
Samokov BG 17 D5
Samora Correia P .154 C2
Šamorín SK 111 A4
Samos
  E 141 B3
  GR 188 B1
Samoš SRB 126 B2
Samothraki GR . . .183 C7
Samper de Calanda E 153 A3
Sampéyre I 133 A3
Sampieri I 177 C3
Sampigny F 92 C1
Samplawa PL. 69 B4
Samproniano I . . .168 A1
Samtens D. 66 B2
Samugheo I 179 C2
San Adrián E 144 B2
San Agustín E . . .164 C2
San Agustin de Guadalix E 151 B4
Sanaigmore GB. . . .34 C1
San Alberto I 135 A5
San Amaro E 140 B2
Sânandrei RO 126 B3
San Andrés del Rabanedo E 142 B1
San Antolín de Ibias E 141 A4
San Arcángelo I . . .174 A2
Sanary-sur-Mer F .132 B1
San Asensio E . . .143 B4
San Bartoloméde las Abiertas E 150 C3
San Bartolomé la Torre E 161 B2
San Bartoloméde Pinares E 150 B3
San Bartolomeo in Galdo I 170 B3
San Benedetto del Tronto I 136 C2
San Benedetto in Alpe I 135 B4
San Benedetto Po I 121 B3
San Benito E 156 B3
San Benito de la Contienda E 155 C3
San Biágio Plátani I 176 B2
San Biágio Saracinisco I 169 B3

San Bonifacio I . . .121 B4
San Calixto E 156 C2
San Cándido I 109 C3
San Carlo
  CH 119 A5
  I 176 B2
San Carlos del Valle E 157 B4
San Casciano dei Bagni I 135 C4
San Casciano in Val di Pesa I 135 B4
San Cataldo
  Puglia I 173 B4
  Sicilia I 176 B2
San Cebrián de Castro E 149 A4
Sancergues F 104 B1
Sancerre F 103 B4
San Cesário di Lecce I 173 B4
Sancey-le-Long F .105 B5
Sanchiorian E 150 B3
San Chirico Raparo I 174 A2
Sanchonuño E . . .151 A3
San Cibrao das Viñas E 140 B3
San Cipirello I . . .176 B2
San Ciprián E 141 A3
San Clemente E . . .158 B1
San Clodio E 141 B3
Sancoins F 104 C1
San Colombano al Lambro I 120 B2
San Costanzo I . . .136 B2
San Crisóbal de Entreviñas E 142 B1
San Cristóbal de la Polantera E 141 B5
San Cristóbal de la Vega E 150 A3
San Cristovo E . . .141 B3
Sancti-Petri E 162 B1
Sancti-Spiritus E . .149 B3
Sand
  Hedmark N 48 B3
  Rogaland N . . .52 A2
Sanda S. 57 C4
San Damiano d'Asti I 119 C5
San Damiano Macra I 133 A3
Sandane N. 198 D3
San Daniele del Friuli I 122 A2
Sandanski BG 183 B5
Sandared S 60 B2
Sandarne S 51 A4
Sandau D. 73 B5
Sandbach
  D 96 C1
  GB 38 A4
Sandbank GB 34 C3
Sandbanks GB . . .43 B5
Sandbukt N 192 C5
Sandby DK. 65 B4
Sande
  D 71 A5
  Sogn og Fjordane N. 46 A2
  Vestfold N 54 A1
Sandefjord N. 54 A1
Sandeid N 52 A1
San Demétrio Corone I 174 B2
San Demétrio né Vestini I 169 A3
Sandersleben D . . .82 A3
Sanderstølen N . . .47 B6
Sandes N 53 B3
Sandesneben D . . .65 C3
Sandhead GB 36 B2
Sandhem S 60 B3
Sandhorst D 71 A4
Sandhurst GB 44 B3
Sandıklı TR 189 A5
Sandillon F 103 B4
Sandl A. 96 C2
Sandnes N 52 B1
Sandness GB 33 A5
Sandnessjøen N . .195 D3
Sando E 149 B3
Sandomierz PL . . .87 B5
San Dónaci I 173 B3
San Donàdi Piave I 122 B1
San Donato Val di Comino I 169 B3
Sándorfalva H 126 A2
Sandown GB 44 C2
Sandøysund N 54 A1
Sandrigo I 121 B4
Sandsele S 195 E8
Sandset N 194 B5
Sandsjöfors S 62 A2
Sandstad N 198 B6
Sandvatn N 52 B2
Sandvig-Allinge DK 67 A3
Sandvika
  Akershus N 48 C2
  Hedmark N 48 B3
  Nord-Trøndelag N 199 B9
Sandviken S 51 B3
Sandvikvåg N 46 C2
Sandwich GB. 45 B5
Sandy GB. 44 A3
San Emiliano E . . .141 B5
San Enrique E 162 B2
San Esteban E . . .141 A4
San Esteban de Gormaz E 151 A4
San Esteban de la Sierra E 149 B4
San Esteban de Litera E 145 C4
San Esteban del Molar E 142 C1

San Esteban del Valle E 150 B3
San Esteban de Valdueza E 141 B4
San Fele I 172 B1
San Felice Circeo I 169 B3
San Felices E 143 B4
San Felices de los Gallégos E 149 B3
San Felice sul Panaro I 121 C4
San Ferdinando di Púglia I 171 B4
San Fernando E . .162 B1
San Fernando de Henares E 151 B4
San Fili I 174 B2
San Foca I 173 B4
San Fratello I 177 B3
Sangatte F 78 B1
San Gavino Monreale I 179 C2
San Gémini Fonte I 168 A2
Sangerhausen D . .82 A3
San Germano Vercellese I 119 B5
San Giácomo
  Trentino Alto Adige I 108 C2
  Umbria I 136 C1
San Gimignano I . .135 B4
San Ginésio I 136 B2
Sanginto Lido I . . .174 B2
San Giórgio a Liri I 169 B3
San Giorgio della Richinvelda I 122 A1
San Giórgio del Sánnio I 170 B2
San Giórgio di Lomellina I 120 B1
San Giórgio di Nogaro I 122 B2
San Giorgio di Piano I 121 C4
San Giórgio Iónico I 173 B3
San Giovanni a Piro I 172 B1
San Giovanni Bianco I 120 B2
San Giovanni di Sinis I 179 C2
San Giovanni in Croce I 120 B3
San Giovanni in Fiore I 174 B2
San Giovanni in Persiceto I 121 C4
San Giovanni Reatino I 169 A2
San Giovanni Rotondo I 171 B3
San Giovanni Suérgiu I 179 C2
San Giovanni Valdarno I 135 B4
Sangis S 196 D6
San Giuliano Terme I 134 B3
San Giustino I 135 B5
San Godenzo I . . .135 B4
Sangonera la Verde E 165 B3
San Gregorio Magno I 172 B1
Sangüesa E 144 B2
Sanguinet F 128 B1
San Guiseppe Jato I 176 B2
Sanica BIH 124 C2
Sanitz D. 65 B5
San Javier E 165 B4
San Jorge P 154 B2
San José E 164 C2
San Juan E 143 B3
San Juan de Alicante E 165 A4
San Juan de la Nava E 150 B3
San Justo de la Vega E 141 B4
Sankt Aegyd am Neuwalde A 110 B2
Sankt Andrä A 110 C1
Sankt Andreasberg D 82 A2
Sankt Anna S 56 B2
Sankt Anna am Aigen A 110 C2
Sankt Anton am Arlberg A 107 B5
Sankt Anton an der Jessnitz A 110 B2
Sankt Augustin D . .80 B3
Sankt Blasien D . .106 B2
Sankt Englmar D . .95 B4
Sankt Gallen
  A. 110 B1
  CH 107 B4
Sankt Gallenkirch A. 107 B4
Sankt Georgen
  A 96 C2
  D 106 A3
Sankt Georgen am Reith A 110 B1
Sankt Georgen ob Judenburg A 110 B1
Sankt Georgen ob Murau A 109 B5
Sankt Gilgen A . . .109 B4
Sankt Goar D 81 B3
Sankt Goarshausen D 81 B3
Sankt Ingbert D . . .92 B3
Sankt Jacob A . . .109 C4

ankt Jakob in
Defereggen A 109 C3
ankt Johann am
Tauern A 110 B1
ankt Johann am
Wesen A 109 A4
ankt Johann im
Pongau A 109 B4
ankt Johann in Tirol
A. 109 B3
ankt Katharein an der
Laming A. 110 B2
ankt Kathrein am
Hauenstein A 110 B2
ankt Lambrecht
A. 110 B1
ankt Leonhard am
Forst A 110 A2
ankt Leonhard im
Pitztal A 108 B1
ankt Lorenzen A .109 C3
ankt Marein
  Steiermark A 110 B2
  Steiermark A 110 B3
ankt Margarethen im
Lavanttal A 110 C1
ankt Margrethen
CH 107 B4
ankt Michael A. . .110 B2
ankt Michael im
Burgenland A . . .111 B3
ankt Michael im
Lungau A. 109 B4
ankt Michaelisdonn
D 64 C2
ankt Niklaus CH .119 A4
ankt Nikolai im
Sölktal A 109 B5
ankt Olof S 63 C2
ankt Oswald D. . .96 C1
ankt Paul
A. 110 C1
A. 132 A2
ankt Peter D 106 A3
ankt Peter am
Kammersberg A .110 B1
ankt-Peterburg = St
Petersburg RUS. . .9 C7
ankt Peter-Ording
D 64 B1
ankt Pölten A 110 A2
ankt Radegund
A. 110 B2
ankt Ruprecht an der
Raab A 110 B2
ankt Salvator A . .110 C1
ankt Stefan A 110 C1
ankt Stefan an der
Gail A. 109 C4
ankt Stefan im
Rosental A. 110 C2
ankt Valentin A. . .110 A1
ankt Veit an der Glan
A. 110 C1
ankt Veit an der
Gölsen A 110 A2
ankt Veit in
Defereggen A . . .109 C3
ankt Wendel D. . .92 B3
ankt Wolfgang
A. 109 B4
D 108 A3
an Lazzaro di Sávena
I 135 A4
an Leo I 135 B5
an Leonardo de
Yagüe E 143 C3
an Leonardo in
Passiria I 108 C2
an Lorenzo al Mare
I 133 B3
an Lorenzo a Merse
I 135 B4
an Lorenzo Bellizzi
I 174 B2
an Lorenzo de
Calatrava E 157 B4
an Lorenzo de El
Escorial E 151 B3
an Lorenzo de la
Parrilla E 158 B1
an Lorenzo di Sebato
I 108 C2
an Lorenzo in Campo
I 136 B2
an Lorenzo Nuovo
I 168 A1
an Lourenço P .160 A1
San Luca I 175 C2
Sanlúcar de Barrameda
E 161 C3
Sanlúcar de Guadiana
E 160 B2
Sanlúcar la Mayor
E 161 B3
San Lúcido I 174 B2
Sanluri I 179 C2
San Marcello I . . .173 B3
San Marcello Pistoiese
I 135 A3
San Marcial E . . .149 A4
San Marco I 170 C2
San Marco Argentano
I 174 B2
San Marco dei Cavoti
I 170 B2
San Marco in Lámis
I 171 B3
San Marino RSM .136 B1
San Martin de
Castañeda E . . .141 B4
San Martín de la Vega
E 151 B4
San Martín de la Vega
del Alberche E . .150 B2
San Martín del Tesorillo
E 162 B2
San Martin de Luiña
E 141 A4

San Martin de
Montalbán E . . .157 A3
San Martin de Oscos
E 141 A4
San Martin de Pusa
E 150 C2
San Martin de Unx
E 144 B2
San Martin de
Valdeiglesias E. .150 B3
San Martino di
Campagna I 122 A1
San Martino di
Castrozza I 121 A4
San-Martino-di-Lota
F. 180 A2
San Martino in Pénsilis
I 170 B3
San Mateo de Gallego
E 144 C3
San Máuro Forte I .172 B2
San Michele all'Adige
I 121 A4
San Michele di
Ganzaria I 177 B3
San Michele Mondov ì
I 133 A3
San Miguel de Aguayo
E 142 A2
San Miguel de Bernuy
E 151 A4
San Miguel del Arroyo
E 150 A3
San Miguel de Salinas
E 165 B4
Sânmihaiu Roman
RO. 126 B3
San Millán de la
Cogolla E 143 B4
San Miniato I 135 B3
San Muñoz E 149 B3
Sänna S 55 B5
Sannazzaro
de'Burgondi I . . .120 B1
Sanne D 73 B4
Sannicandro di Bari
I 171 B4
Sannicandro
Gargánico I 171 B3
San Nicola del'Alto
I 174 B2
San Nicolás del Puerto
E 156 C2
Sânnicolau Mare
RO. 126 A2
San Nicolò I 121 C4
San Nicolò Gerrei
I 179 C3
Sannidal N. 53 B5
Sanniki PL. 77 B4
Sanok PL. 12 D5
San Pablo de los
Montes E. 157 A3
San Pancrázio
Salentino I 173 B3
San Pantaleo I . . .178 A3
San Páolo di Civitate
I 171 B3
Santa Comba de
Rossas P. 149 A3
Santa Cristina I . .120 B2
Santa Cristina de la
Polvorosa E 141 B5
San Pawl il-Bahar
M 175 C3
San Pedro
  Albacete E. 158 C1
  Oviedo E 141 A4
San Pedro de
Alcántara E. . . .162 B3
San Pedro de Ceque
E 141 B4
San Pedro del Arroyo
E 150 B3
San Pedro del Pinatar
E 165 B4
San Pedro del Romeral
E 143 A3
San Pedro de Merida
E 156 B1
San Pedro de
Valderaduey E . .142 B2
San Pedro Manrique
E 144 B1
San Pellegrino Terme
I 120 B2
San Piero a Sieve
I 135 B4
San Piero in Bagno
I 135 B4
San Piero Patti I . .177 A3
San Pietro in Casale
I 121 C4
San Pietro in Gu I .121 B4
San Pietro in Palazzi
I 134 B2
San Pietro in Volta
I 122 B1
San Pietro Vara I . .134 A2
San Pietro Vernótico
I 173 B3
San Polo d'Enza I .121 C3
Sanquhar GB. . . .36 A3
San Quírico d'Órcia
I 135 B4
San Rafael del Rio
E 153 B4
San Remo I 133 B3
San Román de
Cameros E 143 B4
San Roman de Hernija
E 150 A2
San Román de la Cuba
E 142 B2
San Roman de los
Montes E. 150 B3
San Romao P. . . .155 C3
San Roque E 162 B2
San Roque de Riomera
E 143 A3
San Rufo I 172 B1

San Sabastián de los
Ballesteros E . . .162 A3
San Salvador de
Cantamuda E . . .142 B2
San Salvo I. 170 A2
San Salvo Marina
I 170 A2
San Sebastián de los
Reyes E. 151 B4
San Sebastiano Curone
I 120 C2
San Secondo
Parmense I 120 C3
Sansepolcro I . . .135 B5
San Serverino Marche
I 136 B2
San Severino Lucano
I 174 A2
San Severo I 171 B3
San Silvestre de
Guzmán E 161 B2
Sanski Most BIH . .124 C2
San Sosti I 174 B2
San Stéfano di Cadore
I 109 C3
San Stino di Livenza
I 122 B1
Santa Agnès E. . .166 B1
Santa Amalia E . . .156 A1
Santa Ana
  Cáceres E 156 A2
  Jaén E 163 A4
Santa Ana de Pusa
E 150 C3
Santa Barbara E . .153 B4
Santa Bárbara P . .160 B1
Santa Barbara de Casa
E 161 B2
Santa Bárbara de
Padrões P. 160 B2
Santacara E 144 B2
Santa Catarina P . .160 B2
Santa Caterina di
Pittinuri I 178 B2
Santa Caterina
Villarmosa I. 177 B3
Santa Cesárea Terme
I 173 B4
Santa Clara-a-Nova
P 160 B1
Santa Clara-a-Velha
P 160 B1
Santa Clara de Louredo
P 160 B2
Santa Coloma de
Farners E 147 C3
Santa Coloma de
Gramenet E. . . .147 C3
Santa Coloma de
Queralt E. 147 C2
Santa Colomba de
Curueño E. 142 B1
Santa Colomba de
Somoza E 141 B4
Santa Comba E . . .140 A2
Santa Comba Dáo
P 148 B1
Santa Comba de
Rossas P. 149 A3
Santa Cristina I . .120 B2
Santa Cristina de la
Polvorosa E 141 B5
Santa Croce Camerina
I 177 C3
Santa Croce di
Magliano I 170 B2
Santa Cruz
E 140 A2
P 154 B1
Santa Cruz de Alhama
E 163 A4
Santa Cruz de
Campezo E 143 B4
Santa Cruz de Grio
E 152 A2
Santa Cruz de la
Salceda E 151 A4
Santa Cruz de la Sierra
E 156 A2
Santa Cruz de la Zarza
E 151 C4
Santa Cruz del Retamar
E 151 B3
Santa Cruz del Valle
E 150 B2
Santa Cruz de Moya
E 159 B2
Santa Cruz de Mudela
E 157 B4
Santa Cruz de
Paniagua E 149 B3
Santadi I 179 C2
Santa Doménica Talao
I 174 B1
Santa Doménica
Vittória I. 177 B3
Sant'Ángelo dei
Lombardi I. 172 B1
Sant'Angelo in Vado
I 136 B1
Sant'Angelo Lodigiano
I 120 B2
Santa Ninfa I 176 B1
Sant'Antíoco I . . .179 C2
Sant'Antoni de Calonge
E 147 C4
Santa Eláia I 152 B2
Santa Eulália P . . .155 C3
Santa Eulalia de Oscos
E 141 A3
Santa Eulàlia des Riu
E 166 C1
Santa Fe E 163 A4
Sant'Ágata dei Goti
I 170 B2
Sant'Ágata di Ésaro
I 174 B1
Sant'Ágata di Puglia
I 171 B3
Sant'Agata Feltria
I 135 B5

Sant'Ágata Militello
I 177 A3
Santa Gertrude I .108 C1
Santa Giustina I . .121 A5
Sant Agust ide
Lluçanès I 147 B3
Santa Iria P 160 B2
Santa Leocadia P .148 A1
Santa Lucia del Mela
I 177 A4
Santa Lucia-de-Porto-
Vecchio I. 180 B2
Santa Luzia P 160 B1
Santa Maddalena
Vallalta I 108 C3
Santa Magdalena de
Polpis E. 153 B4
Santa Margalida E .167 B3
Santa Margarida
P 154 B2
Santa Margarida do
Sado P. 160 A1
Santa Margaridao de
Montbui E. 147 C2
Santa Margherita
I 179 D2
Santa Margherita di
Belice I 176 B2
Santa Margherita
Ligure I 134 A2
Santa Maria
  CH 108 C1
  I 179 B3
Santa Maria al Bagno
I 173 B3
Santa Maria Cápua
Vétere I 170 B2
Santa Maria da Feira
P 148 B1
Santa Maria de Cayón
E 143 A3
Santa Maria de Corco
E 147 B3
Santa Maria de Huerta
E 152 A1
Santa Maria de la
Alameda E 151 B3
Santa Maria de las
Hoyas E. 143 C3
Santa Maria del Camí
E 167 B2
Santa Maria del Campo
E 143 B3
Santa Maria del Campo
Rus E. 158 B1
Santa Maria della Versa
I 120 C2
Santa Maria del
Páramo E 142 B1
Santa Maria del Taro
I 134 A2
Santa Maria de
Mercadillo E 143 C3
Santa Maria de Nieva
E 164 B3
Santa Maria de
Trassierra E 156 C3
Santa Maria di Licodia
I 177 B3
Santa Maria-di-
Rispéscia E 168 A1
Santa Maria la Palma
I 178 B2
Santa María la Real de
Nieva E 150 A3
Santa Maria Maggiore
I 119 A5
Santa Maria
Ribarredonda E .143 B3
Santa Marina del Rey
E 141 B5
Santa Marinella I . .168 A1
Santa Marta
  Albacete E. 158 B1
  Badajoz E 155 C4
Santa Marta de
Magasca E 156 A1
Santa Marta de
Penaguião P. . . .148 A2
Santa Marta de Tormes
E 150 B2
Santana
  Évora P 154 C2
  Setúbal E. 154 C1
Sântana RO. 126 A3
Santana da Serra
P 160 B1
Santana do Mato
P 154 C2
Sant'Anastasia I .170 C2
Santander E 143 A3
Sant'Andrea Frius
I 179 C3
Sant'Ángelo dei
Lombardi I. 172 B1
Santanyí E 167 B3
Santa Olalla
  Huelva E. 161 B3
  Toledo E. 150 B3
Santa Pau E 147 B3
Santa Pola E 165 A4
Santa Ponça E . . .166 B2
Santarcángelo di
Romagna I 136 A1
Santarém P 154 B2

Santa Severa
F. 180 A2
I 168 A1
Santa Severina I .175 B2
Santas Martas E . .142 B1
Santa Sofia I 135 B4
Santa Susana P. . .154 C2
Santa Suzana P. . .155 C3
Santa Teresa di Riva
I 177 B4
Santa Teresa Gallura
I 178 A3
Santa Uxía E 140 B2
Santa Valburga I . .108 C1
Santa Vittória in
Matenano I 136 B2
Sant Boi de Llobregat
E 147 C3
Sant Carles de la
Ràpita E 153 B4
Sant Carlos E 166 B1
Sant'Caterina I . . .135 C4
Sant Celoni E. . . .147 C3
Sant Climent E . . .167 B4
Sant'Egídio alla Vibrata
I 136 C2
Sant'Elia a Pianisi
I 170 B2
Sant'Elia Fiumerapido
I 169 B3
Sant'Elpídio a Mare
I 136 B2
Santéramo in Colle
I 171 C4
Santervas de la Vega
E 142 B2
Sant' Eufemia
Lamezia. 175 C2
Sant Feliu E 147 C3
Sant Feliu de Codines
E 147 C3
Sant Feliu de Guíxols
E 147 C4
Sant Feliu Sasserra
E 147 C3
Sant Ferran E . . .166 C1
Sant Francesc de
Formentera E . . .166 C1
Sant Francesc de ses
Salines E. 166 C1
Santhià I 119 B5
Sant Hilari Sacalm
E 147 C3
Sant Hipólit de
Voltregà E 147 B3
Santiago de Alcántara
E 155 B3
Santiago de Calatrava
E 163 A3
Santiago de
Compostela E. . .140 B2
Santiago de la Espade
E 164 A2
Santiago de la Puebla
E 150 B2
Santiago de la Ribera
E 165 B4
Santiago del Campo
E 155 B4
Santiago del Litem
P 154 B2
Santiago do Cacém
P 160 B1
Santiago do Escoural
P 154 C2
Santiago Maior P. .155 C3
Santibáñez de Béjar
E 149 B4
Santibáñez de la Peña
E 142 B2
Santibáñez de Murias
E 142 A1
Santibáñez de
Vidriales E. 141 B4
Santibáñez el Alto
E 149 B3
Santibáñez el Bajo
E 149 B3
Santillana E 142 A2
Santiponce E. . . .162 A1
San Tirso de Abres
E 141 A3
Santisteban del Puerto
E 157 B4
Santiuste de San Juan
Bautiste E 150 A3
Santiz E 149 A4
Sant Jaume dels
Domenys E. 147 C2
Sant Joan Baptista
E 166 B1
Sant Joan de les
Abadesses E . . .147 B3
Sant Jordi E 153 B4
Sant Josep de sa Talaia
E 166 C1
Sant Juliáde Loria
AND. 146 B2
Sant'Ilario d'Enza
I 121 C3
Sant Llorençde
Morunys E 147 B2
Sant Llorençdes
Carctassar E . . .167 B3
Sant Llorenç Savall
E 147 C3
Sant Luis E 167 B4
Sant Mart ide Llemaná
E 147 B3
Sant Marti de Maldá
E 147 C2
Sant Marti Sarroca
E 147 C2
Sant Mateu E 153 B4
Sant Miquel E 166 B1
Santo Aleixo I 161 A2
Santo Amado P . . .161 A2

Santo Amaro P . . .155 C3
Santo André P . . .160 A1
Santo Domingo E .155 C3
Santo Domingo de la
Calzada E 143 B4
Santo Domingo de
Silos E. 143 C3
Santo Estêvão
  Faro P 160 B2
  Santarém P 154 C2
Santok PL. 75 B4
Santomera E 165 A3
Santoña E 143 A3
Santo-Pietro-di Tenda
F. 180 A2
Sant'Oreste I 168 A2
Santo Spirito I . . .171 B4
Santo Stefano d'Aveto
I 134 A2
Santo Stéfano di
Camastra I 177 A3
Santo Stefano di Magra
I 134 A2
Santo Stéfano
Quisquina I 176 B2
Santo Tirso P. . . .148 A1
Santotis E 142 A2
Santo Tomé E . . .164 A1
Santovenia
  Burgos E. 143 B3
  Zamora E 142 C1
Sant Pau de Seguries
E 147 B3
Santpedor E. 147 C2
Sant Pere de
Riudebitles E . . .147 C2
Sant Pere Pescador
E 147 B4
Sant Pere Sallavinera
E 147 C2
Sant Quirze de Besora
E 147 B3
Sant Rafel E 166 C1
Sant Ramon E . . .147 C2
Santu Lussurgiu I .178 B2
Santutzi E 143 A3
Sant Vincençde
Castellet E 147 C2
San Valentino alla Muta
I 108 C1
San Venanzo I . . .135 C5
San Vicente de
Alcántara E. . . .155 B3
San Vicente de Arana
E 144 B1
San Vicente de la
Barquera E 142 A2
San Vicente de la
Sonsierra E. . . .143 B4
San Vicente de Toranzo
E 143 A3
San Vietro E 149 A3
San Vigílio I 108 C2
San Vincente del
Raspeig E 165 A4
San Vincenzo I . . .134 B3
San Vito I 179 C3
San Vito al Tagliamento
I 122 B1
San Vito Chietino
I 169 A4
San Vito dei Normanni
I 173 B3
San Vito di Cadore
I 108 C3
San Vito lo Capo I .176 A1
San Vito Romano
I 169 B2
Sanxenxo E 140 B2
Sanza I 172 B1
São Aleixo P 155 C3
São Barnabé P . . .160 B1
São Bartoloméda Serra
P 160 A1
São Bartolomeu de
Messines P. 160 B1
São Bento P 140 C2
São Brás P. 160 B2
São Brás de Alportel
P 160 B2
São Braz do
Reguedoura P . .154 C2
São Cristóvão P . .154 C2
São Domingos P . .160 B1
São Geraldo P . . .154 C2
São Jacinto P 148 B1
São João da Madeira
P 148 B1
São João da Pesqueira
P 148 A2
São João da Ribeira
P 154 B2
São João da Serra
P 148 B1
São João da Venda
P 160 B2
São João dos
Caldeireiros P. . .160 B2
São Julião P 155 B3
São Leonardo P . .155 C3
São Luis P 160 B1
São Manços P . . .155 C3
São Marcos da
Ataboeira P. 160 B2
Saõ Marcos da Serra
P 160 B1
São Marcos de Campo
P 155 C3
São Martinho da
Cortiça P. 148 B1
São Martinho das
Amoreiras P. . . .160 B1
São Martinho do Porto
P 154 B1
São Matias
  Beja P 160 A2
  Évora P 154 C2
São Miguel d'Acha
P 155 A3

São Miguel de
Machede P 155 C3
São Pedro da Torre
P 140 C2
São Pedro de Cadeira
P 154 B1
São Pedro de Moel
P 154 B1
São Pedro de Solis
P 160 B2
São Pedro do Sul
P 148 B1
Saorge F 133 B3
São Romão P. . . .154 C2
São Sebastião dos
Carros P. 160 B2
São Teotónio P . . .160 B1
São Torcato P 148 A1
Sapataria P 154 C1
Sapes GR. 183 B7
Sapiãos P. 148 A2
Sa Pobla E. 167 B3
Sappada I. 109 C3
Sappen N. 192 C5
Sapri I. 174 A1
Sarajärvi FIN 197 D10
Sarajevo BIH 139 B4
Saramon F. 129 C3
Sarandë AL. 182 D2
Saranovo SRB. . . .127 C2
Saraorci SRB. . . .127 C3
Sa Rapita E 167 B3
Saray TR. 186 A2
Saraycık TR. 187 C4
Saraydüzü TR 188 B3
Saraylar TR. 186 B2
Sarayönü TR 189 A7
Sarbia PL. 75 B5
Sarbinowo
  Zachodnio-Pomorskie
  PL 67 B4
  Zachodnio-Pomorskie
  PL 74 B3
Sárbogárd H 112 C2
Sarcelles F. 90 B2
Sarche I 121 A3
Sardara I 179 C2
Sardoal P. 154 B2
Sardón de Duero
E 150 A3
Sare F. 144 A2
S'Arenal E 166 B2
Šarengrad HR 125 B5
Sarentino I. 108 C2
Sarezzo I 120 B3
Sargans CH 107 B4
Sári H. 112 B3
Saríbeyler TR. . . .186 C2
Saricakaya TR 187 B5
Sari-d'Orcino F . . .180 A2
Sarigöl TR 188 A3
Sarikaya TR 23 B8
Sarıköy TR 186 B2
Sarilhos Grandes
P 154 C2
Sariñena E 145 C3
Sarioba TR. 187 C7
Sárisáp H 112 B2
Sariyer TR 186 A4
Sarkad H 113 C5
Sárkeresztes H . . .112 B2
Sárkeresztúr H . . .112 B2
Särkijärvi FIN 196 B6
Şarkikaraağaç TR .189 A6
Sarköy TR 186 B2
Sarlat-la-Canéda
F 129 B4
Sarliac-sur-l'Isle F .129 A3
Sármellék H 111 C4
Särna S 199 D10
Sarnadas P 155 B3
Sarnano I 136 B2
Sarnen CH. 106 C3
Sarnesfield GB . . .39 B4
Sárnico I 120 B2
Sarno I 170 C2
Sarnonico I 121 A4
Sarnow D. 74 A2
Sarny UA 13 C7
Särö S 60 B1
Saronno I 120 B2
Sárosd H 112 B2
Šarovce SK 112 A2
Sarpoil F 117 B3
Sarpsborg N 54 A2
Sarracín E 143 B3
Sarral E 147 C2
Sarralbe F 92 B3
Sarrancolin F. . . .145 B4
Sarras F 117 B4
Sarre I 119 B4
Sarreaus E 140 B3
Sarrebourg F 92 C3
Sarreguemines F . .92 B3
Sárrétudvari H . . .113 B5
Sarre-Union F . . .92 C3
Sarria E 141 B3
Sarriàde Ter E . . .147 B3
Sarrión E 153 B3
Sarroca de Lleida
E 153 A4
Sarroch I 179 C3
Sarron F. 128 C2
Sársina I. 135 B5
Særslev DK 59 C3
Sarstedt D. 72 B2
Sárszentlörinc H. .112 C2
Sárszentmihaly H .112 B2
Sárszentmiklós
H 112 C2
Sarteano I 135 C4
Sartène F 180 B1
Sartilly F 88 B2
Sartirana Lomellina
I 120 B1
Saruhanlı TR 186 D2
Sárvár H 111 B3

Sarvisvaara S . . . 196 C4
Sarzana I . . . 134 A2
Sarzeau F . . . 101 B3
Sarzedas P . . . 155 B3
Sasalli TR . . . 188 A1
Sasamón E . . . 142 B2
Sa Savina E . . . 166 C1
Sásd H . . . 125 A4
Sasino PL . . . 68 A2
Sássari I . . . 178 B2
Sassello I . . . 133 A4
Sassenberg D . . . 71 C5
Sassetta I . . . 134 B3
Sassnitz D . . . 66 B2
Sassocorvaro I . . . 136 B1
Sasso d'Ombrone
 I . . . 135 C4
Sassoferrato I . . . 136 B1
Sassoleone I . . . 135 A4
Sasso Marconi I . . . 135 A4
Sassuolo I . . . 135 A3
Sástago E . . . 153 A3
Šaštinske Stráže
 SK . . . 98 C1
Sas van Gent NL . . . 79 A3
Såtåhaugen N . . . 199 C7
Satão P . . . 148 B2
Såtenäs S . . . 55 B3
Säter S . . . 50 B2
Sätila S . . . 60 B2
Satillieu F . . . 117 B4
Satnica Đakovačka
 HR . . . 125 B4
Sátoraljaújhely H . . . 16 A4
Satow D . . . 65 C4
Sätra-brunn S . . . 50 C3
Sætre N . . . 54 A1
Satrup D . . . 64 B2
Satteins A . . . 107 B4
Satu Mare RO . . . 17 B5
Saturnia I . . . 168 A1
Saucats F . . . 128 B2
Saucelle E . . . 149 A3
Sauda N . . . 52 A2
Sauðarkrókur IS . . . 190 B6
Saudasjøen N . . . 52 A2
Sauerlach D . . . 108 B2
Saugues F . . . 117 C3
Sauherad N . . . 53 A5
Saujon F . . . 114 C3
Sauland N . . . 53 A4
Saulces Monclin F . . . 91 B4
Saulgau D . . . 107 A4
Saulgrub D . . . 108 B3
Saulieu F . . . 104 B3
Saulnot F . . . 106 B1
Sault F . . . 131 A4
Sault-Brénaz F . . . 118 B2
Sault-de-Navailles
 F . . . 128 C2
Saulx F . . . 105 B5
Saulxures-sur-
Moselotte F . . . 106 B1
Saulzais-le-Potier
 F . . . 103 C4
Saumos F . . . 128 B1
Saumur F . . . 102 B1
Saunavaara FIN . . . 197 B10
Saundersfoot GB . . . 39 C2
Saurat F . . . 146 B2
Saurbær
 Borgarfjarðarsýsla
 IS . . . 190 C4
 Dalasýsla IS . . . 190 B4
 Eyjafjarðarsýsla
 IS . . . 191 B7
Sáuris I . . . 109 C3
Sausset-les-Pins
 F . . . 131 B4
Sauteyrargues F . . . 131 B2
Sauvagnat F . . . 116 B2
Sauve F . . . 131 B2
Sauveterre-de-Béarn
 F . . . 144 A3
Sauveterre-de-Guyenne
 F . . . 128 B2
Sauviat-sur-Vige
 F . . . 116 B1
Sauxillanges F . . . 117 B3
Sauzet
 Drôme F . . . 117 C4
 Lot F . . . 129 B4
Sauzé-Vaussais F . . . 115 B4
Sauzon F . . . 100 B2
Sava I . . . 173 B3
Sävar S . . . 200 C6
Sævareid N . . . 46 B2
Savarsin RO . . . 16 B5
Sävast S . . . 196 D4
Savaştepe TR . . . 186 C2
Savci SLO . . . 111 C3
Säve S . . . 60 B1
Savelletri I . . . 173 B3
Savelli I . . . 174 B2
Savenay F . . . 101 B4
Saverdun F . . . 146 A2
Saverne F . . . 93 C3
Savières F . . . 91 C3
Savigliano I . . . 119 C4
Savignac-les-Eglises
 F . . . 129 A3
Savignano Irpino I . . . 171 B3
Savignano sul
Rubicone I . . . 136 A1
Savigny-sur-Braye
 F . . . 102 B2
Saviñán E . . . 152 A2
Savines-le-lac F . . . 132 A2
Savino Selo SRB . . . 126 B1
Saviol I . . . 135 A5
Sävja S . . . 51 C4
Šavnik MNE . . . 139 C5
Savognin CH . . . 107 C4
Savona I . . . 133 A4
Savonlinna FIN . . . 9 B6
Savournon F . . . 132 A1
Sævråsvåg N . . . 46 B2

Sävsjö S . . . 62 A2
Savsjön S . . . 50 C1
Sävsjöström S . . . 62 A3
Savudrija HR . . . 122 B2
Savukoski FIN . . . 197 B11
Sawbridgeworth
 GB . . . 45 B4
Sawtry GB . . . 44 A3
Sax E . . . 159 C3
Saxdalen S . . . 50 B1
Saxilby GB . . . 40 B3
Saxmundham GB . . . 45 A5
Saxnäs S . . . 195 F6
Saxthorpe GB . . . 41 C5
Sayalonga E . . . 163 B3
Sayatón E . . . 151 B5
Sayda D . . . 83 B5
Säytsjärvi FIN . . . 193 C11
Šazava CZ . . . 97 B3
Sázava CZ . . . 96 B2
Scaër F . . . 100 A2
Scafa I . . . 169 A4
Scalasaig GB . . . 34 B1
Scalby GB . . . 40 A3
Scalea I . . . 174 B1
Scaletta Zanclea I . . . 177 A4
Scalloway GB . . . 33 A5
Scamblesby GB . . . 41 B3
Scandale I . . . 175 B2
Scandiano I . . . 121 C3
Scandicci I . . . 135 B4
Scandolara Ravara
 I . . . 120 B3
Scanno I . . . 169 B3
Scansano I . . . 168 A1
Scanzano Jónico
 I . . . 174 A2
Scarborough GB . . . 40 A3
Scardovari I . . . 122 C1
Scardoy GB . . . 32 D2
Scarperia I . . . 135 B4
Scarriff IRL . . . 28 B3
Scey-sur-Saône et St
Albin F . . . 105 B4
Schachendorf A . . . 111 B3
Schaffhausen CH . . . 107 B3
Schafstädt D . . . 83 A3
Schafstedt D . . . 64 B2
Schäftlarn D . . . 108 B2
Schagen NL . . . 70 B1
Schalkau D . . . 82 B3
Schangnau CH . . . 106 C2
Schapbach D . . . 93 C4
Scharbeutz D . . . 65 B3
Schärding A . . . 96 C1
Scharnitz A . . . 108 B2
Scharrel D . . . 71 A4
Schattendorf A . . . 111 B3
Scheemda NL . . . 71 A3
Scheessel D . . . 72 A2
Schéggia I . . . 136 B1
Scheibbs A . . . 110 A2
Scheibenberg D . . . 83 B4
Scheidegg D . . . 107 B4
Scheifling A . . . 110 B1
Scheinfeld D . . . 94 B2
Schelklingen D . . . 94 C1
Schenefeld
 Schleswig-Holstein
 D . . . 64 B2
 Schleswig-Holstein
 D . . . 72 A2
Schenklengsfeld D . . . 82 B1
Scherfede D . . . 81 A5
Schermbeck D . . . 80 A2
Scherpenzeel NL . . . 70 B2
Schesslitz D . . . 94 B3
Scheveningen NL . . . 70 B1
Schiedam NL . . . 79 A4
Schieder-Schwalenberg
 D . . . 72 C2
Schierling D . . . 95 C4
Schiers CH . . . 107 C4
Schildau D . . . 83 A4
Schillingen D . . . 92 B2
Schillingsfürst D . . . 94 B2
Schilpário I . . . 120 A3
Schiltach D . . . 93 C4
Schiltigheim F . . . 93 C3
Schio I . . . 121 B4
Schirmeck F . . . 92 C3
Schirnding D . . . 83 B4
Schkeuditz D . . . 83 A4
Schkölen D . . . 83 A3
Schladen D . . . 73 B3
Schladming A . . . 109 B4
Schlangen D . . . 81 A4
Schleiden D . . . 80 B2
Schleiz D . . . 83 B3
Schleswig D . . . 64 B2
Schleusingen D . . . 82 B2
Schlieben D . . . 83 A5
Schliengen D . . . 106 B2
Schliersee D . . . 108 B2
Schlitz D . . . 81 B5
Schloss Neuhaus
 D . . . 81 A4
Schlossvippach D . . . 82 A3
Schlotheim D . . . 82 A2
Schluchsee D . . . 106 B3
Schlüchtern D . . . 81 B5
Schmallenberg D . . . 81 A4
Schmelz D . . . 92 B2
Schmidmühlen D . . . 95 B3
Schmiedeberg D . . . 84 B1
Schmiedefeld D . . . 82 B2
Schmirn A . . . 108 B2
Schmölln
 Brandenburg D . . . 74 A3
 Sachsen D . . . 83 B4
Schnackenburg D . . . 73 B4
Schnaittach D . . . 95 B3
Schneeberg D . . . 83 B4
Schneizlreuth D . . . 109 B3
Schnéverdingen D . . . 72 A2
Schöder A . . . 109 B5
Schoenburg B . . . 80 B2
Schollene D . . . 73 B5
Schöllkrippen D . . . 81 B5
Schomberg D . . . 107 A3

Schönach D . . . 95 C4
Schönau
 Baden-Württemberg
 D . . . 106 B2
 Bayern D . . . 95 C4
Schönbeck D . . . 74 A2
Schönberg
 Bayern D . . . 96 C1
 *Mecklenburg-
Vorpommern* D . . . 65 C3
 Schleswig-Holstein
 D . . . 65 B3
Schönebeck D . . . 73 B4
Schöneck D . . . 83 B4
Schönecken- D . . . 80 B2
Schönermark D . . . 74 A2
Schönewalde D . . . 83 A5
Schongau D . . . 108 B1
Schöngrabern A . . . 97 C4
Schönhagen D . . . 81 A5
Schönhausen D . . . 73 B5
Schöningen D . . . 73 B3
Schönkirchen D . . . 64 B3
Schönsee D . . . 95 B4
Schöntal D . . . 94 B1
Schönthal D . . . 95 B4
Schonungen D . . . 94 A2
Schönwalde D . . . 65 B3
Schoondijke NL . . . 79 A3
Schoonebeek NL . . . 71 B3
Schoonhoven NL . . . 79 A4
Schopfheim D . . . 106 B2
Schöppenstedt D . . . 73 B3
Schörfling A . . . 109 B4
Schorndorf D . . . 94 C1
Schortens D . . . 71 A4
Schotten D . . . 81 B5
Schramberg D . . . 106 A3
Schraplau D . . . 83 A3
Schrattenberg A . . . 97 C4
Schrecksbach D . . . 81 B5
Schrems A . . . 96 C3
Schrobenhausen D . . . 95 C3
Schröcken A . . . 107 B5
Schrozberg D . . . 94 B1
Schruns A . . . 107 B4
Schüpfheim CH . . . 106 C3
Schüttorf D . . . 71 B4
Schwaan D . . . 65 C5
Schwabach D . . . 94 B3
Schwäbisch Gmünd
 D . . . 94 C1
Schwäbisch Hall D . . . 94 B1
Schwabmünchen
 D . . . 108 A1
Schwadorf A . . . 111 A3
Schwagstorf D . . . 71 B4
Schwaigern D . . . 93 B5
Schwalmstadt D . . . 81 B5
Schwanberg A . . . 110 C2
Schwanden CH . . . 107 C4
Schwandorf D . . . 95 B4
Schwanebeck D . . . 73 C4
Schwanenstadt A . . . 109 A4
Schwanewede D . . . 72 A1
Schwanfeld D . . . 94 B2
Schwangau D . . . 108 B1
Schwarmstedt D . . . 72 B2
Schwarza D . . . 82 B2
Schwarzach im Pongau
 A . . . 109 B4
Schwarzau im Gebirge
 A . . . 110 B2
Schwarzenau A . . . 97 C3
Schwarzenbach D . . . 83 B3
Schwarzenbach am
Wald D . . . 83 B3
Schwarzenbek D . . . 72 A3
Schwarzenberg D . . . 83 B4
Schwarzenburg
 CH . . . 106 C2
Schwarzenfeld D . . . 95 B4
Schwarz-heide D . . . 84 A1
Schwaz A . . . 108 B2
Schwechat A . . . 111 A3
Schwedt D . . . 74 A3
Schwei D . . . 71 A5
Schweich D . . . 92 B2
Schweighausen D . . . 106 A2
Schweinfurt D . . . 94 A2
Schweinitz D . . . 83 A5
Schweinrich D . . . 74 A1
Schwelm D . . . 80 A3
Schwemsal D . . . 83 A4
Schwendt A . . . 109 B3
Schwenningen D . . . 107 A3
Schwepnitz D . . . 84 A1
Schwerin D . . . 73 A4
Schwerte D . . . 81 A3
Schweskau D . . . 73 B4
Schwetzingen D . . . 93 B4
Schwyz CH . . . 107 B3
Sciacca I . . . 176 B2
Scicli I . . . 177 C3
Ściechów PL . . . 75 B3
Scigliano I . . . 175 B2
Scilla I . . . 175 C1
Ścinawa PL . . . 85 A4
Scionzier F . . . 118 A3
Scoglitti I . . . 177 C3
Scole GB . . . 45 A5
Sconser GB . . . 31 B2
Scopello
 Piemonte I . . . 119 B5
 Sicília I . . . 176 A1
Scordia I . . . 177 B3
Scorzè I . . . 121 B5
Scotch Corner GB . . . 37 B5
Scotter GB . . . 40 B3
Scourie GB . . . 32 C1
Scousburgh GB . . . 33 B5
Scrabster GB . . . 32 C3
Screeb IRL . . . 28 A2
Scremerston GB . . . 37 A5
Scritto I . . . 136 B1
Scúrcola Marsicana
 I . . . 169 A3
Seaford GB . . . 45 C4

Seaham GB . . . 37 B5
Seahouses GB . . . 37 A5
Seascale GB . . . 36 B3
Seaton GB . . . 43 B3
Sebazac-Concourès
 F . . . 130 A1
Seben TR . . . 187 B6
Sebersdorf A . . . 110 B2
Sebezh RUS . . . 8 D6
Sebnitz D . . . 84 B2
Seborga I . . . 133 B3
Seby S . . . 63 B4
Seč
 Vychodočeský
 CZ . . . 97 B3
 Západočeský CZ . . . 71 A5
Sečanj SRB . . . 126 B2
Secemin PL . . . 87 B3
Séchault F . . . 91 B4
Seckau A . . . 110 B1
Seclin F . . . 78 B3
Secondigny F . . . 114 B3
Seda P . . . 155 B3
Sedan F . . . 91 B4
Sedano E . . . 143 B3
Sedbergh GB . . . 37 B4
Sedella I . . . 163 B3
Sédico I . . . 121 A5
Sédilo I . . . 178 B2
Sédini I . . . 178 B2
Sedlarica HR . . . 124 B3
Sedlčany CZ . . . 96 B2
Sedlec-Prčice CZ . . . 96 B2
Sedlice CZ . . . 96 B1
Sędziejowice PL . . . 86 A3
Sędziszów PL . . . 87 B4
Sędziszów Małopolski
 PL . . . 87 B5
Seebach F . . . 93 C3
Seeboden A . . . 109 C4
Seefeld
 Brandenburg D . . . 74 B2
 Niedersachsen D . . . 71 A5
Seefeld in Tirol A . . . 108 B2
Seeg D . . . 108 B1
Seehausen
 Sachsen-Anhalt
 D . . . 73 B4
 Sachsen-Anhalt D . . . 73 B4
Seeheim-Jugenheim
 D . . . 93 B4
Seelbach D . . . 93 C3
Seelow D . . . 74 B3
Seelze D . . . 72 B2
Seerhausen D . . . 83 A5
Sées F . . . 89 B4
Seesen D . . . 82 A2
Seeshaupt D . . . 108 B2
Seewalchen A . . . 109 B4
Seferihisar TR . . . 188 A1
Segård N . . . 48 B2
Segarcea RO . . . 17 C6
Segerstad S . . . 55 A4
Segesd H . . . 124 A3
Seglinge FIN . . . 51 B7
Segmon S . . . 55 A4
Segonzac F . . . 115 C3
Segorbe E . . . 159 B3
Segovia E . . . 151 B3
Segré F . . . 101 B5
Segura
 E . . . 144 B1
 P . . . 155 B3
Segura de León E . . . 161 A3
Segura de los Baños
 E . . . 152 B3
Ségur-les-Villas F . . . 116 B2
Segurrilla E . . . 150 B3
Sehnde D . . . 72 B2
Seia P . . . 148 B2
Seiches-sur-le-Loir
 F . . . 102 B1
Seifhennersdorf D . . . 84 B2
Seignelay F . . . 104 B2
Seijo E . . . 140 C2
Seilhac F . . . 116 B1
Seilles B . . . 79 B5
Seim N . . . 46 B2
Seinäjoki FIN . . . 8 A3
Seissan F . . . 145 A4
Seitenstetten Markt
 A . . . 110 A1
Seixal P . . . 154 C1
Seiz A . . . 110 B1
Seizthal A . . . 110 B1
Sejerslev DK . . . 58 B1
Seksna RUS . . . 9 C11
Selárdalur IS . . . 190 B1
Selárgius I . . . 179 C3
Selb D . . . 83 B4
Selby GB . . . 40 B2
Selca HR . . . 138 B2
Selce HR . . . 123 B3
Selçuk TR . . . 188 B2
Selde DK . . . 58 B2
Selenča SRB . . . 126 B1
Selendi
 Manisa TR . . . 186 D2
 Manisa TR . . . 186 D3
Selenicë AL . . . 182 C1
Sélestat F . . . 106 A2
Seleuš SRB . . . 126 B2
Selevac SRB . . . 127 C2
Selfoss IS . . . 190 D5
Selgua E . . . 145 C4
Selice SK . . . 112 A1
Seligenstadt D . . . 93 A4
Seligenthal D . . . 82 B2
Selimiye TR . . . 188 B2
Selizharovo RUS . . . 9 D8
Selja N . . . 50 A1
Selje N . . . 198 C2
Seljelvnes N . . . 192 C3
Seljord N . . . 53 A4
Selkirk GB . . . 35 C5
Sella E . . . 159 C3
Sellano I . . . 136 C1
Selles-St Denis F . . . 103 B3
Selles-sur-Cher F . . . 103 B3

Sellières F . . . 105 C4
Sellin D . . . 66 B2
Sellye H . . . 125 B3
Selm D . . . 80 A3
Selnica ob Dravi
 SLO . . . 110 C2
Selongey F . . . 105 B4
Selonnet F . . . 132 A2
Selow D . . . 65 C4
Selsey GB . . . 44 C3
Selsingen D . . . 72 A2
Selters D . . . 81 B3
Seltz F . . . 93 C4
Selva I . . . 167 B2
Selva di Cadore I . . . 108 C3
Selva di Val Gardena
 I . . . 108 C2
Selvik
 Sogn og Fjordane
 N . . . 46 A2
 Vestfold N . . . 54 A1
Selvino I . . . 120 B2
Selyatyn UA . . . 17 B6
Sem N . . . 54 A1
Semeljci HR . . . 125 B4
Semič SLO . . . 123 B4
Semide
 F . . . 91 B4
 P . . . 148 B1
Semily CZ . . . 84 B3
Seminara I . . . 175 C1
Semlac RO . . . 126 A3
Semlacu Mare RO . . . 126 B3
Semmen-stedt D . . . 73 B3
Šempeter SLO . . . 123 A4
Semriach A . . . 110 B2
Semur-en-Auxois
 F . . . 104 B3
Sena E . . . 145 C3
Sena de Luna E . . . 141 B5
Senarpont F . . . 90 B1
Sénas F . . . 131 B4
Senčur SLO . . . 123 A3
Senden
 Bayern D . . . 94 C2
 Nordrhein-Westfalen
 D . . . 80 A3
Sendenhorst D . . . 81 A3
Sendim P . . . 149 A3
Senec SK . . . 111 A4
Seneffe B . . . 79 B4
Séneghe I . . . 178 B2
Senés E . . . 164 B2
Senez F . . . 132 B2
Senftenberg D . . . 84 A1
Sengouagnet F . . . 145 B4
Sengwarden D . . . 71 A5
Senica SK . . . 98 C1
Senice na Hané CZ . . . 98 B1
Senigállia I . . . 136 B2
Senirkent TR . . . 189 A5
Senj HR . . . 123 C3
Senje SRB . . . 127 D3
Senjehopen N . . . 194 A8
Senjski Rudnik
 SRB . . . 127 D3
Senlis F . . . 90 B2
Sennan S . . . 60 C2
Sennecey-le-Grand
 F . . . 105 C3
Sennen GB . . . 42 B1
Senno BY . . . 13 A8
Sénnori I . . . 178 B2
Sennwald CH . . . 107 B4
Sennybridge GB . . . 39 C3
Senonches F . . . 89 B5
Senones F . . . 92 C2
Senorbì I . . . 179 C3
Senovo SLO . . . 123 A4
Senožeče SLO . . . 123 B3
Senožeti SLO . . . 123 A4
Sens F . . . 104 A2
Sens-de-Bretagne
 F . . . 101 A4
Senta SRB . . . 126 B2
Senterada E . . . 145 B4
Šentjernej SLO . . . 123 B4
Šentjur SLO . . . 123 A4
Senumstad N . . . 53 B4
Seoane E . . . 141 B3
Seon CH . . . 106 B3
Sépeaux F . . . 104 B2
Sépey CH . . . 119 A4
Sepino I . . . 170 B2
Sępólno Krajeńskie
 PL . . . 76 A2
Seppenrade D . . . 80 A3
Seppois F . . . 106 B2
Septemvri BG . . . 183 A6
Septeuil F . . . 90 C1
Sepúlveda E . . . 151 A4
Sequals I . . . 122 A1
Sequeros E . . . 149 B3
Seraincourt F . . . 91 B4
Seraing B . . . 80 B1
Seravezza I . . . 134 B3
Sered' SK . . . 98 C1
Seredka RUS . . . 8 C6
Şereflikoçhisar TR . . . 23 B7
Seregélyes H . . . 112 B2
Seregno I . . . 120 B2
Sérent F . . . 101 B3
Serfaus A . . . 108 B1
Sergiev Posad
 RUS . . . 9 D11
Seriate I . . . 120 B2
Sérifontaine F . . . 90 B1
Serifos GR . . . 185 B5
Sérignan F . . . 130 B2
Serik TR . . . 189 C6
Serina I . . . 120 B2
Serinhisar TR . . . 188 B4
Sermaises F . . . 90 C2

Sermaize-les-Bains
 F . . . 91 C4
Sérmide I . . . 121 C4
Sermoneta I . . . 169 B2
Sernache de Bonjardim
 P . . . 154 B2
Sernancelhe P . . . 148 B2
Serock PL . . . 77 B6
Serón E . . . 164 B2
Serón de Najima
 E . . . 152 A1
Serooskerke NL . . . 79 A3
Seròs E . . . 153 A4
Serpa P . . . 160 B2
Serpukhov RUS . . . 9 E10
Serra de Outes E . . . 140 B2
Serradifalco I . . . 176 B2
Serradilla E . . . 155 B4
Serradilla del Arroyo
 E . . . 149 B3
Serradilla del Llano
 E . . . 149 B3
Serramanna I . . . 179 C2
Serramazzoni I . . . 135 A3
Serranillos E . . . 150 B3
Serrapetrona I . . . 136 B2
Serra San Bruno I . . . 175 C2
Serra San Quirico
 I . . . 136 B2
Serrastretta I . . . 175 B2
Serravalle
 Piemonte I . . . 119 B5
 Umbria I . . . 136 C2
Serravalle di Chienti
 I . . . 136 B1
Serravalle Scrivia
 I . . . 120 C1
Serre I . . . 172 B1
Serrejón E . . . 150 C2
Serres
 F . . . 132 A1
 GR . . . 183 B5
Serrières F . . . 117 B4
Serrières-de-Briord
 F . . . 118 B2
Sersale I . . . 175 B2
Sertã P . . . 154 B2
Sertig Dörfli CH . . . 107 C4
Servance F . . . 106 B1
Serverette F . . . 117 C3
Servia GR . . . 182 C4
Servian F . . . 130 B2
Serviers F . . . 131 A3
Servigliano I . . . 136 B2
Serzedelo P . . . 148 A1
Sesa E . . . 145 B3
Seseña Nuevo E . . . 151 B4
Sesimbra P . . . 154 C1
Seskarö S . . . 196 D6
Seskinore GB . . . 27 B3
Sesma E . . . 144 B1
Sessa Aurunca I . . . 170 B1
Ses Salines E . . . 167 B3
Sesta Godano I . . . 134 A2
Šestanovac HR . . . 138 B2
Sestao E . . . 143 A4
Sestino I . . . 135 B5
Sesto I . . . 109 C3
Sesto Calende I . . . 120 B1
Sesto Fiorentino I . . . 135 B4
Sèstola I . . . 135 A3
Sesto San Giovanni
 I . . . 120 B2
Sestriere I . . . 119 C3
Sestri Levante I . . . 134 A2
Sestroretsk RUS . . . 9 B7
Sestu I . . . 179 C3
Sesvete HR . . . 124 B2
Setcases E . . . 146 B3
Sète F . . . 130 B2
Setenil E . . . 162 B2
Setermoen N . . . 194 B9
Setonje SRB . . . 127 C3
Setskog N . . . 54 A2
Settalsjølia N . . . 199 C7
Settimo Torinese
 I . . . 119 B4
Settimo Vittone I . . . 119 B4
Settle GB . . . 40 A1
Setúbal P . . . 154 C2
Seubersdort D . . . 95 B3
Seúl I . . . 179 C3
Seúlo I . . . 179 C3
Seurre F . . . 105 C4
Sevel DK . . . 58 B1
Sevenoaks GB . . . 45 B4
Sévérac-le-Château
 F . . . 130 A2
Sever do Vouga P . . . 148 B1
Severin HR . . . 123 B4
Severomorsk RUS . . . 3 B13
Séveso I . . . 120 B2
Ševětín CZ . . . 96 B2
Sevettijärvi FIN . . . 193 C12
Sévigny F . . . 91 B4
Sevilla E . . . 162 A2
Sevilla la Nueva E . . . 151 B3
Seville = Sevilla E . . . 162 A2
Sevilleja de la Jara
 E . . . 156 A3
Sevlievo BG . . . 17 D6
Sevnica SLO . . . 123 A4
Sevojno SRB . . . 127 D1
Sevrier F . . . 118 B3
Sexdrega S . . . 60 B3
Seyches F . . . 129 B3
Seyda D . . . 83 A4
Seydişehir TR . . . 189 B6
Seyðisfjörður IS . . . 191 B12
Seyitgazi TR . . . 187 C5
Seyitömer TR . . . 187 C4
Seymen TR . . . 186 A2
Seyne F . . . 132 A2
Seynes F . . . 131 A3
Seyssel F . . . 118 B2
Sézanne F . . . 91 C3
Sezana SLO . . . 122 B2
Sezulfe P . . . 149 A2
Sezze I . . . 169 B3

Sfântu Gheorghe
 RO . . . 17 C6
Sforzacosta I . . . 136 B2
Sgarasta Mhor GB . . . 31 B1
's-Gravendeel NL . . . 79 A4
's-Gravenhage = The
Hague NL . . . 70 B1
's-Gravenzande NL . . . 79 A4
Shaftesbury GB . . . 43 A4
Shaldon GB . . . 43 B3
Shalskiy RUS . . . 9 B9
Shanagolden IRL . . . 29 B2
Shanklin GB . . . 44 C2
Shap GB . . . 37 B4
Sharpness GB . . . 43 B4
Shawbury GB . . . 38 B4
's-Heerenberg NL . . . 80 A2
Sheerness GB . . . 45 B4
Sheffield GB . . . 40 B2
Shefford GB . . . 44 A3
Shëmri AL . . . 182 A2
Shenfield GB . . . 45 B4
Shëngjergj AL . . . 182 B2
Shepshed GB . . . 40 C2
Shepton Mallet GB . . . 43 A4
Sherborne GB . . . 43 B4
Shercock IRL . . . 27 C4
Sheringham GB . . . 41 C5
's-Hertogenbosch
 NL . . . 79 A5
Shiel Bridge GB . . . 32 D2
Shieldaig GB . . . 31 B3
Shijak AL . . . 182 B1
Shillelagh IRL . . . 30 B2
Shimsk RUS . . . 9 C7
Shipston-on-Stour
 GB . . . 44 A2
Shklow BY . . . 13 A9
Shkodër AL . . . 182 A1
Shoeburyness GB . . . 45 B4
Shoreham-by-Sea
 GB . . . 44 C3
Shotley Gate GB . . . 45 B5
Shrewsbury GB . . . 38 B4
Shugozero RUS . . . 9 C9
Shumen BG . . . 17 D7
Siabost GB . . . 31 A2
Siamanna I . . . 179 C2
Sianów PL . . . 67 B5
Siatista GR . . . 182 C3
Siauges-St Romain
 F . . . 117 B3
Šiauliai LT . . . 8 E3
Sibari I . . . 174 B2
Sibbhult S . . . 63 B2
Šibenik HR . . . 138 B1
Siberstedt D . . . 64 B2
Sibinj HR . . . 125 B3
Sibiu RO . . . 17 C6
Sibnica SRB . . . 127 C2
Sibsey GB . . . 41 B4
Siculiana I . . . 176 B2
Šid SRB . . . 125 B5
Sidari I . . . 182 D1
Siddeburen NL . . . 71 A3
Sidensjö S . . . 200 C4
Siderno I . . . 175 C2
Sidirokastro GR . . . 183 B5
Sidmouth GB . . . 43 B3
Sidzina PL . . . 99 B3
Siebe N . . . 192 D7
Siebenlehn D . . . 83 A5
Siedlce PL . . . 12 B5
Siedlice PL . . . 75 A4
Siedlinghausen D . . . 81 A4
Siedlisko PL . . . 75 B5
Siegburg D . . . 80 B3
Siegen D . . . 81 B4
Siegenburg D . . . 95 C3
Sieghartskirchen
 A . . . 111 A3
Siegsdorf D . . . 109 B3
Siekierki PL . . . 74 B3
Sielpia PL . . . 87 A4
Siemiany PL . . . 69 B4
Siena I . . . 135 B4
Sieniawka PL . . . 84 B2
Sienno PL . . . 87 A5
Sieppijärvi FIN . . . 196 B7
Sieradz PL . . . 86 A2
Sieraków
 Śląskie PL . . . 86 B2
 Wielkopolskie PL . . . 75 B5
Sierakowice PL . . . 68 A2
Sierck-les-Bains F . . . 92 B2
Sierentz F . . . 106 B2
Sierning A . . . 110 A1
Sierpc PL . . . 77 B4
Sierra de Fuentes
 E . . . 155 B4
Sierra de Luna E . . . 144 B3
Sierra de Yeguas
 E . . . 162 A3
Sierre CH . . . 119 A4
Siestrzeń PL . . . 77 B5
Sietamo E . . . 145 B3
Siewierz PL . . . 86 B3
Sigdal N . . . 48 B1
Sigean F . . . 130 B1
Sigerfjord N . . . 194 B6
Sighetu-Marmatiei
 RO . . . 17 B5
Sighişoara RO . . . 17 B6
Sigillo I . . . 136 B1
Siglufjörður IS . . . 191 A7
Sigmaringen D . . . 107 A4
Signa I . . . 135 B4
Signes F . . . 132 B1
Signy-l'Abbaye F . . . 91 B4
Signy-le-Petit F . . . 91 B4
Sigri GR . . . 183 D7
Sigtuna S . . . 57 A3
Sigüeiro E . . . 140 B2
Sigüenza E . . . 151 A5
Sigües E . . . 144 B2
Sigulda LV . . . 8 D4
Siilinjärvi FIN . . . 8 A5
Sikenica SK . . . 112 A2

ikfors S 196 D4
ikia GR 183 C5
ikinos GR 185 C6
ikkilsdalseter N 47 A6
iklós H 125 B4
ikórz PL 77 B4
ikselet S 195 D8
ilandro I 108 C1
ilánus I 178 B2
ilbaš SRB 126 B1
ile TR 187 A4
iles E 164 A2
ilgueiros P 148 B2
ilifke TR 23 C7
iliqua I 179 C2
ilistra BG 17 C7
ilivri TR 186 A3
iljan N 53 A5
iljansnäs S 50 B1
ilkeborg DK 59 B2
illa E 159 B3
illamäe EST 8 C5
illeda E 140 B2
illé-le-Guillaume
F 102 A1
illenstede D 71 A4
illerud S 54 A3
illian A 109 C3
illoth GB 36 B3
ilno PL 68 B2
ilnowo PL 68 B1
ilo HR 123 B3
ils E 147 C3
ilsand N 194 A8
ilte S 57 C4
ilute LT 12 A4
ilvalen N 195 E3
ilvaplana CH 107 C4
ilvares P 148 B2
ilvberg S 50 B2
ilverdalen S 62 A3
ilvermines IRL 28 B3
ilverstone GB 44 A2
ilverton GB 43 B3
ilves P 160 B1
ilvi Marina I 169 A4
imandre F 105 C3
imanovci SRB 127 C2
imard F 105 C4
imat de Valldigna
E 159 B3
imav TR 186 C3
imbach
Bayern D 95 C4
Bayern D 95 C5
imbário I 175 C2
imeonovgrad BG 183 A7
imeria RO 17 C5
imi GR 188 C2
imićevo SRB 127 C3
imitli BG 183 B5
imlångsdalen S 60 C3
immerath D 80 B2
immerberg D 107 B4
immern D 93 B3
imo FIN 197 D8
imonovce SK 99 C4
imonsbath GB 43 A3
imonstorp S 56 B2
imontornya H 112 C2
implon CH 119 A5
imrishamn S 63 C2
inaia RO 17 C6
inalunga I 135 B4
inarcas E 159 B2
incan TR 187 C7
incanlı TR 187 D5
indal DK 58 A3
indelfingen D 93 C5
india I 178 B2
ındırgı TR 186 C3
inekli TR 186 A3
ines P 160 B1
inetta FIN 197 C8
ineu E 167 B3
ingen D 107 B3
ingleton GB 44 C3
ingsås N 199 C7
iniscóla I 178 B3
inj HR 138 B2
inlabajos E 150 A3
inn D 81 B4
innai I 179 C3
innes N 52 B2
inop TR 23 A8
ins CH 106 B3
insheim D 93 B4
int Annaland NL 79 A4
int Annaparochie
NL 70 A2
int Athonis NL 80 A1
int Nicolaasga NL 70 B2
int Oedenrode NL 79 A5
intra P 154 C1
inzheim D 93 C4
inzig D 80 B3
iófok H 112 C2
ion CH 119 A4
ion Mills GB 27 B3
iorac-en-Périgord
F 129 B3
ipanska Luka HR 139 C3
ipovo BIH 138 A3
ira N 52 B2
iracusa I 177 B4
iret RO 17 B7
irevåg N 52 B1
irig SRB 126 B1
irkka FIN 196 B7
irmione I 121 B3
irniö FIN 197 D11
irok H 113 B4
iroké SK 99 C4
iroki Brijeg BIH 139 B3
irolo I 136 B2
iruela E 156 B2
isak HR 124 B2
isante E 158 B1
išljavić HR 123 B4
issach CH 106 B2
Sissonne F 91 B3
Sistelo P 140 C2
Sisteron F 132 A1
Sistiana I 122 B2
Sistranda N 198 B5
Sitasjaurestugorna
S 194 C8
Sitges E 147 C2
Sitia GR 185 D7
Sittard NL 80 A1
Sittensen D 72 A2
Sittingbourne GB 45 B4
Sitzenroda D 83 A4
Sivac SRB 126 B1
Sivaslı TR 189 A4
Siverić HR 138 B2
Sivrihisar TR 187 C6
Sixt-Fer-á-Cheval
F 119 A3
Siziano I 120 B2
Sizun F 100 A1
Sjenica SRB 16 D3
Sjoa N 198 D6
Sjøåsen N 199 A8
Sjöbo S 61 D3
Sjøenden
Hedmark N 48 A3
Hedmark N 48 B3
Sjøholt N 198 C3
Sjøli N 48 A3
Sjølstad N 199 A9
Sjölunda S 56 A1
Sjømarken S 60 B2
Sjørring DK 58 B1
Sjötofta S 60 B3
Sjötorp S 55 B4
Sjoutnäset S 199 A11
Sjøvegan N 194 B8
Sjuntorp S 54 B3
Skåbu N 47 A6
Skafså N 53 A4
Skaftafell IS 191 D9
Skagaströnd IS 190 B5
Skagen DK 58 A3
Skagersvik S 55 B5
Skaiå N 53 B3
Skaidi N 193 B8
Skala GR 184 A1
Skała PL 87 B3
Skaland N 194 A8
Skala Oropou GR 185 A4
Skala-Podilska UA 13 D7
Skalat UA 13 D6
Skalbmierz PL 87 B4
Skålevik N 53 B4
Skalica SK 98 C1
Skalité SK 98 B2
Skällinge S 60 B2
Skalná CZ 83 B4
Skals DK 58 B2
Skælskør DK 65 A4
Skalstugan S 199 B9
Skanderborg DK 59 B2
Skånes-Fagerhult
S 61 C3
Skåne-Tranås S 61 D3
Skånevik N 52 A1
Skänninge S 55 B6
Skanör med Falsterbo
S 66 A1
Skåpafors S 54 A3
Skąpe PL 75 B4
Skara S 55 B4
Skærbæk DK 64 A1
Skarberget N 194 B7
Skärblacka S 56 B1
Skarð IS 190 B3
Skarda S 200 B4
Skare N 46 C3
Skåre S 55 A4
Skärhamn S 60 B1
Skarnes N 48 B3
Skärplinge S 51 B4
Skarpnatö FIN 51 B6
Skarp Salling DK 58 B2
Skarrild DK 59 C1
Skarstad N 194 B7
Skärstad S 62 A2
Skarsvåg N 193 A9
Skarszewy PL 69 A3
Skårup DK 65 A3
Skärvången S 199 B11
Skarvsjöby S 195 F8
Skaryszew PL 87 A5
Skarżysko-Kamienna
PL 87 A4
Skarzysko Ksiazece
PL 87 A4
Skatøy N 53 B5
Skattkärr S 55 A4
Skattungbyn S 50 A1
Skatval N 199 B7
Skaulo S 196 B4
Skave DK 59 B1
Skawina PL 99 B3
Skebobruk S 51 C5
Skebokvarn S 56 A2
Skedala S 61 C2
Skedevi S 56 B1
Skedsmokorset N 48 B3
Skee S 54 B2
Skegness GB 41 B4
Skei N 46 A3
Skela SRB 127 C2
Skelani BIH 127 D1
Skellefteå S 2 D7
Skelleftehamn S 2 D7
Skelmersdale GB 38 A4
Skelmorlie GB 34 C3
Skelund DK 58 B3
Skender Vakuf
BIH 138 A3
Skene S 60 B2
Skępe PL 77 B4
Skepplanda S 60 B2
Skeppshult S 60 B3
Skerries IRL 30 A2
Ski N 54 A1
Skiathos GR 183 D5
Skibbereen IRL 29 C2
Skibotn N 192 C4
Skidra GR 182 C4
Skien N 53 A5
Skierniewice PL 77 C5
Skillingaryd S 60 B4
Skillinge S 63 C2
Skillingmark S 49 C4
Skilloura CY 181 A2
Skinnardai S 57 A4
Skinnskatteberg S 50 C2
Skipmannvik N 195 C6
Skipness GB 34 C2
Skipsea GB 41 B3
Skipton GB 40 B1
Skiptvet N 54 A2
Skiros GR 183 E6
Skivarp S 66 A2
Skive DK 58 B2
Skjånes N 193 B12
Skjærhalden N 54 A2
Skjeberg N 54 A2
Skjeggedal N 46 B3
Skjeljanger N 46 B1
Skjeljavik N 46 C2
Skjern DK 59 C1
Skjervøy N 192 B4
Skjold
Rogaland N 52 A1
Troms N 192 C3
Skjoldastraumen N 52 A1
Skjolden N 47 A4
Skjønhaug N 54 A2
Skjøtningsberg
N 193 A11
Škocjan SLO 123 B4
Skoczów PL 98 B2
Skodborg DK 59 C2
Škofja Loka SLO 123 A3
Škofljica SLO 123 B3
Skog S 51 A3
Skoganvarre N 193 C9
Skogen S 54 A3
Skogfoss N 193 C13
Skoghall S 55 A4
Skogly N 193 C13
Skogn N 199 B8
Skognes N 192 C3
Skogstorp
Halland S 60 C2
Södermanland S 56 A2
Skoki PL 76 B2
Skokloster S 57 A3
Sköldinge S 56 A2
Skole UA 13 D5
Skollenborg N 53 A5
Sköllersta S 56 A1
Skomlin PL 86 A2
Skonseng N 195 D5
Skopelos GR 183 D5
Skopje MK 182 A3
Skoppum N 54 A1
Skórcz PL 69 B3
Skorogoszcz PL 86 B1
Skoroszów PL 85 A5
Skorovatn N 199 A10
Skorped S 200 C3
Skørping DK 58 B2
Skotfoss N 53 A5
Skotniki PL 87 A3
Skotselv N 48 C1
Skotterud N 49 C4
Skottorp S 61 C2
Skovby DK 64 B2
Skövde S 55 B4
Skovsgård DK 58 A2
Skrad HR 123 B3
Skradin HR 138 B1
Skradnik HR 123 B4
Skråmestø N 46 B1
Škrdlovice CZ 97 B3
Skrea S 60 C2
Skreia N 48 B2
Skrolsvik N 194 A7
Skruv S 63 B3
Skrwilno PL 77 A4
Skrydstrup DK 59 C2
Skucani BIH 138 B2
Skudeneshavn N 52 A1
Skui N 48 C2
Skulsk PL 76 B3
Skultorp S 55 B4
Skultuna S 56 A2
Skuodas LT 8 D2
Skurup S 66 A2
Skute N 48 B2
Skuteč CZ 97 B3
Skutskär S 51 B4
Skutvik N 194 B6
Skvyra UA 13 D8
Skwierzyna PL 75 B4
Skýcov SK 98 C2
Skyllberg S 55 B5
Skyttmon S 200 C1
Skyttorp S 51 B4
Sládkovičovo SK 111 A4
Slagelse DK 61 D1
Slagharen NL 71 B3
Slagnäs S 195 E9
Slaidburn GB 40 B1
Slane IRL 30 A2
Slangerup DK 61 D2
Slano HR 139 C3
Slantsy RUS 8 C6
Slaný CZ 84 B2
Slap SLO 122 A2
Šlapanice CZ 97 B4
Slåstad N 48 B3
Slatina
BIH 139 B3
HR 125 B3
RO 17 C6
Slatiňany CZ 97 B3
Slatinice CZ 98 B1
Slättberg S 50 A1
Slattum N 48 C2
Slavičin CZ 98 B1
Slavkov CZ 98 C1
Slavkovica SRB 127 C2
Slavkov u Brna CZ 97 B4
Slavonice CZ 97 C3
Slavonski Brod
HR 125 B4
Slavonski Kobas
HR 125 B3
Slavōsovce SK 99 C4
Slavskoye RUS 69 A5
Slavuta UA 13 C7
Sława
Lubuskie PL 85 A4
Zachodnio-Pomorskie
PL 67 C4
Slawharad BY 13 B9
Sławków PL 86 B3
Sławno
Wielkopolskie PL 76 B2
Zachodnio-Pomorskie
PL 68 A1
Sławoborze PL 67 C4
Sl'ažany SK 98 C2
Sleaford GB 40 C3
Sleðbrjótur IS 191 B11
Sledmere GB 40 A3
Sleights GB 37 B6
Slemmestad N 54 A1
Ślesin PL 76 B3
Sliač SK 99 C3
Sliema M 175 C3
Sligo IRL 26 B2
Slite S 57 C4
Slitu N 54 A2
Sliven BG 17 D7
Śliwice PL 68 B3
Slobozia RO 17 C7
Slochteren NL 71 A3
Slöinge S 60 C2
Słomniki PL 87 B4
Slonim BY 13 B6
Słońsk PL 75 B3
Slootdorp NL 70 B1
Slottsbron S 55 A4
Slough GB 44 B3
Slövag N 46 B2
Slovenj Gradec
SLO 110 C2
Slovenska Bistrica
SLO 123 A4
Slovenská L'upča
SK 99 C3
Slovenská-Ves SK 99 B4
Slovenské Darmoty
SK 112 A3
Slovenske Konjice
SLO 123 A4
Słubice PL 74 B3
Sluderno I 108 C1
Sluis NL 78 A3
Šluknov CZ 84 A2
Slunj HR 123 B4
Słupca PL 76 B2
Słupia PL 87 A3
Słupiec PL 85 B4
Słupsk PL 68 A2
Slutsk BY 13 B7
Smålandsstenar S 60 B3
Smalåsen N 195 E4
Smardzewo PL 75 B4
Smarhon BY 13 A7
Smarje SLO 123 A4
Šmarjeta SLO 123 B4
Šmartno SLO 123 A3
Smečno CZ 84 B2
Smedby S 63 B4
Smědec CZ 96 C2
Smederevo SRB 127 C2
Smederevska Palanka
SRB 127 C2
Smedjebacken S 50 B2
Smęgorzów PL 87 B5
Smeland N 53 B4
Smidary CZ 84 B3
Śmigiel PL 75 B5
Smilde NL 71 B3
Smiřice CZ 85 B3
Smithfield GB 36 B4
Śmitowo PL 75 A5
Smögen S 54 B2
Smogulec PL 76 A2
Smołdzino PL 68 A2
Smolenice SK 98 C1
Smolensk RUS 13 A10
Smolník SK 99 C4
Smolyan BG 183 B6
Smuka SLO 123 B3
Smygehamn S 66 A2
Smykow PL 87 A4
Snainton GB 40 A3
Snaith GB 40 B2
Snaptun DK 59 C3
Snarby N 192 C3
Snarum N 48 B1
Snåsa N 199 A9
Snedsted DK 58 B1
Sneek NL 70 A2
Sneem IRL 29 C2
Snejbjerg DK 59 B1
Snillfjord N 198 B6
Šnjegotina BIH 125 C3
Snøde DK 65 A3
Snøfjord N 193 B8
Snogebaek DK 67 A4
Snyatyn UA 13 D6
Soave I 121 B4
Sober E 140 B3
Sobernheim D 93 B3
Soběslav CZ 96 B2
Sobota
Dolnośląskie PL 85 A3
Łódzkie PL 77 B4
Sobotište SK 98 C1
Sobotka CZ 84 B3
Sobótka
Dolnośląskie PL 85 B4
Wielkopolskie PL 86 A1
Sobra HR 139 C3
Sobrado
Coruña E 140 A2
Lugo E 141 B3
Sobral da Adica P 161 A2
Sobral de Monte
Agraço P 154 C1
Sobreira Formosa
P 154 B3
Søby DK 64 B3
Soca SLO 122 A2
Sochaczew PL 77 B5
Sochos GR 183 C5
Socodor RO 113 C5
Socol RO 127 C3
Socovos E 164 A3
Socuéllamos E 158 B1
Sodankylä FIN 197 B9
Soderåkra S 63 B4
Söderala S 51 A3
Söderås S 50 B2
Söderbärke S 50 B2
Söderby-Karl S 51 C5
Söderfors S 51 B4
Söderhamn S 51 A4
Söderköping S 56 B2
Söderö S 56 B1
Södertälje S 57 A3
Södingberg A 110 B2
Södra Finnö S 56 B2
Södra Ny S 55 A4
Södra Råda S 55 A5
Södra Sandby S 61 D3
Södra Vi S 62 A3
Sodražica SLO 123 B3
Sodupe E 143 A3
Soengas P 148 A1
Soest
D 81 A4
NL 70 B2
Sofades GR 182 D4
Sofia BG 17 D5
Sofikon GR 184 B4
Şofronea RO 126 A3
Sögel D 71 B4
Sogliano al Rubicone
I 135 A5
Sogndalsfjøra N 46 A4
Søgne N 53 B3
Söğütköy TR 188 C3
Soham GB 45 A4
Sohland D 84 A2
Sohren D 93 B3
Soignies B 79 B4
Soissons F 90 B3
Söjtör H 111 C3
Sokal' UA 13 C6
Söke TR 188 B2
Sokna N 48 B1
Sokndal N 52 B2
Soknedal N 199 C7
Soko BIH 125 C4
Sokolac BIH 139 B4
Sokółka PL 13 B5
Sokolov CZ 83 B4
Sokołowo PL 76 B3
Sokołów Podlaski
PL 12 B5
Sola N 52 B1
Solana de los Barros
E 155 C4
Solana del Pino E 157 B3
Solánas I 179 C3
Solares E 143 A3
Solarino I 177 B4
Solarussa I 179 C2
Solas GB 31 B1
Solberg S 200 C3
Solberga S 62 A2
Solber-gelva N 53 A6
Solbjørg N 46 B2
Solčany SK 98 C2
Solčava SLO 123 A3
Solda I 108 C1
Sölden A 108 C2
Solec Kujawski PL 76 A3
Soleils F 132 B2
Solenzara F 180 B2
Solera E 163 A4
Solesmes F 79 B3
Soleto I 173 B4
Solgne F 92 C2
Solheim N 46 B2
Solheimsvik N 52 A2
Solignac F 115 C5
Solihull GB 44 A2
Solin HR 138 B2
Solingen D 80 A3
Solivella E 147 C2
Solkan SLO 122 B2
Söll A 108 B3
Sollana E 159 B3
Sollebrunn S 54 B3
Sollefteå S 200 C3
Sollenau A 111 B3
Sollen-tuna S 57 A3
Sóller E 166 B2
Sollerön S 50 B1
Søllested DK 65 B4
Solliès-Pont F 132 B2
Sollihøgda N 48 C2
Solnechnogorsk
RUS 9 D10
Solnice CZ 85 B4
Solofra I 170 C2
Solomiac F 129 C3
Solopaca I 170 B2
Solórzano E 143 A3
Solothurn CH 106 B2
Solre-le-Château F 79 B4
Solsona E 147 C2
Solsvik N 46 B1
Solt H 112 C3
Soltau D 72 B2
Soltsy RUS 9 C7
Soltszentimre H 112 C3
Soltvadkert H 112 C3
Solumsmoen N 48 C1
Solund N 46 A1
Solva GB 39 C1
Sölvesborg S 63 B2
Solymár H 112 B2
Soma TR 186 C2
Somain F 78 B3
Somberek H 125 A4
Sombernon F 104 B3
Sombor SRB 125 B5
Sombreffe B 79 B4
Someren NL 80 A1
Somero FIN 8 B3
Somersham GB 44 A3
Somerton GB 43 A4
Sominy PL 68 A2
Somma Lombardo
I 120 B1
Sommariva del Bosco
I 119 C4
Sommarøy N 192 C2
Sommarset N 194 C6
Sommatino I 176 B2
Sommeilles F 91 C4
Sommen S 55 B5
Sommepy-Tahure
F 91 B4
Sömmerda D 82 A3
Sommerfeld D 74 B2
Sommersted DK 59 C2
Sommesous F 91 C4
Somme-Tourbe F 91 B4
Sommières F 131 B3
Sommières-du-Clain
F 115 B4
Somo E 143 A3
Somogyfajsz H 111 C4
Somogyjád H 111 C4
Somogysámson
H 111 C4
Somogysárd H 125 A3
Somogyszil H 112 C2
Somogyszob H 124 A3
Somogyvár H 111 C4
Somontin E 164 B2
Somosiero E 151 A4
Somosköújifalu
H 113 A3
Sompolno PL 76 B3
Sompuis F 91 C4
Son N 54 A1
Son Bou E 167 B4
Sonceboz CH 106 B2
Soncillo E 143 B3
Soncino I 120 B2
Sóndalo I 120 A3
Søndeled N 53 B5
Sønder Bjert DK 59 C2
Sønderborg DK 64 B2
Sønderby DK 64 B2
Sønder Felding DK 59 C1
Sønderho DK 59 C1
Sønder Hygum DK 59 C1
Sønder Omme DK 59 C1
Sondershausen D 82 A2
Søndersø DK 59 C3
Søndervig DK 59 B1
Søndre Enningdal
Kappel N 54 B2
Sóndrio I 120 A2
Soneja E 159 B3
Son en Breugel NL 80 A1
Songe N 53 B5
Songeons F 90 B1
Sonkamuotka FIN 196 A6
Sonkovo RUS 9 D10
Sönnarslöv S 61 D4
Sonneberg D 82 B3
Sonnefeld D 82 B3
Sonnewalde D 84 A1
Sonnino I 169 B3
Sonogno CH 120 A1
Sonsbeck D 80 A2
Sonseca E 157 A4
Son Servera E 167 B3
Sønsterud N 49 B4
Sonstorp S 56 B1
Sonta SRB 125 B5
Sontheim D 94 C2
Sonthofen D 107 B5
Sontra D 82 A1
Sopelana E 143 A4
Sopje HR 125 B3
Šoporňa SK 111 A4
Sopot
PL 69 A3
SRB 127 C2
Sopotnica MK 182 B3
Sopron H 111 B3
Šor SRB 127 C1
Sora I 169 B3
Soragna I 120 C3
Söråker S 200 D3
Sorano I 168 A1
Sorbara I 121 C4
Sorbas E 164 B2
Sórbolo I 121 C3
Sörbygden S 200 D2
Sordal N 52 B3
Sordale GB 32 C3
Sore F 128 B2
Sörenberg CH 106 C3
Soresina I 120 B2
Sorèze F 146 A3
Sörforsa S 200 E3
Sorges F 115 C4
Sórgono I 179 B3
Sorgues F 131 A3
Sorgun TR 23 B8
Soria E 143 C4
Soriano Cálabro I 175 C2
Soriano nel Cimino
I 168 A2
Sorihuela del
Guadalimar E 164 A1
Sorisdale GB 34 B1
Sørkjosen N 192 C4
Sorli N 199 A10
Sormás H 111 C3
Sörmjöle S 200 C6
Sørmo N 194 B9
Sornac F 116 B2
Sorø DK 61 D1
Soroca MD 17 A8
Sørreisa N 194 A9
Sorrento I 170 C2
Sorsele S 195 E8
Sörsjön S 49 A5
Sorso I 178 B2
Sort E 146 B2
Sortavala RUS 9 B7
Sortino I 177 B4
Sortland N 194 B6
Sørum N 48 B2
Sørumsand N 48 C3
Sorunda S 57 A3
Sörup D 64 B2
Sørvågen N 194 C3
Sørvær N 192 B6
Sorvik S 50 B2
Sørvika N 199 C8
Sos F 128 B3
Sösdala S 61 C3
Sos del Rey Católico
E 144 B2
Sošice HR 123 B4
Sośnica PL 75 A5
Sośnicowice PL 86 B2
Sośno PL 76 A2
Sosnovyy Bor RUS 9 C6
Sosnowiec PL 86 B3
Sospel F 133 B3
Šoštanj SLO 123 A4
Sotaseter N 198 D4
Sotillo de Adrada
E 150 B3
Sotillo de la Ribera
E 143 C3
Sotin HR 125 B5
Sotkamo FIN 3 D11
Sotobañado y Priorato
E 142 B2
Soto de la Marina
E 143 A3
Soto del Barco E 141 A4
Soto de los Infantes
E 141 A4
Soto de Real E 151 B4
Soto de Ribera E 141 A5
Sotoserrano E 149 B3
Soto y Amío E 141 B5
Sotresgudo E 142 B2
Sotrondio E 142 A1
Sotta F 180 B2
Sottomarina I 122 B1
Sottrum D 72 A2
Sottunga FIN 51 B7
Sotuelamos E 158 B1
Souain F 91 B4
Soual F 146 A3
Soucy F 104 A2
Souda GR 185 D5
Soudron F 91 C4
Souesmes F 103 B4
Soufflenheim F 93 C3
Soufli GR 186 A1
Souillac F 129 B4
Souilly F 91 B5
Soulac-sur-Mer F 114 C2
Soulaines-Dhuys F 91 C4
Soulatgé F 146 B3
Soultz-Haut-Rhin
F 106 B2
Soultz-sous-Forêts
F 93 C3
Soumagne B 80 B1
Soumoulou F 145 A3
Souppes-sur-Loing
F 103 A4
Souprosse F 128 C2
Sourdeval F 88 B3
Soure P 154 A2
Sournia F 146 B3
Souro Pires P 149 B2
Sourpi GR 182 D4
Sours F 90 C1
Sousceyrac F 116 C2
Sousel P 155 C3
Soustons F 128 C1
Söğüt
Bilecik TR 187 B5
Burdur TR 189 B4
Soutelo de Montes
E 140 B2
Southam GB 44 A2
Southampton GB 44 C2
Southborough GB 45 B4
South Brent GB 42 B3
South Cave GB 40 B3
Southend GB 34 C2
Southend-on-Sea
GB 45 B4
South Hayling GB 44 C3
South Molton GB 42 A3
South Ockendon
GB 45 B4
South Petherton
GB 43 B4
Southport GB 38 A3
South Shields GB 37 B5
South Tawton GB 42 B3
Southwell GB 40 B3
Southwold GB 45 A5
South Woodham
Ferrers GB 45 B4
Söğütlu TR 187 B5
Souto P 148 B2
Soutochao E 141 C3
Souto da Carpalhosa
P 154 B2
Souvigny F 104 C2
Souzay-Champigny
F 102 B1
Soverato I 175 C2
Soveria Mannelli I 175 B2
Sövestad S 66 A2
Sovetsk RUS 12 A4
Sovići BIH 138 B3
Sovicille I 135 B4
Søvik N 198 C3
Sowerby GB 37 B5
Soyaux F 115 C4
Sozopol BG 17 D7
Spa B 80 B1
Spadafora I 177 A4
Spaichingen D 107 A3
Spakenburg NL 70 B2

Spalding GB 41 C3
Spálené Poříčí CZ .96 B1
Spalt D 94 B2
Spangenberg D ..82 A1
Spangereid N 52 B3
Spantekow D 74 A2
Sparanise I 170 B2
Sparbu N 199 B8
Sparkær DK 58 B2
Sparkford GB 43 A4
Sparreholm S 56 A2
Sparta = Sparti
  GR 184 B3
Spartà I 177 A4
Sparti = Sparta
  GR 184 B3
Spean Bridge GB .34 B3
Speicher D 92 B2
Speichersdorf D ..95 B3
Speke GB 38 A4
Spello I 136 C1
Spenge D 72 B1
Spennymoor GB ..37 B5
Spentrup DK 58 B3
Sperenberg D 74 B2
Sperlinga I 177 B3
Sperlonga I 169 B3
Spetalen N 54 A1
Spetses GR 184 B4
Speyer D 93 B4
Spézet F 100 A2
Spezzano Albanese
  I 174 B2
Spezzano della Sila
  I 174 B2
Spiddle IRL 28 A2
Spiegelau D 96 C1
Spiekeroog D 71 A4
Spiez CH 106 C2
Spigno Monferrato
  I 133 A4
Spijk NL 71 A3
Spijkenisse NL ...79 A4
Spilamberto I ...135 A4
Spili GR 185 D5
Spilimbergo I ...122 A1
Spilsby GB 41 B4
Spinazzola I ...172 B2
Spincourt F 92 B1
Spind N 52 B2
Spindleruv-Mlyn
  CZ 84 B3
Spinoso I 174 A1
Špišic Bukovica
  HR 124 B3
Spišská Belá SK .99 B4
Spišská Nová Ves
  SK 99 C4
Spišská Stará Ves
  SK 99 B4
Spišské-Hanušovce
  SK 99 B4
Spišské Podhradie
  SK 99 C4
Spišské Vlachy SK .99 C4
Spišský-Štvrtok
  SK 99 C4
Spital A 110 B1
Spital am Semmering
  A 110 B2
Spittal an der Drau
  A 109 C4
Spittle of Glenshee
  GB 35 B4
Spitz A 97 C3
Spjald DK 59 B1
Spjærøy N 54 A1
Spjelkavik N ...198 C3
Spjutsbygd S 63 B3
Split HR 138 B2
Splügen CH 107 C4
Spodsbjerg DK ...65 B3
Spofforth GB 40 B2
Spohle D 71 A5
Spoleto I 136 C1
Spoltore I 169 A4
Spondigna I ...108 C1
Sponvika N 54 A2
Spornitz D 73 A4
Spotorno I 133 A4
Spraitbach D 94 C1
Sprakensehl D ...72 B3
Spręcowo PL 69 B5
Spremberg D 84 A2
Spresiano I 122 B1
Sprimont B 80 B1
Springe D 72 B2
Sproatley GB 41 B3
Spydeberg N 54 A2
Spytkowice PL ...99 B3
Squillace I 175 C2
Squinzano I 173 B4
Sračinec HR 124 A2
Srbac BIH 124 B3
Srbobran SRB ...126 B1
Srebrenica BIH ..127 C1
Srebrenik BIH ...125 C4
Sredets BG 17 D7
Središče SLO ...124 A2
Šrem PL 76 B2
Sremska Mitrovica
  SRB 127 C1
Sremski Karlovci
  SRB 126 B1
Srní CZ 96 B1
Srnice Gornje BIH 125 C4
Šrock PL 86 A3
Šroda Śląska PL ..85 A4
Šroda Wielkopolski
  PL 76 B2
Srpska Crnja SRB 126 B2
Srpski Itebej SRB .126 B2
Srpski Miletić
  SRB 125 B5
Staatz A 97 C4
Stabbursnes N ..193 B8
Staberdorf D 65 B4

Stabroek B 79 A4
Stachy CZ 96 B1
Staðarfell IS ...190 B3
Stade D 72 A2
Staden B 78 B3
Stadl an der Mur
  A 109 B4
Stadskanaal NL ..71 B3
Stadtallendorf D ..81 B5
Stadthagen D 72 B2
Stadtilm D 82 B3
Stadtkyll D 80 B2
Stadtlauringen D .82 B2
Stadtlengsfeld D .82 B2
Stadtlohn D 71 C3
Stadtoldendorf D .82 A1
Stadtroda D 83 B3
Stadtsteinach D ..82 B3
Stäfa CH 107 B3
Staffanstorp S ...61 D3
Staffelstein D 82 B2
Staffin GB 31 B2
Stafford GB 40 C1
Stainach A 110 B1
Staindrop GB 37 B5
Staines-upon-Thames
  GB 44 B3
Stainville F 91 C5
Stainz A 110 C2
Staithes GB 37 B6
Staiti I 175 D2
Stäket S 57 A3
Stakroge DK 59 C1
Štalcerji SLO ...123 B3
Stalden CH 119 A4
Stalham GB 41 C5
Stalheim N 46 B3
Stallarholmen S ..56 A3
Ställberg S 50 C1
Ställdalen S 50 C1
Stallhofen A 110 B2
Stalon S 195 F6
Stalowa Wola PL ..12 C5
Stamford GB 40 C3
Stamford Bridge
  GB 40 B3
Stamnes N 46 B2
Stams A 108 B1
Stamsried D 95 B4
Stamsund N 194 B4
Stanford le Hope
  GB 45 B4
Stånga S 57 C4
Stange N 48 B3
Stanghella I 121 B4
Stanhope GB 37 B5
Staniši SRB 125 B5
Staňkov CZ 95 B5
Stankovci HR ...137 B4
Stanley GB 37 B5
Stans CH 106 C3
Stansted Mountfitchet
  GB 45 B4
Stanzach A 108 B1
Stapar SRB 125 B5
Staphorst NL 70 B3
Staplehurst GB ...45 B4
Stąporków PL 87 A4
Stara Baška HR ..123 C3
Starachowice PL ..87 A5
Stara Fužina SLO .122 A2
Stara Kamienica
  PL 84 B3
Stara Kiszewa PL .68 B3
Stará Ľubovňa SK .99 B4
Stara Moravica
  SRB 126 B1
Stara Novalja HR .137 A3
Stara Pazova SRB 127 C2
Stará Turá SK 98 C1
Staraya Russa RUS .9 D7
Stara Zagora BG ..17 D6
Stärbsnäs S 51 C6
Starčevo SRB ...127 C2
Staré Dlutowo PL .77 A4
Staré Hamry CZ ..98 B2
Staré Jablonki PL .69 B5
Staré Mesto CZ ..98 B1
Stare Pole PL 69 A4
Stare Sedlo CZ ...96 B2
Stare Stracze PL ..85 A4
Stargard Szczeciński
  PL 75 A4
Stårheim N 198 D2
Stari Banovci
  SRB 127 C2
Starigrad
  Ličko-Senjska
  HR 123 C3
  Splitsko-Dalmatinska
  HR 138 B2
Stari Gradac HR .124 B3
Starigrad-Paklenica
  HR 137 A4
Stari Jankovci HR .125 B4
Stari Majdan BIH .124 C2
Stari-Mikanovci
  HR 125 B4
Staritsa RUS 9 D9
Starkenbach A ...108 B1
Starnberg D 108 B2
Starogard D 75 A4
Starogard Gdański
  PL 69 B3
Starokonstyantyniv
  UA 13 D7
Staro Petrovo Selo
  HR 124 B3
Staro Selo
  HR 124 B1
  SRB 127 C2
Stary Brzozów PL .77 B5
Stary Dzierzgoń PL 69 B4
Starý Hrozenkov
  CZ 98 C1
Stary Jaroslaw PL .68 A1
Stary Plzenec CZ .96 B1
Stary Sącz PL 99 B4
Starý Smokovec
  SK 99 B4

Staryy Chartoriysk
  UA 13 C6
Staškov SK 98 B2
Stassfurt D 82 A3
Staszów PL 87 B5
Stathelle N 53 A5
Staufen D 106 B2
Staunton GB 39 C4
Stavang N 46 A2
Stavanger N 52 B1
Stavåsnäs S 49 B4
Stavby S 51 B5
Staveley GB 40 B2
Stavelot B 80 B1
Stavenisse NL ...79 A4
Stavern N 53 B6
Stavnäs S 55 A3
Stavoren NL 70 B2
Stavros
  CY 181 A1
  GR 183 C5
Stavroupoli GR ..183 B6
Stavseng N 47 A6
Stavsjø N 48 B2
Stavsnäs S 57 A4
Stawiszyn PL 76 C3
Steane N 53 A4
Steblevë AL 182 B2
Stechelberg CH ..106 C2
Stechovice CZ ...96 B2
Stechow D 73 B5
Steckborn CH ...107 B3
Stede Broek NL ..70 B2
Steeg A 107 B5
Steenbergen NL ..79 A4
Steenvoorde F ...78 B2
Steenwijk NL 70 B3
Štefanje HR 124 B2
Steffisburg CH ..106 C2
Stegaurach D 94 B2
Stege DK 65 B5
Stegelitz D 74 A2
Stegersbach A ...111 B3
Stegna PL 69 A4
Steimbke D 72 B2
Stein D 94 B3
Steinach
  A 108 B2
  Baden-Württemberg
  D 106 A3
  Bayern D 82 B2
  Thüringen D 82 B2
Stein an Rhein CH 107 B3
Steinau
  Bayern D 81 B5
  Niedersachsen D. 64 C1
Steinbeck D 74 B2
Steinberg am Rofan
  A 108 B2
Steindorf A 109 C5
Steine N 46 B2
Steinen D 106 B2
Steinfeld
  A 109 C4
  D 71 B5
Steinfurt D 71 B4
Steingaden D ...108 B1
Steinhagen D 72 B1
Steinheid D 82 B3
Steinheim
  Bayern D 107 A5
  Nordrhein-Westfalen
  D 81 A5
Steinhöfel D 74 B3
Steinhorst D 72 B3
Steinigtwolmsdorf
  D 84 A2
Steinkjer N 199 A8
Steinsholt N 53 A5
Stekene B 79 A4
Stelle D 72 A3
Stellendam NL ...79 A4
Stenåsa S 63 B4
Stenay F 91 B5
Stenberga S 62 A3
Stendal D 73 B4
Stenhammar S ...55 B4
Stenhamra S 57 A3
Stenhousemuir GB 35 B4
Stenløse DK 61 D2
Stensätra S 50 B3
Stensele S 195 E8
Stenstorp S 55 B4
Stenstrup DK 65 A3
Stenudden S 195 D8
Stenungsund S ...54 B2
Štěpánov CZ 98 B1
Stephanskirchen
  D 108 B3
Stepnica PL 74 A3
Stepojevac SRB ..127 C2
Stepping DK 59 C2
Sterbfritz D 82 B1
Sternberg D 65 C4
Šternberk CZ 98 B1
Sterup D 64 B2
Stes Maries-de-la-Mer
  F 131 B3
Stęszew PL 75 B5
Štěti CZ 84 B2
Stevenage GB ...44 B3
Stewarton GB ...36 A2
Steyerburg D 72 B2
Steyning GB 44 C3
Steyr A 110 A1
Stężyca PL 68 A2
Stezzano I 120 B2
Stia I 135 B4
Stibb Cross GB ..42 B2
Sticciano Scalo I .135 C4
Stidsvig S 61 C3
Stiens NL 70 A2
Stige DK 59 C3
Stigen S 54 B3
Stigliano I 174 A2
Stigtomta S 56 B2
Stilida GR 182 E4
Stilla N 192 C7
Stillington GB ...40 A2
Stilo I 175 C2

Stintino I 178 B2
Stio I 172 B1
Štip MK 182 B4
Stira GR 185 A5
Stirling GB 35 B4
Štitnik SK 99 C4
Štity CZ 97 B4
Stjärnhov S 56 A3
Stjärnsund S 50 B3
Stjørdalshalsen N 199 B7
Stobnica PL 87 A3
Stobno PL 75 A5
Stobreč HR 138 B2
Stochov CZ 84 B1
Stockach D 107 B4
Stöckalp CH 106 C3
Stockaryd S 62 A2
Stockbridge GB ..44 B2
Stockerau A 97 C4
Stockheim D 82 B3
Stockholm S 57 A4
Stockport GB 40 B1
Stocksbridge GB ..40 B2
Stockton-on-Tees
  GB 37 B5
Stod CZ 96 B1
Stöde S 200 D2
Stødi N 195 D6
Stöðvarfjörður
  IS 191 C12
Stoer GB 32 C1
Stoholm DK 58 B2
Stoke Ferry GB ...41 C4
Stoke Fleming GB .43 B3
Stoke Mandeville
  GB 44 B3
Stoke-on-Trent GB .40 B1
Stokesley GB 37 B5
Stokke N 54 A1
Stokkemarke DK ..65 B4
Stokken N 53 B4
Stokkseyri IS ...190 D4
Stokkvågen N ...195 D4
Stokmarknes N ..194 B5
Štoky CZ 97 B3
Stolac BIH 139 B3
Stolberg D 80 B2
Stolin BY 13 C7
Stollberg D 83 B4
Stöllet S 49 B5
Stollhamm D 71 A5
Stolno PL 76 A3
Stolpen D 84 A2
Stolzenau D 72 B2
Stompetoren NL ..70 B1
Ston HR 139 C3
Stonařov CZ 97 B3
Stone GB 40 C1
Stonehaven GB ..33 E4
Stonehouse GB ..36 A3
Stongfjorden N ..46 A2
Stonndalen N 47 B4
Stony Stratford GB 44 A3
Stopnica PL 87 B4
Storå S 56 A1
Storås N 198 B6
Storby FIN 51 B6
Stordal
  Møre og Romsdal
  N 198 C4
  Nord-Trøndelag
  N 199 B8
Store GB 33 B4
Storebø N 46 B2
Storebro S 62 A3
Store Damme DK .65 B5
Store Heddinge DK 65 A5
Store Herrestad S .66 A2
Store Levene S ...55 B3
Storelv N 192 B6
Store Molvik N ..193 B12
Støren N 199 B7
Store Skedvi S ...50 B2
Store Vika S 57 B3
Storfjellseter N ..199 D7
Storfjord N 192 C3
Storfjorden N ...198 C3
Storfors S 55 A5
Storforshei N ...195 D5
Storhøliseter N ..47 A6
Storjord N 195 D6
Storkow
  Brandenburg D ..74 B2
  Mecklenburg-
  Vorpommern D .74 A3
Storli N 198 C6
Storlien S 199 B9
Stornara I 171 B3
Stornoway GB ...31 A2
Storo I 121 B3
Storozhynets UA ..17 A6
Storrington GB ...44 C3
Storseleby S 200 B2
Storsjön S 50 A3
Storslett N 192 C5
Storsteinnes N ..192 C3
Storsund S 196 D3
Storuman S 195 E8
Störvattnet S ...199 C9
Storvik
  N 195 D4
  S 50 B3
Storvorde DK 58 B3
Storvreta S 51 C4
Štos SK 99 C4
Stössen D 83 A3
Stotel D 72 A1
Stötten D 108 B1
Stotternheim D ..82 A3
Stouby DK 59 C2
Stourbridge GB ..40 C1
Stourport-on-Severn
  GB 39 B4
Støvring DK 58 B2
Stow GB 35 C5
Stowbtsy BY 13 B7
Stowmarket GB ..45 A4
Stow-on-the-Wold
  GB 44 B1
Straach D 73 C5

Strabane GB 27 B3
Strachan GB 33 D4
Strachur GB 34 B2
Stracin MK 182 A4
Strackholt D 71 A4
Stradbally IRL ...29 B1
Stradella I 120 B2
Straelen D 80 A2
Stragari SRB 127 C2
Strakonice CZ ...96 B1
Strålsnäs S 55 B6
Stralsund D 66 B2
Strand N 48 A3
Stranda N 198 C3
Strandby DK 58 A3
Strandebarm N ..46 B3
Strandhill IRL 26 B2
Strandlykkja N ...48 B3
Strandvik N 46 B2
Strangford GB ...27 B5
Strängnäs S 56 A3
Strängsjö S 56 B2
Stráni CZ 98 C1
Stranice SLO ...123 A4
Stranorlar IRL ...26 B3
Stranraer GB 36 B1
Strasatti I 176 B1
Strasbourg F 93 C3
Strasburg D 74 A2
Strašice CZ 96 B1
Strässa S 56 A1
Strassburg A 110 C1
Strass im Steiermark
  A 110 C2
Strasskirchen D ..95 C4
Strasswalchen A .109 B4
Stratford-upon-Avon
  GB 44 A2
Strathaven GB ...36 A2
Strathdon GB 32 D3
Strathkanaird GB .32 D1
Strathpeffer GB ..32 D2
Strathy GB 32 C3
Strathyre GB 34 B3
Stratinska BIH ..124 C2
Stratton GB 42 B2
Straubing D 95 C4
Straulas I 178 B3
Straume N 53 A5
Straumen
  Nordland N 194 C6
  Nord-Trøndelag
  N 199 B8
Straumsjøen N ..194 B5
Straumsnes N ...194 C6
Straupitz D 74 C3
Strausberg D 74 B2
Straussfurt D 82 A3
Strawczyn PL 87 B4
Straža
  SLO 123 B4
  SRB 127 C3
Stražnad Nezárkou
  CZ 96 B2
Strážnice CZ 98 C1
Strážný CZ 96 C1
Stráž Pod Ralskem
  CZ 84 B2
Štrbské Pleso SK .99 B4
Strečno SK 98 B2
Street GB 43 A4
Strehla D 83 A5
Strekov SK 112 B2
Strem A 111 B3
Stremska-Rača
  SRB 127 C1
Strengberg A 110 A1
Strengelvåg N ...194 B6
Stresa I 119 B5
Streufdorf D 82 B2
Strib DK 59 C2
Striberg S 55 A5
Stříbro CZ 95 B4
Strichen GB 33 D4
Strigno I 121 A4
Strigova HR 111 C3
Strijen NL 79 A4
Strizivojna HR ...125 B4
Strmica HR 138 A2
Strmilov CZ 97 B3
Ströhen D 72 B1
Strokestown IRL ..28 A3
Stromberg
  Nordrhein-Westfalen
  D 81 A4
  Rheinland-Pfalz D .93 B3
Stromeferry GB ...31 B3
Strömnäs S 200 B2
Stromness GB ...33 C3
Strömsberg S 51 B4
Strömsbruk S ...200 E3
Strömsfors S 56 B2
Strömsnäsbruk S .61 C3
Strömstad S 54 B2
Strömsund
  Jämtland S 199 B12
  Västerbotten S ..195 E7
Stronachlachar GB 34 B3
Stróngoli I 174 B3
Stronie Śląskie PL .85 B4
Strontian GB 34 B2
Stroppiana I 119 B5
Stroud GB 43 A4
Stroumbi CY 181 B1
Stróża PL 99 B3
Strücklingen D ...71 A4
Struer DK 58 B1
Struga MK 182 B2
Strugi Krasnyye
  RUS 9 C6
Strumica MK 182 B4
Strumien PL 98 B2
Struy GB 32 D2
Stružec HR 124 B2
Stryków PL 77 C4
Stryn N 198 D3
Stryy UA 13 D5
Strzegocin PL 77 B5
Strzegom PL 85 B4

Strzegowo PL 77 B5
Strzelce PL 77 B4
Strzelce Krajeńskie
  PL 75 B4
Strzelce Kurowo
  PL 75 B4
Strzelce Opolskie
  PL 86 B2
Strzelin PL 85 B5
Strzelno PL 76 B3
Strzepcz PL 68 A3
Strzybnica PL 86 B2
Strzygi PL 77 A4
Stubbekøbing DK .65 B5
Stuben A 107 B5
Stubenberg A 110 B2
Stubline SRB 127 C2
Studená CZ 97 B3
Studenci HR 138 B3
Studenka CZ 98 B2
Studenzen A 110 B2
Studienka SK 98 C1
Studland GB 43 B5
Studley GB 44 A2
Studzienice PL ...68 A2
Stuer D 73 A5
Stugudal N 199 C8
Stugun S 200 C1
Stuhr D 72 A1
Stukenbrock D ...81 A4
Stülpe D 74 B2
Stupava SK 111 A4
Stupnik HR 124 B1
Stupsk PL 77 A5
Sturkö S 63 B3
Sturminster Newton
  GB 43 B4
Šturovo SK 112 B2
Sturton GB 40 B3
Stuttgart D 94 C1
Stvolny CZ 96 A1
Stykkishólmur IS .190 B3
Styri N 48 B3
Stysö S 60 B1
Suances E 142 A2
Subbiano I 135 B4
Subiaco I 169 B3
Subotica SRB ...126 A1
Subotište SRB ...127 C1
Sučany SK 98 B2
Suceava RO 17 B7
Sucha-Beskidzka
  PL 99 B3
Suchacz PL 69 B4
Suchań PL 75 A4
Suchdol nad Lužnice
  CZ 96 C2
Suchedniów PL ...87 A4
Suchorze PL 68 A2
Suchteln D 80 A2
Sucina E 165 B4
Suckow D 73 A4
Sućuraj HR 138 B3
Süderbrarup D ...64 B2
Süderlügum D ...64 B1
Sudoměřice u Bechyně
  CZ 96 B2
Sudovec HR 124 A2
Suðureyri IS 190 A2
Sueca E 159 B3
Suelli I 179 C3
Sugenheim D 94 B2
Sugères F 117 B3
Sugny B 91 B4
Suhl D 82 B2
Suhlendorf D 73 B3
Suhopolje HR ...124 B3
Suho Polje BIH ..125 C5
Şuhut TR 189 D5
Šuica BIH 138 B3
Suippes F 91 B4
Sukošan HR 137 A4
Sükösd H 125 A4
Sukow D 73 A4
Šul'a SK 99 C3
Suldalsosen N ...52 A2
Suldrup DK 58 B2
Sulechów PL 75 B4
Sulęcin PL 75 B4
Sulęczyno PL 68 A2
Sulejów PL 87 A3
Sulejówek PL 77 B6
Süleymanlı TR ..186 D2
Sulgen CH 107 B4
Sulibórz PL 75 A4
Sulina RO 17 C8
Sulingen D 72 B1
Suliszewo PL 75 A4
Sulitjelma N 195 C7
Sułkowice PL 99 B3
Süller TR 189 A4
Sully-sur-Loire F .103 B4
Sulmierzyce
  Łódzkie PL 86 A3
  Wielkopolskie PL .85 A5
Sulmona I 169 A3
Sülöğlu TR 186 A1
Sułów PL 85 A5
Sulsdorf D 65 B4
Sultandağı TR ...189 A6
Sülüklü TR 187 D7
Suluova TR 23 A8
Sulvik S 54 A3
Sülysáp H 112 B3
Sülz D 93 C4
Sulzbach
  Baden-Württemberg
  D 94 B1
  Baden-Württemberg
  D 94 C1
  Bayern D 93 B5
  Saarland D 92 B2
Sulzbach-Rosenberg
  D 95 B3
Sülze D 72 B3
Sulzfeld D 82 B2

Sumartin HR 138 B2
Sumburgh GB 33 B6
Sümeg H 111 C4
Sumiswald CH ...106 B2
Šumná CZ 97 C4
Šumperk CZ 97 B4
Šumvald CZ 98 B1
Sunbilla E 144 A2
Sünching D 95 C4
Sund
  FIN 51 B7
  S 54 A2
Sundborn S 50 B2
Sundby DK 58 B1
Sunde N 46 C2
Sunde bru N 53 B5
Sunderland GB ..37 B5
Sundern D 81 A4
Sundhultsbrunn S 62 A2
Sundnäs S 195 D8
Sundom S 196 D6
Sunds DK 59 B2
Sundsfjord N ...195 D5
Sundsvall S 200 D3
Sungurlu TR 23 A8
Suni I 178 B2
Sunja HR 124 B2
Sunnansjö S 50 B2
Sunnaryd S 60 B3
Sunndalsøra N ..198 C5
Sunne S 49 C5
Sunnemo S 49 C5
Sunnersberg S ...55 B4
Suolovuopmio N .192 C7
Suomussalmi FIN .3 D11
Suoyarvi RUS 9 A9
Super Sauze F ...132 A2
Supetar HR 138 B2
Supetarska Draga
  HR 123 C3
Supino I 169 B3
Šuplja Stijena
  MNE 139 B5
Surahammar S ...56 A2
Šurany SK 112 A2
Surazh BY 13 A9
Surbo I 173 B4
Surčin SRB 127 C2
Surgères F 114 B3
Surhuisterveen NL .70 A2
Súria E 147 C2
Surin F 115 B4
Surka N 48 B2
Surnadalsøra N ..198 C5
Sursee CH 106 B3
Surte S 60 B2
Surwold D 71 B4
Sury-le-Comtal F .117 B4
Susa I 119 B5
Šušara SRB 127 C3
Susch CH 107 C5
Susegana I 122 B1
Süsel D 65 B3
Sušice CZ 96 B1
Šušnjevica HR ...123 B3
Sussen D 94 C1
Susurluk TR 186 C3
Susz PL 69 B4
Sütçüler TR 189 B5
Sutivan HR 138 B2
Sutjeska SRB 126 B2
Sutri I 168 A2
Sutton GB 44 B3
Sutton Coldfield
  GB 40 C2
Sutton-in-Ashfield
  GB 40 B2
Sutton-on-Sea GB .41 B4
Sutton-on-Trent
  GB 40 B2
Sutton Scotney GB 44 B2
Sutton Valence GB .45 B4
Suvaja BIH 124 C2
Suvereto I 135 B3
Suze-la-Rousse F .131 A3
Suzzara I 121 C3
Svabensverk S ...50 A2
Svalbard IS 191 A10
Svalöv S 61 D3
Svanabyn S 200 B2
Svanberga S 51 C5
Svaneke DK 67 A4
Svanesund S 54 B2
Svanstein S 196 C6
Svappavaara S ...196 B4
Svärdsjö S 50 B3
Svarstad N 53 A5
Svärta S 56 B3
Svarta S 55 A5
Svartå S 55 A5
Svartbyn S 196 C5
Svärtinge S 56 B2
Svartlå S 196 D3
Svartnäs S 50 B3
Svartnes N 195 C6
Svarttjärn S 195 E7
Svatsum N 48 A1
Svätý Jur SK 111 A4
Svätý Peter SK ...112 B2
Svedala S 61 D3
Sveg S 199 C11
Sveindal N 52 B3
Sveio N 52 A1
Svejbæk DK 59 B2
Svelgen N 198 D2
Svelvik N 54 A1
Svendborg DK ...65 A3
Svene N 53 A5
Svenljunga S 60 B3
Svennevad S 56 A1
Svenstavik S 199 C11
Svenstrup DK 58 B2
Švermov CZ 84 B1
Sveti Ivan Zabno
  HR 124 B2

Ivan Zelina 124 B2
Nikole MK. 182 B3
Rok HR. 137 A4
a nad Sázavou 97 B3
yy RUS 69 A5
vinčenat HR 122 B2
a HR 123 C4
nik SK. 12 D4
ov CZ. 96 B1
jnac SRB 127 C3
ngrad BG 183 B8
dal N 54 A2
nult S 62 A3
na SK 98 C2
ninge 61 D1
....57 A4
tsa RUS 9 B8
ntov BG 17 D6
ach BY 13 B6
SK. 99 B4
vy CZ. 97 B4
lin SK 112 B2
vær N 194 B5
temyr N 46 A2
tland N 52 A1
cka CZ. 97 B4
novec SK. 98 B2
rya N 49 B4
tlahorsk BY 13 B8
tlincote GB 40 C2
fham GB 41 C4
nage GB 43 B5
nley GB. 45 B4
llinbar IRL 26 B3
nsea GB 39 C3
zędz PL 76 B2
ragh GB 27 B4
tki PL 69 B5
nica
nośląskie PL. 85 B4
uskie PL. 84 A3
nik PL. 12 C5
win PL. 67 C4
bodzice PL. 85 B4
bodzin PL. 75 B4
cie PL. 76 A3
dziebnia PL 77 A4
radów Zdrój 84 B3
rki PL. 85 B4
rzawa PL 85 A3
rozu PL. 67 C3
ta PL. 74 A3
ta Anna PL. 86 B3
tno PL. 75 B5
terbant NL 70 B2
don GB 44 B2
eshead GB 41 C3
ford IRL 26 C2
oujście PL. 66 C3
ton GB 35 C5
nica PL. 74 A3
rds IRL 30 A2
negacie PL 68 B2
S 56 B1
stroy RUS 9 B8
wice PL. 68 A1
evka RUS 9 E9
w PL. 86 A1
wice PL. 75 B4
eland N 52 A1
eland N 46 B2
D 72 B1
ylven N 198 C3
ng N 48 C2
N 198 C4
pister GB 33 A5
ngton GB. 36 A3
onds Yat GB. 39 C4
awsko-Pomorskie 76 A2
elkopolskie PL. 68 B1
rum S. 62 A4
lebäck S. 49 B4
äjärvi FIN. 197 B8
adbattyán H 112 B2
adegyháza H 112 B2
adszállás H 112 C3
lek PL. 86 A2
ol H 113 B4
ály H. 112 C2
cs H 112 C2
már H. 112 C3
anta H. 125 B4
sa PL. 87 A4
kszentmárton 112 C3
onna H 99 C4
nocin PL. 76 A2
notuły PL. 75 B3
y H 111 B4
vas H 113 C4
vaskó H 113 B4
zvár H. 125 A4
halombatta 112 B2
awa PL. 99 B4
awnica PL 99 B4
ecin PL. 74 A3
ecinek PL. 68 B1
ekociny PL. 87 B3
erców PL. 86 A3
ucin PL. 87 B5
uczarz PL 75 A5
uki PL. 77 B5
urowa PL. 87 B4
zyrk PL. 99 B3
ytna PL. 85 B4
ysу PL. 77 A5
zyty PL. 86 A2
csény H 112 A3
derkény H 125 B4
dres H 112 C2
ged H 126 A2
ghalom H 113 B5
gvár H. 113 C4

Székesfehérvár H 112 B2
Székkutas H 113 C4
Szekszárd H 125 A4
Szemplino Czarne PL. 77 A5
Szemud PL. 68 A3
Szendehely H 112 B3
Szendrő H 99 C4
Szentendre H. 112 B3
Szentes H 113 C4
Szentgotthárd H 111 C3
Szentlászló H 125 A3
Szentlőrinc H. 125 A3
Szentmártonkáta H 113 B3
Szenyér H 111 C4
Szeremle H 125 A4
Szerencs H 113 A5
Szerep H 113 B5
Szigetszentmiklós H 112 B3
Szigetvár H 125 A3
Szikáncs H. 126 A2
Szikszó H. 113 A4
Szil H 111 B4
Szilvásvárad H 113 A4
Szklarska Poreba PL. 84 B3
Szlichtyngowa PL. 85 A4
Szob H 112 B2
Szolnok H 113 B4
Szombathely H 111 B3
Szorosad H 112 C2
Szpetal Graniczny PL. 77 B4
Szprotawa PL 84 A3
Szreńsk PL. 77 A5
Sztum PL. 69 B4
Sztutowo PL. 69 A4
Szubin PL. 76 A2
Szücsi H. 113 B3
Szulmierz PL. 77 B5
Szulok H 124 A3
Szumanie PL. 77 B4
Szwecja PL 75 A5
Szydłów
Łódzkie PL. 86 A3
Świętokrzyskie PL 87 B5
Szydłowiec PL. 87 A4
Szydlowo PL. 77 A5
Szydłowo PL. 75 A5
Szymanów PL. 77 B5
Szynkielów PL. 86 A2

T
Taastrup DK 61 D2
Tab H 112 C2
Tabanera la Luenga E 151 A3
Tabaqueros E 158 B2
Tábara E 149 A4
Tabenera de Cerrato E 142 B2
Taberg S. 62 A2
Tabernas E 164 B2
Taboada E 140 B3
Taboadela E 140 B3
Tábor CZ 96 B2
Táborfalva H 112 B3
Taborište HR 124 B2
Tábua P 148 B1
Tabuaco P 148 A2
Tabuenca E 152 A2
Tabuyo del Monte E 141 B4
Täby S 57 A4
Tác H 112 B2
Tachov CZ. 95 B4
Tadcaster GB. 40 B2
Tadley GB 44 B2
Tafalla E 144 B2
Tafjord N 198 C4
Taganheira P 160 B1
Tågarp S 61 D2
Tággia I 133 B3
Tagliacozzo I 169 A3
Táglio di Po I 121 B5
Tagnon F 91 B4
Tahal E 164 B2
Tahitótfalu H 112 B3
Tahtaköprü TR. 187 C4
Tailfingen D 107 A4
Taillis F 101 A4
Tain GB 32 D2
Tain-l'Hermitage F. 117 B4
Taipadas P 154 C2
Taivalkoski FIN 197 D11
Takene S 55 A4
Takovo SRB. 127 C2
Taksony H 112 B3
Tal E 140 B2
Talachyn BY. 13 A8
Talamello I 135 B5
Talamone I 168 A1
Talant F 105 B3
Talarrubias E 156 A2
Talaván E 155 B4
Talavera de la Reina E 150 C3
Talavera la Real E 155 C4
Talayuela E 150 C2
Talayuelas E 159 B2
Talgarth GB 39 C3
Talgje N 52 A1
Talhadas P 148 B1
Táliga E 155 C3
Talizat F 116 B3
Tálknafjörður IS 190 B2
Talla I 135 B4
Talladale GB 31 B3
Tallaght IRL 30 A2
Tallard F 132 A2
Tällberg S. 50 B1
Tallberg S. 196 C5
Tallinn EST 8 C4

Talloires F 118 B3
Tallow IRL 29 B3
Tallsjö S. 200 B4
Tallvik S. 196 C5
Talmay F 105 B4
Talmont-St Hilaire F 114 B2
Talmont-sur-Gironde F. 114 C3
Talne UA. 13 D9
Talsano I 173 B3
Talsi LV. 8 D3
Talvik N 192 B6
Talybont GB. 39 B3
Tal-Y-Llyn GB. 38 B3
Tamajón E 151 B4
Tamame E 149 A4
Tamames E 149 B4
Tamarit de Mar E. 147 C2
Tamarite de Litera E 145 C4
Tamariu E. 147 C4
Tamási H 112 C2
Tambach-Dietharz D 82 B2
Tameza E 141 A4
Tammisaari FIN. 8 B3
Tampere FIN 8 B3
Tamsweg A 109 B4
Tamurejo E 156 B3
Tamworth GB. 40 C2
Tana bru N 193 B12
Tañabueyes E 143 B3
Tanakajd H. 111 B3
Tananger N 52 B1
Tanaunella I 178 B3
Tancarville F 89 A4
Tandsjöborg S. 199 D11
Tånga S 61 C2
Tangelic H 112 C2
Tangen N 48 B3
Tangerhütte D 73 B4
Tangermünde D. 73 B4
Tanhua FIN 197 B10
Taninges F 118 A3
Tankavaara FIN 197 A10
Tann D 82 B2
Tanna D 83 B3
Tannadice GB 35 B5
Tannåker S. 60 C3
Tännäs S 199 C9
Tannay
Ardennes F 91 B4
Nièvre F 104 B2
Tannenbergsthal D 83 B4
Tännesberg D 95 B4
Tannheim A 108 B1
Tannila FIN. 197 D8
Tanowo PL. 74 A3
Tanum S. 54 B2
Tanumshede S 54 B2
Tanus F 130 A1
Tanvald CZ. 84 B3
Taormina I 177 B4
Tapa EST 8 C4
Tapia de Casariego E 141 A4
Tapio F 146 A2
Tápióbicske H. 112 B3
Tápiógyörgye H 113 B3
Tápióság H. 112 B3
Tápiószecső H 112 B3
Tápiószele H. 113 B3
Tápiószentmárton H 113 B3
Tapolca H. 111 C4
Tapolcafő H 111 B4
Tar HR 122 B2
Tarabo S. 60 B2
Taradell E 147 C3
Taraklı TR. 187 B5
Taramundi E 141 A3
Tarancón E 151 B4
Táranto I 173 B3
Tarare F 117 B4
Tarascon F. 131 B3
Tarascon-sur-Ariège F. 146 B2
Tarashcha UA 13 D9
Tarazona E 144 C2
Tarazona de la Mancha E 158 B2
Tarbena E 159 C3
Tarbert
GB 34 C2
IRL 29 B2
Tarbes F. 145 A4
Tarbet GB. 34 B3
Tarcento I 122 A2
Tarczyn PL. 77 C5
Tardajos E 143 B3
Tardelcuende E 151 A5
Tardets-Sorholus F. 144 A3
Tardienta E 145 C3
Tärendö S 196 B5
Tarifa E 162 B2
Tariquejas E. 161 B2
Tarján H 112 B2
Tárkany H 112 B2
Tarland GB. 33 D4
Tarlow PL. 87 A5
Tarm DK. 59 C1
Tarmstedt D. 72 A2
Tärnaby S 195 E6
Tarnalelesz H 113 A4
Tarnaörs H. 113 B4
Tárnáveni RO 17 B6
Tärnet N. 193 C14

Tarnobrzeg PL. 87 B5
Tarnos F 128 C1
Tarnów
Lubuskie PL. 75 B3
Małopolskie PL 87 B4
Tarnowo Podgórne PL. 75 B5
Tarnowskie Góry PL. 86 B2
Tärnsjö S. 51 B3
Tårnvik N 194 C6
Tarouca P 148 A2
Tarp D 64 B2
Tarquinia I 168 A1
Tarquinia Lido I. 168 A1
Tarragona E 147 C2
Tårrajaur S. 196 C2
Tàrrega E 147 C2
Tarrenz A 108 B1
Tårs
Nordjyllands DK. 58 A3
Storstrøms DK. 65 B4
Tarsia I 174 B2
Tarsus TR. 23 C8
Tartas F 128 C2
Tartu EST. 8 C5
Tarves GB 33 D4
Tarvisio I 109 C4
Taşağıl TR 189 C6
Tåsjö S 200 C1
Tasköprü TR 23 A8
Tasov CZ. 97 B4
Tasovčići BIH. 139 B3
Taşucuo TR. 23 C7
Tát H. 112 B2
Tata H. 112 B2
Tatabánya H. 112 B2
Tataháza H. 126 A1
Tåtanfor S 61 C2
Tatarbunary UA. 17 C8
Tatárszentgyörgy H 112 B3
Tatranská-Lomnica SK. 99 B4
Taucha D. 83 A4
Taufkirchen D 95 C4
Taufkirchen an der
Pram A. 96 C1
Taulé F. 100 A2
Taulignan F 131 A3
Taulov DK. 59 C2
Taunton GB. 43 A4
Taunusstein D. 81 B4
Tauragė LT. 12 A5
Taurianova I. 175 C2
Taurisano I. 173 C4
Tauste E 144 C2
Tauves F 116 B2
Tavankut SRB 126 A1
Tavannes CH. 106 B2
Tavarnelle val di Pesa I 135 B4
Tavas TR 188 B4
Tavaux F 105 B4
Tävelsås S. 62 B2
Taverna I 175 B2
Taverne CH 120 A1
Tavernelle I 135 B5
Tavernes de la
Valldigna E 159 B3
Tavérnola Bergamasca I 120 B3
Taverny F 90 B2
Tavescan E 146 B2
Taviano I 173 C4
Tavira P 160 B2
Tavistock GB 42 B2
Tavşanlı TR 187 C4
Taynuilt GB. 34 B2
Tayport GB. 35 B5
Tázlár H. 112 C3
Tazones E 142 A1
Tczew PL. 69 A3
Tczów PL. 87 A5
Teangue GB. 31 B3
Teano I 170 B2
Teba E 162 B3
Tebay GB. 37 B4
Techendorf A 109 C4
Tecklenburg D. 71 B4
Tecko-matorp S. 61 D3
Tecuci RO 17 C7
Tefenni TR. 189 B4
Tegelsmora S 51 B4
Tegernsee D 108 B2
Teggiano I 172 B1
Tegoleto I 135 B4
Teichel D. 82 B3
Teignmouth GB. 43 B3
Teillay F 101 B4
Teillet F 130 B1
Teisendorf D 109 B3
Teistungen D 82 A2
Teixeiro E 140 A2
Tejada de Tiétar E 150 B2
Tejado E 152 A1
Tejares E 150 B2
Tejn DK. 67 A3
Teke TR 187 A4
Tekirdağ TR. 186 B2
Tekovské-Lužany SK 112 A2
Telavåg N 46 B1
Telč CZ. 97 B3
Telese Terme I 170 B2
Telford GB 38 B4
Telfs A. 108 B2
Telgárt SK 99 C4
Telgte D 71 C4
Tellingstedt D 64 B2
Telšiai LT 8 E3
Telti I 178 B3
Teltow D. 74 B2
Tembleque E 157 A4
Temelin CZ. 96 B2
Temerin SRB 126 B1
Temiño E 143 B3

Témpio Pausánia I 178 B3
Templederry IRL 28 B3
Templemore IRL 28 B4
Temple Sowerby GB 37 B4
Templin D. 74 A2
Temse B 79 A4
Tenay F 118 B2
Ten Boer NL 71 A3
Tenbury Wells GB 39 B4
Tenby GB 39 C2
Tence F 117 B4
Tende F 133 A3
Tenhult S 62 A2
Tenja HR 125 B4
Tenneville B. 92 A1
Tennevoll N 194 B8
Tensta S 51 B4
Tenterden GB 45 B4
Teo E 140 B2
Teora I 172 B1
Tepasto FIN 196 B7
Tepelenë AL. 182 C2
Teplá CZ. 95 B4
Teplice CZ. 84 B1
Teplička nad Váhom SK 98 B2
Tepsa FIN. 197 B8
Tera E 143 C4
Téramo I. 169 A3
Ter Apel NL 71 B4
Terborg NL. 71 C3
Terchová SK 99 B3
Terebovlya UA. 13 D6
Teremia Mare RO 126 B2
Terena P. 155 C3
Terešov CZ. 96 B1
Terezin CZ. 84 B2
Terezino Polje HR 124 B3
Tergnier F 90 B3
Teriberka RUS 3 B11
Terlizzi I 171 B4
Termas de Monfortinho P 155 A4
Terme di Súio I 169 B3
Terme di Valdieri I 133 A3
Termens E 145 C4
Termes F 116 C3
Términi Imerese I 176 B2
Terminillo I. 169 A2
Térmoli I. 170 B3
Termonfeckin IRL. 27 C4
Ternberg A. 110 B1
Terndrup DK. 58 B3
Terneuzen NL 79 A3
Terni I 168 A2
Ternitz A. 111 B3
Ternopil UA. 13 D6
Terpni GR. 183 C5
Terracina I 169 B3
Terråk N 195 E3
Terralba I 179 C2
Terranova di Pollino I 174 B2
Terranova di Sibari I 174 B2
Terras do Bouro P 148 A1
Terrasini I 176 A2
Terrassa E 147 C3
Terrasson-Lavilledieu F. 129 A4
Terrazos E 143 B3
Terriente E 152 B2
Terrugem P 155 C3
Tertenía I 179 C3
Teruel E 152 B2
Tervola FIN 196 C7
Tervuren B 79 B4
Terzaga E. 152 B2
Tešanj BIH 125 C3
Tésáske-Mlyňany SK 98 C2
Teslić BIH. 125 C3
Tessin D 66 B1
Tessy-sur-Vire F. 88 B2
Tét H 111 B4
Tetbury GB. 43 A4
Teterchen F 92 B2
Teterow D. 65 C5
Teteven BG. 17 D6
Tetiyev UA. 13 D8
Tetovo MK. 182 A2
Tettau D 82 B3
Tettnang D 107 B4
Teublitz D. 95 B4
Teuchern D. 83 A4
Teulada
E 159 C4
I 179 D2
Teupitz D. 74 B2
Teurajärvi S. 196 C5
Teutschenthal D 83 A3
Tevel H 112 C2
Teviothead GB. 36 A4
Tewkesbury GB. 39 C4
Thale D. 82 A3
Thalfang D. 92 B2
Thalgau A. 109 B4
Thalkirch CH. 107 C4
Thalmässing D 95 B3
Thalwil CH. 107 B3
Thame GB. 44 B3
Thann F 106 B2
Thannhausen D. 94 C2
Thaon-les-Vosges F. 105 A5
Tharandt D. 83 B5
Tharsis E 161 B2
Thasos GR. 183 C6
Thatcham GB. 44 B2
Thaxted GB. 45 B4
Thayngen CH 107 B3
Theale GB. 44 B2
The Barony GB. 33 B3
Thebes = Thiva GR. 185 A4

Theding-hausen D 72 B2
Theessen D. 73 B5
The Hague = 's-Gravenhage NL. 70 B1
Themar D. 82 B2
The Mumbles GB. 39 C3
Thénezay F 102 C1
Thenon F 129 A4
Therouanne F. 78 B2
Thessaloniki = Salonica GR. 182 C4
Thetford GB. 45 A4
Theux B 80 B1
Thézar-les-Corbières F. 146 A3
Thèze F 145 A3
Thiberville F 89 A4
Thibie F 91 C4
Thiéblemont-Farémont F. 91 C4
Thiendorf D 84 A1
Thiene I 121 B4
Thierrens CH 106 C1
Thiers F 117 B3
Thiesi I 178 B2
Thiessow D 66 B2
Thiezac F 116 B2
Þingeyri IS 190 B2
Þingvellir IS 190 C4
Thionville F 92 B2
Thira GR 185 C6
Thiron-Gardais F. 89 B4
Thirsk GB. 37 B5
Thisted DK. 58 B1
Thiva = Thebes GR. 185 A4
Thivars F 90 C1
Thiviers F 115 C4
Thizy F 117 A4
Tholen NL 79 A4
Tholey D 92 B3
Thomas Street IRL. 28 A3
Thomastown IRL. 30 B1
Thônes F 118 B3
Thonnance-les-Joinville F 91 C5
Thonon-les-Bains F. 118 A3
Thorame-Basse F 132 A2
Thorame-Haute F. 132 A2
Thorens-Glières F 118 A3
Thorigny-sur-Oreuse F. 91 C3
Thörl A. 110 B2
Þorlákshöfn IS 190 D4
Thornaby on Tees GB. 37 B5
Thornbury GB 43 A4
Thorne GB. 40 B3
Thornhill
Dumfries & Galloway GB. 36 A3
Stirling GB 35 B3
Thornthwaite GB. 36 B3
Thornton-le-Dale GB. 40 A3
Þórshöfn IS 191 A10
Thouarcé F 102 B1
Thouars F. 102 C1
Thrapston GB. 44 A3
Threlkeld GB. 36 B3
Thrumster GB 32 C3
Thueyts F 117 C4
Thuin B 79 B4
Thuir F 146 B3
Thumau D 95 A3
Thun CH. 106 C2
Thuret F 116 B3
Thurey F 105 C4
Thüringen A. 107 B4
Thurins F 117 B4
Thürkow D. 65 C5
Thurles IRL 29 B4
Thurmaston GB. 40 C2
Thurø By DK. 65 A3
Thursby GB. 36 B3
Thurso GB. 32 C3
Thury-Harcourt F. 89 B3
Thusis CH. 107 C4
Þykkvibær IS. 190 D5
Thyregod DK. 59 C2
Tibi E 159 C3
Tibro S. 55 B5
Tidaholm S. 55 B4
Tidan S. 55 B5
Tidersrum S. 62 A3
Tiedra E. 150 A2
Tiefenbach D. 95 B4
Tiefencastel CH. 107 C4
Tiefenort D. 82 B2
Tiefensee D. 74 B2
Tiel NL 79 A5
Tielmes E 151 B4
Tielt B. 78 A3
Tienen B. 79 B4
Tiengen D. 106 B3
Tiercé F 102 B1
Tierga E. 152 A2
Tiermas E. 144 B2
Tierp S. 51 B4
Tierrantona E. 145 B4
Tighina MD. 17 B8
Tighnabruaich GB. 34 C2
Tignes F. 119 B3
Tigy F. 103 B4
Tihany H. 112 C1
Tijnje NL. 70 A2
Tijola E. 164 B2
Tikhvin RUS. 9 C8
Til Châtel F 105 B4
Tilh F 128 C2
Tillac F. 145 A4
Tillberga S. 56 A2
Tille F. 90 B2
Tillicoultry GB. 35 B4
Tilloy Bellay F. 91 B4
Tilly F 115 B5
Tilly-sur-Seulles F. 88 A3

Tim DK 59 B1
Timau I 109 C4
Timbaki GR 185 D5
Timi CY 181 B1
Timişoara RO 126 B3
Timmele S. 60 B3
Timmendorfer Strand D 65 C3
Timmernabben S. 62 B4
Timmersdala S 55 B4
Timoleague IRL 29 C3
Timolin IRL 30 B2
Timrå S. 200 D3
Timsfors S. 61 C3
Timsgearraidh GB. 31 A1
Tinajas E 152 B1
Tinalhas P 155 B3
Tinchebray F 88 B3
Tincques F. 78 B2
Tineo E. 141 A4
Tinglev DK. 64 B2
Tingsryd S. 63 B2
Tingstäde S. 57 C4
Tingvoll N 198 C5
Tinlot B. 79 B5
Tinnoset N 53 A5
Tinos GR. 185 B6
Tintagel GB 42 B2
Tinténiac F. 101 A4
Tintern GB. 39 C4
Tintigny B 92 B1
Tione di Trento I 121 A3
Tipperary IRL. 29 B3
Tiptree GB. 45 B4
Tirana = Tiranë AL. 182 B1
Tiranë = Tirana AL. 182 B1
Tirano I. 120 A3
Tiraspol MD. 17 B8
Tire TR 188 A2
Tires I. 108 C2
Tiriez E. 158 C1
Tirig E. 153 B4
Tiriolo I. 175 C2
Tírnavos GR. 182 D4
Tirrénia I. 134 B3
Tirschenreuth D. 95 B4
Tirstrup DK. 59 B3
Tirteafuera E. 157 B3
Tisno HR. 137 B4
Tišnov CZ. 97 B4
Tisovec SK. 99 C3
Tisselskog S. 54 B3
Tistedal N. 54 A2
Tistrup DK. 59 C1
Tisvildeleje DK. 61 C2
Tiszaalpár H. 113 C3
Tiszabö H. 113 B4
Tiszacsége H. 113 B5
Tiszadorogma H. 113 B4
Tiszaföldvár H. 113 C4
Tiszafüred H. 113 B4
Tiszajenő H. 113 B4
Tiszakécske H. 113 C4
Tiszakeszi H. 113 B4
Tiszakürt H. 113 C4
Tiszalök H. 113 A5
Tiszalúc H. 113 A5
Tiszanána H. 113 B4
Tiszaörs H. 113 B4
Tiszaroff H. 113 B4
Tiszasüly H. 113 B4
Tiszasziget H. 126 A2
Tiszaszőlős H. 113 B4
Tiszaújváros H. 113 B5
Tiszavasvári H. 113 B5
Titaguas E 159 B2
Titel SRB 126 B2
Titisee-Neustadt D. 106 B3
Tito I. 172 B1
Titova Korenica HR. 123 C4
Titran N 198 B5
Tittling D. 96 C1
Tittmoning D. 109 A3
Titz D. 80 A2
Tiurajärvi FIN. 196 B7
Tived S. 55 B5
Tiverton GB. 43 B3
Tivisa E 153 A4
Tívoli I 168 B2
Tizsadob H. 113 A5
Tjällmo S. 56 B1
Tjåmotis S. 195 D9
Tjæreborg DK. 59 C1
Tjautjas S. 196 B3
Tjøme N. 54 A1
Tjong N 195 D4
Tjonnefoss N. 53 B4
Tjörn IS. 190 B5
Tjörnarp S. 61 D3
Tjøtta N 195 E3
Tkon HR. 137 B4
Tleń PL. 68 B3
Tlmače SK. 98 C2
Tłuchowo PL. 77 B4
Tlumačov CZ. 98 B1
Tóalmas H. 112 B3
Toano I. 134 A3
Toba D. 82 A2
Tobarra E. 158 C2
Tobermore GB. 27 B4
Tobermory GB. 34 B1
Toberonochy GB. 34 B2
Tobha Mor GB. 31 B1
Tobo S. 51 B4
Tocane-St Apre F 129 A3
Tocha P 148 B1
Tocina E 162 A2
Töcksfors S. 54 A2
Tocón E 163 A4
Todal N. 198 C5
Todi I. 136 C1
Todmorden GB. 40 B1
Todorici BIH. 138 A3
Todtmoos D 106 B3

Todtnau D 106 B2
Toén E 140 B3
Tofta
　Gotland S 57 C4
　Skaraborg S 55 B4
Toftbyn S 50 B2
Tofte N 54 A1
Töftedal S 54 B2
Tofterup DK 59 C1
Toftlund DK 59 C2
Tófü H 125 A4
Tohmo FIN 197 C10
Tokaj H 113 A5
Tokarnia PL 87 B4
Tokary PL 76 C3
Tokod H 112 B2
Tököl H 112 B2
Tolastadh bho Thuath
　GB 31 A2
Toledo E 151 C3
Tolentino I 136 B2
Tolfa I 168 A1
Tolg S 62 A2
Tolga N 199 C8
Tolkmicko PL 69 A4
Tollarp S 61 D3
Tollered S 60 B2
Tølløse DK 61 D1
Tolmachevo RUS . . . 9 C6
Tolmezzo I 122 A2
Tolmin SLO 122 A2
Tolna H 112 C2
Tolnanémedi H . . . 112 C2
Tolob GB 33 B5
Tolosa
　E 144 A1
　P 155 B3
Tolox E 162 B3
Tolpuddle GB 43 B4
Tolva
　E 145 B4
　FIN 197 C11
Tolve I 172 B2
Tomar P 154 B2
Tomaševac SRB . . 126 B2
Tomašica BIH . . . 124 C2
Tomášikovo SK . . . 111 A4
Tomašouka BY . . . 13 C5
Tomášovce SK . . . 99 C3
Tomaszów Mazowiecki
　PL 87 A4
Tomatin GB 32 D3
Tombeboeuf F . . . 129 B3
Tomdoun GB 32 D1
Tomelilla S 66 A2
Tomellosa E 151 B5
Tomelloso E 157 A4
Tomiño E 140 C2
Tomintoul GB 32 D3
Tomislavgrad BIH 138 B3
Tomisław PL 84 A3
Tomisławice PL . . . 76 B3
Tomnavoulin GB . . 32 D3
Tompa H 126 A1
Tompaládony H . . 111 B3
Tomra N 198 C3
Tomter N 54 A1
Tona E 147 C3
Tonara I 179 B3
Tonbridge GB 45 B4
Tondela P 148 B1
Tønder DK 64 B1
Tongeren B 79 B5
Tongue GB 32 C2
Tönisvorst D 80 A2
Tønjum N 47 A4
Tonkopuro FIN . . 197 C11
Tonnay-Boutonne
　F 114 C3
Tonnay-Charente
　F 114 C3
Tonneins F 129 B3
Tonnerre F 104 B2
Tonnes N 195 D4
Tönning D 64 B1
Tonsåsen N 47 B6
Tønsberg N 54 A1
Tonstad N 52 B2
Toomyvara IRL . . . 28 B3
Toormore IRL 29 C2
Topares E 164 B2
Topas E 150 A2
Toplița RO 17 B6
Topola SRB 127 C2
Topolčani MK . . . 182 B3
Topol'čany SK . . . 98 C2
Topol'čianky SK . . . 98 C2
Topolje HR 124 B2
Topólka PL 76 B3
Topol'niky SK . . . 111 B4
Topolovățu Mare
　RO 126 B3
Toponár H 125 A3
Toporów PL 75 B4
Topsham GB 43 B3
Topusko HR 124 B1
Toques E 140 B3
Torà E 147 C2
Toral de los Guzmanes
　E 142 B1
Toral de los Vados
　E 141 B4
Torbalı TR 188 A2
Torbjörntorp S . . . 55 B4
Torbole I 121 B3
Torchiarolo I 173 B4
Torcross GB 43 B3
Torcy-le-Petit F . . . 89 A5
Torda SRB 126 B2
Tørdal N 53 A4
Tordehumos E . . . 142 C1
Tordera E 147 C3
Tordesillas E 150 A2
Tordesilos E 152 B2
Töre S 196 D5
Töreboda S 55 B5
Toreby DK 65 B4

Torekov S 61 C2
Torella dei Lombardi
　I 170 C3
Torelló E 147 B3
Toreno E 141 B4
Torfou F 114 A2
Torgau D 83 A5
Torgelow D 74 A3
Torgueda P 148 A2
Torhamn S 63 B3
Torhop N 193 B11
Torhout B 78 A3
Torigni-sur-Vire F . . 88 A3
Torija E 151 B4
Toril E 152 B2
Torino = Turin I . . . 119 B4
Toritto I 171 C4
Torkovichi RUS . . . 9 C7
Torla E 145 B3
Tormac RO 126 B3
Törmänen FIN . . 193 D11
Tormestorp S 61 C3
Tórmini I 121 B3
Tornada P 154 B1
Tornal'a SK 99 C4
Tornavacas E . . . 150 B2
Tornby DK 58 A2
Tornesch D 72 A2
Tornes GB 32 D2
Torniella I 135 B4
Tornimparte I . . . 169 A3
Tornio FIN 196 D7
Tornjoš SRB 126 B1
Toro E 150 A2
Törökszentmiklós
　H 113 B4
Toropets RUS 9 D7
Torpa S 61 C3
Torpè I 178 B3
Torphins GB 33 D4
Torpo N 47 B5
Torpoint GB 42 B2
Torpsbruk S 62 A2
Torquay GB 43 B3
Torquemada E . . . 142 B2
Torralba de Burgo
　E 151 A5
Torralba de Calatrava
　E 157 A4
Torrão P 154 C2
Torre Annunziata
　I 170 C2
Torreblacos E . . . 143 C4
Torreblanca E . . . 153 B4
Torreblascopedro
　E 157 B4
Torrecaballeros E 151 A3
Torrecampo E . . . 156 B3
Torre Canne I . . . 173 B3
Torre Cardela E . . 163 A4
Torrecilla E 152 B1
Torrecilla de la Jara
　E 156 A3
Torrecilla de la Orden
　E 150 A2
Torrecilla del Pinar
　E 151 A3
Torrecilla en Cameros
　E 143 B4
Torrecillas de la Tiesa
　E 156 A2
Torre das Vargens
　P 154 B3
Torre de Coelheiros
　P 154 C3
Torre de Dom Chama
　P 149 A2
Torre de Juan Abad
　E 157 B4
Torre de la Higuera
　E 161 B3
Torre del Bierzo E 141 B4
Torre del Burgo E 151 B4
Torre del Campo
　E 163 A4
Torre del Greco I . 170 C2
Torre del Lago Puccini
　I 134 B3
Torre dell'Orso I . 173 B4
Torre del Mar E . . 163 B3
Torredembarra E . 147 C2
Torre de Miguel
　Sesmero E . . . 155 C4
Torre de Moncorvo
　P 149 A2
Torre de Santa Maria
　E 156 A1
Torredonjimeno E 163 A4
Torre do Terranho
　P 148 B2
Torre Faro I 177 A4
Torregrosa E . . . 147 C1
Torreira P 148 B1
Torrejoncillo E . . 155 B4
Torrejón de Ardoz
　E 151 B4
Torrejón de la Calzada
　E 151 B4
Torrejón del Rey
　E 151 B4
Torrejon el Rubio
　E 156 A1
Torrelaguna E . . . 151 B4
Torrelapaja E . . . 152 A2
Torre la Ribera E 145 B4
Torrelavega E . . . 142 A2
Torrelobatón E . . 150 A2
Torrelodones E . . 151 B4
Torre los Negros
　E 152 B2
Torremanzanas E 159 C3
Torremayor E . . . 155 C4
Torremezzo di
　Falconara I . . . 174 B2
Torremocha E . . . 156 A1
Torremolinos E . . 163 B3
Torrenieri I 135 B4

Torrenostra E . . . 153 B4
Torrenova I 168 B2
Torrent E 159 B3
Torrente de Cinca
　E 153 A4
Torrenueva
　Ciudad Real E . 157 B4
　Granada E . . . 163 B4
Torreorgaz E . . . 155 B4
Torre Orsáia I . . . 172 B1
Torre-Pacheco E . 165 B4
Torre Péllice I . . . 119 C4
Torreperogil E . . . 157 B4
Torres E 163 A4
Torresandino E . . 143 C3
Torre Santa Susanna
　I 173 B3
Torres-Cabrera E . 163 A3
Torres de la Alameda
　E 151 B4
Torres Novas P . . 154 B2
Torres Vedras P . 154 B1
Torrevieja E 165 B4
Torricella I 173 B3
Torri del Benaco I 121 B3
Torridon GB 31 B3
Torriglia I 134 A2
Torrijos E 151 C3
Torrita di Siena I . 135 B4
Torroella de Montgri
　E 147 B4
Torrox E 163 B4
Torrskog S 54 A3
Torsåker S 50 B3
Torsang S 50 B2
Torsås S 63 B4
Torsby S 49 B4
Torsetra N 48 B2
Torshälla S 56 A2
Tórshavn FO 4 A3
Torslanda S 60 B1
Torsminde DK 59 B1
Torsnes N 46 B3
Törtel H 113 B3
Tórtoles E 150 B2
Tórtoles de Esgueva
　E 142 C2
Tortol I 179 C3
Tortona I 120 C1
Tórtora I 174 B1
Tortoreto Lido I . . 136 C2
Tortorici I 177 A3
Tortosa E 153 B4
Tortosendo P . . . 148 B2
Tortuera E 152 B2
Tortuero E 151 B4
Toruń PL 76 A3
Torup S 60 C3
Tor Vaiánica I . . . 168 B2
Torver GB 36 B3
Tørvikbygde N . . . 46 B3
Torviscón E 163 B4
Torzym PL 75 B4
Tosbotn N 195 E3
Toscolano-Maderno
　I 121 B3
Tosno RUS 9 C7
Tossa de Mar E . . 147 C3
Tossåsen S 199 C10
Tosse F 128 C1
Tösse S 54 B3
Tossicia I 169 A3
Tostedt D 72 A2
Tosya TR 23 A8
Tószeg H 113 B4
Toszek PL 86 B2
Totana E 165 B3
Totebo S 62 A4
Tôtes F 89 A5
Tótkomlós H 113 C4
Totland N 198 D2
Tøtlandsvik N 52 A2
Totnes GB 43 B3
Tótszerdahely H . 124 A2
Tøttdal N 199 A8
Totton GB 44 C2
Touça P 149 A2
Toucy F 104 B2
Toul F 92 C1
Toulon F 132 B1
Toulon-sur-Allier
　F 104 C2
Toulon-sur-Arroux
　F 104 C3
Toulouse F 129 C4
Tourcoing F 78 B3
Tour de la Parata
　F 180 B1
Tourlaville F 88 A2
Tournai B 78 B3
Tournan-en-Brie F . 90 C2
Tournay F 145 A4
Tournon-d'Agenais
　F 129 B3
Tournon-St Martin
　F 115 B4
Tournon-sur-Rhône
　F 117 B4
Tournus F 105 C3
Touro
　E 140 B2
　P 148 B2
Tourouvre F 89 B4
Tourriers F 115 C4
Tours F 102 B2
Tourteron F 91 B4
Tourves F 132 B1
Toury F 103 A3
Touvedo P 148 A1
Touvois F 114 B2
Toužim CZ 83 B4
Továčov CZ 98 B1
Tovariševo SRB . . 126 B1
Tovarnik HR 125 B5
Tovdal N 53 B4
Towcester GB . . . 44 A3
Town Yetholm GB . 35 C5

Tråastølen N 47 B4
Trabada E 141 A3
Trabadelo E 141 B4
Trabanca E 149 A3
Trabazos E 149 A3
Traben-Trarbach D . 92 B3
Trabia I 176 B2
Tradate I 120 B1
Trädet S 60 B3
Trafaria P 154 C1
Tragacete E 152 B2
Tragwein A 96 C2
Traiguera E 153 B4
Trainel F 91 C3
Traisen A 110 A2
Traismauer A 97 C3
Traitsching D 95 B4
Trákhonas CY . . . 181 A2
Tralee IRL 29 B2
Tramacastilla de Tena
　E 145 B3
Tramagal P 154 B2
Tramariglio I . . . 178 B2
Tramatza I 179 B2
Tramelan CH . . . 106 B2
Tramonti di Sopra
　I 122 A1
Tramore IRL 30 B1
Trampot F 92 C1
Trana I 119 B4
Tranås S 55 B5
Tranbjerg DK 59 B3
Tranby N 54 A1
Trancoso P 148 B2
Tranebjerg DK . . . 59 C3
Tranekær DK 65 B3
Tranemo S 60 B3
Tranent GB 35 C5
Tranevåg N 52 B2
Trängslet S 49 A5
Tranhult S 60 B3
Trani I 171 B4
Trans-en-Provence
　F 132 B2
Transtrand S 49 A5
Tranum DK 58 A2
Tranvik S 57 A4
Trápani I 176 A1
Trappes F 90 C2
Traryd S 61 C3
Trasacco I 169 B3
Trasierra E 156 B1
Träslövsläge S . . . 60 B2
Trasmiras E 140 B3
Traspinedo E . . . 150 A3
Trate SLO 110 C2
Trauchgau D 108 B1
Traun A 110 A1
Traunreut D 109 B3
Traunstein D 109 B3
Traunwalchen D . . 109 B3
Tråvad S 55 B4
Travemünde D . . . 65 C3
Traversétolo I . . . 120 C3
Travnik
　BIH 139 A3
　SLO 123 B3
Travo
　F 180 B2
　I 120 C2
Trawsfynydd GB . . 38 B3
Trbovlje SLO . . . 123 A4
Trbušani SRB . . . 127 D2
Treban F 116 A3
Trebatsch D 74 B3
Trebbin D 74 B2
Třebechovice pod
　Orebem CZ . . . 85 B3
Trebel D 73 B4
Třebenice CZ 84 B1
Trébeurden F . . . 100 A2
Trebgast D 82 B3
Trebinje BIH 139 C4
Trebisacce I 174 B2
Trebitz D 83 A4
Trebnje SLO 123 B4
Třeboň CZ 96 B2
Třebovice CZ 97 B4
Trebsen D 83 A4
Trebujena E 161 C3
Trecastagni I . . . 177 B4
Trecate I 120 B1
Trecenta I 121 B4
Tredegar GB 39 C3
Tredózio I 135 A4
Treffen A 109 C4
Treffort F 118 A2
Treffurt D 82 A2
Trefnant GB 38 A3
Tregaron GB 39 B3
Trégastel-Plage F . 100 A2
Tregnago I 121 B4
Tregony GB 42 B2
Tréguier F 100 A2
Trégunc F 100 B2
Treharris GB 39 C3
Trehörningsjö S . . 200 C4
Tréia I 136 B2
Treignac F 116 B1
Treignat F 116 A2
Treignes B 91 A4
Treis-Karden D . . . 80 B3
Trekanten S 63 B4
Trélazé F 102 B1
Trelech GB 39 C2
Trélissac F 129 A3
Trelleborg S 66 A2
Trélon F 91 A4
Trélou-sur-Marne F . 91 B3
Tremblay-le-Vicomte
　F 89 B5
Tremés P 154 B2
Tremezzo I 120 B2
Tremošná CZ 96 B1
Tremp E 145 B4
Trenčianska Stankovce
　SK 98 C1
Trenčianska Turná
　SK 98 C2

Trenčianske Teplá
　SK 98 C2
Trenčianske Teplice
　SK 98 C2
Trenčín SK 98 C2
Trendelburg D . . . 81 A5
Trengereid N 46 B2
Trensacq F 128 B2
Trent D 66 B2
Trento I 121 A4
Treorchy GB 39 C3
Trept F 118 B2
Trepuzzi I 173 B4
Trescore Balneário
　I 120 B2
Tresenda I 120 A3
Tresfjord N 198 C4
Tresigallo I 121 C4
Trešnjevica SRB . 127 D3
Tresnurághes I . . 178 B2
Trespaderne E . . . 143 B3
Třešt CZ 97 B3
Trestina I 135 B5
Tretower GB 39 C3
Trets F 132 B1
Tretten N 48 A2
Treuchtlingen D . . 94 C2
Treuen D 83 B4
Treuenbrietzen D . 74 B1
Treungen N 53 A4
Trevelez E 163 B4
Trevi I 136 C1
Treviana E 143 B3
Treviglio I 120 B2
Trevignano Romano
　I 168 A2
Trevi nel Lázio I . 169 B3
Treviso I 122 B1
Trévoux F 117 B4
Trézelles F 117 A3
Trezzo sull'Adda I 120 B2
Trhová Kamenice
　CZ 97 B3
Trhové Sviny CZ . . 96 C2
Triacastela E . . . 141 B3
Triaize F 114 B2
Trianda GR 188 C3
Triaucourt-en-Argonne
　F 91 C5
Tribanj Kruščica
　HR 137 A4
Triberg D 106 A3
Tribsees D 66 B1
Tribuče SLO 123 B4
Tricárico I 172 B2
Tricase I 173 C4
Tricésimo I 122 A2
Trieben A 110 B1
Triebes D 83 B4
Triepkendorf D . . . 74 A2
Trier D 92 B2
Trieste I 122 B2
Trie-sur-Baïse F . 145 A4
Triggiano I 173 A2
Triglitz D 73 A5
Trignac F 101 B3
Trigueros E 161 B3
Trigueros del Valle
　E 142 C2
Trikala GR 182 D3
Trikeri GR 183 D5
Trikomo CY 181 A2
Trilj HR 138 B2
Trillo E 152 B1
Trilport F 90 C2
Trim IRL 30 A2
Trimdon GB 37 B5
Trindade
　Beja P 160 B2
　Bragança P . . . 149 A2
Třinec CZ 98 B2
Tring GB 44 B3
Trinità d'Agultu I 178 B2
Trinitápoli I 171 B4
Trino I 119 B5
Trinta P 148 B2
Triora I 133 B3
Tripoli GR 184 B3
Triponzo I 136 C1
Triptis D 83 B3
Triste E 144 B3
Trittau D 72 A3
Trivento I 170 B2
Trivero I 119 B5
Trivigno I 172 B1
Trn BIH 124 C3
Trnava
　HR 125 B4
　SK 98 C1
Trnovec SK 112 A1
Trnovo BIH 139 B4
Trnovska vas
　SLO 110 C2
Troarn F 89 A3
Trochtelfingen D . . 94 C1
Trödje S 51 B4
Troense DK 65 A3
Trofa P 148 A1
Trofaiach A 110 B2
Trofors N 195 E4
Trogir HR 138 B2
Trøgstad N 54 A2
Tróia I 171 B3
Troia P 154 C2
Troina I 177 B3
Troisdorf D 80 B3
Trois-Ponts B 80 B1
Trois-Vierges L . . . 92 A2
Trojane SLO 123 A3
Troldhede DK 59 C1
Trollhättan S 54 B3
Trólog BIH 138 B2
Tromello I 120 B1
Tromøy N 53 B4
Tromsø N 192 C3
Trondheim N . . . 199 B7
Tronget F 116 A3
Trönninge S 61 C2
Trönningeby S . . . 60 B2

Trönö S 51 A3
Tronzano-Vercellese
　I 119 B5
Trôo F 102 B2
Troon GB 36 A2
Tropea I 175 C1
Tropy Sztumskie
　PL 69 B4
Trosa S 57 B3
Trösken S 50 B3
Trossingen D . . . 107 A3
Trostberg D 109 A3
Trouville-sur-Mer F 89 A4
Trowbridge GB . . . 43 A4
Troyes F 104 A3
Trpanj HR 138 B3
Trpinja HR 125 B4
Tršće HR 123 B3
Tršice CZ 98 B1
Trstená SK 99 B3
Trstenci BIH 125 B3
Trsteno HR 139 C3
Trstice SK 111 A4
Trstin SK 98 C1
Trubia E 141 A5
Trubjela MNE . . . 139 C4
Truchas E 141 B4
Trujillanos E 155 C4
Trujillo E 156 A2
Trumieje PL 69 B4
Trun
　CH 107 C3
　F 89 B4
Truro GB 42 B1
Trusetal D 82 B2
Truskavets' UA . . . 13 D5
Trustrup DK 59 B3
Trutnov CZ 85 B3
Tryserum S 56 B2
Trysil N 49 A4
Tryszczyn PL 76 A2
Trzcianka PL 75 A5
Trzciel PL 75 B4
Trzcińsko Zdrój PL 74 B3
Trzebiatów PL . . . 67 B4
Trzebiel PL 84 A2
Trzebielino PL . . . 68 A2
Trzebień PL 84 A3
Trzebież PL 74 A3
Trzebinia PL 86 B3
Trzebnica PL 85 A5
Trzebnice PL 85 A4
Trzeciewiec PL . . . 76 A3
Trzemeszno PL . . . 76 B2
Trzemeszno-Lubuskie
　PL 75 B4
Trzetrzewina PL . . 99 B4
Tržič SLO 123 A3
Tsamandas GR . . 182 D2
Tschagguns A . . . 107 B4
Tschernitz D 84 A2
Tsebrykove UA . . . 17 B9
Tsyelyakhany BY . . 13 B6
Tua P 148 A2
Tuam IRL 28 A3
Tubbercurry IRL . . 26 B2
Tubbergen NL . . . 71 B3
Tubilla del Lago E 143 C3
Tübingen D 93 C5
Tubize B 79 B4
Tučapy CZ 96 B2
Tučepi HR 138 B3
Tuchan F 146 B3
Tüchen D 73 A5
Tuchola PL 76 A2
Tuchomie PL 68 A2
Tuchów PL 99 B5
Tuczno PL 75 A5
Tuddal N 53 A4
Tudela E 144 B2
Tudela de Duero
　E 150 A3
Tudweiliog GB . . . 38 B2
Tuejar E 159 B2
Tuffé F 102 A2
Tufsingdalen N . . 199 C8
Tuhaň CZ 84 B2
Tui E 140 B2
Tukhkala RUS . . 197 D13
Tukums LV 8 D3
Tula I 178 B2
Tulcea RO 17 C8
Tul'chyn UA 13 D8
Tulette F 131 A3
Tuliszków PL 76 B3
Tulla IRL 28 B3
Tullamore IRL . . . 30 A1
Tulle F 116 B1
Tullins F 118 B2
Tulln A 97 C4
Tullow IRL 30 B2
Tułowice PL 85 B5
Tulppio FIN 197 B12
Tulsk IRL 28 A3
Tumba S 57 A3
Tummel Bridge GB 35 B3
Tun S 55 B3
Tuna
　Kalmar S 62 A4
　Uppsala S 51 B5
Tuna Hästberg S . . 50 B2
Tunçbilek TR . . . 187 C4
Tunes P 160 B1
Tungelsta S 57 A4
Tunnerstad S 55 B5
Tunnhovd N 47 B5
Tunstall GB 45 A5
Tuohikotti FIN 8 B5
Tuoro sul Trasimeno
　I 135 B5
Tupadly PL 76 B3
Tupanari BIH . . . 139 A4
Tupik RUS 9 E8
Tuplice PL 84 A2
Tura H 112 B3
Turany SK 99 B3
Turanj HR 137 B4
Turba BIH 139 A3
Turbe BIH 139 A3
Turbenthal CH . . . 107 B3

Turcia E . . . . . . 141 ..
Turčianske Teplice
　SK . . . . 9..
Turcifal P . . . . 15..
Turckheim F . . . . . 10..
Turda RO . . . .
Turégano E . . . . 1..
Turek PL 7
Turgutlu TR . . . . . 17..
Turi I . . . . 17..
Turin = Torino I . . . 11..
Turis E . . . . 15..
Türje H . . . . 11..
Turka UA 1
Túrkeve H 1
Türkheim D . . . . . . 10..
Türkmenli TR . . . . 18..
Turku FIN . . . .
Turleque E . . . . . . 15..
Turňa nad Bodvou
　SK . . . . 9..
Turnberry GB 3
Turnhout B 7
Türnitz A . . . . 11..
Turnov CZ . . . .
Turnu RO . . . . 12..
Turnu Măgurele
　RO 1
Turón E . . . . 16..
Turoszów PL 8
Turowo PL 7
Turquel P . . . . 15..
Turri I . . . . 17..
Turries F . . . . 13..
Turriff GB 3
Tursi I . . . . 17..
Turtmann CH . . . . 11..
Turtola FIN . . . . . 19..
Turze PL 8
Turzovka SK . . . . . . 9..
Tusa I . . . . 17..
Tuscánia I . . . . . . 16..
Tuse DK 6
Tušilovic HR 1
Tuszyn PL 8
Tutow D 6
Tutrakan BG 1
Tuttlingen D . . . . . 10..
Tutzing D . . . . 10..
Tuzla
　BIH . . . . 12..
　TR 2
Tuzlucku TR . . . . 18..
Tvååker S 6
Tväralund S . . . . . 20..
Tvärskog S 6
Tvedestrand N . . . . . 5..
Tveit
　Hordaland N . . . . 4..
　Rogaland N . . . . . 5..
Tver RUS . . . .
Tverrelvmo N . . . . . 19..
Tversted DK . . . . . . 5..
Tving S 6
Tvrdošin SK . . . . . . 9..
Tvrdošovce SK . . . 11..
Twardogóra PL . . . . 8..
Twatt GB 3
Twello NL 7
Twimberg A . . . . . 11..
Twist D 7
Twistringen D . . . . . 7..
Tworóg PL 8
Twyford
　Hampshire GB . . . 4..
　Wokingham GB . . . 4..
Tyachiv UA 1
Tychówka PL 6
Tychowo PL 7
Tychy PL 8
Tydal N . . . . 1..
Týec nad Labem
　CZ . . . .
Tyfors S . . . . 4..
Tygelsjö S 6
Tylldal N . . . . 19..
Tylstrup DK . . . . . . 5..
Tymbark PL . . . . . . 9..
Tymowa PL . . . . . . 9..
Tyndrum GB . . . . . . 3..
Týnec nad Sázavou
　CZ . . . .
Tynemouth GB . . . . 3..
Tyngsjö S . . . . 4..
Týniště nad Orlicí
　CZ . . . .
Týn nad Vltavou
　CZ . . . . 9..
Tynset N . . . . 19..
Tyreső S . . . . 5..
Tyringe S . . . .
Tyrislöt S . . . . 5..
Tyristrand N . . . . . . 4..
Tyrrellspass IRL . . . 3..
Tysnes N . . . . 4..
Tyssebotn N . . . . . . 4..
Tyssedal N . . . . 4..
Tystberga S . . . . . . 5..
Tysvær N . . . . 5..
Tywyn GB . . . . 3..
Tzermiado GR . . . 18..
Tzummarum NL . . . . 7..

U

Ub SRB . . . . 12..
Ubby DK . . . . 6..
Úbeda E . . . . 15..
Überlingen D . . . . 10..
Ubidea E . . . . . . 14..
Ubli HR . . . . 13..
Ubrique E . . . . . . 16..
Ucero E . . . . 14..
Uchaud F . . . . . . 13..
Uchte D 7
Uckerath D . . . . . . 8..
Uckfield GB . . . . . . 4..
Ucklum S . . . . 5..

s E. 151 C5
. . . . .177 A3
na HR. 137 A4
ebo S. 60 B3
eholm S. 49 B5
evalla S. 54 B2
neden S. 49 C4
NL 80 A1
. . . . .82 A2
a SK 98 B2
H 122 A2
rt H 125 B4
kermünde D . .74 A3
en D 71 B3
en D 73 B3
ndorf CH 106 C2
en D 72 A2
D 72 B3
lme GB 43 B3
heim D 94 B2
ana E 143 A4
to I. 173 C4
ldse DK 61 D1
erby DK. 58 A3
rslev DK 59 C3
ano la Chiesa
. . . . .173 B4
r E 164 C1
r F 118 B3
jevik BIH. 125 C5
nes N 46 B2
ch RUS 9 D11
ane HR 138 B2
d H 111 B4
ské Hradiště
. . . . .98 B1
ský Brod CZ . .98 B1
ský Ostroh
. . . . .98 C1
gen D 94 C1
ské-Janovice
. . . . .96 B3
nèves CZ 96 A2
st D 84 A2
GB 31 B2
eest NL 70 B1
orn N. 70 B1
uizen NL 71 A3
uizermeeden
. . . . .71 A3
RO 126 B2
zkie PL. 87 A3
olskie PL. 86 B2
d u Brna D 97 B4
rtyán H 112 B3
yós H 113 C5
re H 125 B4
e PL 75 A5
it H 112 C3
entmargita H .113 B6
E 144 B2
c SLO 122 A2
ergé LT 13 A6
. . . . .56 B2
. . . . .188 B3
aka SK 99 C3
TR 186 A2
sai I 179 C3
erg DK 58 B2
er GB 32 C3
by GB 40 B3
j MNE 16 E3
m DK 59 C2
oss N 53 A5
a del Campo
. . . . .164 B2
AL 182 B1
org DK 59 B1
a SRB 127 B3
ager S 200 C4
ool GB 32 C1
ed S 60 B2
un N 196 B4
. . . . .52 A2
cona E 153 B4
emolins E 147 C1
slev DK. 59 C3
vad S 55 B4
. . . . .126 A1
H. 112 B3
. . . . .94 C1
e F 154 B2
en D. 80 B2
en N 47 B6
BIH 139 B4
en S 60 B3
hstein D 81 B5
a S 56 B1
sfors S 200 C1
en NL 71 A4
erg N. 198 C6
a GB. 33 A5
er DK 58 A3
einvik N 198 C2
. . . . .59 C3
org Amt. DK . .59 B2
en H 194 B6
ey TR 188 A4
orlu TR 189 A5
. . . . .23 C8
rston GB. 36 B3
. . . . .46 B3
g HR 122 B2
a RUS 13 D9
. . . . .3 C14
értide I 135 B5
riático I 174 B2
ari SRB 127 C2
s S 200 C6
ransele S 200 B4
ausen A 108 B1
a SRB 127 C4
anovic HR 138 B2
äs S 195 E7
rbey TR 186 B1
ósdalur IS 190 A3

Unapool GB 32 C1
Unari FIN 197 B8
Unbyn S. 196 D4
Uncastillo E 144 B2
Undenäs S. 55 B5
Undersaker S . . .199 B10
Undredal N 46 B4
Unešić HR 138 B2
Úněšov CZ. 96 B1
Ungheni MD. 17 B7
Unhais da Serra P .148 B2
Unhošť CZ. 84 B2
Unichowo PL. 68 A2
Uničov CZ. 98 B1
Uniejów PL. 76 C3
Unisław PL. 76 A3
Unkel D 80 B3
Unken A. 109 B3
Unna D. 81 A3
Unnaryd S 60 C3
Unquera E 142 A2
Unterach A. 109 B4
Unterägeri CH . . .107 B3
Unterammergau D .108 B2
Unterhaching D. . .108 A2
Unteriberg CH . . .107 B3
Unterkochen D . . .94 C2
Unter Langkampfen
A. 108 B3
Unterlaussa A . . .110 B1
Unterlüss D 72 B3
Untermünkheim D. .94 B1
Unterschächen
CH 107 C3
Unterschleissheim
D 95 C3
Unterschwaningen
D 94 B2
Untersiemau D . . .82 B2
Unter-steinbach D. .94 B2
Unterweissenbach
A. 96 C2
Unterzell D. 95 B4
Upavon GB 44 B2
Úpice CZ. 85 B4
Upilka PL. 68 B2
Upphärad S 54 B3
Uppingham GB . . .40 C3
Upplands-Väsby S .57 A3
Uppsala S 51 C4
Uppsjøhytta N. . . .48 A1
Upton-upon-Severn
GB 39 B4
Ur F 146 B2
Uras I 179 C2
Uraz PL. 85 A4
Urbánia I 136 B1
Urbino I 136 B1
Urçay F 103 C4
Urda E 157 A4
Urdax E 144 A2
Urdilde E 140 B2
Urdos F 145 B3
Urk NL 70 B2
Úrkút H. 111 B4
Urla TR. 188 A1
Urlingford IRL 30 B1
Urnäsch CH 107 B4
Urnes N. 47 A4
Uroševac KOS. . . .16 D4
Urracal E. 164 B2
Urries E 144 B2
Urroz E 144 B2
Ursensollen D 95 B3
Urshult S. 63 B2
Uršna Sela SLO . .123 B4
Urszulewo PL 77 B4
Ury F 90 C2
Urzicen RO 17 C7
Urzulei I 178 B3
Usagre E 156 B1
Uşak TR 187 D4
Usedom D 66 C2
Useldange L. 92 B1
Uséllus I 179 C2
Ushakovo RUS . . .69 A5
Usingen D 81 B4
Usini I 178 B2
Usk GB. 39 C4
Uskedal N 46 C2
Üsküdar TR 186 A4
Uslar D 82 A1
Úsov CZ. 97 B5
Usquert NL. 71 A3
Ussássai I 179 C3
Ussé F 102 B2
Usséglio I 119 B4
Ussel
Cantal F. 116 B2
Corrèze F. 116 B2
Usson-du-Poitou
F. 115 B4
Usson-en-Forez F .117 B3
Usson-les-Bains
F. 146 B3
Ustaoset N 47 B5
Ustaritz F 144 A2
Uštěk CZ 84 B2
Uster CH 107 B3
Ústí CZ. 98 B1
Ustikolina BIH . . .139 B4
Ústí nad Labem CZ .84 B2
Ústí nad Orlicí CZ. .97 B4
Ustiprača BIH . . .139 B5
Ustka PL. 68 A1
Ust Luga RUS 8 C6
Ustroń PL. 98 B2
Ustronie Morskie
PL. 67 B4
Ustyuzhna RUS. . .9 C10
Uszód H. 112 C2
Utåker N 46 C2
Utansjö S 200 D3
Utebo E 152 A3
Utena LT. 13 A6
Utery CZ. 95 B5
Uthaug N 198 B6
Utiel E 159 B2
Utne N 46 B3
Utö S 57 B4

Utrecht NL 70 B2
Utrera E 162 A2
Utrillas E 153 B3
Utsjoki FIN. 193 C11
Utstein kloster N . .52 A1
Uttendorf A 109 B3
Uttenweiler D 107 A4
Utterslev DK 65 B4
Uttoxeter GB 40 C2
Utvälinge S 61 C2
Utvorda N. 199 A7
Uusikaarlepyy FIN . .3 E8
Uusikaupunki FIN. . .8 B2
Uvaly CZ. 96 A2
Uvdal N 47 B5
Uza F 128 B1
Uzdin SRB 126 B2
Uzdowo PL. 77 A5
Uzein F. 145 A3
Uzel F. 100 A3
Uzerche F 116 B1
Uzès F 131 A3
Uzhhorod UA. 12 D5
Uzhok UA. 12 D5
Užice SRB 127 D1
Uznach CH. 107 B3
Üzümlü
Konya TR 189 B6
Muğla TR 188 C4
Uzunköprü TR . . .186 A1

V

Vaalajärvi FIN . . .197 B9
Vaas F 102 B2
Vaasa FIN. 8 A2
Vaasen NL 70 B2
Vabre F. 130 B1
Vác H 112 B3
Vacha D 82 B2
Váchartyán H . . .112 B3
Väckelsång S 63 B2
Vacqueyras F . . .131 A3
Vad S 50 B2
Vada I 134 B3
Väddö S 51 C5
Väderstad S. 55 B5
Vadheim N 46 A2
Vadillo de la Sierra
E. 150 B2
Vadillos E. 152 B1
Vadla N. 52 A2
Vado I 135 A4
Vado Lígure I . . .133 A4
Vadsø N 193 B13
Vadstena S 55 B5
Vadum DK 58 A2
Vaduz FL 107 B4
Vafos N 53 B5
Våg N 111 B4
Vågåmo N 198 D6
Væggerløse DK. . .65 B4
Vaggeryd S 62 A2
Vaghia GR 184 A4
Váglio Basilicata I .172 B1
Vagney F 106 A1
Vagnhärad S. 57 B3
Vagnsunda S 57 A4
Vagos P 148 B1
Vai GR 185 D7
Vaiano I 135 B4
Vaiges F 102 A1
Vaihingen D 93 C4
Vaillant F 105 B4
Vailly-sur-Aisne F. .91 B3
Vailly-sur Sauldre
F. 103 B4
Vairano Scalo I . .170 B2
Vaison-la-Romaine
F. 131 A4
Vaïte F 105 B4
Väjern S 54 B2
Väjszló H 125 B3
Vaksdal N. 46 B2
Vál H. 112 B2
Valaam RUS. 9 B7
Valada P 154 B2
Vålådalen S 199 B10
Valadares P 148 A1
Valado P 154 B1
Valandovo MK . . .182 B4
Valašská SK. 99 C3
Valaská Belá SK . .98 C2
Valašská Dubová
SK 99 B3
Valašská Polanka
CZ 98 B1
Valašské Klobouky
CZ 98 B2
Valašské Meziříčí
CZ 98 B1
Valberg F 132 A2
Vålberg S 55 A4
Valbo S 51 B4
Valbom P 148 A1
Valbondione I . . .120 A3
Valbonnais F 118 C2
Valbuena de Duero
E 142 C2
Vălcani RO. 126 B2
Valdagno I 121 B4
Valdaracete E . . .151 B4
Valday RUS 9 D8
Valdealgorfa E . .153 B3
Valdecaballeros E .156 A2
Valdecabras E . . .152 B1
Valdecarros E . . .150 B2
Valdeconcha E . .151 B5
Valdefresno E . . .142 B1
Valdeganga E . . .158 B2
Valdelacasa E . . .150 B2
Valdelacasa de Tajo
E 156 A2
Valdelarco E 161 B3
Valdelosa E 149 A4
Valdeltormo E . . .153 B4

Valdelugeros E . . .142 B1
Valdemanco de Esteras
E. 156 B3
Valdemarsvik S . . .56 B2
Valdemorillo E. . .151 B3
Valdemoro E 151 B4
Valdemoro Sierra
E 152 B2
Valdenoceda E . .143 B3
Valdeobispo E . . .149 B3
Valdeolivas E. . . .152 B1
Valdepeñas E . . .157 B4
Valdepeñas de Jaén
E 163 A4
Valdepiélago E . .142 B1
Valdepolo E 142 B1
Valderas E 142 B1
Valdérice I 176 A1
Valderrobres E . .153 B4
Valderrueda E . . .142 B2
Val de San Lorenzo
E 141 B4
Val de Santo Domingo
E 150 B3
Val d'Esquières F .132 B2
Valdestillas E. . . .150 A3
Valdetorres E . . .156 B1
Valdetorres de Jarama
E. 151 B4
Valdeverdeja E . .150 C2
Valdevimbre E . . .142 B1
Valdieri I. 133 A3
Valdilecha E. 151 B4
Val-d'Isère F 119 B3
Valdobbiádene I . .121 B4
Valdocondes E . .143 C3
Valdoviño E. 140 A2
Vale de Açor
Beja P 160 B2
Portalegre P. . .154 B3
Vale de Agua P . .160 B1
Vale de Cambra P .148 B1
Vale de Lobo P . .160 B1
Vale de Prazeres
P 148 B2
Vale de Reis P . .154 C2
Vale de Rosa P . .160 B2
Vale de Santarém
P 154 B2
Vale de Vargo P. .160 B2
Vale do Peso P . .155 B3
Valega P. 148 B1
Valéggio sul Mincio
I 121 B3
Valeiro P. 154 C2
Valença P 140 B2
Valençay F 103 B3
Valence
Charente F. . . .115 C4
Drôme F. 117 C4
Valence d'Agen F .129 B3
Valence d'Albigeois
F. 130 A1
Valence-sur-Baise
F 129 C3
Valencia E 159 B3
Valencia de Alcántara
E 155 B3
Valencia de Don Juan
E 142 B1
Valencia de las Torres
E 156 B1
Valencia del Ventoso
E 161 A3
Valencia de Mombuey
E 161 A2
Valenciennes F . . .79 B3
Valensole F 132 B1
Valentano I 168 A1
Valentigney F . . .106 B1
Valentine F 145 A4
Valenza I 120 B1
Valenzuela E 163 A3
Valenzuela de
Calatrava E. . .157 B4
Våler
Hedmark N 48 B3
Østfold N 54 A1
Valera de Abajo E .158 B1
Valeria E 158 B1
Valestrand N 46 B2
Valestrandsfossen
N 46 B2
Valevåg N. 52 A1
Valfabbrica I 136 B1
Valflaunes F 131 B2
Valga EST. 8 D5
Valgorge F 131 A3
Valguarnera Caropepe
I 177 B3
Valhelhas P 148 B2
Valjevo SRB. 127 C1
Valka LV 8 D4
Valkeakoski FIN . . .8 B4
Valkenburg NL. . . .80 B1
Valkenswaard NL. .79 A5
Valko H. 112 B3
Valla S. 56 A2
Valladа E 159 C3
Valladolid E 150 A3
Vallakra S 61 D2
Vallata I 172 A1
Vallberga S 61 C3
Vall d'Alba E 153 B3
Valldemossa E . . .166 B2
Valle 52 A3
Valle Castellana I .136 C2
Valle de Abdalajís
E. 163 B3
Valle de Cabuérniga
E 142 A2
Valle de la Serena
E 156 B2
Valle de Matamoros
E. 155 C4
Valle de Santa Ana
E. 155 C4

Valledolmo I. 176 B2
Valledoria I. 178 B2
Vallelado E. 150 A3
Vallelunga Pratameno
I. 176 B2
Valle Mosso I . . .119 B5
Vallendar D 81 B3
Vallentuna S 57 A4
Vallerás S. 49 B5
Valleraugue F . . .130 A2
Vallermosa I. 179 C2
Vallet F 101 B4
Valletta M. 175 C3
Valley GB. 38 A2
Vallfogona de Riucorb
E 147 C2
Valli del Pasúbio I .121 B4
Vallo della Lucánia
I 172 B1
Valloire F 118 B3
Vallombrosa I . . .135 B4
Vallon-Pont-d'Arc
F. 131 A3
Vallorbe CH 105 C5
Vallouise F 118 C3
Valls E 147 C2
Vallset N. 48 B3
Vallsta S. 50 A3
Vallstena S. 57 C4
Valmadrid E 153 A3
Valmiera LV 8 D4
Valmojado E 151 B3
Valmont F 89 A4
Valmontone I 169 B2
Valö S 51 B5
Valognes F 88 A2
Valonga P. 148 B1
Valongo P 148 A1
Válor E 164 C1
Valoria la Buena
E 142 C2
Våløy N 199 A7
Valozhyn BY 13 A7
Valpaços P. 148 A2
Valpelline I 119 B4
Valpiana I 135 B3
Valpovo HR 125 B4
Valras-Plage F . .130 B2
Valréas F 131 A3
Vals CH 107 C4
Valsavarenche I . .119 B4
Vålse DK 65 B4
Valsequillo E 156 B2
Valsjöbyn S 199 A11
Vals-les-Bains F. .117 C4
Valsonne F 117 B4
Valstagna I 121 B4
Valtablado del Río
E 152 B1
Valthorens IS .191 B11
Val Thorens F . . .118 B3
Váltice CZ. 97 C4
Valtiendas E 151 A4
Valtierra E 144 B2
Valtopina I 136 B1
Valtorta I 120 B2
Valtournenche I . .119 B4
Valverde E 144 C2
Valverde de Burguillos
E 155 C4
Valverde de Júcar
E 158 B1
Valverde de la Vera
E 150 B2
Valverde de la Virgen
E 142 B1
Valverde del Camino
E 161 B3
Valverde del Fresno
E 149 B3
Valverde de Llerena
E 156 B2
Valverde de Mérida
E 156 B1
Valvträsk S. 196 C4
Vamberk CZ. 85 B4
Vamdrup DK 59 C2
Våmhus S 50 A1
Vamlingbo S 57 D4
Vammala FIN 8 B3
Vamos GR. 185 D5
Vámosmikola H. .112 B2
Vámosszabadi H. .111 B4
Vandel DK 59 C2
Vandenesse F . . .104 C2
Vandenesse-en-Auxois
F. 104 B3
Vandóies I 108 C2
Väne-Åsaka S . . .54 B3
Vänersborg S 54 B3
Vänersnäs S 54 B3
Vang N 47 A5
Vänge S. 51 C4
Vangsnes N. 46 A3
Vathia GR. 184 C3
Vatican City = Cittádel
Vaticani I 168 B2
Vatili CY 181 A2
Vatin SRB. 126 B3
Vatland N 52 B3
Vatnar N. 53 A5
Vatnås N 48 C1
Vatne N. 198 C3
Vatnestrøm N 53 B4
Vätö S 51 C5
Vatra-Dornei RO . .17 B6
Vatry F 91 C4
Vattholma S 51 B4
Vättis CH 107 C4
Vauchamps F 91 C3
Vauchassis F . . .104 A2
Vaucouleurs F . . .92 C1
Vaudoy-en-Brie F .90 C3
Vaulen N 52 B1
Vaulruz CH 106 C1
Vaulx Vraucourt F .90 A2
Vaumas F. 104 C2
Vausseroux F . . .115 B3

Vauvenargues F . .132 B1
Vauvert F. 131 B3
Vauvillers F 105 B5
Vaux-sur-Sure B . .92 B1
Vawkavysk BY . . .13 B6
Vaxholm S 57 A4
Vaxjö S. 62 B2
Våxtorp S. 61 C3
Vayrac F 129 B4
Važec SK 99 B3
Veberöd S 61 D3
Vechelde D 72 B3
Vechta D 71 B5
Vecinos E. 149 B4
Vecsés H 112 B3
Vedavågen N 52 A1
Veddige S 60 B2
Vedersø DK 59 B1
Vedeseta I 120 B2
Vedevåg S 56 A1
Vedra E 140 B2
Vedum S 55 B3
Veendam NL 71 A3
Veenendaal NL . . .70 B2
Vega
Asturias E 142 A1
Asturias E 142 A1
Vega de Espinareda
E 141 B4
Vega de Infanzones
E 142 B1
Vegadeo E 141 A3
Vega de Pas E . .143 A3
Vega de Valcarce
E 141 B4
Vega de Valdetronco
E 150 A2
Vegårshei N 53 B4
Vegas de Coria E .149 B3
Vegas del Condado
E 142 B1
Vegby S 60 B3
Vegger DK 58 B2
Veggli N 47 B6
Veghel NL. 80 A1
Veglast D 66 B1
Véglie I 173 B3
Veguillas E 151 B4
Vegusdal N 53 B4
Veidholmen N . . .198 B4
Veidnes N 193 B10
Veikåker N 48 B1
Veinge S 61 C3
Vejbystrand S 61 C2
Vejen DK 59 C2
Vejer de la Frontera
E 162 B2
Vejle DK 59 C2
Vejprty CZ 83 B5
Velada E. 150 B3
Vela Luka HR. . . .138 C2
Velayos E 150 B3
Velbert D 80 A3
Velburg D 95 B3
Velde N 199 A8
Velden
Bayern D 95 B3
Bayern D 95 C4
Velden am Wörther See
A. 109 C5
Velefique E 164 B2
Velen D 80 A2
Velenje SLO 123 A4
Veles MK 182 B3
Velesevec HR . . .124 B2
Velešín CZ. 96 C2
Velestino GR 182 D4
Velez Blanco E . .164 B2
Vélez de Benaudalla
E 163 B4
Vélez-Málaga E . .163 B3
Vélez Rubio E . . .164 B2
Veliika Radinci
SRB 127 B1
Velika HR 125 B3
Velika Gorica HR .124 B2
Velika Grdevac
HR 124 B3
Velika Greda SRB .126 B3
Velika Ilova BIH . .125 C3
Velika Kladuša
BIH 124 B1
Velika Kopanica
HR 125 B4
Velika Krsna SRB .127 C2
Velika Obarska
BIH 125 C5
Velika Pisanica
HR 124 B3
Velika Plana SRB. .127 C3
Velika Zdenci HR. .124 B3
Velike Lašče SLO .123 B3
Velike Središte
SRB 126 B3
Veliki Gaj SRB . .126 B3
Veliki Popović
SRB 127 C3
Velikiye Luki RUS . .9 D7
Veliko Gradište
SRB 127 C3
Veliko Orašje
SRB 127 C3
Veliko Selo SRB .127 C3
Veliko Tarnovo BG .17 D6
Velilla del Río Carrió
E 142 B2
Velilla de San Antonio
E 151 B4
Veli Lošinj HR . . .137 A3
Velingrad BG . . .183 A5
Velizh RUS 9 E7
Veljun HR 123 B4
Velká Bíteš CZ. . .97 B4
Velká Hleď'scbe CZ .95 B4
Velká Lomnica SK. .99 B4
Velkánad Veličkou
CZ 98 C1

270 Vel–Vil

Velké Bystřice CZ . . 98 B1
Velké Heraltice CZ . . 98 B1
Velké Karlovice CZ . 98 B2
Vel'ke'Kostol'any SK . . . 98 C1
Vel'ké Leváre SK . . 97 C5
Velké Losiny CZ . . . 98 A1
Velké Meziříčí CZ . . 97 B4
Velké Pavlovice CZ . . . 97 C4
Vel'ké Rovné SK . . . 98 B2
Vel'ké Uherce SK . . 98 C2
Vel'ké Zálužie SK . . 98 C1
Vel'ký Blahovo SK . 99 C4
Velky Bor CZ . . . 96 B1
Vel'ký Cetin SK . . 112 A2
Vel'ký Krtíš SK . . . 112 A3
Vel'ký Meder SK . . 111 B4
Velky Ujezd CZ . . . 98 B1
Vellahn D . . . 73 A3
Vellberg D . . . 94 B1
Velles F . . . 103 C3
Velletri I . . . 168 B2
Vellinge S . . . 66 A2
Vellisca E . . . 151 B5
Velliza E . . . 150 A3
Vellmar D . . . 81 A5
Velp NL . . . 70 B2
Velten D . . . 74 B2
Velvary CZ . . . 84 B2
Velvendos GR . . . 182 C4
Vemb DK . . . 59 B1
Vemdalen S . . . 199 C10
Veme N . . . 48 B2
Véménd H . . . 125 A4
Vemmedrup DK . . . 61 D2
Vena S . . . 62 A3
Venaco F . . . 180 A2
Venafro I . . . 169 B4
Venarey-les-Laumes F . . . 104 B3
Venaría I . . . 119 B4
Venasca I . . . 133 A3
Venčane SRB . . . 127 C2
Vence F . . . 132 B3
Venda Nova
Coimbra P . . . 154 A2
Leiria P . . . 154 B2
Vendas Novas P . 154 C2
Vendays-Montalivet F . . . 114 C2
Vendel S . . . 51 B4
Vendelso S . . . 57 A4
Vendeuil F . . . 91 B3
Vendeuvre-sur-Barse F . . . 104 A3
Vendoeuvres F . . . 115 B5
Vendôme F . . . 103 B3
Venelles F . . . 131 B4
Veness GB . . . 33 B4
Venézia = Venice I . . . 122 B1
Venialbo E . . . 150 A2
Venice = Venézia I . . . 122 B1
Vénissieux F . . . 117 B4
Venjan S . . . 49 B5
Venlo NL . . . 80 A2
Vennesla N . . . 53 B3
Vennesund N . . . 195 E3
Vennezey F . . . 92 C2
Venn Green GB . . . 42 B2
Venosa I . . . 172 B1
Venray NL . . . 80 A1
Vent A . . . 108 C1
Venta de Baños E . 142 C2
Venta del Moro E . . 158 B2
Venta de los Santos E . . . 157 B4
Venta las Ranas E 142 A1
Ventanueva E . . . 141 A4
Ventas de Huelma E . . . 163 A4
Ventas de Zafarraya E . . . 163 B3
Ventavon F . . . 132 A1
Ventimíglia I . . . 133 B3
Ventnor GB . . . 44 C2
Ventosa de la Sierra E . . . 143 C4
Ventosilla E . . . 143 C4
Ventspils LV . . . 8 D2
Venturina I . . . 134 B3
Venzolasca F . . . 180 A2
Venzone I . . . 122 A2
Vép H . . . 111 B3
Vera
E . . . 164 B3
N . . . 199 B9
Vera Cruz P . . . 160 A2
Vera de Bidasoa E . . . 144 A2
Vera de Moncayo E . . . 144 C2
Verbánia I . . . 119 B5
Verberie F . . . 90 B2
Verbicaro I . . . 174 B1
Verbier CH . . . 119 A4
Vercelli I . . . 119 B5
Vercel-Villedieu-le-Camp F . . . 105 B5
Verchen D . . . 66 C1
Vercheny F . . . 118 C2
Verclause F . . . 131 A4
Verdalsøra N . . . 199 B8
Verden D . . . 72 B2
Verdens Ende N . . . 54 A1
Verdikoussa GR . . 182 D3
Verdille F . . . 115 C3
Verdú E . . . 147 C2
Verdun F . . . 92 B1
Verdun-sur-Garonne F . . . 129 C4
Verdun-sur-le-Doubs F . . . 105 C4
Veresegyház H . . . 112 B3
Verfeil F . . . 129 C4
Vergato I . . . 135 A4
Vergel E . . . 159 C4
Vergeletto CH . . . 120 A1
Verges E . . . 147 B4
Vergiate I . . . 120 B1
Vergt F . . . 129 A3
Veria GR . . . 182 C4
Verín E . . . 141 C3
Veringenstadt D . . 107 A4
Verl D . . . 81 A4
Verma N . . . 198 C5
Vermand F . . . 90 B3
Vermelha P . . . 154 B1
Vermenton F . . . 104 B2
Vernago I . . . 108 C1
Vernante I . . . 133 A3
Vernantes F . . . 102 B2
Vernár SK . . . 99 C4
Vernasca I . . . 120 C2
Vernayaz CH . . . 119 A4
Vernazza I . . . 134 A2
Vern-d'Anjou F . . . 102 B1
Verneřice CZ . . . 84 B2
Vernet F . . . 146 A2
Vernet-les-Bains F . . . 146 B3
Verneuil F . . . 91 B3
Verneuil-sur-Avre F . . . 89 B4
Vernier CH . . . 118 A3
Vérnio I . . . 135 A4
Vérnole I . . . 173 B4
Vernon F . . . 90 B1
Vernoux-en-Vivarais F . . . 117 C4
Veróce H . . . 112 B3
Verolanuova I . . . 120 B3
Véroli I . . . 169 B3
Verona I . . . 121 B4
Verpelét H . . . 113 B4
Verrabotn N . . . 199 B7
Verrès I . . . 119 B4
Verrey-sous-Salmaise F . . . 104 B3
Verrières F . . . 115 B4
Versailles F . . . 90 C2
Versam CH . . . 107 C4
Verseg H . . . 112 B3
Versmold D . . . 71 B5
Versoix CH . . . 118 A3
Verteillac F . . . 115 C4
Vértesacsa H . . . 112 B2
Vertou F . . . 101 B4
Vertus F . . . 91 C3
Verviers B . . . 80 B1
Vervins F . . . 91 B3
Verwood GB . . . 43 B5
Veryan GB . . . 42 B2
Veržej SLO . . . 111 C3
Verzuolo I . . . 133 A3
Verzy F . . . 91 B4
Vescovato F . . . 180 A2
Vése H . . . 124 A3
Veselie BG . . . 17 D7
Veselínad Lužnicí CZ . . . 96 B2
Veselínad Moravou CZ . . . 98 C1
Vésime I . . . 119 C5
Veskoniemi FIN . 193 D11
Vesoul F . . . 105 B5
Vespolate I . . . 120 B1
Vessigebro S . . . 60 C2
Vestbygd N . . . 52 B2
Vestenanova I . . . 121 B4
Vester Husby S . . . 56 B2
Vester Nebel DK . . 59 C2
Vesterøhavn DK . . 58 A3
Vester Torup DK . . 58 A2
Vester Vedsted DK . 59 C1
Vestervig DK . . . 58 B1
Vestfossen N . . . 53 A5
Vestmannaeyjar IS . . . 190 D5
Vestmarka N . . . 48 C3
Vestnes N . . . 198 C4
Vestone I . . . 120 B3
Vestre Gausdal N . . 48 A2
Vestre Jakobselv N . . . 193 B13
Vestre Slidre N . . . 47 A5
Vesyegonsk RUS . 9 C10
Veszprém H . . . 112 B1
Veszprémvarsány H . . . 112 B1
Vésztő H . . . 113 C5
Vetlanda S . . . 62 A3
Vetovo HR . . . 125 B3
Vetralla I . . . 168 A2
Větrný Jeníkov CZ . 97 B3
Vétroz CH . . . 119 A4
Vetschau D . . . 84 A2
Vettasjärvi S . . . 196 B4
Vetto I . . . 134 A3
Vetulónia I . . . 135 C3
Veules-les-Roses F 89 A4
Veulettes-sur-Mer F . . . 89 A4
Veum N . . . 53 A4
Veurne B . . . 78 A2
Veverská Bítýška CZ . . . 97 B4
Vevey CH . . . 106 C1
Vevi GR . . . 182 C3
Vevring N . . . 46 A2
Vex CH . . . 119 A4
Veynes F . . . 132 A1
Veyre-Monton F . . 116 B3
Veyrier F . . . 118 B3
Vézelay F . . . 104 B2
Vézelise F . . . 92 C2
Vézenobres F . . . 131 A3
Vezins F . . . 102 B1
Vézins-de-Lévézou F . . . 130 A1
Vezirhan TR . . . 187 B5
Vezirköprü TR . . . 23 A8
Vezza di Óglio I . . 120 A3
Vezzani F . . . 180 A2
Vezzano I . . . 121 A4
Vezzano sul Cróstolo I . . . 121 C3
Vi S . . . 200 D3
Viadana I . . . 121 C3
Via Gloria P . . . 160 B2
Viana E . . . 143 B4
Viana do Alentejo P . . . 154 C2
Viana do Bolo E . . 141 B3
Viana do Castelo P . . . 148 A1
Vianden L . . . 92 B2
Viannos GR . . . 185 D6
Viaréggio I . . . 134 B3
Viator E . . . 164 C2
Vibble S . . . 57 C4
Viborg DK . . . 58 B2
Vibo Valéntia I . . . 175 C2
Vibraye F . . . 102 A2
Vic E . . . 147 C3
Vícar E . . . 164 C2
Vicarello I . . . 134 B3
Vicari I . . . 176 B2
Vicchio I . . . 135 B4
Vicdesses F . . . 146 B2
Vic-en-Bigorre F . . 145 A4
Vicenza I . . . 121 B4
Vic-Fézensac F . . 129 C3
Vichy F . . . 117 A3
Vickan S . . . 60 B2
Vickerstown GB . . . 36 B3
Vic-le-Comte F . . . 116 B3
Vico F . . . 180 A1
Vico del Gargano I . . . 171 B3
Vico Equense I . . . 170 C2
Vicopisano I . . . 134 B3
Vicosoprano CH . . 120 A2
Vicovaro I . . . 169 A2
Vic-sur-Aisne F . . . 90 B3
Vic-sur-Cère F . . . 116 C2
Victoria = Rabat M . . . 175 C3
Vidago P . . . 148 A2
Vidauban F . . . 132 B2
Vide P . . . 148 B2
Videbæk DK . . . 59 B1
Videm SLO . . . 123 B3
Videseter N . . . 198 D4
Vidigueira P . . . 160 A2
Vidin BG . . . 16 D5
Vidlin GB . . . 33 A5
Vidsel S . . . 196 D3
Vidzy BY . . . 13 A7
Viechtach D . . . 95 B4
Vieille-Brioude F . 117 B3
Vieira P . . . 154 B2
Vieira do Minho P . 148 A1
Vieiros P . . . 155 C3
Vielha E . . . 145 B4
Vielle-Aure F . . . 145 B4
Viellespesse F . . . 116 B3
Viellevigne F . . . 114 B2
Vielmur-sur-Agout F . . . 130 B1
Vielsalm B . . . 80 B1
Viels Maison F . . . 91 C3
Vienenburg D . . . 73 C3
Vienna = Wien A . . 111 A3
Vienne F . . . 117 B4
Vieritz D . . . 73 B5
Viernheim D . . . 93 B4
Vierraden D . . . 74 A3
Viersen D . . . 80 A2
Vierville-sur-Mer F . 88 A3
Vierzon F . . . 103 B4
Vieselbach D . . . 82 B3
Vieste I . . . 171 B4
Vietas S . . . 194 C9
Vieteren B . . . 78 B2
Vietri di Potenza I . 172 B1
Vietri sul Mare I . . 170 C2
Vieux-Boucau-les-Bains F . . . 128 C1
Vif F . . . 118 B2
Vig DK . . . 61 D1
Vigásio I . . . 121 B3
Vigaun A . . . 109 B4
Vigeland N . . . 52 B3
Vigeois F . . . 116 B1
Vigévano I . . . 120 B1
Viggianello I . . . 174 B2
Viggiano I . . . 174 A1
Vigliano I . . . 169 A3
Vigmostad N . . . 52 B3
Vignale I . . . 119 B5
Vignanello I . . . 168 A2
Vigneulles-lès-Hattonchâtel F . . 92 C1
Vignevieille F . . . 146 B3
Vignola I . . . 135 A4
Vignory F . . . 105 A4
Vignoux-sur Barangeon F . . . 103 B4
Vigo E . . . 140 B2
Vigo di Fassa I . . . 121 A4
Vigone I . . . 119 C4
Vigrestad N . . . 52 B1
Vihiers F . . . 102 B1
Viitasaari FIN . . . 8 A4
Vík IS . . . 190 D6
Vik
Nordland N . . . 195 E3
Rogaland N . . . 52 B1
Sogn og Fjordane N . . . 46 A3
S . . . 63 C2
Vika S . . . 50 B2
Vikajärvi FIN . . . 197 C9
Vikane N . . . 54 A1
Vikarbyn S . . . 50 B2
Vike N . . . 46 B2
Vikedal N . . . 52 A1
Vikeland N . . . 53 B3
Viken
Jämtland S . . . 199 A10
Skåne S . . . 61 C2
Viker N . . . 48 B2
Vikersund N . . . 48 C1
Vikeså N . . . 52 B2
Vikevåg N . . . 52 A1
Vikingstad S . . . 56 B1
Vikmanshyttan S . . 50 B2
Vikna N . . . 199 A7
Vikøy N . . . 46 B3
Vikran
Troms N . . . 192 C2
Troms N . . . 194 B7
Viksjö S . . . 200 D3
Viksøyri N . . . 46 A3
Viksta S . . . 51 B4
Vila Boim P . . . 155 C3
Vila Chãde Ourique P . . . 154 B2
Viladamat E . . . 147 B4
Vila de Cruces E . . 140 B2
Vila de Rei P . . . 154 B2
Vila do Bispo P . . . 160 B1
Vila do Conde P . . . 148 A1
Viladrau E . . . 147 C3
Vila Flor P . . . 149 A2
Vila Franca das Navas P . . . 149 B2
Vilafranca del Maestrat E . . . 153 B3
Vilafranca del Penedès E . . . 147 C2
Vila Franca de Xira P . . . 154 C1
Vila Fresca P . . . 154 C1
Vilagarcía de Arousa E . . . 140 B2
Vilajuiga E . . . 147 B4
Vilamarin E . . . 140 B3
Vilamartín de Valdeorras E . . . 141 B3
Vila Nogueira P . . . 154 C1
Vila Nova da Baronia P . . . 154 C2
Vilanova de Castelló E . . . 159 B3
Vila Nova de Cerveira P . . . 140 C2
Vila Nova de Famalicão P . . . 148 A1
Vila Nova de Foz Côa P . . . 149 A2
Vila Nova de Gaia P . . . 148 A1
Vila Nova de Milfontes P . . . 160 B1
Vila Nova de Paiva P . . . 148 B2
Vila Nova de São Bento P . . . 161 B2
Vilanova de Sau E 147 C3
Vilanova i la Geltrú E . . . 147 C2
Vilapedre E . . . 140 A3
Vila Pouca de Aguiar P . . . 148 A2
Vila Praja de Ancora P . . . 148 A1
Vilarandelo P . . . 148 A2
Vilar de Santos E . . 140 B3
Vilardevós E . . . 141 C3
Vila Real P . . . 148 A2
Vila-real de los Infantes E . . . 159 B3
Vila Real de Santo António P . . . 160 B2
Vilar Formosa P . . 149 B3
Vila-Rodona E . . . 147 C2
Vila Ruiva P . . . 160 A2
Vilasantar E . . . 140 A2
Vilaseca E . . . 147 C2
Vila Seca P . . . 148 B1
Vilassar de Mar E . 147 C3
Vilasund S . . . 195 D5
Vila Velha de Ródão P . . . 155 B3
Vila Verde
Braga P . . . 148 A1
Lisboa P . . . 154 B1
Vila Verde de Filcalho P . . . 161 B2
Vila Viçosa P . . . 155 C3
Vilches E . . . 157 B4
Vildbjerg DK . . . 59 B1
Vilémov CZ . . . 97 B3
Vileyka BY . . . 13 A7
Vilhelmina S . . . 200 B2
Vilia GR . . . 184 A4
Viljandi EST . . . 8 C4
Villabáñez E . . . 150 A3
Villablanca E . . . 161 B2
Villablino E . . . 141 B4
Villabona E . . . 144 A1
Villabragima E . . . 142 C1
Villabuena del Puente E . . . 150 A2
Villacadima E . . . 151 A4
Villacañas E . . . 157 A4
Villacarriedo E . . . 143 A3
Villacarrillo E . . . 164 A1
Villa Castelli I . . . 173 B3
Villacastín E . . . 150 B3
Villach A . . . 109 C4
Villacidro I . . . 179 C2
Villaconejos E . . . 151 B4
Villaconejos de Trabaque E . . . 152 B1
Villa Cova de Lixa P . . . 148 A1
Villada E . . . 142 B2
Villadangos del Páramo E . . . 141 B5
Villadecanes E . . . 141 B4
Villa del Prado E . . 150 B3
Villa del Río E . . . 157 C3
Villadepera E . . . 149 A3
Villa de Peralonso E . . . 149 A3
Villa di Chiavenna I . . . 120 A2
Villadiego E . . . 142 B2
Villadompardo E . . 163 A3
Villadóssola I . . . 119 A5
Villaeles de Valdavia E . . . 142 B2
Villaescusa de Haro E . . . 158 B1
Villafáfila E . . . 142 C1
Villafeliche E . . . 152 A2
Villaflores E . . . 150 A2
Villafrades de Campos E . . . 142 B2
Villafranca
Avila E . . . 150 B2
Navarra E . . . 144 B2
Villafranca de Córdoba E . . . 157 C3
Villafranca del Bierzo E . . . 141 B4
Villafranca de los Barros E . . . 155 C4
Villafranca de los Caballeros E . . . 157 A4
Villafranca di Verona I . . . 121 B3
Villafranca in Lunigiana I . . . 134 A2
Villafranca-Montes de Oca E . . . 143 B3
Villafranca Tirrena I . . . 177 A4
Villafranco del Campo E . . . 152 B2
Villafranco del Guadalquivir E . . 161 B3
Villafrati I . . . 176 B2
Villafrechós E . . . 142 C1
Villafruela E . . . 143 C3
Villagarcia de las Torres E . . . 156 B1
Villaggio Mancuso I . . . 175 B2
Villagonzalo E . . . 156 B1
Villagotón E . . . 141 B4
Villagrains F . . . 128 B2
Villaharta E . . . 156 B3
Villahermosa E . . . 158 C1
Villaherreros E . . . 142 B2
Villahoz E . . . 143 B3
Villaines-la-Juhel F 89 B3
Villajoyosa E . . . 159 C3
Villalago I . . . 169 B3
Villalba
E . . . 140 A3
I . . . 176 B2
Villalba de Calatrava E . . . 157 B4
Villalba de Guardo E . . . 142 B2
Villalba del Alcor E . . . 161 B3
Villalba de la Sierra E . . . 152 B1
Villalba de los Alcores E . . . 142 C2
Villalba de los Barros E . . . 155 C4
Villalba del Rey E . 151 B5
Villalcampo E . . . 149 A3
Villalcázar de Sirga E . . . 142 B2
Villalengua E . . . 152 A2
Villalgordo del Júcar E . . . 158 B1
Villalgordo del Marquesado E . . 158 B1
Villalmóndar E . . . 143 B3
Villalón de Campos E . . . 142 B1
Villalonga E . . . 159 C3
Villalonso E . . . 150 A2
Villalpando E . . . 142 C1
Villaluenga E . . . 151 B4
Villalumbroso E . . . 142 B2
Villálvaro E . . . 143 C3
Villamalea E . . . 158 B2
Villamanán E . . . 142 B1
Villamanín E . . . 142 B1
Villamanrique E . . . 157 B5
Villamanrique de la Condesa E . . . 161 B3
Villamanta E . . . 151 B3
Villamantilla E . . . 151 B3
Villamar I . . . 179 C2
Villamartín E . . . 162 B2
Villamartín de Campos E . . . 142 B2
Villamartin de Don Sancho E . . . 142 B1
Villamassárgia I . . 179 C2
Villamayor E . . . 142 A1
Villamayor de Calatrava E . . . 157 B3
Villamayor de Campos E . . . 142 C1
Villamayor de Santiago E . . . 157 A5
Villamblard F . . . 129 A3
Villamejil E . . . 141 B4
Villamesias E . . . 156 A2
Villaminaya E . . . 157 A4
Villa Minozzo I . . . 134 A3
Villamor de los Escuderos E . . . 150 A2
Villamoronta E . . . 142 B2
Villamuelas E . . . 151 C4
Villamuriel de Cerrato E . . . 142 C2
Villandraut F . . . 128 B2
Villanova I . . . 173 B3
Villanova d'Asti I . . 119 C4
Villanova del Battista I . . . 171 B3
Villanova Mondov i I . . . 133 A3
Villanova Monteleone I . . . 178 B2
Villante E . . . 143 B3
Villantério I . . . 120 B2
Villanubla E . . . 142 C2
Villanueva de Alcardete E . . . 157 A4
Villanueva de Alcorón E . . . 152 B1
Villanueva de Algaidas E . . . 163 A3
Villanueva de Argaña E . . . 143 B3
Villanueva de Bogas E . . . 157 A4
Villanueva de Córdoba E . . . 156 B3
Villanueva de Gállego E . . . 144 C3
Villanueva del Aceral E . . . 150 A3
Villanueva de la Concepcion E . . 163 B3
Villanueva de la Fuente E . . . 158 C1
Villanueva de la Jara E . . . 158 B2
Villanueva de la Reina E . . . 157 B4
Villanueva del Arzobispo E . . . 164 A2
Villanueva de la Serena E . . . 156 B2
Villanueva de la Sierra E . . . 149 B3
Villanueva de las Manzanas E . . . 142 B1
Villanueva de las Peras E . . . 141 C5
Villanueva de las Torres E . . . 164 B1
Villanueva de la Vera E . . . 150 B2
Villanueva del Campo E . . . 142 C1
Villanueva del Duque E . . . 156 B3
Villanueva del Fresno E . . . 155 C3
Villanueva del Huerva E . . . 152 A2
Villanueva de los Castillejos E . . . 161 B2
Villanueva de los Infantes E . . . 157 B5
Villanueva del Rey E . . . 156 B2
Villanueva del Rio E . . . 162 A2
Villanueva del Río y Minas E . . . 162 A2
Villanueva del Rosario E . . . 163 B3
Villanueva del Trabuco E . . . 163 A3
Villanueva de Mesia E . . . 163 A4
Villanueva de Nía E . . . 142 B2
Villanueva de Oscos E . . . 141 A4
Villanueva de San Carlos E . . . 157 B4
Villanueva de San Juan E . . . 162 A2
Villanueva de Tapia E . . . 163 A3
Villanueva de Valdegovia E . . . 143 B3
Villány H . . . 125 B4
Villaputzu I . . . 179 C3
Villaquejida E . . . 142 B1
Villaquilambre E . . 142 B1
Villaquiran de los Infantes E . . . 142 B2
Villaralto E . . . 156 B3
Villarcayo E . . . 143 B3
Villard-de-Lans F . 118 B2
Villar de Barrio E . . 140 B3
Villar de Cañas E . . 158 B1
Villar de Chinchilla E . . . 158 C2
Villar de Ciervo E . 149 B3
Villardeciervos E . . 141 C4
Villar de Domingo Garcia E . . . 152 B1
Villardefrades E . . 142 C1
Villar del Arzobispo E . . . 159 B3
Villar del Buey E . . 149 A3
Villar del Cobo E . . 152 B2
Villar del Humo E . . 158 B2
Villar de los Navarros E . . . 152 A2
Villar del Pedroso E . . . 156 A2
Villar del Rey E . . . 155 B4
Villar del Rio E . . . 143 B4
Villar del Saz de Navalón E . . . 152 B1
Villar de Rena E . . . 156 A2
Villarejo E . . . 151 A4
Villarejo de Fuentes E . . . 158 B1
Villarejo de Orbigo E . . . 141 B5
Villarejo de Salvanes E . . . 151 B4
Villarejo-Periesteban E . . . 158 B1
Villares del Saz E . 158 B1
Villaretto I . . . 119 B4
Villargordo del Cabriel E . . . 158 B2
Villarino E . . . 149 A3
Villarino de Conso E . . . 141 B3
Villarluengo E . . . 153 B3
Villarobe E . . . 143 B3
Villarosa I . . . 177 B3
Villar Perosa I . . . 119 C4
Villarramiel E . . . 142 B2
Villarrasa E . . . 161 B3
Villarreal de San Carlos E . . . 150 C1
Villarrin de Campos E . . . 142 C1
Villarrobledo E . . . 158 B1
Villarroya de la Sierr
E . . . 15
Villarroya de los Pinares E . . . 15
Villarrubia de los Ojo
E . . . 15
Villarrubia de Santiag
E . . . 15
Villarrubio E . . . 15
Villars-les-Dombes F . . . 11
Villarta E . . . 15
Villarta de los Monte
E . . . 15
Villarta de San Juan E . . . 15
Villasana de Mena E . . . 14
Villasandino E . . . 14
Villa San Giovanni I . . . 17
Villa Santa Maria I 16
Villasante E . . . 14
Villa Santina I . . . 12
Villasarracino E . . 14
Villasayas E . . . 15
Villasdardo E . . . 14
Villaseca de Henares
E . . . 15
Villaseca de Laciana E . . . 14
Villaseca de la Sagra E . . . 15
Villaseco de los Gamitos E . . . 14
Villaseco de los Reye
E . . . 14
Villasequilla de Yepe
E . . . 15
Villasimíus I . . . 17
Villasmundo I . . . 17
Villasor I . . . 17
Villastar E . . . 15
Villastellone I . . . 11
Villatobas E . . . 15
Villatorp E . . . 15
Villatoya E . . . 15
Villavaliente E . . . 15
Villavelayo E . . . 14
Villavella E . . . 14
Villaver de de Guadalimar E . . 15
Villaverde del Rio E . . . 16
Villaviciosa E . . . 14
Villaviciosa de Córdoba E . . . 15
Villaviciosa de Odón E . . . 15
Villavieja de Yeltes E . . . 14
Villayón E . . . 14
Villé F . . . 9
Villebois-Lavalette F . . . 11
Villecerf F . . . 9
Villecomtal F . . . 13
Villedieu-les-Poêles F . . . 8
Villedieu-sur-Indre F . . . 10
Ville-di-Pietrabugno F . . . 18
Villedômain F . . . 10
Villefagnan F . . . 11
Villefontaine F . . . 11
Villefort F . . . 13
Villefranche-d'Albigeois F . . 13
Villefranche-d'Allier F . . . 11
Villefranche-de-Lauragais F . . . 14
Villefranche-de-Lonchat F . . . 12
Villefranche-de-Pana
F . . . 13
Villefranche-de-Rouergue F . . . 13
Villefranche-du-Périgord F . . . 12
Villefranche-sur-Che
F . . . 10
Villefranche-sur-Mer F . . . 13
Villefranche-sur-Saô
F . . . 11
Villegenon F . . . 10
Villel E . . . 15
Villemaur-sur-Vanne F . . . 10
Villemontais F . . . 11
Villemur-sur-Tarn F . . . 12
Villena E . . . 15
Villenauxe-la-Grande F . . . 9
Villenave-d'Ornon F . . . 12
Villeneuve
CH . . . 11
F . . . 12
Villeneuve-d'Ascq F . . . 7
Villeneuve-de-Berg F . . . 13
Villeneuve-de-Marsa
F . . . 12
Villeneuve-de-Rivière F . . . 14
Villeneuve-la-Guyard F . . . 9
Villeneuve-l'Archevêque F . . 10
Villeneuve-le-Comte F . . . 9
Villeneuve-lès-Avign
F . . . 13
Villeneuve-les-Corbières F . . . 14

neuve-St Georges
. . . . .90 C2
neuve-sur-Allier
. . . . .104 C2
neuve-sur-Lot
. . . . .129 B3
éal F. 129 B3
ias E. 142 C2
romain F 103 B3
s-Bocage
vados F 88 A3
nme F. 90 B2
s-Bretonneux
. . . . .90 B2
s-Carbonnel F 90 B2
s-Cotterêts F. .90 B3
sexel F. 105 B5
s-Farlay F 105 C4
. . . . .79 B4
s-le-Gambon
. . . . .79 B4
s-le-Lac F 106 B1
s-sur-Mer F . . .89 A3
upt F. 92 B1
ville F. 89 A4
seneux F. 91 C4
sous-la-Ferté
. . . . .105 A3
sur-Illon F 105 A5
sur-Tourbe F . .91 B4
run F 103 B3
ta Barrea I 169 B3
urbanne F. 117 B4
veyrac F. 130 B2
vocance F. 117 B4
rs-St Benoit
. . . . .104 B2
rs-St Georges
. . . . .91 C3
gen D 106 A3
ar D 81 B4
do E 142 B2
n F. 104 B3
ria E. 150 B2
s N 46 A1
us LT 13 A6
. . . . .108 B1
. . . . .58 B1
iburg D. 95 C4
ck D 95 B3
ofen D 96 C1
ult S. 63 B2
i MNE 139 C4
stre B 149 A3
orde B 79 B4
iro P. 154 B1
rcate I. 120 B2
anzo E. 140 A1
oso P 149 A3
nerby S 62 A3
utiers F 89 B4
erk CZ 96 B1
. . . . .78 B2
di CH. 108 C1
dio I. 133 A3
ixa E 147 C1
rós E 153 B4
s S. 50 B1
y F 118 B2
erg S 60 C2
a F 146 B3
a SRB 127 C2
hiaturo I 170 B2
i I. 135 B3
eby DK 65 A3
elgransele S. .195 E9
eln S. 200 B5
erup DK 58 B1
svik N 52 A2
ts F 91 C4
uil F. 103 B3
a RO 126 A3
åker S 56 A1
nes N 48 A2
rau F 146 B3
rom N 48 A2
ais F 149 A3
a
. . . . .124 A2
. . . . .182 B4
. . . . .112 A3
. . . . .123 B4
o
egra de Arriba
. . . . .143 B4
rdaland N 46 B3
r-Trøndelag N .198 B6
emark N 53 A3
ovci HR. 125 B4
den S 200 B3
inga S. 55 B4
ytsya UA. 13 D8
n F. 103 B4
n-sur-Verdon
. . . . .132 B1
löv S 61 C3
tra N 48 A1
ärn S. 50 B3
rosa S 55 A5
ela I 163 B3
ela de Sayago
. . . . .149 A4
elas E 151 B4
esa E. 143 C4
elberg D 73 B4
D 64 B2
I. 133 A3
y F 117 B4
va SLO 122 B2
teno I 108 C2
erow D 74 A1
. . . . .138 B3
. . . . .137 A4
CH. 120 A1
. . . . .88 B3
da S. 62 A2

Vireux F 91 A4
Virgen A 109 B3
Virgen de la Cabeza
E 157 B3
Virginia IRL 27 C3
Virieu F. 118 B2
Virieu-le-Grand F. .118 B2
Virje HR 124 A2
Virkkunen FIN . . .197 D10
Virklund DK 59 B2
Virovitica HR 124 B3
Virsbo S 50 C3
Virserum S 62 A3
Virtaniemi FIN . . .193 D12
Virton B 92 B1
Virtsu EST 8 C3
Viry F. 118 A3
Vis HR 138 B2
Visbek D. 71 B5
Visby
DK 64 A1
S 57 C4
Visé F 80 B1
Višegrad BIH 139 B5
Viserba I 136 A1
Viseu P. 148 B2
Visiedo E 152 B2
Viskafors S 60 B2
Visland N 52 B2
Vislanda S 62 B2
Visnes N. 52 A1
Višnja Gora SLO .123 B3
Višnjan HR. 122 B2
Višnové CZ 97 C4
Visnums-Kil S 55 A5
Viso del Marqués
E 157 B4
Visoko
BIH. 139 B4
SLO 123 A3
Visone I 119 C5
Visp CH 119 A4
Vissefjärda S 63 B3
Visselhövede D . . .72 B2
Vissenbjerg DK . . .59 C3
Vistabella del Maestrat
E 153 B3
Vistheden S 196 D3
Vita I. 176 B1
Vitanje SLO 123 A4
Vitebsk = Vitsyebsk
BY 13 A9
Viterbo I 168 A2
Vitez BIH 139 A3
Vithkuq AL 182 C2
Vitigudino E. 149 A3
Vitina
BIH. 138 B3
GR 184 B3
Vitis A 97 C3
Vitkov CZ. 98 B1
Vitoria-Gasteiz E .143 B4
Vitré F. 101 A4
Vitrey-sur-Mance
F 105 B4
Vitry-en-Artois F . .78 B2
Vitry-le-François F .91 C4
Vitry-sur-Seine F. .90 C2
Vitsand S 49 B4
Vitsyebsk = Vitebsk
BY 13 A9
Vittangi S 196 B4
Vittaryd S. 60 C3
Vitteaux F 104 B3
Vittel F 105 A4
Vittinge S 51 C4
Vittória I 177 C3
Vittório Véneto I . .122 B1
Vittsjö S 61 C3
Viù I 119 B4
Viul N 48 B2
Vivario F. 180 A2
Viveiro E 140 A3
Vivel del Rio Martin
E 152 B3
Viver E 159 B3
Viverols F. 117 B3
Viveros E. 158 C1
Viviers F 131 A3
Vivonne F 115 B4
Vivy F 102 B1
Vize TR. 186 A2
Vizille F 118 B2
Viziñada HR. 122 B2
Viziru RO 17 C7
Vizovice CZ. 98 B1
Vizvár H 124 A3
Vizzavona F 180 A2
Vizzini I. 177 B3
Vlachiotis GR 184 C3
Vlachovice CZ. . . .98 B1
Vlachovo SK 99 C4
Vláchovo Březi CZ 96 B1
Vladimirci SRB . . .127 C1
Vladimirovac SRB 127 B2
Vladislav CZ 97 B3
Vlagtwedde NL . . .71 A4
Vlajkovac SRB. . .127 B3
Vlasenica BIH 139 A4
Vlašim CZ 96 B2
Vlatkovići BIH. . . .138 A3
Vledder NL 70 B3
Vlissingen NL 79 A3
Vlkolinec SK 99 B3
Vlorë AL 182 C1
Vlotho D. 72 B1
Vnanje Gorice
SLO 123 B3
Vobarno I 121 B3
Vočin HR 124 B3
Vöcklabruck A . . .109 A4
Vöcklamarkt A . . .109 B4
Vodanj SRB 127 C2
Voderady SK 98 C1
Vodice
Istarska HR 123 B3
Šibenska HR . . .137 B4
SLO 123 B3
Vodňany CZ. 96 B2

Vodnjan HR 122 C2
Vodskov DK 58 A3
Voe GB 33 A5
Voerså DK 58 A3
Voghera I. 120 C2
Vogogna I. 119 A5
Vogué F 131 A3
Vohburg D 95 C3
Vohenstrauss D . . .95 B4
Vöhl D 81 A4
Vöhrenbach D . . .106 A3
Vöhringen D 94 C2
Void-Vacon F 92 C1
Voiron F 118 B2
Voise F. 90 C1
Voisey F. 105 B4
Voiteg RO. 126 B3
Voiteur F 105 C4
Voitsberg A 110 B2
Vojakkala FIN. . . .196 D7
Vojens DK 59 C2
Vojka SRB 127 C2
Vojlovica SRB . . .127 C2
Vojnić HR. 123 B4
Vojnice SK 112 B2
Vojnik SLO 123 A4
Vojvoda Stepa
SRB 126 B2
Volada GR 188 D2
Volargne I. 121 B3
Volary CZ. 96 C1
Volče SLO 122 A2
Volda N. 198 C3
Volendam NL 70 B2
Volga RUS 9 C11
Volimes GR 184 B1
Volissos GR. 185 A6
Volkach D. 94 B2
Völkermarkt A 110 C1
Volkhov RUS. 9 C8
Völklingen D 92 B2
Volkmarsen D 81 A5
Voll N 198 C4
Vollenhove NL 70 B2
Vollore-Montagne
F 117 B3
Vollsjö S. 61 D3
Volodymyr-Volyns'kyy
UA 13 C6
Volokolamsk RUS. . .9 D9
Volos GR 182 D4
Volosovo RUS. 9 C6
Volovets UA. 13 D5
Voltággio I 120 C1
Volta Mantovana I 121 B3
Volterra I 135 B3
Voltri I. 133 A4
Volturara Áppula I 170 B3
Volturara Irpina I . .170 C2
Volvic F 116 B3
Volx F 132 B1
Volyně CZ. 96 B1
Vonitsa GR. 182 E2
Vönöck H. 111 B4
Vonsild DK. 59 C2
Voorschoten NL . . .70 B1
Vopnafjörður IS . .191 B11
Vorau A. 110 B2
Vorbasse DK 59 C2
Vorchdorf A 109 B4
Vorden
D. 71 B5
NL 71 B3
Vordernberg A . . .110 B1
Vordingborg DK . . .65 A4
Vorë AL 182 B1
Voreppe F 118 B2
Vorey F. 117 B3
Vorgod DK 59 B1
Vormsund N. 48 B3
Võru EST 8 D5
Voskopojë AL. . . .182 C2
Voss N. 46 B3
Votice CZ. 96 B2
Voué F. 91 C4
Vouillé F. 115 B4
Voulx F. 90 C2
Voussac F 116 A3
Vouvray F. 102 B2
Vouvry CH 119 A3
Vouzela P. 148 B1
Vouziers F 91 B4
Voves F 103 A3
Voxna S 50 A2
Voy GB 33 B3
Voynitsa RUS 3 D12
Voznesenye RUS. . . .9 B9
Vrå
DK 58 A2
S 60 C3
Vráble SK. 98 C2
Vračenovići MNE. .139 C4
Vračev Gaj SRB. .127 C3
Vračevsnica SRB .127 C2
Vrådal N 53 A4
Vrakneika GR 184 A2
Vrana HR 123 C3
Vranduk BIH 139 A3
Vrångö S 60 B1
Vrani RO 127 B3
Vranić SRB 127 C2
Vraniči BIH. 139 B4
Vranja HR. 123 B3
Vranjak BIH 125 C4
Vranje SRB 16 D4
Vranovice CZ. 97 C4

Vrbnik continued
Zadarsko-Kninska
HR. 138 A2
Vrbno pod Pradědem
CZ 85 B5
Vrboska HR 138 B2
Vrbov SK. 99 B4
Vrbovce SK 98 C1
Vrbové SK. 98 C1
Vrbovec HR 124 B2
Vrbovski SRB 127 C2
Vrbovsko HR 123 B4
Vrchlabí CZ. 84 B3
Vrčin SRB 127 C2
Vrdy CZ. 97 B3
Vrebac HR 137 A4
Vreden D 71 B3
Vreoci SRB 127 C2
Vretstorp S 55 A5
Vrginmost HR 124 B1
Vrgorac HR 138 B3
Vrhnika SLO 123 B3
Vrhovine HR 123 C4
Vrhpolje SRB 127 C1
Vriezenveen NL . . .71 B3
Vrigne-aux-Bois F .91 B4
Vrigstad S 62 A2
Vrlika HR 138 B2
Vrnograč BIH 124 B1
Vron F 78 B1
Vroomshoop NL . . .71 B3
Vroutek CZ. 83 B5
Vrpolje HR 125 B4
Vršac SRB 126 B3
Vrsar HR 122 B2
Vrsi HR. 137 A4
Vrtoče BIH 124 C2
Vrútky SK. 98 B2
Všeruby CZ 95 B4
Všestary CZ. 85 B3
Vsetin CZ. 98 B1
Vučkovica SRB . .127 D2
Vught NL 79 A5
Vuillafans F 105 B5
Vukovar HR 125 B5
Vuku N. 199 B8
Vulcan RO 17 C5
Vulcănești MD. . . .17 C8
Vuoggatjålme S . .195 D7
Vuojärvi FIN 197 B9
Vuolijoki FIN 3 D10
Vuollerim S 196 C3
Vuotso FIN. 197 A10
Vuzenica SLO 110 C2
Vyartsilya RUS 9 A7
Vyborg RUS. 9 B6
Výčapy-Opatovce
SK 98 C2
Východna SK 99 B3
Vydrany SK 111 A4
Vyerkhnyadzvinsk
BY 13 A7
Vyhne SK 98 C2
Vy-lès Lure F 105 B5
Vylkove UA 17 C8
Vynohradiv UA 17 A5
Vyshniy Volochek
RUS 9 D9
Vyškov CZ 97 B5
Vysoké nad Kysucou
SK 98 B2
Vysoké Mýto CZ. . .97 B4
Vysokovsk RUS . . .9 D10
Vyšší Brod CZ. 96 C2
Vytegra RUS 9 B10

W

Waabs D. 64 B2
Waalwijk NL 79 A5
Waarschoot B 79 A3
Wabern D. 81 A5
Wąbrzeźno PL. . . .69 B3
Wachock PL. 87 A5
Wachow D. 74 B1
Wachów PL. 86 B2
Wächtersbach D . . .81 B5
Wackersdorf D 95 B4
Waddington GB. . . .40 B3
Wadebridge GB. . . .42 B2
Wadelsdorf D. 84 A2
Wädenswil CH . . .107 B3
Wadern D 92 B2
Wadersloh D 81 A4
Wadlew PL. 86 A3
Wadowice PL. 99 B3
Wagenfeld D 72 B1
Wageningen NL. . . .70 C2
Waghäusel D. 93 B4
Waging D. 109 B3
Wagrain A 109 B4
Wagrowiec PL 76 B2
Wahlsdorf D. 74 C2
Wahlstedt D. 64 C3
Wahrenholz D 73 B3
Waiblingen D 94 C1
Waidhaus D. 95 B4
Waidhofen an der
Thaya A 97 C3
Waidhofen an der Ybbs
A. 110 B1
Waimes B 80 B2
Wainfleet All Saints
GB. 41 B4
Waizenkirchen A. . .96 C1
Wakefield GB. 40 B2
Wałbrzych PL. 85 B4
Walchensee D 108 B2
Walchsee A 109 B3
Wałcz PL. 76 A1
Wald CH 107 B3
Waldachtal D 93 C4
Waldbach A 110 B2
Waldböckelheim D .93 B3
Waldbröl D 81 B3
Waldeck D. 81 A5
Waldenburg D 83 B4

Waldfischbach-
Burgalben D 93 B3
Waldheim D 83 A5
Waldkappel D 82 A1
Waldkirch D. 106 A2
Waldkirchen D. . . .96 C1
Waldkirchen am Wesen
A. 96 C1
Waldkraiburg D. . .109 A3
Wald-Michelbach D 93 B4
Waldmohr D. 93 B3
Waldmünchen D . . .95 B4
Waldring A. 109 B3
Waldsassen D. 95 A4
Waldshut D 106 B3
Waldstatt CH 107 B4
Waldwisse F 92 B2
Walenstadt CH . .107 B4
Walentynów PL . . .87 A5
Walichnowy PL . . .86 A2
Walincourt F 90 A3
Walkenried D 82 A2
Walkeringham GB. .40 B3
Wallasey GB 38 A3
Walldürn D. 94 B1
Wallenfells D 82 B3
Wallenhorst D 71 B5
Wallers F 78 B3
Wallersdorf D 95 C4
Wallerstein D. 94 C2
Wallingford GB 44 B2
Wallitz D. 74 A1
Walls GB 33 A5
Wallsbüll D 64 B2
Walmer GB. 45 B5
Walsall GB 40 C2
Walshoutem B 79 B5
Walsrode D 72 B2
Waltenhofen D . . .107 B5
Waltershausen D . .82 B2
Waltham Abbey GB 45 B4
Waltham on the Wolds
GB. 40 C3
Walton-on-Thames
GB. 44 B3
Walton-on-the-Naze
GB. 45 B5
Wamba E 142 C2
Wanderup D 64 B2
Wandlitz D. 74 B2
Wanfried D 82 A2
Wangen im Allgäu
D 107 B4
Wangerooge D 71 A4
Wangersen D 72 A2
Wängi CH. 107 B3
Wanna D 64 C1
Wansford GB. 40 C3
Wantage GB. 44 B2
Wanzleben D 73 B4
Waplewo PL. 77 A5
Wapnica PL. 75 A4
Wapno PL. 76 B2
Warburg D 81 A5
Wardenburg D 71 A5
Ware GB. 44 B3
Waregem B 79 B3
Wareham GB. 43 B4
Waremme B 79 B5
Waren D 74 A1
Warendorf D 71 C4
Warga NL 70 A2
Warin D 65 C4
Wark GB. 37 A4
Warka PL 87 A5
Warkworth GB 37 A5
Warlubie PL. 69 B3
Warminster GB 43 A4
Warnemünde D . . .65 B5
Warnow D 65 C4
Warnsveld NL 70 B3
Warrenpoint GB . . .27 B4
Warrington GB 38 A4
Warsaw = Warszawa
PL. 77 B6
Warsingsfehn D . . .71 A4
Warsow D 73 A4
Warstein D 81 A4
Warszawa = Warsaw
PL. 77 B6
Warta PL. 86 A2
Wartberg A. 110 B1
Warth A. 107 B5
Warwick GB. 44 A2
Warza D. 82 B2
Wasbister GB 33 B3
Washington GB. . . .37 B5
Wąsosz PL. 85 A4
Wasselonne F 93 C3
Wassen CH 107 C3
Wassenaar NL. . . .70 B1
Wasserauen CH . .107 B4
Wasserburg D 108 A3
Wassertrüdingen
D. 94 B2
Wassy F. 91 C4
Wasungen D. 82 B2
Watchet GB. 43 A3
Waterford IRL 30 B1
Watergrasshill IRL. .29 B3
Waterloo B 79 B4
Waterville IRL 29 C1
Watford GB. 44 B3
Wathlingen D 72 B3
Watten
F. 78 B2
GB. 32 C3
Wattens A. 108 B2
Watton GB 41 C4
Wattwil CH. 107 B4
Waunfawr GB 38 A2
Wavignies F. 90 B2
Wavre B 79 B4
Wearhead GB 37 B4
Wechadłow PL. . . .87 B4
Węchadlow PL. . . .87 B4
Wedel D 72 A2
Wedemark D. 72 B2
Weedon Bec GB . . .44 A2
Weener D 71 A4
Weert NL 80 A1

Weesp NL. 70 B2
Weeze D. 80 A2
Weferlingen D 73 B4
Wegeleben D. 82 A3
Weggis CH. 106 B3
Węgierska-Górka
PL. 99 B3
Węgorzyno PL. . . .75 A4
Węgrzynice PL 75 B4
Wegscheid D. 96 C1
Wehdel D. 72 A1
Wehr D 106 B2
Wehretten D 80 B2
Weibersbrunn D . . .94 B1
Weichering D 95 C3
Weida D 83 B4
Weiden D 95 B4
Weidenberg D 95 B3
Weidenhain D 83 A4
Weidenstetten D . . .94 C1
Weierbach D 93 B3
Weikersheim D 94 B1
Weil D 108 A1
Weil am Rhein D . .106 B2
Weilburg D 81 B4
Weil der Stadt D . . .93 C4
Weilerswist D 80 B2
Weilheim
Baden-Württemberg
D 94 C1
Bayern D 108 B2
Weilmünster D. . . .81 B4
Weiltensfeld A 110 C1
Weimar D. 82 B3
Weinberg D 94 B2
Weinfelden CH . . .107 B4
Weingarten
Baden-Württemberg
D 93 B4
Baden-Württemberg
D 107 B4
Weinheim D 93 B4
Weinstadt D. 94 C1
Weismain D. 82 B3
Weissbriach A 109 C4
Weissenbach A . . .108 B1
Weissenberg D 84 A2
Weissenbrunn D . . .82 B3
Weissenburg D 94 B2
Weissenfels D 83 A3
Weissenhorn D 94 C2
Weissenkirchen A. .97 C3
Weissensee D 82 A3
Weissenstadt D. . . .83 B3
Weisskirchen im
Steiermark A . . .110 B1
Weisstannen CH . .107 C4
Weisswasser D . . .84 A2
Weitendorf D. 65 C5
Weitersfeld A 97 C3
Weitersfelden A. . . .96 C2
Weitnau D 107 B5
Wéitra S 96 C2
Weiz A. 110 B2
Wejherowo PL. . . .68 A3
Welkenraedt B 80 B1
Wellaune D 83 A4
Wellin B 91 A5
Wellingborough
GB. 44 A3
Wellington
Somerset GB. . . .43 B3
Telford & Wrekin
GB. 38 B4
Wellingtonbridge
IRL. 30 B2
Wells GB. 43 A4
Wells-next-the-Sea
GB. 41 C4
Wels A 109 A5
Welschenrohr CH .106 B2
Welshpool GB 38 B3
Welver D 81 A3
Welwyn Garden City
GB. 44 B3
Welzheim D 94 C1
Welzow D. 84 A2
Wem GB. 38 B4
Wembury GB 42 B2
Wemding D 94 C2
Wenden D 81 B3
Wendisch Rietz D . .74 B3
Wendlingen D 94 C1
Weng A. 109 A4
Weng bei Admont
A. 110 B1
Wengen CH 106 C2
Wenigzell A 110 B2
Wennigsen D 72 B2
Wenns A. 108 B1
Wenzenbach D 95 B4
Weppersdorf A. . . .111 B3
Werben D 73 B4
Werbig D 74 C2
Werdau D 83 B4
Werder D 74 B1
Werdohl D 81 A3
Werfen A 109 B4
Werkendam NL . . .79 A4
Werl D 81 A3
Werlte D. 71 B4
Wermelskirchen D .80 A3
Wermsdorf D. 83 A4
Wernberg Köblitz
D. 95 B4
Werne D 81 A3
Werneck D 94 B2
Werneuchen D 74 B2
Wernigerode D 82 A2
Wertach D 108 B1
Wertheim D 94 B1
Wertingen D 94 C2
Weseke D 80 A2
Wesel D. 80 A2
Wesenberg D 74 A1
Wesendorf D 73 B3
Wesołowo PL. 77 A5
Wesselburen D 64 B1
Wesseling D 80 B2
West Bridgford GB .40 C2

West Bromwich
GB. 40 C2
Westbury
Shropshire GB. . .38 B4
Wiltshire GB. 43 A4
Westbury-on-Severn
GB. 39 C4
Westendorf A. . . .108 B3
Westensee D 64 B2
Westerbork NL 71 B3
Westerburg D. 81 B3
Westerhaar NL. . . .71 B3
Westerholt D 71 A4
Westerkappeln D . .71 B4
Westerland D. 64 B1
Westerlo B. 79 A4
Westerstede D. . . .71 A4
West Haddon GB. . .44 A2
Westheim D. 94 B2
Westhill GB 33 D4
Westkapelle
B. 78 A3
NL 79 A3
West Kilbride GB . . .34 C3
West Linton GB . . .35 C4
West Lulworth GB. .43 B4
West Mersea GB . . .45 B4
Westminster GB . . .44 B3
Weston GB. 40 C1
Weston-super-Mare
GB. 43 A4
Westport IRL 28 A2
Westruther GB. . . .35 C5
West-Terschelling
NL 70 A2
Westward Ho! GB . .42 A2
West Woodburn
GB. 37 A4
Wetheral GB 37 B4
Wetherby GB. 40 B2
Wetter
Hessen D. 81 B4
Nordrhein-Westfalen
D. 80 A3
Wetteren B. 79 A3
Wettin D. 83 A3
Wettringen D 71 B4
Wetzikon CH 107 B3
Wetzlar D. 81 B4
Wewelsfleth D 64 C2
Wexford IRL. 30 B2
Weybridge GB. 44 B3
Weyerbusch D. 81 B3
Weyer Markt A . . .110 B1
Weyersheim F 93 C3
Weyhe D. 72 B1
Weyhill GB. 44 B2
Weymouth GB. 43 B4
Weyregg A 109 B4
Wezep NL. 70 B3
Węzyska PL. 75 B3
Whalton GB. 37 A5
Whauphill GB. 36 B2
Wheatley GB. 44 B2
Whickham GB. 37 B5
Whipsnade GB 44 B3
Whitburn GB 35 C4
Whitby GB 37 B6
Whitchurch
Hampshire GB. . .44 B2
Herefordshire GB. .39 C4
Shropshire GB. . .38 B4
White Bridge GB . . .32 D2
Whitegate IRL. 29 C3
Whitehaven GB. . . .36 B3
Whitehead GB. 27 B5
Whithorn GB. 36 B2
Whitley Bay GB. . . .37 A5
Whitstable GB. 45 B5
Whittington GB. . . .38 B4
Whittlesey GB 41 C3
Wiązów PL. 85 B5
Wick GB. 32 C3
Wickede D. 81 A3
Wickford GB. 45 B4
Wickham GB 44 C2
Wickham Market
GB. 45 A5
Wicklow IRL. 30 B2
Wicko PL. 68 A2
Widawa PL. 86 A2
Widdrington GB . . .37 A5
Widecombe in the Moor
GB. 42 B3
Widemouth GB. . . .42 B2
Widnes GB. 38 A4
Widuchowo PL. . . .74 A3
Więcbork PL 76 A2
Wiefelstede D 71 A5
Wiehe D. 82 A3
Wiehl D. 81 B3
Wiek D. 66 B2
Większyce PL 86 B1
Wielbark PL 77 A5
Wiele PL. 68 B2
Wieleń PL. 75 B5
Wielgie
Kujawsko-Pomorskie
PL. 77 B4
Łódzkie PL. 86 A3
Mazowieckie PL. .87 A5
Wielgomłyny PL. . .87 A3
Wielichowo PL. . . .75 B5
Wieliczka PL. 99 B4
Wielka Łąka PL. . .76 A3
Wielowies PL. 86 B2
Wieluń PL. 86 A2
Wien = Vienna A . .111 A3
Wiener Neustadt
A. 111 B3
Wiepke D. 73 B4
Wierden NL 71 B3
Wieren D 73 B3
Wieruszów PL 86 A2
Wierzbica
Mazowieckie PL. .77 B6
Mazowieckie PL. .87 A5
Wierzbie PL. 86 A2

272 Wie–Zyy

Wierzbięcin PL 75 A4
Wierzchowo PL 75 A5
Wierzchucino PL. . .68 A3
Wierzchy PL. 86 A2
Wies A 110 C2
Wiesau D 95 B4
Wiesbaden D. 93 A4
Wieselburg A. 110 A2
Wiesen CH. 107 C4
Wiesenburg D. 73 B5
Wiesenfelden D. . . .95 B4
Wiesensteig D. 94 C1
Wiesentheid D. 94 B2
Wiesloch D 93 B4
Wiesmath A 111 B3
Wiesmoor D 71 A4
Wietmarschen D . . .71 B4
Wietze D. 72 B2
Wigan GB. 38 A4
Wiggen CH. 106 C2
Wigston GB 40 C2
Wigton GB. 36 B3
Wigtown GB. 36 B2
Wijchen NL 80 A1
Wijhe NL. 70 B3
Wijk bij Duurstede
  NL 70 C2
Wil CH 107 B4
Wilamowice PL 99 B3
Wilczęta PL. 69 A4
Wilczkowice PL. . . .77 B4
Wilczna PL. 76 B3
Wilczyn PL. 76 B3
Wildalpen A 110 B1
Wildbad D 93 C4
Wildberg
  Baden-Württemberg
  D. 93 C4
  Brandenburg D . .74 B1
Wildegg CH 106 B3
Wildendürnbach A .97 C4
Wildeshausen D . . .72 B1
Wildon A 110 C2
Wilfersdorf A 97 C4
Wilhelmsburg
  A. 110 A2
  D 74 A2
Wilhelmsdorf D . . .107 B4
Wilhelmshaven D . .71 A5
Wilków PL 77 B5
Willebadessen D. . .81 A5
Willebroek B 79 A4
Willgottheim F. 93 C3
Willhermsdorf D . . .94 B2
Willich D. 80 A2
Willingen D 81 A4
Willington GB 37 B5
Willisau CH 106 B3
Wilmslow GB. 40 B1
Wilsdruff D. 83 A5
Wilster D 64 C2
Wilsum D 71 B3
Wilton GB. 44 B2
Wiltz L 92 B1
Wimborne Minster
  GB 43 B5
Wimereux F 78 B1
Wimmenau F. 93 C3
Wimmis CH 106 C2
Wincanton GB. 43 A4
Winchcombe GB. . .44 B2
Winchelsea GB 45 C4
Winchester GB 44 B2
Windermere GB . . .36 B4
Windischeschenbach
  D 95 B4
Windischgarsten
  A. 110 B1
Windorf D. 96 C1
Windsbach D 94 B2
Windsor GB 44 B3
Wingene B 78 A3
Wingham GB. 45 B5
Winkleigh GB. 42 B3
Winklern A 109 C3
Winnenden D. 94 C1
Winnica PL. 77 B5
Winnigstedt D. 73 B3
Winnweiler D 93 B3
Winschoten NL 71 A4
Winsen
  Niedersachsen D. .72 A3
  Niedersachsen D. .72 B2
Winsford GB 38 A4
Wińsko PL. 85 A4
Winslow GB 44 B3
Winsum
  Friesland NL 70 A2
  Groningen NL 71 A3
Winterberg D 81 A4
Winterfeld D. 73 B4
Winterswijk NL 71 C3
Winterthur CH 107 B3
Wintzenheim F 106 A2
Winzer D. 95 C5
Wipperdorf D 82 A2
Wipperfürth D 80 A3
Wirksworth GB 40 B2
Wisbech GB. 41 C4
Wischhafen D 64 C2
Wishaw GB 35 C4
Wisła PL. 98 B2
Wisła Wielka PL. . . .98 B2
Wislica PL. 87 B4
Wismar D. 65 C4
Wisniewo PL 77 A5
Wiśniowa PL 99 B4
Wissant F. 78 B1
Wissembourg F 93 B3
Wissen D 81 B3
Witanowice PL 99 B3
Witham GB. 45 B4
Withern GB 41 B4
Withernsea GB 41 B4
Witkowo PL 76 B2
Witney GB 44 B2

Witnica PL 75 B3
Witonia PL. 77 B4
Witry-les-Reims F . .91 B4
Wittdün D. 64 B1
Wittelsheim F 106 B2
Witten D. 80 A3
Wittenberge D 73 A4
Wittenburg D 73 A4
Wittenheim F 106 B2
Wittingen D 73 B3
Wittichenau D 84 A2
Wittighausen D 94 B1
Wittlich D. 92 B2
Wittislingen D 94 C2
Wittmannsdorf A . .110 C2
Wittmund D 71 A4
Wittorf D 72 A2
Wittstock D 73 A5
Witzenhausen D . . .82 A1
Wiveliscombe GB . .43 A3
Wivenhoe GB 45 B4
Władysławowo PL . .69 A3
Wleń PL 84 A3
Włocławek PL 77 B4
Włodawa PL. 13 C5
Włodzimierzów PL .87 A3
Włosień PL. 84 A3
Włostow PL 87 B5
Włoszakowice PL . .75 C5
Włoszczowa PL 87 B3
Wöbbelin D 73 A4
Woburn GB 44 B3
Wodzisław PL 87 B4
Wodzisław Śląski
  PL. 98 B2
Woerden NL. 70 B1
Woerth F 93 C3
Wohlen CH 106 B3
Woippy F 92 B2
Wojcieszów PL 85 B3
Wojkowice Kościelne
  PL. 86 B3
Wojnicz PL. 99 B4
Woking GB. 44 B3
Wokingham GB. . . .44 B3
Wola Jachowa PL . .87 B4
Wola Niechcicka
  PL. 86 A3
Wolbórz PL 87 A3
Wolbrom PL 87 B3
Wołczyn PL. 86 A2
Woldegk D 74 A2
Wolfach D 93 C3
Wolfegg D 107 B4
Wolfen D. 83 A4
Wolfenbüttel D 73 B3
Wolfersheim D. 81 B4
Wolfhagen D 81 A5
Wolfratshausen D 108 B2
Wolfsberg A 110 C1
Wolf's Castle GB . . .39 C2
Wolfshagen D 74 A2
Wolfstein D 93 B3
Wolfurt A 107 B4
Wolgast D 66 B2
Wolhusen CH 106 B3
Wolin PL. 67 C3
Wolka PL. 87 A4
Wolkenstein D. 83 B5
Wolkersdorf A 97 C4
Wöllersdorf A. 111 B3
Wollin D 73 B5
Wöllstadt D 81 B4
Wolmirstedt D 73 B4
Wolnzach D 95 C3
Wołów PL. 85 A4
Wolsztyn PL 75 B5
Wolvega NL 70 B2
Wolverhampton
  GB 40 C1
Wolverton GB 44 A3
Wombwell GB 40 B2
Woodbridge GB. . . .45 A5
Woodhall Spa GB . .41 B3
Woodstock GB 44 B2
Wookey Hole GB . . .43 A4
Wool GB. 43 B4
Woolacombe GB . . .42 A2
Wooler GB 37 A4
Woolwich GB. 45 B4
Wooperton GB 37 A5
Worb CH 106 C2
Worbis D 82 A2
Worcester GB 39 B4
Wördern A 97 C4
Wörgl A 108 B3
Workington GB 36 B3
Worksop GB 40 B2
Workum NL 70 B2
Wörlitz D 83 A4
Wormer NL. 70 B1
Wormhout F 78 B2
Wormit GB 35 B5
Worms D 93 B4
Worpswede D 72 A1
Wörrstadt D. 93 B4
Wörschach A 110 B1
Worsley GB 38 A4
Wörth
  Bayern D. 93 B5
  Bayern D. 95 B4
  Bayern D. 95 C4
  Rheinland-Pfalz D.93 B4
Worthing GB 44 C3
Woudsend NL 70 B2
Woumen B 78 A2
Woźniki PL. 86 B3
Wragby GB 41 B3
Wrangle GB 41 B4
Wręczyca Wlk. PL. .86 B2
Wredenhagen D . . .73 A5
Wremen D 72 A1
Wrentham GB 45 A5
Wrexham GB 38 A3
Wriedel D 72 A3
Wriezen D 74 B3
Wrist D. 64 C2
Wróblewo
  Mazowieckie PL. .77 B5

Wróblewo continued
  Wielkopolskie PL .75 B5
Wrocki PL. 69 B4
Wrocław PL 85 A5
Wronki PL 75 B5
Wroxham GB 41 C5
Września PL 76 B2
Wrzosowo PL 67 B4
Wschowa PL. 85 A4
Wulfen D 80 A3
Wülfen D 83 A3
Wulkau D 73 B5
Wünnenberg D 81 A4
Wünsdorf D. 74 B2
Wunsiedel D 95 A4
Wunstorf D 72 B2
Wuppertal D 80 A3
Wurmannsquick D .95 C4
Würselen D 80 B2
Wurzbach D 82 B3
Würzburg D 94 B1
Wurzen D. 83 A4
Wust D 74 B1
Wusterhausen D . . .73 B5
Wusterwitz D 73 B5
Wustrau-Altfriesack
  D. 74 B1
Wustrow D 66 B1
Wuustwezel B 79 A4
Wye GB. 45 B4
Wyględów PL 87 A5
Wyk D 64 B1
Wykroty PL 84 A3
Wylye GB 43 A5
Wymiarki PL 84 A3
Wymondham GB . . .41 C5
Wyrzysk PL 76 A2
Wyśmierzyce PL . . .87 A4
Wysoka
  Dolnośląskie PL. .85 A3
  Wielkopolskie PL .76 A2
Wyszanów PL 86 A2
Wyszogród PL 77 B5

X

Xanten D 80 A2
Xanthi GR 183 B6
Xarrë AL. 182 D2
Xátiva E 159 C3
Xeraco E 159 B3
Xert E 153 B4
Xerta E 153 B4
Xertigny F 105 A5
Xilagani GR 183 C7
Xilokastro GR 184 A3
Xinzo de Limia E . .140 B3
Xixón = Gijón E . . .142 A1
Xove E 140 A3
Xubia E 140 A2
Xunqueira de Ambia
  E 140 B3
Xunqueira de
  Espadañedo E . .140 B3
Xylophagou CY . . .181 B2

Y

Yablanitsa BG 17 D6
Yağcılar TR 186 C3
Yahyalı TR 23 B8
Yakoruda BG 183 A5
Yalova TR 187 B4
Yalvaç TR. 189 A6
Yambol BG 17 D7
Yampil UA 13 D8
Yaniskoski RUS .193 D12
Yantarnyy RUS 69 A4
Yarbasan TR 186 D3
Yarcombe GB 43 B3
Yaremcha UA. 13 D6
Yarm GB. 37 B5
Yarmouth GB 44 C2
Yarrow GB 35 C4
Yasinya UA 17 A6
Yatağan TR 188 B3
Yate GB 43 A4
Yatton GB 43 A4
Yavoriv UA. 13 D5
Yaxley GB 41 C3
Yazıca TR 187 B6
Yazıköy TR 188 C2
Ybbs A 110 A2
Ybbsitz A 110 B1
Ydby DK 58 B1
Yddal N 46 B2
Ydes F 116 B2
Yealmpton GB 42 B3
Yebra de Basa E . .145 B3
Yecla E 159 C2
Yecla de Yeltes E . .149 B3
Yelsk BY. 13 C8
Yelverton GB 42 B2
Yena RUS. 197 B14
Yenice
  Ankara TR 23 B7
  Aydın TR 188 B3
  Çanakkale TR . . .186 C2
  Edirne TR. 183 C8
Yeniçağa TR 187 B7
Yeniçiftlik TR. 186 D1
Yenifoça TR 186 D1
Yenihisar TR 188 B2
Yeniköy Plaji TR . .186 B3
Yenipazar TR. 188 B3
Yenişarbademli
  TR 189 B6
Yenişehir TR 187 B4
Yenne F 118 B2
Yeovil GB 43 B4
Yepes E 151 C4
Yerköy TR 23 B8
Yerólakkos CY. . . .181 A2
Yeroskipos CY. . . .181 B1
Yerseke NL 79 A4
Yerville F 89 A4
Yeşildağ TR. 189 B6
Yeşilhisar TR 23 B8
Yeşilköy TR 186 B3
Yeşilova TR 189 B4

Yeşilyurt TR. 188 A3
Yeste E 164 A2
Yezerishche BY. 9 E6
Y Felinheli GB 38 A2
Ygos-St Saturnin
  F. 128 C2
Ygrande F 104 C1
Yialousa CY 181 A3
Yığılca TR 187 B6
Yli-Ii FIN. 197 D8
Yli-Kärppä FIN. . . .197 D8
Yli-Muonio FIN. . . .196 A6
Ylitornio FIN. 196 C6
Ylivieska FIN 3 D9
Ylläsjärvi FIN 196 B7
Ymonville F. 103 A3
Yngsjö S 63 C2
York GB 40 B2
Youghal IRL 29 C4
Yoğuntaş TR 186 A2
Yozgat TR 23 B8
Yport F 89 A4
Ypres = Ieper B . . .78 B2
Yssingeaux F 117 B4
Ystad S 66 A2
Ystalyfera GB 39 C3
Ystebrød N 52 B1
Ystradgynlais GB . .39 C3
Ytre Arna N 46 B2
Ytre Enebakk N 54 A2
Ytre Rendal N 199 D8
Ytteran S 199 B11
Ytterhogdal S 199 C11
Yttermalung S 49 B5
Yunak TR 187 D6
Yuncos E 151 B4
Yunquera E 162 B3
Yunquera de Henares
  E 151 B4
Yushkozero RUS . . .3 D13
Yverdon-les-Bains
  CH 106 C1
Yvetot F 89 A4
Yvignac F. 101 A3
Yvoir B 79 B4
Yvonand CH 106 C1
Yxnerum S 56 B2
Yzeure F. 104 C2

Z

Zaamslag NL 79 A3
Zaanstad NL 70 B1
Žabalj SRB. 126 B2
Žabar H 113 A4
Žabari SRB 127 C3
Zabiče SLO. 123 B3
Zabierzów PL 87 B3
Ząbki PL. 77 B6
Ząbkowice Śląskie
  PL. 85 B4
Zablaće HR 138 B1
Žabljak MNE 139 B5
Żabno PL 87 B4
Zabok HR 124 A1
Żabokreky SK 98 C2
Zabor PL 75 C4
Żabowo PL 75 A4
Zabrdje BIH 125 C4
Zábřeh CZ 97 B4
Zábřezje SRB. 127 C2
Ząbrowo PL 67 C4
Zabrze PL. 86 B2
Zabrzeż PL 99 B4
Zacharo GR 184 B2
Zadar HR 137 A4
Zadzim PL 86 A2
Zafarraya E 163 B3
Zafferana Etnea . .177 B4
Zafra E 155 C4
Žaga SLO 122 A2
Zagajica SRB. 127 C3
Žagań PL 84 A3
Zaglav HR 137 B4
Zaglavak SRB 127 C1
Zagnańsk PL 87 B4
Zagora GR 183 D5
Zagorć SLO 110 C2
Zagorićani BIH 138 B3
Zagorje SLO 123 A4
Zagórów PL 76 B2
Zagradje SRB 127 C2
Zagrilla E 163 A3
Zagvozd HR 138 B3
Zagwiździe PL 86 B1
Zagyvarékas H 113 B4
Zagyvaróna H 113 A3
Zahara E 162 B2
Zahara de los Atunes
  E 162 B2
Zahinos E 155 C4
Zahna D. 83 A4
Záhoří CZ 96 B2
Zahrádka CZ 97 B3
Zahrensdorf D 73 A3
Zaidín E 153 A4
Zaječar SRB 16 D5
Zákamenné SK 99 B3
Zákány H 124 A2
Zákányszék H 126 A1
Zakliczyn PL 99 B4
Zakopane PL 99 B3
Zakroczym PL 77 B5
Zakrzew PL 87 A5
Zakrzewo PL 76 B3
Zakupy CZ 84 B2
Zakynthos GR 184 B1
Zalaapáti H 111 C4
Zalabaksa H 111 C3
Zalaegerszeg H . . .111 C3
Zalakomár H 111 C4
Zalakoppány H . . .111 C4
Zalalövő H 111 C3
Zalamea de la Serena
  E. 156 B2
Zalamea la Real E .161 B3
Zalaszentgrót H . .111 C4
Zalaszentiván H . . .111 C3

Zalău RO. 17 B5
Zalavár H 111 C4
Zalcsie E 86 A3
Zaldibar E 143 A4
Zalec SLO 123 A4
Zalesie PL 77 A5
Zalewo PL 69 B4
Zalishchyky UA. . . .13 D6
Zalla E 143 A3
Zaltbommel NL. 79 A5
Zamárdi H 112 C1
Zamarte PL 68 B2
Zamberk CZ. 85 B4
Zambra E 163 A3
Zambugueira do Mar
  P 160 B1
Zámoly H 112 B2
Zamora E 149 A4
Zamość PL 13 C5
Zamoście PL 86 A3
Zams A 108 B1
Zandhoven B 79 A4
Žandov CZ 84 B2
Zandvoort NL. 70 B1
Zangliveri GR 183 C5
Zánka H 111 C4
Zaorejas E 152 B1
Zaovine SRB 127 D1
Zapadnaya Dvina
  RUS 9 D8
Zapfend D 94 A2
Zapole PL. 86 A2
Zapolyarnyy
  RUS 193 C14
Zapponeta I 171 B3
Zaprešić HR. 124 B1
Zaragoza E 153 A3
Zarasai LT 13 A7
Zarautz E 144 A1
Zarcilla de Ramos
  E 164 B3
Zaręby PL 77 A6
Żarki PL 86 B3
Zarko GR 182 D4
Zarnow PL 87 A4
Zarnowiec PL. 68 A3
Zarošice CZ 97 B4
Żarów PL 85 B4
Zarrentin D 73 A3
Žary PL 84 A3
Zarza Capilla E . . .156 B2
Zarza de Alange E .156 B1
Zarza de Granadilla
  E 149 B3
Zarza de Tajo E . . .151 B4
Zarzadilla de Totana
  E 164 B3
Zarza la Mayor E . .155 B4
Zarzuela del Monte
  E 150 B3
Zarzuela del Pinar
  E 151 A3
Zas E 140 A2
Zasavica SRB 127 C1
Zasieki PL 84 A2
Zásmuky CZ 96 B3
Žatec CZ 83 B5
Zaton HR 139 C4
Zatonie PL 84 A3
Zator PL 99 B3
Zauchwitz D 74 B2
Zavala BIH 139 C3
Zavalje BIH 124 C1
Zavattarello I 120 C2
Zavidovići BIH 139 A4
Zavlaka SRB 127 C1
Zawady PL 77 C5
Zawadzkie PL 86 B2
Zawdy PL 86 A2
Zawidów PL 84 A3
Zawidz PL 77 B4
Zawiercie PL 86 B3
Zawoja PL 99 B3
Zawonia PL. 85 A5
Žažina HR 124 B2
Zázrivá SK 99 B3
Zbarazh UA. 13 D6
Zbąszyń PL 75 B4
Zbąszynek PL 75 B4
Zbehy SK 98 C2
Zbiersk PL 76 C3
Zbiroh CZ. 96 B1
Zblewo PL 69 B3
Zbójno PL 77 A4
Zbrachlin PL 76 A3
Zbraslav CZ 96 B2
Zbraslavice CZ 97 B3
Ždala HR 124 A3
Ždánice CZ 98 B1
Žďár nad Sázavou
  CZ 97 B3
Zdbice PL 75 A5
Zdenci HR 125 B3
Ždiar SK. 99 B4
Ždice CZ 96 B2
Zdirec nad Doubravou
  CZ 97 B3
Zdolbuniv UA. 13 C7
Zdounky CZ. 98 B1
Zdrelo SRB 127 C3
Zduńska Wola PL . .86 A2
Zduny
  Łódzkie PL. 77 B4
  Wielkopolskie PL .85 A5
Żdżary PL 87 A4
Zdziechowice
  Opolskie PL. 86 A2
Zdzieszowice PL . .86 B2
Zdziszowice PL 86 B2
Zeberio E 143 A4
Žebrák CZ 96 B1
Zebreira P 155 B3
Zebrzydowa PL 84 A3
Zechlin D. 74 A1
Zederhaus A 109 B4
Žednik SRB 126 B1
Zeebrugge B 78 A3

Zegrze PL. 77 B6
Zehdenick D 74 B2
Zehren D 83 A5
Zeil D 94 A2
Zeilarn D 95 C4
Zeist NL 70 B2
Zeithain D 83 A5
Zeitz D 83 A4
Želatava CZ 97 B3
Zele B 79 A4
Zelenoborskiy RUS 3 C13
Zelenogorsk RUS . . .9 B6
Zelenograd RUS . . .9 D10
Zelenogradsk RUS .12 A4
Železná Ruda CZ. . .96 B1
Železnice CZ 84 B3
Železnik SRB 127 C2
Železniki SLO 123 A3
Železny Brod CZ . . .84 B3
Zelhem NL 71 B3
Želiezovce SK 112 A2
Želkowo PL 68 A2
Zell
  CH 106 B2
  Baden-Württemberg
  D. 93 C4
  Baden-Württemberg
  D. 106 B2
  Rheinland-Pfalz D .92 A3
Zella-Mehlis D 82 B2
Zell am See A. 109 B3
Zell am Ziller A. . . .108 B2
Zell an der Pram A .96 C1
Zell bei Zellhof A . . .96 C2
Zellerndorf A 97 C3
Zellingen D 94 B1
Zelów PL 86 A3
Zeltweg A 110 B1
Zelzate B 79 A3
Zemberovce SK. . . .98 C2
Zembrzyce PL 99 B3
Zemianske-Kostol'any
  SK 98 C2
Zemitz D 66 C2
Zemné SK 112 B1
Zemst B 79 B4
Zemun SRB 127 C2
Zemunik Donji HR 137 A4
Zennor GB 42 B1
Zenson di Piave . . .122 B1
Zerbst D 73 C5
Zerf D 92 B2
Zerind RO 113 C5
Żerków PL 76 B2
Zermatt CH 119 A4
Zernez CH 107 C5
Zerpen-schleuse D .74 B2
Zestoa E. 144 A1
Zetel D 71 A4
Zeulenroda D. 83 B3
Zeven D 72 A2
Zevenaar NL 70 C3
Zevenbergen NL . . .79 A4
Zévio I 121 B4
Zeytinbağı TR 186 B3
Zeytindağ TR 186 D2
Zgierz PL 86 A3
Zgorzelec PL. 84 A3
Zgošča BIH 139 A4
Zhabinka BY 13 B6
Zharkovskiy RUS . . .9 E8
Zhashkiv UA 13 D9
Zhlobin BY 13 B9
Zhmerynka UA 13 D8
Zhodzina BY 13 A8
Zhytomyr UA 13 C8
Žiar nad Hronom
  SK 98 C2
Zicavo F 180 B2
Zickhusen D 65 C4
Zidani Most SLO . .123 A4
Ziddorf D 73 A5
Židlochovice CZ . . .97 B4
Ziębice PL. 85 B5
Ziegendorf D 73 A4
Ziegenrück D 83 B3
Zielona PL 77 A4
Zielona Góra PL . . .75 C4
Zieluń-Osada PL . . .77 A4
Ziemetshausen D . .94 C2
Zierenberg D 81 A5
Zierikzee NL. 79 A3
Ziersdorf A 97 C3
Zierzow D 73 A4
Ziesar D 73 B5
Ziesendorf D 65 C5
Ziethen D 74 B2
Žihle CZ 96 A1
Žilina SK. 98 B2
Ziltendorf D. 74 B3
Zimandu Nou RO .126 A3
Zimna Woda PL 77 A5
Zimnicea RO 17 D6
Zinal CH 119 A4
Zinasco I 120 B2
Zingst D 66 B1
Zinkgruvan S 55 B6
Zinnowitz D. 66 B2
Žinkovy CZ 96 B1
Zirc H 112 B1
Žiri SLO 123 A3
Zirl A. 108 B2
Zirndorf D 94 B2
Žirovnica SRB 127 C3
Žirovnice CZ 97 B3
Zisterdorf A 97 C4
Žitište SRB 126 B2
Zitsa GR. 182 D2
Zittau D 84 B2

Živaja HR 1
Živinice BIH 1
Zlatar HR 1
Zlatar Bistrica HR 12
Zlate Hory CZ . . . .
Zlaté Klasy SK. 1
Zlaté Moravce SK . .
Zlatná na Ostrove
  SK . . . .
Zlatniky SK . . . .
Zlatograd BG 1
Žlebič SLO. . . . .
Zlín CZ . . . .
Złocieniec PL. . . . . .
Złoczew PL . . . .
Złotniki Kujawskie
  PL. . . . .
Złotoryja PL. . . . . . .
Złotów PL. . . . .
Złoty Stok PL. . . . . .
Zlutice CZ . . . .
Zmajevac BIH 12
Zmajevo SRB. . . . .
Żmigród PL . . . .
Zmijavci HR. . . . . . .
Žminj HR . . . .
Żnin PL. . . . .
Znojmo CZ. . . . .
Zöblitz D . . . .
Zocca I . . . .
Zoetermeer NL. . . . .
Zofingen CH 1
Zogno I. . . . .
Zohor SK . . . .
Zolling D . . . .
Zolochiv UA. . . . . . .
Zomba H . . . .
Zomergem B . . . . . .
Zoñan E . . . .
Zonguldak TR . . . . .
Zonhoven B . . . .
Zonza F . . . .
Zörbig D . . . .
Zorita E . . . .
Żory PL. . . . .
Zossen D . . . .
Zottegem B . . . .
Zoutkamp NL. . . . . .
Zovi Do BIH 13
Zrenjanin SRB. . . .12
Žrnovica HR . . . . . .
Zručnad Sazavou
  CZ . . . .
Zsadány H 1
Zsámbék H 1
Zsámbok H 1
Zsana H 1
Zschopau D . . . .
Zuberec SK . . . .
Zubia E 1
Zubiri E . . . .
Zubtsov RUS. . . . . .
Zucaina E 1
Zudar D . . . .
Zuera E 1
Zufre E 1
Zug CH. 10
Zuheros E 1
Zuidhorn NL. 7
Zuidlaren NL 7
Zuidwolde NL 7
Zújar E 1
Żukowo PL. . . . .
Żuljana HR. 13
Žulová CZ 8
Zülpich D 8
Zumaia E 1
Zumárraga E 1
Zundert NL. 7
Županja HR 12
Zurgena E 1
Zürich CH 10
Żuromin PL . . . .
Zurzach CH 1
Zusmarshausen D .9
Zusow D. . . . .
Züssow D . . . .
Žuta Lovka HR 12
Zutphen NL 7
Žužemberk SLO . . .1
Zvenyhorodka UA. .1
Zvikovské Podhradi
  CZ . . . .
Zvolen SK . . . .
Zvolenská Slatina
  SK . . . .
Zvornik BIH 1
Zwartsluis NL 7
Zweibrücken D 9
Zweisimmen CH . .10
Zwettl A. . . . .
Zwettl an der Rodl
  A. . . . .
Zwickau D. . . . .
Zwiefalten D 10
Zwierzyn PL. . . . . . .
Zwierzno PL . . . . . .
Zwiesel D . . . .
Zwieselstein A 10
Zwoleń PL . . . .
Zwolle NL. . . . .
Zwönitz D. . . . .
Zychlin PL . . . .
Zydowo
  Wielkopolskie PL .7
  Zachodnio-Pomors…
Żyrardów PL . . . . . .
Żytno PL . . . .
Żywiec PL . . . .
Zyyi CY. 18